Company Law Handbook: the Fundamentals

Company Law Handbook: the Fundamentals

Dr Saleem Sheikh
LLB (Hons), LLM (Lond), PhD (Lond)

Bloomsbury Professional
LONDON • DUBLIN • EDINBURGH • NEW YORK • NEW DELHI • SYDNEY

BLOOMSBURY PROFESSIONAL

Bloomsbury Publishing Plc
50 Bedford Square, London, WC1B 3DP, UK
1359 Broadway, New York, NY 10018, USA
Bloomsbury Publishing Ireland Ltd
29 Earlsfort Terrace, Dublin 2, Ireland

2

Printed 2022, Reprinted 2026

British Library Cataloguing-in-Publication Data

A catalogue record for this book is available from the British Library.

ISBN: PB: 978 1 52651 559 9
Epdf: 978 1 52651 560 5
Epub: 978 1 52651 558 2

Typeset by Evolution Design and Digital (Kent)
Printed and bound in Great Britain by TJ Books, Padstow, Cornwall

MIX
Paper | Supporting responsible forestry
FSC® C013056

For product safety related questions contact productsafety@bloomsbury.com

Preface

Company Law Handbook: the Fundamentals reflects the impact of emerging significant developments in English company law, through case law, statutory regulation, and other influential authorities and organisations responsible for regulating the company law regime in England.

The Handbook has the following objectives:

(i) to set out the essential regulatory framework, with reference to principal legislation and statutory instruments governing English companies;

(ii) to highlight the principal case law influencing the continuous development of English company law;

(iii) to provide practical checklists on key areas impacting English companies; and

(iv) to consider the interrelationship between other interrelated areas of law and their impact on English company law.

The *Handbook* charts the life of a company from pre-incorporation through to its incorporation and continuing obligations. It considers the essential requirements for establishing an English company, including the legal and practical steps, procedures and documents required during the existence and operation of the corporation. It also addresses the role of the key officers in the company, their general duties within the corporate governance structure, and the governance relationship between management and shareholders. Consideration is also given to the capital requirements, financing aspects and the role of auditors. *The Handbook* aims to serve the legal and practical needs of various users and practitioners including lawyers, accountants, directors, industrialists, entrepreneurs, company secretaries, academics and law students.

English company law is constantly changing, evolving, developing and adapting through legislative reforms and landmark cases. Subsequent editions will take account of the key legal and practical changes impacting companies.

For a further detailed reference guide to English company law, see the online version of *Company Law Handbook*, available as part of Bloomsbury Professional's Company and Commercial Law online service. For a free trial, please email professionalsales@bloomsbury.com.

The law is stated as at 31 December 2021.

Dr Saleem Sheikh
London
February 2022

Acknowledgements

I owe profound gratitude and appreciation to the many people, companies, entities and organisations who encouraged me to write *Company Law Handbook: the Fundamentals*.

I owe sincere appreciation to my family for their relentless encouragement and support. I pay particular tribute to my wife, Shabena, for her wonderful sense of humour, and always being there for me; my daughter Iram, in successfully completing her MPharm and who is now a successful pharmacist; and my three sons, Kamil who achieved the top grade for his business management course at university, and is now on an accelerated career ladder; to Sohail who aspires to be a lawyer and currently studying law at university, and aspiring to be a high profile lawyer; and to my son, Hamza, for diligently completing his higher legal academic studies towards a prosperous future career.

I pay tribute to my late mother, Fahmida and father, Tahir Jamil, for their efforts in encouraging me in life, for loving me, for giving me determination, hope and confidence in life. I also thank my aunt, Saeeda Khan, for being there for me when I most needed her, and to my dear friends, Akram Mughal and Mubashar Lone. To Afifa who has joined the family and wishing her much success in her career. I also dedicate this book and pay tribute to the late Professor Lord Wedderburn of Charlton and late Professor John Parkinson.

I am also grateful to the many institutions that assisted me in my research for this book, including The Institute of Advanced Legal Studies, and the London School of Economics and Political Science.

These acknowledgements would not be complete without reference to my publishers, Bloomsbury Professional, who provided me with an exciting opportunity to write this book. I owe gratitude and appreciation to Andy Hill. Thank you also immensely to Ellie Coull and Jane Bradford for all their continuous assistance, patience and hard work in preparation of this book. I am very fortunate to have worked with a team who displayed the highest professional standards in bringing their experience and skills to this book.

Contents

Introduction

Aims and objectives

Company Law Handbook: the Fundamentals serves as a reference guide for all significant developments at a national level impacting on English company law. It takes account of the legislative and regulatory changes including key case law interpretation.

The *Handbook* is intended to serve as a useful guide for various groups of users ranging from the practitioner, director, secretary, industrialist, academic or student, and to anyone else who has an interest in company law and practice. The *Handbook* addresses the needs of these users in various ways. First, by analysing company law from the pre-incorporation stage to incorporation and continuing obligations. Second, each chapter provides an Introduction to the topic under consideration and the key issues that will be addressed in that chapter. The paragraphs are numbered in sequential order for ease of reference. Third, some chapters also set out key cases that further explain and interpret various legislative provisions of the Companies Act 2006 and other legislation impacting on companies. Finally, in appropriate contexts, a checklist of main aspects of the topic are provided with reference to the primary legislative provisions.

The chapters

Chapter 1 addresses the pre-incorporation phase before a company is established. It examines the concept of a 'promoter'. It also looks at the fiduciary duties of promoters, their liability at common law, pre-incorporation contracts; and how CA 2006 addresses liability in such situations.

The company, once incorporated, is considered to be a legal entity distinct from its shareholders. The concept of corporate personality is examined in *Chapter 2*, with reference to landmark decisions impacting on the independent personality of the corporation. The concept of 'lifting' or 'piercing' the veil is considered, with an analysis of the leading Supreme Court decisions.

Chapter 3 considers the legal and practical aspects of company formation, with reference to the steps and procedures involved in forming a private company limited by shares, including registration and its effect.

One of the significant constitutional documents for a company is its articles of association regulating the company's internal governance. The nature of articles of some companies that can be established under CA 2006 is considered in *Chapter 4*, including model form articles of association and enforceability issues between the shareholders and the company concerning the articles, and alteration of articles.

The ability of a company to engage in activities depends upon its corporate capacity. *Chapter 5* addresses the powers of directors to bind the company and any constitutional limitations on their powers. It examines the *ultra vires* doctrine in its application to corporate capacity, execution of documents and application of the company seal.

Depending upon the circumstances, companies may re-register or convert into another form of corporate entity such as a private, public or an unlimited company. These aspects of re-registration are considered from a legal and practical perspective in *Chapter 6* by way of checklists and the documentation required.

Corporate governance has now become one of the key aspects at the heart of the operation of English company law. *Chapter 7* addresses the key committees that were established to look into various aspects of corporate governance in the UK, and also considers the latest versions of the UK Corporate Governance Code and the Stewardship Code.

Chapter 8 looks at types of directors and their appointment and removal. The various categories of directors are considered with reference to their position within the company, and the leading cases on the directors, particularly the interrelationship between *de facto* and shadow directors.

Before 2006, the general duties of directors were fragmented, and the legal position was largely governed by case law on the fiduciary and common law duties of directors which were applied in random fashion. CA 2006 has codified some of the directors' duties commonly found under the fiduciary and common law principles. *Chapter 9* examines the general statement of directors' duties as set out in CA 2006.

Chapter 10 continues the theme of directors' duties with particular reference to directors' specific statutory duties and liabilities, and situations where shareholders' consent is also required before directors can enter into a transaction for shareholder and corporate protection.

Chapter 11 looks at directors' disqualification, and examines the grounds on which a disqualification order or undertaking may be made, including the disqualification periods under the Company Directors Disqualification Act 1986, and key case law.

Within the corporate governance system, shareholders' interests may need protection. CA 2006 provides redress for aggrieved shareholders in certain circumstances including specific remedies available. *Chapter 12* considers a derivative claim, and the grounds for such application, including the courts' powers to consider a derivative claim.

Another key remedy for an aggrieved shareholder is to petition the court on the grounds of unfair prejudicial conduct, and the various orders that the court may make in this regard. *Chapter 13* addresses of the judicial perspectives towards 'unfair prejudicial conduct', and the cases interpreting the legislative.

For public limited companies, the role of the company secretary is significant, in ensuring corporate compliance with various rules and regulations. *Chapter 14* looks at the secretary's role in this context, with a checklist of key points to consider in the appointment of the secretary.

Decisions within a company are made through resolutions and meetings, unless written resolutions apply in some circumstances. *Chapter 15* considers the different types of resolutions under CA 2006 and the board and shareholders' meetings that may be convened.

Chapter 16 looks at the duties, role and function of auditors and their liability.

The topic of shares and share capital is examined in *Chapter 17* which considers different types of shares and rights (if any) attaching to such shares. This chapter also looks at the power of directors to allot shares and pre-emption rights, including waivers and alteration of share capital as well as reduction of share capital.

Chapter 18 considers acquisition by a company of its own shares. It also addresses the redemption procedure.

The concept of company charges is examined in *Chapter 19,* and the types of charges commonly found in English company law.

Chapter 20 looks at certification and transfer of securities, with reference to procedural aspects and people with significant control of a company's shares.

Chapter 21 considers information about interests in a company's shares and key cases in this area.

In some situations, a company may be dissolved with its removal from the register at Companies House under various grounds as set out in CA 2006. *Chapter 22* considers the position on dissolution of a company and circumstances giving rise to its restoration at Companies House.

Chapter 23 considers role of the Registrar of Companies in English company law including the Registrar's powers, with reference to some key case law decisions on the Registrar's negligence.

Companies may also be regulated through the process of company investigations, leading to company inspectors being appointed with wide powers to investigate the company's affairs and its officers. This has given rise to key case law addressing issues such as natural justice, and the use of evidence obtained by the inspectors in subsequent proceedings against the company officers; and the implications under the European Convention of Human Rights, including the human rights of key corporate officers. These aspects are considered in *Chapter 24*.

Closely aligned to corporate governance are the social responsibilities of companies. In *Chapter* 25, the legal aspects of the concept are examined, including judicial and statutory regulation.

Abbreviations

AC	Appeals Cases
AGM	Annual General Meeting
All ER	All England Law Reports
App Cas	Law Reports Appeal Cases (1875-1890)
ARD	Accounting Reference Date
BCC	Butterworths Company Cases
BCLC	Butterworths Company Law Cases
BEIS	Department for Business, Energy & Industrial Strategy
BOT	Board of Trade
CA	Court of Appeal
CA 1985	Companies Act 1985
CA 1989	Companies Act 1989
CA 2006	Companies Act 2006
CDDA 1986	Company Directors Disqualification Act 1986
CEO	Chief Executive Officer
CFO	Chief Financial officer
ChD	Law Reports Chancery Division (1876-1890)
CIB	BEIS Companies Investigation Branch
CLR	Commonwealth Law Reports
CPD	Common Pleas Division
CPD	Common Pleas Division (1875-1880)
CSIH	Court of Session (Inner House)
D&O Insurance	Directors' and Officers' Liability Insurance
DRR	Directors' Remuneration Report
DTI	Department of Trade and Industry
DTR	Disclosure and Transparency Rule
E & B	Ellis and Blackburn's Queen's Bench Reports (1852-1858)
EGM	Extraordinary General Meeting
Ex D	Exchequer Division (1875-1880)
FLR	Family Law Reports
FRC	Financial Reporting Council
GAAP	Generally Accepted Accounting Principles
Hare	Hare's Vice-Chancellor's Reports (1841-1853)
HL	House of Lords
HL Cas	House of Lords Cases (Clark) (1847-1866)

IA 1986	Insolvency Act 1986
IAS	International Accounting Standards
ICAEW	Institute of Chartered Accountants in England and Wales
ICSA	Institute of Chartered Secretaries and Administrators
KB	Law Reports King's Bench
LLP	Limited Liability Partnership
LLPA 2000	Limited Liability Partnership Act 2000
LP	Limited Partnership
LR CP	Law Reports, Common Pleas (1865-1875)
LR Eq	Law Reports, Equity (1865-1875)
LR Ex	Law Reports, Exchequer (1865-1875)
LR HL	Law Reports, English and Irish Appeal Cases (1865-1875)
LR QB	Law Reports, Queen's Bench (1865-1875)
LT	Law Times
Ltd	Limited
MCA 1973	Matrimonial Causes Act 1973
OFR	Operating and Financial Review
NED	Non-Executive Director
NI	Northern Ireland
PC	Privy Council
PLC	Public Limited Company
PSC	People with Significant Control
SBEEA 2015	Small Business, Enterprise and Employment Act 2015
SFO	Serious Fraud Office
SI	Statutory Instrument
TLR	Times Law Reports
WLR	Weekly Law Reports
UKLA	UK Listing Authority

Table of Statutes

[All references are to paragraph number.]

Table of Statutory Instruments

[All references are to paragraph number.]

Table of Cases

[*All references are to paragraph number.*]

B

D

E

M

N

O

P

Q

R

S

T

U

1 Pre-incorporation

Introduction

1.1 This chapter considers the promoters who undertake the preliminary formalities required to establish the company. It addresses the following aspects:

- the identity of the promoters;
- the characteristics of the promoters;
- how the courts have defined promoters, and judicial attitudes towards promoters;
- the duties and obligations of promoters;
- remedies for breach of promoters' duties and obligations;
- the position on pre-incorporation contracts both at common law and under CA 2006; and
- includes a checklist on promoters.

Promoters

1.2 This section considers the definition of a promoter with reference to case law, including the characteristics and attributes of promoters. Their duties and obligations are addressed, as are judicial attitudes towards promoters.

Who is a promoter?

1.3 The term 'promoter' is not defined in CA 2006, and reference is often made to case law for guidance on the definition including the duties of promoters. Although there is no general consensus in English company law as to the definition of a promoter, there are some practical features and characteristics that distinguish a promoter from others:

- The term covers a broad spectrum of persons embarking on the purpose of setting up an entity for a particular project assignment. The project may be *bona fide* or a sham depending upon the promoter's intentions: *Twycross v Grant* (1877) 2 CPD 469.
- A promoter may be actively involved in the company formation, but a person who has also been passively involved in the company formation may still be a promoter. According to Cockburn in *Twycross v Grant* (1877) 2 CPD 469, the promoters not only provisionally formed the company, but were, in fact, to the end its creators; they found the directors, and qualified them; they prepared the prospectus; they paid for printing and advertising, and the expenses incidental to

the establishment of the company. So long as the work of company formation continued, those who carried on that work had retained the character of promoters. Their duties may come to an end once the directors are appointed and take over the company's management.

See too: *Emma Silver Mining Co v Grant* (1879) 11 Ch D 918; *Jubilee Cotton Mills v Lewis* [1924] AC 958.

- A promoter need not necessarily be involved in the establishment of the company, but will still be regarded as one if the promoter is in any way involved in the negotiation or obtaining of potential finance or negotiating agreements on behalf of the company that is to be established: *Lagunas Nitrate Co v Lagunas Syndicate* [1899] 2 Ch 392.
- A person advising promoters in a professional capacity will not be considered as a promoter: *Re Great Wheal Polgooth Co* (1883) 53 LJ Ch 42. However, if the professional goes beyond professional advice and becomes involved in becoming a director or obtaining potential investors, he may be considered as a promoter: *Lydney & Wigpool Iron Ore Co v Bird* (1886) 33 Ch D 85; *Bagnall v Carlton* (1877) 6 Ch D 371.
- One of the principal objectives of a promoter is to comply with the initial formalities required to establish a company, and to register the company at Companies House.
- The determination as to whether or not a person is a promoter is one of fact: the courts will look at all the factual circumstances in determining what role the promoter played in the establishment of the company, including any dealings with third parties before the company was established. This includes entering into pre-incorporation contracts for the company's purposes and future activities. In a public company, where securities are to be offered to the public, the promoter will usually be involved in preparing and issuing the prospectus.
- In some cases, promoters may not be involved in the initial stages of forming the company but may still be considered as promoters even if they are involved at the tail-end of company establishment: *Lagunas Nitrate Co v Lagunas Syndicate* [1899] 2 Ch 392 The promoter's role will continue until the company has been incorporated or directors have been appointed: *Twycross v Grant* (1877) 2 CPD 396.
- In some instances, promoters may seek potential funding from investors to ensure the viability and financial success of the company once it is established. Depending on the circumstances, these investors may take a passive or active part in the company's management and operations, or they may nominate their potential directors to sit on the company's board to oversee the activities of the company and guide the company in the early stages of its set up.
- Promoters may themselves become directors/shareholders in the company, but it is not a prerequisite that they do so. They may simply be arranging and co-ordinating the process of bringing together other investors into a company, without any involvement in the functional and operational aspects of the company.
- Promoters who become directors and/or shareholders in a company will be interested in ensuring the long-term success of the company, which may include profit maximisation and corporate social responsibilities towards wider stakeholders.

- Promoters usually tend to be individuals. They may also include a general partnership, a limited liability partnership, a limited partnership, an unincorporated association, or any other entity or organisation seeking to establish a company.
- Promoters may identify and purchase business assets on the company's behalf before incorporation, enter into contracts with third parties, and hire potential personnel to work for the company once it is established.
- A promoter may also a person who holds himself out or represents himself to be acting on behalf of a company that will be incorporated.

Judicial definitions of promoters

1.4 Although the term 'promoter' is referred to in CA 2006 (see for example, CA 2006, s 762(1)(c) on obtaining a trading certificate), there is no statutory definition of the term. Over the years, however, the English courts have developed certain features and attributes of promoters to highlight the various activities in which they are involved in the company's incorporation.

1.5 The courts have traditionally been reluctant to set out a detailed definition of a promoter capturing all aspects and features of his duties and obligations. This is because the courts preferred to keep the term flexible, in order to catch potential rogues attempting to abuse the companies legislation by using the company as a cloak for their fraudulent and deceitful activities. The cases on promoters have, therefore, concentrated largely on the standards of behaviour that promoters were required to display in their dealings with the public and third parties, including upholding standards of moral probity. The courts have applied various areas of law in imputing liability to promoters, including misrepresentation, fraud, unjust enrichment, negligence and contractual liability. This has also included at times applying equitable principles and imposing fiduciary duties on promoters. Although CA 2006 sets out the duties of directors, it does not provide for such duties for promoters and reliance is therefore placed on common law cases to identify the duties.

1.6 A promoter's legal existence is determined by fact not law. As long ago as 1879, in *Emma Silver Mining Co Ltd v Lewis,* 4 CPD, 36 (CP 1879), the court stated that the term 'promoter,' did not have a very definite meaning, but involved the idea of exertion for the purpose of floating a company, and also the idea of some duty towards the company, imposed by or arising from the position which the so-called promoter assumed toward it. The persons who form a company have duties towards it before it comes into existence.

1.7 One of the earliest attempts to define the term 'promoter' was set out in *Twycross v Grant* (1877) 2 CPD 469 at p 541, where Cockburn CJ stated:

> 'A promoter, I apprehend, is one who undertakes to form a company with reference to a given project and to set it going, and who takes the necessary steps to accomplish that purpose … and so long as the work of formation continues, those who carry on the work must, I think, retain the character of promoters. Of course, if a governing body, in the shape of directors, has once been formed, and they take … what remains to be done in the way of forming the company, into their own hands, the functions of a promoter are at an end.'

On occasions, the courts equated the position of a promoter to that of a person discharging trustee-like functions in the course of his duties in establishing the company. In *Bagnall v Carlton* (1877) 6 Ch D 371, Cotton LJ described promoters as almost akin to trustees, but not identical to them: similar to trustees, promoters had fiduciary duties to discharge and could not secretly make to themselves a profit in the transaction in which they were trustees.

In Whaley & Bridge Calico Printing Co v Green (1880) 5 QBD 109, Bowen J stated:

> 'The term promoter is a term not of law, but of business, usefully summing up in a single word a number of business operations familiar to the commercial world by which a company is generally brought into existence.'

1.8 It is not always the position that the promoter should personally be involved in the company formation: this aspect could be delegated to others yet the person who delegated could still be a promoter: *Lagunas Nitrate Co v Lagunas Syndicate* [1899] 2 Ch 392.

In establishing a company, the promoter may seek the assistance of a lawyer, accountant or a company formation agent. It has been held that such professionals, in undertaking their duties in that capacity, cannot be considered as the company's promoters: *Re Great Wheal Poolgooth Co Ltd* (1883) 53 LJ Ch 42.

1.9 In subsequent cases, the courts have tended to retreat from defining the term in any further detail or even using the term 'promoter', but they have instead addressed the relationship of the promoter vis-à-vis the company that is being established.

A promoter cannot be an agent of a company that does not exist: *Lydney and Wigpool Iron Ore Co v Bird* (1886) 33 ChD 85. However, the Court of Appeal stated that the principles of agency or trustee could still apply to a promoter. Lindley LJ thought that the term 'promoter' was ambiguous in the context of company law. Instead, it was necessary to ascertain in each case what the so-called promoter really did before his legal liabilities could be accurately ascertained. This would entail looking at the facts and circumstances surrounding the promoter's actions. The court would in appropriate circumstances extend the concepts of agency and trusteeship in their application to promoters for the purposes of attributing liability.

Promoters' duties

1.10 Promoters' duties and liabilities are generally regulated by equity and common law unlike the statutory duties of directors. When discharging their duties and responsibilities through the process of establishing a company, promoters occupy a special relationship in their dealings with third parties and the company they are setting up. Promoters have not been immune from the scrutiny of the courts, for the very reason that the courts perceive promoters as individuals, who have the capacity to enter into contracts and commercial dealings with third parties at a time when the company has not been formed.

1.11 Further, promoters also have full knowledge, understanding and intention as to the motives for setting up the company. Accordingly, the courts consider that some liability ought to be imposed on promoters for any of their acts or activities which are in breach of the law. The objective of the courts has also been to protect the public and third parties dealing with promoters from using any deceptive or fraudulent activities perpetrated by the promoters. Promoters cannot, therefore, shield behind the cloak of a company that is in the process of being formed, and expect to be exonerated from any liabilities that they may incur while acting in that capacity. Generally, a promoter has capacity to enter into contractual relations with third parties; to sue and be sued; as well being subject to criminal penalties and sanctions.

A promoter's existence does not necessarily end on the formation of the company, but any liability or accountability may still continue until all issues have been resolved between the promoter and the company: *Eden v Ridsdales Rwy, Lamp & Lighting Co* (1889) 23 QBD 368.

1.12 Recognising that promoters are able to operate with unfettered powers and thereby the potential to engage in abuses of a fraudulent and deceitful nature in establishing the company, the courts have adapted the fiduciary principles applicable to trustees and directors, by applying them to promoters in order to minimise the scope of any potential abuses, and to demonstrate that promoters must be scrupulously honest and display exemplary behaviour in the conduct of their duties: *Hichens v Congreve* (1828) 4 Russ 562. Any wrongdoing conducted by the promoter in setting up the company is a wrong done to the company, and the company is the proper claimant to such action against the promoter: *Foss v Harbottle* (1843) 2 Hare 461; and see too the derivative action under the Companies Act 2006, Pt 11.

Owing to the position occupied by the promoters, the courts have developed some duties that are applicable to promoters. The next section considers some of their important duties.

Fiduciary duty

1.13 CA 2006 does not address the duties and obligations of promoters but only considers their personal liability under a pre-incorporation context. Many of their duties are therefore common law based rather than statutory. The duties were developed by the courts largely in the nineteenth century to deal with the types of conduct and actions undertaken by promoters. The courts have traditionally applied equitable principles to promoters when addressing their duties and obligations, when determining the liability of the promoter in the steps leading to the company's establishment. As the company has no legal existence before it is established and is therefore a lifeless creature, the courts have been of the view that a promoter is not an agent of an entity which is not yet in existence, as there is no principal who can give instructions to an agent.

1.14 In law, the term 'fiduciary' refers to an obligation to act in a specified way towards the entity, organisation or person to whom the obligation is owed. The fiduciary is therefore placed in a special position of trust towards the person to whom he owes duties or in his dealings with various parties. The fiduciary's intentions to act in that capacity must be *bona fide* and demonstrated by his actions towards the person he represents. Fiduciary obligations are often manifested in a duty of loyalty, honesty, good faith, the 'no profit' rule, the duty not to make secret profits, the 'no conflict' rule, or acting in any manner which may otherwise prejudicially affect the best interests of the person, entity or organisation for whom the fiduciary acts. A fiduciary is required to operate with moral probity and display exemplary standards of behaviour and professionalism in dealings with others. Fiduciaries are also required to display the utmost good faith in their dealings with third parties.

1.15 Over the years, the courts have applied these fiduciary principles borrowed from the law of trusts (based on the trustee–beneficiary relationship) towards promoters.

They have considered that promoters occupy a fiduciary position: the fiduciary position is not owed so much to the directors and shareholders of the company that is ultimately formed, but towards third parties with whom promoters have dealings. This is because promoters will have knowledge as to the potential company that will be established, its objectives, activities, the amount of capital required, the identity of the potential investors that are to be targeted, any business plans that have been developed by the promoters, dealings with third parties, and in some cases, the expertise and skill that promoters may bring to the company. These aspects place the promoters in a fiduciary and advantageous position such that, should any liabilities ensue, the promoters should bear the burden of such liabilities if they are found to have breached any of the fiduciary duties that the law imposes on them.

1.16 The promoter is subject to a fiduciary duty while he is a promoter of the entity that is being formed, and therefore liable for any secret profits he has made. The psychological make-up and motive for establishing the company are important factors in the consideration of any secret profits made by the promoter. In the course of their dealings, promoters are required to make full disclosure to the company that is ultimately established of all profits made, including all material matters that affect the setting up of the company. They are also jointly and severally liable in respect of the secret profits made.

A promoter must not make any secret profit from his position: *Re British Seamless Paper Box Co* (1881) 17 Ch D 467. See on appeal [1902] 2 Ch 809, p 825, where the Court of Appeal stated that promoters who became directors of companies they formed, stood in a fiduciary duty in relation to their company.

In some circumstances, promoters can be subject to fiduciary obligations. In *Re Leeds and Hanley Theatres of Varieties Ltd* [1902] 2 Ch 809, it was held that the promoters stood in a fiduciary position towards the persons who were invited to take shares in the company, and that it was their duty to disclose to those persons the fact that they were the real owners of the company.

1.17 Promoters usually engage in transactions for and on behalf of a company to be formed. One of the main issues arising here is a situation where the promoter acquires an asset or property and then sells it to the company, without declaring an interest in the transaction, thereby making an undisclosed profit. This is known as a 'secret profit'. The courts have on occasions decided that a full disclosure of a secret profit made must be to an independent board of directors.

Full disclosure of a secret profit must be made to an independent board. In *Erlanger v New Sombrero Phosphate Co* [1874–1880] All ER Rep 271, the House of Lords held that promoters who purchase property and then created a company to purchase from them the property they owned, stood in a fiduciary position towards that company, and they must faithfully state to the company the facts which applied to the property, and would influence the company in deciding on the reasonableness of acquiring it. According to Lord Penzance, the company never had an opportunity of exercising, through independent directors, a fair and independent judgment in respect of the transaction in question. The promoters fell below the standards of moral probity through their conduct and connivance. Lord Cairns considered that any disclosure of a transaction by promoters should be to an independent board of directors who were the competent and partial judges as to whether or not the transaction should be entered into.

In *Gluckstein v Barnes* [1900] AC 240, the House of Lords held that the promoters should have disclosed to the company the profit they had made from the transaction.

The fact that the company could not now rescind the transaction was not a bar to relief, and that the promoter in question was personally liable to account to the company for the profits made. The Earl of Halsbury LC was of the view that the company should have been informed of the transaction and consulted as to whether the company would have allowed such profit to be made. The promoters were under a duty of good faith and honesty to disclose the transaction, particularly as they had used ingenious arrangements and deception to trap investors investing in the company. According to Lord MacNaghten stated that the promoters were dishonest, using the company as a cloak to commit their fraud and making secret profits.

A liquidator could seek to recover secret profits made by the promoter: *Re Darby* [1911] 1 KB 95

1.18 A failure to disclose an interest in the transaction or contract renders the contract voidable at the company's option: *Re Lady Forrest (Murchison) Gold Mines Ltd* [1901] 1 Ch 582

In *Lydney and Wigpool Iron Ore Company Ltd v Bird* [1886–90] All ER Rep Ext 1686, the Court of Appeal decided that a promoter of a company was accountable for any money obtained by him from the funds of the company without the knowledge of the company, as, although before the company was formed, he could not be considered as agent or trustee for it, yet the principles of the law of agency and trusteeship apply. Although the term 'promoter' was ambiguous, it was necessary to ascertain in each case what the so-called 'promoter' really did before his legal liabilities could be accurately ascertained. In every case, it was preferable to look at the facts, and ascertain and describe them as they are.

See too *Beck v Kantorowicz* (1857) 3 K & J 230; and *Bagnall v Carlton* (1877) 6 Ch D 371.

1.19 However, the *Erlanger* case imposed a strict approach towards disclosure by the promoters to an independent board including the mechanisms and composition of such a board and determining the degree of 'independency' of the board of directors. This rule was subsequently relaxed to require disclosure instead to the shareholders in a general meeting: see *Salomon v Salomon & Co Ltd* [1897] AC 22. Indeed, in *Lagunas Nitrate Co v Lagunas Syndicate* [1899] 2 CH 392, Lindley LJ stated: 'After *Salomon's* case, I think it impossible to hold that it is the duty of promoters of a company to provide it with an independent board of directors if the real truth is disclosed to those who are induced by the promoters to join the company'. Any disclosure of the actions of the promoters must be to all shareholders with a full and frank disclosure and not just to some shareholders: *Gluckstein v Barnes* [1900] AC 240.

It will not be sufficient for the disclosure of the secret profit to be made to close associates or relatives of the promoter in the company that is established, particularly where directors are charged with duties and responsibilities to act in the best interests of the company in discharging their duties.

1.20 Promoters also must not deliberately place themselves in a position where their personal interests conflict with their duty to establish the company: *Lagunas Nitrate Co v Lagunas Syndicate* [1899] 2 Ch 442. According to Lindley MR: '... in equity the promoters of a company stand in a fiduciary relation to it, and to those persons whom they induce to become shareholders in it, and cannot in equity bind the company by any contract with themselves without fully and fairly disclosing to the company all material facts which the company ought to know'.

1.21 In order to avoid liability for any potential actions, promoters would attempt to contract out of their fiduciary duties by including a 'waiver' clause in the company's articles of association. The effect of this clause was that both the company and the shareholders were denied any right of action against the promoters: *Omnium Electric Palaces v Baines* [1914] 2 Ch 332.

Remedies

1.22 Under English law, there are various remedies available where a promoter is found to be in breach of his fiduciary obligations. The two main remedies in this area have focused on rescission of the contract entered into by the promoter; and the promoter accounting for the secret profits namely for breach of his fiduciary duties, with the remedy of tracing available.

Rescission

1.23 This may arise where there is a transfer or disposal of an asset to the company, and the promoter fails to disclose the secret profit he has made from the transaction. In this situation, the company may be able to rescind the contract. In order for rescission to apply and be effective, the company must not have ratified or affirmed the contract otherwise rescission may be lost: *Erlanger v New Sombrero Phosphate Co* [1874–1880] All ER Rep 271: *Steedman v Frigidaire Corp* [1933] 1 DLR 161; *Re Leeds & Hanley Theatre of Variety* [1902] 2 Ch 809.

1.24 If there is a delay by the company in rescinding the contract, the company may not thereafter be able to rescind the contract: *Long v Lloyd* [1958] 1 WLR 753; and *Leaf v International Galleries* [1950] 2 KB 86. A bona fide third party without notice who obtains rights in respect of the contract, will be able to enforce such rights against the company if the company has not rescinded the contract: *Re Leeds and Hanley Theatres of Varieties Ltd* [1902] 2 Ch 809. The effect of rescission is to place the parties in their original position as if the transaction had not taken place, unless this is not possible owing to the actions and conduct of the promoter: *Lagunas Nitrate Co v Lagunas Syndicate* [1899] 2 Ch 392.

1.25 Rescission will not be possible if the original asset cannot be returned back to its previous state: *Ladywell Mining Co v Brookes* (1887) 35 Ch D 400; *Smith New Court Securities v Scrimgeour Vickers (Asset Management) Limited* [1977] AC 254 per Lord Browne-Wilkinson.

Action of deceit

1.26 The parties who have been subject to fraud, may also be able to sue by an action of deceit: *Whaley Bridge Calico Printing Co v Green* (1879) 5 QBD 109. See too *Re Olympia Limited* [1898] 1 Ch 153 under name of *Gluckstein v Barnes* [1900] AC 240.

Trusteeship

1.27 It may be possible for the company to enforce the promoter's claim on the basis of the trusteeship principle, particularly where the promoter has been promised monies, bribes or other commissions, but which have not been received by the promoter from a third party or promisor. The trusteeship principle would operate on the basis that the promoter was a trustee for the monies that he would have received from the promisor or the third party: *Whaley Bridge Calico Printing Co v Green* (1879) 5 QBD 109.

A promoter may also be liable in respect of bribes under the Bribery Act 2010.

Damages for breaches of fiduciary duties

1.28 In *Leeds and Hanley Theatres of Varieties Ltd* [1902] 2 Ch 809, the Court of Appeal stated that it may be possible for the company to claim damages against the promoter for breach of his fiduciary duties: see too *Jacobus Marler Estates Ltd v Marler* (1913) 85 LJPC 167n, PC. Damages for breaches of equitable obligations such as fiduciary duties, have also been awarded by the courts: *Target Holdings Ltd v Redferns* [1996] AC 421; *Knight v Frost* [1999] 1 BCLC 364 at p 373.

Compensation

1.29 The courts may be prepared to make an order holding the promoter liable to pay compensation to members of the public who subscribed for shares. This action is based on the information provided in the information memorandum, the prospectus or similar document, which information later proves to be false in a material particular, and where the whole objective of the scheme is to defraud the potential investors for the purposes of obtaining monies.

Account of profits

1.30 A promoter may be required by the court to account for the profits made in a transaction which has not been disclosed to the company, particularly where a secret profit has been made and rescission of the transaction is not possible to recover the secret profit: *Emma Silver Mining Co v Grant* (1879) 11 Ch D 918; and *Lydney and Wigpool Iron Ore Co v Bird* (1886) 33 Ch D 85. The courts have not generally permitted account of profits where rescission has not been available: *Re Ambrose Lake Tin Co* (1880) 14 Ch D 390; *Lady Forrest (Murchison) Gold Mine* [1901] 1 Ch 582; *Jacobus Marler Estates v Marler* (1913) 85 LJPC 167. In such cases, it will not be open to the company to require the promoter to account for the profits made from the transaction, on the basis that it would not be possible to quantify the profit or commission made by the promoter: *Re Cape Breton Co* (1885) 29 Ch D 795; and *Ladywell Mining Co v Brookes* (1887) 35 Ch D 400.

1.31 The courts have shown some reluctance to value the asset in question, and then require the promoter to account for profits, on the basis that this would be tantamount to re-writing the contract between the parties: *Re Cape Breton* (1885) 29 Ch D 795.

If it could be shown that the original purchase of the asset by the promoter was in fact for the company itself, the courts may in equity allow for account of profits, based on the initial purchase by the promoter of the asset and resale to the company: *Omnium Electric Palaces v Baines* [1914] 2 Ch 322 per Sargant J.

Action for misrepresentation

1.32 It may be possible to bring an action against the promoter for misrepresentation under the Misrepresentation Act 1967 and claim damages. It must be shown that the promoter made a false statement of fact, which induced others to enter into the contract. There is a defence if the promoter establishes that he had reasonable grounds to believe and did believe up to the time of making the contract, that the facts that were represented were true in the circumstances. The Misrepresentation Act 1967 allows for damages instead of rescission.

1.33 Under the Misrepresentation Act 1967, s 3, any exclusion clause in connection with the misrepresentation must satisfy the requirement of reasonableness under s 11(1) of the Unfair Contract Terms Act 1977 (UCTA 1977); and it is for those claiming that the term satisfies that requirement to show that it does. UCTA 1977, s 11(1) states that 'the term shall have been a fair and reasonable one to be included having regard to the circumstances which were, or ought reasonably to have been, known to or in the contemplation of the parties when the contract was made'.

Pre-incorporation contracts

1.34 As part of their functional and operational duties in establishing the company, promoters will also be dealing with third parties by, for example, entering into contracts, before the company is established. Such contracts may be of a diverse nature, but include contracts for leasing office premises, buildings, ordering goods or equipment, or entering into contracts for the provision of services and utilities. The issue which the courts have addressed is to identify who should be liable in the event the promoter defaults or is in breach of his obligations under the contract with a third party. The issue of liability is significant, particularly where the company simply has no existence at the time the contracts are entered into by the promoter. This is because a company only acquires a separate legal personality upon incorporation – once the certificate of incorporation has been issued by the Registrar of Companies at Companies House.

In the absence of a company's legal existence, the courts have sought to impose personal liability on the promoter. This has been achieved through the application of various legal devices, including the use of contractual and agency principles.

Common law position

1.35 Under the contractual principles in English law, a contract can only be entered into with a person, entity or organisation that is in existence. A party cannot therefore contract with a non-existent being: *Rover International Ltd v Cannon Film Sales Ltd* (No 3) [1987] BCLC 540 per Harman J: 'If somebody does not exist, he cannot contract'.

1.36 Where a promoter signs a contract 'for and on behalf of a company' before the company has been established, the court is likely to impute personal liability to the promoter. However, where a promoter signs in the potential company's name with his name as a director, the courts may not impute personal liability on the basis there was no contract in existence. These contrasting principles are illustrated in *Kelner* and *Newborne* cases. In *Kelner v Baxter* (1866) LR 2 CP 174, the promoters were personally liable on the contract entered into by them.In *Newborne v Sensolid (GB) Ltd* [1953] 1 All ER 708, the contract was entered into by the company which was thereby liable.

1.37 Once the company is formed, it will be considered as a third party to the contract between the promoter and another person, entity or organisation, and will not be able to obtain any benefits from such contract; nor can any obligations be imposed on the company on the basis of privity of contract. Further, the Contracts (Rights of Third Parties) Act 1999 has no application to pre-incorporation contracts, and only allows enforcement by third parties where the contractual term provides some benefit being conferred to the unformed company. For some consideration, the parties could agree that once the company is formed, it will have the option of entering into a contract with the third party on terms agreed in advance.The 1999 Act only applies in respect of enforcement of rights by a third party and is not concerned with the imposition of obligations.

1.38 An agent or promoter who has not contracted personally may be liable to the other party to the contract in damages for a breach of warranty of authority: *Collen v Wright* (1857) 8 E & B 647.The personal liability arises on the basis that the promoter or agent impliedly warrants to the other party to the contract that an entity exists, when in fact it has no existence: *McRae v Commonwealth Disposals Commission* (1950) 84 CLR 377; and *Black v Smallwood* [1966] ALR 744.

The position under CA 2006

1.39 Section 51 of CA 2006 states that a contract which purports to be made by or on behalf of a company at a time when the company has not been formed has effect, subject to any agreement to the contrary, as one made with the person purporting to act for the company or as agent for it, and he is personally liable on the contract accordingly.

The promoters can therefore be personally liable on the contract entered into: *Phonogram Ltd v Lane* [1982] QB 938.

1.40 Subsequent cases have considered the scope of CA 2006, s 51.

In *Oshkosh B'Ghosh Inc v Dan Marbel Inc* [1989] BCLC 507, the company was carrying on business under a name other than its registered name.This was because the company was purchased off-the-shelf and its change of name did not take effect until later on when the altered name was entered at Companies House. The issue was whether a director of the company was liable for the debts of the company.The Court of Appeal held that there was no basis for finding the defendant liable under CA 2006, s 51, as the company had been duly formed in 1979, before the contracts with the claimant had been entered into, and the issue of a new certificate on the alteration of the company's name could not be taken to re-form or reincorporate the company.

Section 51 does not apply to a company that has been previously struck off: *Cotronic (UK) Ltd v Dezonie* [1991] BCLC 721.

1.41 Section 51 of CA 2006 has no application where the company had already been established, but referred to by an incorrect name: *Badgerhill Properties Ltd v Cottrell* [1991] BCLC 805.

1.42 In *Hellmuth, Obata & Kassabaum Incorporated, T/a HOK Sport v King* [2000] All ER 1394, the court was required to consider the liability of a person purporting to act as agent for an unformed company by signing a letter of intent on behalf of such company. The court decided that although no contractual document had ever been signed by the parties, however, sufficient agreement had been reached between them as to the terms of the proposed contract so as to impose contractual obligations. The defendant had acted on behalf of the intended joint venture company during the negotiations. Accordingly, the defendant was personally liable under CA 2006, s 51 for sums due under the agreement to the claimant. Further, for the purposes of s 51, individuals who purported to act on behalf of an unincorporated company could be liable under that section for quasi-contractual obligations upon that company: *British Steel Corporation v Cleveland Bridge & Engineering Co Ltd* [1984] 1 All ER 504.

In some situations, general common law principles may apply for pre-incorporation contract formation: *Braymist Ltd v Wise Finance Co Ltd* [2002] 1 BCLC 415. See too: *Gibbons v Doherty* [2013] IEHC 109.

Checklist

1.43 *The following checklist addresses the essential issues for consideration, where promoters propose to establish a company and engage in the preliminary formalities for its establishment, including contractual dealings with third parties and liability aspects before incorporation.*

No	Issue	Reference
1	Who is establishing the company?	
2	Are the promoters involved in the company formation?	
3	What are the intentions of the promoters in setting up the company?	
4	What are the objects of the company? A company must not be set up for an unlawful purpose.	CA 2006, s 31 CA 2006, s 7(2)
5	Will the promoters become the directors and shareholders in the company?	
6	What will be the duties and responsibilities of the promoters?	Common law
7	Will promoters be entering into any contracts with third parties before the company is established?	CA 2006, s 51 and the common law
8	Will promoters be contracting with third parties on behalf of an unformed company, or in their own name? Consider personal liability aspects.	CA 2006, s 51 and *Kelner v Baxter* (1886) LR 2 C P 174; and *Newborne v Sensolid (Great Britain) Limited* [1954] 1 QB 45
9	Will the contract with the third parties provide for a release of liability for the promoter by the third party?	Terms of novation agreement
10	Once the company has been established, will the promoters novate any pre-incorporation contracts? Will the promoters:	Terms of novation agreement

No	Issue		Reference
	(a)	To declare any interests to the company's board of directors if they are appointed directors?	CA 2006, ss 177 and 182
	(b)	To declare any "secret" profits to the company's board of directors if they are appointed directors?	CA 2006, s 176
11	Are the promoters required to account to the company for any profits made?		

2 Corporate personality

Introduction

2.1 This chapter addresses the following aspects:

- defining 'corporate personality', and the circumstances in which the company is treated as a distinct legal entity from its shareholders;
- the landmark decision in *Salomon v A Salomon & Co Ltd* with legal and practical implications;
- the relationship between a controlling shareholder and his employment connection with the company;
- application of the corporate personality principle to family companies and matrimonial disputes, with reference to *Prest v Petrodel Resources Ltd* [2013] All ER 90; and
- the circumstances in which the courts will pierce or lift the corporate veil to impose liability on the shareholders or directors, having regard to *VTB Capital plc v Nutritek International* [2013] 1 BCLC 179*;* and *Prest v Petrodel Resources.*

Corporate personality

2.2 In English company law, the concept of 'separate legal personality' or 'corporate personality' signifies that a company is distinct from its shareholders. The company has the liability and not the shareholders. The company has a legal but not a physical existence. It is neither an agent nor a trustee for its shareholders. A company acquires certain attributes upon incorporation. It is treated as a 'person' in its own right.

Upon incorporation, the company has a unique identity. It has a certificate of incorporation with its distinct registration number, which distinguishes it from other corporate entities. The certificate signifies the company's incorporation.

The courts have, on occasions, resorted to anthropomorphic references to companies who are likened to a human being. In such situations, a company may be compared to a natural person. In *HL Bolton (Engineering) Co Ltd v TJ Graham & Sons Ltd* [1957] 1 QB 159 at p 172, Denning LJ (as he was then) stated: 'A company may in many ways be likened to a human being. It has a brain and a nerve centre which controls what it does. It also has hands which hold the tools and act in accordance with directions from the centre.'

In *Jetivia SA v Bilta (UK) Ltd* [2015] UKSC 23, however, the Supreme Court disapproved of such anthropomorphic references, as unhelpful in identifying the concept of corporate personality.

A company cannot act on its own and requires others for its functioning and operation. The nature of the corporation was also considered in *Lennard's Carrying Co Ltd v Asiatic Petroleum Co Ltd* [1915] AC 705, where the House of Lords decided that liability could be imposed on corporations for the directors' acts as they were the controlling minds within the corporation. The legal fiction of the corporation was set out by Viscount Haldane when he stated:

> '… a corporation is an abstraction. It has no mind of its own any more than it has a body of its own; its active and directing will must consequently be sought in the person of somebody who for some purposes may be called an agent, but who is really the directing mind and will of the corporation, the very ego and centre of the personality of the corporation.

A company can only act through others to carry out its intentions: *Welton v Saffrey* [1897] AC 299; *Gas Lighting Improvement Co Ltd v Commissioners of Inland Revenue* [1923] AC 723.

In *Tesco Supermarkets Ltd v Nattrass* [1972] AC 153, Lord Reid considered the nature of the personality which by a fiction, the law attributed to a corporation. Lord Reid stated:

> 'A living person has a mind which can have knowledge or intention or be negligent and he has hands to carry out his intentions. A corporation has none of these: it must act through living persons, though not always one or the same person. Then the person who acts is not speaking or acting for the company. He is acting as the company and his mind which directs his acts is the mind of the company. There is no question of the company being vicariously liable. He is not acting as a servant, representative, agent or delegate. He is an embodiment of the company or, one could say, he hears and speaks through the persona of the company, within his appropriate sphere, and his mind is the mind of the company. If it is a guilt mind then that guilt is the guilt of the company.'

However, the Supreme Court in *Bilta* [2015] stated that knowledge of a breach of duty and wrongdoing by a director, was not to be attributed to the company, even if the director was the sole shareholder or member, but this depended upon the context of the situation in which action against directors arose, such as an agency relation or where there was a breach of duty by directors. See further **9.77**.

The *Salomon* case

From rags to riches

2.3 The principles legitimising one-man companies and establishing that the company was not an agent for its shareholders were established in *Salomon v Salomon & Co Ltd* [1897] AC 22.

2.4 Aron Salomon set up a sole trader as a leather merchant, hide factor, wholesale and export shoe manufacturer in the East End of London, in Whitechapel High Street. With very little capital, he built up extensive warehouses and a large establishment. Aron's business was inextricably associated with and revolved around his family. He and his wife had a family of five sons and one daughter. Four of the sons were working with him in the business, but they were dissatisfied with their position as employees of the business. They wanted a share of the business The sons kept pressing their father to give them a share of the business. According to Aron, 'they troubled me, all the while'. He agreed to give his family a share of the business. Although a promoter of the company at that time, Aron still maintained control and established the terms upon which the company would be established. In July 1892, he converted his business into a limited liability company, and named it "A Salomon & Co Ltd".

2.5 All the formalities under the Companies Act 1862 (at that time) for establishing Aron's limited liability company were complied with; the Act, *inter alia*, required seven members to establish a company. The company had a memorandum of association with a capital of £40,000 in 40,000 shares of £1 each. The subscribers to the memorandum were Aron, his wife and five of his children. One share each was allotted to his four sons and one each for his wife and daughter. Aron received 20,000 shares in the company. The Salomon family convened a meeting and appointed Aron and his two elder sons as the company's directors. The company also had articles of association setting out the procedure for nominating the first directors with the usual powers given to directors including a borrowing power prohibiting directors from exceeding £10,000. When Aron's business was transferred to the company on 1 June 1892, the consideration paid for the transfer was £39,000 – 'a sum which represented the sanguine expectations of a fond owner rather than anything that can be called a business-like or reasonable estimate of value' per Lord Macnaghten in *Salomon v Salomon & Co Ltd* [1897] AC 22. The consideration was paid as follows: (i) £20,000 of income received from the business was paid to Aron who then returned this to the company in exchange for fully-paid shares; (ii) As part payment, Aron took up £10,000 in debentures in the company; (iii) the balance (with the exception of £1,000 which Aron seemed to have retained), went to discharge the debts and liabilities of the business at the time of the transfer. As a result, Aron received £1,000 for his business, £10,000 in debentures. and half of the nominal capital of the company in fully paid shares.

Hard times

2.6 The company did not trade for long. It fell upon 'evil days'. Shortly after the company was established, there was a period of economic recession. Aron's warehouses became full of unsaleable stock. He and his wife tried desperately to save the company's business from recession and collapse. They lent the company money to try and ensure its survival. During the early part of 1893, in an effort to revive the collapsing business, Aron borrowed £5,000 from a creditor, Edmund Broderip, who charged the company 10% interest. In order to obtain security for this loan to the company, the £10,000 worth of debentures (which Aron had received when the business was converted into a company) to pay off the debts were transferred to Broderip at 8% interest. The company struggled to pay off its debts and Broderip's interest was not paid when it was due, along with other business expenses. Broderip immediately took proceedings and appointed a receiver. The company was ultimately forced into liquidation. It was compulsorily wound up in October 1893. An order for the sale of its assets was granted in March 1894.

House of Lords: legitimisation of one-man companies

2.7 The House of Lords held that a one-man company was a legitimate creation under the Companies Act, provided it was validly formed and complied with all the formalities required under the Act. Further, the company was neither an agent nor a trustee for its shareholders. The House of Lords accepted that the Companies Act allowed for the establishment of a 'one-man company', even though control was practically vested in one person, who was the company's controlling shareholder.

2.8 Lord Halsbury stated that once a company had been legally incorporated, it must be treated like any other independent person with rights and liabilities: see too *Prest v Petrodel Resources Ltd* [2013] All ER 90. The motives of those who took part in the promotion of the company were irrelevant in addressing those rights and liabilities.

2.9 According to Lord Macnaghten, provided all the formalities of the Companies Act were complied with, it did not matter whether the shareholders were strangers or were related to each other. The Companies Act did not require, as a condition for establishing a company, that the shareholders should be independent or unconnected, or that any one of them should take a substantial interest in the company, or that they should have a mind or will of their own, or that there should be a balance of power in the company's constitution. When all the formalities for setting up a company had been complied with, the company was thereafter capable of exercising all the functions of an incorporated company with a separate personality. A company attained maturity on its birth. There was no period of minority nor an interval of incapacity. The company was at law a different person from the company's shareholders, and though it may be that after incorporation, the business was precisely the same as it was before, the same persons were managers and the same hands received the profits, the company was not at law the agent of the subscribers or trustees for them. Nor were the subscribers as members liable, in any shape or form, except to the extent and manner provided by the Companies Act.

The *Salomon* decision legitimised the establishment of one-man companies under the Companies Act. It did not matter whether the shareholders were independent of one another, related or 'mere dummies' or nominees for the controlling shareholders. It did not matter that the shareholders were family members. It did not matter that the majority of the shareholders had only a very minority stake in the company. Providing all the formalities for establishing a company were complied with, a one-man company was a valid legal vehicle under the Companies Act.

One-man company contracting with its employee: the controlling shareholder concept

2.10 Following the *Salomon* decision, an issue which has arisen in the context of company and employment law has been whether a one-man company can validly enter into an employment relationship with its employee, such that the employee is able to obtain the benefits and advantages of employment protection legislation or other legislation (such as insurance). This would only be possible if the person employed by the one-man company, could be treated as an 'employee' or a 'worker' within the meaning of the employment law legislation.

It has been held in *Lee v Lee's Air Farming Ltd* [1960] 3 All ER 420, that a company could validly enter into a contract with its sole employee, as the company and employee are distinct persons at law. *Lee's* case is authority for two propositions: first, that an individual who owned all or almost all of the shares in the company and was its sole director with total dominion over the company, could also be employed by the company under a contract of service. Second, the issue as to whether the 'control' condition had been satisfied was irrelevant in the creation of the contract of employment. The company and the employee were not in law the same person. They were distinct in their own right. It was the company that exercised the relevant control.

The controlling shareholder concept and English employment legislation

2.11 The relationship between company law and employment law can be seen in the context of a controlling shareholder, who has a contract of employment with the company. The issue arises whether such a person is an employee of the company for the purposes of protections and rights under the English employment law legislation.

The courts usually consider as a starting point, the genuineness of the contract of employment between the employer and employee, having regard to all facts. If no sham or illegality is involved, the next stage is to demonstrate that the contract was one of employment, as opposed to a contract for services.

In *Secretary of State for Business, Enterprise and Regulatory Reform v Neufeld and Howe* [2009] EWCA Civ 280, the Court of Appeal held that having regard to all the facts and circumstances (including genuineness of contract between the company and employee; absence of sham; employer and employee/worker relationship), a controlling shareholder could be an employee of the company.

Company can own property

2.12 The independent legal personality of the company, means that the company can own property as a natural person. The property belongs to the company and not its shareholders. The company can acquire or dispose of property in its own name. Generally, the shareholders have no interest in the company's property: *Macaura v Northern Assurance Co Ltd* [1925] All ER Rep 51. See too *Daimler Co Ltd v Continental Tyre and Rubber Co (Great Britain) Ltd* [1916] 2 AC 307.

Company can sue and be sued

2.13 A company can sue its own directors and officers as well as third parties. This includes the company's capacity to sue for libel or slander, in respect of loss of business reputation: *South Hetton Coal Co v North-Eastern News Association* [1894] 1 QB 133; and *D & L Caterers v D'Ajou* [1945] KB 364.

As the company is a separate legal entity, the legal rights belong to the company and not to its shareholders. Shareholders have separate rights of action, which include an action for unfair prejudicial conduct (CA 2006, s 994), or pursuing a derivative claim (Part 11 CA 2006).

2.14 Generally, a company can also be vicariously liable for the torts committed by its agents in the course of their employment or business on the company's behalf. This includes negligence or fraudulent misrepresentation: *Citizen's Life Assurance Co Ltd v Brown* [1904] AC 423; *Lister v Hesley Hall Ltd* [2002] 1 AC 215. See, however, two Supreme Court cases setting out the tests for vicarious liability to apply: *Barclays Bank plc v Various Claimants* [2020] UKSC 13; and *Morrison Supermarkets plc v Various Claimants* [2020] UKSC 12.

In general, a company can be prosecuted for its criminal acts, such as breaches of health and safety at the workplace, namely the Health and Safety at Work etc Act 1974; conspiracy to defraud (*R v ICR Haulage Ltd* [1944] KB 551) or attempted fraud (*Purcell Meats (Scotland) Ltd v McLeod* 1987 SLT 528). Although the acts are performed by the company's agents such as its directors and officers, their acts are the acts of the company. However, there are limitations on the criminal sanctions that the court may impose on the company. Although a company may be fined for its criminal acts, it cannot be imprisoned. It cannot also be prosecuted for perjury or indecent conduct: *Dean v John Menzies (Holdings) Ltd* 1981 SLT 50; and *Chuter v Freeth & Pocock Ltd* [1911] 2 KB 832. See too the impact on companies of the Corporate Manslaughter and Corporate Homicide Act 2007.

Perpetual succession

2.15 A company has the ability to outlive its directors and shareholders. It may be established for a fixed term or indefinitely. Unlike natural persons, a company does not suffer from any incapacitation, such as mental illness or other physical defects. It is omnipresent. However, its existence may come to an end upon its dissolution on a winding up – whether on a voluntary or compulsory winding up. As long ago as 1937, Greer LJ in *Stepney Corporation v Osofsky* [1937] 3 All ER 289 stated that the corporation had 'no soul to be saved or body to be kicked'

Statutory effects of incorporation

2.16 The CA 2006, s 16 provides that upon registration, the following are the effects of incorporation:

- The subscribers to the memorandum, together with such other persons as may from time to time become members of the company, are a body corporate by the name stated in the certificate of incorporation: CA 2006, s 16(2).
- That body corporate is capable of exercising all the functions of an incorporated company: CA 2006, s 16(3).
- The status and registered office of the company are as stated in, or in connection with, the application for registration: CA 2006, s 16(4).
- In the case of a company having a share capital, the subscribers to the memorandum become holders of the shares specified in the statement of capital and initial shareholdings: CA 2006, s 16(5).
- The persons named in the statement of proposed officers:

  (a) as director, or

  (b) as secretary or joint secretary of the company,

  are deemed to have been appointed to that office: CA 2006, s 16(6).

Piercing the corporate veil

2.17 This section considers the concept of piercing the corporate veil. It then proceeds to examine the circumstances where the courts have pierced the corporate veil, and the modern judicial approaches towards the concept.

Defining the concept

2.18 On occasions, the courts have ignored the separate personality of the company. This has been achieved by piercing or lifting the veil of incorporation, to identify issues such as, for example, those who evade their legal obligations and responsibilities;

or those who may conceal their personal assets from third parties, because such assets are held by the company; those who are the real controllers of the company; or for what purposes or motives the company was formed; or the extent of corporate abuse being perpetrated, and the identity of the persons engaged in the corporate abuse or impropriety. In other situations, the courts have pierced the corporate veil to confer certain benefits and advantages to the company or group of companies. The term 'piercing the corporate veil' has traditionally been used to describe exceptions to the corporate personality concept. In this situation, the courts will look behind the company, to ascertain the intention and motives of the directors or shareholders, in respect of particular transactions or activities where wrongdoing or abuse is taking place.

2.19 In *Prest v Petrodel Resources Ltd* [2013] All ER 90, the Supreme Court stated that the term 'piercing the corporate veil' (which was the preferred term as opposed to 'lifting the corporate veil'), referred to disregarding the separate legal personality of the company. The doctrine was to be used as a last resort. There were limited circumstances for the operation of this doctrine to apply.

2.20 According to the Supreme Court in *Prest v Petrodel Resources Ltd* [2013] All ER 90, the starting point for analysis of piercing the veil was to consider the general proposition that subject to very limited circumstances (most of which were statutory), a company was a legal entity distinct from its shareholders. It had rights and liabilities of its own which were distinct from those of its shareholders. Its property was its own, and not that of its shareholders: *Salomon v A Salomon and Co Ltd* [1897] AC 22; *Macaura v Northern Assurance Co Ltd* [1925] AC 619; *Lonrho Ltd v Shell Petroleum Co Ltd* [1980] 1 WLR 627. In this regard, the Supreme Court reinforced the separate legal personality of the company which was distinct from its shareholders.

The Supreme Court decided that there was a principle of English law which enabled a court in very limited circumstances to pierce the corporate veil. It applied when a person was under an existing legal obligation or liability, or subject to an existing legal restriction which he deliberately evaded, or whose enforcement he deliberately frustrated by interposing a company under his control. The court may then pierce the corporate veil, but only for the purpose of depriving the company or its controller of the advantage which they would otherwise have obtained by the company's separate legal personality. The principle should be used as a last resort. In most cases, the facts necessary to establish this would disclose a legal relationship between the company and its controller giving rise to legal or equitable rights of the controller over the company's property, thus making it unnecessary to pierce the veil. In these cases, there was no public policy imperative justifying piercing the corporate veil. However, there was recognition of a small residual category of cases where the abuse of the corporate veil to evade or frustrate the law could be addressed only by disregarding the legal personality of the company was consistent with authority and long-standing principles of legal policy. The principle had no application in *Prest*, because the husband's actions did not evade or frustrate any legal obligation to his wife, nor was he concealing or evading the law in relation to the distribution of assets of the marriage upon its dissolution.

Lord Sumption stated that the corporate veil may be pierced only to prevent the abuse of corporate legal personality. It may be an abuse of the separate legal personality of a company to use it to evade the law or to frustrate its enforcement. However, it was not an abuse to cause a legal liability to be incurred in the first place. It was not an abuse to rely upon the fact that a liability was not the controllers because it was the company's.

2.21 There are two distinct principles which were recognised in *Prest* as associated with piercing the corporate veil: the 'concealment' and the 'evasion' principles.

The 'concealment' principle does not involve piercing the veil. It was concerned with the interposition of a company or several companies so as to conceal the identity of the real actors. However, this would not deter the courts from identifying them, assuming that their identity was legally relevant. In such cases, the court was not disregarding the 'facade', but only looking behind it to discover the facts which the corporate structure was concealing.

Under the 'evasion' principle, the court may disregard the corporate veil if there is a legal right against the person in control of it which existed independently of the person's involvement, and a company was interposed so that the separate legal personality of the company will defeat the right or frustrate its enforcement. According to Lord Sumption, some cases may fall into both the concealment and evasion principles, and in some circumstances, the difference between them may be critical. Cases such as *Gilford Motor Co Ltd v Horne* [1933] Ch 935 and *Jones v Lipman* [1962] 1 All ER 442 displayed characteristics of the evasion principle. *Gencor ACP Ltd v Dalby* [2000] 2 BCLC 734 and *Trustor AB v Smallbone (No 2)* [2001] 3 All ER 987, represented the concealment principle. These considerations reflected the broader principle that the corporate veil may be pierced only to prevent the abuse of corporate legal personality. It may be an abuse of the separate legal personality of a company to use it to evade the law or to frustrate its enforcement. It was not an abuse to cause a legal liability to be incurred by the company in the first place. It was not an abuse to rely upon the fact that a liability was not the controller's but the company's.

2.22 Lord Sumption concluded that there was a limited principle of English law which applied when a person was under an existing legal obligation or liability subject to an existing legal restriction, which he deliberately evaded or whose enforcement he deliberately frustrated by interposing a company under his control. The court may then pierce the corporate veil for the purpose, and only for the purpose, of depriving the company or its controller of the advantage that they would otherwise have obtained by the company's separate legal personality. The principle was properly described as a limited one, because in almost every case where the test was satisfied, the facts would in practice disclose a legal relationship between the company and its controller which would make it unnecessary to pierce the corporate veil.

See too *Persad v Singh* (Privy Council decision) [2017] UKPC 32.

2.23 Following the *Prest* decision, in M v M [2013] All ER 133, King J held that the court could order assets in the name of the company to be transferred to the other spouse, on the basis that the assets were held by the husband by way of a resulting trust. The court did not pierce the corporate veil to reach this result.

However, see *Smith v Bottomley* [2013] EWCA Civ 953.

2.24 In *Pennyfeathers Ltd v Pennyfeathers Property Co Ltd* [2013] EWHC 3530 (Ch), based on the concealment principle established in *Prest*, directors were liable for breaches of their fiduciary duties towards the company; and it was not appropriate to apply the evasion principle.

2.25 The Supreme Court in *Hurstwood Properties v Rossendale Borough Council* [2021] UKSC 16, inter alia, considered piercing the corporate veil. The court doubted the coherence of the 'evasion' principle as applied in *Prest*, and held that piercing the corporate veil did not apply on the facts of the case. This was because on the facts the rates liability accrued day by day. Thus, before the lease was granted, the respondent companies were liable for any accrued rates, and once the lease was granted, only the SPV was liable. Accordingly, the interposition of the SPV was not itself an abuse of corporate personality, as the SPV did not evade enforcement of a legal obligation. The *Hurstwood* case suggests that the Supreme Court could in the future decline to follow the 'evasion' principle in *Prest* and formulate a simple, rational test for the remnants of the piercing the corporate veil principle.

Attribution of liability to a non-contracting party

2.26 The Supreme Court has considered the position of whether lifting the corporate veil could be extended to attribute liability to a non-contracting party. In *VTB Capital plc v Nutritek International Corp* [2013] 1 BCLC 179, the court held that there was no justification for extending the principle of piercing the corporate veil to impose liability on a non-contracting party.

According to Lord Neuberger, there is a case for retaining the principle of piercing the corporate veil in certain circumstances 'in order to defeat injustice', though it is not clear what aspects of 'injustice' are being referred to that would allow for such piercing. It resonates to some extent with cases that have considered piercing the corporate veil in the interests of justice. This suggests a broader category of situations where the court may pierce the corporate veil.

Piercing the veil by legislation

Misfeasance

2.27 Section 212 of the Insolvency Act 1986 (IA 1986) is concerned with misfeasance, and only has application in the course of a company's winding up. It applies to an officer of the company, liquidator, or any other person who has been concerned or has taken part in the promotion, formation or management of the company: IA 1986, s 212(1). The offences apply to misapplication or retention or becoming accountable for any money or other property of the company, any misfeasance or breach of any fiduciary or other duty in relation to the company. On the application of a liquidator or of any creditor or contributory, the court may look into the conduct of the person alleged to be involved in misfeasance, and can compel him to repay, restore or account for the money or property or any part of it with interest at such rate as the court thinks just; or to contribute such sum to the company's assets by way of compensation in respect of the misfeasance or breach of the fiduciary or other duty as the court thinks just: IA 2006, s 212(3).

Fraudulent trading

2.28 Section 213 of the IA 1986 is concerned with fraudulent trading. It applies where in the course of a company's winding up, it appears that any business of the company has been carried on with intent to defraud the company's creditors or creditors of any other person, or for any other fraudulent purpose: IA 1986, s 213(1). On the application of the liquidator, the court may declare that any persons who were knowingly parties to the carrying on of the business are liable to make such contribution (if any) to the company's assets as the court thinks proper: IA 1986, s 213(2). The term 'intent' is used in the sense that a person must have been taken to intend the natural or foreseen consequences of his act: see Oliver J in *Re Murray-Watson Ltd* (unreported, 6 April 1977). Section 213 of the IA 1986 requires an intention on the part of the person to defraud creditors. In *Re Patrick & Lyon Ltd* [1933] Ch 786 at 790–791, the court stated that this required actual dishonesty which involved according to current notions of fair trading among commercial men 'real moral blame'. An intention to defraud creditors may be demonstrated where the company carries on business with no prospect of paying off its debts *Re William C Leitch Bros Ltd* [1932] 2 Ch 71. It is sufficient if only one creditor is defrauded.

2.29 The Companies Act 2006 creates a criminal offence of fraudulent trading, but there is no requirement for fraudulent trading to have been conducted in the course of a company's winding up. Section 993 of the Companies Act 2006 states that, if any business of a company is carried on with intent to defraud the company's creditors or creditors of any other persons or for any fraudulent purpose, then every person who was knowingly a party to the carrying on of the business in that manner is liable to imprisonment or a fine or both. This applies whether or not the company is in the course of being wound up. On conviction on indictment, the imprisonment term must not exceed ten years, or a fine can be imposed, or both: CA 2006, s 993(3)(a). In *R v Grantham* [1984] BCLC 270, the Court of Appeal stated that a person could be convicted of fraudulent trading, if he took part in the management of the company's affairs, and obtained credit for the company, knowing that there was no prospect of paying the debt when it became due or shortly thereafter. See too *Re Augustus Barnett & Son Ltd* [1986] BCLC 170.

Wrongful trading

2.30 Section 214 of the IA 1986 is concerned with wrongful trading. It applies where some time before commencement of the winding up, the person against whom the order is sought knew or ought to have concluded that there was no reasonable prospect that the company would avoid going into insolvent liquidation. The facts which a director of a company ought to know or ascertain, the conclusions which he ought to reach and the steps which he ought to take are those which would be known or ascertained or reached or taken by a reasonably diligent person having both: (a) the general knowledge, skill and experience that may reasonably be expected for a person carrying out the same functions as are carried out by that director in relation to the company; and (b) the general knowledge, skill and experience that the director has. The company would be in an insolvent liquidation if there are insufficient assets for payment of the company's debts and other liabilities and expenses of winding up. The liquidator can apply to the court for an order that the person is liable to make such contribution (if any) to the company's assets as the court thinks proper. There is a defence for the person against whom wrongful trading is alleged, to show that he took every step with a view to minimising the potential loss to the company's creditors as he ought to have taken.

Checklist

2.31 *This checklist sets out the current law on piercing the corporate veil and practical implications based on the decisions in VTB Capital plc v Nutritek International Corp [2013]*

1 BCLC 179 and Prest v Petrodel Resources Ltd [2013] All ER 90, particularly in identifying circumstances when the courts will pierce the corporate veil to impose liability, including the consequences of a company's separate legal personality.

No	Issue	Reference
1	The starting position for establishing the separate legal personality of a company is the Companies Act 2006. A company is a legal entity distinct from its shareholders.	CA 2006, ss 1–5 and 16
2	*Salomon v A Salomon and Co Ltd* legitimised the establishment of 'one-man' companies provided there is compliance with the Companies Acts on registration formalities.	[1897] AC 22
3	The effect of a separate legal personality is that a company has rights and liabilities of its own; it can sue and be sued; it can enter into contracts.	CA 2006, s 16
4	The separate legal personality also applies to a sole owner and controller of a company, who can contract with his company as an employee.	*Macaura v Northern Assurance Co Ltd* [1925] AC 619; *Lee v Lee's Air Farming Limited* [1960] 3 All ER 420
5	The term 'piercing the corporate veil' means disregarding the separate personality of the company.	*Petrodel Resources Ltd v Prest* [2013] 1 BCLC 30
6	The court may be justified in piercing the corporate veil, if the company's separate legal personality is being abused for the purpose of some relevant wrongdoing.	*Petrodel Resources Ltd* v Prest [2013] 1 BCLC 30
8	A distinction can be made between two principles in determining when piercing the corporate veil applies: the 'concealment principle' and the 'evasion principle'. The concealment principle does not involve the application of piercing the corporate veil. Under this principle, the company is used to conceal the real actors in the company, and the courts can look to see who these persons are to discover the facts which the corporate structure is concealing. The evasion principle allows the court to disregard the corporate veil. This will apply if there is a legal right against the person in control of it, which exists independently of the company's involvement, and a company is interposed, so that the separate legal personality of the company will defeat the right or frustrate its enforcement. There is recent Supreme Court dicta to suggest that there are some doubts about application of the "evasion" principle as applied in *Prest* to piercing the veil concept.	See *Jones v Lipman* [1962] 1 WLR 832; *Gencor ACP Ltd v Dalby* [2000] 2 BCLC 734; and *Trustor AB v Smallbone (No 2)* [2001] 1 WLR 1177 on the concealment principle See *Gilford Motor Co Ltd v Horne* [1933] Ch 935 on application of the evasion principle *Hurstwood Properties v Rossendale Borough Council* [2021] UKSC 16
9	The corporate veil may not be pierced to impose liability on a non-contracting party.	*VTB Capital plc v Nutritek International Corp* [2013] 1 BCLC 179

3 Formation and registration of a company

Introduction

3.1 The aim of this chapter is to consider the following issues:

- the differences between 'off-the-shelf' companies and 'tailor-made' companies;
- how to establish a private company limited by shares or a public limited company;
- how a company can change its registered address;
- the forms and documents required to register a company; and
- checklists for steps and procedures on incorporation.

Off-the-shelf companies

3.2 Off-the-shelf companies are companies that have already been established, but typically remain dormant until purchased.

Some of the issues to consider are:

Costs

3.3 It is often cheaper to purchase an off-the-shelf company than one which is specifically formed for the purpose. Costs differ depending upon the incorporation history of the company, including suitability of the name as this type of company will already have a name as evidenced by the certificate of incorporation. However, this should be balanced against the cost and procedures involved in the event that, for example, the name needs to be changed, capital needs to be increased or the articles of association require amendment.

Name

3.4 The company has already been established with a name and is able to function with immediate effect upon purchase. The purchasers of the company may need to change the company name to one suited for their purposes, provided the name is not similar or identical to one already registered at Companies House. Also, consideration should be given to any common law actions for passing off in the use of the name.

Articles

3.5 The articles of an off-the-shelf company may not be suitable for the company's internal management and administration. Once purchased, the company's articles of association may require changes with the adoption of model articles or amendment to these articles or the company may wish to draft a new set of articles specifically suited for its purposes: see Chapter 4.

Capital

3.6 The capital clause may need to be amended as the share capital may not be adequate for the company. It may need to be increased.

Registered office

3.7 The company's registered office will need to change as the current registered office of the founding shareholders will not suffice. Accordingly, Companies House will need to be notified: see **3.13**.

Directors' residential addresses

3.8 Directors' residential addresses will need to be changed, and if required, for such residential addresses not to be disclosed by the registrar to Companies House.

Tailor-made company

3.9 A tailor-made company is one which is formed in the very initial stages of setting up a new company. Some of the essential features to consider are:

Name

3.10 The name will be selected by promoters provided it is not similar to or identical to one already registered at Companies House. The selected name may be suited to the company's activities. Consideration should also be given to any common law actions for passing off.

Articles

3.11 These can be specifically tailored to the needs and requirements of the promoters, or it may adopt the Model Articles or a combination of such articles and specific articles suited for the company's particular purposes.

Cost

3.12 It will cost more to form a tailor-made company than an off-the-shelf company because of the specific requirements of the company's promoters which require adaptation.

Registered office

3.13 The promoters will select their own registered office for receipt of correspondence and notices. See too The Companies (Address of Registered Office) Regulations 2016 (SI 2016/423).

Capital

3.14 The promoters will determine the amount of capital best suited to the company's operations.

Time

3.15 It will take longer to form a tailor-made company depending upon the complexities involved in the articles of association, and any other factors that may delay the company formation.

Purposes of the company

3.16 A company cannot be formed for an 'unlawful purpose': CA 2006, s 7(2). The term 'unlawful purpose' is not defined. However, case law provides some guidance.

According to *R v Registrar of Joint Stock Companies, ex parte More* [1931] 2 KB 197, an 'unlawful purpose' is one which is contrary to the general law or illegal.

3.17 The court will have regard to the purpose and activity carried on by the company under its name. In *R v Registrar of Companies ex parte Bowen* [1914] 3 KB 1611, an order was made against the registrar on the basis that the activity in question was lawful, and that all the statutory conditions had been complied with by the proposed company and its founders. The registrar was therefore bound to register the company. According to Lord Reading CJ, generally the Registrar also has discretion to refuse to register a company which is not formed for a lawful purpose, which would include names that contained 'scandalous' or 'obscene' words.

3.18 A company cannot be established if it offends the general law. In *R v Registrar of Joint Stock Companies, ex parte More* [1931] 2KB 197, the Court of Appeal upheld the registrar's decision to refuse to register the company, on the basis that the proposed company's activities were not lawful. According to Greer LJ: 'The question is whether the persons proposing to register the company are persons associated for a lawful purpose.' Slesser LJ stated: 'It is clear that a company cannot be formed whose proposed constitution necessarily involves an offence against the general law.'

3.19 The court will have regard to the specific objects of the company to determine whether or not they are lawful: *Bowman v Secular Society* [1917] AC 406. The House of Lords considered that the term 'unlawful purpose' would apply to the object, or activities in which the company is engaged. The activities may be considered illegal or contrary to public interest or law or public morals, either upon incorporation or after the company has been established. The registrar's discretion can be subject to judicial review, even where the company has already been registered at Companies House.

3.20 A company's objects which are considered sexually immoral by the courts may be illegal and for an unlawful purpose: *R v Registrar of Companies, ex parte Attorney General* [1991] BCLC 476. In such situations, the court would grant judicial review of the registrar's decision to register the company, and would strike it off the register if it was registered for unlawful purposes.

Registration documents

3.21 The company must deliver the following documents to the Registrar:

- memorandum of association;
- an application for registration of the company;
- the documents mentioned below; and
- a statement of compliance: CA 2006, s 9(1).

The application for registration must state:

(a) the company's proposed name;

(b) whether the company's registered office is to be situated in England and Wales (or in Wales), in Scotland or in Northern Ireland;

(c) whether the liability of the members of the company is to be limited, and if so whether it is to be limited by shares or by guarantee; and

(d) whether the company is to be a private or a public company: CA 2006, s 9(2).

If the application is delivered by a person as agent to the subscribers to the memorandum of association, it must state his name and address.

3.22 The following additional documents must also be lodged with the Registrar:

(a) in the case of a company that is to have a share capital, a statement of capital and initial shareholdings (see s 10): CA 2006, s 9(4);

(b) in the case of a company that is to be limited by guarantee, a statement of guarantee (see s 11);

(c) a statement of the company's proposed officers (see s 12): CA 2006, s 9(5);

(d) a statement of initial significant control: CA 2006, s 9(4)(d) (as inserted by SBEEA 2015, Sch 3, Pt 2) (see s 12A).The application must also contain

(e) a statement of the intended address of the company's registered office: CA 2006, s 9(5)(a);

(f) a copy of any proposed articles of association (to the extent that these are not supplied by the default application of model articles: see s 20); and

(g) a statement of the type of company it is to be and its intended principal business activities: CA 2006, s 9(5)(c) (as inserted by the SBEEA 2015, s 93).

3.23 The information as to the company's type must be given by reference to the classification scheme prescribed for the purposes of CA 2006, s 5A: CA 2006, s 9(5A) (as inserted by SBEEA 2015, s 93).

The information as to the company's intended principal business activities may be given by reference to one or more categories of any prescribed system of classifying business activities: CA 2006, s 9(5B) (as inserted by the SBEEA 2015, s 93).

The application must be delivered to the Registrar of Companies for England and Wales, if the registered office of the company is to be situated in England and Wales (or in Wales): s.9(6) CA 2006.

Statement of capital and initial shareholdings

3.24 Where a company is to have a share capital, a statement of capital and initial shareholdings is required to be delivered to the registrar. The statement must set the following details: CA 2006, s 10(1):

- the total number of shares of the company to be taken on formation by the subscribers to the memorandum of association;
- the aggregate nominal value of those shares;
- the aggregate amount (if any) to be unpaid on those shares (whether on account of their nominal value or by way of premium); and
- for each class of shares:
  - (i) the prescribed particulars of the rights attached to the shares;
  - (ii) the total number of shares that class;
  - (iii) the aggregate nominal value of the shares that class: CA 2006, s 10(2) (as inserted by SBEEA 2015, Sch 6);
- such information as may be prescribed for the purpose of identifying the subscribers to the memorandum of association: CA 2006, s 10(3).

3.25 With respect to each subscriber to the memorandum of association, the statement must also contain the following details:

- The number, nominal value (of each share) and class of shares to be taken by him on formation. Further, where the subscriber to the memorandum of association is to take shares of more than one class, the information that is required (as to the number, nominal value and class of shares), for each class of shares, CA 2006, s 10(4) and (5).
- The amount to be paid up and the amount of (if any) to be unpaid on each share (whether on account of the nominal value of the share or by way of premium): CA 2006, s 10(3).

Statement of guarantee

3.26 A statement of guarantee is required to be delivered to the registrar for a company limited by guarantee: CA 2006, s 11(1).

The statement must provide such information as may be prescribed for the purposes of identifying the subscribers to the memorandum of association – this includes: the names and addresses of the subscribers to the memorandum of association.

It must also state that each member undertakes that, if the company is wound up while he is a member, or within one year after he ceases to be a member, he will contribute to the assets of the company such amounts as may be required for the following:

(i) payment of the debts and liabilities of the company contracted before he ceases to be a member:

(ii) payment of the costs, charges and expenses of winding up; and

(iii) adjustment of the rights of the contributories among themselves,

not exceeding a specified amount: CA 2006, s.11(3).

Statement of proposed officers

3.27 The statement of proposed officers of the company which is required to be delivered to the registrar must contain the required particulars of the following: CA 2006, s 12(1):

- the person who is, or persons who are, to be the first director or directors of the company;
- where a company is to be a private company, any person who is (or the persons who are) to be the first secretary (or joint secretary) of the company;
- where the company is to be a public company, the person who is (or the persons who are) to be the first secretary (or joint secretaries) of the company).

3.28 References to 'required particulars' are to the required particulars that will be required (or in the absence of an election under ss167A or 279A, would be required) in the company's register of directors and register of directors' residential addresses (see CA 2006, ss 162–166) or, as the case may be for a secretary, its register of secretaries (see CA 2006, ss 277–279): CA 2006, s12(2) (as inserted by the SBEEA 2015, Sch 5, Pt 1).

3.29 The statement must also include a statement by the subscribers to the memorandum of association that each of the persons named as a director, as secretary or as one of the joint secretaries has consented to act in the relevant capacity. If all the partners in a firm are to be joint secretaries, consent may be given by one partner on behalf of all of them: CA 2006, s 12(3) (as inserted by the SBEEA 2015, s 100(2)).

Statement of initial significant control

3.30 The statement of initial significant control required to be delivered to the registrar must:

(a) state whether, on incorporation, there will be anyone who will count for the purposes of s 790M (register of people with significant control over a company) as either a registrable person or a registrable relevant legal entity in relation to the company;

(b) include the required particulars of anyone who will count as such; and

(c) include any other matters that on incorporation will be required (or, in the absence of an election under s 790X, would be required) to be entered in the company's PSC register by virtue of s 790M: CA 2006, s 12A(1) (as inserted by the SBEEA 2015, Sch 3, Pt 2).

3.31 It is not necessary to include under sub-s (1)(b) the date on which someone becomes a registrable person or a registrable relevant legal entity in relation to the company: CA 2006, s 12A(2) (as inserted by the SBEEA 2015, Sch 3, Pt 2).

If the statement includes required particulars of an individual, it must also contain a statement that those particulars are included with the knowledge of that individual: CA 2006, s 12A(3) (as inserted by SBEEA 2015, Sch 3, Pt 2).

'Registrable person', 'registrable relevant legal entity' and 'required particulars' have the meanings given in Pt 21A (see ss 790C and 790K): CA 2006, s 12A(4) (as inserted by the SBEEA 2015, Sch 3, Pt 2).

Statement of compliance

3.32 The statement of compliance required to be delivered to the registrar of companies is a statement that the requirements of CA 2006 as to registration have been complied with: CA 2006, s 13(1).

The registrar may accept the statement of compliance as sufficient evidence of compliance: CA 2006, s 13(2).

Memorandum of Association

3.33 The memorandum of association is not part of the company's constitution. Its function is to provide details of the company's subscribers at the date of the company's formation. It cannot be amended or updated. The memorandum of association must be authenticated by each subscriber, which will provide validity by adding their signatures next to their names: CA 2006, s 8(2). It is therefore a much shorter document. It is a registerable document and must be delivered to the registrar at Companies House for formal registration of a company.

3.34 For companies formed under CA 2006, the memorandum of association will contain limited information evidencing the intention to form the company. For companies formed before CA 2006, the memorandum will contain key constitutional information of a type which will in future be set out in the articles of association, or provided to the registrar in another format. Such material is treated for the future as part of the company's articles of association: CA 2006, s 28.

A company's memorandum must be in a prescribed form as set out under SI 2008/3014.

Articles of Association

3.35 The articles of association are the internal regulations of the company setting out the governance aspects and regulating the relationship between directors and shareholders. Every company must have articles of association. See Chapter 4 on the Company's Constitution.

Registration

3.36 If he is satisfied that the requirements of CA 2006 are complied with, the registrar must register the documents delivered to him: CA 2006, s 14.

Issue of certificate of incorporation

3.37 On the registration of a company, the registrar of companies must provide a certificate that the company is incorporated: CA 2006, s 15(1).

The certificate must state:

(i) the name and registered number of the company;

(ii) the date of its incorporation;

(iii) whether it is a limited or unlimited company, and if it is limited, whether it is limited by guarantee;

(iv) whether it is a private or a public company;

(v) whether the company's registered office is situated in England and Wales: CA 2006, s 15(2).

The certificate must be signed by the registrar or authenticated by the registrar's official seal: CA 2006, s 15(3). Under s 15(4), it is conclusive evidence that requirements of the Act as to registration have been complied with and that the company is duly registered.

3.38 The word 'conclusive' means what it says – the registrar's certificate is conclusive and unassailable and it is not possible to go behind the certificate: *Re CL Nye Ltd* [1971] Ch 442; *Bank of Beirut SAL v HRH Prince Adel El-Hashemite* [2015] EWHC 1451 (Ch). The issue of 'conclusive evidence' of the certificate of incorporation has the effect that all registration formalities for establishing a company have been complied with notwithstanding any issues discovered subsequently, unless exceptions can be found to declare the company a nullity. This could apply where, for example, the company was set up for an unlawful purpose: *Bowman v Secular Society* [1971] AC 406; and *R v Registrar of Companies, ex p Attorney General* [1991] BCLC 476. However, in *Exeter Trust v Screenways Ltd* [1991] BCC 477, the Court of Appeal refused to order rectification of the register of charges at Companies House on the basis that the registrar's certificate was conclusive evidence that the requirements as to registration had been satisfied.

3.39 One issue in this regard has been whether an exception to the conclusiveness of the certificate can apply where there is fraud on the basis of the principle that 'fraud unravels all'? See *HIH Casualty & General Insurance v Chase Manhattan Bank* [2003] UKHL 6. The effect of fraud is to vitiate 'judgments, contracts and all transactions whatsoever': *Lazarus Estates Ltd v Beasley* [1956] 1 QB 702; and *Arab National Bank v The Registrar of Companies* [2005] EWHC 3047 (Ch).

In *Bank of Beirut SAL v HRH Prince Adel El-Hashemite* [2015] EWHC 1451 (Ch), Nugee J was of the view that the principle that fraud unravels all was not a sufficient basis to go behind the conclusiveness of a certificate of incorporation as this would be adding provisos to the provisions on conclusiveness, which were not intended by applicable legislation. This was particularly so as the registrar at Companies House would have acted in good faith in registering a legal entity, even though any mistake by the registrar in registering the entity's documents were procured by fraud by an applicant. The position is less clear where, for example, the registration of documents is effected by the registrar fraudulently and not mistakenly.

Company: registered office and change of address

3.40 Associated with the establishment of a company, is the company's registered office.

A company must at all times have a registered office to which all communications and notices may be addressed: CA 2006, s 86. This is particularly important for service of documents. Under s 1139(1), a document may be served on a company registered under CA 2006 by leaving it at, or sending it by post to, the company's registered office. The term 'registered address' is defined as any address for the time being shown as a current address in relation to that person in the part of the register available for public inspection: CA 2006, s 1139(3).

3.41 A company may change the address of its registered office by giving notice to the registrar: CA 2006, s 87. The change takes effect upon the notice being registered by the registrar, but until the end of the period of 14 days, beginning with the date on which it is registered, a person may validly serve any document on the company at the address properly registered.

3.42 For the purpose of any duty of a company:

- to keep available for inspection at its registered office any register, index, or other documents; or
- to mention the address of its registered office in any document: CA 2006, s 87(3)

a company that has given notice to the registrar of a change in the address of its registered office, may act on the change as from such date, not more than 14 days after the notice is given, as it may determine: CA 2006, s 87(4).

3.43 There is a defence for the company if it cannot perform its duties within the time period to change its registered office address. Where a company unavoidably ceases to perform at its registered office any such duty as is mentioned in s 87(3)(a), in circumstances in which it was not practicable to give prior notice to the registrar of a change in the address of its registered office, but:

(a) resumes performance of that duty at other premises as soon as practicable, and

(b) gives notice accordingly to the registrar of a change in the situation of its registered office within 14 days of doing so,

it is not to be treated as having failed to comply with that duty: CA 2006, s 87(4).

Checklist: incorporation of a private company limited by shares

3.44 *The following checklist sets out the steps and procedures required to establish a private company limited by shares, including the documentation involved both during incorporation and post-incorporation.*

No	*Issue*	*Reference*
1	Who will form the private limited company? It may be formed by a sole subscriber and be a single member company. Any enactment or rule of law applicable to companies formed by two or more persons or having two or more members applies with any necessary modification in relation to a company formed by one person or having only one person as a member.	CA 2006, s 7 CA 2006, s 38
2	The company must not be formed for an unlawful purpose.	CA 2006, s 7(2)
3	Search in index of names for existing company names and choice of name. Ensure that name proposed to be registered is not the same as or identical to one already registered at Companies House. Consider any sensitive names and whether any consent is required from a government/regulatory body or organisation. Take account of any potential passing-off issues. Consider any exemption for company to use 'limited' (Ltd) as part of its name.	CA 2006, Pt 5 and Pt 41
4	Prepare a memorandum of association for subscribers to the company. Ensure signature by subscriber(s) and witnessed by at least one witness.	CA 2006, s 8
5	There must be at least one director.	CA 2006, s 154
6	A company secretary may be appointed but this is not a requirement.	CA 2006, s 270
7	Prepare articles of association. Either specifically tailored or model articles for a company limited by shares or a combination. Ensure articles are signed by subscriber(s) and witnesses.	CA 2006, s 18
8	Prepare statement of capital and initial shareholdings and, if appropriate, a statement of initial significant control.	CA 2006, s 10, CA 2006, s 12A(1)
9	Prepare statement of proposed officers.	CA 2006, s 12
10	Prepare statement of compliance (either by proposed officer or secretary or solicitor) that the requirements of CA 2006 as to registration have been complied with.	CA 2006, s 13
11	Prepare Form IN01 setting out the following details: • company name; • any restrictions on company name; • company type; • registered office address; • articles of association; • proposed officers; • secretary (if required); • statement of capital; • statement of initial shareholdings; • statement of compliance.	Form IN01

No	*Issue*	*Reference*
12	Lodge at Companies House: • Form IN01; • Pay applicable fee for filing; • memorandum of association; • articles of association (unless model articles adopted then no need to lodge as accepted by Companies House by default); • If required Form NE01 (exemption from requirement to use 'Limited'); • Consent of government authority/regulatory body or organisation on name use.	
13	Obtain certificate of incorporation from the registrar which will set out: • registered number; • name of company; • private company limited by shares; • date of incorporation.	CA 2006, s 15
14	Call a board meeting. Prepare letterhead including invoices with company's name, registered address and company registration number.	
15	Notify tax authorities of incorporation for tax purposes.	
16	Appoint company chairman.	
17	Appoint company bankers. Ensure bank mandate prepared with appropriate signatories.	
18	Appoint auditors and accountants.	CA 2006, s 485
19	Fix the company's accounting reference date.	Form AA01
20	Allot shares to the shareholders and issue share certificates.	CA 2006, s 188
21	If required, prepare service contracts for directors and seek approval if required under CA 2006.	
22	Obtain directors' indemnity insurance and employers' liability insurance.	
23	Do directors need to declare any interests in contracts or any other proposed interests?	CA 2006, ss 177, 182
24	Update: • register of directors; • register of directors' interests; • register of secretary (if appropriate); • register of charges (if appropriate); • register of members.	
25	Notify registrar if service contract or statutory books will be kept at a location other than at the company's registered office.	

Checklist: differences between a private and a public company

3.45 The following checklist sets out some of the key differences between a private and a public company under CA 2006.

Issue	*Private*	*Public*
Name	Must end with Ltd or Limited (or Welsh equivalent) unless exempt	Must end with plc or public limited company (or Welsh equivalent) unless exempt
Securities	Cannot offer securities to the public	Can offer securities to the public
Trading certificate	No need for a trading certificate. The company can start business immediately upon obtaining the certificate of incorporation	Trading certificate required
Share capital	No minimum share capital	The nominal value of the company's share capital must not be less than the authorised minimum £50,000
Secretary	No requirement	Required and with appropriate qualifications
Directors	One director required	Two directors required of whom one must be a natural person
Accounting/ audit requirement	Exemptions apply for small or medium-sized companies	No exemptions
Annual general meetings	No requirement for AGMs	Must hold AGMs
Written resolutions	Can be used	Cannot be used
Allotment of shares	May allot shares in accordance with its capital requirements	A public company may not allot shares unless at least one-quarter of their nominal value and the whole of any premium has been paid up
Non-cash consideration for shares		A public company may not allot shares as fully or partly paid up (as to their nominal value or any premium on them), otherwise than in cash if the consideration for the allotment is or includes an undertaking which is to be, or may be, performed more than five years after the date of the allotment. If the allotment for non-cash consideration is permissible, then an expert's prior valuation and report on the consideration given is usually required. Further, a public company may not allot shares in consideration of an undertaking to do work or perform services
Pre-emption rights	May disapply	Limited period for disapplication of pre-emptive rights
Dividends distribution	No restrictions apply	Prohibition from making a distribution if its net assets are less than the aggregate in value of its called-up share capital and its undistributable reserves

Issue	*Private*	*Public*
Loss of capital	No particular restrictions where losses suffered	Where the company's net assets are reduced to half or less of its called-up share capital, directors are obliged to convene an extraordinary general meeting, for shareholders to determine what steps should be taken to address the losses
Dormant company	Where a private company is classified as a 'small' company, it need not appoint auditors but must file an abbreviated balance sheet	No such requirement
Financial assistance	Exemption for private companies (subject to certain conditions) to give financial assistance for the acquisition of its shares	Cannot give financial assistance for acquisition of its shares
Purchase or redemption of shares	Exemption for private companies (subject to certain conditions) for a private company to redeem or purchase its shares	No such exemption
Interest in shares	No requirement of disclosure of interest in shares	Disclosure required including keeping a register of interest in shares
Proxy	A proxy who attends a general or class meeting of shareholders in a private company has the same right as the shareholder appointing him to speak at such meeting	No such requirement

4 The company's constitution

Introduction

4.1 This chapter addresses the following issues:

- the statutory definition of the term 'constitution' and the contexts in which the term is used;
- the company's articles of association;
- an overview of the standard company's model articles of association;
- the procedure for amending the company's articles of association and the test applied on alteration;
- the contractual status of the articles of association;
- the status of the memorandum of association; and
- construction of the articles of association.

The company's constitution

4.2 The Companies Act 2006 refers to a 'company's constitution' to include:

- the company's articles of association; and
- any resolutions and agreements affecting a company's constitution: CA 2006, s 17. CA 2006, s 29 defines these as:
  - any special resolution;
  - any resolution or agreement agreed to by all the members of a company that, if not so agreed to, would not have been effective for its purpose unless passed by a special resolution;
  - any resolution or agreement agreed to by all the members of a class of shareholders that, if not agreed to, would not have been effective for its purpose unless passed by some particular majority or otherwise in some particular manner;
  - any resolution or agreement that effectively binds all members of a class of shareholders though not agreed to by all those members; any other resolution or agreement to which Chapter 3 of Part 3 applies.

4.3 The term 'company's constitution' as used in CA 2006, s 17 is not exhaustive and will apply throughout the Companies Acts, 'unless the context requires otherwise'. Therefore, a wider or restricted meaning could be attributed to the term under specific provisions of the Companies Acts.

Under s 257, however, the definition of a 'company's constitution' has a wider significance for the purpose of Part 10 of the Act, in respect of company directors. The definition includes resolutions and decisions made by members of the company.

In addition to the provisions of a company's articles of association, and the resolutions and agreements, the contents of certain other documents will be of constitutional relevance for certain purposes. For example, a company's certificate of incorporation summarises key information applicable to the company, by setting out whether it is a public or a private company.

Articles of association

4.4 Under CA 2006, the company's constitution includes its articles of association. The company's articles are rules governing the internal function and operation of the company: *Gunewardena v Conran Holdings Limited* [2016] EWHC 2983 (Ch). They form a statutory contract between the company and its shareholders, and between each of the shareholders. They are an integral part of the company's constitution, and legally binding on the company and its shareholders. Articles of association establish the division of power and responsibility between the directors and the shareholders, creating a separation of management and ownership between them.

4.5 As the company's memorandum of association is no longer part of a company's constitution, the articles of association will contain all the essential powers, objects and activities of the company. The articles are intended to provide some flexibility for both directors and shareholders to facilitate effective governance of the company. They provide some transparency in the relationship between directors and shareholders for the proper functioning of the company.

4.6 If companies do not provide for their own articles, then by default, they may adopt model articles for a private or public company under the Companies (Model Articles) Regulations 2008, SI 2008/3229. The model articles do not set out the provisions of the Companies Act 2006, and consideration should be given to any amendments that a company may need to make, to ensure that the provisions are suitably adapted for the company's purposes. See Chapter 3.

The nature of the company's articles of association

4.7 A company must have articles of association setting out relevant internal regulations: CA 2006, s 18(1). Unless it is a limited company to which the default model articles apply (Companies (Model Articles) Regulations 2008, SI 2008/3229), it must register the articles of association with the Registrar of Companies at Companies House.

The articles of association registered by a company must be contained in a single document and be divided into paragraphs numbered consecutively:) CA 2006, s 18(3).

4.8 The adoption of the model articles by companies formed under CA 2006 will be a matter for individual companies. They are able to incorporate provisions from the model articles (with or without amendment); and/or add to those provisions; and/or exclude such provisions as they think fit.

Companies can also adopt the provisions of model articles by reference. This is a common practice, which enables a company that wishes to incorporate specific provisions to do so, without the necessity of having to copy out the provisions in question.

4.9

Example:

A company's registered articles may have the following variations in its articles of association:

- 'The Model Articles apply except for articles x, y and z'; or
- 'The company's articles are a, b and c, plus model articles 'g, p and q''; or
- 'Model article 'n' applies but it is amended as follows …'

Alteration of articles of association

4.10 The company may amend its articles of association by special resolution: CA 2006, s 21(1). This is subject to the rules on entrenchment as set out in s 22. Private companies can, however, amend their articles by a written resolution procedure.

Judicial attitudes towards alteration of articles of association

4.11 Over the years, there has developed a principle in English company law, that subject to any restrictions under statute or any entrenchment provision and where appropriate, the interests of minority shareholders, a company is generally free to amend its articles of association. The principle has also been based on majority rule – if the majority of the shareholders have decided on a particular transaction, the minority must accept majority decisions based on the rule in *Foss v Harbottle* (1843) 2 Hare 46, subject to certain exceptions (such as fraud or illegality). See, however, the derivative action under CA 2006, Pt 11.

4.12 Traditionally, English courts have stated the power to alter the articles of association under the CA 2006 must be exercised 'bona fide for the benefit of the company as a whole'. This expression appears to have been inextricably linked to CA 2006, s 21 and its predecessors. This concept derives from partnership law, and was enshrined in English company law to ensure that the majority did not abuse its powers of expulsion to the detriment of the minority. In some cases, this has been based on the ability of the majority shareholders to bind the minority.

There has been no clear explanation in English case law as to the meaning of the term 'bona fide'. Subsequent cases have, therefore, developed other tests applicable to alteration of articles, while still retaining aspects of the bona fide test. The cases also demonstrate judicial reluctance by the courts to intervene in commercial business decisions of companies, in determining the bona fides of their decisions, based on principles established in *Foss v Harbottle* (1843) 2 Hare 461, that where wrongs are done to the company, then only the company is the proper claimant, and the majority control over corporate decisions: see too *Burland v Earle* [1902] AC 83; and *MacDougall v Gardiner* (1875) 1 Ch D 13; and *Edwards v Halliwell* [1950] 2 All ER 1064. Articles of association can be the subject of challenge even if passed by the requisite majority of shareholders. as being invalid in certain circumstances.

One of the earliest cases to set out the 'bona fide' test was *Allen v Gold Reefs of West Africa Ltd* [1900] 1 Ch 656. The Court of Appeal decided that any power to alter the articles of association must be exercised 'bona fide for the benefit of the company', and must not be exceeded.

4.13 Although *Allen's* case was not concerned with compulsory transfer provisions (or 'expropriation clauses' or 'exclusion' clauses), which compels a majority shareholder to purchase some or all shares of the minority shareholder, with a view to excluding any further participation by the minority shareholder, some subsequent cases have involved compulsory transfer provisions, which have applied the *Allen* test. However, the courts have never clearly articulated the concept of 'bona fide for the benefit of the company'

There have been some cases that have associated alteration of articles with aspects of conscience, equity, natural justice, oppressiveness and fair play. The courts would consider it unconscionable for majority shareholders to alter articles of association where minority shareholders would be subjected to a detriment or oppression. In this regard, the courts addressed the subjective intentions of the shareholders as decision makers, and whether such intentions were tainted with any bad faith or mala fides on their part, in effecting the alteration, including purely selfish motives, desires or intentions on the part of the majority shareholders: *Brown v British Abrasive Wheel Co* [1919] 1 Ch 290.

4.14 Subsequent cases have been critical of and distinguished *Brown v British Abrasive Wheel Co.* by upholding the bona fide test established in *Allen*. In *Sidebottom v Kershaw, Leese & Co Ltd* [1920] 1 Ch 154, the Court of Appeal upheld an alteration to the articles, as it was for the company's benefit as a whole. This could be determined by addressing issues such as: whether the proposed alteration was calculated to directly harm the shareholder? Were the motives malicious or in bad faith? What would be the detriment to the company if the alteration was not effected?

4.15 From time to time, the courts have also considered concepts such as honesty and real intention behind the proposed alteration of the articles of association: *Dafen Tinplate Co Ltd v Llanelly Steel Co (1907) Ltd* [1920] 2 Ch 124.

However, it is for the company to decide what is in its best interests of the company regarding alteration to the articles of association, and not the court: *Shuttleworth v Cox Bros & Co (Maidenhead) Ltd* [1927] 2 KB 9. in this regard, the Court of Appeal in *Shuttleworth* disapproved of *Dafen Tinplate Co Ltd v Llanelly Steel Co Ltd* [1920] 2 Ch 124.

4.16 The test to be applied in expropriation cases is whether the alteration is bona fide for the company's benefit: *Constable v Executive Connections Ltd* [2005] 2 BCLC 638. Shareholders must collectively decide what in their honest opinion is for the company's benefit as a whole: *Greenhalgh v Arderne Cinemas Ltd* [1950] 2 All ER 1120.

Provided the power to alter the articles of association is exercised bona fide by the shareholders, the courts will be reluctant to interfere in such decisions: *Rights & Issues Investment Trust Ltd v Stylo Shoes Ltd* [1965] Ch 250; *Citco Banking Corp NV v Pusser's Ltd* [2007] 2 BCLC 483. However, the test for alterations to articles of association cannot solely be based on bona fide for the company's benefit. In *Hutton v West Cork Rly Co* (1893) 23 Ch D 654, Bowen LJ stated: 'Bona fides cannot be the sole test, otherwise you might have a lunatic conducting the affairs of the company, and paying away its money with both hands in a manner perfectly bona fide yet perfectly irrational'.

4.17 In the leading case of *Arbuthnott v Bonnyman* [2015] All ER (D) 218 (*Re Charterhouse Capital Limited*), the issues concerned transfer of shares and the validity of the transfer. The claimant owned shares in the company. Other shareholders formed a new corporate vehicle to acquire the company and sold their shares to the new corporate vehicle. The claimant refused to sell his shares claiming: (a) unfair prejudicial conduct; and (b) that the company had sought to expropriate his shares at a gross undervalue. The Court of Appeal considered the construction of the 'drag' rights (compulsory sale of shares of a minority shareholder if majority sell their shares), and of the amendment to the company's articles of association. It dismissed the claimant's claim. It set out the following principles from some of the key cases on the conditions for effecting a challenge to an alteration to the articles of association:

(1) The limitations on the exercise of the power to amend a company's articles arise because, as in the case of all powers, the manner of their exercise is constrained by the purpose of the power and because the framers of the power of a majority to bind a minority will not, in the absence of clear words, have intended the power to be completely without limitation. These principles may be characterised as principles of law and equity or as implied terms: *Allen v Gold Reefs of West Africa Ltd* [1900] Ch 656 at 671; *Assenagon Asset Management SA v Irish Bank Resolution Corpn Ltd* [2013] Bus LR 266 at 278–280.

(2) A power to amend will be validly exercised if it is exercised in good faith in the interests of the company: *Sidebottom v Kershaw Leese and Co Ltd* [1920] 1 Ch 154 at 163.

(3) It is for the shareholders, and not the court, to say whether an alteration of the articles is for the benefit of the company but it will not be for the benefit of the company if no reasonable person would consider it to be such: *Shuttleworth* at 18–19, 23–24, 26–27; *Peters' American Delicacy Co v Heath* (1939) 61 CLR 457 at 488.

(4) The view of shareholders acting in good faith that a proposed alteration of the articles is for the benefit of the company, and which cannot be said to be a view which no reasonable person could hold, is not impugned by the fact that one or more of the shareholders was actually acting under some mistake of fact or lack of knowledge or understanding: *Peters' American Delicacy Co* at 491. In other words, the court will not investigate the quality of the subjective views of such shareholders.

(5) The mere fact that the amendment adversely affects, and even if it is intended adversely to affect, one or more minority shareholders and benefit others does not, of itself, invalidate the amendment if the amendment is made in good

faith in the interests of the company: *Sidebottom* at 161, 163–167, 170–173; *Shuttleworth*; *Citco* at 490, 493; *Peters' American Delicacy Co* at 480, 486.

(6) A power to amend will also be validly exercised, even though the amendment is not for the benefit of the company, because it relates to a matter in which the company as an entity has no interest, but rather is only for the benefit of shareholders as such or some of them, provided that the amendment does not amount to oppression of the minority or is otherwise unjust or is outside the scope of the power: *Peters' American Delicacy Co* at 481, 504, 513, 515; *Assenagon*.

(7) The burden is on the person impugning the validity of the amendment of the articles to satisfy the court that there are grounds for doing so: *Citco* at 491; *Peters' American Delicacy Co* at 482.

It is clear from *Re Charterhouse Capital Ltd*, that the courts will not generally interfere in shareholders' decisions when effecting an alteration to the company's articles of association, provided the alteration is exercised in good faith. The term 'good faith' signifies that the alteration must be for the company's benefit. The circumstances in which a minority shareholder may successfully mount a challenge to the articles of association are, however, limited to demonstrating: (a) lack of good faith; (b) unfair prejudicial conduct; (c) the amendment was outside the scope of power or beyond the company's capacity. The minority shareholder also has the burden of showing that the alteration was not in good faith, and when requesting the court to set aside the alteration. The *Re Charterhouse Capital Ltd* case demonstrates the court's unwillingness to intrude in corporate affairs where shareholders make a decision in the company's best interests, unless circumstances arise which require intervention by the court. The Court of Appeal was persuaded by the following factors in upholding the drag rights by way of amendment to the articles of association: (a) there would be a better alignment of ownership as part of the management buyout and achieving such alignment was in the company's best interests; (b) the drag rights were not specifically targeted at the claimant nor was he singled out, but applied to all shareholders: the claimant was entitled to be bought out on the same terms as the exiting majority shareholders; (c) the company's shareholder's agreement and its articles of association when read together, already contained drag rights, which formed one of the bases of the original commercial bargain between the shareholders.

4.18 In *Staray Capital Limited v Yang* [2017] UKPC 43, the Privy Council (non-binding on English courts), summarised the following principles applicable to the amendment of articles which reflect the principles in *Re Charterhouse Capital Ltd*, and the limited circumstances a claimant can successfully challenge alteration of the articles.

- A power to amend will be validly exercised if it is exercised in good faith in the interests of the company.
- It is for the shareholders, and not for the court, to say whether an alteration of the articles is for the benefit of the company, but it will not be for the benefit of the company if no reasonable person would consider it to be such.
- The mere fact that the amendment adversely affects, and even if it is intended adversely to affect, one or more minority shareholders and benefit others does not, of itself, invalidate the amendment, if the amendment is made in good faith in the interests of the company.
- The burden is on the person impugning the validity of the amendment of the articles to satisfy the court that there are grounds for doing so.

Further effects of alteration of articles of association on company members

4.19 CA 2006, s 25 states that a company's shareholder is not bound by an alteration to its articles after the date on which he became a shareholder in the following circumstances:

- if and so far as the alteration requires him to take or subscribe for more shares in the company, than the number held by him at the date on which the alteration was made; or
- the alteration has the effect in any way of increasing his liability to the company as at that date, to contribute to the company's share capital or otherwise to pay money to the company: CA 2006, s 25(1).

A shareholder may, however, give his written consent to such an alteration and, where he does so, he will be bound by the alteration: CA 2006, s 25(2).

Registrar to be sent a copy of amended articles

4.20 Once a company amends its articles, it must send a copy of the amended articles to the registrar not later than 15 days after the amendment takes effect: CA 2006, s 26(1). Failure to comply can result in a criminal offence and fine: CA 2006, s 26(3).

Registrar's notice to comply in case of failure with respect to amended articles

4.21 Where the registrar believes that a company has failed to comply with any CA 2006 provision requiring it to send to the registrar a document, making or evidencing an alteration in the company's articles; or to send to the registrar a copy of the company's articles as amended, the registrar may give notice to the company requiring it to comply: CA 2006, s 27(1). The notice must state the date on which it was issued; and require the company to comply within 28 days of the date of the notice: CA 2006, s 27(2). If the company complies with the notice within the specified time, it will not be subject to legal proceedings. However, if it does not so comply, it will be liable to a civil penalty of £200 and any criminal proceedings: CA 2006, s 27(3). The fine may be recovered by the registrar and is then paid into the Consolidated Fund: CA 2006, s 27(4).

Shareholders' agreement

4.22 Although the articles of association are the principal internal rules governing the company, they may from time to time be supplemented by other rules and regulations, which may elaborate further on the articles of association. A shareholders' agreement may be supplemental to a company's articles of association, and will set out further provisions governing relations between the shareholders on issues such as voting, capital, transfer of shares, possible 'lock in' periods for shareholders, detailed governance aspects and exit provisions. Shareholders' agreements are usually drafted to ensure consistency with the articles. The shareholders' agreement may prevail over the company's articles of association, provided it is not inconsistent with CA 2006.

As the shareholders' agreement is a private document, it does not require registration at Companies House.

Typically, new shareholders joining the shareholders' agreement will do so by a deed of adherence, where they agree to comply with all aspects of the shareholders' agreement.

Model articles of association

4.23 Companies have the freedom to draft and set out their internal rules, but in some cases they can rely on a standard prescribed set of articles to govern their relationships, with adaptations to such articles specifically applicable to their particular situation. Under CA 2006, companies have the option to adopt model articles of association, which are set out in standard form. These model articles may be adopted either in their entirety, or in part depending upon the company's requirements.

4.24 Under the Companies (Model Articles) Regulations 2008, SI 3228/3229 the three model articles enacted are:

- Model Articles for Private Companies Limited by Shares: reg 2, Sch 1 to the Companies (Model Articles) Regulations 2008;
- Model Articles for Private Companies Limited by Guarantee: reg 3 of the Companies (Model Articles) Regulations 2008;
- Model Articles for Public Companies: reg 4 of the Companies (Model Articles) Regulations 2008.

Contractual status of the articles of association: 'insider' and 'outsider' rights – a statutory contract

4.25 The provisions of the company's constitution bind the company and its members, to the same extent as if there were covenants on the part of the company and of each member to observe those provisions: CA 2006, s 33(1). The effect of s 33(1) is that the articles of association are a statutory contract created by the Companies Act 2006 (and its predecessors): *Bratton Seymour Service Co Ltd v Oxborough* [1992] BCLC 693. This contract is also enforceable between the shareholders. However, under this statutory contract, certain provisions under the articles of association may not be enforceable, unlike a typical contractual document, as enforceability depends upon the capacity in which a person brings an action, as considered below. The contractual status of the articles is likely to arise on a transfer of shares, on a right of pre-emption, or where an obligation is placed on the directors to purchase the shares of a shareholder who is leaving the company: *Borland's Trustees v Steel* [1901] 1 Ch 279.

However, s 33 does not clearly define the relationship between the members, or the relationship between the company and its members.

4.26 Over the years, there have been a number of cases that have considered the effect of s 33(1) (previously CA 1985, s 14) as to the enforcement rights between the different parties, depending on whether a person is an 'insider' and able to enforce the provisions of the articles of association, or an 'outsider' who is excluded from enforceability. At common law, only those who are parties to a contract can enforce it, having regard to the doctrine of privity of contract. In the context of company law, a shareholder may enforce terms in the articles of association as an 'insider', but a director may be excluded from enforcing the articles of association, even where he is closely involved with the company, because the law treats him/her as outsider owing to the capacity in which the person brings an action.

It should be noted that the Contracts (Rights of Third Parties) Act 1999 does not apply to the company's constitution: s 6(2).

This section considers four different situations where enforceability has been considered by the courts.

(i) A company's enforcement of the articles of association against a shareholder

4.27 Section 33(1) of CA 2006 allows a company to enforce the articles against a shareholder, as both are parties to such contract as set out in the articles. The articles bind the members in their capacity as members of the company.

A company can enforce provisions of the articles against shareholders: *Hickman v Kent or Romney Marsh Sheepbreeders' Association* [1915] 1 Ch 881. According to the company's articles of association, any disputes between the shareholders were to be referred to arbitration. One of the company's shareholders was in a dispute with the company and issued legal proceedings. The company applied to prevent such legal proceedings from going ahead, and to refer the dispute to arbitration in accordance with the company's articles of association. The court decided that the shareholder was bound by the provisions of the articles of association and that the dispute be referred to arbitration. Further, a member can only enforce provisions of the articles in his capacity as a member, and not in any other capacity; and the articles create rights and obligations between members and between members and the company.

4.28 However, *in Beattie v Beattie* [1938] Ch 708, the articles provided that any dispute between a company and a shareholder should be referred to arbitration. The Court of Appeal applied *Hickman's* case, and held that a dispute between the company and a director who was also a member, was not subject to the articles. This was because the dispute was simply concerned with the company and its director, and not the company with its shareholder.

In *Quinn & Axtens Ltd v Salmon* [1909] 1 Ch 311, the Court of Appeal held that although the dispute in question affected the director in question, it was possible to sidestep the *Hickman* case, and for the managing director in his capacity as a shareholder to bring such proceedings.

4.29 A substantive procedural irregularity may entitle a shareholder to bring an action against the company: *Edwards v Halliwell* [1950] 2 All ER 1064.

However, a mere internal irregularity may not entitle a shareholder to bring proceedings, if the majority can cure the irregularity. In *MacDougall v Gardiner* (1875) 1 Ch D 13, in breach of the company's articles, the chairman of the meeting refused to request a poll by the shareholders. It was held this was an internal irregularity and the shareholders had no right of action. The decision was based on the majority rule principle. However, see now, CA 2006, Pt 11 derivative actions.

A shareholder may bring proceedings where personal rights are infringed: *Pender v Lushington* (1877) 6 Ch D 70.

(ii) A shareholder may enforce provisions of the articles of association against another shareholder

4.30 A shareholder may be able to enforce articles against another shareholder: *Rayfield v Hands* [1960] Ch 1. According to Vaisey J, the article in dispute was concerned with the relationship between a shareholder and other shareholders, even though it provided for the directors to purchase the shares of the outgoing shareholder.

(iii) Can a shareholder enforce the articles of association against the company?

4.31 Some of the cases in this area provide conflicting positions as to whether a shareholder can enforce the articles against the company. It may not always be possible for a shareholder to enforce articles of association against the company.

In *Hickman v Kent or Romney Marsh Sheepbreeders' Association* [1915] Ch 881, Astbury J stated that it may be possible for a shareholder to enforce provisions of the articles of association in his capacity only as a shareholder in the company, and not in any other capacity. See also *Re Severn and Wye and Severn Bridge Railway Co* [1896] 1 Ch 559 (a shareholder's right to have his vote recorded by the company).

In *Pender v Lushington* (1877) 6 Ch D 70, the company's chairman failed to follow proper procedure in recording the votes of the shareholders. This affected the rights of shareholders. The shareholders in their capacity as such succeeded in obtaining an injunction to prevent the passing of any resolution.

A shareholder may bring proceedings against a company for declaration of dividends. In *Wood v Odessa Waterworks Co* (1889) 42 Ch D 636, a shareholder in his capacity as such was able to bring proceedings against the company to compel declaration of a dividend, as provided by the articles: see too *Kaye v Croydon Tramways* [1898] 1 Ch 358; *Baillie v Oriental Telephone and Electric Co Ltd* [1915] 1 Ch 503.

4.32 Section 33(1) of CA 2006 creates a contract which is enforceable by a shareholder against the company. A shareholder may bring proceedings against the company where directors propose to take certain action that could threaten or jeopardise the interests of the company, by a potential breach of the articles of association: *Irvine v Union Bank of Australia* (1877) 2 App Cas 366.

(iv) Outsiders cannot enforce the articles of association

4.33 A person who is not suing in his capacity as a member is considered as an 'outsider'. Some cases have not allowed a shareholder to sue in any capacity other than as a member of the company. The courts have usually prevented 'outsider rights' from being enforced, on the basis that the statutory contract is between the company and its shareholders, who are entitled to enforce against each other. Any rights of the outsider are likely to be governed by another contractual arrangement, and not the articles of association:

A professional adviser is considered as an 'outsider' and cannot enforce under the company's articles: *Eley v Positive Life Association* (1876) 1 Ex D 88.

A seller of a mine was considered as an 'outsider' and could not enforce under the company's articles: *Pritchard's Case* L R 8 Ch 956.

In some situations, outsiders' rights may be enforceable under another agreement and not the articles: *Re New British Iron Co, ex p Beckwith* [1898] 1 Ch 324, where the court held that remuneration owing to a director, could not be enforced under the company's articles of association, but under another contract between the company and the director.

Status of the memorandum of association

4.34 Companies established under the Companies Act 2006, on or after 1 October 2009, will adopt a new format for the memorandum of association. However, the memorandum of association does not fall within the definition of a company's constitution. It simply represents a 'snapshot' of the company at the time of incorporation, compared to the wider format of the memorandum of association under the Companies Act 1985. Its function is only to set out the agreement of the shareholders to establish the company.

4.35 Section 81(1) of CA 2006 provides that a memorandum of association is a memorandum stating that the subscribers (the founding shareholders) wish to engage in two respects:

- They agree to form a company under CA 2006. This evidences their intention to form a company in compliance with the formalities under the Act.
- The subscribers also agree to become members of the company and, in the case of a company that is to have a share capital, to take at least one share each. By taking their respective allocation of shares, the subscribers will be shareholders in the company.

4.36 The memorandum of association must, however, be in a prescribed form and must be authenticated by each member. The prescribed format for the memorandum of association is set out in the Companies (Registration) Regulations 2008 (2008/3014). Companies are not required to set out any objects clauses in the memorandum of association, as the objects clause is unrestricted, unless the company specifically restricts the objects clause in its articles of association: CA 2006, s 31(1). The objects clause, including any restrictions in the objects, will now be contained in the articles of association. For any company incorporated before 1 October 2009, its objects are deemed to be contained in the articles of association, and if they previously contained restrictions, then such restrictions can be removed by special resolution to make the objects unrestricted. This also includes any entrenching provisions that were set out in the memorandum of association. These are now deemed to be contained in the articles of association: CA 2006, s 28.

4.37 The memorandum of association will not be required to set out the company's authorised share capital. This is now deemed to be contained in the articles of association. This clause may be removed by the company's shareholders by an ordinary resolution.

4.38 With regards to whether the liability of the shareholders is limited, whether by shares or guarantee, these provisions are now deemed to be contained in the company's articles of association, and in the model articles for both a private and a public company. If a company chooses not to adopt the model articles, it must include a limited liability statement in its articles of association.

Construction of the articles of association

4.39 Ever since the enactment of the Companies Acts in the UK, the articles of association have been a fundamental part of the company's constitution. The articles become more significant because they are required to be registered at Companies House. They are open to inspection, so that a third party can identify the procedural rules of internal governance within the company, and any limits of authority placed on the company's directors.

4.40 A company's articles of association are its internal regulations. They regulate the governance of the company: how it will function, operate and manage the day to day activities of the company, including management by directors. The provisions of the articles of association are contractual but a special form of contract. They are a statutory contract between various parties involved: a statutory contract with its own distinctive features. The articles of association also contain all the necessary elements for a contract to come into existence. An offer is made to a prospective shareholder by the company/existing shareholders to join the company. The offer is accepted by the in-coming shareholder for a consideration, being the share price for the shares subscribed. The parties therefore intend to create a binding legal relationship. Some of the provisions in the articles contain covenants and others in the form of undertakings on various parties to comply with its terms. The statutory contractual effect of the articles signifies a deeper relationship between the parties involved. The provisions bind the company and the shareholder together. They also bind the shareholders *inter se* depending upon the particular article provision: CA 2006, s 31.

4.41 By entering into a unique statutory contractual relationship, some of the parties may have legitimate expectations which are expected to be honoured and implemented. Where, for example, dividends are declared by the directors, the directors are expected to pay the shareholders their entitlement by virtue of the statutory contract.

The position becomes problematic when the 'legitimate expectations' of one party do not accord with the 'reality' of the situation under the statutory contact. This can arise in the context of 'quasi-partnerships', where small companies operate in a partnership format and convene meetings on an ad hoc basis. Although the quasi-partnership company has articles of association in place, however, the 'partners' may agree to certain matters orally, and which are not subsequently transposed either in the form of minutes or amendments to the articles of association. Quasi-partnership agreements can therefore be characterised as a loose form of arrangement between the parties, that may take the form of oral agreements or a 'gentlemen's agreement' between the parties. These types of agreements are characteristically based upon the trust and confidence in each of the parties to deliver their part of the bargain. Typically, a shareholder is promised participation in the company's management or some assumption of responsibility. Once they have struck a bargain, there are legitimate expectations that the bargain will be honoured by one or more of the parties. Issues arise when the agreements between the parties are not implemented in practice. As the company progresses, the participation by the aggrieved shareholder becomes a distant reality, leading the shareholder to bring proceedings for unfair prejudicial conduct, or a derivative action or a personal action against the company. These disputes between the parties can also lead to a construction of the articles of association, and whether any terms can be implied into the articles, because the articles may be construed as a commercial agreement between the parties and the company.

In connection with the construction of commercial contracts generally, Lord Neuberger in the leading Supreme Court case of *Arnold v Britton* [2015] UKSC 36, identified the following factors that should be taken into account:

(i) the reliance placed in some cases on commercial common sense and surrounding circumstances should not be invoked to undervalue the importance of the language of the provision to be construed;

(ii) the less clear the relevant words were the more ready the court could be to depart from their natural meaning. That did not, however, justify the court embarking on an exercise of searching for, let alone constructing, drafting infelicities in order to facilitate a departure from the natural meaning;

(iii) commercial common sense should not be invoked retrospectively. The fact that a contractual arrangement had worked out badly, or even disastrously, for one of the parties was not a reason for departing from the natural language. Commercial common sense was only relevant as at the date the contract was made;

(iv) while commercial common sense was a very important factor, a court should be very slow to reject the natural meaning of a provision as correct simply because it appeared to be a very imprudent term for one of the parties to have agreed, even ignoring the benefit of hindsight;

(v) when interpreting a contractual provision, account could only be taken of facts or circumstances which existed at the time the contract was made, and which were known or reasonably available to both parties; and

(vi) in some cases, an event might subsequently occur which was plainly or not intended or contemplated by the parties. In such a case, if it was clear what the parties would have intended, the court would give effect to that intention.

Construing articles of association

4.42 The articles of association are a business document. In *Holmes v Keyes* [1959] Ch 199, Jenkins LJ was of the view that a company's articles of association served a commercial purpose when he stated: '…the articles of association of the company should be regarded as a business document and should be construed so as to give them reasonable business efficacy, where a construction tending to that result is admissible on the language, in preference to a result which would or might prove unworkable'.

In *Re Hartley Baird Ltd* [1955] Ch 143, Wynn-Parry J, stated: 'In the interpretation of such a commercial document as articles of association, the maxim *ut res magis valeat quam pereat* should be applied, namely "It is better for a thing to have effect than to be made void".'

In *BWE International Ltd v Jones* [2004] 1 BCLC 406, the Court of Appeal was required to consider the construction of an article requiring notice to be given to the company by any member of a desire to sell or transfer shares, specifying the price at which he was willing to sell or transfer the shares. The transfer notice fixed the price by reference to a formula whose operations depended upon future events. The issue was whether the notice was one 'specifying the price at which the [Transferor] is willing to sell or transfer the shares'.

The Court of Appeal held that the approach to be adopted in interpreting articles of association was the same approach to other commercial documents. The articles should be construed so as to give them reasonable business efficacy where that was admissible on the language. However, the articles should not be construed so as to cut down the shareholder's rights as to his property, unless that was a fair interpretation of the articles. On the facts, the transfer notice was invalid because the price was required to be stated in detail, wholly and completely. According to Arden LJ, although the articles of association should be construed as a business document, they should also be construed so as to make them workable.

4.43 In construing the articles of association, the court also consider the practicalities of the situation. In *Dashfield v Davidson* [2009] 1 BCLC 220, Lewison J stated that the articles should be interpreted in a business-like manner, which produced a workable result in a variety of possible factual scenarios, rather than being interpreted in a way that was tailor-made to the particular facts of the case.

4.44 A plain and ordinary interpretation and construction should be given to the articles unless this produced a commercial absurdity. In *Thompson v Goblin Hill Hotels Ltd* [2011] 1 BCLC 587, the company's articles of association stated that the maintenance charges for the villas were to be borne by 'each member' of the company. The company levied maintenance charges on the leaseholder shareholders, and not the investor shareholders. The case turned on the construction of the words in the articles of association. The Privy Council applied the principle that the plain and ordinary meaning of the words used in a commercial contract could only be displaced if it produced a commercial absurdity. The provision under the company's articles was to be given its plain and ordinary meaning that the amount assessed for maintenance was to be borne by each member of the company, including the investor shareholders, in the proportion that his shareholding bore to the entire issued share capital of the company, since the respondents, on whom the onus lay, had not shown that such an interpretation resulted in a commercial absurdity. As a matter of ordinary language the particular provision in the articles of association could only reasonably be understood to bear their literal meaning so that 'each member' meant exactly that, namely each shareholder and not just leaseholder shareholders. Furthermore, in the face of the plain and ordinary meaning, it was impossible to imply a term that the assessments should be borne only by leaseholder shareholders.

The Privy Council preferred the approach taken by Lord Diplock in *Antaios Cia Naviera SA v Salen Rederierna AB, The Antaios* [1985] AC 191:

> 'If a detailed semantic and syntactical analysis of words in a commercial contract is going to lead to a conclusion that flouts business common sense, it must be made to yield to business common sense'.

Rectification

4.45 Errors or mistakes can sometimes occur in a company's articles of association, which were not intended by the incorporators at the time the company was being incorporated. The simplest course of action would be to pass a special resolution to amend the error or mistake, and to lodge the resolution together with the amended articles of association at Companies House. However, some shareholders may not wish to convene a meeting to effect the rectification, which may lead to the detriment of a shareholder or group of shareholders. The aggrieved shareholder then resorts to litigation seeking the court's assistance in the rectification of the mistake or error.

4.46 In *Evans v Chapman* [1902] W.N. 78, the court was required to determine whether a provision in the company's articles of association could be rectified. The mistake to be rectified was solely due to a clerical error. Joyce J held that although a mistake was made, it could only be rectified by the company passing a special resolution at the general meeting. The court had no jurisdiction to rectify mistakes or errors in the context of the articles of association.

In *Scott v Frank F. Scott (London) Ltd* [1940] Ch 794, one of the issues before the Court of Appeal was whether the articles of association could be rectified. It was held that the articles could not subsequently be rectified to give effect to the intention of the founder members at the time the company was established. Luxmoore LJ was of the view that the power to amend or rectify the articles was purely statutory and shareholders were required to comply with the statutory procedures for amending the articles under the Companies Acts.

Possible rectification under CA 2006, s 994

4.47 CA 2006, s 994 is concerned with a petition by a company member who may apply to the court on the ground that:

(a) The company's affairs are being or have been conducted in a manner that is unfairly prejudicial to the interests of the members generally or of some part of its members (including at least himself); or

(b) That an act or proposed act or omission of the company (including an act or omission on its behalf) is or would be so prejudicial.

Section 994 may allow a member to bring unfair prejudicial proceedings that may have the effect of rectification of the company's constitution. However, there are procedural obstacles that would need to be surmounted. The member would have to show that the conduct was either unfair to the members (or some part), or that some act or omission would be so prejudicial. In the event that the member is able to overcome this hurdle, it may be possible for the member to request rectification by way of an order under CA 2006, s 996. The list of orders are not exhaustive, and the court has a discretion to make such order as it thinks fit for giving relief in the matters complained of. One order may require the company not to make any, or any specified alterations in its articles, without the leave of the court: CA 2006, s 996(2)(d). This order could apply to rectification of the articles by the court.

Implied terms in the articles of association

4.48 As the articles of association are a special form of statutory contracts, the courts have shown unwillingness to add or subtract provisions. Typically, the articles are construed as expressly written.

Extrinsic Circumstances

4.49 One issue which has arisen is whether the courts can imply terms into the articles of association, having regard to the extrinsic circumstances in order to reconstruct a particular provision of the articles?

In *Bratton Seymour Service Co Ltd v Oxborough* [1992] BCLC 693, the issue before the Court of Appeal was whether it was possible to imply into the articles of association of a company, set up to manage a development of flats. A term provided that the shareholders, who were the owners of the flats, should make contributions for the upkeep of the amenity areas of the development. The Court of Appeal held that although the Court might be able to infer a term purely by way of constructional implication, it was not possible to go further and to imply a term from extrinsic evidence of surrounding circumstances. On the facts, it was not possible to imply a term that the shareholders of the company should be under an obligation to make an additional financial contribution, since this went well beyond the language of the articles of association.

According to Dillon LJ, the articles of association did not follow the conventional pattern of a contractual document. They differed considerably from a typical contract. The articles had statutory force and a statutory form of contract, and accordingly, the court had no power to imply terms into the articles.

4.50 The rationale of the courts in this area lend support to the conclusiveness of the certificate of incorporation. Under CA 2006, s 15(4), the certificate is conclusive evidence that the requirements of the Companies Act 2006 as to registration have been complied with, and that the company is duly registered under the Act. This means that the Registrar will not check for errors or mistakes in, for example, the articles of association, nor rectify them. The objective of conclusiveness is also to protect third parties who rely on documents available for public inspection at Companies House, such as the articles of association.

4.51 In some cases, the distinction between refusing to imply terms and construing the articles of association can become blurred. In *Folkes Group plc v Alexander* [2002] 2 BCLC 254, the court provided five words to be added to the articles of association, as the absence of those words would have produced an absurd result. Rimer J accepted that his insertion of the words came close towards the maximum limits allowed for construction of articles of association.

4.52 In *AG of Belize v Belize Telecom* [2009] 2 BCLC 148(Privy Council), there were various classes of shareholders with ability to appoint and remove directors. However, the articles made no express provision as to what would be the position for appointment of directors, where a shareholder's shareholding fell below a certain threshold.

Lord Hoffmann set out some basic principles of implication of terms:

- The court had no power to improve upon an instrument which it was called upon to construe, whether it was a contract, a statute or articles of association.
- It was concerned only to discover what the instrument meant.
- When an instrument did not provide expressly for what was to happen when some event occurred, the most usual inference was that nothing was to happen.
- Although in certain cases the court would imply a term, the purpose of such an implication was to spell out the meaning of the instrument, not to make an addition to the instrument.
- In every case in which it was said that some provision ought to be implied in an instrument, the question for the court was whether such a provision would spell out in express words what the instrument, read against the relevant background,

> would reasonably be understood to mean. That question could be reformulated in various ways which a court might find helpful in providing an answer – the implied term had to 'go without saying', it had to be 'necessary to give business efficacy to the contract' and so on – but those were not to be treated as different or additional tests. There was only one question: was that what the instrument, read as a whole against the relevant background, would reasonably be understood to have meant.

Lord Hoffmann decided that the implication was also required in such a case to avoid defeating what appeared to be the overriding purpose of the machinery of appointment and removal of directors, namely to ensure that the board reflected the appropriate shareholder interests in accordance with the scheme laid out in the articles. The implication as to the composition of the board was based not on extrinsic evidence known to a limited number of persons, but upon the scheme of the articles themselves and, to a limited extent, such background as was apparent from the memorandum and the fact that all in *Belize* knew that telecommunications was a state monopoly. See too *Stena Line Ltd v Merchant Navy Ratings Pension Fund Trustees Ltd* [2011] EWCA Civ 543.

4.53 In *Marks and Spencer plc v BNP Paribas Securities Services Trust Company (Jersey) Ltd* [2015] UKSC 72, Lord Neuberger further amplified on the test established by Lord Hoffmann in *Belize*. According to Lord Neuberger, the notion that a term will be implied if a reasonable reader of the contract, knowing all its provisions and surrounding circumstances would understand it to be implied, was acceptable provided that: (a) the reasonable reader was treated as reading the contract at the time it was made; and (b) he would consider the term to be so obvious as to go without saying or to be necessary for business efficacy.

Lord Neuberger also considered whether the process of implying a term was part of the exercise of interpretation. See *Banque Bruxelles Lambert SA v Eagle Star Insurance Co Ltd* [1997] AC 191, where Lord Hoffmann suggested that the issue of whether to imply a term into the contract was one of construction of the agreement as a whole in its commercial setting. In *Belize*, Lord Hoffmann took this further when he stated that 'the implication of the term is not an addition to the instrument. It only spells out what the instrument means' He also referred to the danger of detaching the phrase 'necessary to give business efficacy' from the basic process of construction. Lord Neuberger accepted that both: (i) construing the words which the parties have used in their contract; and (ii) implying terms into the contract, involved determining the scope and meaning of the contract. However, construing the words used and implying additional words were different processes governed by a different set of rules.

Shareholders' informal consent

4.54 In the event of a mistake or an error, the usual procedure is to convene a general meeting and to pass a special resolution to rectify the matter in question and lodge the documents at Companies House. However, the practice in some quasi-partnership companies is to proceed by way of an informal unanimous consent of shareholders without formally convening a general meeting. The effect of this procedure is that while changes may be made to the articles of association, they may not have been registered at Companies House, and do not reflect the reality of the situation between the document registered at Companies House, and the changes made within the corporation, but which are not registered: *Cane v Jones* [1980] 1 WLR 1451 (see **15.85**).

Checklist: alteration of articles of association

4.55 *This checklist sets out the law, practice and procedure for amending articles of association.*

No	Issue	Reference
1	Prepare an agenda for the board meeting	Articles and Agenda
2	Draft appropriate amendments to the company's articles of association – check also whether any specific requirements may be set out in any shareholders' agreement	Articles and Shareholders' Agreement
3	Send notice of the board meeting to the company's directors giving date, time and place of the meeting	Articles
4	Can directors dispense with a board meeting by a written resolution procedure?	Articles
5	Is a quorum present?	Articles
6	Has a chairman been appointed for the board meeting?	Articles
7	Directors to vote on the resolution to amend the company's articles of association on a show of hands	Articles
8	Prepare minutes of the board meeting	Minutes
9	Company or secretary to send notice of extraordinary general meeting to the shareholders. Meeting to state date, time, place and proxy	Notice
10	Can the EGM be dispensed with?	Articles
11	Is a quorum present at the EGM?	Articles
12	Appoint chairman for the EGM	CA 2006, s 21(1)
13	Shareholders to vote on the special resolution on a show of hands or on a poll	CA 2006, s 26(1)
14	Prepare minutes of the EGM	CA 2006, s 355
15	Lodge the special resolution at Companies House	CA 2006, s 26(1)
16	Lodge the amended articles of association at Companies House within 15 days after the amendments have been made	CA 2006, s 26(1)

Checklist: model articles for private company limited by shares

4.56 *This checklist sets out in summary form the Model Articles of Association for a company limited by shares.*

No	Issue	Articles
1	*Defined Terms* – sets out the main interpretation terms used in these Model Articles	Part 1, article 1
2	*Liability of Members* – the liability of members is limited to the amount, if any, unpaid on the shares held by them	Part 1, article 2
3	*Directors' General Authority* – directors are responsible for management of the company's business for which purpose they may exercise all powers of the company, subject to the articles	Part 2, article 3

No	Issue	Articles
4	*Shareholders' Reserve Power* – shareholders have residual authority by special resolution which can direct the directors to take or refrain from taking specified action	Part 2, article 4
5	*Directors May Delegate* – directors may delegate their powers to certain persons on such terms as thought fit, subject to the articles	Part 2, article 5
6	*Committees* – where directors delegate any of their powers to committees, such committees must follow procedures within the articles governing the taking of decisions by directors. Directors can also make procedural rules for committees	Part 2, article 6
7	*Directors to take decisions collectively* – any decision of directors should be by majority decision or under article 8. If only one director, he may take decisions without regard to any of the provisions in the articles on directors' decision making	Part 2, article 7
8	*Unanimous Decisions* – directors may take unanimous decisions where they share a common view on a matter and in this case, a written resolution procedure may be used	Part 2, article 8
9	*Calling a Directors' Meeting* – any director can call a board meeting or by authorising the company secretary (if any) to give notice of the meeting with specific contents of the notice	Part 2, article 9
10	*Participation in Directors' Meetings* – subject to the articles, directors may participate in Board meetings or in part	Part 2, article 10
11	*Quorum for Directors' Meetings* – two directors unless otherwise determined by directors	Part 2, article 11
12	*Chairing of Directors' Meetings* – directors may appoint a director to chair meetings of the board which appointment can be terminated any time	Part 2, article 12
13	*Casting Vote* – chairman has casting vote in the event of a deadlock	Part 2, article 13
14	*Conflicts of Interest* – in the event that a director is involved in a proposed or actual conflict of interest that director cannot vote or count in a quorum subject to exceptions	Part 2, article 14
15	*Record of Decisions to be Kept* – all unanimous or majority decisions of directors to be kept for ten years by directors	Part 2, article 15
16	*Directors' discretion to make further rules* – directors can make further rules as thought fit as to how they take decisions and how rules are recorded or communicated to directors	Part 2, article 16
17	*Method of Appointing Directors* – a director can be appointed by ordinary resolution or by a decision of the directors	Part 2, article 17
18	*Termination of directors' appointment* – sets out the circumstances when a person ceases to be a director	Part 2, article 18
19	*Directors' remuneration* – directors are entitled to remuneration as they determine	Part 2, article 19
20	*Directors' expenses* – the company may pay any reasonable expenses which the directors properly incur in respect of their meetings	Part 2, article 20

No	Issue	Articles
21	*All shares to be fully paid up* – a share cannot be issued for less than the aggregate of its nominal value	Part 3, article 21
22	*Powers to issue different classes of share* – a company may issue shares with such rights or restrictions as determined by ordinary resolution, subject to the articles and rights attached to any existing share	Part 3, article 22
23	*Company not bound by less than absolute interests* – company is not bound by and need not recognise any interest in a share other than the holder's absolute ownership	Part 3, article 23
24	*Share certificates* – the company must issue share certificates to each shareholder free of charge with specific details set out in the share certificate	Part 3, article 24
25	*Replacement of share certificates* – in certain circumstances a shareholder can obtain a replacement share certificate upon indemnity and payment of a reasonable fee to the directors	Part 3, article 25
26	*Share transfers* – shares may be transferred by instrument of transfer or as determined by directors	Part 3, article 26
27	*Transmission of shares* – sets out the procedure where shares are transmitted on death of a shareholder or on bankruptcy	Part 3, article 27
28	*Exercise of transmittees' rights* – sets out the procedure for transmittees to hold shares in the company	Part 3, article 28
29	*Transmittees bound by prior notices* – where notice is given to a shareholder in respect of shares and transmittee is entitled to those shares, transmittee bound by the notice if given to the shareholder before transmittee's name entered in register of members	Part 3, article 29
30	*Procedure for declaring dividends* – by ordinary resolution and the directors may decide to pay interim dividends	Part 3, article 30
31	*Payment of dividends and other distributions* – addresses how a dividend will be paid once declared	Part 3, article 31
32	*No interest on distributions* – general rule that a company will not pay interest on dividends subject to exceptions	Part 3, article 32
33	*Unclaimed distributions* – deals with procedure where dividends unclaimed by shareholders	Part 3, article 33
34	*Non-cash distributions* – subject to ordinary resolution, company may decide to pay all or part of dividends by non-cash assets	Part 3, article 34
35	*Waiver of distributions* – deals with circumstances when dividends may be waived	Part 3, article 35
36	*Authority to capitalise and appropriation of capitalised sums* – directors may decide to capitalise the company's profits subject to ordinary resolution	Part 3, article 36
37	*Attendance and speaking at general meetings* – the right of a person to attend and speak, communicate any information or opinions concerning that meeting	Part 4, article 37
38	*Quorum for general meetings* – no business can be conducted at a general meeting unless quorum is present except appointment of chairman	Part 4, article 38

No	Issue	Articles
39	*Chairing general meetings* – the chairman will chair general meetings if appointed and the procedure where a chairman has not been appointed and who can chair	Part 4, article 39
40	*Attendance and speaking by directors and non-shareholders* – directors may attend and speak at general meetings whether or not they are shareholders. At chairman's discretion, others may be entitled to attend and speak	Part 4, article 40
41	*Adjournment* – where a meeting is not quorate within half an hour of the meeting time, it may be adjourned in circumstances set out	Part 4, article 41
42	*Voting: general* – on a show of hands unless poll demanded	Part 4, article 42
43	*Errors and disputes* – An objection as to the qualification of the person voting at a general meeting can only be raised at the general meeting or adjourned meeting	Part 4, article 43
44	*Poll votes* – deals with circumstances when a poll vote is taken	Part 4, article 44
45	*Content of proxy notices* – sets out what is required in a proxy notice	Part 4, article 45
46	*Delivery of proxy notices* – deals with appointment and revocation of proxy notices	Part 4, article 46
47	*Amendments to resolutions* – deals with procedure for amendments to ordinary and special resolutions	Part 4, article 47
48	*Means of communication to be used* – this is subject to the articles and means of communication prescribed under CA 2006 in respect of notices or documents	Part 4, article 48
49	*Company seals* – any common seal may only be used by authority of the directors	Part 4, article 49
50	*No right to inspect accounts and other records* – accounting or other records cannot be inspected by a shareholder unless authorised by directors or by ordinary resolution	Part 4, article 50
51	*Provision for employees on cessation of business* – directors may make provision for the benefit of employees or former employees of the company on a cessation or transfer of business	Part 4, article 51
52	*Indemnity* – deals with indemnifying a director in certain circumstances and form of indemnity	Part 4, article 52
53	*Insurance* – directors may decide to take out insurance in respect of any loss or liability incurred by the director	Part 4, article 53

Checklist: articles of association

4.57

No	Issue	Reference
1	Articles are defined as part of the company's 'constitution' and are registered at Companies House	CA 2006, s 17

No	Issue	Reference
2	The company's 'constitution' also includes resolutions of directors and shareholders	CA 2006, s 29
3	The memorandum of association is not part of the company's constitution	CA 2006, s 8
4	Articles regulate the internal relations between the company, directors and the shareholders and every company must have articles	CA 2006, s 18
5	A company may either have tailor-made articles, or adopt the default Model Articles or combine both the Model Articles and its own articles	Articles
6	Articles may be supplemented by a shareholders' agreement setting out in more detail the governance between shareholders and directors including exit mechanisms and restrictive covenants	Shareholders' Agreement
7	Certain provisions of the articles may be entrenched for the protection of certain shareholders	CA 2006, s 22(1)
8	A company may alter its articles of association	CA 2006, s 21(1)
9	Judicial attitudes towards articles of association range from various tests employed for the alteration including: (i) bona fide for the benefit of the company; (ii) notions of conscience, oppression and (iii) shareholders to consider the alteration honestly as to whether for the company's benefit.	*Allen v Gold Reefs of West Africa Ltd* [1900] 1 Ch 656; *Brown v British Abrasive Wheel* [1919] 1 Ch 290; *Sidebottom v Kershaw, Leese & Co Ltd* [1920] 1 Ch 154.
10	Provisions of the company's constitution bind the company and its members to the same extent as if there were covenants on the part of the company and of each member to observe those provisions	CA 2006, s 33(1)
11	A company may enforce articles against a shareholder	*Hickman v Kent or Romney Marsh Sheepbreeders' Association* [1915] Ch 881
12	A shareholder may enforce provisions of the articles of association against another shareholder	Ch 851; *Rayfield v Hands* [1960] Ch 1
13	A shareholder may be able to enforce some of the provisions of the articles against the company	*Pender v Lushington* (1877) 6 Ch D 70
14	Outsiders cannot enforce the articles of association	*Eley v Positive Life Association* (1876) 1 Ex D 88
15	The courts will not usually imply terms into the articles of association, except in very limited circumstances	*AG of Belize v Belize Telecom* [2009] 2 BCLC 148 *Marks and Spencer plc v BNP Paribas Securities Services Trust Company (Jersey) Ltd* [2015] UKSC 72

5 Corporate capacity and related matters

Introduction

5.1 This section addresses the following issues:

- consideration of corporate capacity;
- how corporate capacity may be restricted;
- the effect of corporate capacity;
- the powers of directors to bind the company; and
- related matters including execution of documents by companies.

Background to corporate capacity

5.2 As the company is considered a separate legal entity distinct from its shareholders, it has legal capacity to enter into contracts with third parties, and internally with shareholders and directors: CA 2006, s 16; *Salomon v Salomon & Co Ltd* [1897] AC 22.

Previously, a company's capacity to enter into transactions was strictly regulated by various mechanisms, including restricting or expanding its ability to enter into certain transactions, through provisions contained in the objects clause in the memorandum of association. Corporate capacity could also be restricted through judicial intervention by the use of the doctrine of *ultra vires*. The aim of the *ultra vires* doctrine, as it applied to companies, was to protect investors and creditors against unauthorised corporate activities and depletion of their funds. In the strict sense of the term, any transaction which was beyond the company's capacity as defined in its objects clause in the memorandum of association would be void, and could not be ratified by the members: *Ashbury Railway Carriage and Iron Company v Riche* (1875) LR 7 HL 653.

5.3 At times, the *ultra vires* doctrine created obstacles for companies and third parties by restricting their commercial freedom to enter into transactions, and progressively the practice grew of expanding a companies' objects clauses to allow them to undertake a wide range of business activities without invoking the *ultra vires* doctrine: *Bell Houses Ltd v City Wall Properties Ltd* [1966] 1 QB 207. This technique of expanding the objects clauses as widely as possible to allow for any activity by a company, was at times met with judicial disapproval. Although the House of Lords in *Cotman v Brougham* [1918] AC 514 viewed this activity as 'pernicious practice: confusing power with purpose', Lord Wrenbury felt he had to 'yield to it'.

However, the application of the *ultra vires* doctrine created judicial uncertainty owing to the confusion between corporate capacity and a company's powers. In *Rolled Steel Products v British Steel Corporation* [1985] 3 All ER 52, the Court of Appeal stated that the term *ultra vires* was only applicable to acts beyond the company's capacity, as opposed to corporate powers.

5.4 Corporate capacity is now regulated by CA 2006 and the company's articles of association.

Corporate capacity

Nature of corporate capacity

5.5 A company's capacity refers to its ability to carry out specific activities or enter into transactions, through the board of directors, the shareholders or third parties for the purposes of the company's business. Historically, the activities were governed by the company's objects clause, and powers that were supplementary to the company's objects, as set out in the company's memorandum of association.

However, there is no longer a requirement for a company to provide an objects clause in its constitution, subject to an exception. Section 31 of CA 2006 states that a company will have unlimited objects, unless the objects are specifically restricted by the articles. In practice, this means that unless a company makes a deliberate choice to restrict its objects or activities, the objects will have no bearing on what a company can do. This allows freedom for companies to engage in commercial dealings, without any impediment or restrictions in the objects clause. Any restrictions or limitations in the company's articles of association will not affect the company's capacity to engage in transactions, but it may impact on the powers and duties of directors who enter into the prohibited transaction or activity, which may be expressly prohibited in the company's articles of association.

5.6

Example:

Company A decides to restrict its objects clause in its articles of association with the following provision:

> 'Notwithstanding any other provision in the Company's Articles of Association, the Company shall not at any time engage in any philanthropic activities or provide any donations to any organisations, persons, charities or entities without the unanimous consent of the shareholders.'

In breach of the restrictions in its articles, Company A provides financial donations to charities, and seconds some of its employees to local organisations to discharge its corporate social responsibilities, and to demonstrate that it is a good, responsible and caring corporate citizen.

The effects of CA 2006, ss 31 and 39 are that Company A's capacity to enter into the transaction cannot be challenged. The external effects of the *ultra vires* doctrine, therefore, have no application. The directors may be in breach of their general duties set out in CA 2006, Pt 10, unless they can demonstrate that they acted in good faith to promote the company's success. They may consider CA 2006, s 1157 (relief from liability) as exoneration from liability for breach of duty, if they acted reasonably and honestly. Internally within the company, shareholders may have an action against the directors for exceeding their powers, or acting in breach of their general duties, or in breach of the contractual provisions of the articles of association. The internal effects of the *ultra vires* doctrine may therefore still apply.

5.7 Under CA 2006, s 31(2) where a company changes its articles to add, remove or alter a statement of the company's objects, it must give notice to the registrar at Companies House. The registrar must register the notice, and the alteration will not take effect until the notice has been registered.

Section 31(3) of CA 2006 ensures that any such amendment to the company's articles of association will not affect any rights or obligations of the company, or render defective any legal proceedings by or against it.

Under CA 2006, directors still have a duty to observe the company's constitution. Section 171 requires directors to act within their powers. However, restrictions in a company's objects will have little effect outside of the internal operations of the company because of the effect of s 39 (company's capacity) and s 40 (power of directors to bind the company).

Effect of corporate capacity

5.8 Part 4 of CA 2006 is concerned with the company's capacity and related matters. Section 39(1) of CA 2006 applies to a company's capacity to enter into obligations or to carry out a transaction with third parties. It states that the validity of a company's acts will not be called into question, on the ground of lack of capacity by reason of anything in a company's constitution.

The effect of s 39 is that there are no limits to a company's capacity to enter into transactions or undertake various acts, and the company has full contractual and commercial freedom in its dealings with third parties. Therefore, whatever the 'act' in which the company engages, it cannot be called into question. However, the company cannot engage in unlawful or illegal activities or activities that are contrary to public policy or morals. Section 7(2) of CA 2006 states that a company cannot be established for an unlawful purpose.

Also, the courts may in limited circumstances, question a company's capacity to enter into transactions or undertake acts, by piercing the corporate veil to identify any evasive wrongdoing: *Prest v Petrodel Ltd* [2013] All ER 90.

Although CA 2006 has abolished the external effects of the ultra vires doctrine (as between the company and third parties), the internal effects of the doctrine still survive as between the company and the director, thereby imposing liabilities on directors.

In *Ceredigion Recycling & Furniture Team v Pope* [2022] EWCA Civ 22, the Court of Appeal stated that the fact that CA 2006, s 39 had abolished the ultra vires doctrine as between the company and third parties, did not relieve the directors from liability to the company for their breach of duty or wrongdoing merely because, qua members, they agreed with the course which was taken. Not only is that liability of the directors expressly preserved by CA 2006, s 40(5), but *Bilta (UK) Ltd v Nazir (No 2)*

[2015] UKSC 23 in the Supreme Court, stated that knowledge of the breach of duty and wrongdoing by a director, was not to be attributed to the company, even if the director is the sole shareholder or member.

Powers of directors to bind the company

5.9 Section 40(1) of CA 2006 provides that in favour of a person dealing with the company in good faith, the power of the directors to bind the company, or authorise others to do so, is deemed not to be constrained by the company's constitution. The internal aspects of the *ultra vires* doctrine still survive as between the shareholders and directors, which means that directors' powers may be open to challenge by the shareholders.

The concept of 'good faith'

5.10 The effect of CA 2006, s 40(1) is that a third party dealing with a company in good faith need not be concerned about whether a company is acting within its constitution. The term 'good faith' is not defined by CA 2006. Instead, there is a presumption of good faith in favour of the third party. Therefore, only some third parties will benefit from CA 2006, s 40. The third party is presumed to have acted in good faith unless the contrary is proved. The third party is not to be regarded as acting in bad faith, by reason only of his knowing that an act is beyond the powers of the directors under the company's constitution.

5.11 In practice, it may be difficult to demonstrate bad faith owing to the protections given to the third party in the following circumstances:

- There is no obligation on the third party to enquire into the limitations on the powers of directors to bind the company. Therefore, the doctrine of constructive notice does not apply: *Royal British Bank v Turquand* (1856) 6 E & B 327.
- The onus is on the company to show that the third party was not acting in good faith unless the contrary is proved.
- A third party who knows that the act in question is beyond the powers of directors under the company's constitution, will not be considered to have acted in bad faith.

The concept of 'good faith' was considered in *Barclays Bank v TOSG Trust Fund Ltd* [1984] BCLC 1. Nourse J stated that a person had to act 'genuinely and honestly in the circumstances of the case'. This case proceeded on appeal to the Court of Appeal on other grounds. See too *Sargespace Ltd v Natasha Anastasia Eustace* [2013] EWHC 2944 (QB).

A third party who is put on notice cannot benefit from CA 2006, s 40: *Wrexham Associated Football Club Ltd v Crucialmove* [2007] BCC 139.

A third party will not be acting in bad faith by knowing of the limitations on directors' powers: *Ford v Polymer Vision Ltd* [2009] 2 BCLC 160.

'Person dealing with the company'

5.12 CA 2006, s 40(2) states that a person 'deals with' a company if he is a party to any transaction or other act to which the company is a party. The 'transaction' referred to may be a contract or an obligation that is entered into. The term 'act' may refer to consideration paid for the transaction or services performed, with our without consideration. This section has given rise to some case law as to what meaning is to be given to 'person' and 'dealing with the company'. In this regard, the courts have stated that a third party is a constructive trustee for monies knowingly improperly received: *International Sales and Agencies Ltd v Marcus* [1982] 3 All ER 551. See too Ungoed-Thomas J in *Selangor United Rubber Estates Ltd v Cradock (a bankrupt) (No 3)* [1968] 2 All ER 1073, and Lord Dunpark in *Thompson v J Barke & Co (Caterers) Ltd* 1975 SLT 67; and *Belmont Finance Corp v Williams Furniture Ltd (No 2)* [1980] 1 All ER 393.

The position of directors under CA 2006, s 40

5.13 CA 2006, s 40 concerns directors and allows any limitations on their powers to bind the company or authorise others to do so to be removed. A person must be a director to fall within CA 2006, s 40: *Smith v Henniker-Major & Co (a firm)* [2002] 2 BCLC 655. The references to limitations on the directors' powers under the company's constitution include limitations deriving from a resolution of the company, or of any class of shareholders; or from any agreement between the members of the company or any class of shareholders: CA 2006, s 40(3).

The internal effects of the *ultra vires* doctrine still survive. Despite directors exceeding the limitations on their powers, shareholders can still take action. CA 2006, s 40(4) provides that it does not affect any right of a member of a company to bring proceedings to restrain the doing of an action that is beyond the powers of the directors. This procedure allows shareholders to bring an action (usually seeking an injunction), to prevent directors from entering into future obligations that are beyond their powers. However, no such proceedings lie in respect of an act to be done in fulfilment of a legal obligation arising from a previous act of the company.

5.14 Further, s 40 does not affect any liability incurred by the directors, or any other person, by reason of the directors exceeding their powers: CA 2006, s 40(5): *Ceredigion Recycling & Furniture Team v Pope* [2022] EWCA Civ 22. Section 40 is also subject to s 41 (transactions with directors or their associates), and s 42 (companies that are charities).

Constitutional limitations: transactions involving directors or their associates

5.15 Section 41 of CA 2006 applies to a transaction if, or to the extent that, its validity depends on s 40. It provides that nothing in s 41 is to be read as excluding the operation of any other enactment or rule of law by virtue of which the transaction may be called into question or any liability to the company may arise: s 41(1). The term 'transaction' includes any act: CA 2006, s 41(7).

This section also addresses the position of the nature of the transaction between the company and its director or connected persons. Where a company enters into a transaction of the type contemplated under s 41(1), and the parties to the transaction include a director of the company or of its holding company, or a person connected with any such director, the transaction is voidable at the instance of the company. The reference to a person connected with a director has the same meaning as in Part 10 (company directors): CA 2006, s 41(7).

Section 41 of CA 2006 refers to a transaction with an 'insider', such as a director or person connected with a director. Irrespective of whether the transaction is voided, the 'insider' and any director of the company who authorised the transaction, is liable to account to the company for any gain he has made directly or indirectly as a result of the transaction, and to indemnify the company for any loss or damage that the company has incurred resulting from the transaction.

5.16 Under s 41(4) a transaction will cease to be voidable in certain circumstances:

- if restitution of any money or assets that have been lost as a result of the transaction is no longer possible; or
- the company is indemnified for any loss or damage resulting from the transaction; or
- rights acquired bona fide for value without actual notice of the directors exceeding their powers by a person who is not a party to the transaction would be affected by voiding the transaction; or
- the transaction is affirmed by the company.

However, where the 'insider' is not a director of the company, it may be possible for him to avoid liability under s 41(3), if he can show that at the time he entered into the transaction with the company, he did not know that the directors were exceeding their authority: CA 2006, s 41(5).

However, nothing in the preceding provisions of s 41 affects the rights of any party to the transaction not within s 41(2)(b)(i) or (ii). But the court may, on the application of the company or any such party, make an order affirming, severing or setting aside the transaction, on such terms as appear to the court to be just: CA 2006, s 41(6). See too *Re Torvale Group Ltd* [1999] 2 BCLC 605.

Formalities of doing business under the law of England and Wales

5.17 This section considers related matters concerning corporate capacity where a company undertakes business activities.

Company contracts

5.18 Under the law of England and Wales a contract may be made by a company, by writing under its common seal; or on behalf of a company, by a person acting under its authority, express or implied: CA 2006, s 43(1).

Any formalities required by law in the case of a contract made by an individual also apply, unless a contrary intention appears, to a contract made by or on behalf of a company: CA 2006, s 43(2).

Execution of documents

5.19 Under the law of England and Wales, a document is executed by a company by the affixing of its common seal; or by signature in accordance with the following provisions: CA 2006, s 44(1).

5.20 A document is validly executed by a company if it is signed on behalf of the company by two authorised signatories; or by a director of the company in the presence of a witness who attests the signature: CA 2006, s 44(2).

5.21 The following are 'authorised signatories' for the purposes of CA 2006, s 44(2):

(a) every director of the company; and

(b) in the case of a private company with a secretary or a public company, the secretary (or any joint secretary) of the company: CA 2006, s 44(3).

5.22 A document signed in accordance with s 44(2) and expressed, in whatever words, to be executed by the company, has the same effect as if executed under the common seal of the company: CA 2006, s 44(4): *Williams v Redcard Ltd* [2011] 2 BCLC 350.

In favour of a purchaser, a document is deemed to have been duly executed by a company if it purports to be signed in accordance with s 44(2). A 'purchaser' means a purchaser in good faith for valuable consideration and includes a lessee, mortgagee or other person who for valuable consideration acquires an interest in property: CA 2006, s 44(5).

Where a document is to be signed by a person on behalf of more than one company, it is not duly signed by that person for the purposes of this section unless he signs it separately in each capacity: CA 2006, s 44(6).

5.23 The references to a document being (or purporting to be) signed by a director or secretary are to be read, in a case where that office is held by a firm, as references to its being (or purporting to be) signed by an individual authorised by the firm to sign on its behalf: CA 2006, s 44(7).

This section applies to a document that is (or purports to be) executed by a company, in the name of or on behalf of another person whether or not that person is also a company: CA 2006, s 44(8).

Common seal

5.24 A company may have a common seal, but need not have one: CA 2006, s 45(1). If a company has a common seal, it must have its name engraved in legible characters on the seal: CA 2006, s 45(2). If a company fails to comply with s 45(2), an offence is committed by the company; and every officer of the company who is in default: CA 2006, s 45(3).

An officer of a company, or a person acting on behalf of a company, commits an offence if he uses, or authorises the use of, a seal purporting to be a seal of the company on which its name is not engraved as required by s 45(2): CA 2006, s 45(4). A person can be fined if found guilty of this offence: CA 2006, s 45(5).

Execution of deeds

5.25 A document is validly executed by a company as a deed for the purposes of s 1(2)(b) of the Law of Property (Miscellaneous Provisions) Act 1989 and for the purposes of the law of Northern Ireland if, and only if it is duly executed by the company; and it is delivered as a deed: CA 2006, s 46(1).

For the purposes of s 46(1)(b) a document is presumed to be delivered upon its being executed, unless a contrary intention is proved: CA 2006, s 46(2).

See too Law Commission Report, "Execution of Electronic Documents" (2019) (Law Com No 386).

Execution of deeds or other documents by attorney

5.26 Under the law of England and Wales a company may, by instrument executed as a deed, empower a person, either generally or in respect of specified matters, as its attorney to execute deeds or other documents on its behalf: CA 2006, s 47(1). A deed or other document which is executed, whether in the UK or elsewhere, applies as if executed by the company: CA 2006, s 47(2).

Official seal for share certificates etc

5.27 A company that has a common seal may have an official seal for use for sealing securities issued by the company; or for sealing documents creating or evidencing securities so issued: CA 2006, s 50(1).

5.28 The official seal must be a facsimile of the company's common seal, with the addition on its face of the word 'Securities'; and when duly affixed to the document has the same effect as the company's common seal: CA 2006, s 50(2).

Checklist

5.29 *This checklist sets out the key issues governing corporate capacity and matters that need to be considered where corporate capacity is challenged. It also addresses the main provisions and case law impacting on corporate capacity*

No	Issue	Reference
1	Previously, a company's objects clause was set out in its memorandum of association.	Memorandum of association
2	Acts outside the company's objects were considered *ultra vires* the company.	*Ashbury Railway Carriage and Iron Company v Riche* (1875) LR 7 HL 653
3	A practice grew of mitigating the effects of the *ultra vires* doctrine by expanding the objects clause, to enable the widest interpretation to be given to each activity of the objects clause, including those incidental or conducive to the company's objects.	*Bell Houses Ltd v City Wall Properties Ltd* [1966] 1 QB 207
4	The combined effects of the reforms in 1972 and 1989 led to a short-form objects clause in the memorandum of association.	European Communities Act 1972 Previously Companies Act 1989, s 3A (see now CA 2006, s 31)

No	Issue	Reference
5	Under CA 2006, companies no longer need an objects clause.	CA 2006, s 31
6	If a company chooses to have an objects clause, it will appear in the articles of association.	Articles of association
7	A company is deemed to have unrestricted objects, unless it chooses to place limitations or restrictions on its activities.	CA 2006, s 31
8	A company cannot be established for an unlawful purpose.	CA 2006, s 7(2)
9	A company's capacity refers to its ability to carry out acts or transactions whether through its board, directors, shareholders or third parties.	CA 2006, s 39
10	A company has unlimited capacity to enter into transactions. The validity of an act done by a company cannot be called into question on the ground of lack of capacity by reason of anything in the company's constitution. Although the external effects of the ultra vires doctrine have been abolished (as between the company and third parties), the doctrine still has application internally as between directors and the company.	CA 2006, s 39 *Ceredigion Recycling & Furniture Team v Pope* [2022] EWCA Civ 22
11	Where a person deals with the company in good faith, the powers of the directors to bind the company or authorise others to do so, is deemed not to be constrained by the company's constitution.	CA 2006, s 40
12	Transactions between the company and its directors or their associates are voidable at the instance of the company but there are exceptions where the transaction ceases to be voidable.	CA 2006, s 41
13	There are certain formalities to be observed for company contracts.	CA 2006, s 43
14	There are certain formalities to be observed for the execution of documents by a company.	CA 2006, s 44
15	A company need not have a common seal.	CA 2006, s 45
16	There are certain formalities to be observed for the execution of deeds by a company.	CA 2006, s 46

6 Company re-registration

Introduction

6.1 This chapter addresses the following issues:

- the companies that may be allowed to re-register to enable them to alter their status;
- the steps and procedures that are required to alter their status; and
- a checklist of legal and practical issues in connection with the re-registration process.

CA 2006 provides a procedure allowing companies to alter their legal status, by converting into another corporate legal form. This allows for flexibility and convenience, and avoids the process of having to dissolve one company, and to establish the desired company.

Companies that may alter their status

6.2 The following companies may re-register to alter their status: CA 2006, s 89:

- from a private company to a public company: CA 2006, ss 90–96;
- from a public company to a private company: CA 2006, ss 97–101;
- from a private limited company to an unlimited company: CA 2006, ss 102–104;
- from an unlimited private company to a limited company: CA 2006, ss 105–108;
- from a public company to an unlimited private company: CA 2006, ss 109–111.

Checklist: private company becoming public

6.3 A private company (whether limited or unlimited) may be re-registered as a public company limited by shares (CA 2006, s 90(1)).

This checklist sets out the procedures required to effect a change of status where a private company wishes to convert its status to a public company.

6.3 *Company re-registration*

No	Issue	Reference
1	Ensure the proposed public company has a minimum of at least two directors	CA 2006, s. 154(2)
2	Ensure that the company meets the authorised minimum share capital requirements (see below)	CA 2006, s 90
3	Ensure that a suitably qualified company secretary is appointed (see below)	CA 2006, s 273
4	The private company must pass a special resolution for re-registration as a public company. The procedure will be:	CA 2006, s 90(1)(a)
	• call a board meeting upon reasonable notice;	Articles of association/ Notice to board members
	• prepare an agenda for the meeting including any background papers and briefs particularly on responsibilities and obligations of a public company including directors;	Agenda
	• board meeting may be dispensed with if written resolution used;	Written resolution
	• ensure quorum present;	
	• ensure all five conditions present for alteration of status (see below);	CA 2006, s 90
	• board meeting votes on altering the status of the private company to a public company;	
	• prepare minutes of the board meeting;	
	• call an EGM by notice to the shareholders setting out date, time and place of the meeting including nature of special resolution and reference to appointment of a proxy, or consent to short notice;	CA 2006, s 307(1) Notice to shareholders
	• consider if written resolution may be used;	
	• ensure quorum present;	
	• voting on a show of hands (unless poll demanded) – 75% required for approval by majority;	
	• prepare minutes of the EGM for circulation;	Minutes
	• lodge the special resolution/written resolution at Companies House;	CA 2006, s 307(5) Written resolution
	• lodge statement of compliance;	Compliance statement
	• lodge form at Companies House;	Form R01 (Application by a private company for re-registration as a public company)

No	Issue	Reference
	• printed copy of the articles of association; • copy of balance sheet dated no more than seven months before receipt of Form RR01; • auditor's statement; • auditor's report; • fee for re-registration; • change company headed notepaper/business cards to reflect plc status; • change company signage at Head Office; • notify suppliers/third parties/banks/HMRC/VAT/PAYE. • revise, draft and lodge a memorandum of association for a public company limited by shares (see below) • obtain a certificate of re-registration from the Registrar of Companies • if required, obtain a new company seal • change company's bank account details	
5	The following five conditions for altering the status from private company to public company must be satisfied: • the company must have a share capital; • the requirements of CA 2006, s 91 are met as regards share capital (see below); • the requirements of CA 2006, s 92 are met as regards its net assets; • compliance with CA 2006, s 93 (recent allotment of shares for non-cash consideration if this section applies); and • the company has not previously re-registered as unlimited.	CA 2006, s 90(1)(b) and (2)
6	The company must make such changes in its name and in its articles as are necessary in connection with it becoming a public company (articles of association for plc to be prepared and reference to 'plc' or 'public liability company' or Welsh equivalent).	CA 2006, s 90(3)
7	If the company is unlimited, it must also make such changes in its articles of association as are necessary in connection with it becoming a company limited by shares.	CA 2006, s 90(4)
8	The following requirements as to share capital must be met at the time the special resolution is passed that the company should be re-registered as a public company:	CA 2006, s 91(1)

No	Issue	Reference
	(a) the nominal value of the company's allotted share capital must not be less than the authorised minimum; (b) each of the company's allotted shares must be paid up at least as to one-quarter of the nominal value of that share and the whole of any premium on it; (c) if any shares in the company or any premium on them have been fully or partly paid up by an undertaking given by any person that he or another should do work or perform services (whether for the company or any other person), the undertaking must have been performed or otherwise discharged; and (d) if the shares have been allotted as fully or partly paid up as to their nominal value or any premium on them otherwise than in cash, and the consideration for the allotment consists of or includes an undertaking to the company, then either: (i) the undertaking must have been performed or otherwise discharged; or (ii) there must be a contract between the company and some person pursuant to which the undertaking is to be performed within five years from the time the special resolution is passed. For the purpose of determining whether the above requirements under (b), (c) and (d) are met, the following may be disregarded: (i) shares allotted before 22 June 1982 in the case of a company then registered in Great Britain; or (ii) shares allotted before 31 December 1984 in the case of a company then registered in Northern Ireland; (iii) shares allotted in pursuance of an employee's share scheme by reason of which the company, but for CA 2006, s 91(2)(b), be precluded under CA 2006, s 91(1)(b) (but not otherwise) from being re-registered as a private company.	
	• No more than one-tenth of the nominal value of the company's allotted share capital is to be disregarded under CA 2006, s 91(2)(b). The allotted share capital is treated as not including shares disregarded under CA 2006, s 91(2)(b).	CA 2006, s 91(3)
	• Shares disregarded under CA 2006, s 91(2) are treated as not forming part of the allotted share capital for the purposes of CA 2006, s 91(1)(a).	CA 2006, s 91(4)
	• A company must not be re-registered as a public company if it appears to the registrar that:	CA 2006, s 91(5)

No	Issue	Reference
	(a) the company has resolved to reduce its share capital; (b) the reduction is made under CA 2006, s 626 (reduction in connection with the redenomination of share capital). It is supported by a solvency statement in accordance with CA 2006, s 643; or it has been confirmed by an order of the court under CA 2006, s 648; and the effect of the reduction is, or will be, that the nominal value of the company's allotted share capital is below the authorised minimum.	
9	With regard to the requirement as to net assets, a company applying to re-register as a public company must obtain: (a) a balance sheet prepared as at a date not more than seven days before the date on which the application is delivered to the registrar; (b) an unqualified report by the company's auditor on that balance sheet; and (c) a written statement by the company's auditor that it is his opinion at the balance sheet date that the amount of the company's net assets was not less than aggregate of its called up share capital and undistributable reserves. ● Between the balance sheet date and the date on which the application for re-registration is delivered to the registrar, there must be no change in the company's financial position that results in the amount of its net assets becoming less than the aggregate of its called up share capital and distributable reserves. ● The term 'unqualified report' means: (a) if the balance sheet was prepared for a financial year of the company, a report stating without material qualification the auditor's opinion that the balance sheet has been properly prepared in accordance with the requirements of CA 2006; or	CA 2006, s 92(1)
	(b) if the balance sheet was not prepared for a financial year of the company, a report stating without material qualification the auditor's opinion that the balance sheet has been properly prepared in accordance with the provisions of CA 2006 which would have applied if it had been prepared for a financial year of the company.	CA 2006, s 92(3)
	● For the purpose of an auditor's report on the balance sheet that was not prepared for a financial year of the company, the provisions of CA 2006 apply with such modifications as are necessary by reason of the fact.	CA 2006, s 92(4)

No	Issue	Reference
	• For the purposes of CA 2006, s 92(3), a qualification is material unless the auditor states in his report that the matter giving rise to the qualification is not material for the purpose of determining (by reference to the company's balance sheet) whether, at the balance sheet date, the amount of the company's net assets were less than the aggregate of its called-up share capital and 'undistributable reserves'.	
10	With regard to recent allotment shares for non-cash consideration, this is governed by CA 2006, s 93 which applies where: (a) shares are allotted by the company in the period between the date as to which the balance sheet required by CA 2006, s 92 is prepared and the passing of the resolution that the company should re-register as a public company; and (b) the shares are allotted as fully or partly paid up as to their nominal value or any premium on them otherwise than in cash.	CA 2006, s 93(1)
	• The registrar must not entertain an application by the company for re-registration as a public company unless: (a) the requirements of s 593(1)(a) and (b) have been complied with (independent valuation of non-cash consideration: valuer's report to company not more than six months before allotment); or (b) the allotment is in connection with: (i) a share exchange (see sub-ss (3)–(5) below); or (ii) a proposed merger with another company (see sub-s (6) below).	CA 2006, s 93(2)
	• An allotment is in connection with a share exchange if: (a) the shares are allotted in connection with an arrangement under which the whole or part of the consideration for the shares allotted is provided by: (i) the transfer to the company allotting the shares of shares (or shares of a particular class) in another company; or (ii) the cancellation of shares (or shares of a particular class) in another company; and (b) the allotment is open to all the holders of the shares of the other company in question (or, where the arrangement applies only to shares of a particular class, to all the holders of the company's shares of that class) to take part in the arrangement in connection with which the shares are allotted.	CA 2006, s 93(3)

No	Issue	Reference
	• In determining whether a person is a holder of shares for the purposes of sub-s (3), there shall be disregarded: (a) shares held by, or by a nominee of, the company allotting the shares; (b) shares held by, or by a nominee of: (i) the holding company of the company allotting the shares; (ii) a subsidiary of the company allotting the shares; or (iii) a subsidiary of the holding company of the company allotting the shares.	CA 2006, s 93(4)
	• It is immaterial, for the purposes of deciding whether an allotment is in connection with share exchange, whether or not the arrangement in connection with which the shares are allotted involves the issue to the company allotting the shares of shares (or shares of a particular class) in the other company.	CA 2006, s 93(5)
	• There is a proposed merger with another company if one of the companies concerned proposed to acquire all the assets and liabilities of the other in exchange for the issue of its shares or other securities to shareholders of the other (whether or not accompanied by a cash payment). 'Another company' includes anybody corporate.	CA 2006, s 93(6)
	• For the purposes of CA 2006, s 93: (a) the consideration for an allotment does not include any amount standing to the credit of any of the company's reserve accounts, or of its profit and loss account, that has been applied in paying up (to any extent) any of the shares allotted or any premium on those shares; and (b) 'arrangement' means any agreement, scheme or arrangement, including an arrangement sanctioned in accordance with: (i) Part 26 CA 2006 (arrangement and reconstruction); or (ii) s 110 of the Insolvency Act 1986 (c 45) or art 96 of the Insolvency (Northern Ireland) Order 1989 (SI 1989/2405 (NI 19)) (liquidator in winding up accepting shares as consideration for sale of company's property)).	CA 2006, s 93(7)
11	An application for re-registration as a public company must contain:	CA 2006, s 94(1)
	(a) a statement of the company's proposed name on re-registration; and	

No	Issue	Reference
	(b) in the case of a company without a secretary, a statement of the company's proposed secretary under CA 2006, s 95.	
	• The application must be accompanied by:	CA 2006, s 94(2) CA 2006 (as inserted by SBEEA 2015, s 98(2))
	(a) a copy of the special resolution that the company should re-register as a public company unless a copy has already been forwarded to the registrar under CA 2006, Pt 3, Ch 3;	
	(b) a copy of the company's articles as proposed to be amended;	
	(c) a copy of the balance sheet and other documents referred to in CA 2006, s 92(1);	
	(d) if CA 2006, s 93 applies (recent allotment of shares for non-cash consideration), a copy of the valuation report (if any) under CA 2006, s 93(2)(a); and	
	(e) a statement of the aggregate amount paid up on the shares of the company on account of their nominal value.	
	• The statement of compliance required to be delivered together with the application is a statement that the requirements so as to re-registration as a public company have been complied with.	CA 2006, s 94(3)
	• The registrar may accept the statement of compliance as sufficient evidence that the company is entitled to be re-registered as a public company.	CA 2006, s 94(4)
12	The statement of the company's proposed secretary must contain the required particulars of the person who is or the persons who are to be the secretary or joint secretaries of the company.	CA 2006, s 95(1)
	• The required particulars are the particulars that will be required to be stated in the company's register of secretaries (CA 2006, ss 277–279).	CA 2006, s 95(2)
	• The statement must also include a statement by the company that the person named as secretary, or each of the persons named as joint secretaries, has consented to act in the relevant capacity. If all the partners in the firm are to be joint secretaries, consent may be given by one partner on behalf of all of them.	CA 2006, s 95(3) (as inserted by SBEEA 2015, s 100(3))

No	Issue	Reference
13	With regard to the issue of a certificate of incorporation on re-registration, if on the application for re-registration as a public company, the registrar is satisfied that the company is entitled to be so re-registered the company shall be re-registered accordingly.	CA 2006, s 96(1)
	• The registrar must issue a certificate of incorporation altered to meet the circumstances of the case.	CA 2006, s 96(2)
	• The certificate must state that it is issued on re-registration and the date on which it is issued.	CA 2006, s 96(3)
	• On the issue of the certificate the following take effect:	CA 2006, s 96(4)
	(a) the company becomes a public company;	
	(b) the changes in the company's name and articles take effect; and	
	(c) where the application contained a statement under CA 2006, s 95 (Statement of proposed secretary), the person or persons named in the statement as secretary or joint secretary of the company are deemed to have been appointed to that office.	

Checklist: public company becoming private

6.4 *A public company may re-register as a private company under CA 2006. This checklist sets out the conditions, steps and procedures required to effect such re-registration.*

No	Issue	Reference
1	A public company may be re-registered as a private company limited by shares or by guarantee if the following are satisfied:	CA 2006, s 97(1)
	(a) A special resolution that the public company should be re-registered as a private company is passed.	
	(b) An application for re-registration is delivered to the registrar in accordance with CA 2006, s 100 together with other documents required by that section and a statement of compliance.	
	• Call a board meeting upon reasonable notice.	Notice
	• Prepare an agenda for the meeting including any background papers and briefs.	Agenda
	• Ensure quorum present.	
	• Ensure all conditions present for alteration of status (see below).	
	• Board meeting votes on altering the status of the public company to a private company.	
	• Prepare minutes of the board meeting.	Minutes

No	Issue	Reference
	• Call an EGM by notice to the shareholders setting out date, time and place of the meeting including nature of special resolution and reference to appointment of a proxy.	Notice
	• Ensure quorum present.	
	• Voting on a show of hands (unless poll demanded).	
	• Prepare minutes of the EGM for circulation.	Minutes
	• Lodge the special resolution at Companies House and copy court order (if appropriate).	CA 2006, s 30
	• Lodge statement of compliance.	Statement of compliance
	• Lodge Form RR02 or RR05 at Companies House with fee.	Form RRO2 (Application by a public company for registration as a private limited company)
	• Lodge printed copy of articles of association and memorandum of association	Companies House
	• Obtain certificate of re-registration from the Registrar of Companies	
	• If required, obtain a new company seal	
	• Notify suppliers/third parties/banks/HMRC/VAT/PAYE.	
	• Printed copy of the amended articles of association.	Articles of association
	• Fee for re-registration.	
	• Change company headed notepaper/business cards.	
	• Change company signage at Head Office.	
	• The following conditions must be complied with: (a) where no application under CA 2006, s 98 for cancellation of the resolution has been made: (i) having regard to the number of members who consented to or voted in favour of the resolution, no such application may be made; or (ii) the period within which such an application could be made has expired; (a) where such an application has been made – (i) the application has been withdrawn; or (ii) an order has been made confirming the resolution and a copy of that order has been delivered to the registrar.	CA 2006, s 97(2)
	• The company must make such changes in its name and in its articles as are necessary in connection with its becoming a private company limited by shares, or as the case may be, by guarantee.	CA 2006, s 97(3)

No	Issue	Reference
2	Where a special resolution by a public company to be re-registered as a private limited company has been passed, and application to the court for the cancellation of the resolution may be made: (a) by the holders of not less in the aggregate than 5% in nominal value of the company's issued share capital on any class of the company's issued share capital (disregarding any shares held by the company at treasury shares); (b) if the company is not limited by shares, by not less than 5% of its members; or (c) by not less than 50 of the company's members. However, the above do not apply to a person who has consented to or voted in favour of the resolution.	CA 2006, s 98(1)
	• The application must be made within 28 days after the passing of the resolution and may be made on behalf of the persons entitled to make it by such one or more of their number as they may appoint for the purpose.	CA 2006, s 98(2)
	• On the hearing of the application, the court must make an application either cancelling or confirming the resolution.	CA 2006, s 98(3)
	• The court may: (a) make an order on such terms and conditions as it thinks fit; (b) if it thinks fit, adjourn the proceedings in order that an arrangement may be made to the satisfaction of the court for the purchase of the interests of dissentient members; and (c) give such directions and make such orders, as it thinks expedient for facilitating or carrying into effect any such arrangement.	CA 2006, s 98(4)
	• The court's order may if the court thinks fit: (a) provide for the purchase by the company of the shares of any of its members and for the reduction accordingly of the company's capital; and (b) make such other alteration in the company's articles as may be required in consequence of that provision.	CA 2006, s 98(5)
	• The court's order may, if the court thinks fit, require the company not to make any, or any specified, amendments to its articles without the leave of the court.	CA 2006, s 98(6)
3	• On making an application under CA 2006, s 98 (application to court to cancel resolution) the applicants or the person making the application on their behalf, must immediately give notice to the registrar. This is without prejudice to any provisions of rules of court as to service of notice of the application.	CA 2006, s 99(1)

No	Issue	Reference
	• On being served with notice of any such application, the company must immediately give notice to the registrar.	Form RR05 (Notice by the applicants of application to the court for cancellation of resolution for re-registration) CA 2006, s 99(2)
	• Within 15 days of making of the court's order on the application, or such other longer period as the court may at any time direct, the company must deliver to the registrar a copy of the order.	CA 2006, s 99(3)
	• If a company fails to comply with CA 2006, s 99(2) or (3), the offence is committed by the company and every officer of the company who is in default.	CA 2006, s 99(4)
	• A person guilty of an offence under CA 2006, s 99 is liable on summary conviction to a fine not exceeding level 3 on the standard scale and, for continued contravention, a daily default fine not exceeding one-tenth of level 3 on the standard scale.	CA 2006, s 99(5)
4	• An application for re-registration as a private limited company must contain a statement of the company's proposed name on re-registration.	CA 2006, s 100(1)
	• The application must be accompanied by: (a) a copy of the resolution that the company should re-register as a private limited company (unless a copy has already been forwarded to the registrar under Chapter 3 of Part 3); and (b) a copy of the company's articles as proposed to be amended.	CA 2006, s 100(2)
	• The statement of compliance required to be delivered together with the application is a statement that the requirements as to re-registration as a private limited company have been complied with.	CA 2006, s 100(3)
	• The registrar may accept the statement of compliance as sufficient evidence that the company is entitled to be re-registered as a private limited company.	CA 2006, s 100(4)
	• If, on an application for re-registration as a private limited company, the registrar is satisfied that the company is entitled to be so re-registered, the company shall be re-registered accordingly.	CA 2006, s 101(1)
	• The registrar must issue a certificate of incorporation altered to meet the circumstances of the case.	CA 2006, s 101(2)
	• The certificate must state that it is issued on re-registration and the date on which it is issued.	CA 2006, s 101(3)
	• On the issue of the certificate: (a) the company becomes a private limited company and;	CA 2006, s 101(4)

No	Issue	Reference
	(b) the changes in the company's name and articles take effect.	
	• The certificate is conclusive evidence that the requirements of CA 2006, as to re-registration have been complied with.	CA 2006, s 101(5)

Checklist: private limited company becoming unlimited

6.5 *This checklist sets out the legal and practical steps and procedures for altering the status of a private limited company to become unlimited. This process of re-registration is not common in practice, but some companies may become unlimited to keep their accounts private without the need to file them at Companies House. Advantage of this re-registration may also include ease of distribution of funds to the shareholders under an unlimited company than a private limited liability company.*

No	Issue	Reference
1	A private limited company may be re-registered as an unlimited company if: (a) all the members of the company have assented to its being so re-registered; (b) an application for re-registration is delivered to the registrar in accordance with CA 2006, s 103, together with the other documents required by that section and a statement of compliance; and (c) there is compliance with the condition that the company has not been previously re-registered as limited.	CA 2006, s 102(1) CA 2006, s 102(2)
2	• The company must make such changes in its name and its articles as are necessary in connection with its becoming an unlimited company; and if it is to have a share capital, as are necessary, in connection with its becoming an unlimited company having a share capital.	CA 2006, s 102(3)
3	• Call a board meeting upon reasonable notice.	Notice
4	• Prepare agenda for the meeting including any background papers and briefs.	Agenda
5	• Board meeting may be dispensed with if written resolution used.	Written resolution
6	• Ensure quorum present for the board meeting.	
7	• Board meeting votes on altering the status of the limited liability company to an unlimited company.	
8	• Prepare minutes of the board meeting.	Minutes
9	• Call an EGM by notice to the shareholders setting out date, time and place of the meeting including nature of special resolution and reference to appointment of a proxy.	Notice

No	Issue	Reference
10	• Consider if written resolution may be used.	
11	• Make appropriate changes to the articles of association and memorandum of association.	
12	• Ensure quorum present for the EGM.	
13	• Voting on a show of hands (unless poll demanded). Unanimous consent required.	
14	• Prepare minutes of the EGM for circulation.	Minutes
15	• Lodge the written resolution at Companies House.	CA 2006, s 30
16	• Lodge Form RR05 at Companies House.	Form RR05 (Application by a private limited company for re-registration as an unlimited company)
17	• Printed copy of the amended articles of association for an unlimited company and memorandum of association.	Articles and memorandum
18	• Fee for re-registration.	Fee
19	• Change company headed notepaper/business cards.	
20	• Change company signage at Head Office.	
21	• Notify suppliers/third parties/banks/HMRC/VAT/ PAYE.	
22	• Obtain certificate of re-registration from the Registrar of Companies	
23	• If required, obtain a new company seal	
24	• Change company's bank account details	
25	• A trustee in bankruptcy of a member of the company is entitled, to the exclusion of the member, to assent to the company's becoming an unlimited company. The personal representative of a deceased member of the company may assert on behalf of the deceased.	CA 2006, s 102(4)
26	• The reference to a 'trustee in bankruptcy of a member of the company' includes: (a) a permanent trustee or an interim trustee (within the meaning of the Bankruptcy (Scotland) Act 1985 (c 66)) on the sequestrated estate of a member of the company; and (b) a trustee under a protected trustee deed (within the meaning of the Bankruptcy (Scotland) Act 1985) granted by a member of the company.	CA 2006, s 102(5)
27	• An application for re-registration as an unlimited company must contain a statement of the company's proposed name on re-registration.	CA 2006, s 103(1)

No	Issue	Reference
28	● The application must be accompanied by the following: (a) the prescribed form of assent to the company being registered as an unlimited company authenticated by or on behalf of all the members of the company; (b) a copy of the company's articles as proposed to be amended.	CA 2006, s 103(2)
29	● The statement of compliance delivered together with the application is a statement that the requirements as to re-registration as an unlimited company have been complied with.	CA 2006, s 103(3)
30	● The statement must contain a statement on the directors of the company: (a) that the persons by whom or on whose behalf the form of assent is authenticated constitute the whole membership of the company; and (b) if any of the members have not authenticated that form themselves, that the directors have taken all reasonable steps to satisfy themselves that each person who authenticated it on behalf of a member was lawfully empowered to do so.	CA 2006, s 103(4)
31	● The registrar may accept the statement of compliance as sufficient evidence that the company is entitled to be re-registered as an unlimited company.	CA 2006, s 103(5)
32	● If, on an application for re-registration of a private limited company as an unlimited company, the registrar is satisfied that the company is entitled to be so re-registered, the company shall be registered accordingly.	CA 2006, s 104(1)
33	● The registrar must issue a certificate of incorporation altered to meet the circumstances of the case.	CA 2006, s 104(2)
34	● The certificate must state that it is issued on re-registration and the date on which it is issued.	CA 2006, s 104(3)
35	● On the issue of the certificate: (a) the company becomes an unlimited company; and (b) the changes in the company's name and articles take effect.	CA 2006, s 104(4)
36	● The certificate is conclusive evidence that the requirements of CA 2006, as to re-registration, have been complied with.	CA 2006, s 104(5)

Checklist: unlimited private company becoming limited

6.6 *This checklist sets out how an unlimited private company may alter its status to become a limited company – whether limited by shares or guarantee. It considers the steps and procedures required to effect the change.*

No	Issue	Reference
1	An unlimited company may be re-registered as a private limited company if: (a) a special resolution that it should be so re-registered is passed; (b) the application for re-registration is delivered to the registrar in accordance with CA 2006, s 106 together with the other documents required by that section; and a statement of compliance; and (c) there is compliance with the condition that the company has not previously re-registered as an unlimited company.	CA 2006, s 105(1); CA 2006, s 105(2)
2	● Call a board meeting upon reasonable notice.	Notice
3	● Prepare agenda for the meeting including any background papers and briefs.	Agenda
4	● A board meeting may be dispensed with if written resolution used.	
5	● Ensure quorum present at the Board Meeting.	
6	● Board meeting votes on altering the status of the unlimited company to a limited liability company (whether limited by shares or guarantee).	
7	● Prepare minutes of the board meeting.	Minutes
8	● Call an EGM by notice to the shareholders setting out date, time and place of the meeting including nature of special resolution and reference to appointment of a proxy. The special resolution must state whether the company is to be limited by shares or guarantee.	Notice, CA 2006, s 105(3)
9	● Consider if written resolution may be used.	Written resolution
10	● Make appropriate changes to the articles of association and memorandum of association.	
11	● Ensure quorum present at the EGM	
12	● Voting on a show of hands (unless poll demanded).	
13	● Prepare minutes of the EGM for circulation.	Minutes
14	● Lodge the special resolution at Companies House.	CA 2006, s 30
15	● Lodge Form RR06 at Companies House.	Form RR06
16	● Printed copy of the amended articles of association for a limited company and memorandum of association.	Articles and memorandum
17	● Fee for re-registration.	
18	● Statement of compliance.	
19	● Change company headed notepaper/business cards.	

No	Issue	Reference
20	• Change company signage at head office.	
21	• Notify suppliers/third parties/banks/HMRC/VAT/PAYE.	
22	• The company must make such changes in its name and in its articles, as are necessary in connection with its becoming a company limited by shares, or as the case may be, by guarantee.	CA 2006, s 105(4)
23	• An application for re-registration as a limited company must contain a statement of the company's proposed name on re-registration.	CA 2006, s 106(1)
24	• The application must be accompanied by: (a) a copy of the resolution that the company should re-register as a private limited company (unless a copy has already been forwarded to the registrar under CA 2006, Pt3, Ch 3); (b) if the company is to be limited by guarantee, a statement of guarantee; and (c) a copy of the company articles as proposed to be amended.	CA 2006, s 106(2)
25	• The statement of guarantee required to be delivered in the case of a company that is to be limited by guarantee must state that each member undertakes that, if the company is wound up while he is a member, or within one year after he ceases to be a member, he will contribute to the assets of the company such amount as may be required for: (a) Payment of the debts and liabilities of the company contracted before he ceases to be a member; (b) Payment of the costs, charges and expenses of winding up; and (c) adjustment of the rights of the contributories among themselves not exceeding a specified amount.	CA 2006, s 106(3)
26	• The statement of compliance required to be delivered together with the application is a statement that the requirements as to re-registration as a limited company have been complied with.	CA 2006, s 106(4)
27	• The registrar may accept the statement of compliance as sufficient evidence that the company is entitled to be re-registered as a limited company.	CA 2006, s 106(5)
28	• If, on an application for registration of an unlimited company as a limited company, the registrar is satisfied that the company is entitled to be re-registered, the company shall be re-registered accordingly.	CA 2006, s 107(1)
29	• The registrar must issue a certificate of incorporation altered to meet the circumstances of the case.	CA 2006, s 107(2)
30	• The certificate must state that it is issued on re-registration and the date on which it is issued.	CA 2006, s 107(3)

No	Issue	Reference
31	• On the issue of the certificate, the company becomes an unlimited company; the changes in the company's name and articles take effect.	CA 2006, s 107(4)
32	• The certificate is conclusive evidence that the requirements for re-registration have been complied with.	CA 2006, s 107(5)
33	• A company, which on re-registration under CA 2006, s 107 already has allotted share capital, must deliver a statement of capital to the registrar within 15 days after the re-registration.	CA 2006, s 108(1)
34	• The requirement under CA 2006, s 108(1) does not apply if the information which would be included in the statement has already been sent to the registrar in: (a) a statement of capital and initial shareholdings (see s.10 CA 2006); or (b) (if different) the last statement of capital sent by the company.	CA 2006, s 108(2) (as inserted by SBEEA 2015, s 93(4))
35	• The statement of capital must state with respect to the company's share capital on re-registration: (a) the total number of shares of the company; (b) the aggregate nominal value of those shares; (c) for each class of shares: (i) prescribed particulars of the rights attached to the shares; (ii) the total number of shares of that class; and (iii) the aggregate nominal value of shares of that class, and (d) the amount paid up and the amount (if any) unpaid on each share (whether on account of the nominal value of the share or by way of premium).	CA 2006, s 108(3)
36	• If default is made in complying with CA 2006, s 108, an offence is committed by the company and every officer of the company who is in default.	CA 2006, s 108(4)
37	• A person guilty of an offence under CA 2006, s 108 is liable, on summary conviction, to a fine not exceeding level 3 on the standard scale and for continued contravention, a daily default fine not exceeding one-tenth of level 3 on the standard scale	CA 2006, s 108(5)

Checklist: public company becoming private and unlimited

6.7 *This checklist sets out the legal steps and procedures required to effect an alteration in the status from a public company becoming private and unlimited.*

No	Issue	Reference
1	• A public company limited by shares may be re-registered as an unlimited private company with a share capital if: (a) all the members of the company have assented to its being so re-registered; (b) the application for re-registration is delivered to the registrar in accordance with CA 2006, s 110 together with the other documents required by that section; and a statement of compliance; and (c) the satisfaction of the condition that the company has not previously been registered as limited or unlimited.	CA 2006, s 109(1) CA 2006, s 109(2)
2	• The company must make such changes in its name and in its articles as are necessary in connection with its becoming an unlimited private company.	CA 2006, s 109(3)
3	• Call a board meeting upon reasonable notice.	Notice
4	• Prepare an agenda for the meeting.	Agenda
5	• Include any background papers to the Agenda.	
6	• Ensure quorum present.	
7	• The board meeting votes on altering the status of the public company to an unlimited private company.	
8	• Prepare minutes of the board meeting.	Minutes
9	• Call an EGM by notice to the shareholders setting out the date, time and place of the meeting including the appointment of a proxy.	
10	• Consider if written resolution may be used.	Written resolution
11	Make appropriate changes to the articles of association and memorandum of association for the private unlimited company.	CA 2006, s 109(3)
12	• Voting by a show of hands (unless poll demanded).	
13	• Prepare minutes of the EGM for circulation.	Minutes
14	• Lodge the written resolution at Companies House.	CA 2006, s 30
15	• Lodge Form RR07 at Companies House.	Form RR07 (Application by a public company for re-registration as a private unlimited company)
16	• Printed copy of the amended articles of association for the private unlimited company and memorandum of association	
17	• Fee for re-registration	

No	Issue	Reference
18	• Statement of compliance.	
19	• Change company headed notepaper/business cards.	
20	• Change company signage at head office.	
21	• Notify suppliers/third parties/banks/HMRC/VAT/ PAYE.	
22	• or the purpose of CA 2006, s 109: (a) a trustee in bankruptcy of a member of the company is entitled to the exclusion of the member to assent the company's re-registration; and (b) the personal representative of a deceased member of the company may assent on behalf of the deceased.	CA 2006, s 109(4)
23	• The reference to 'a trustee in bankruptcy of a member of a company' includes: (a) a permanent trustee or an interim trustee (within the meaning of the Bankruptcy (Scotland) Act 1985 (c 66) on the sequestered estate of a member of the company; and (b) a trustee under a protected trustee deed (within the meaning of the Bankruptcy (Scotland) Act 1985) granted by a member of the company.	CA 2006, s 109(5)
24	• An application for re-registration of a public company as an unlimited private company must contain a statement of the company's proposed name on re-registration.	CA 2006, s 110(1)
25	• The application must be accompanied by: (a) the prescribed form of assent to the company's being registered as an unlimited company authenticated by or on behalf of all the members of the company; and (b) a copy of the company's articles as proposed to be amended.	CA 2006, s 110(2)
26	• The statement of compliance required to be delivered together with the application is a statement to re-registration as an unlimited private company have been complied with.	CA 2006, s 110(3)
27	• The statement must contain a statement by the directors of the company: (a) that the persons by whom or on whose behalf the form of assent is authenticated constitute the whole membership of the company; and (b) if any of the members have not authenticated that form themselves, that the directors have taken all reasonable steps to satisfy themselves that each person who authenticated it on behalf of a member was lawfully empowered to do so.	CA 2006, s 110(4)

No	Issue	Reference
28	• The registrar may accept the statement of compliance as sufficient evidence that the company is entitled to be re-registered as an unlimited private company.	CA 2006, s 110(5)
29	• If, on an application for re-registration of a public company as an unlimited private company, the registrar is satisfied that the company is entitled to be so re-registered, the company shall be re-registered accordingly.	CA 2006, s 111(1)
30	• The registrar must issue a certificate of incorporation altered to meet the circumstances of the case.	CA 2006, s 111(2)
31	• The certificate must state that it is issued on a re-registration and the date on which it is so issued.	CA 2006, s 111(3)
32	• On issue of the certificate, the company becomes an unlimited private company, and the changes in the company's name and articles take effect.	CA 2006, s 111(4)
33	• The certificate is conclusive evidence that the requirements under the CA 2006, as to re-registration have been complied with.	CA 2006, s 111(5)

7 Corporate governance and the code

Introduction

7.1 This chapter addresses the following issues:

- defining 'corporate governance';
- the development of corporate governance in England;
- the separation of ownership from control;
- the establishment of various committees on corporate governance;
- consideration of the UK Corporate Governance Code; and
- the Stewardship Code.

Definition of corporate governance

7.2 The term 'corporate governance' can be described as the system by which companies are directed and controlled. Within the corporate governance system, the board of directors are responsible for the governance of their companies. The shareholders' role in the governance is to appoint the directors, and the auditors and to satisfy themselves that an appropriate governance structure is in place. The responsibilities of the board include setting the company's strategic aims, providing the leadership to put them into effect, supervising the management of the business and reporting to shareholders on their stewardship. The board's actions are subject to laws, regulations and the shareholders' resolutions in a general meeting.

As a system, corporate governance is concerned with the boards and key executives who control, manage and operate the company. These executives are driven by corporate values, corporate ethics, norms and beliefs, and manage the operational aspects of the company's daily interaction with its internal and external stakeholders. The corporate governance system also addresses how a board can add value to a company, ensuring that its long-term strategy is not only profit maximisation and long-term success, but also discharging its corporate social responsibilities towards wider stakeholders in society.

7.3 An effective corporate governance system should provide mechanisms for regulating directors' duties to prevent them from abusing their powers, and to ensure that they act in the best interests of the company in its broad sense. There are various methods of regulating directors' duties. In English company law, this is achieved in a somewhat random fashion by employing the following control mechanisms:

(1) By legislation: under CA 2006, certain safeguards (eg unfair prejudicial conduct and the derivative action) exist for the protection of shareholders and creditors. The Insolvency Act 1986 provides further protection and safeguards for the company's creditors who invest in the company. Directors bear a high level of responsibility to the company's creditors to ensure that a company is not involved in fraudulent or wrongful trading.

(2) The application of other common law and fiduciary duties to directors that have not been codified under CA 2006 on the general duties of directors.

(3) Directors may also be subject to civil liability for breach of their fiduciary duties.

(4) Compliance with the UK Code of Corporate Governance. Companies are subject to the City Code on Takeovers and Mergers and SARs and the Listing Rules.

(5) Shareholders are given some rights to monitor directors' actions under the articles of association as well as some statutory rights under CA 2006.

(6) Auditors ensure that the risk of financial irregularities is minimised by auditing the company's accounts and ensuring that a company's accounts provide a 'true and fair view' of its financial position.

A brief overview of the development of corporate governance in the UK

7.4 The development of corporate governance in the UK owes its historical origins to a number of company law committees that were established to examine the efficiency, effectiveness, operational and functional aspects of corporate governance, and how the system could be better improved to ensure more accountability and transparency by directors, in managing the corporation as well as their dealings with shareholders.

This section briefly considers the key origins of corporate governance dating back to the 1990s and traces the developments over the years culminating in the publication of the UK Code on Corporate Governance.

The principle of profit maximisation

7.5 In England, the concept of corporate governance was largely entrenched in the traditional theory of the firm, which advocated that the only objective of companies was to maximise profits with shareholders' welfare as their paramount consideration. This structure of corporate governance mandated directors to carry out the shareholders' directions. Directors were, therefore, perceived as agents for their shareholders.

Adam Smith, in *An Inquiry into the Causes of the Wealth of Nations* (first published 1776, published by The Modern Library in 1937), believed that individual entrepreneurs, who relied on their own efforts and market forces, would be led by an 'invisible hand' to achieve the rewards which the markets were prepared to offer. The success of the entrepreneur was conditional on risk taking. He was not complimentary to directors when he wrote:

> 'The directors of such companies, however, being the managers of other people's money than of their own, it cannot well be expected, that they should watch over it with the same anxious vigilance with which the partners in a private co-partnery frequently watch over their own … Negligence and profusion, therefore, must always prevail more or less, in the management of the affairs of such a company.'

Smith also observed that directors:

> 'seldom pretend to understand anything of the business of the company; and when the spirit of faction happens not to avail among them, give themselves no trouble about it, but receive contentedly such half yearly or yearly dividend, as the directors think proper to make to them'.

English company law has clearly reinforced the profit maximisation principle within the corporate governance system. In *North-West Transportation v Beatty* (1887) 12 App Cas 589, the claimant, Henry Beatty, sued the directors of the company and claimed an order to set aside a sale made to the company of his steamer *The United Empire*, which he had owned before she was sold. Sir Richard Baggallay stated that the resolution of a majority of the shareholders, duly adopted, upon any question coming under the pinnacle of a company's mandate, was binding upon the majority, and consequently upon the company. Further, every shareholder had a right to vote on any such question, although he might have a personal interest in the subject matter opposed to, or different from, the general or particular interests of the company.

The rule in *North-West Transportation* seems to have gained solid ground in England, as it is in conformity with the traditional notion on which English company law is based. It is not, therefore, surprising that initiatives for amending companies' legislation in England prior to 1980 were sporadic, unconstructed and akin to the traditional notion that social responsibilities must not enter the realm of the company's activities.

The separation of ownership from control

7.6 During the 19th century, the English courts considered directors as agents of the shareholders: the shareholders could give directions by an ordinary resolution which would be binding on the directors. This had the effect that directors' powers could be controlled and regulated from time to time, as dictated by the shareholders. The shareholders reigned supreme. Two lines of authorities governed the principle that the courts would not interfere in the decisions of the shareholders. First, the courts could declare that that any breach of articles was a mere irregularity, that could be cured by the shareholders: *MacDougall v Gardiner* (1875) 1 Ch D 13. Secondly, the courts considered that a breach of articles infringed the personal rights of shareholders: *Pender v Lushington* (1877) 6 Ch D 70.

Earlier judicial authorities were of the view that shareholders could mandate directors to act in a certain manner. In *Isle of Wight Railway v Tahourdin* (1883) 25 Ch D 320, the Court decided that the shareholders were entitled to intervene and interfere in the company's management, if they believed that the course of action taken by directors was not for the company's benefit.

7.7 The decision of the Court of Appeal in the *Tahourdin* case demonstrated that shareholder power was dominant within the corporate decision making functions. The shareholders were considered as active participants within the company, with powers to mandate directors to comply with shareholders' mandate. It also signalled the court's desire not to interfere in the internal management of the company's affairs, unless required to do so in the company's interests. The courts accepted that the shareholders' authority was final, ultimate and binding on the directors.

7.8 Subsequently, some judicial authorities considered that the articles of association governed the powers vested in directors and the shareholders. Where the articles provided for directors to manage the company's affairs, the shareholders could not interfere with such powers. In *Automatic Self Cleansing Filter Syndicate Co v Cunninghame* [1906] 2 Ch 34, the Court of Appeal held that on the construction of the company's articles of association, the shareholders had delegated wide powers to the directors on the day to day management of the company, and that directors were not agents for the shareholders. The Court of Appeal distinguished the *Tahourdin* case on the grounds that the wording in that company's articles of association was different from the present case.

7.9 Some English law cases have considered that directors were not agents for the shareholders: they had powers to conduct the day-to-day operations of the company.

The principles established in *Automatic Self Cleansing Filter Syndicate Co* were subsequently considered by the Court of Appeal in *Gramaphone & Typewriter Ltd v Stanley* [1908] 2 KB 89. Fletcher Moulton LJ cited with approval the *Automatic* case, and the fact that directors were not agents of their shareholders, and were not required to comply with shareholder directions, unless required by the company's constitution and resolutions passed at general meetings. According to Buckley LJ, as the shareholders had delegated a significant degree of control to the directors, and they could not interfere with the powers delegated to them.

7.10 The *Automatic* case, however, did not gain support from some subsequent cases, as the effect of the case would be that directors may act on their own volition, with their powers becoming uncontrollable. In this situation, shareholders would simply be perceived as passive with no voice, and accepting all decisions made by directors, whether or not in the company's best interests. *Marshalls Valve Gear Co v Manning Wardle & Co* [1909] 1 Ch 267 distinguished the *Automatic* case, and asserted that shareholders had the ultimate residual authority to control directors' actions.

However, in *Quin & Axtens Ltd v Salmon* [1909] 1 Ch 311, the Court of Appeal reverted to the position established in the *Automatic* case, thereby maintaining a complete separation of ownership from control. The effect of this was to prevent shareholders from generally interfering in the day-to-day management of the company.

7.11 The prevailing view expressing the separation of ownership from control was established in *Shaw & Sons (Salford) Ltd v Shaw* [1935] 2 KB 113. The Court of Appeal decided that if powers of management were vested in the directors of a company, they alone could exercise those powers. The only way in which the general body of the shareholders could control the exercise of powers vested by the articles in the directors, was by altering the articles of the company, or refusing to re-elect the directors of whose actions they disapproved. They could not usurp the powers which, by the articles, were vested in the directors.

See too *Rose v McGivern* [1998] 2 BCLC 593 per Neuberger J; and *Scott v Scott* [1943] 1 All ER 582.

7.12 The Model Articles for a private company limited by shares vests authority in directors to manage the day-to-day affairs of the company, but this is 'subject to the articles'. The Model Articles also provide for ultimate residual power ('members reserve') vested in the shareholders to mandate directors to act in a particular manner by way of a special resolution.

(Model Articles of Association of a Private Company Limited by Shares)

PART 2

DIRECTORS

DIRECTORS' POWERS AND RESPONSIBILITIES

Directors' general authority

3. Subject to the articles, the directors are responsible for the management of the company's business, for which purpose they may exercise all the powers of the company.

Shareholders' reserve power

4.—(1) The shareholders may, by special resolution, direct the directors to take, or refrain from taking, specified action.

(2) No such special resolution invalidates anything which the directors have done before the passing of the resolution.

The establishment of corporate governance committees

Cadbury Committee

7.13 The Cadbury Committee was established in May 1991 under the chairmanship of Sir Adrian Cadbury by the Financial Reporting Council (FRC), the London Stock Exchange and the accountancy profession to address the financial aspects of corporate governance, and produced a report on 1 December 1992 on *The Financial Aspects of Corporate Governance.* The principal recommendations of the Cadbury Committee included that all boards of listed companies registered in the UK should comply with a Code of Best Practice which the Committee had developed. The Code was designed to achieve high standards of corporate behaviour expected of such companies. Its principles were based on openness, integrity and accountability. The Code addressed various aspects such as the role of auditors, the board of directors, shareholders and non-executive directors (NEDs) including reporting and controls.

Greenbury Committee

7.14 In January 1995, a Study Group on Directors' Remuneration was established on the initiative of the CBI, in response to public and shareholder concerns about the pay and other remuneration of company directors in the UK. This group became known as the 'Greenbury Committee' as it was headed by Sir Richard Greenbury, whose terms of reference were 'to identify good practice in determining directors' remuneration and prepare a Code of such practice for use by UK plcs'.

On 17 July 1995, the Greenbury Committee published a report on 'Directors' Remuneration' which focused exclusively on plc directors' remuneration in listed companies. The report was published against a background of concerns about executive remuneration, with large pay increases and large gains from share options in privatised utility industries, including the amounts of compensation paid to some departing directors. The Committee did not recommend statutory controls, but action to strengthen accountability and encourage enhanced performance coupled with proper reporting to shareholders and transparency about directors' remuneration.

The Committee published a new Code of Best Practice on Directors' Remuneration which recommended that all listed companies in the UK should comply with the Code, and report annually to the shareholders about their compliance. The Code required boards to establish a remuneration committee to address the executive compensation of directors independently monitored by NEDs.

Hampel Committee

7.15 The Hampel Committee on Corporate Governance was established in November 1995 by the Financial Reporting Council (FRC). The Committee published its Final Report in January 1998. It published a Combined Code on Corporate Governance which applied to listed plcs.

Turnbull – Internal Control: Guidance for Directors on the Combined Code

7.16 In September 1999, Nigel Turnbull, as Chairman of the Internal Control Working Party of the Institute of Chartered Accountants in England and Wales, published a report entitled *Internal Control: Guidance for Directors on the Combined Code.*

The Turnbull guidance emphasised the following aspects:

- *The need to maintain a sound system of internal control.*
- *Reviewing the effectiveness of internal control.*
- *The board's statement on internal control.*

Higgs – Review of the Role and Effectiveness of Non-executive Directors

7.17 In January 2003, Derek Higgs published a report entitled *Review of the Role and Effectiveness of Non-executive Directors*. It addressed the role of the board and the participation of non-executive directors (NEDs) within it. Higgs emphasised the need for board collectivity, in promoting the company's success by directing and supervising its affairs. The board's role is to provide entrepreneurial leadership of the company within a framework of prudent and effective controls which enables risk to be assessed and managed.

Smith – Report on Audit Committees – Combined Code Guidance

7.18 In January 2003, Sir Robert Smith published a report entitled *Report on Audit Committees – Combined Code Guidance* which set out guidance designed to assist company boards in making suitable arrangements for their audit committees and to assist directors serving on audit committees in carrying out their role. The report highlighted the fact that the audit committee had a particular role, acting independently from the executive, to ensure that the interests of shareholders were properly protected in relation to financial reporting and internal control.

Walker – a Review of Corporate Governance in UK Banks and other Financial Industry Entities

7.19 On 26 November 2009, David Walker published a report entitled *A Review of Corporate Governance in UK Banks and other Financial Industry Entities* in the light of the experience of critical loss and failure of the banking system during the period of economic recession.

It made a number of recommendations including to strengthen the role of Non-Executive Directors; a greater accountability role of the chairman; and the need for the board to undertake a formal and vigorous evaluation of its performance.

Regulatory framework of corporate governance in the UK

7.20 In the UK, corporate governance is subject to the following principal regulations:

- the Companies Act 2006 and its regulations;
- the Listing Rules of the London Stock Exchange under the aegis of the Financial Conduct Authority;
- the Disclosure and Transparency Rules;
- the UK Corporate Governance Code; and
- the Stewardship Code.

These aspects are considered in relation to the UK Corporate Governance Code. The Stewardship Code is considered separately.

For small and medium-sized enterprises, the Quoted Companies Alliance has published the *Corporate Governance Code for Small and Mid-Size Quoted Companies* (QCA Code) which helps quoted companies put into practice appropriate corporate governance arrangements and encourage positive engagement between companies and shareholders. The QCA Code is widely recognised as an industry standard for those growing companies for which the UK Corporate Governance Code is not applicable. This includes standard listed companies, those on the AIM and the ICAP Securities and Derivatives Exchange.

The UK Corporate Governance Code

Introduction

7.21 A revised UK Corporate Governance Code (the Code) was published by the Financial Reporting Council ('FRC') in July 2018 (replacing the previous Code in April 2016). The FRC has the responsibility for revisions to the Code. Previous reviews of the Code were in 2005, 2007, 2008, 2010, 2012, 2014 and 2016. The 2018 Code applies to accounting periods beginning on or after 1 January 2019.

The Code applies to all companies with a Premium Listing of equity shares regardless of whether they are incorporated in the UK or elsewhere.

The Code is based on the 'comply or explain' principle for good corporate governance in the UK. Since its inception, it has never been a rigid set of rules, but comprises a set of principles on effective governance with main principles and supporting provisions. The Code effectively represents a guide to a number of aspects for effective board practice. Owing to its flexibility, it is also recognised by the Code that there may be reasons justifying departure from the principles of the Code in particular circumstances if good governance can be achieved by other effective means.

Objectives of the Code

7.22 The objective of the Code is to facilitate effective, entrepreneurial and prudent management that can deliver the long-term success of the company. It is a guide to key components of effective board practice. It is based on the underlying principles of all good governance: accountability, transparency, probity and focus on the sustainable success of an entity over the longer term.

The comply or explain approach

7.23 At the heart of the Code is the 'comply or explain' approach which is required to be undertaken by all companies with a premium listing. The Code consists of Principles and provisions with the latter clarifying and supplementing the Principles.

The Listing Rules require companies to apply the main principles and report to shareholders about how they have done so. The principles are the core of the Code and the way in which they are applied should be the central question for a board as it determines how it is to operate.

It is recognised that an alternative to following a provision may be justified in particular circumstances if good governance can be achieved by other means. A condition of so doing is that the reasons for it should be explained clearly and carefully to shareholders, who may wish to discuss the position with the company and whose voting intentions may be influenced as a result.

In providing an explanation, the company should aim to illustrate how its actual practices are consistent with the principle to which the particular provision relates, contribute to good governance and promote the delivery of business objectives. It should set out the background, provide a clear rationale for the action it is taking and describe any mitigating actions being taken to address any additional risk and maintain conformity with the relevant principle. Where deviation from a particular provision is intended to be limited in time, the explanation should indicate when the company expects to comply with the provision.

7.24 In their response to explanations, shareholders should pay due regard to companies' individual circumstances and should bear in mind the size and complexity of the company and the nature of the risks and challenges it faces. Whilst shareholders have every right to challenge companies' explanations if they are unconvincing, they should not be evaluated in a mechanistic way; departures from the Code should not be automatically treated as breaches. Shareholders should be careful to respond to the statements from companies in a manner that supports the 'comply or explain' process bearing in mind the purpose of good corporate governance. They should put their views to the company and both parties should be prepared to discuss the position.

Smaller listed companies, in particular those new to listing, may judge that some of the provisions are disproportionate or less relevant in their case. Some of the provisions do not apply to companies below the FTSE 350. Such companies may nonetheless consider that it would be appropriate to adopt the approach in the Code and they are encouraged to do so. Externally managed investment companies typically have a different board structure which may affect the relevance of particular provisions; the Association of Investment Companies' *Corporate Governance Code and Guide* can assist them in meeting their obligations under the Code.

7.25 Under the Listing Rules, there is a requirement to include in their annual report and accounts:

'(5) a statement of how the listed company has applied the Main Principles set out in the UK Corporate Governance Code, in a manner that would enable shareholders to evaluate how the principles have been applied;

(6) a statement as to whether the listed company has:

(a) complied throughout the accounting period with all relevant provisions set out in the UK Corporate Governance Code; or

(b) not complied throughout the accounting period with all relevant provisions set out in the UK Corporate Governance Code and if so, setting out:

(i) those provisions, if any it has not complied with;

(ii) in the case of provisions whose requirements are of a continuing nature, the period within which, if any, it did not comply with some or all of those provisions; and

(iii) the company's reasons for non-compliance; and

(7) a report to the shareholders by the board which contains all the matters set out in LR 9.8.8 R.' (This latter aspect is in connection with directors' remuneration.)

Under the Disclosure and Transparency Rules (DTR 7.2), the following aspects apply in respect of corporate governance statements:

'DTR 7.2.1: An issuer to which this section applies must include a corporate governance statement in its directors' report. That statement must be included as a specific section of the directors' report and must contain at least the information set out in DTR 7.2.2R to DTR 7.2.7R and, where applicable, DTR 7.2.10R.

DTR 7.2.2: The corporate governance statement must contain a reference to:

(1) the corporate governance code to which the issuer is subject; and/or

(2) the corporate governance code which the issuer may have voluntarily decided to apply; and/or

(3) all relevant information about the corporate governance practices applied beyond the requirements under national law.

DTR 7.3.3:

(1) An issuer which is complying with DTR 7.2.2R(1) or DTR 7.2.2R(2) must:

(a) state in its directors' report where the relevant corporate governance code is publicly available; and

(b) to the extent that it departs from that corporate governance code, explain which parts of the corporate governance code it departs from and the reasons for doing so.

(2) Where DTR 7.2.2R(3) applies, the issuer must make its corporate governance practices publicly available and state in its directors' report where they can be found.

(4) If an issuer has decided not to apply any provisions of a corporate governance code referred to under DTR 7.2.2R(1) and DTR 7.2.2R(2), it must explain its reasons for that decision.

DTR 7.2.4: A listed company which complies with LR 9.8.6R(6) (the 'comply or explain' rule in relation to the UK Corporate Governance Code) will satisfy the requirements of DTR 7.2.2R and DTR 7.2.3R.

DTR 7.2.5: The corporate governance statement must contain a description of the main features of the issuer's internal control and risk management systems in relation to the financial reporting process.

DTR 7.2.6: The corporate governance statement must contain the information required by paragraph 13(2)(c), (d), (f), (h) and (i) of Schedule 7 to the Large and Medium-sized Companies and Groups (Accounts and Reports) Regulations 2008 (SI 2008 No 410) (information about share capital required under Directive 2004/25/EC (the Takeover Directive)) where the issuer is subject to the requirements of that paragraph.

DTR 7.2.7: The corporate governance statement must contain a description of the composition and operation of the issuer's administrative, management and supervisory bodies and their committees.

DTR 7.2.8: In the FCA's view, the information specified in provisions A.1.1, A.1.2, B.2.4, D.2.11 and C.3.3 of the UK Corporate Governance Code will satisfy the requirements of DTR 7.2.7R.

DTR: 7.2.9: An issuer may elect that, instead of including its corporate governance statement in its directors' report, the information required by DTR 7.2.1R to DTR 7.2.7R may be set out:

(1) in a separate report published together with and in the same manner as its annual report. In the event of a separate report, the corporate governance statement must contain either the information required by DTR 7.2.6 R or a reference to the directors' report where that information is made available; or

(2) by means of a reference in its directors' report to where such document is publicly available on the issuer's website.

DTR: 7.2.10: Subject to DTR 7.2.11R, an issuer which is required to prepare a group directors' report within the meaning of s 415(2) of CA 2006 must include in that report a description of the main features of the group's internal control and risk management systems in relation to the process for preparing consolidated accounts. In the event that the issuer presents its own annual report and its consolidated annual report as a single report, this information must be included in the corporate governance statement required by DTR 7.2.1R.

DTR 7.2.11: An issuer that elects to include its corporate governance statement in a separate report as permitted by DTR 7.2.9R(1) must provide the information required by DTR 7.2.10R in that report.'

Approval and signing of separate corporate governance statement

7.26 Under s 419A of CA 2006, any separate corporate governance statement must be approved by the board of directors and signed on behalf of the board by a director or the secretary of the company: see *The Companies Act 2006 (Accounts, Reports and Audit) Regulations 2009*, SI 2009/1581, reg 2 (with application as stated in reg 1(3)).

The main principles of the UK Corporate Governance Code

7.27 The Code is based on five sections that set out the Principles. Each main principle is followed by Code Provisions that further clarify and elucidate on the Principles.

Principles

1: Board Leadership and Company Purpose

A. A successful company is led by an effective and entrepreneurial board, whose role is to promote the long-term sustainable success of the company, generating value for shareholders and contributing to wider society.

B. The board should establish the company's purpose, values and strategy, and satisfy itself that these and its culture are aligned. All directors must act with integrity, lead by example and promote the desired culture.

C. The board should ensure that the necessary resources are in place for the company to meet its objectives and measure performance against them. The board should also establish a framework of prudent and effective controls, which enable risk to be assessed and managed.

D. In order for the company to meet its responsibilities to shareholders and stakeholders, the board should ensure effective engagement with, and encourage participation from, these parties.

E. The board should ensure that workforce policies and practices are consistent with the company's values and support its long-term sustainable success. The workforce should be able to raise any matters of concern.

2: Division of Responsibilities

F. The chair leads the board and is responsible for its overall effectiveness in directing the company. They should demonstrate objective judgement throughout their tenure and promote a culture of openness and debate. In addition, the chair facilitates constructive board relations and the effective contribution of all non-executive directors, and ensures that directors receive accurate, timely and clear information.

G. The board should include an appropriate combination of executive and non-executive (and, in particular, independent non-executive) directors, such that no one individual or small group of individuals dominates the board's decision-making. There should be a clear division of responsibilities between the leadership of the board and the executive leadership of the company's business.

H. Non-executive directors should have sufficient time to meet their board responsibilities. They should provide constructive challenge, strategic guidance, offer specialist advice and hold management to account.

I. The board, supported by the company secretary, should ensure that it has the policies, processes, information, time and resources it needs in order to function effectively and efficiently.

3: Composition, Succession and Evaluation

J. Appointments to the board should be subject to a formal, rigorous and transparent procedure, and an effective succession plan should be maintained for board and senior management. Both appointments and succession plans should be based on merit and objective criteria and, within this context, should promote diversity of gender, social and ethnic backgrounds, cognitive and personal strengths.

K. The board and its committees should have a combination of skills, experience and knowledge. Consideration should be given to the length of service of the board as a whole and membership regularly refreshed.

L. Annual evaluation of the board should consider its composition, diversity and how effectively members work together to achieve objectives. Individual evaluation should demonstrate whether each director continues to contribute effectively.

4: Audit, Risk and Internal Control

M. The board should establish formal and transparent policies and procedures to ensure the independence and effectiveness of internal and external audit functions and satisfy itself on the integrity of financial and narrative statements.

N. The board should present a fair, balanced and understandable assessment of the company's position and prospects.

O. The board should establish procedures to manage risk, oversee the internal control framework, and determine the nature and extent of the principal risks the company is willing to take in order to achieve its long-term strategic objectives.

5: Remuneration

P. Remuneration policies and practices should be designed to support strategy and promote long-term sustainable success. Executive remuneration should be aligned to company purpose and values, and be clearly linked to the successful delivery of the company's long-term strategy.

Q. A formal and transparent procedure for developing policy on executive remuneration and determining director and senior management remuneration should be established. No director should be involved in deciding their own remuneration outcome.

R. Directors should exercise independent judgement and discretion when authorising remuneration outcomes, taking account of company and individual performance, and wider circumstances.

The Stewardship Code 2020 – An overview

7.28 The FRC first published *The Stewardship Code* which was revised in September 2012 and implemented 1 October 2012. The objective was to improve long-term returns to beneficiaries by enhancing the quantity and quality of engagement between investors and companies. The origins of the Code date back to a publication by the Institutional Shareholders Committee (ISC) of *The Responsibilities of Institutional Shareholders and Agents: Statements of Principles* which was first published in 2002 and subsequently converted into a code in 2009. Following the Walker Review of corporate governance in UK banks and other financial industry entities, the FRC was invited to take responsibility for the Code and that the FRC's remit be extended to develop and encourage best practice stewardship of UK-listed companies by institutional investors.

The FRC has published the latest Stewardship Code 2020, that sets substantially higher expectations for investor stewardship policy and practice. The 2020 Code focuses on how effective stewardship delivers sustainable value for beneficiaries, the economy and society. The Code aims to increase demand for more effective stewardship and investment decision-making which is better aligned to the needs of institutional investors' clients and beneficiaries. The 2020 Code sets out more rigorous requirements for reporting, focusing on how stewardship activities deliver outcomes against objectives. The reporting is subject to increased oversight by the FRC to ensure that the Code is effective in raising the quality of stewardship across the investor community.

The 2020 Code

7.29 The 2020 Code defines 'stewardship' as the responsible allocation and management of capital across the institutional investment community to create sustainable value for beneficiaries, the economy and society. Stewardship activities include monitoring assets and service providers, engaging issuers and holding them to account on material issues, and publicly reporting on the outcomes of these activities. The primary purpose of stewardship is to look after the assets of beneficiaries that have been entrusted to the care of others. The scope of the Code is broadened to include investment decision-making and investment in assets other than listed equity.

The Code is applicable to a range of different entities in the investment community – asset managers, owners and service providers. Institutional investors cannot delegate their responsibility for stewardship. They remain responsible for ensuring those activities are carried out in a manner consistent with their own approach to stewardship. All signatories to the Code are required to provide more detailed reporting on their stewardship activities and how effectively they have achieved their stated objectives. The Code remains underpinned by the FCA's Conduct of Business Sourcebook and incorporates the requirements of the EU Shareholder Rights Directive 2017/828.

The Code is written for asset owners, asset managers and entities providing services to the institutional investment community including investment consultants, proxy advisers and other service providers that want to demonstrate their commitment to stewardship. The Code does not prescribe a single approach, but allows signatories to demonstrate high-quality stewardship that is aligned with each signatory's business model, objectives and activities to fulfil obligations to beneficiaries and clients.

Key Principles of the 2020 Code

7.30 The 2020 Code sets out the following key Principles:

Principles for Asset Owners and Asset Managers

Principle 1: Purpose, strategy and culture

Signatories' purpose, investment beliefs, strategy, and culture enable stewardship that creates long-term value for clients and beneficiaries leading to sustainable benefits for the economy, the environment and society.

Principle 2: Governance, resources and incentives

Signatories' governance, resources and incentives support stewardship.

Principle 3: Conflicts of interest

Signatories manage conflicts of interest to put the best interests of clients and beneficiaries first.

Principle 4: Promoting well-functioning markets

Signatories identify and respond to market-wide and systemic risks to promote a well-functioning financial system.

Principle 5: Review and assurance

Signatories review their policies, assure their processes and assess the effectiveness of their activities.

Principle 6: Client and beneficiary needs

Signatories take account of client and beneficiary needs and communicate the activities and outcomes of their stewardship and investment to them.

Principle 7: Stewardship, investment and ESG Integration

Signatories systematically integrate stewardship and investment, including material environmental, social and governance issues, and climate change, to fulfil their responsibilities.

Principle 8: Monitoring managers and service providers

Signatories monitor and hold to account managers and/or service providers.

Principle 9: Engagement

Signatories engage with issuers to maintain or enhance the value of assets.

Principle 10: Collaboration

Signatories, where necessary, participate in collaborative engagement to influence issuers.

Principle 11: Escalation

Signatories, where necessary, escalate stewardship activities to influence issuers.

Principle 12: Exercising Rights and Responsibilities

Signatories actively exercise their rights and responsibilities.

Principles for Service Providers

Principle 1: Purpose, strategy and culture

Signatories' purpose, strategy and culture enable them to promote effective stewardship.

Principle 2: Governance, resources and incentives

Signatories' governance, workforce, resources and incentives enable them to promote effective stewardship.

Principle 3: Conflicts of interest

Signatories identify and manage conflicts of interest and put the best interests of clients first.

Principle 4: Promoting well-functioning markets

Signatories identify and respond to market-wide and systemic risks to promote a well-functioning financial system.

Principle 5: Supporting client's stewardship

Signatories support clients' integration of stewardship and investment, taking into account, material environmental, social and governance issues, and communicating what activities they have undertaken.

Principle 6: Review and assurance

Signatories review their policies and assure their processes

Structure of the Code

7.31 The Stewardship Code 2020 sets high stewardship standards for asset owners and asset managers, and for the service providers that support them. The structure of the 2020 Code provides for Principles and Reporting Expectations in the form of 'activity' and 'outcome'. Separate principles apply to asset managers and owners and separate principles apply to service providers. The Code does not prescribe a single approach to effective stewardship. Instead, it allows organisations to meet the expectations in a manner that is aligned with their own business model and strategy.

Application of the Code

7.32 All the Principles are supported by reporting expectations. These set out the information that organisations should include in their Stewardship Report and will form the basis of assessment of reporting quality. When applying the Principles, signatories should consider the following, among other issues:

- the effective application of the UK Corporate Governance Code and other governance codes;
- directors' duties, particularly those matters to which they should have regard under CA 2006, s 172;
- capital structure, risk, strategy and performance;
- diversity, remuneration and workforce interests;
- audit quality;
- environmental and social issues, including climate change; and
- compliance with covenants and contracts.

Reports should be engaging, succinct and in plain English. They should be as specific and as transparent as possible without compromising effective stewardship.

The Report should be a single document structured to give a clear picture of how the organisation has applied the Code. Relevant data, diagrams, tables, examples and case studies should be used appropriately. It should focus on activities and outcomes and provide enough information to enable the reader to have a good understanding of the application of the Code without having to refer to information elsewhere. However, the Report may link to more detailed policies and disclosures, including against other reporting requirements. Any additional information should be clear and accessible.

Reports should be fair, balanced and understandable. For example, reporting should acknowledge setbacks experienced and lessons learned, as well as successes. Activities to achieve desired outcomes may take more than a year and may not be completed within an organisation's reporting period. Where this is the case, this should be indicated and progress reported.

The Code recognises that signatories differ by size, type, business model and investment approach, and do not exercise stewardship in an identical way. The reporting expectations do not require disclosure of stewardship activities on a fund-by-fund basis or for each investment strategy. However, the information provided should give a clear indication of how stewardship activities differ across funds, asset classes and geographies proportionately to their operations.

Reports must be reviewed and approved by the applicant's governing body, and signed by the chair, chief executive or chief investment officer.

Once the applicant has been accepted as a Code signatory and the Report is approved by the FRC, the Report will be a public document and must be made available on the signatory's website or, if they do not have a website, in another accessible form.

See also *The Wates Corporate Governance Principles for Large Private Companies* (FRC, December 2018).

Checklist: corporate governance framework

7.33 *This checklist sets out an overview of the regulatory framework governing corporate governance in the United Kingdom*

No	Issue	Reference
1	There is no universally accepted definition of 'corporate governance'. It may be described as the system by which companies are directed and controlled.	See Cadbury Committee on the Financial Aspects of Corporate Governance (1992)
2	Traditionally in the UK, corporate governance had been concerned with the drive by companies towards profit maximisation	*North-West Transportation v Beatty* (1887) 12 App Cas 589
3	The UK corporate governance system is based on the separation of ownership from control: directors control the management of the company and shareholders are the owners	See Model Articles

4	The traditional view was that shareholders could mandate directors to act in a certain manner	*Isle of Wight v Tahourdin* (1883) 25 Ch D 320
5	However, the traditional view gave way to a modern view that since shareholders had delegated some of their powers to the directors under the company's constitution, they could not interfere with such powers	*Automatic Self Cleansing Filter Syndicate Co v Cunninghame* [1906] 2 Ch 34; *Shaw & Sons (Salford) Ltd v Shaw* [1935] 2 KB 113
6	Since the 1990s, various committees were established to address issues concerning corporate governance – the key ones being: • Cadbury Committee • Greenbury Committee • Hampel Committee • Turnbull • Higgs • Smith • Walker	
7	In the UK, the UK Corporate Governance Code applies to all companies with a Premium Listing of equity shares	2018 edition published by FRC
8	The Stewardship Code applies to institutional investors	2020 edition published by FRC
9	The Wates Corporate Governance Principles apply to large private companies based on six principles: • Purpose and leadership • Board composition • Director responsibilities • Opportunity and risk • Remuneration • Stakeholder relationships and engagement	December 2018

8 Directors: types, appointment and removal

Introduction

8.1 This chapter addresses the following issues:

- identifying who is a 'director' of the company;
- distinguishing between different types of directors;
- the requirement to have a director(s);
- the minimum requirements to be satisfied before a person can become a director;
- the register of directors and the particulars of directors to be registered;
- appointing a director; and
- removing a director from office.

Definition of director

8.2 Under CA 2006, the term 'director' includes any person occupying the position of director, by whatever name called: CA 2006, s 250. The term is similarly used in the Insolvency Act 1986 (IA 1986), s 251 and the Company Directors Disqualification Act 1986 (CDDA 1986), s 22(4). However, this definition is not exhaustive and does not properly identify who is a director of the company. The title occupied by a person is not the determining factor in identifying whether that person is a director of a company. A person need not be called a 'director' to act in that capacity. In some cases, a person may occupy the position of a 'manager' or a 'governor', but could still exercise the functions of a director under CA 2006. The term 'director' is sometimes used in a misleading way in employment law, where some personnel are described as 'marketing director' or 'operations director', but do not perform the essential management functions of a director as contemplated under CA 2006.

8.3 A director can be described as a person who has ultimate control of management or any part of the company's business: *Smithton Ltd v Naggar* [2015] 2 BCLC 22. Arden LJ considered that having regard to the usual split of powers between directors and shareholders, and shareholders' delegation of day to day management powers to directors (which can be intervened by the exercise of a special resolution), a director was a person 'who either alone or with others has ultimate control of the management or any part of the company's business …it does not include a purely negative role of giving or receiving permission for some business activity'.

8.4 In *Re Eurostem Maritime Ltd* [1987] PCC 190, Mervyn Davies J considered that the words in s 250(1) 'occupying the position of director' covered any *de facto* director. However, *Re Lo-Line Electric Motors Ltd* [1988] BCLC 698 took a different approach, where the court stated that the definition of 'director' is inclusive and not exhaustive, and may include a *de facto* director.

Distinguishing between various types of directors

8.5 In company law and practice, a distinction is often made between the following types of directors:

- *de jure* director;
- *de facto* director;
- shadow director; and
- directors of corporate directors.

De jure director

8.6 A *de jure* director ('director in law') is a person who has been validly and formally appointed to the company's board, following the proper procedures for appointment under the company's constitution and CA 2006. He agrees to become a director of the company, and has not been disqualified as a director under the CDDA 1986.

The *de jure* director will also be registered at Companies House, and his name entered in the register of directors.

De facto director

8.7 A distinction has often been made between *de jure* and *de facto* directors and their responsibilities and duties on the board of directors. Although the term *de jure* director has a generally accepted meaning, the concept of a *de facto* director has been problematic, and has given rise to a number of cases, particularly in relation to directors' disqualification proceedings. A *de facto* director (director 'in fact') is a term applied to a person who assumes the position of a *de jure* director within the corporate governance structure, without having been validly appointed as a *de jure* director. He is then treated or assumes some or all of the functions of a *de jure* director, including any liabilities that may ensue.

8.8 The essential nature of the distinction often arises where a *de facto* director has become liable to a claim, penalty or fine, and attempts to evade liability by claiming that he was not properly appointed. The cases have shown that this distinction usually arises in disqualification, misfeasance, wrongful trading and fraudulent trading proceedings, or when things go wrong within the company, and liability is imputed to the *de facto* director. Judicial cases have not often been consistent in their approach towards determining whether a person was, in reality, a *de facto* or a *de jure* director or indeed a shadow director, and what tests or factors should be taken into account in distinguishing between a *de facto* director and a shadow director, and whether in practice there was any real distinction between the two. Until *Re Paycheck Services 3 Ltd; Revenue and Customs Commissioners v Holland* [2011] 1 BCLC 141, there were differing and conflicting judicial interpretations as to who was a *de facto* director, the tests used to identify such director in law and practice, and how a *de facto* director differed from a shadow director. As Lord Collins remarked in the leading case of *Re Paycheck*, that for over 150 years, *de facto* directors in English law were persons who assumed their position, role and functions as directors, but whose appointment was defective, or had come to an end, but nevertheless acted or continued to act as directors. Many of the earlier cases on *de facto* directors were concerned with the validity of their acts: *Charles Edward Mangles v Grand Collier Dock Co* (1840) 10 Sim 519; *Foss v Harbottle* (1843) 2 Hare 4; *Re County Life Assurance Co* (1870) 5 Ch App 288; *Murray v Bush* (1873) LR 6 HL 37; *Mahony v East Holyford Mining Co* (1875) LR 7 HL 869; *Rama Corp Ltd v Proved Tin and General Investments Ltd* [1952] 1 All ER 554; *Royal British Bank v Turquand* (1856) 6 El & Bl 327; 119 ER 886; *Freeman and Lockyer (a firm) v Buckhurst Park Properties (Mangal) Ltd* [1964] 1 All ER 630; *John Morley Building Co v Barras* [1891] 2 Ch 386 and *Channel Collieries Trust Ltd v Dover St Margaret's and Martin Mill Light Rly Co* [1914] 2 Ch 506; *Morris v Kanssen* [1946] 1 All ER 586.

The modern approach to de facto directors

8.9 The modern concept of a *de facto* director emerged from a 19th century principle that a person whose appointment as a director was defective, but who acted as if properly appointed, could not rely on the invalidity of his appointment to escape his responsibilities as a director: *Popely v Popely* [2019] EWHC 1507. See too *Carlyle Capital Corporation Ltd v Conway*, Judgment 38/2017 of the Royal Court of Guernsey. Although previous cases on *de facto* directors were principally concerned with the defective appointment of a director or those who had ceased to be a director and their liability, the modern concept of *de facto* directors has extended to disqualification proceedings, insolvency including wrongful trading by directors: see *Re Eurostem Maritime Ltd* (1987) PCC 190.

The acts of de facto directors extend to liability in disqualification proceedings: *Re Lo-Line Electric Motors Ltd* [1988] BCLC 698.

In *Re Hydrodam (Corby) Ltd* [1994] 2 BCLC 180, Millett J stated that a *de jure* director is one who has been validly appointed by the board of directors with proper authority and powers to manage the company's business. Millett J considered that a *de facto* director was a person who assumed to act as a director. He was held out as a director of the company and claimed and purported to be a director, although he was never actually or validly appointed as such. To establish that a person was a *de facto* director, it was necessary to show that he undertook functions in relation to the company, which could properly be discharged only by a director. It was not sufficient to show that he was concerned in the management of the company's affairs, or undertook tasks in relation to its business which could properly be performed by a manager below board level:

> 'Those who assume to act as directors and who thereby exercise the powers and discharge the functions of a director, whether validly appointed or not, must accept the responsibilities which are attached to the office.'

Re Hydrodam raised questions as to whether it was a necessary ingredient of *de facto* directorship that the person in question should have been held out by the company.

Authorities subsequent to *Re Hydrodam* have tended to downplay this aspect as being a useful indicator, but not an essential requirement.

8.10 Since *Hydrodam*, there have been a number of cases that have considered the position of a *de facto* director. Some of these cases have been concerned with directors' disqualification proceedings. They have treated *Hydrodam* as the starting position, before applying the principles to the facts in question. However, some of the previous judicial decisions (mainly first instance decisions) applied different tests in determining whether a person was a *de facto* director, with no consistency nor uniformity.

8.11 Some cases have been of the view that holding out and the label of 'director' were not a necessary precondition in identifying a *de facto* director. However, carrying out the role as director was an important factor: *Re Moorgate Metals* [1995] BCC 143. See too *Secretary of State for Trade and Industry v Hollier* [2007] BCC 11; *SSTI v Tjolle* [1998] BCC 282; and *Re H Laing Demolition Building Contractors Ltd, Secretary of State for Trade and Industry v Laing* [1996] 2 BCLC 324.

8.12 Some cases have demonstrated that it was necessary to show that the de facto director was the sole person directing the affairs of the company or, if there were others who were true directors, that he acted on an equal footing with such persons in directing the affairs of the company ("equal footing" test): *Re Richborough Furniture Limited* [1996] 1 BCLC 507; but see *Secretary of State for Trade and Industry v Ashby (No 1915 of 1992)* (unreported), where Anthony Mann QC considered that it was not a requirement in all respects for a de facto director to be on an exactly equal footing to all the other directors.

The 'equal footing' test was also applied by His Honour Judge Cooke in *Secretary of State for Trade and Industry v Elms* (16 January 1997, unreported) who considered that the test was not so much about equality of power, but 'equality of ability' to participate in the notional board room. In this regard, it is necessary to ask:

> 'Is he somebody who is simply advising and, as it were, withdrawing having advised, or somebody who joins the other directors, de facto or de jure, in decisions which affect the future of the company?'

He stated that in determining whether a person was a shadow director, consideration should be given to the following:

- Was he directing others?
- Was he committing the company to major obligations?
- Was he taking part in an equally based collective decision-making process at board level (ie at the level of a director with a foot in the board room)?

8.13 There was no one test in identifying a de facto director and consideration must be given to various factors: *Secretary of State for Trade and Industry v Tjolle* [1998] 1 BCLC 333. Jacob J stated that it was difficult to postulate one decisive test of whether a person was a *de facto* director. The court had to take account of all the relevant factors, including whether or not there was a holding out by the company of the individual as a director, whether the individual used the title, whether the individual had proper information (eg management accounts) on which to base decisions, and whether the individual had to make major decisions. The question was whether the individual was part of the corporate governing structure.

A de facto director's actions may be directorial and either acting in an individual capacity or as a director of the company: *Secretary of State for Trade and Industry v Jones* [1999] BCC 336.

Assuming of the status and functions of a company director were important elements in identifying whether or not a person was a de facto director: *Re Kaytech International plc, Secretary of State for Trade and Industry v Kaczer* [1999] 2 BCLC 351. See too *IRC v McEntaggart* [2006] 1 BCLC 476.

On occasions, the courts have stated that various factors should be taken into account. These include the functions performed by a person in identifying whether or not a person was a de facto director: *Gemma Ltd v Davies* [2008] 2 BCLC 281.

8.14 A person may still be a *de facto* director even if he does not have day-to-day control over the company's affairs, and even though he acts as a director only in relation to part of the company's activities: *Secretary of State for Trade and Industry v Deverell* [2001] Ch 340.

The actions of the de facto director in practice can be indicative in determining the capacity in which he acts, and that he is part of a corporate governance structure: *Secretary of State for Trade and Industry v Hollier* [2007] BCC 618. Etherton J stated that in considering whether a person 'assumes to act as a director', the important aspect was not what he called himself but what he did, and that he had been part of the corporate governance structure. *See too Secretary of State for Trade and Industry v Hall* [2009] BCC 190.

8.15 In the leading Supreme Court case considering de facto directors, the Court decided that assumption of responsibility and involvement in the corporate governance structure, were significant indications of participation by a de facto director in corporate matters: *In Re Paycheck Services 3 Ltd, Revenue and Customs Commissioners v Holland* [2011] 1 BCLC 141,the Supreme Court stated that there was no one test for determining and identifying whether a person was a *de facto* director and this was a matter of fact and degree. All the relevant factors had to be taken into account. Those who assumed to act as directors and who thereby exercised the powers and discharged the functions of a director, whether validly appointed or not, had to accept the responsibilities of the office. Accordingly, one had to look at what the person had actually done to see whether he had assumed those responsibilities in relation to the subject company. The question was one of law and it was a question of principle. The guiding principle could be expressed in that way, unless and until Parliament provided otherwise. So long as the relevant acts had been done by the individual entirely within the ambit of the discharge of his duties and responsibilities as a director of the corporate director, it was to that capacity that his acts had to be attributed. The term could not be universally applied to all situations and statutory provisions which imposed liability on a director. The court would look at the purpose for the rule being applied, whether the director was acting alone and directing the company's affairs or on an equal footing with other directors in directing the company's affairs, whether there was any holding out by that person, and whether, having regard to all the facts and circumstances, the person was part of the company's governance structure.

See now CA 2006, s 156A(1) (as inserted by SBEEA 2015, s 87(4)) which prevents the appointment of corporate directors). See too *Re Idessa (UK) Ltd (in liquidation); Burke and another v Morrison* [2012] 1 BCLC 80; *Re Snelling House Ltd* [2012] EWHC 440 (Ch); *Re UKLI Ltd; Secretary of State for Business, Innovation and Skills v Chohan* [2013] EWHC 680 (Ch).

In order to determine whether a person was a de facto director, it was necessary to consider that person's role within the corporate governance process. Following *Paycheck*, in *Smithton Ltd v Naggar* [2015] 2 BCLC 22, the Court of Appeal was required to consider the test that should be applied in identifying whether a person was a de facto director. It held that having regard to the usual split of powers between shareholders and directors under Table A of the Companies (Tables A to F) Regulations 1985 on the basis that the powers of management of the company's business were delegated to the directors and the shareholders could not intervene except by special resolution, a director was a person who either alone or with others had ultimate control of the management of any part of the company's business. In the usual case a purely negative role of giving or receiving permission for some business activity or being consulted about directorial decisions or for approval did not make a person a director.

Further, whether a person was a de facto or shadow director depended on whether he was part of the system of corporate governance of the company, and if so, in what capacity he acted in relation to the corporate governance structure and whether, objectively, he had assumed the status and function of a director so as to assume responsibility to act as a director. The assessment of the capacity in which a person acted was one of fact and degree and all the circumstances had to be taken into account but relevant factors included whether the company considered him to be a director, whether it held him out as such, and whether third parties considered him to be a director.

Arden LJ set out the following factors in identifying whether or not a person could be a de facto director:

- The concepts of shadow director and de facto are different but there is some overlap.
- A person may be de facto director even if there was no invalid appointment. The question is whether he has assumed responsibility to act as a director.
- To answer that question, the court may have to determine in what capacity the director was acting (as in *Holland*).
- The court will in general also have to determine the corporate governance structure of the company so as to decide in relation to the company's business whether the defendant's acts were directorial in nature.
- The court is required to look at what the director actually did and not any job title actually given to him.
- A defendant does not avoid liability if he shows that he in good faith thought he was not acting as a director. The question whether or not he acted as a director is to be determined objectively and irrespective of the defendant's motivation or belief.
- The court must look at the cumulative effect of the activities relied on. The court should look at all the circumstances 'in the round' (per Jonathan Parker J in *Secretary of State for Trade and Industry v Jones* [1999] BCC 336).
- It is also important to look at the acts in their context. A single act might lead to liability in an exceptional case.
- Relevant factors include:

  (i) whether the company considered him to be a director and held him out as such;

(ii) whether third parties considered that he was a director.

- The fact that a person is consulted about directorial decisions or his approval is sought for such decisions does not in general make him a director because he is not making the decision.
- Acts outside the period when he is said to have been a de facto director may throw light on whether he was a de facto director in the relevant period.
- The question whether a director is a de facto or shadow director is a question of fact and degree.

See too *Popely v Popely* [2019] EWHC 1507 (Ch).

Directors: types, appointment and removal

8.16 The tests identified in *Holland* in respect of a de facto director, are more appropriate where there is a formal corporate governance structure in place. The issue arises as to what is the legal position where there is only an informal corporate governance structure? This includes situations where a person is given a title in the company (such as a deputy managing director), but this does not contribute towards any aspect of the actual governance structure. In *Re Mumtaz Properties Ltd* [2012] 2 BCLC 109, Arden LJ stated that in these situations, the test would be whether the person was 'one of the nerve centres from which the activities of the company radiated'. In I*ngram v Singh* [2020] EWHC 2473, it was explained by HH Judge Hodge QC, that the focus on corporate governance structure in *Holland* was less relevant in identifying a de facto director, where a formal structure did not exist, in other words, where there was a loose, informal governance arrangement. The *Re Mumtaz* approach has been followed in *Umbrella Care Ltd v Nisa* [2022] EWHC 86, where Johnson J. applied the "nerve centre" test to determine whether the person concerned was a de facto director.

Shadow director

8.17 Under CA 2006, a 'shadow director' means a person in accordance with whose directions or instructions the directors of the company are accustomed to act: CA 2006, s 251(1).

The following are not regarded as shadow directors:

- A person is not a shadow director by reason only of the fact that the directors act:
  - (a) on advice given by that person in a professional capacity;
  - (b) in accordance with instructions, a direction, guidance or advice given by that person in the exercise of a function conferred by or under an enactment;
  - (c) in accordance with guidance or advice given by that person in that person's capacity as a Minister of the Crown (within the meaning of the Ministers of the Crown Act 1975): CA 2006, s 251(2) (as inserted by s 90(3) SBEEA 2015).
- A body corporate is not to be regarded as a shadow director of any of its subsidiary companies for the purposes of:

- Chapter 2 (general duties of directors);
- Chapter 4 (transactions requiring members' approval); or
- Chapter 6 (contract with sole member who is also a director),

by reason only that the directors of the subsidiary are accustomed to act in accordance with its directions or instructions: CA 2006, s 251(3).

8.18 Various provisions of CA 2006 and the Insolvency Act 1986 (s 251 as amended by SBEEA 2015, s 90(1)) make references to a shadow director in the regulation and disclosure of transactions. These Acts impute liability to a person if he is influential in running the company's affairs through other directors, while not himself on the company board; and if the directors are accustomed to acting in accordance with that person's directions and instructions. The issue concerning shadow directors also arises in the context of CDDA 1986 proceedings including the insolvency proceedings dealing with wrongful trading. Section 22(5) of the CDDA 1986 (as inserted by SBEEA 2015, s 90(2)) provides an identical definition of a 'shadow director' as s 251 of CA 2006.

8.19 Various cases have considered the statutory definition of 'shadow director' and the test to be applied in determining whether a person was a shadow director.

A shadow director has been considered as the ***éminence*** grise controlling the directors: In *Re Lo-Line Electric Motors Ltd* [1988] BCLC 698, Browne-Wilkinson V-C was concerned with an allegation that the person in question was a *de facto* director, not a shadow director. He said of the latter that the definition presupposes that there is a board of directors 'who act in accordance with instructions from someone else, the éminence grise or shadow director'.

8.20 At times, the courts have stated that the shadow director is a puppet master controlling the Board actions: *Re Unisoft Group Ltd (No 3)* [1994] 1 BCLC 609

In *Re Hydrodam (Corby) Limited* [1994] 2 BCLC 180. Millett J stated:

> 'A shadow director … does not claim or purport to act as a director. On the contrary, he claims not to be a director. He lurks in the shadows, sheltering behind others who, he claims, are the only directors of the company to the exclusion of himself. He is not held out as a director by the company. To establish that a defendant is a shadow director of a company it is necessary to allege and prove: (1) who are the directors of the company, whether de facto or de jure; (2), that the defendant directed those directors how to act in relation to the company or that he was one of the persons who did so; (3) that those directors acted in accordance with such directions; and (4) that they were accustomed so to act. What is needed is first, a board of directors claiming and purporting to act as such; and secondly, a pattern of behaviour in which the board did not exercise any discretion or judgment of its own, but acted in accordance with the directions of others.'

8.21 However, this graphic view of a passive shadow director may not necessarily accord with the position in practice. A shadow director is likely to be proactive, planning, scheming his instructions or directions to the directors. He may also be impulsive – acting on the spur of the moment, catching directors off-guard and requiring them to act immediately in respect of a particular matter or transaction.

8.22 In determining the position of the shadow director, the court will also enquire as to the locus for effective decision making: *Australian Securities Commission v AS Nominees Ltd* (1995) 133 ALR 1.

Various factors may be identified in determining whether or not a person was a shadow director: *Secretary of State for Trade and Industry v Deverell* [2000] 2 BCLC 133. In the course of his judgment, Morritt LJ stated the following propositions that would be applicable to a shadow director:

'(1) The definition of a shadow director is to be construed in the normal way to give effect to the parliamentary intention ascertainable from the mischief to be dealt with and the words used.

(2) The purpose of the legislation is to identify those, other than professional advisers, with real influence in the corporate affairs of the company. But it is not necessary that such influence should be exercised over the whole field of its corporate activities …

(3) Whether any particular communication from the alleged shadow director, whether by words or conduct, is to be classified as a direction or instruction must be objectively ascertained by the court in the light of all the evidence. In that connection I do not accept that it is necessary to prove the understanding or expectation of either giver or receiver. In many, if not most, cases it will suffice to prove the communication and its consequence … Certainly the label attached by either or both parties then or thereafter cannot be more than a factor in considering whether the communication came within the statutory description of direction or instruction.

(4) Non-professional advice may come within that statutory description. The proviso excepting advice given in a professional capacity appears to assume that advice generally is or may be included. Moreover the concepts of "direction" and "instruction" do not exclude the concept of "advice" for all three share the common feature of "guidance".

(5) It will, no doubt, be sufficient to show that in the face of "directions or instructions" from the alleged shadow director the properly appointed directors or some of them cast themselves in a subservient role or surrendered their respective discretions. But I do not consider that it is necessary to do so in all cases … Such a requirement would be to put a gloss on the statutory requirement that the board are "accustomed to act in accordance with" such directions or instructions … .'

On the facts, the Court of Appeal held that the two individuals concerned, who claimed that they were the company's consultants, were, in fact, shadow directors who were involved at a senior level in the governance of the company's affairs.

8.23 A pattern of conduct of accepting instructions was an important factor in identifying a shadow director – one single event will not suffice: *Secretary of State for Trade and Industry v Becker* [2003] 1 BCLC 555.

Also, the level of influence exerted over directors was significant in identifying a shadow director: *Re Mea Corporation, Secretary of State for Trade and Industry v Aviss* [2007] 1 BCLC 618.

A shadow director must also exercise real influence in the corporate affairs of the company: *Coroin Ltd (sub nom Mckillen v Misland (Cyprus) Investments Ltd)* [2012] EWHC 1158 (Ch).

Do shadow directors owe fiduciary duties?

8.24 There appears to be a position, now taken by the courts that shadow directors owe a duty, like directors, to act in the best interests of the company. The position is supported by CA 2006, s 170(5) (as amended by SBEEA 2015, s 89) which states that the general duties of directors apply to a shadow director of a company where and to the extent that they are capable of so applying.

In *Ultraframe (UK) Limited v Fielding* [2005] EWHC 1638 (Ch), Lewison J was of the view that the fact that a person was determined to be a shadow director did not imply that he owed fiduciary duties to the company similarly to those imposed on directors. He stated:

> 'The indirect influence exerted by a paradigm shadow director who does not directly deal with or claim the right to deal directly with the company's assets will not usually, in my judgment, be enough to impose fiduciary duties upon him; although he will, of course, be subject to those statutory duties and disabilities that the Companies Act creates. The case is the stronger where the shadow director has been acting throughout in furtherance of his own, rather than the company's, interests. However, on the facts of a particular case, the activities of a shadow director may go beyond the mere exertion of indirect influence.'

Lewison J went on to stress that the real question was as to the nature of the activities undertaken, and not a label attached to their perpetrator.

However, in *Re Mea Corporation, Secretary of State for Trade and Industry v Aviss* [2007] 1 BCLC 618, Lewison J appeared to have assumed that a shadow director owed duties to the company to act in the best interests of the company.

Significance of the distinction between a de facto director and a shadow director

8.25 In *Re Hydrodam (Corby) Ltd* [1994] 2 BCLC 180, Millett J was of the view that that the *de facto* and shadow directorships did not overlap and that there were clear distinctions between the two. They were alternatives and in most and perhaps all cases, are mutually exclusive.

However, according to Lord Collins in *Re Paycheck Services 3 Ltd; Revenue and Customs Commissioners v Holland* [2011] 1 BCLC 141, over the years the distinction between de facto directors and shadow directors has become blurred and eroded, and impossible to maintain. This is owing to the extension of the *de facto* directorship concept and the consideration of such matters, as the taking of major decisions by the individual, which might be through instructions to the de jure directors, and the evaluation of his real influence in the company's affairs: see *Re Kaytech International plc, Secretary of State for Trade and Industry v Kaczer* [1999] 2 BCLC 351.

8.26 Another consequence has been that the courts were confronted with the very difficult problem of identifying what functions were in essence the sole responsibility of a director or board of directors. In this regard, a number of tests have been suggested of which the following are the most relevant:

- First, whether the person is the sole person directing the affairs of the company (or acting with others equally lacking in a valid appointment), or if there are others who are true directors, whether he is acting on an equal footing with the others in directing its affairs: *Re Richborough Furniture Ltd*.
- Secondly, whether there is a holding out by the company of the individual as a director, and whether the individual used the title: *Secretary of State for Trade and Industry v Tjolle*.
- Thirdly, taking all the circumstances into account, whether the individual is part of 'the corporate governing structure': *Secretary of State for Trade and Industry v Tjolle*, approved in *Re Kaytech International plc, Secretary of State for Trade and Industry v Kaczer*, where Robert Walker LJ also approved the way in which Jacob

J in *Secretary of State for Trade and Industry v Tjolle* declined to formulate a single test. He also said that the concepts of shadow director and *de facto* director had in common 'that an individual who was not a *de jure* director is alleged to have exercised real influence (otherwise than as a professional adviser) in the corporate governance of a company' (at 424). See also especially *Re Mea Corp Ltd, Secretary of State for Trade and Industry v Aviss* [2006] EWHC 1846 (Ch), [2007] 1 BCLC 618 (Lewison J); *Ultraframe (UK) Ltd v Fielding, Northstar Systems Ltd v Fielding* [2005] EWHC 1638 (Ch), [2005] All ER (D) 397 (Jul) (Lewison J); *Secretary of State for Trade and Industry v Hollier* [2006] EWHC 1804 (Ch), [2007] BCC 11 (Etherton J). In fact it is just as difficult to define 'corporate governance' as it is to identify those activities which are essentially the sole responsibility of a director or board of directors, although perhaps the most quoted definition is that of the Cadbury Report: 'Corporate governance is the system by which companies are directed and controlled' (Report of the Committee on the Financial Aspects of Corporate Governance, 1992, para 2.5).

The modern judicial attitude is to look more towards various factors in determining the degree of control exercised over the company's affairs, by either the de facto director or the shadow director. Indeed, it may be possible for a person to be both a shadow director and a *de facto* director in certain circumstances. The distinction may matter in respect of a shadow director who will be liable only under the statutory provisions that impose obligations on a shadow director. It would seem that the *de facto* director will be liable to a larger extent than a shadow director, and that more cases are likely to be brought against a *de facto* director than a shadow director based on the extent of control exercised over the company's governing structure.

Directors of corporate directors

8.27 Can a *de jure* director of one company, while acting in that role, become a *de facto* director of another company? Does the *de jure* role in one company protect against liability to the other?

These issues were raised in the leading case of *Re Paycheck Services 3 Ltd; Revenue and Customs Commissioners v Holland* [2011] 1 BCLC 141, the husband and wife established an intricate structure of companies (composite companies) whose activities included the administration of the business and tax affairs of contracting workers in different sectors. Each of the contractors became an employee of one of the composite companies and was given a share which carried no voting rights. This meant that the employees received both a salary and a dividend. The structure of the composite companies was such that each company was only liable to pay corporation tax at the small companies' rate. However, under UK legislation, these composite companies were in reality associated companies, which meant that each company was liable to pay corporation tax at the main rate. Provision had not been made for the payment of tax at the main rate. Further, each company had, throughout its life, declared and paid dividends that should not have been paid because there were insufficient distributable reserves to permit them. All the composite companies stopped trading and went into liquidation and thereafter into a creditors' voluntary liquidation. The Revenue was the only creditor.

HMRC applied to the court in respect of each composite company alleging that, as *de facto* directors of the composite companies, it had been guilty of misfeasance and breaches of duty in causing the payments of unlawful dividends.

A majority of the Supreme Court (Lord Walker and Lord Clarke dissenting) decided that it was clear from established authority, that the circumstances in which a person could be held to be a *de facto* director for the purposes of s 212 of the Insolvency Act 1986 varied widely from case to case, and was very much a question of fact and degree. All the relevant factors had to be taken into account.

The objective of s 212 of the Insolvency Act 1986 was to impose liability on those who had been in a position to prevent damage to creditors by taking proper steps to protect their interests. Those who assumed to act as directors and who thereby exercised the powers and discharged the functions of a director, whether validly appointed or not, had to accept the responsibilities of the office.

Accordingly, one had to look at what the person had actually done to see whether he had actually assumed those responsibilities in relation to the subject company. The question was one of law and it was a question of principle. The guiding principle could be expressed in that way unless and until Parliament provided otherwise.

As long as the relevant acts had been done by the individual entirely within the discharge of his duties as the director of the corporate director, it was to that capacity that his acts had to be attributed.

In the present case, he had been doing no more than discharging his duties as a director of the composite companies. Everything that he had done had been done under that umbrella.

Further, the Revenue had been unable to point to anything that he had done which could not be said to have been done by him in his capacity as a director of the corporate director. It had not been shown that he had been acting as *de facto* director of the composite companies so as to make him responsible for the misuse of the assets.

8.28 The statutory position on corporate directors is governed by s 156A(1) of CA 2006 (as inserted by SBEEA 2015, s 87(4)). This provides that a person may not be appointed a director of a company unless the person is a natural person. However, this does not prohibit the holding of the office of director by a natural person as a corporation sole or otherwise by virtue of an office: s 156A(2). An appointment made in contravention of s 156A of CA 2006 is void. Nothing in s 156A affects any liability of a person under any provision of the Companies Acts or any other enactment if the person:

(a) purports to act as a director; or

(b) acts as a shadow director,

although the person could not, by virtue of s 156A, be validly appointed as a director: CA 2006, s 156A(4).

Section 156A is subject to s 156B (power to provide for exceptions from requirement that each director be a natural person): CA 2006, s 154(5).

8.29 If a purported appointment is made in contravention of s 156A, an offence is committed by:

(a) the company purporting to make the appointment;

(b) where the purported appointment is of a body corporate or a firm that is a legal person under the law by which it is governed, that body corporate or firm; and

(c) every officer of a person falling within paragraph (a) or (b) who is in default.

8.30 For this purpose, a shadow director is treated as an officer of a company: CA 200, s 156A(6).

A person guilty of an offence under CA 2006, s 156A is liable on summary conviction in England and Wales to a fine: CA 2006, s 156A(7).

Director's appointment

8.31 CA 2006 does not address in any detail how directors may be appointed and the procedure for such appointment. Much is therefore left to the company's articles of association to set out the mechanism for such appointment. Under Model Article 17 for private companies limited by shares, a person may be appointed as a director provided he is 'willing to act as a director' and is permitted by law to do so. The appointment may be by ordinary resolution or a decision of the directors. The person must agree to the appointment: *Re British Empire Match Co Ltd* (1888) 59 LT 291. In *Re CEM Connections Limited* [2000] BCC 917, Registrar Rawson stated that for the appointment of a director of a company to be valid it was necessary that the person appointed should give informed consent of that appointment. The fact that a person signed a form of consent was strong prima facie evidence that consent was given, but it was not conclusive, and may be rebutted by evidence which indicates that the signature was obtained without the person signing the document appreciating what he or she was doing.

The power to appoint a director for public companies is contained in Model Articles for public companies Article 20, with the director holding office only until the next annual general meeting: Article 21(2).

Others who may appoint the directors

8.32 Under CA 2006, s 154(1), every private company must have at least one director; and a public company must have at least two directors: CA 2006, s 154(2). Where a public company's directors is reduced to one, that sole director cannot act on his own, and he must then appoint another director if such power exists under the articles: *Channel Collieries Trust Ltd v Dover St Margaret's and Martin Hill Light Railway Co* [1914] 2 Ch 506. Such power is provided for under Article 11(3)(a) of the Model Articles for a private company, and Article 17(1)(b) Model Articles for a public company. In relation to a private company, Model Article 17(2) provides that in any case where, as a result of death, the company has no shareholders and no directors, the personal representatives of the last shareholder to have died have the right, by notice in writing, to appoint a person to be a director.

8.33 It is also possible for the Secretary of State under CA 2006, s 156 to require the company to appoint a director within a period of one to three months, where the company has less than the statutory minimum number of directors, or there is no natural director appointed. Failure to comply with s 156 will be an offence with the imposition of a fine: CA 2006, s 156(7).

Minimum age

8.34 A person may not be appointed a director of a company unless he has attained the age of 16: CA 2006, s 157(1). However, this does not affect the validity of an appointment that is not to take effect until the person attained that age: CA 2006, s 157(2).

Where the office of a company is held by a corporation sole, or otherwise by virtue of another office, the appointment to that other office of a person who has not attained the age of 16 is not effective also to make him a director of the company until he attains the age of 16 years: CA 2006, s 157(3).

Any appointment made in contravention of s 157 is void: CA 2006, s 157(4).

The Secretary of State may by regulation specify the cases in which a person who has not attained the age of 16 may be appointed a director of a company: CA 2006, s 158(1).

Validity of acts of directors

8.35 The acts of a person acting as a director are valid notwithstanding that it is afterwards discovered that:

- there was a defect in his appointment;
- he was disqualified from holding office;
- he had ceased to hold office;
- he was not entitled to vote on the matter in question: CA 2006, s 160(1).

This applies even if the resolution for his appointment is void under s 160: CA 2006, s 161(2).

8.36 This section addresses defective appointments of directors that may have arisen during the company's existence which are then validated: see *Morris v Kanssen* [1946] AC 459. A person seeking to rely on the validation provisions must ensure he has acted in good faith to invoke such provisions: *Channel Collieries Trust Ltd v Dover, St Margaret's and Martin Hill Light Railway Co* [1914] 2 Ch 506.

In *British Asbestos Co Ltd v Boyd* [1903] 2 Ch 439, Farwell stated that the aim of the validation provision was 'to make the honest acts of *de facto* directors as good as the honest acts of *de jure* directors … although there may be some slip which has been overlooked, if it has been bona fide overlooked, then the acts of the *de facto* directors are as good as the acts of the *de jure* directors.'

Register of directors

8.37 Every company is required to keep a register of its directors: CA 2006, s 162(1).

The register must contain the required particulars (see ss 163–165) of each person who is a director of the company: CA 2006, s 162(2).

The register must be kept available for inspection:

- at the company's registered office; or
- at a place specified in regulations under s 1136: CA 2006, s 162(3).

The company must give notice to the registrar:

- of the place at which the register is kept available for inspection; and
- of any change of that place: CA 2006, s 162(4),

unless it has, at all times, been kept at the company's registered office: CA 2006, s 162(4).

The register must be open to the inspection:

- of any member of the company without charge; and
- of any other person on payment on such fee as may be prescribed: CA 2006, s 162(5).

8.38 If default is made in complying with s 162(1), (2), or (3) or if default is made in complying with s 162(4), or if an inspection required under s 162(5) is refused, an offence is committed by:

- the company; and
- every officer of the company who is in default: CA 2006, s 162(6).

A person guilty of an offence under s 162 is liable on summary conviction to a fine: CA 2006, s 162(7).

In case of refusal of inspection of the register, the court may, by order, compel an immediate inspection of it: CA 2006, s 162(8).

An issue has arisen as to whether there is an obligation to register a shadow director as part of the register of directors under CA 2006, s 162. In *Bagri Services Ltd v HMRC* [2021] UKFTT 482 (TC), the Tribunal decided that there was no requirement to do so (unlike its predecessor under CA 1985, s 288(6)).

Particulars of directors to be registered – individuals

8.39 A company's register of directors must contain the following particulars in the case of an individual:

- name and any former name;
- service address;
- country and state (or part of the UK) in which he usually resides;
- nationality;
- business occupation (if any); and
- date of birth: CA 2006, s 163(1).

8.40 The term 'name' means a person's Christian name (or any forename) and surname, except in the case of:

- a peer; or
- an individual usually known by a title.

In these situations, the title may be stated instead of his Christian name (or other forename) and surname or in addition to either or both of them: CA 2006, s 163(2).

8.41 The term 'former name' means a name by which the individual was formerly known for business purposes: CA 2006, s 163(3). Where a person is, or was, formerly known by more than one such name, each of them must be stated.

It is not necessary for the register to contain particulars of a former name in the following cases:

- In the case of a peer or an individual normally known by a British title, where the name is one by which the person was known previous to the adoption of or succession to the title.
- In the case of any person, where the former name:
  - was changed or disused before the person attained the age of 16; or
  - has been changed or disused for 20 years or more: CA 2006, s 163(4)(b).

A person's service address may be stated to be 'The company's registered office': CA 2006, s 163(5).

Register of directors' residential addresses

8.42 Every company must keep a register of directors' residential addresses: CA 2006, s 165(1). This must state the usual residential address of each of the company's directors: CA 2006, s 165(2).

If a director's usual residential address is the same as his service address (as stated in the company's register of directors), the register of directors' residential addresses need only contain an entry to that effect: CA 2006, s 165(2). This does not apply if his service address is stated to be 'The company's registered office'.

If default is made in complying with s 165, an offence is committed by the company, and every officer of the company who is in default. For this purpose a shadow director is treated as an officer of the company: CA 2006, s 165(4).

8.43 A person guilty of an offence under s 165 is liable, on summary conviction, to a fine not exceeding level 5 on the standard scale and, for continued contravention, a daily default fine not exceeding one-tenth of level 5 on the standard scale: CA 2006, s 165(5).

Section 165 applies only to directors who are individuals, not where the director is a body corporate or a firm that is a legal person under the law by which it is governed: CA 2006, s 165(6).

8.44 Under s 166, the Secretary of State has the power to make regulations in respect of the particulars of directors to be registered including amendments, adding and removing items from the particulars required to be contained in the company's register of directors' residential addresses. This has been enacted under the Companies (Disclosure of Address) Regulations 2009, SI 2009/214 (as amended by the Companies (Disclosure of Address) (Amendment) Regulations 2018, SI 2018/528), which removes the requirement that individuals must show that there is a serious risk that they, or a person living with them, will be subject to violence or intimidation as a result of the activities of a company with which they are involved. Applications to make their address unavailable for public inspection can now be made in respect of information filed before 1 January 2003; and the Companies (Disclosure of Address) (Amendment) Regulations 2015, SI 2015/842.

Protected information

8.45 Chapter 8 of Part 10 to the CA 2006 makes provision for protecting an individual company director regarding information as to his usual residential address; and the information that his service address is his usual residential address.

This type of information is categorised as 'protected information': CA 2006, s 240(2). The information does not cease to be protected information on the individual ceasing to be a director of the company: CA 2006, s 240(3).

Chapter 8 applies to both the current director of a company and, where appropriate, to a former director: CA 2006, s 240(3).

Protected information: restriction on use or disclosure by company

8.46 A company must not use or disclose protected information about any of its directors except for the following situations:

- for communicating with the director concerned;
- in order to comply with any requirement of the Companies Acts as to the particulars to be sent to the registrar; and
- in accordance with CA 2006, s 244 (disclosure under court order): CA 2006, s 241(1).

Section 241(1), however, does not prohibit any use or disclosure of protected information with the consent of the director concerned: CA 2006, s 241(2). The reference to a director includes, to that extent, a former director.

Protected information: restriction on use or disclosure by registrar

8.47 The registrar must omit protected information from the material on the register that is available for inspection where:

- it is contained in a document delivered to him in which such information is required to be stated; and
- in the case of a document having more than one part, it is contained in a part of the document in which such information is required to be stated: CA 2006, s 242.

The registrar is not required to check other documents or (as the case may be) other parts of the document to ensure the absence of protected information; or to omit from the material that is available for public inspection anything registered before 1 October 2008: CA 2006, s 242(2).

The registrar must not use or disclose protected information except as permitted by s 243 (permitted use or disclosure by registrar); or in accordance with s 244 (disclosure under court order): CA 2006, s 242(3).

Permitted use or disclosure by the registrar

8.48 Section 243 of CA 2006 sets out the circumstances where the registrar may use the protected information.The protected information may be used and disclosed by the registrar for communicating with the director in question: CA 2006, s 243(1). The registrar may disclose protected information to a public authority under regulations made by the Secretary of State, or to a credit reference agency: CA 2006, s 243(2). The term 'credit reference agency' means a person carrying on a business comprising the furnishing of information relevant to the financial standing of individuals, being information collected by the agency for that purpose: CA 2006, s 243(7). The registrar may disclose protected information to a public authority under regulations made by the Secretary of State, or to a credit reference agency: CA 2006, s 243(2).

8.49 The Secretary of State may make provision by regulations:

(a) specifying conditions for the disclosure of protected information in accordance with s 243, and

(b) providing for the charging of fees: CA 2006, s 243(3).

The Secretary of State may make provision by regulations requiring the registrar, on application, to refrain from disclosing protected information relating to a director to a credit reference agency: CA 2006, s 243(4). The Secretary of State has enacted the *Companies (Disclosure of Address) Regulations 2009 (SI 2009/214)* which came into force on 1 October 2009; and the Companies (Disclosure of Address) (Amendment) Regulations 2015, SI 2015/ 842.

Disclosure under court order

8.50 The court may make an order for the disclosure of protected information by the company or by the registrar if:

(a) there is evidence that service of documents at a service address other than the director's usual residential address is not effective to bring them to the notice of the director, or

(b) it is necessary or expedient for the information to be provided in connection with the enforcement of an order or decree of the court,

and the court is otherwise satisfied that it is appropriate to make the order: CA 2006, s 244(1).

8.51 An order for disclosure by the registrar is to be made only if the company:

(a) does not have the director's usual residential address, or

(b) has been dissolved: CA 2006, s 244(2).

The order may be made on the application of a liquidator, creditor or member of the company, or any other person appearing to the court to have a sufficient interest: CA 2006, s 244(3).

The order must specify the persons to whom, and purposes for which, disclosure is authorised: CA 2006, s 244(4).

Circumstances in which registrar may put the address on the public record

8.52 The registrar may put a director's usual residential address on the public record if:

(a) communications sent by the registrar to the director and requiring a response within a specified period remain unanswered, or

(b) there is evidence that service of documents at a service address provided in place of the director's usual residential address is not effective to bring them to the notice of the director: CA 2006, s 245(1).

8.53 The registrar must give notice of the proposal:

(a) to the director, and

(b) to every company of which the registrar has been notified that the individual is a director: CA 2006, s 245(2).

8.54 The notice must:

(a) state the grounds on which it is proposed to put the director's usual residential address on the public record, and

(b) specify a period within which representations may be made before that is done: CA 2006, s 245(3).

It must be sent to the director at his usual residential address, unless it appears to the registrar that service at that address may be ineffective to bring it to the individual's notice, in which case it may be sent to any service address provided in place of that address: CA 2006, s 245(4).

The registrar must take account of any representations received within the specified period: CA 2006, s 245(5).

What is meant by putting the address on the public record is explained in section 246: CA 2006, s 245(6).

Putting the address on the public record

8.55 The registrar, on deciding in accordance with section 245 that a director's usual residential address is to be put on the public record, shall proceed as if notice of a change of registered particulars had been given:

(a) stating that address as the director's service address, and

(b) stating that the director's usual residential address is the same as his service address: CA 2006, s 246(1).

The registrar must give notice of having done so:

(a) to the director, and

(b) to the company: CA 2006, s 246(2).

8.56 On receipt of the notice the company must:

(a) enter the director's usual residential address in its register of directors as his service address, and

(b) state in its register of directors' residential addresses that his usual residential address is the same as his service address: CA 2006, s 246(3). But:

(a) s 246(3)(a) does not apply if an election under s 167A is in force in respect of the company's register of directors, and

(b) s 246(3)(b) does not apply if an election under s 167A is in force in respect of the company's register of directors' residential addresses: CA 2006, s 246(3A) (as inserted by SBEEA 2015, Sch 5, Pt 2).

If the company has been notified by the director in question of a more recent address as his usual residential address, it must:

(a) enter that address in its register of directors as the director's service address, and

(b) give notice to the registrar as on a change of registered particulars: CA 2006, s 246(4).

If an election under s 167A is in force in respect of the company's register of directors, the company must, in place of doing the things mentioned in sub-s (4)(a) and (b), deliver the particulars to the registrar in accordance with s 167D: CA 2006, s 246(4A) (as inserted by SBEEA 2015, Sch 5, Pt 2).

If a company fails to comply with s 246(3), (4) or (4A), an offence is committed by:

(a) the company, and

(b) every officer of the company who is in default: CA 2006, s 246(5) (as inserted by SBEEA 2015, Sch 5, Pt 2).

A person guilty of an offence under s 246(5) is liable on summary conviction to a fine and, for continued contravention and a daily default fine: CA 2006, s 246(6).

A director whose usual residential address has been put on the public record by the registrar under this section, may not register a service address other than his usual residential address for a period of five years from the date of the registrar's decision: CA 2006, s 246(7).

Duty to notify registrar of change

8.57 A company must within the period of 14 days from:

- a person becoming or ceasing to be a director; or
- the occurrence of any change in the particulars contained in its register of directors or its register of directors' residential addresses;

give notice to the registrar of the change and of the date on which it occurred: CA 2006, s 167(1).

Notice of a person having become a director of the company must contain a statement of the particulars of the new director that are required to be included in the company's register of directors and its register of directors' residential addresses, and be accompanied by a statement by the company that the person has consented to act in that capacity CA 2006, s 167(2) (as inserted by SBEEA 2015, s 100(4)). For newly appointed directors and secretaries, a statement will be added by Companies House to the relevant appointment and incorporation forms (paper and electronic) that the person has consented to act in their relevant capacity. Companies will be required to agree to this statement. As part of this, Companies House will write to all newly appointed directors to make them aware that their appointment has been filed on the public register and explain their statutory general duties.

8.58 Where a company gives notice of a change of a director's service address as stated in the company's register of directors, and the notice is not accompanied by notice of any resulting change in the particulars contained in the company's register of directors' residential addresses, the notice must be accompanied by a statement that no such change is required: CA 2006, s 167(3).

If default is made in complying with this section, an offence will be committed by the company, and every officer of the company who is in default: CA 2006, s 167(4). For this purpose, a shadow director is treated as an officer of the company.

A person guilty of an offence under s 167 will be liable, on summary conviction, to a fine: CA 2006, s 167(5).

Removing a director

8.59 A company may, by ordinary resolution, at a meeting remove a director before the expiration of his period of office, notwithstanding anything in any agreement between it and him: CA 2006, s 168.

Special notice is required of a resolution to remove a director under s 168 or to appoint somebody instead of a director so removed at the meeting at which he is removed: CA 2006, s 168(2).

A vacancy created by the removal of a director, if not filled at the meeting at which he is removed, may be filled as a casual vacancy: CA 2006, s 168(3).

8.60 A person appointed director in place of a person removed under s 168 is treated, for the purpose of determining the time at which he or any other director is to retire, as if he had become director on the day on which the person in whose place he is appointed was last appointed a director: CA 2006, s 168(4).

Section 168 is not to be taken:

(a) as depriving a person removed under it of compensation or damages payable to him in respect of the termination of his appointment as director or of any appointment terminating with that as director; or

(b) as derogating from any power to remove a director that may exist apart from s 168.

The Model Articles of Association for a private company limited by shares only sets out the grounds for termination of a director's appointment: Article 18. However, some articles of association may require a director to resign following a request from the other directors of the company.

The expulsion provisions in the articles of association were valid and effective in removing a director: *Lee v Chou Wen Hsien* [1984] 1 WLR 1202. Although the power of expulsion vested in the directors was a fiduciary power and accordingly, in exercising it, they had to act in what they believed to be the best interests of the company and not for ulterior purposes, the expulsion provision in the company's articles of association was so drafted as to require a director to vacate immediately his office once he had been requested to do so by all the other directors. Lord Brightman was of the view that the courts could not interfere in the management of the company's affairs, where bad faith was pleaded by the aggrieved director against other directors.

8.61 In some cases, it is possible for the removal of a director to be blocked where a director who is also a shareholder can exercise his weighted voting rights to prevent his removal from office.

Weighted voting rights may validly and effectively prevent the removal of a director: *Bushell v Faith* [1970] AC 1099. Article 9 of the articles of association of a private company provided that, in the event of a resolution being proposed at a general meeting of the company for the removal of a director, any shares held by that director should carry three votes per share. It was held by the House of Lords (Lord Morris dissenting) that Article 9 was valid and applicable, despite the provisions of CA 2006, s 168, since Parliament was only seeking to make an ordinary resolution sufficient to remove a director, and had not sought to fetter a company's right to issue a share with such rights or restrictions as it thought fit and these need not be of general application, but could be attached to special circumstances and particular types of resolution.

8.62 It may also be possible to use the entrenchment provisions under CA 2006, s 22 which provides that a company's articles may contain provision ('provision for entrenchment') to the effect that specified provisions of the articles may be amended or repealed only if conditions are met, or procedures are complied with, that are more restrictive than those applicable in the case of a special resolution. This may be a basis for circumventing the removal provisions under CA 2006, s 168.

Another basis on which CA 2006, s 168 may be circumvented is that an agreement may be made between the directors and the shareholders which has the effect of preventing the removal of a director. This is because s 168 deals with an agreement between the company and its director so that s 168 overrides such agreement: *Walker v Standard Chartered Bank plc* [1992] BCLC 535.

8.63 It may be possible for the director who may also be the shareholder to petition on grounds of unfair prejudicial conduct under CA 2006, s 994 based on the view that the director had a legitimate expectation of participating in the company's management: see *Re Westbourne Galleries Limited* [1973] AC 360.

Assuming there is a service contract in place, a director may be entitled to compensation where there is a breach of the service contract by the company. Companies Act 2006, s 168(5)(a) removal of a director does not deprive him of compensation or damages payable to him. The company would therefore be advised to check the provisions of the service contract (if any) with the director to identify the extent of any compensation payable to the director. It applies to termination of his appointment as director or of any appointment terminating with that as director. The director may be entitled to damages for breach of contract where the service contract was for a fixed term which has not expired, or that compensation is payable to the director as part of his terms under the service contract on termination of office.

A director's appointment and termination provisions may be set out in the company's articles of association. In this case, the ordinary contractual principles would apply and provided proper procedures were followed under the articles, it would appear that the director may not have entitlement to claim for damages.

The director's appointment could be terminated by ordinary resolution: *Read v Astoria Garage (Streatham) Ltd* [1952] Ch 637. See too: *Swabey v Port Darwin Gold Mining Co* (1889) 1 Meg 385.

8.64 In other cases, a director may have a service contract with the company which has been breached because, for example, termination occurred within the fixed term period of the contract. In such cases, the director may be entitled to damages.

In some circumstances, the courts may imply terms between the parties. In *Southern Foundries (1926) Ltd v Shirlaw* [1940] AC 701, it was held by the House of Lords, (Viscount Maugham and Lord Romer dissenting), that it was an implied term of the agreement of 21 December 1933, that Southern should not remove the respondent from his position as director during the term of years for which he was appointed managing director. Further, that in respect of the breach of the agreement, the respondent was entitled to the damages awarded by the trial judge.

Resignation

8.65 A director may leave office by an act of resignation. This may be effected by a notice served on the company setting out the date of resignation. Such notice when once given cannot be withdrawn without the consent of the company: *Glossop v Glossop* [1907] 2 Ch 370. Typically, the service contract between a director and the company will set out the notice period required to be given and much will depend upon the executive position occupied by the director in the company: the more senior the executive, the longer the notice period required: *CMS Dolphin Ltd v Simonet* [2001] 2 BCLC 704.

Director's right to protest against removal

8.66 On receipt of notice of an intended resolution to remove a director under s 168, the company must send a copy of the notice to the director concerned: CA 2006, s 169(1). The director (whether or not a member of the company) is entitled to be heard on the resolution at the meeting: CA 2006, s 169(2).

- Where notice is given of an intended resolution to remove a director under s 169, and the director concerned makes representations in writing to the company (not exceeding a reasonable length) and requests their notification to members of the company, the company must notify the shareholders, unless the representations are received by too late for it to do so:

- In any notice of the resolution given to members of the company, the company must state the fact of the representations having been made; and

- The company must send a copy of the representations to every member of the company to whom notice of the meeting is sent (whether before or after receipt of the representations by the company): CA 2006, s 169(3).

If a copy of the representations is not sent as required by s 169(3), because it was received too late, or because of the company's default, the director may (without prejudice to his right to be heard orally), require that the representations be read out at the meeting: CA 2006, s 169(4).

Copies of the representations need not be sent out and the representations need not be read out at the meeting if, on the application either of the company or of any other person who claims to be aggrieved, the court is satisfied that the rights conferred by s 169 are being abused: CA 2006, s 169(5).

The court may order the company's costs on an application under s 165(5) to be paid in whole or in part by the director, notwithstanding that he is not a party to the application: CA 2006, s 169(6).

Checklist: Appointment of a director

8.67 *This checklist sets out the steps and procedures for appointing a director. Notwithstanding the CA 2006 provisions which partially address the appointment of a director, check the company's articles of association on procedure and practice.*

No	**Issue**	**Reference**
1	Prepare an agenda for the board meeting	Agenda
2	Check articles of association on procedure for appointing a director – whether by directors or shareholders. Ensure proposed director not disqualified and check Companies House on register of directors' disqualifications; undertake World Check if necessary. See articles on number of directors (minimum/maximum that may be appointed). Check also any provisions of a shareholders' agreement/joint venture agreement on procedure for nomination and appointment of directors.	Articles of association or Model Articles/ Shareholders' Agreement
3	Ensure director is at least 16 years of age	CA 2006, s 157(1)
4	Send notice of the board meeting to the company's directors of date, time and place of the meeting.	Notice
5	Can directors dispense with a board meeting by a written resolution procedure? Is a quorum present?	Articles of association
6	Has a chairman been appointed for the board meeting?	Articles of Association
7	Directors to vote on the resolution to appoint the director. Voting will be on a show of hands by simple majority.	Articles of Association
8	Prepare minutes of the board meeting.	Minutes
9	Is shareholders' approval required to appoint a director? Company or company secretary to send notice of extraordinary general meeting to the shareholders. Meeting to state date, time, place and proxy.	Articles of Association
10	Can the EGM be dispensed with?.	Articles of Association
11	Is a quorum present at the EGM?	
12	Appoint chairman for the EGM.	Articles of Association
13	Shareholders to vote on the appointment of the director on a show of hands or on a poll.	
14	Prepare minutes of the EGM.	Minutes
15	File Form AP01 (Appointment of Director) or AP02 (Appointment of Corporate Director) at Companies House.	Form APO1/APO2

No	Issue	Reference
16	Inform bank, insurers, HMRC, company personnel, change letterhead/invoices to include director's name. Consider whether obligation to notify if listed company	
17	Will director be entering into service contract? Consider terms. Does service contract require approval of shareholders?	CA 2006, s 188
18	Update register of directors and register of directors' residential addresses.	Company's register
19	Lodge the amended articles of association at Companies House within 15 days after the amendments have been made.	Articles
20	Consider whether director has any interest in contracts or dealings that require disclosure?	CA 2006, ss 177, 182
21	Consider providing director with induction on company obligations and duties in law.	

Checklist: Removal of a director

8.68 *This checklist sets out the steps and procedures required to remove a director from office under the CA 2006. References are also made to the model articles of association though companies should consider their own articles of association governing the procedures for convening the meetings.*

No	Issue	Reference
	Steps and procedures	
1	Consider any service contract entered into between company and director and consequences of termination including any compensation payable.	Model Articles 9(1) and 18
2	Convene a board meeting on reasonable notice (or such notice as required by the articles of association).	Model Article 9(2)
3	Notice to set out the date, time and place of the board meeting.	Agenda
4	Prepare an agenda for the board meeting setting out the proposed removal of the director.	Model Article 9(4)
5	A written resolution cannot be used at the board meeting to remove director.	Model Article 10
6	Ensure quorum is present. Consider the voting at the board meeting – usually by simple majority on a show of hands unless the articles of association provide otherwise.	Model Article 11
7	Directors to put the ordinary resolution to remove the director to the shareholders. Is Chairman appointed? Does Chairman have a casting vote? Are there any conflicts of interest?	Model Articles 12, 13 and 14
8	After the board meeting, prepare minutes of the board meeting.	Model Article 15
9	Prepare ordinary resolution to remove a director and notice to shareholders.	CA 2006, s 168

No	Issue	Reference
10	Notice to set out the date, time, place of meeting and resolution proposed including a note on proxy.	CA 2006, s 169
11	Consider providing the director to be removed from office an opportunity to make representations in respect of proposed dismissal. Representation must be of reasonable length.	Model Articles 37, 38, 39, 40, 42, 44, 45 CA 2006, s 169
12	Ensure quorum present. Has Chairman been appointed? Shareholders to vote on the resolution. Voting is on a show of hands unless a poll is demanded.	
13	After the EGM, prepare minutes of the meeting.	Minutes
14	Update Register of Directors and Register of Directors' residential addresses.	
15	Ensure any authorities given to directors (bank mandate etc) are revoked immediately and check any personal guarantees given to bank.	
16	Remove name of director from all letterheads, invoices.	
17	Inform insurance company where director's name is on the directors' indemnity policy.	
18	File Form TM01 (Termination of appointment of director) to Companies House within 14 days.	Form TM01
19	Inform the company's auditors.	
20	Inform HMRC.	
21	Check director's service contract/contract of employment on obligations – reminding director (if applicable) of post-termination covenants; duty of confidentiality; non-solicitation clause; non-dealing; intellectual property aspects; use of company name and logo; prohibition on making disparaging remarks. Consider whether any compensation payable to director arising from the service contract?	CA 2006, s 172(a) and (b)
22	Consider whether director is entering into a settlement agreement? Was independent advice taken?	
23	Consider whether any Stock Exchange obligations are to be satisfied for notification on director's removal.	

9 Directors: general duties

Introduction

9.1 This chapter addresses the following issues:

- the trusteeship of directors based on the law of trusts;
- the concept of a 'fiduciary' and its application to directors' duties;
- the general duties of directors and attribution of liability;
- a consideration of the proper purpose rule;
- the remedies available under the CA 2006, the common law and equity including the proprietary nature of claims; and
- an examination of relief from liability available for directors.

Are corporate managers trustees?

9.2 In English company law, the courts have sometimes referred to directors as 'trustees' or 'fiduciaries' of the company. This section considers the 'trusteeship' of directors and their 'fiduciary' duties, as these concepts has been used by the courts, to impose obligations on directors.

The concept of 'fiduciary'

9.3 The concept of 'fiduciary', 'fiduciary duties' and 'fiduciary undertaking' are familiar to the law of trusts: they are equitable principles developed over a period of time by the Chancery Courts, in their application to trustees who administered assets on behalf of the beneficiaries of a trust. The concept involved notions of conscience: acting in good faith; a sense of loyalty; acting selflessly; and ensuring the best interests of the beneficiaries at all times. The trustees acted with a moral conscience, to ensure that trust assets were not misapplied, misappropriated, nor trust funds depleted unnecessarily without cause or reason. Trustees were required to undertake their fiduciary obligations with a sense of moral and legal purpose and objective, which became fundamental to the status of a trustee. They generally acted voluntarily in the performance of their duties, without expectation of any remuneration or reimbursement: *Robinson v Pett* (1734) 3 P Wms 249; *Re Barber* (1886) 34 Ch D 77. Such remuneration or reimbursement was only claimable, if trustees could demonstrate a specific entitlement. Further, trustees were required to ensure that they did not place themselves in a position where their duties and interests might conflict. There are various types of fiduciary relationships existing in law and practice, extending 'to the most intimate and confidential relations which can possibly exist between one party and another, where the one is wholly in the hands of the other because of his infinite trust in him': *Coomber v Coomber* [1911] 1 Ch 723, Fletcher Moulton LJ.

9.4 *Lehtimaki v Cooper* [2020] UKSC 33, is the leading Supreme Court authority on the applicability of the 'fiduciary' principle as applied to charity members: the duties of such members are not just limited to acting in a fiduciary capacity (though a member of a charity does not always have to owe a fiduciary duty to further the aims and purposes of the charitable company), but extend to contractual and legislative duties too. According to Lady Arden, the distinguishing characteristic of a 'fiduciary' is that he owes a single-minded duty of loyalty in matters covered by his duty: see too Finn, P D *Fiduciary Obligations* (1977) A member of a charitable company in principle owes this duty. A charitable company itself is analogous to a charitable trustee, in the sense that it holds its assets, subject to a binding obligation to apply them for charitable purposes only. The practical objections to members being fiduciaries (with duties to make their own investigations before voting and so on), are met by the fact that trust law allows such duties to be shaped by contract, and in this case, the members' duties are shaped by the company's constitution, as well as relevant legislation. Accordingly, the duty is essentially a contract-and-statute-based model. The notion that a member is a fiduciary, does not mean that there may not be matters on which a member can vote, which only concern him personally, and not the charity. Lady Arden further stated that it did not matter that a member would not be subject to the full range of fiduciary duties. As long as they owed the 'irreducible core' of a fiduciary duty to perform their role honestly and in good faith for the benefit of the charity, the fiduciary duty could still be shaped by the charitable company's constitution and the relevant company law legislation. Further, the law already recognised exceptions to the general principle under company law that shareholders did not owe fiduciary duties to the company or other members.

9.5 From time to time, the courts have held that a fiduciary is liable to account for breach of his fiduciary duty. In *Boardman v Phipps* [1967] 2 AC 46, Viscount Dilhorne advocated that equity, may, where there has been some impropriety of conduct on the part of a person in a fiduciary relationship (eg a trustee purchasing trust property), require that person to account.

A person in a fiduciary position must not make any secret profit or put himself in a conflict of interest situation: *Bray v Ford* [1896] AC 44. The concept of "fiduciary" signifies that the person occupying a fiduciary position must not personally profit from that position, to the detriment of the beneficiary. In *Keech v Sandford* (1726) Sel Cas T King 61, the court held that a trustee could not personally benefit from a renewal of a lease, and that the benefit must be held on trust for the beneficiary. See too *Chan v Zacharia* (1984) 154 CLR 178; *Don King Productions Inc v Warren* [2000] Ch 291; and *Thompson's Trustee in Bankruptcy v Heaton* [1974] 1 WLR 605.

The extension of trusteeship to directors as fiduciaries

9.6 In his book, *Fiduciary Obligations* (1977), Paul Finn sets out various situations in which the 'fiduciary' obligations can arise. These include trustee–beneficiary, solicitor–client and director–shareholder relationships: see *Imperial Mercantile Credit Association v Coleman* (1873) LR 6 HL 189. According to Finn: 'For a person to be a fiduciary he must first and foremost have bound himself in some way to protect and/

or to advance the interests of another.' In *Grimaldi v Chameleon Mining NL (No 2)* [2012] 287 ALR 22, Finn J gave an authoritative definition of a 'fiduciary' and stated that '… a person will be in a fiduciary relationship with another when and insofar as that person has undertaken to perform such a function for, or has assumed such a responsibility to, another as would thereby reasonably entitle that other to expect that he or she [the fiduciary] will act in that other's interest to the exclusion of his or her own or a third party's interest'. See too Millett LJ in *Bristol and West Building Society v Mothew* [1998] Ch 1.

9.7 Another aspect of the fiduciary relationship is the concept of 'legitimate expectations', in that one party is entitled to expect that the other will act in his interests in and for the purposes of the relationship. Aspects such as ascendancy, influence, vulnerability, trust confidence or dependency are only evidence of a relationship suggesting that entitlement: *Arklow Investments Ltd v Maclean* [2000] 1 WLR 594.

Fiduciary relationships may also have the characteristics of 'vulnerability and discretion' *Frame v Smith* [1987] 2 SCR 99. However, the concept of vulnerability is now considered by the courts as only an indicator of fiduciary status rather than its defining feature: *Hodgkinson v Simms* [1994] 3 SCR 377.

9.8 In *Bairstow v Queens Moat Houses plc* [2001] 2 BCLC 531, the Court of Appeal considered the trusteeship nature of directors' duties. Robert Walker LJ stated that the fiduciary obligations undertaken in this case by the former directors, involved heavy and continuing responsibilities for the stewardship of the company's assets. They were not strictly speaking trustees, as title to the assets was not vested in them; but they had trustee-like responsibilities, because they had the power and the duty to manage the company's business in the interests of all its members.

There is a principle at common law that directors owe continuing fiduciary duties to their company: *Gwembe Valley Development Co Ltd v Koshy* [1998] 2 BCLC 613. However, in some cases a director may not owe fiduciary duties to the company. In *Plus Group Ltd v Pyke* [2002] 2 BCLC 201, the Court of Appeal held that although the fiduciary duty of a director to his company was uniform and universal, there was no completely rigid rule that a director could not be involved in the business of another company, which was in competition with a company of which he was a director. Every decision whether a fiduciary relationship existed in relation to the matter complained of was fact-specific, and in exceptional circumstances, where a director had been effectively excluded from the company, it was not a breach of fiduciary duty for him to work for a competing company.

In *First Subsea Ltd v Balltec Ltd* [2018] 1 BCLC 20, the Court of Appeal held that a director was at all times a fiduciary and trustee in respect of the company and its assets. This applied even if he was not in possession of trust property, and there had been no misappropriation of company property. This was because he belonged to the class of constructive trusts which arose where a defendant was in receipt of trust property under a transaction in which a trust was intended to be created from the outset, and it was intended that he was to be a trustee.

9.9 In the context of company law and practice, the courts have applied the trusteeship principle to directors based on the view that directors' duties were similar to those of a trustee: *York and North-Midland Rly v Hudson* (1853) 16 Beav 485; *Charitable Corp v Sutton* (1742) 2 Atk 400.

9.10 Some cases have decided that although company directors are not strictly speaking trustees, they are in a closely analogous position, because of the fiduciary duties which they owe to the company: *Great Eastern Rly Co v Turner* (1872) 8 Ch App 149; *Re Forest of Dean Coal Mining Co* (1878) 10 Ch D 450; *Imperial Hydropathic Hotel Co v Hampson* (1882) 23 Ch D 1.

9.11 At common law, directors stand in a fiduciary relationship to their company: *Re City Equitable Fire Insurance Co Ltd* [1924] All ER Rep 485; approved by the Court of Appeal [1925] Ch 407.

The statutory regime: scope and nature of general duties of directors under CA 2006

Duty to the company

9.12 Section 170(1) of CA 2006 establishes that directors owe their duties to the company and not to its individual shareholders, nor to its employees, or any other person or third party: *Percival v Wright* [1902] 2 Ch 421. These duties can only be enforced by those who act for or on behalf of the company, including bringing a derivative action under Pt 11 of the CA 2006. The duties are also owed by a *de facto* director in the same way and to the same extent they are owed by a properly appointed (*de jure*) director: CA 2006, s 170(1). The duties will apply to a *de facto* director, where it can be shown that the person was part of the corporate governing structure, and had assumed a role in the company sufficient to impose a duty on him: *Re Paycheck Services 3 Ltd, Revenue and Customs Commissioners v Holland* [2011] 1 BCLC 141.

9.13 This duty is owed collectively to the shareholders as a group and not to individual shareholders generally: *Re Chez Nico (Restaurants) Ltd* [1992] BCLC 192. Although the duty is owed to the company rather than the shareholders, the interests of the company are synonymous with the interests of the shareholders as a general body, both present and future: *Greehalgh v Arderne Cinemas Limited* [1951] Ch 286.

Directors are also required to balance a long-term view against short-term interests of present members: *Gaiman v National Association for Mental Health* [1971] Ch 317. This follows the fiduciary principle that directors must act bona fide in the best interest of the company. In *Re Smith & Fawcett* [1942] Ch 304, the court stated that directors must act at all times bona fide in which they consider (not what the court may consider) to be in the best interest of the company. This principle reflects the court of equity's reluctance to interfere with or second-guess the commercial judgement of directors. The requirement that directors owe a duty to the company, means that when taking any decision concerning the management of a company, they must positively apply their minds to the question of what are the best interests of the company. If they fail to carry out the task, the court may intervene and imposed the decision: *Inland Revenue Commissioners v Richmond* [2003] EWHC 999 (Ch).

Duty towards individual shareholders?

9.14 The CA 2006 does not address the issue as to whether directors may owe duties towards individual shareholders. At common law, there was reluctance by the courts towards recognising that directors owed duties towards individual shareholders, owing to the cohesion of shareholders who are treated as a collective group within the company.

However, in some situations, directors may owe duties towards shareholders through the implied terms under the company's articles of association: *Towcester Racecourse Co Ltd v The Racecourse Association* [2003] 1 BCLC 260.

Directors may also owe duties towards individual shareholders, if they act as agents for the shareholders in the sale of their shares: *Allen v Hyatt* (1914) 30 TLR 444. In *Coleman v Myers* (1977) 2 NZLR 225, the Court of Appeal decided that a fiduciary duty was established between directors and shareholders in view of the 'special circumstances' that existed between them, namely: the company was a private company with shares held largely by members of one family; the other members of the family had habitually looked to the defendants for business advice; the information affecting the true value of the shares had been withheld from shareholders by the defendants. See too *Re Chez Nico (Restaurants) Limited* [1992] BCLC 192; and *Stein v Blake and Others (No 2)* [1998] 1 BCLC 573.

Directors may also be personally liable to the shareholders where they misrepresent or provide misleading advice or abuse their position: *Gething v Kilner* [1972] 1 All ER 1166; *Briess v Woolley* [1954] AC 333; and *Dawson International plc v Coats Paton plc* [1989] BCLC 233. In *Peskin v Anderson* [2001] 1 BCLC 372, the Court of Appeal stated that fiduciary duties owed by directors to shareholders only arose if there was a special factual relationship between the directors and the shareholders in the particular case, capable of generating fiduciary obligations. This would include as a duty of disclosure of material facts, or an obligation to use confidential information and valuable commercial opportunities for the benefit of shareholders, and not to prefer and promote the directors' own interests at the expense of shareholders.

Applicability of certain general duties to former directors

9.15 Some of the directors' general duties continue to apply even where a person is no longer a director of the company. The objective is to ensure that former directors do not easily avoid their fiduciary duties after having left the company, and that such specific duties continue to apply to them. This is particularly the case in respect of the following two of the seven general directors' duties to former directors:

- The duty to avoid conflicts of interest under CA 2006, s 175, with particular regard to exploitation of any property, information or opportunity of which he became aware at a time when he was director: CA 2006, s 170(2)(a); and

- The duty not to accept benefits from third parties under s 176, with particular regard to things done or omitted by him before he ceased to be a director: CA 2006, s 170(2)(b).

The term 'exploitation' is not defined, but suggests use of the property, information or opportunity for personal benefit, or for another person's benefit. It is immaterial whether the company could take advantage of the property, information, or opportunity.

There is no definition of 'benefits' and a wide interpretation will be given to the term, including gratuitous benefits, pecuniary advantages, services performed, secret profits, or any gains received whether directly or indirectly in his capacity as a director of the company.

The 'benefits' must be received from 'third parties'. The term 'third party' means a person other than the company, an associate body, corporate, or a person or an associate body corporate: CA 2006, s 176(2).

The duty not to accept benefits from third parties applies to 'things done or omitted by him' before a person ceased to be a director of the company. This refers to positive action undertaken by the director or any lack of action on the director's part. It may also include any preparatory work undertaken by the former director. The word 'omissions' would refer to inaction, lack of action, inactivity, failure to act, or silence, where the matter required some effort on the part of the director to avoid receipt of the benefit.

The specific statement of general duties that are applicable to a former director are subject to any 'necessary adaptations'. This recognises the fact that any such duties on a former director must not be too onerous, as they would apply to an existing director of the company. For example, where the former director may not have up-to-date knowledge concerning the company or its detailed functioning since he left. Depending on the circumstances, a lower or higher standard may be expected of a former director depending on the degree of his involvement in respect of the above specific duties before he left the company.

In *Allfiled UK Ltd v Eltis* [2015] EWHC 1300 (Ch), Hildyard J accepted that the rigour of fiduciary accountability may occasionally be abated where resignation has been forced upon the director, and he or she has not actively sought to solicit the company's customers, or to exploit any opportunity belonging to it: see too *Hunter Kane Ltd v Watkins* [2003] EWHC 186 (Ch), approved by the Court of Appeal in *Foster Bryant Surveying Ltd v Bryant* [2007] EWCA Civ 200.

Application of common law rules and equitable principles

9.16 The general duties of directors are based on certain common law rules and equitable principles as they apply in relation to directors. The general duties have effect in place of those rules and principles: CA 2006, s 170(3).

The general duties must be interpreted and applied in the same way as common law rules or equitable principles. Consideration will also be taken of the corresponding common law rules and equitable principles in interpreting and applying the general duties: CA 2006, s 170(4). The courts will therefore still have regard to existing case law on directors' duties in the common law and the fiduciary duties in equity, in the interpretation of the statement of the general duties of directors. Further, where future developments in common law or equity take place, the courts will have regard to such new developments as they occur. This will be the case in particular regarding developments in equity, trusts and fiduciaries, and other areas of law that may impact upon directors' duties, particularly, for example, in the analogy that the courts have used at common law between the law of trusts and its application to directors as trustees for the company, which area may be developed further by the courts.

9.17 The scope and nature of general duties of directors as set out in ss 171–177 of CA 2006, apply to a shadow director of a company where and to the extent that they are capable of so applying: CA 2006, s 170(5) (as amended by SBEEA 2015, s 89). The Secretary of State can make regulations about the application of the general duties of directors to shadow directors. The regulations may make provision for prescribed general duties of directors to apply to shadow directors with such adaptations as may be prescribed; and for prescribed general duties of directors not to apply to shadow directors. This provision inserted by SBEEA 2015, s 89 recognises that the starting point with shadow directors is that all the general duties as set out in ss 171–177 of CA 2006 will apply to them, and no general distinction is maintained. However, the words 'where and to the extent that they are capable of so applying' has several effects: first, not all the general duties are suited to applying to shadow directors. Second, the Secretary of State may by regulations, directly apply or disapply one or more of the general duties to shadow directors with or without modifications, to facilitate their applying to shadow directors. The rationale of this provision is to ensure that the shadow directors are made accountable for their actions and activities on the same level as directors (unless some of the provisions do not apply or are excluded). Once the shadow director is identified, he must comply with the general duties to the extent applicable.

Duty to act within powers

9.18 There are two aspects in this duty that must be observed by a director of a company:

A director must:

(a) act in accordance with the company's constitution; and

(b) only exercise powers for the purposes for which they conferred: CA 2006, s 171.

Acting in accordance with the company's constitution

9.19 The term 'constitution' is defined for the purposes of directors' general duties under CA 2006, s 257 to include the following:

(a) any resolution or other decision come to in accordance with the constitution: CA 2006, s 257(1); and

(b) any decision by the members of the company, or class of members, that is treated by virtue of any enactment or rule of law as equivalent to a decision by the company. This is in addition to the matters set out in CA 2006, s 17 (general provision as to matter contained in the company's constitution): CA 2006, s 257(2).

9.20 Under CA 2006, s 171(a), the duty to act in accordance with the company's constitution, means that the directors must observe any limitations or restrictions on their powers. They cannot usurp the powers of the shareholders. The objective of s 171(a) is to ensure that the demarcation of responsibilities between directors and shareholders is maintained under the corporate governance system as set out in the company's constitution. While directors will manage the day-to-day operations of the company, they are ultimately responsible to their shareholders who have residual authority on major matters affecting the company.

Exercising powers for the purposes conferred

9.21 Prior to s 171, the position at common law was that directors were required to ensure that they exercised their powers for a proper and not any collateral purpose.

This latter duty was known as the 'proper purpose' doctrine. Under this doctrine at common law, where directors acted beyond their powers, this was considered ultra vires the company: *Re Lands Allotment Company* [1894] 1 Ch 616; *Re Oxford Benefit Building and Investment Society* (1886) 35 Ch D 502; and *Leeds Estate Building and Investment Company v Shepherd* (1886) 36 Ch D 502. This rule has now been codified under the CA 2006, and amplified further in *Eclairs Group Ltd v JKX Oil & Gas plc; Glengary Overseas Ltd v JKX Oil & Gas plc* [2015] UKSC 71 (see **9.26** below).

9.22 Section 171(b) of CA 2006 also imposes a duty on directors only to exercise powers for the purposes for which they were conferred. Some of the leading cases decided before CA 2006 considered the proper purposes doctrine and its application to directors' powers. In such cases, the improper purposes typically involved directors maintaining control of the company for personal advantage to the detriment of the shareholders: *Fraser v Whalley* (1864) 2 Hem & M 10. The nature of improper purposes arises because directors exercise powers outside their limits for which they were conferred: in effect, it is an abuse of authority by the director who misuses his authority to usurp power and position within the company. The court will not consider the subjective intentions of the director concerned who has exercised the powers for improper purposes – the test is objective: *Howard Smith Ltd v Ampol Petroleum Ltd* [1974] AC 821. Where directors have exercised their powers for a proper purposes, the courts are unlikely to second-guess such decisions based on the reasonableness or unreasonableness of directors' decisions: *Edge v Pensions Ombudsman* [2000] Ch 602.

9.23 On occasions, the courts have held that the issuing of new shares was an abuse of power by directors: *Punt v Symons Co Ltd* [1903] 2 Ch 506. In *Piercy v Mills & Co Ltd* [1920] 1 Ch 77, the directors decided to allot shares with the intention of preventing the majority shareholders from exercising control of the company. This was held to be an improper exercise of directors' powers.

In *Re Smith & Fawcett Ltd* [1942] Ch 304, the court stated that directors must act for a proper purpose. Where directors act for an improper or 'collateral' purpose, the court will intervene and set aside the act in question. See too *Hogg v Cramphorn* [1967] Ch 254.

In *Harlowe's Nominees Ptd Ltd v Woodside Oil Co* [1968] 123 Ch 483 and *Teck Corp Ltd v Millar* [1972] 33 ALR 3 at 288, the High Court of Australia and the Canadian Court respectively upheld directors' decisions to prevent a takeover.

Bamford v Bamford [1970] Ch 212, also illustrates an improper exercise of power by directors in the context of a takeover of the company.

The raising of capital and issuing shares was considered by the Privy Council as an abuse of power by directors, where the predominant purpose was to thwart a takeover attempt: *Howard Smith Ltd v Ampol Petroleum* [1974] AC 821. According to Lord Wilberforce, when considering the powers to directors, it was:

> '… necessary to start with consideration of the power whose exercise is in question; in this case, a power to issue shares. Having ascertained, on a fair view, the nature of this power and having defined as can best be done in the light of the modern conditions, or some, limits within which it may he exercised, it is then necessary for the court, if a particular exercise of it is challenged, to examine the substantial purpose for which it was to be exercised, and to reach a conclusion whether that purpose was proper or not. In doing so, it will necessarily give credit to the bona fide opinion of the directors, if such is found to exist, and will respect their judgment as to the matter of the management having done this, the ultimate conclusion has to be as to the side of a fairly broad time on which the case falls.'

In determining whether directors have acted for improper purposes, the court will consider the powers conferred for directors and the limitations placed upon them in the exercise of that power. The court will then consider the actual purpose for which the power was exercised. In this regard, the court is entitled to '... look at the situation objectively, in order to estimate how critical or pressing a substantial, as per contra insubstantial an alleged requirement may have been.'

9.24 In some cases, the courts have considered that it may be a legitimate use of power by directors to forestall a takeover bid: *Criterion Properties plc v Stratford UK Properties LLC* [2002] 2 BCLC 151 and [2003] 2 BCLC 129.

9.25 Once a breach of CA 2006, s 171(a) is found, directors cannot establish a defence that they were unaware of the limitations under the company's constitution: they are required to have read and fully understood the provisions of the articles of association and any restrictions on their powers. The common law position where directors acted for improper purposes was that any such exercise of their powers was void; and where misuse of the company's capital was concerned or unlawful distribution of dividends, directors are treated as constructive trustees owing to a breach of trust and liable to account to the company.

Where directors act in breach of CA 2006, s 171(b), the position at common law is that their actions are voidable and liable to set aside by the company, unless third party rights apply: *Hunter v Senate Support Services Ltd* [2004] EWHC 1085 (Ch). The company may also consider ratification of directors' actions in such situations: *Bamford v Bamford* [1970] Ch 212; *Criterion Properties plc v Stratford UK Properties LLC* [2004] 1 WLR 1846.

9.26 In *Eclairs Group Ltd v JKX Oil & Gas plc; Glengary Overseas Ltd v JKX Oil & Gas plc* [2015] UKSC 71, although the Supreme Court decided that the proper purpose rule applied to an article provision (Article 42 of *JKX Oil & Gas plc* articles of association), which imposed restrictions on rights attaching to shares, there was no unanimity on the appropriate test that should be applied in identifying, whether or not directors acted for a proper purpose within the powers conferred on them, particularly where multiple purposes were involved.

According to the Supreme Court, one of the fiduciary duty of directors is to ensure that they exercise their powers for proper purposes under s 171(b) of CA 2006. The proper purpose rule is not concerned with excess of power by doing an act which is beyond the scope of the instrument creating it, as a matter of construction or implication. It is concerned with an abuse of power by directors – by doing acts which are within the scope of authority but carried out for an improper reason. The exercise of directors' powers is limited to the purpose for which they were conferred. A company director must not, subjectively, act for an improper purpose. Where the instrument conferring a power is silent as to its purpose, this can be deduced from the mischief of the provision, its express terms and their effect, and the court's understanding of the business context.

Under article 42, the power to restrict the rights attaching to shares was ancillary to the statutory power to call for information under s 793. Article 42 has three closely related purposes: (i) to induce a shareholder to comply with a disclosure notice; (ii) to protect the company and its shareholders against having to make decisions about their respective interests in ignorance of relevant information; and (iii) as a punitive sanction for a failure to comply with a disclosure notice. Seeking to influence the outcome of shareholders' resolutions or the company's general meetings is no part of those proper purposes.

According to the Supreme Court, the proper purpose rule was the principal means by which equity enforced directors' proper conduct: it was fundamental to the constitutional distinction between board and shareholder. Typically, a battle for control of the company was probably the context where the proper purpose rule had the most valuable part to play. Lord Sumption and Lord Hodge considered that where the directors had multiple concurrent purposes, the relevant purpose or purposes were those without which the decision would not have been made. If that purpose or those purposes were improper, the decision was ineffective. The court found that four of the six directors were concerned only with the effect of the restriction notices on the outcome of the general meeting. They acted for an improper purpose.

Duty to promote the success of the company

9.27 Under CA 2006, s 172, a director of a company must act in the way he considers, in good faith, would be the most likely, to promote the success of the company for the benefit of its members as a whole, and in doing so, have regard (amongst other matters) to:

(a) the likely consequence of any decision in the long term;

(b) the interests of the company's employees;

(c) the need to foster the company's business relationships with suppliers, customers and others;

(d) the impact on the company's operations on the community and the environment;

(e) the desirability of the company maintaining a reputation for high standards of business conduct; and

(f) the need to act fairly as between members of the company: CA 2006, s 172(1).

9.28 At common law directors were required to act in good faith in the interests of the company. This was a fundamental duty of loyalty that a director owed to his company. This aspect of duty towards the company has now been reformulated under s 171 of the CA 2006. However, the common law requirement that directors act in the interests of the company did not address clearly in whose interests, owing to the inanimate legal entity nature of the corporation – whether of shareholders individually or collectively or other broader stakeholders? In *Gaiman v National Association for Mental Health* [1971] Ch 317, Sir Robert Megarry VC was of the view that the interests of the association could not be considered in isolation: they referred to the interests of members both present and future. Similarly, in *Brady v Brady* [1988] BCLC 20, Nourse LJ was of the view that 'the interests of a company, as an artificial person, cannot be distinguished from the interests of the persons who are interested in it'. The common law position also at times recognised the interests of other stakeholders such as employees: *Parke v Daily News (No 2)* [1962] Ch 927; *Hutton v West Cork Railway Co* (1883) 23 Ch D 654.

Directors must act bona fide in the company's interests: *Smith & Fawcett Ltd* [1942] Ch 304. This means the interests of the shareholders collectively as a whole, which has as its objective the need to balance the interests of the present shareholders, against the long-term interests of future shareholders. Directors 'must exercise their discretion bona fide in what they consider– not what a court may consider – to be in the interests of the company, and not for any collateral purpose'.

The term 'bona fide in the interests of the company' is reflected in CA 2006, s 172: *Re Southern Counties Fresh Foods Limited* [2008] All ER 195.

9.29 Section 172 of CA 2006 upholds the primacy of shareholder consideration in promoting the company's success. It is based on the premise of profit maximisation in the shareholders' interests as the primary objective of the company. However, in undertaking this objective, directors must have regard to consideration of other stakeholders, though not on equal par to the shareholders, as only shareholders, not other stakeholders, may enforce directors' duties. There is no requirement for the directors to balance the interests of the stakeholder groups under s 172 in determining the success of the company, particularly as these stakeholders do not have enforceable rights under the section, which they can bring against the company or the directors. In practice, it may be difficult to demonstrate that the directors did not act in good faith when taking account of the interests of various stakeholders under s 172.

The duty to promote the success of the company codifies the fiduciary principle imposed on a director having regard to 'enlightened shareholder value'. This has two elements:

(1) the director must act in a way he considers in good faith, would be most likely to promote the success of the company for the benefit of the members as a whole; and

(2) in doing so, the director must have regard, *inter alia*, to the factors listed in CA 2006, s 172(1).

A duty to act in good faith

9.30 The first aspect of CA 2006, s 172(1) is the requirement for directors to act in good faith. It is addressed to each director who 'must act in the way he considers' in good faith to promote the company's success. The duty is subjective: *Regentcrest plc v Cohen* [2001] 2 BCLC 80. The promotion of the success of the company is based on the business judgment decision of directors: they are best placed to decide what will constitute the company's success having regard to the various factors. The duty must be considered as a whole, together with the factors set out. This is one of the core duties that will apply in any aspect of directors' day-to-day management of the company; in their decision-making functions; in the closure of a branch of a business; in their conduct of all company affairs. There is no objectivity test involved in what a reasonable director would have done in the circumstances.

9.31 Directors must also have a 'good faith' belief that they acted to promote the company's success. They are required to address their minds to the issue in question and demonstrate some supporting reasoning how they had acted in good faith. A director may not be in breach of his duties if he acted honestly in the circumstances: *Extrasure Travel Insurances Limited v Scattergood* [2003] 1 BCLC 598.

Usually the courts will not second-guess the decisions of directors

9.32 Although the courts will not second-guess directors' business decisions (see *Burland v Earle* [1902] AC 83; *Carlen v Drury* (1812) 1 Ves & B 154), they are still required to determine whether directors have satisfied the aspect of good faith under s 172. This would require the courts to determine not only directors' acting bona fide, but a demonstration (whether active or otherwise) that they addressed their minds honestly to the issue in question.

In addressing the issue of good faith, the court will also consider whether any bad faith was exercised by the directors in considering the promotion of the company's interests. In *Primlake v Matthews Associates* [2007] 1 BCLC 666, Lawrence Collins J, was of the view that on the facts, the directors acted in bad faith in making excessive payments by way of directors' remuneration to another director: the directors had not held an honest belief that such excessive payments should be made. See too *Simtel Communications Ltd v Rebak* [2006] 2 BCLC 571.

Directors must have regard to the purposes for which the company was formed under CA 2006, s 172 in considering its long term success: *Southern Private Landlords Association* [2010] BCC 387.

The term 'good faith' is not defined but the directors' intentions and motives will be taken into account, as well as whether they acted bona fide in arriving at their decision. Bad faith may apply where directors acted illegally, fraudulently, or where an improper motive or intent is enacted and embraces high expectation of such type of behaviour. Aspects of good faith also include integrity, ethical behaviour, professionalism, honour, respect, adherence to the company's values. Good faith is a wide term and should be interpreted broadly, to embrace such well-intentioned types of behaviour.

The concept of 'success'

9.33 Section 172(1) of CA 2006 requires a director to act in good faith in a way he considers '... would be most likely to promote the success of the company for the benefit of its members as a whole ...'. There is no definition of 'success'. It is, however, considered as the pivotal factor in directors exercising their discretion under s 172. For some companies, the term success would be measured in terms of profit maximisation for the benefit of shareholders. Indeed, some shareholders would view this as the primary objective of commercially driven companies. However, not all companies that are established have as their objective profit maximisation: for some companies, the distribution of dividends is not the main motive – they may be charitable companies, or shareholders forming a management company for the operation of flats. Their motives are not profit maximisation and success would be measured in terms of the objectives they have established at the outset in operating such companies. This aspect is addressed in s 172(2) of CA 2006 which states that:

> 'where or to the extent that the purposes of the company consist of or include purposes other than the benefit of its members, [s 172(1) CA 2006] has effect as if the reference to promoting the success of the company for the benefit of its members were to achieving those purposes'.

9.34 The legal effect of CA 2006, s 172 is that it will be the shareholders who will define the company's success whether measured in terms of profitability or value, and for directors to implement the concept of success in practice. The purpose of objectives of the company may be either established in the company's constitutional documents or communicated to the directors through, for example, a shareholders' agreement. Although directors are given a degree of flexibility in promoting the company's success, they are still ultimately responsible and accountable to the company's shareholders for the decisions that they reach.

It requires the director(s) in question (and not a reasonable or a prudent director since the concept is applied to the particular company under consideration) to determine how to promote the long-term success of the company. The words 'most likely' suggest that the director address his mind by projecting forward in determining whether the decisions that he makes will be for the long-term success of the company. The term 'promote' would suggest an enhancement or furtherance of the company's interest. Therefore, promoting the success of the company signifies profit maximisation and enlightened shareholder value. The primary objective is to ensure optimal shareholder maximisation of wealth, as a result of the capital contribution made by its shareholders collectively.

9.35 According to the ministerial statements of the government on the concept 'success', Lord Goldsmith stated that the starting point was that it was essentially for the members of the company is define the objectives they wanted to achieve. Success meant what the members collectively wanted the company to achieve. For a commercial company, success normally means 'long-term' increase in value: *Pantiles Investments Ltd v Winckler* [2019] EWHC 1298 (Ch). For certain companies such as charities and community interim companies, it will mean the attainment of the objective for which the company has been established.

Although, for a commercial company, 'success' will normally mean long-term increase of its value, the company, constitution and the decisions made under it, will also lay down the appropriate success model for the company. Shareholders should, therefore, define the success that they wish to achieve.

9.36 The decision to promote the success of the company must be for the benefit of the members as a whole. This clearly prohibits directors from favouring one class of shareholders over another, or starting one class inequitably or unfairly, in arriving at a decision or treating minority shareholders with prejudice or oppression as compared to majority shareholders. The term applies to shareholders as a group.

For some companies, success may be measured in terms of the company's wider social responsibilities, as part of the wider objectives of companies and not just profit maximisation. This is envisaged by CA 2006, s 172(2) which states that where or to the extent that the purposes of the company consist of or include purposes other than the benefit of its members, s 172(1) has effect as if the reference to promoting the success of the company for the benefit of its members were to achieving those purposes.

The six factors

Factor (a) – 'the likely consequences of any decision in the long term'

9.37 This factor requires a director to address his mind by acting positively or proactively, in determining the likely consequence of any decision in the long term. The decision must not be reached on a short-term basis or for short-term gains or benefits.

Directors will apply their mind to the likely future consequences of any decision they reach. They are not required to be certain about the consequences, as this would be onerous. They will ask themselves: 'What is likely to result from the decisions we make today in the long term?'

Factor (b) – 'the interests of the company's employees'

9.38 Previously CA 1985, s 309 addressed the requirement for directors to have regard to the interests of the company's employees. In some cases, where directors were challenged on certain decisions by the shareholders, they would invoke s 309 as a defensive measure against an attack by the shareholders: *Re Saul D Harrison & Sons plc* [1995] 1 BCLC 14.

Judicial attitudes towards directors considering the interests of employees have varied, and the law has not been applied consistently by the courts. Legal issues have arisen where a company has engaged in corporate philanthropy or gratuitous distributions of an altruistic nature towards, for example, its employees. Some cases have shown that the courts have viewed gratuitous payments by companies to employees with no great enthusiasm; and in other cases, the courts have permitted gratuitous payments to employees as a recognition of directors taking account of employees' interests within the corporation: *Hampson v Price's Patent Candle Co* (1876) 45 LJ Ch 437; *Hutton v West Cork Railway Co* (1883) 23 Ch D 654; *Parke v Daily News Limited* [1962] Ch 927.

The 'interests of the company's employees' has wide meaning and significance, and would include their well-being; consideration, where practicable, of retraining and redeployment of employees in the event of potential redundancies; health and safety; potential mergers, acquisitions and takeovers; consultations affecting employees in connection with company operations; involvement in a company's strategic policies and implementation.

With regard to employees, CA 2006, s 247 deals with the power for directors to make gratuitous provision for employees on cessation or transfer of business. The powers of the directors of a company include (if they would not otherwise do so) power to make provision for the benefit of persons employed or formerly employed by the company, or any of its subsidiaries, in connection with the cessation or the transfer to any person of the whole or part of the undertaking of the company or that subsidiary: CA 2006, s 247(1).

This power is exercisable notwithstanding the general duty imposed by s 172 (duty to promote the success of the company): CA 2006, s 247(2).

In the case of a company that is a charity it is exercisable notwithstanding any restrictions on the directors' powers (or the company's capacity) flowing from the objects of the company: CA 2006, s 247(3).

9.39 The power may only be exercised if sanctioned by a resolution of the company; or by a resolution of the directors: CA 2006, s 247(4).

A resolution of the directors must be authorised by the company's articles; and is not sufficient sanction for payments to or for the benefit of directors, former directors or shadow directors: CA 2006, s 247(5).

Any other requirements of the company's articles as to the exercise of the power conferred by s 247 must be complied with: CA 2006, s 247(6).

Any payment under s 247 must be made before the commencement of any winding up of the company; and out of profits of the company that are available for dividend: CA 2006, s 247(7).

Factor (c) – 'the need to foster the company's business relationship with suppliers, customers and others'

9.40 A company will have business dealings with various third parties. This factor provides for directors to address the requirement to foster the company's business relationships with suppliers, customers and others. The word 'foster' would suggest the need to promote growth or develop business relationships with such third parties. Developing such business relationships is vital for the company's sustainability and viability to ensure growth and success. It signifies the need to have a business understanding with the company's suppliers, customers and others: how the parties can work together for mutual benefit and gain. A company cannot operate or function in a vacuum: it has dealings with other businesses and in some cases, relies on suppliers and customers for its very existence. It signifies the need for a regular dialogue with such third parties on how the company can conduct better and ethical business in society. For example, the dialogue with customers will be how the company can provide a better service or a better product. What will it take to extract a sense of loyalty from customers towards the company? How does the company better promote its services or products? How does the company effectively address customer complaints or grievances? Is the after-sales service provided effectively to customers? Does the company carry out frequent visits to its suppliers to ensure the suppliers are complying with their ethical duties, obligations in supplying products and services (see for example 'Independent Review into the boohoo Group PLC's Leicester supply chain', A Levitt QC, 2020). The list set out in factor (c) is not exhaustive and the category is not closed, as it includes, 'others'. This may include lenders, creditors, professional advisers and other third parties with whom the company has dealings.

Factor (d) – 'the impact of the company's operations on the community and the environment'

9.41 This requires directors to have regard, *inter alia*, to the environment and to avoid any pollution or harm to the local community through the company's activities or operations; to for example, prevent any leakage of hazardous substances into the community that could cause harm or damage or reasonable foreseeability of such harm or damage occurring. In this regard, the company would need to assess the magnitude of risk involved and have in place effective measures to address the level of risk.

Another situation may involve the proposed closure of the company's operations in a particular district location, where the local community is heavily dependent upon local businesses for employment. The closure of the company's branch could lead to redundancies and reflect poorly on the company's image. In such circumstances, the directors must have regard to the impact the closure would have on the local community.

The term 'operations' is not defined but would signify its activities, functions and procedures. Although under separate legislation, the Corporate Manslaughter and Corporate Homicide Act 2007 has significant implications for a company conducting or organising its operations and activities in the wider community.

The impact of the company's operations on the community and the environment also suggests that the company should exercise it social responsibilities in society as a good corporate citizen, and also for sustainability purposes.

Factor (e) – 'the desirability of the company maintaining a reputation for high standards of business conduct'

9.42 This factor is concerned with business ethics and conduct – the manner, behaviour and values of a company implemented in practice. The ethics may be enshrined in various forms ranging from mission statements, vision statements or codes of conduct. In some cases, companies may also be affiliated to various organisations to demonstrate high standards of business conduct.

The wording under factor (e) only requires 'desirability' – this is voluntary and not an obligation for companies. The term 'maintain' suggests regularising a specific standard and keeping up with such standard by, for example, frequent reviews or updates. Some companies have international standards in place that regularise their systems and procedures, as well as compliance standards. The standard is not an ordinary or reasonable one – but it is a high standard. Factor (e) also displays characteristics of corporate social rectitude, which is concerned with the ethical aspects of corporate social behaviour – the need to adopt ethical values towards shareholders, creditors, employees and other wider potential claimants and stakeholders of the company.

Factor (f) – 'the need to act fairly as between members of the company'

9.43 Directors must not take advantage of one group of shareholders to the detriment of the others. They must be transparent with all members concerned and not engage in partial disclosure of information to one group to the exclusion of the other.

The key term is 'fairly': directors must exercise impartial judgment and decisions affecting various groups of members: *Mutual Life Insurance Co of New York v Rank Organisation Limited* [1985] BCLC 11; *Re BSB Holdings Ltd* [1996] 1 BCLC 155. See too: *Re Sunrise Radio Ltd, Kohli v Lit* [2010] 1 BCLC 367; and *Re McCarthy Surfacing Ltd; Hequet v McCarthy* [2009] 1 BCLC 622.

This factor may give rise to litigation because of the potential for enforcement by the members concerned, and may give rise to a judicial review on the rights and interests of the shareholders within the company.

Combination of the factors

9.44 In some cases, the courts may have regard to a combination of factors when considering the long term success of the company, as set out in CA 2006, s 172(2): *Shepherd v Williamson* [2010] All ER 142.

Interests of creditors?

9.45 CA 2006, s 172 does not address the interests of creditors. This aspect will continue to be governed by the common law position and the Insolvency Act 1986. Of particular importance is IA 1986, s 214 which is concerned with wrongful trading. It imposes upon directors a duty of care to take account of the interests of creditors to take all reasonable steps to minimise further loss to the company's creditors, where there is no reasonable prospect of the company avoiding insolvent liquidation. Section 214 is enforceable by the company's liquidator. Under CA 2006, s 172(3), the duty imposed by IA 1986, s 214 'has effect subject to any enactment…requiring directors, in certain circumstances, to consider or act in the interests of creditors of the company'. Therefore, in exercising their duties under s 172, directors must also have regard to the provision on wrongful trading under IA 1986, s 214.

At common law, directors have a duty to consider the interests of creditors where the company is insolvent or near insolvency: *Walker v Wimborne* (1976) 137 CLR 1. This approach was followed in *West Mercia Safetywear Ltd v Dodd* [1988] BCLC 250; *Re Welfab Engineers Limited* [1990] BCLC 833; *Lonrho Ltd v Shell Petroleum Co* [1980] 1 WLR 627.

9.46 In some situations, the interests of creditors may need to be taken into account well before the company's suspected insolvency: *Brady v Brady* [1988] BCLC 20. In *Nicholson v Permakraft (NZ) Ltd* [1985] 1 NZLR 242, the court was of the view that the duty of care by directors towards creditors would apply by 'a course of action which would jeopardise solvency'. The courts have also stated at common law that the duty by the directors is not owed to creditors individually, but is rather a duty owed to the company: *Winkworth v Edward Baron Development Co Ltd* [1986] 1 WLR 1512; and *Yukong Line Ltd of Korea v Rendsburg Investment Corp of Liberia* [1998] 1 WLR 294. Further, directors may still continue to trade even though the company may be in financial problems provided they continue to take account of creditors' interests in these circumstances: *Facia Footwear Ltd v Hinchcliffe* [1998] 1 BCLC 218.

In *LCC v Sequana S.A.* [2016] EWHC 1686 (Ch), Rose J was of the view that the creditors' interest duty could arise in circumstances where the company was not actually insolvent. Something short of actual insolvency was sufficient. The essence of the test in determining the creditors' interest duty was that the directors ought in the conduct of the company's business, to be anticipating the company's insolvency because when that occurred, the creditors had a greater claim to the company's assets than the shareholders. See too: *Re Horsley & Weight Ltd* [1982] Ch 442; *Kinsela v Russell Kinsela Pty Ltd (in liq)* (1986) 10 ACLR 395; *Grove v Flavel* (1986) 11 ACLR 161. Other cases demonstrate the need for doubtful solvency or where the company is on the verge of a collapse: *Colin Gwyer & Associates Ltd v London Wharf (Limehouse) Ltd* [2002] EWHC 2748 (Ch); *MDA Investment Management Ltd* [2003] EWHC 2277 (Ch); *Re Loquitur Ltd* [2003] 2 BCLC 442; *GHLM Trading Ltd v Maroo* [2012] EWHC 61 (Ch); *Vivendi SA v Richards* [2013] EWHC 3006 (Ch); *Roberts (liquidator of Onslow Ditchling Ltd) v Frohlich* [2011] EWHC 257 (Ch); and *Re HLC Environmental Projects Ltd (in liq)* [2013] EWHC 2876 (Ch); *Wessely v White* [2018] EWHC 1499 (Ch) (compliance with CA 2006, s 172 and consideration of interests of creditors meant there was no breach of the director's statutory duties). See too *Re PV Solar Solutions Ltd (in liquidation), Ball v Hughes* [2018] 1 BCLC 58 (where a company was insolvent or of dubious solvency, the directors' duty under CA 2006, s 172(3) to act in the best interests of the company was regarded as a duty to act in the interests of the creditors as a whole, since the interests of the company were regarded as the interests of the creditors alone and their interests were paramount).

BTI 2014 LLC v Sequana S.A. [2019] EWCA Civ 112, is the leading case on the duty of directors to have regard to the interests of creditors, including the circumstances when it arises. Richards LJ stated that in the context of companies that are normally and necessarily risk-taking, the primacy of the interests of shareholders involves risks for those dealing with companies, in particular creditors. To a large extent, those risks come with the fact of dealing with the company, and in the case of most creditors voluntarily assumed. Therefore, creditors can be assumed to look after their own interests when deciding to deal with a company and there are a range of protective measures, such as the taking of security, for which they can bargain.

The Court of Appeal also stated that the duty to have regard to creditors' interests, may be triggered prior to actual insolvency to include something close to actual established insolvency. It further held that the duty is engaged from the point at which directors know or should know that the company is or is likely (in the sense of probable) to become insolvent.

Duty to exercise independent judgement

9.47 A director of a company must exercise independent judgement: CA 2006, s 173(1).

Section 173 does not prevent directors from seeking advice from other advisers or professional advisers in arriving at an informed decision.

Directors must act in good faith in respect of the contract they have entered into to vote at board meetings in order to carry out the provisions of the contract into effect: *Thorby v Goldberg* (1964) 112 CLR 597.

In some situations, directors could bind themselves to fetter their future discretion: *Fulham Football Club Ltd v Cabra Estates plc* [1994] 1 BCLC 363.

9.48 The duty to exercise independent judgement under CA 2006, s 173 is not infringed by a director acting:

(a) in accordance with an agreement duly entered into by the company that restricts the future exercise of discretion by its directors; or

(b) in a way authorised by the company's constitution: CA 2006, s 173(2). The definition of 'constitution' is set out in s 257.

Section 173(2)(a) captures the principle in *Fulham Football Club*, and reference to 'duly entered into' suggest that directors must act bona fide, and in good faith in the best interests of the company in the future exercise of their discretion. Further, s 173(2)(b) requires directors to also have regard to the company's constitution to identify any restrictions or limitations on their powers. They will not be in breach of s 173 if they act in a manner authorised by the company's articles of association.

Duty to exercise reasonable care, skill and diligence

9.49 A director of a company must exercise reasonable care, skill and diligence: CA 2006, s 174(1). This means the care, skill and diligence that would be exercised by a reasonably diligent person with:

(a) the general knowledge, skill and experience that may reasonably be expected of a person carrying out the functions carried out by the director in relation to the company; and

(b) the general knowledge, skill and experience that the director has: CA 2006, s 174(2).

Section 174 of CA 2006 codifies the common law position for directors to exercise reasonable skill and care in the exercise of their functions. This was a common law duty, as opposed to a fiduciary one: CA 2006, s 178(2). The position at common law was to ascertain the standard of skill and care required of a director in discharging his duty. At common law, a lower standard of duty was required of a director, which explains why many directors were not held liable for decisions that they made. The courts applied a subjective test in the application of this duty, namely what the director did in the circumstances, and not what a reasonable director would have done: *Re City Equitable Fire Fire Insurance Co* [1924] All ER Rep 485 and [1925] Ch 407. At common law, directors engaging in business ventures which proved disastrous were not in breach of their duty of skill and care: *Re Brazilian Rubber Plantations and Estates Ld* [1911] 1 Ch 425; *Overend & Gurney Co v Gibb* (1871–72) LR 5 HL 480; and *Re Cardiff Savings Bank* [1892] 2 Ch 100.

9.50 The common law position changed subsequently when the courts began to address the test for determining the standard of skill and care that should be exercised by a director in the performance of his duties. In *Dorchester Finance Co v Stebbing* [1989] BCLC 498, the non-executive director had fallen below the duty of skill and care expected of him. Similarly, in *Norman v Theodore Goddard* [1991] BCLC 1028, Hoffmann J equated the standard of skill and care to that of IA 1986, s 214(4), as an objective test and not a subjective one. As to the distinction between the duties at common law and equity, see: *Bristol & West Building Society v Mothew* [1996] 4 All ER 698.

9.51 Under CA 2006, s 174 there is a collective and individual responsibility on directors to exercise reasonable care, skill and diligence. However, in practice there will be a difference in the functions carried on by an executive and non-executive director, including the types of companies in which they operate so that liability under s 174 may not be imputed to all types of directors: much will depend upon the functions that were discharged by different types of directors and the nature of their duties for s 174 to apply. For example, in the Australian case of *Daniels v Anderson* (1995) 16 ACSR 607, the non-executive directors were held not liable for their failure to discover fraud committed by an employee. The Court of Appeal also stated however that an objective approach required non-executive directors to 'take reasonable steps to place themselves in a position to guide and monitor the management of a company'.

9.52 Further, any delegation by the director to another person, for example, an employee, does not absolve that director from the application of s 174 to supervise and monitor the activities of the person to whom the delegation has been made: *Equitable Life Assurance Society v Bowley* [2004] 1 BCLC 180; and *Re Barings plc (No 5)* [1999] 1 BCLC 433.

9.53 However, on occasions the courts have stated that directors 'have a continuing duty to acquire and maintain a sufficient knowledge and understanding of the company's business, to enable them properly to discharge their duties as directors': *Lexi Holdings plc v Luqman* [2009] 2 BCLC 1.

9.54 The test and the standard under CA 2006, s 174 is an objective one which must be discharged: *Re Brian D Pierson (Contractors) Ltd* [2001] 1 BCLC 275; and *Re Continental Assurance Co of London plc* [2007] 2 BCLC 287.

The nature of the duties exercised by a director was considered by Jonathan Parker in *Re Barings plc (No 5) Secretary of State for Trade and Industry v Baker (No 5)* [1999] 1 BCLC 433 stated the following propositions:

(a) Each individual director owed duties to the company to inform himself about its affairs, and to join with his co-directors in supervising and controlling them.

(b) Subject to the articles of association of the company, a board of directors might delegate specific tasks and functions. Some degree of delegation was almost always essential if the company's business was to be carried on efficiently: to that extent, there was a clear public interest in delegation by those charged with the responsibility for the management of a business.

(c) The duty of an individual director, however, did not mean that he might not delegate. Having delegated a particular function it did not mean he was no longer under any duty in relation to the discharge of that function, notwithstanding that the person to whom the function had been delegated appeared both trustworthy and capable of discharging the function.

(d) Where delegation had taken place the board (and the individual directors) remained responsible for the delegated function or functions and retained a residual duty of supervision and control. The precise extent of that residual duty will depend on the facts of each particular case, as will the question of whether it had been breached.

(e) A person who accepted the office of director of a particular company undertook the responsibility of ensuring that he understood the nature of the duty a director was called upon to perform. That duty would vary according to the size and business of that particular company and the experience or skills that the director held himself out to have in support of appointment to the office. The duty included that of acting collectively to manage the company.

(f) Where there was an issue as to the extent of a director's duties and responsibilities in any particular case, the level of reward which he was entitled to receive or which he might reasonably have expected to receive from the company might be a relevant fact in resolving that issue. It was not that the unfitness depended on how much he was paid. The point was that the higher the level of reward, the greater the responsibilities which might reasonably be expected (prima facie, at least) to go with it.

(g) The following general propositions could be stated with respect to the director's duties:

   (i) Directors had, both collectively and individually, a continuing duty to acquire and maintain a sufficient knowledge and understanding of the company's business to enable them properly to discharge their duties as directors.

   Directors must therefore understand the business in which they are involved to discharge their duties effectively: see *Re Queen's Moat Houses plc, Secretary of State for Trade and Industry v Bairstow (No 2)* [2005] 1 BCLC 136; *Re Westmid Packing Services Ltd, Secretary of State for Trade and Industry v Griffiths* [1998] 2 BCLC 646; and *Re Kaytech International plc, Secretary of State for Trade and Industry v Kaczer* [1999] 2 BCLC 351.

   (ii) Whilst directors were entitled (subject to the articles of association of the company) to delegate particular functions to those below them in the management chain, and to trust their competence and integrity to a reasonable extent, the exercise of the power of delegation did not absolve a director from the duty to supervise the discharge of the delegated functions.

   (iii) No rule of universal application can be formulated as to the duty referred to in (ii) above. The extent of the duty, and the question whether it had been discharged, depended on the facts of each particular case, including the director's role in the management of the company.

See too the Court of Appeal decision at [2000] 1 BCLC 523.

9.55 In the event there is a breach of s 174, the appropriate remedy will be compensation for loss caused by the director's negligence towards the company. Under CA 2006, s 178(2), the duties under ss 171–177 of CA 2006 (with the exception of s 174 (duty to exercise reasonable care, skill and diligence)) are, accordingly, enforceable in the same way as any other fiduciary duty owed to a company by its directors. The distinction as to whether compensation is payable under common law and equitable principles has been blurred: *Bristol and West Building Society v Mothew* [1998] Ch 1.

Duty to avoid conflicts of interest

9.56 A director of a company must avoid a situation in which he has, or can have, a direct or indirect interest that conflicts, or possibly may conflict, with the interests of the company: CA 2006, s 175(1). The term 'possibly may conflict' refers to a real sensible possibility of conflict: *Boardman v Phipps* [1966] 3 All ER 721.

The duty to avoid conflicts of interest applies in particular to the exploitation of any property, information or opportunity (and it is immaterial whether the company could take advantage of the property, information or opportunity): CA 2006, s 175(2).

9.57 Under CA 2006, s 175(3), the duty does not apply to a conflict of interest arising in relation to a transaction or arrangement with the company. This excludes self-dealing transactions with the company, which are subject not to the board scrutiny but approval by the shareholders usually by an ordinary resolution: *Bell v Lever Bros Ltd* [1932] AC 161 and *Sinclair Investments (UK) Ltd v Versailles Trade Finance Ltd* [2011] EWCA Civ 347. *Re Dinglis Properties Ltd; Dinglis v Dinglis* [2019] EWHC 1664 (Ch).

The duty under CA 2006, s 175 is not infringed:

(a) if the situation cannot reasonably be regarded as likely to give rise to a conflict of interest – In *Eastford Ltd v Gillespie* [2011] CSIH 12, the court interpreted the word 'likely' as referring to 'a real sensible possibility'; or

(b) if the matter has been authorised by the directors: CA 2006, s 175(4).

Authorisation may be given by the directors:

(a) where the company is a private company and nothing in the company's constitution invalidates such authorisation, by the matter being proposed to and authorised by the directors; or

(b) where the company is a public company and its constitution includes provision enabling the directors to authorise the matter, by the matter being proposed to and authorised by them in accordance with the constitution: CA 2006, s 175(5).

The authorisation is effective only if:

(a) any requirement as to the quorum at the meeting at which the matter is considered is met without counting the director in question or any other interested director; and

(b) the matter was agreed to without their voting or would have been agreed to if their votes had not been counted: CA 2006, s 175(6).

Any reference in s 175 to a conflict of interest includes a conflict of interest and duty and a conflict of duties: CA 2006, s 175(7).

The 'no-conflict' rule applies to various transactions in which a director may be involved including: his dealings with the company; a duty not to receive a benefit from a third party; and a duty for a director not to make personal use of the company's property, information or opportunities (also known as 'corporate opportunities').

A director must not put himself in a position where his interests to the company conflict with his personal interests: *Aberdeen Rly Co v Blaikie Bros* (1854) 1 Macq 461.

The 'no-conflict' rule is designed to prevent any self-interest from arising and is associated in some cases with the 'no-profit' rule: *CMS Dolphin Ltd v Simonet* [2001] 2 BCLC 704; and *Quarter Master UK v Pyke* [2005] 1 BCLC 245.

The no-conflict duty continues until resignation of a director. However, under CA 2006, s 170(2)(a) a former director will be subject to the no-conflict rule regarding exploitation of property, information or opportunity of which he became aware when he was a director.

Section 175 of CA 2006 and the common law has given rise to a number of cases on corporate opportunities arising, where a director diverts an opportunity which properly belonged to the company for his own personal advantage or gain, and where the director property, information or opportunity.

Directors may be in breach of the 'no-conflict' duty where this conflicts between their interests towards the company and his personal interests: *Bhullar v Bhullar* [2003] 2 BCLC 241. In this case, Jonathan Parker LJ held that the rule that a fiduciary was not allowed to enter into engagements in which he had, or could have, a personal interest conflicting, or which might possibly conflict, with the interests of those whom he is bound to protect was universal and inflexible. The test was whether 'reasonable men looking at the facts would think there was a real sensible possibility of conflict' and where a fiduciary, such as the director of a company, exploited a commercial opportunity for his own benefit, the relevant question was not whether the party to whom the duty was owed (ie the company) had some kind of beneficial interest in the opportunity but whether the fiduciary's exploitation of the opportunity was such as to attract the application of the rule.

9.58 The principle behind the no-conflict rule is that the company is entitled to expect the exclusive loyalty of its directors in the pursuit of business opportunities. Earlier cases on conflict of interest have highlighted the conflict between personal interests and the company's interests.

In *Industrial Development Consultants Limited v Cooley* [1972] 2 All ER 162, a director was under a duty to disclose all information which he received in the course of his dealings with another company.

At common law, directors were liable to account to the company for profit made from a transaction unless ratified by the shareholders: *Regal (Hastings) Ltd v Gulliver* [1942] 1 All ER 378. It is irrelevant that the company could not have taken up a business opportunity that came to the company's director: *Gencor ACP Ltd v Dalby* [2000] 2 BCLC 734.

Directors are also obliged to disclose full facts of a transaction to the company: *Sharma v Sharma* [2013] All ER 291. Jackson LJ summarised the position on CA 2006, s 175 by application of the facts as follows:

(a) A company director is in breach of his fiduciary or statutory duty if he exploits for his personal gain:

  (i) opportunities which come to his attention through his role as director; or

  (ii) any other opportunities which he could and should exploit for the benefit of the company.

(b) If the shareholders with full knowledge of the relevant facts consent to the director exploiting those opportunities for his own personal gain, then that conduct is not a breach of the fiduciary or statutory duty.

(c) If the shareholders with full knowledge of the relevant facts acquiesce in the director's proposed conduct, then that may constitute consent. However, consent cannot be inferred from silence unless:

  (i) the shareholders know that their consent is required; or

  (ii) the circumstances are such that it would be unconscionable for the shareholders to remain silent at the time and object after the event.

(d) For the purposes of propositions (b) and (c) full knowledge of the relevant facts does not entail an understanding of their legal incidents. In other words the shareholders need not appreciate that the proposed action would be characterised as a breach of fiduciary or statutory duty.

See too: *Pennyfeathers Ltd v Pennyfeathers Property Company Ltd* [2013] EWHC 3530 (Ch).

However, the intention to resign may in certain situations trigger the no-conflict rule.

See too: *Coleman Taymar Ltd v Oakes* [2001] 2 BCLC 749; and *Shepherds Investments Limited v Walters* [2007] 2 BCLC 202.

9.59 Directors may be in breach of their fiduciary duty in diverting contract opportunities away from the company: *Cook v Deeks* [1916] 1 AC 554; *Canadian Aero Service v O'Malley* [1973] 40 DLR (3d) 371; *Island Export Finance Ltd v Umunna* [1986] BCLC 460.

In *Davies v Ford* [2020] EWHC 686, the High Court decided that the directors had breached their duty under CA 2006, s 175 by taking up the company's business opportunities for their own personal benefit, regardless of whether the company was unable to take up that opportunity itself by reason of its financial position. This decision affirms the strict application of the 'no-conflict duty' to directors in a corporate insolvency or near insolvency situation. The inability of the company to take up the opportunity provided no defence for the directors, who took up the opportunity themselves in their capacity as directors of the company. See too *Keech v Sandford* (1726) Sel Cas 61.

9.60 The no-conflict duty can arise in the context of the exploitation of any property, information or opportunity. Section 175(2) of CA 2006 does not allow for such exploitation by a director.

9.61 The exploitation of property, information or opportunity is illustrated in *CMS Dolphin Ltd v Simonet* [2001] 2 BCLC 704. The director of an advertising agency resigned without giving notice and set up a new business, first in partnership and later through a company controlled by him. He recruited all the staff of the agency, and the principal clients switched their business to him. Further, he diverted the business and the benefit of existing contracts to his partnership/company. He had not personally made profits, as the profits were made by his company. Lawrence Collins J held that the underlying basis of the liability of a director of a company who, following his resignation, exploited a maturing business opportunity of the company of which he had knowledge as a result of his being a director, was that the opportunity was to be treated as if it were property of the company in relation to which the director had fiduciary duties. By seeking to exploit the opportunity after his resignation, he was appropriating that property for himself, and became a constructive trustee of the product of his abuse of the company's property, which he had acquired in circumstances where he knowingly had a conflict of interest, and exploited it by resigning from the company. He was liable to account for the profits made. He compared this to a position of a trustee who has obligations leaving matters unattended without properly accounting for trust property.

A resigning director who had acted honestly and in good faith and whose resignation was forced on him, was not in breach of the no-conflict rule: *Foster Bryant Surveying Ltd v Bryant* [2007] 2 BCLC 239.

9.62 In respect of remedies available under s 175 of CA 2006, where the corporate opportunity has not yet matured, the company may seek an injunction to prevent the director taking up the corporate opportunity. Where the corporate opportunity has been taken by the director, a breach of duty will have been committed with the company claiming compensation for loss occasioned as a result of the exploitation of the corporate property, information or opportunity.

In conflict of interest cases, where exploitation of corporate information, property or information is concerned, the courts have tended to disgorge the director of the profits made, and to account to the company for such profits. Where no profit has been made then there is no liability to account to the company. The court has also considered whether the disgorging of profits is a proprietary remedy or a personal remedy: *FHR European Ventures LLP v Cedar Capital Partners LLC* [2014] UKSC 45. Under the no-conflict cases, however, the company is not entitled generally to recover losses sustained.

Duty not to accept benefits from third parties

9.63 A director of a company must not accept a benefit from a third party conferred by reason of:

(a) his being a director; or

(b) his doing (or not doing) anything as director: CA 2006, s 176(1).

A 'third party' means a person other than the company, an associated body corporate or a person acting on behalf of the company or an associated body corporate: CA 2006, s 176(2). This is an exception to the prohibition set out in s 176(1) which allows the director to perform services for such corporate body.

9.64 Benefits received by a director from a person by whom his services (as a director or otherwise) are provided to the company are not regarded as conferred by a third party: CA 2006, s 176(3). This is an exception to the prohibition set out in s 176(1) in respect of directors' remuneration and service contracts entered into by the director.

This duty is not infringed if the acceptance of the benefit cannot reasonably be regarded as likely to give rise to a conflict of interest: CA 2006, s 176(4). This is also an exception to the prohibition set out in s 176(1).

Any reference in s 176 to a conflict of interest includes a conflict of interest and duty and a conflict of duties: CA 2006, s 176(5).

9.65 Section 176 of CA 2006 does not define the term 'benefits', and it could include gifts as well as bribes, with bribery being a criminal offence under the Bribery Act 2010. English law takes a broad view as to what constitutes a bribe for the purposes of a civil claim: *Fiona Trust & Holding Corp v Privalov* [2010] EWHC 3199 (Comm); *Daraydan Holdings Limited v Solland International Limited* [2005] Ch 119. The rationale for CA 2006, s 176 is that the taking of benefits by a director would conflict with his duty to the company and the benefit received from the third party. Section 176 is not limited to bribes but has wider significance to include payment of monies, or other benefit received by the person concerned which has not been disclosed to the company: *Industries and General Mortgage Co Ltd v Lewis* [1949] 2 All ER 573.

9.66 It is possible for the shareholders to ratify the acceptance of benefits from third parties under CA 2006, s 180(4)(a), which provides that 'the general duties have effect subject to any rule of law enabling the company to give authority, specifically or generally, for anything to be done (or omitted) by the directors, or any of them, that would otherwise be a breach of duty', or as set out in the company's articles of association: see also CA 2006, s 239. However, under the Bribery Act 2010, it is not possible to ratify any giving or receiving of bribes.

9.68 The remedies for breach of s 176 of CA 2006 are set out in s 178 of CA 2006 and the effect is that the common law remedies will be applicable in the circumstances with remedies against the director including the third party. Common law provides a wide range of remedies in these situations, which include rescission of the contract between the company and the third party, where the director has received a third party benefit, and the third party had knowledge of the position of the director: *Taylor v Walker* [1958] 1 Lloyd's Rep 490.

At common law, the director and the third party may also be liable to pay damages where bribery or fraud is involved, subject to the company demonstrating proof of loss: *Mahesan v Malaysia Government Officers' Co-Operative Housing Society Limited* [1979] AC 374.

In other situations, the court may impose a constructive trust on the person concerned who has received the benefit of an asset or interest: *Attorney-General of Hong Kong v Reid* [1994] 1 AC 324. However, the Court of Appeal in *Sinclair Investments (UK) Ltd v Versailles Trade Finance Ltd* [2011] 4 All ER 335 rejected the Privy Council view, but subsequently, *FHR European Ventures LLP v Cedar Capital Partners LLC* [2014] UKSC 45, has overruled *Sinclair*.

Duty to declare interest in proposed transaction or arrangement

9.69 If a director of a company is in any way, directly or indirectly, interested in a proposed transaction or arrangement with the company, he must declare the nature and extent of that interest to the other directors: CA 2006, s 177(1). The disclosure must, therefore, be to the board of directors and not to a committee of directors: *Guinness plc v Saunders* [1990] 2 AC 663. Whereas s 177 addresses disclosure of interest in proposed transactions and therefore a general duty imposed on directors under Pt 10, Ch 2, CA 2006, s 182 is concerned with disclosure of interest in existing transactions and is governed by CA 2006, Pt 10, Ch 3.

The effect of s 177 is to put the company's directors on notice of a proposed interest in a transaction or arrangement. This in turn will enable the directors to put themselves into a position to protect the company's interests for the future. Although section 177 does not set out what steps such directors who are put on notice should take, in practice they will owe a duty of care to the company to act on the notice and take appropriate action.

A director's personal interest must not conflict with the interests of the company: *Aberdeen Rly Co v Blaikie Bros* (1854) 1 Macq 461.

Directors must declare the nature of their personal interest to the company: *Movitext Ltd v Bulfield* [1988] BCLC 104.

9.70 The duty to declare only arises in respect of a proposed arrangement with the company and not otherwise – transactions or arrangements yet to be entered into or contemplated being entered into in the future. The effect is to alert the board of such arrangement or transaction, or such possibility and to provide consent so as to avoid any conflict of interest in due course: the company still has the ability to decide whether or not to proceed with the transaction, because the arrangement or transaction will take place in the future. Section 177 of CA 2006 is not concerned with transactions or arrangements with the holding company or subsidiary – but only the direct company of which the person is a director. It may relate to a contractual arrangement or a non-contractual one, whether by the board of directors or by the director: *Re Duckwari (No 2)* [1998] 2 BCLC 315; *Neptune (Vehicle Washing Equipment) Ltd v Fitzgerald* [1996] Ch 274.

9.71 Section 177 also catches 'indirect' transactions which may not necessarily involve the director in his capacity as such, but possibly as a shareholder or a person connected with the director (as an interest 'in any way'): *Transvaal Lands Co v New Belgian (Transvaal) Land & Development Co* [1914] 2 Ch 488. In *Newgate Stud Co v Penfold* [2008] 1 BCLC 46, the court stated that indirect transactions are caught, such that there is a 'real risk of conflict between duty and personal loyalties'.

Section 177 makes it clear that not only is disclosure required by the director, but also the 'extent' of such disclosure. This refers to providing some detailed content of the information to be disclosed as part of the disclosure requirements.

The duty to declare under s 177 may also apply to a shadow director 'where and to the extent that the corresponding common law rules or equitable principles so apply': CA 2006, s 170(5).

9.72 Section 177 sets out three situations as to how the declaration may be made by the director: the methods of disclosure are not exhaustive and may include other forms of disclosure. The declaration may (but need not) be made:

(a) at a meeting of the directors; or

(b) by notice to the directors in accordance with:

(i) CA 2006, s 184 (notice in writing); or

(ii) s 185 (general notice): CA 2006, s 177(2). Although not expressly stated under CA 2006, this may include situations where even though the director is not interested, but the interest arises between the company and a connected person. The general notice is likely to apply where a specific transaction or arrangement has not yet been identified, but serves as an advance notice with further details still to be provided by the director to the company. A General notice is notice given to the directors of a company to the effect that the director:

> has an interest (as member, officer, employee or otherwise) in a specified body corporate or firm and is to be regarded as interested in any transaction or arrangement that may, after the date of the notice, be made with that body corporate or firm, or
>
> is connected with a specified person (other than a body corporate or firm) and is to be regarded as interested in any transaction or arrangement that may, after the date of the notice, be made with that person. .

The notice must state the nature and extent of the director's interest in the body corporate or firm or, as the case may be, the nature of his connection with the person. Further the general notice is not effective unless: (a) it is given at a meeting of the directors; or (b) the director takes reasonable steps to secure that it is brought up and read at the next meeting of the directors after it is given: CA 2006, s 185.

If a declaration of interest under s 177 proves to be, or becomes, inaccurate or incomplete, a further declaration must be made: CA 2006, s 177(3).

Any declaration required by s 177 must be made before the company enters into the transaction or arrangement: CA 2006, s 177(4).

9.73 There is a requirement to make a full and frank disclosure of the interest, so that the board can make an informed decision.

Section 177 provides certain gateways to the duty of disclosure in existing transactions by the director to the company. It does not require a declaration of an interest of which the director is not aware, or where the director is not aware of the transaction or arrangement in question: CA 2006, s 177(5).

For this purpose, a director is treated as being aware of matters of which he ought reasonably to be aware.

9.74 A director need not declare an interest:

(a) if it cannot reasonably be regarded as likely to give rise to a conflict of interest: *Boardman v Phipps* [1967] 2 AC 46;

(b) if, or to the extent that, the other directors are already aware of it (and for this purpose the other directors are treated as aware of anything of which they ought reasonably to be aware): see *Re Marini Ltd* [2004] BCC 172; and *Lee Panavision Ltd v Lee Lighting Ltd* [1992] BCLC 22; *Runciman v Walter Runciman plc* [1992] BCLC 1084; and *MacPherson v European Strategic Bureau Ltd* [1999] 2 BCLC 203; or

(c) if, or to the extent that, it concerns terms of his service contract that have been or are to be considered:

  (i) by a meeting of the directors; or

  (ii) by a committee of the directors appointed for the purpose under the company's constitution: see *Runciman v Walter Runciman plc* [1992] BCLC 22: CA 2006, s 177(6).

Section 177 does not apply to a single member company: CA 2006, s 231.

9.75 A breach of s 177 is subject to civil consequences as set out in CA 2006, s 178, because it is a breach of a general duty as compared to existing transactions under CA 2006, s 182, which impose criminal sanctions.

The civil consequences that apply are that the proposed transaction or arrangement entered into is voidable at the company's option, subject to any third party rights. The remedy of recission may be available as in the position at common law: *Bentinck v Fenn* (1887) 12 App Cas 652.

9.76 Another consequence is that provided the director declares his interest under CA 2006, s 177, s 180(1)(b) states that the 'the transaction or arrangement is not liable to be set aside by virtue of any common law rule or equitable principle requiring the consent or approval of the members of the company'. This has the effect that the company will not be able to set aside the transaction or arrangement. It may, however, be possible to establish further restrictions in the company's articles of association, on the nature and extent of the disclosure, and to which other body it should be made as additional protections for the company, subject to third party rights under CA 2006, s 40.

Attribution of liability

9.77 The doctrine of attribution is applied generally in a variety of situations and contexts under general agency principles. However, when attributing liability, consideration should be given to the particular factual context and circumstances in which the doctrine is being used. In the company context, a company has independent legal existence separate from its shareholders. However, the company cannot act or function alone: it acts through the directors and agents who control the company's operations. The issue is: where directors are in breach of their duties, can they attribute that breach and state of mind (if appropriate) to the company? In this regard, the attribution doctrine becomes more significant in the particular context of the company/director relationship. Where the company has been the victim of wrong-doing by its directors or of which directors had notice, the wrong-doing or knowledge of the directors cannot be attributed to the company as a defence to a claim brought against the directors by the company's liquidator, in the name of the company and/or on the company's behalf. This principle will apply even where the directors were the only directors and shareholders of the company, and even though the wrong-doing or knowledge of the directors may be attributed to the company in many other ways.

The scope of the doctrine of attribution of liability has been considered in the leading Supreme Court case of *Jetivia SA v Bilta (UK) Ltd* [2015] UKSC 23. One of the issues before the Supreme Court was a consideration of the circumstances in which the knowledge of directors and other persons is attributed to a legal person such as a company ('Attribution').

Attribution

9.78 In *Jetivia SA*, the Supreme Court's starting point on attribution was that that a company had a separate legal personality distinct from its shareholders: *Salomon v Salomon & Co Ltd* [1897] AC 22 and *Prest v Petrodel Resources Limited* [2013] 2 AC 415. A company had a real legal existence regardless of whether it was controlled by one or more persons. However, as a company was not a natural person, it could not operate in vacuum: it must act through its directors and agents who control how the company will function in its day to day existence: *Aberdeen Railway Co v Blaikie Brothers* (1854) 1 Macq 461. They are also accountable to their company and owe fiduciary duties to the company, through common law, equity and their general duties under the Companies Act 2006. The independent existence of the company signifies that the company can incur liabilities; it can enter into contracts; it can sue and be sued, whether in contract, tort or otherwise. Generally, directors can be described as the 'directing mind and will' of the company, in that their acts and state of mind may sometimes be attributed to the company through application of the agency principles at common law. However, this attribution rule was not of general application, but was subject to limitations, and consideration must be given to the very specific and particular context or situation in which the acts and state of mind of the directors could be attributed to the company. In this regard, the court will consider the nature of the agency relationship between the company and its directors, and the nature of the principal's or the other party's claim.

9.79 In *Jetivia SA v Bilta (UK) Ltd*, Bilta was being used by its directors as a vehicle to commit a fraud on a third party, causing losses to the company in breach of the directors' fiduciary duties to the company. Under these particular circumstances, it was not appropriate to attribute to the company the fraud to which the alleged breach of duty related, even if this was being practiced by a person, whose acts and state of mind would be attributed to the company in other contexts. The Supreme Court identified three situations in a civil law context concerning attribution of knowledge to a company:

- In relation to a claim by a defrauded third party against the company. Here under the agency rules, the company should be treated as a perpetrator of the fraud. The acts and state of mind of the director are attributed to the company. The company is treated as an absent human owner of a business who leaves it to his managers to operate the business.
- In respect of a claim between the company against its directors for breach of a duty (whether fiduciary or otherwise), the delinquent directors should not be able to rely on their own breach of duty, nor should their actions or state of mind be attributed to the company. It would also defeat the policy of the Companies Act provisions, which provisions were intended to protect the company including the interests of the company's creditors on where the company is insolvent or near insolvency – the 'statutory policy' argument put forward by Lords Toulson and Hodge.

  Where a company claims against a third party, whether or not there is attribution of the director's act or state of mind, will depend upon the nature of the claim that is in issue.

- The application of the Attribution principles in the context of a company/director relationship, makes it clear that there is no place to hide for a director who breaches his duties. The director cannot attribute his acts and state of mind as those of the company.

According to the court, a company had separate legal personality, but it could act only through its directors and agents. In most circumstances, the acts and state of mind of a company's directors and agents could be attributed to the company by applying the rules of the law of agency. However, whether an act or state of mind could be attributed to a company depended upon the context in which the question arose. Where the question of attribution arose in the context of an agency relationship, the nature of the principal's or other party's claim was highly material. Where an action was for a breach of duty against directors for using the company to commit a fraud on a third party, in a way alleged to have caused the company loss, it was inappropriate to attribute to the company the fraud to which the alleged breach of duty related, even if it was being practised by a person whose acts and state of mind would be attributable to it in other contexts. As between the company and a defrauded third party, the company should be treated as a perpetrator of the fraud, but in the different context of a claim between the company and the directors, the defaulting directors should not be able to rely on their own breach of duty to defeat the operation of the provisions of CA 2006 in cases where those provisions were intended to protect the company. A claim by a company against its directors could be said to be the paradigm case where attribution was inappropriate.

In *Singularis Holdings Ltd (In Official Liquidation) (A Company Incorporated in the Cayman Islands) v Daiwa Capital Markets Europe Ltd* [2019] UKSC 50, the UK Supreme Court stated the accepted principle that a properly incorporated company had a separate legal identity from its shareholders and directors. However, the acts of persons controlling or operating the company can only be attributed to the company in certain circumstances, as stated in the company's constitution or the common law rules of agency or vicarious liability. In *Singularis*, however, the acts of the controller in question concerning his fraud, could not be attributed to the company itself. Therefore, 'to attribute the fraud of a trusted agent of the company to the company, would denude the duty of any value in cases where it is most needed and be a retrograde step'.

Civil consequences of breach of general duties

Application of CA 2006, s 178

9.80 The consequences of breach (or threatened breach) of CA 2006, ss 171–177 are the same as would apply if the corresponding common law rule or equitable principle applied: CA 2006, s 178(1).

The duties in those sections (with the exception of s 174 (duty to exercise reasonable care, skill and diligence)) are, accordingly, enforceable in the same way as any other fiduciary duty owed to a company by its directors: CA 2006, s 178(2). The exception in respect of the duty to exercise reasonable care, skill and diligence, is that this is a common law duty and not a fiduciary one.

The application of s 178 is only to the general duties of directors under Ch 2 of Pt 10 to CA 2006 and not to Chs 3 or 4 of Pt 10 of CA 2006.

Damages

9.81 Most typically the remedy that will be sought by the company will be damages or compensation for the loss sustained. Often, precise measurement of damages or quantification of loss may be problematic for the courts. The damages sought may be in respect of breach of articles of association, or failure by the director to comply with his service contract.

Injunction

9.82 The company may also seek an injunction for any threatened or continuing actions by the director concerned. This is often assessed on the balance of probabilities, and may be effective to prevent the director from further damaging the company.

Setting aside the contract

9.83 A contract or arrangement entered into between the company and the director, may be set aside where it breaches the no-conflict rule, provided it has not been ratified by the company.

Application of the constructive trust principle and tracing

9.84 In some cases, the courts have treated directors as trustees of the company's property or asset, particularly where the asset which belonged to the company, becomes vested or in the possession of the director. In such situations, the court may treat the director as a constructive trustee, so that the asset or property is restored back to the company; and the remedy of tracing may apply to bring the asset back to the company: *JJ Harrison (Properties) Ltd v Harrison* [2002] 1 BCLC 162. Where the asset is with a third party, the court may order the director to restore the asset to the company concerned: *Bairstow v Queen Moat Houses plc* [2001] 2 BCLC 531.

The nature of proprietary versus personal interests

9.85 In other situations, the courts may consider the remedy of accounting for profits (as rescission will not be available) made by the director from a transaction with a third party, which profit may have been made by the company had it entered into the transaction. This may arise from a breach of fiduciary duty in receiving benefits from third parties, or breach of the no-conflict duty. In these cases, the company will not need to demonstrate proof of loss or damage, but to require to account for the profits made from the transaction: *Murad v Al-Saraj* [2005] EWCA Civ 959; *Regal (Hastings) Ltd v Gulliver* [1967] 2 AC 134.

In respect of accounting for profits, the courts have considered whether the duty to account is proprietary or a personal duty. Over the years, the courts have considered the issue of whether a bribe or secret commission received by an agent could be held on trust for his principal, or whether the principal merely had a claim for equitable compensation in a sum equal to the value of the bribe or commission? Judicial attitudes had revealed a number of inconsistent decisions over the years. There are significant legal and practical effects flowing from this question. If the bribe or commission is held on trust, then the principal has a proprietary claim to it. However, if the principal merely has a claim for equitable compensation, then the principal has no proprietary claim. The effect is twofold: first, if the agent becomes insolvent, a proprietary claim would give the principal priority over the agent's unsecured creditors; and if the principal only had a claim for compensation, he would rank equally with other unsecured creditors. Secondly, where the principal has a proprietary claim to the bribe or commission, he may trace and follow it in equity; and if the claim is for equitable compensation, the principal has no right to trace in equity.

9.86 In the leading case of *FHR European Ventures LLP and others v Cedar Capital Partners LLC* [2014] UKSC 45, the issue before the Supreme Court was whether an agent who received a secret commission, held the sum paid on constructive trust for his principal(s), giving rise to proprietary rights, or whether the principal merely had a claim for equitable compensation, in a sum equal to the value of the bribe or commission? The Supreme Court held that where an agent acquires a benefit which came to his notice, as a result of his fiduciary position, or pursuant to an opportunity which results from his fiduciary position, the general equitable rule ('the Rule') is that he is to be treated as having acquired the benefit on behalf of his principal, by way of constructive trust, so it is beneficially owned by the principal. The Rule applies to both bribes and secret commissions received by the agent. The principal, therefore, has a proprietary claim against the agent.

According to the Supreme Court, the following principles applied from a consideration of previous case law:

(1) An agent owed a fiduciary duty to his principal, because he was someone who had undertaken to act for or on behalf of his principal in a particular matter in circumstances, which gave rise to a relationship of trust and confidence.

(2) As a result, an agent must not make a profit out of his trust, and must not place himself in a position in which his duty and his interest may conflict (see *Boardman v Phipps* [1967] 2 AC 46).

(3) A fiduciary who acted for two principals with potentially conflicting interests without the informed consent of both was in breach of the obligation of undivided loyalty, by putting himself in a position where his duty to one principal may conflict with his duty to the other (see Millett LJ in *Bristol and West Building Society v Mothew* [1998] Ch 1.

Another well-established principle, which applied where an agent received a benefit in breach of his fiduciary duty, was that the agent was obliged to account to the principal for such a benefit, and to pay, in effect, a sum equal to profit by way of equitable compensation: see *Regal (Hastings) Ltd v Gulliver* [1967] 2 AC 134. The principal's right to seek an account undoubtedly gave him a right in equitable compensation in respect of the bribe or secret commission, which equalled the quantum of that bribe or commission. In cases to which the Rule applied, the principal had a proprietary remedy in addition to his personal remedy against the agent, and the principal could elect between the two remedies.

The decision in *FHR* effectively allows the principal's claim to rank ahead of ordinary unsecured creditors based on the proprietary claim. The principal can also trace the proceeds of the bribe or secret commission into the hands of a third party, namely those who are not bona fide purchasers for value without notice. The Supreme Court reached the result of prevent the agent from benefiting from the bribe or secret commission which he had obtained in breach of his fiduciary duty and obligation towards the principal, and instead determined that the principal should obtain this benefit rather than set out the circumstances in which the principal should benefit.

Cases within more than one of the general duties

9.87 Except as otherwise provided, more than one of the general duties may apply in any given case: CA 2006, s 179. There have been cases where breaches of more than one of the general duties of directors has been alleged: *Madoff Securities International Ltd (in liquidation) v Raven* [2013] EWHC 3147 (Comm).

Declaration of interest in existing transaction or arrangement

9.88 Where a director of a company is in any way, directly or indirectly, interested in a transaction or arrangement that has been entered into by the company, he must declare the nature and extent of the interest to the other directors in accordance with s 182: CA 2006, s 182(1). This duty applies to existing transactions or arrangements, which a director has recently concluded or acquired. It applies to concluded arrangements or transactions unlike s 177 of CA 2006, which refers to proposed arrangements or transactions.

Section 182 does not apply if or to the extent that the interest has been declared under s 177 (duty to declare interest in proposed transaction or arrangement).

9.89 CA 2006, s 182 sets out three methods for declaration of existing transactions. The declaration must be made:

(a) at a meeting of the directors; or

(b) by notice in writing (see s 184); or

(c) by general notice (see s 185): CA 2006, s 182(2).

If a declaration of interest under this section proves to be, or becomes, inaccurate or incomplete, a further declaration must be made: CA 2006, s 182(3).

9.90 Any declaration required by CA 2006, s 182 must be made as soon as is reasonably practicable.

Failure to comply with this requirement does not affect the underlying duty to make the declaration: CA 2006, s 182(4).

This obligation applies also to shadow directors: CA 2006, s 187(1) but with adaptations. The method of giving notice for declaration at a meeting of directors does not apply. Further, the notice to be given at or brought up and read at meeting of directors does not apply to a shadow director. The general notice by a shadow director is not effective unless given by notice in writing in accordance with s 184: CA 2006, s 187(2)–(4).

A failure by a director to disclose an interest in a transaction, renders the transaction voidable at the option of the company: *Hely-Hutchinson v Brayhead Ltd* [1967] 3 All ER 98; and *Guinness plc v Saunders* [1990] 1 All ER 652 per Lord Goff.

A director owed a duty to declare his interest in a transaction to the company: *Coleman Taymar Ltd v Oakes* [2001] 2 BCLC 749.

9.91 Section 182 of CA 2006 does not require a declaration of an interest of which the director is not aware, or where the director is not aware of the transaction or arrangement in question.

For this purpose a director is treated as being aware of matters of which he ought reasonably to be aware: CA 2006, s 182(5).

A director need not declare an interest under s 182:

(a) if it cannot reasonably be regarded as likely to give rise to a conflict of interest;

(b) if, or to the extent that, the other directors are already aware of it (and for this purpose the other directors are treated as aware of anything of which they ought reasonably to be aware); or

(c) if, or to the extent that, it concerns terms of his service contract that have been or are to be considered:

 (i) by a meeting of the directors; or

 (ii) by a committee of the directors appointed for the purpose under the company's constitution: CA 2006, s 182(6).

9.92 A director who fails to comply with the requirements of CA 2006, s 182 (declaration of interest in existing transaction or arrangement) commits an offence: CA 2006, s 183(1).

A person guilty of an offence under s 183 is liable on conviction on indictment, to a fine; and on summary conviction, to a fine not exceeding the statutory maximum: CA 2006, s 183(2).

Declaration made by notice in writing

9.93 Section 184 of CA 2006 applies to a declaration of interest made by notice in writing: CA 2006, s 184(1).

The director must send the notice to the other directors: CA 2006, s 184(2).

The notice may be sent in hard copy form or, if the recipient has agreed to receive it in electronic form, in an agreed electronic form: CA 2006, s 184(3).

The notice may be sent:

(a) by hand or by post; or

(b) if the recipient has agreed to receive it by electronic means, by agreed electronic means: CA 2006, s 184(4).

Where a director declares an interest by notice in writing in accordance with this section:

(a) the making of the declaration is deemed to form part of the proceedings at the next meeting of the directors after the notice is given; and

(b) the provisions of CA 2006, s 248 (minutes of meetings of directors) apply as if the declaration had been made at that meeting: CA 2006, s 184(5).

General notice treated as sufficient declaration

9.94 General notice in accordance with CA 2006, s 185, is a sufficient declaration of interest in relation to the matters to which it relates: CA 2006, s 185(1).

General notice is notice given to the directors of a company to the effect that the director:

(a) has an interest (as member, officer, employee or otherwise) in a specified body corporate or firm and is to be regarded as interested in any transaction or arrangement that may, after the date of the notice, be made with that body corporate or firm; or

(b) is connected with a specified person (other than a body corporate or firm) and is to be regarded as interested in any transaction or arrangement that may, after the date of the notice, be made with that person: CA 2006, s 185(2).

The notice must state the nature and extent of the director's interest in the body corporate or firm or, as the case may be, the nature of his connection with the person: CA 2006, s 185(3).

General notice is not effective unless it is given at a meeting of the directors; or the director takes reasonable steps to secure that it is brought up and read at the next meeting of the directors after it is given: CA 2006, s 185(4).

Declaration of interest in case of company with sole director

9.95 Where a declaration of interest under CA 2006, s 182 (duty to declare interest in existing transaction or arrangement) is required of a sole director of a company that is required to have more than one director:

(a) the declaration must be recorded in writing;

(b) the making of the declaration is deemed to form part of the proceedings at the next meeting of the directors after the notice is given; and

(c) the provisions of CA 2006, s 248 (minutes of meetings of directors) apply as if the declaration had been made at that meeting: CA 2006, s 186(1).

Section 186 does not affect the operation of s 231 (contract with sole member who is also a director: terms to be set out in writing or recorded in minutes): CA 2006, s 186(2).

Relief from liability

9.96 Where directors or other officers are found to be in breach of their duties, apart from seeking relief from liability from the shareholders, they may be able to apply to the court to seek relief from the impact of Pt 10 of CA 2006.

Section 1157 of CA 2006 is concerned with the power of the courts to grant relief in certain circumstances. It states that if in proceedings for negligence, default, breach of duty or breach of trust against:

(a) an officer of a company, or

(b) a person employed by a company as auditor (whether he is or is not an officer of the company), it appears to the court hearing the case, that the officer or person is or may be liable, but that he acted honestly and reasonably, and that having regard to all the circumstances of the case (including those connected with his appointment), he ought fairly to be excused, the court may relieve him, either wholly or in part, from his liability on such terms as it thinks fit: CA 2006, s 1157(1).

9.97 Further, If any such officer or person has reason to apprehend that a claim will or might be made against him in respect of negligence, default, breach of duty or breach of trust:

(a) he may apply to the court for relief, and

(b) the court has the same power to relieve him as it would have had if it had been a court before which proceedings against him for negligence, default, breach of duty or breach of trust had been brought: CA 2006, s 1157(2).

Where a case to which s 1157(1) applies is being tried by a judge with a jury, the judge, after hearing the evidence, may, if he is satisfied that the defendant ought in pursuance of s 1157(1) to be relieved either in whole or in part from the liability sought to be enforced against him, withdraw the case from the jury and forthwith direct judgment to be entered for the defendant on such terms as to costs or otherwise as the judge may think proper: CA 2006, s 1157(3).

9.98 The effect of s 1157 is to provide relief to a director or officer from past acts or future acts. It provides a wide discretion to the court to provide partial, full or such relief, as the court thinks fit. The starting point is that there has been negligence, default, breach of duty or breach of trust on the part of the director or officer in connection with the company's affairs. The director must show as an absolute precondition that he acted honestly and reasonably: *Bairstow v Queens Moat Houses plc* [2001] 2 BCLC 531, where on the facts the directors had acted dishonestly in falsifying the company's accounts, it was not open to the court to find aspects of honesty. Further, as Lord Nicholls stated in *Royal Brunei Airlines Sdn Bhd v Tan* [1995] 3 All ER 97 at 106:

> 'The standard of what constitutes honest conduct is not subjective. Honesty is not an optional scale, with higher or lower values according to the moral standards of each individual. If a person knowingly appropriates another's property, he will not escape a finding of dishonesty simply because he sees nothing wrong in such behaviour.'

Although the question as to whether a director has acted honestly is tested subjectively, the question whether he has acted reasonably is an objective one: *Coleman Taymar Ltd v Oakes* [2001] 2 BCLC 749; *Inland Revenue Commissioners v Richmond; Re Loquitur Ltd* [2003] 2 BCLC 442.

9.99 The court will have regard to all the circumstances of the case in assessing whether the director 'ought fairly to be excused' from liability. In *Ultraframe (UK) Ltd v Fielding* [2005] EWHC 1638 (Ch), Lewison J stated that 'the expression 'the case' does not mean 'the litigation'; but primarily means the circumstances in which the breach took place … [and] include a review of the director's stewardship of the company; but they do not involve a more wide-ranging inquiry into the director's character and behaviour'.

CA 2006, s 1157 applies to a breach of director's duty of skill and care: *Equitable Life Assurance Society v Bowley* [2004] 1 BCLC 180.

Section 1157 of CA 2006 will not be able to relieve a director who is involved in proceedings such as wrongful trading: *Re Produce Marketing Consortium Ltd* [1989] 1 WLR 745.

Section 1157 of CA 2006 will not be able to relieve a director from liability in respect of ss 216 and 217 of IA 1986 in using a phoenix name: *First Independent Factors & Finance Ltd v Mountford* [2008] 2 BCLC 297. The relief is also not available in respect of disqualification proceedings under s 15 of IA 1986 (liability of disqualified person for debts incurred while disqualified): *IRC v McEntaggart* [2006] 1 BCLC 476.

The court may be unwilling to relieve a director from liability under s 1157 where he has obtained a personal gain or benefit from his actions: *a Flap Envelope Co Ltd* [2004] 1 BCLC 64. See too *Re Marini Ltd* [2004] BCC 172.

The court also may not provide relief to a director under s 1157 at the expense of the company's creditors. In *Inn Spirit Ltd v Burns* [2002] 2 BCLC 780, where Rimer J stated that the court should not excuse directors from liability at the creditors' expense. Similarly, in *First Global Media Group Ltd v Larkin* [2003] EWCA Civ 1765, the Court of Appeal stated it was out of the question to fairly excuse the director from repaying a loan to a creditor. Further, in *Queensway Systems Ltd v Walker* [2007] 2 BCLC 577, Paul Girolami J stated that the defendants who had misapplied company funds were not entitled to be relieved of liability under CA 2006, s 1157 because although they had not acted dishonestly, they had not acted reasonably and the circumstances were not such that they ought fairly to be excused liability. In particular, ignorance of a person's duties as a director and/or that the payments could involve a contravention of CA 2006, or a misapplication of company funds was not a reason for excusing a person from liability, and to do so would prejudice the company's creditors.

Certain factors may apply in considering relief from liability under s 1157

The Northampton Regional Livestock Centre Co Ltd v Cowling [2014] EWHC 30 (QB), involved a director of the company who had placed himself in a position of conflict by acting for both the vendor and purchaser in a commercial property transaction.

Green J considered the application of CA 2006, s 1157 to grant a director relief from liability in respect of negligence, default, breach of duty or breach of trust. He considered the following factors to be appropriate in granting relief:

- good faith and honesty;
- claimant's allegations against the director;
- whether the director sought board approval;
- the severity of the breach involved;
- economic reality of the transaction concerned; and
- the probability of material loss being caused to the company.

Complete inactivity by a director will be a bar to relief under CA 2006, s 1157: *Finch v Finch* [2015] (13 August 2015); *Lexi Holdings Plc v Luqman* [2007] EWHC 2652 (Ch).

Dishonesty will be a bar to any relief under CA 2006, s 1157: *McGivney Construction Ltd v Kaminski* [2015] CSOH 107. The test of honesty is to be judged objectively: *Royal Brunei Airlines* v *Tan Sdn. Bhd* [1995] 2 AC 378. Further, there must be a strong case to allow relief if the director has obtained personal benefit, even if it is relatively trivial: *Towers* v *Premier Waste Management Ltd* CA [2012] BCC 72. See too *Pantiles Investments Ltd v Winckler* [2019] EWHC 1298 (Ch); *Davies v Ford* [2020] EWHC 686 (Ch).

Checklist: directors' general duties

9.100 *The checklist considers the general duties of directors under Pt 10 of CA 2006 based on some of the fiduciary and common law duties of directors which have been codified. Those duties which have not been codified remain to be assessed through developments in common law and equity.*

No	Issue	Reference
1	Directors have sometimes been likened to trustees fulfilling trusteeship and fiduciary duties in the performance of their duties	*Re Forest of Dean Coal Mining Co* (1787) 10 Ch D 450
2	Directors' primary duty is to the company and not to individual shareholders generally	CA 2006, s 170(1); *Peskin v Anderson* [2001] 1 BCLC 372
3	In some situations directors may owe duties towards individual shareholders, particularly where 'special circumstances' may exist to demonstrate such relationship	*Allen v Hyatt* (1914) 30 TLR 444
4	Some of the general duties of directors apply to former directors particularly the duty to avoid conflicts of interest; and the duty not to accept benefits from third parties	CA 2006, s 170(2)
5	The general duties are based on certain common law rules and equitable principles as they apply in relation to directors	CA 2006, s 170(3); *Eclairs Group Ltd v JKX Oil & Gas plc; Glengary Overseas Ltd v JKX Oil & Gas plc* [2015] UKSC 71
6	Directors must act within their powers by: (a) Acting in accordance with the company's constitution; and (b) Exercising powers for the purposes conferred	CA 2006, s 171
7	Directors have a duty to promote the company's success – to act in good faith in considering in good faith what would most likely promote the long term success of the company for the members having regard to the six factors	CA 2006, s 172
8	Directors must exercise independent judgment in the performance of their functions Directors must exercise reasonable care, skill and diligence – the test is both subjective and objective (based on IA 1986, s 214)	CA 2006, s 173 CA 2006, s 174
9	A director must avoid conflicts of interest situation	CA 2006, s 175
10	A director must not accept benefits from third parties	CA 2006, s 176
11	A director must declare interest in a proposed transaction or arrangement	CA 2006, s 177
12	Certain civil consequences flow from breach of the general duties with the application of the common law and equitable principles	CA 2006, s 178

No	Issue	Reference
13	Where an agent acquires a benefit which came to his notice as a result of his fiduciary position, or pursuant to an opportunity which results from his fiduciary position, the general equitable rule ('the Rule') is that he is to be treated as having acquired the benefit on behalf of his principal, so it is beneficially owned by the principal. The Rule applies to both bribes or secret commissions received by the agent	*FHR European Ventures LLP v Cedar Capital Partners LLC [2014] UKSC 45*
14	A director has a duty to declare his interest in an existing transaction or arrangement	CA 2006, s 182
15	In some situations, it may be possible to ratify act of directors amounting to negligence, default, breach of duty or breach of trust in relation to the company	CA 2006, s 239
16	Where directors or other officers are found to be in breach of their duties, apart from seeking relief from liability from the shareholders, they may be able to apply to the court to seek relief from the impact of CA 2006, Pt 10 in respect of negligence, default, breach of duty or breach of trust provided they acted honestly and reasonably	CA 2006, s 1157

10 Directors: specific duties

Introduction

10.1 This chapter addresses the following issues:

- Directors' long-term service contracts;
- Substantial property transactions;
- Loans to directors; and
- Payment for loss of office.

Transactions with directors requiring approval of members

10.2 The CA 2006 contains several provisions designed to deal with particular situations in which a director has or may have a conflict of interest. There is a requirement for shareholders' approval in relation to four different types of transaction by a company with its director, subject to any declaration of interest that may be required by the director involved in the transaction (see CA 2006, ss 177 and 182):

- long-term service contracts;
- substantial property transactions;
- loans, quasi-loans;
- payments for loss of office.

The rules relating to each type of transaction tend to adopt a common structure: they begin with the rule requiring approval from the shareholders; followed by the exceptions to that rule; and then the consequences of breaching that rule.

Service contracts

Directors' long-term service contracts: requirement of members' approval

10.3 Section 188 deals with directors' long-term service contracts requiring members' approval. It applies to a provision under which the 'guaranteed term' of a director's employment (a) with the company of which he is a director; or (b) where he is a director of a holding company, within the group consisting of that company and its subsidiaries, is or may be longer than two years: CA 2006, s 188(1).

10.4 A company may not agree to such provision under CA 2006,s 188(1), unless it has been approved by a shareholders' resolution: CA 2006, s 188(2).

The 'guaranteed term' of a director's employment is:

(a) the period (if any) during which the director's employment:

(i) is to continue, or may be continued otherwise than at the instance of the company (whether under the original agreement or under a new agreement entered into in pursuance of it); and

(ii) it cannot be terminated by the company by notice, or can be so terminated only in specified circumstances; or

(b) in the case of employment terminable by the company by notice, the period of notice required to be given;

or in the case of employment having a period within paragraph (a) and a period within paragraph (b), the aggregate of those periods: CA 2006, s 188(3).

If a company agrees to a provision in contravention of s 188 (directors' long-term service contracts: requirement of members' approval), the provision will be void, to the extent of the contravention. Further, the contract is deemed to contain a term entitling the company to terminate at any time by giving reasonable notice: CA 2006, s 189.

10.5 If more than six months before the end of the guaranteed term of a director's employment, the company enters into a further service contract, s 188 applies if there were added to the guaranteed term of the new contract, the unexpired period of the guaranteed term of the original contract: CA 2006, s 188(4).

A members' resolution must not be passed, unless a memorandum setting out the proposed contract incorporating the provision, is made available to the members in the following circumstances:

(a) in the case of a written resolution, by being sent or submitted to every eligible member at or before the time at which the proposed resolution is sent or submitted to him;

(b) in the case of a resolution at a meeting, by being made available for inspection by members of the company both at the company's registered office, for not less than 15 days ending with the date of the meeting; and at the meeting itself: CA 2006, s 188(5).

10.6 A company must keep available for inspection, a copy of every director's service contract with the company or with a subsidiary of the company. If the contract is not in writing, a written memorandum setting out the terms of the contract: CA 2006, s 228(1).

All the copies and memoranda must be kept available for inspection usually at the company's registered office: CA 2006, s 228(2). The copies and memoranda must be retained by the company for at least one year from the date of termination or expiry of the contract, and must be kept available for inspection during that time: CA 2006, s 228(3).

10.7

- The company must give notice to the registrar of the place at which the copies and memoranda are kept available for inspection; and of any change in that place, unless they have at all times been kept at the company's registered office: CA 2006, s 228(4). The provisions of s 228 apply to a variation of a director's service contract, in the same manner as to the original contract: CA 2006, s 228(7).

Criminal penalties apply for failure to comply with s 288 CA 2006: CA 2006, s 228(6).

10.8 Every copy or memorandum required to be kept under s 228, must be open to inspection by any member of the company without charge: CA 2006, s 229(1).

Any member of the company is entitled, on request and on payment of such fee as may be prescribed, to be provided with a copy of any such copy or memorandum. The copy must be provided within seven days after the request is received by the company: CA 2006, s 229(2).

If an inspection required under s 229(1) is refused, or there is failure to comply with that provision, an offence will be committed by every officer of the company who is in default: CA 2006, s 229(3).

Substantial property transactions

Requirement of members' approval

10.9 Sections 190–196 of CA 2006 deal with substantial property transactions. A company may not enter into an arrangement under which:

(a) a director of the company or of its holding company, or a person connected with such a director, acquires or is to acquire from the company (directly or indirectly) a substantial non-cash asset;

(b) or where the company acquires or is to acquire a substantial non-cash asset (directly or indirectly) from a director or a person so connected): CA 2006, s 190.

The non-cash asset may only be acquired, if the arrangement has been approved by a shareholders' resolution, or is conditional on such approval being obtained: CA 2006, s 190(1).

The main objective of CA 2006, s 190 is to give shareholders specific protection against transactions that may be beneficial to the directors: *Re Duckwari (No 2)* [1998] 2 BCLC 315; and *Re Duckwari (No 3)* [1999] 1 BCLC 168.

10.10 The term 'substantial non-cash asset' means 'any property or interest in property other than cash': CA 2006, ss 191, 1163. The meaning is wide-ranging and may include intellectual property, lease, stock, license or assets: *Ultraframe (UK) Ltd v Fielding* [2005] UKHC 1638 (Ch); and *Re Duckwari plc (No 1)* [1997] 2 BCLC 713. The asset may be described as the benefit of the purchase contract or the beneficial interest in the asset itself. See too *Granada Group Limited v The Law Debenture Pension Trust Corporation plc* [2016] EWCA Civ 1289.

The objective of s 190 of CA 2006 is to safeguard a company from any losses resulting from transactions between a company and a director: *British Racing Drivers' Club Ltd v Hextall Erskine & Co* [1997] 1 BCLC 182.

The *Duomatic* principle of informal unanimous shareholders' assent may be used for the purposes of s 190: *NBH Ltd v Hoare* [2006] 2 BCLC 649.

A company will not be subject to any liability by reason of a failure to obtain the approval required: CA 2006, s 190(3).

Shareholder approval under CA 2006, s 190 was not required where there was only a possibility of acquiring a non-cash asset: *Smithton Ltd v Naggar* [2015] 2 BCLC 22. The Court of Appeal held that shareholder approval under s 190 was only required for arrangements under which a director or a person connected to him, definitely acquired 'or is to acquire' an interest in shares. It was not required for arrangements under which his or their acquisition of an interest in shares was only a possibility.

Meaning of 'substantial'

10.11 An asset is a 'substantial' asset in relation to the company if its value exceeds 10% of the company's assets value, and is more than £5,000; or exceeds £100,000: CA 2006, s 191(2). The 'value' represents the capital value of the asset: *Ultraframe (UK) Limited v Fielding* [2005] EWHC 1638 (Ch). The onus is on the applicant to show that the transaction in question exceeded the financial limits of s 191: *Joint Receivers and Managers of Niltan Carson Ltd v Hawthorne* [1988] BCLC 298 at 321.

Under CA 2006, s 190, the relevant value of the asset is the value to the director, or person connected with him, who acquired the asset, and not the objective market value of the asset: *Micro Leisure Ltd v County Properties and Developments Limited* [2000] BCC 872.

10.12 A company's 'asset value' at any time is the value of the company's net assets determined by reference to its most recent statutory accounts; or if no statutory accounts have been prepared, the amount of the company's called-up share capital: CA 2006, s 191(3).

A company's 'statutory accounts' means its annual accounts prepared in accordance with CA 2006, Pt 15 and its 'most recent' statutory accounts means those in relation to which the time for sending them out to members (see CA 2006, s 424) is most recent: CA 2006, s 191(4).

Whether an asset is a substantial asset must be determined as at the time the arrangement is entered into: CA 2006, s 191(5).

A lease may be a non-cash asset if at a premium: *Ultraframe (UK) Limited v Fielding* [2005] EWHC 1638 (Ch).

A bilateral agreement between the director and the company, can give rise to seeking shareholders' approval under s 190 CA 2006: *Re Duckwari plc (No 1)* [1997] 2 BCLC 713.

Property transactions: civil consequences of transaction

10.13 There are a number of civil remedies available for breach of s 190.

Section 195 of CA 2006 applies where a company enters into an arrangement in contravention of s 190: CA 2006, s 195(1). The arrangement and any transaction entered into in pursuance of the arrangement, (whether by the company or any other person), is voidable at the instance of the company, unless:

(a) restitution of any money or other asset that was the subject matter of the arrangement or transaction is no longer possible;

(b) the company has been indemnified by any other persons for the loss or damage suffered by it;

(c) rights acquired in good faith, for value and without actual notice of the contravention by a person who is not a party to the arrangement or transaction, would be affected by the avoidance: CA 2006, s 195(2).

10.14 Whether or not the arrangement or any such transaction has been avoided, each of the persons specified in s 195(4) is liable:

(a) to account to the company for any gain that has been made directly or indirectly by the arrangement or transaction; and

(b) (jointly and severally with any other person so liable under s 195) to indemnify the company for any loss or damage resulting from the arrangement or transaction: CA 2006, s 195(3).

10.15 The persons who will be liable are:

(a) any director of the company or of its holding company with whom the company entered into the arrangement in contravention of CA 2006, s 190;

(b) any person with whom the company entered into the arrangement in contravention of that section who is connected with a director of the company or of its holding company;

(c) the director of the company or of its holding company with whom any such person is connected; and

(d) any other director of the company who authorised the arrangement or any transaction entered into in pursuance of such an arrangement: CA 2006, s 195(4).

However, sub-ss 195(3) and (4) are subject to sub-ss 195(6), (7): CA 2006, s 195(5).

Loans and quasi-loans

Loans to directors: requirement of members' approval

10.16

- A company may not make a loan to a director of the company or its holding company; or give a guarantee or provide security in connection with a loan or quasi-loan made by any person to such a director, unless the transaction has been approved by a shareholders' resolution: CA 2006, s 197(1).
- A resolution approving a transaction under s 197 must not be passed unless a memorandum setting out the matters in s 197(4) is made available to the shareholders, in the following two circumstances: (a) in the case of a written resolution, by being sent or submitted to every eligible member at or before the time at which the proposed resolution is sent or submitted to him; and (b) in the case of a resolution at a meeting, by being made available for inspection by members of the company both at the company's registered office for not less than 15 days
- Similar provisions apply in respect of a quasi-loan to directors: CA 2006, s 198.

10.17 The matters that must be disclosed in respect of loans and quasi-loans are:

(a) the nature of the transaction;

(b) the amount of the loan and the purpose for which it is required; and

(c) the extent of the company's liability under any transaction connected with the loan: CA 2006, s 197(4).

There is no definition of a 'loan' under this part of the CA 2006. In *Champagne Perrier-Jouet SA v HH Finch Limited* [1982] 3 All ER 713, Walton J was content to use the Oxford Dictionary meaning as 'A sum of money lent for a time to be returned in money or money's worth': see too *Potts's Exors v IRC* [1951] 1 All ER 76. In *First Global Media Group Ltd v Larkin* [2003] EVCA Civ 1765, the Court of Appeal stated: 'A loan ordinarily involves an advance of money pursuant to an agreement providing for its repayment.' In *Currencies Direct Ltd v Ellis* [2002] 2 BCLC 482, the Court of Appeal was required to consider whether a sum of money payable to a director constituted a loan or remuneration for services performed. It held that on the facts, the services performed by the director and payment made, was remuneration and not advances made to a director that were payable.

The consequences of a contravention of CA 2006, s 197 are that it is a breach of the CA 2006, and might constitute a misapplication of the company's funds, including a breach of a director's duty: *Queensway Systems Ltd v Walker* [2007] 2 BCLC 577.

Payments for loss of office

The nature of payments

10.18 The term 'payment for loss of office' refers to a payment made to a director or past director of a company:

(a) by way of compensation for loss of office as the company's director;

(b) by way of compensation for loss, while director of the company or in connection with his ceasing to be a director of it, of:

  (i) any other office or employment in connection with the management of the affairs of the company; or

  (ii) any office (as director or otherwise) or employment in connection with the management of the affairs of any subsidiary undertaking of the company;

(c) as consideration for or in connection with his retirement from his office as director of the company; or

(d) as consideration for or in connection with his retirement, while director of the company or in connection with his ceasing to be a director of it, from:

  (i) any other office or employment in connection with the management of the affairs of the company; or

  (ii) any office (as director or otherwise) or employment in connection with the management of the affairs of any subsidiary undertaking of the company: CA 2006, s 215(1). See *Taupo Totara Timber Co Ltd v Rowe* [1978] AC 537.

The references to 'compensation' and 'consideration' include benefits otherwise than in cash: s 215(2).

Payment by company: requirement of members' approval

10.19 A company may not make a payment for loss of office to a director of the company, unless the payment has been approved by a members' resolution: CA 2006, s 217(1).

10.20 A resolution approving a payment for loss of office, must not be passed, unless a memorandum setting out particulars of the proposed payment (including its amount) is made available to the members of the company, whose approval is sought:

(a) in the case of a written resolution, by being sent or submitted to every eligible member at or before the time at which the proposed resolution is sent or submitted to him;

(b) in the case of a resolution at a meeting, by being made available for inspection by the members both:

  (i) at the company's registered office for not less than 15 days ending with the date of the meeting, and

  (ii) at the meeting itself: CA 2006, s 217(3).

The applicability of CA 2006, s 217 with respect to members of charities, was considered by the Supreme Court in *Lehtimaki v Cooper* [2020] UKSC 33. Lady Arden stated that charities operated within a public law framework, where the court did not in general substitute its own judgment for that of the decision-maker. However, the purpose of s 217 was to ensure adequate disclosure to, and approval by, the company's members, and the right to vote could be restricted by the company's constitution, or by orders made under the CA 2006. In these circumstances, where the matter was internal to the charitable company, the court could, in an appropriate case, direct one of its members how to vote in a particular matter or resolution.

Contracts with sole members who are directors

Contract with sole member who is also a director

10.21 Section 231 of CA 2006 applies where:

(a) a limited company having only one member enters into a contract with the sole member;

(b) the sole member is also a director of the company; and

(c) the contract is not entered into in the ordinary course of the company's business: CA 2006, s 231(1).

The company must, unless the contract is in writing, ensure that the terms of the contract are either set out in a written memorandum; or recorded in the minutes of the first meeting of the directors of the company, following the making of the contract: CA 2006, s 231(2).

10.22 If a company fails to comply with s 231, an offence will be committed by every officer of the company who is in default: CA 2006, s 231(3) with criminal fines being imposed: CA 2006, s 231(4). For the purposes of CA 2006, s 231 a shadow director is also treated as a director: CA 2006, s 231(5).

Failure to comply with s 231 in relation to a contract, does not affect the validity of the contract: CA 2006, s 231(6). Section 231 CA 2006 does not exclude the operation of any other enactment, or rule of law applying to contracts between a company and a director of the company: CA 2006, s 231(7).

Checklist: Approving directors' long-term service contracts

10. 23 *This checklist sets out the steps and procedures involved in approving directors' long-term service contracts under CA 2006, s 188. The practice and procedure will depend upon the Articles of Association adopted by the company, and appropriate adaptations should be made depending upon the circumstances.*

No	Issue	Reference
1	Consider whether the service contract is short term or long term?	CA 2006, ss 188–189 and 227
2	Approval of shareholders is required where the service contract has a 'guaranteed term' and that the period of employment is or may be longer than two years.	CA 2006, s 188(3)
3	The long term service contract may be with the company itself or where he is a director of the holding company, within the group consisting of that holding company and its subsidiaries	CA 2006, s 188(1)
4	Prepare a draft of the service contract or memoranda and ensure all appropriate terms are included (including duties, rights, obligations, restrictions during employment, post-termination covenants, confidentiality, protection of intellectual property, remuneration, pension, expenses, holidays, illness, disciplinary aspects, termination)	
5	Call a Board meeting upon reasonable notice: either a director or secretary (if there is one) may call a board meeting. Set out: • Date • Time • Place • Attach a memorandum of key terms of the service contract	Notice
6	Prepare Agenda for the Board meeting	Agenda
7	At the Board meeting: • Ensure quorum present • Any director to declare interest in the contract • Chairman presides at the Board meeting. Whether Chairman has a casting vote? • Voting on a show of hands to convene an EGM for shareholders' approval to the service contract • Alternatively consider dispensing with a Board meeting and use the written resolution procedure attaching the memorandum to the resolution	CA 2006, ss 177, 182
8	Prepare minutes of the Board meeting	Minutes

9	Call an EGM for every eligible member and set out: • Date • Time • Place • Ordinary resolution • Note on proxy • Attach memorandum of key provisions of the service contract • Ensure memorandum available for inspection by members at least 15 days before the EGM unless consent to short notice applies	Notice
10	At the EGM: • Ensure quorum present • Chairman presides at the EGM. Whether Chairman has a casting vote? • Voting on a show of hands unless a poll is demanded • Shareholders' approval to the service contract • Alternatively consider dispensing with the EGM and use the written resolution procedure attaching the memorandum to the resolution	Articles
	• Where a company agrees to a provision in contravention of CA 2006, s 188, the provision is void to the extent of the contravention. The service contract is deemed to contain a term entitling the company to terminate at any time by giving reasonable notice	CA 2006, s 189
11	After the EGM: • Prepare minutes of the EGM	Minutes
	• Ensure a copy of the director's service contract is kept available for inspection by the company or subsidiary of the company, or a written memorandum setting out terms of the contract	CA 2006, s 228(1)
	• Ensure the copy or memorandum of the service contract is kept available for inspection at the company's registered office or a place specified in the regulations	CA 2006, s 228(2)
	• The copy of the service contract or memoranda must be retained by the company for at least one year from the date of termination or expiry and available for inspection during that time	CA 2006, s 228(3)
	• Company must give notice to the registrar of the place at which copies and memoranda are kept available for inspection; and a change in that place unless at all times kept at the company's registered office	CA 2006, s 228(4)
	• The above aspects apply also to any variation in the director's service contract or memoranda	CA 2006, s 228(7)
	• Ensure that a copy of the service contract or memoranda is available for inspection by a member of the company without charge. If inspection is refused or default is made, the court may compel an immediate inspection or direct that the copy required be sent to the person requiring it.	CA 2006, s 229(1)
	• If a member of the company requests a copy of the service contract or memoranda, the company must send such copy upon payment of such fee as may be prescribed. Ensure a copy is provided within 7 days of request	CA 2006, s 229(2)
	Criminal penalties apply where inspection of the service contract or memoranda is refused.	CA 2006, s 228(6)

11 Directors' disqualification

Introduction

11.1 This chapter addresses the following issues:

- the circumstances when disqualification orders may be applied;
- the use of disqualification undertakings;
- grounds on which the directors' disqualification operates;
- the period of disqualification; and
- foreign directors' disqualification.

Objectives of the Company Directors Disqualification Act 1986

11.2 In the Preamble to the Company Directors Disqualification Act 1986 (CDDA 1986), the objective of the Act is to consolidate certain enactments relating to the disqualification of persons from being directors of companies, and from being otherwise concerned with a company's affairs.

CDDA 1986 applies not only to directors but is wider in scope, and certain provisions apply to a wide range of potential defendants, including company secretaries, liquidators, and other officers within the company.

11.3 The objective of the CDDA was further amplified in *Re Blackspur Group plc, Secretary of State for Trade and Industry v Davies* [1998] 1 BCLC 676, where Lord Woolf MR stated:

> 'The purpose of the 1986 Act is the protection of the public, by means of prohibitory remedial action, by anticipated deterrent effect on further misconduct and by encouragement of higher standards of honesty and diligence in corporate management, from those who are unfit to be concerned in the management of a company.
>
> Parliament has designated the Secretary of State as the proper public officer to discharge the function of making applications to the court for disqualification orders. There is a wide discretion to do so in cases where it appears, in the prescribed circumstances, that "it is expedient in the public interest that a disqualification order should be made". In any particular case it may be decided that the public interest is best served by making and continuing an application to trial; or by not making an application at all; or by not continuing a pending application to trial; or by not contesting at trial points raised by way of defence or mitigation. All these litigation decisions are made by the Secretary of State according to what is considered by her to be "expedient in the public interest". They are not made by the court or by other parties to the proceedings'.

The principal objective is to ensure public protection as well as protection of the creditors. The effect of CDDA 1986 is that directors who are disqualified for a certain period of time, lose the privilege of the limited liability company, owing to their wrongful action or misconduct in acting as a director of the company. In effect, directors who subsequent upon disqualification, conduct business activities on their own account, become personally liable with the threat of bankruptcy if they cannot pay their debts: this is the consequence of abuse of the privilege of incorporation.

11.4 In *Re Tech Textiles Ltd, Secretary of State for Trade and Industry v Vane* [1998] 1 BCLC 259, Arden J stated that protection of 'the public' for this purpose, includes all relevant interest groups, such as shareholders, employees, lenders, customers and other creditors – the stakeholders of the company. Further, in *Hill v Secretary of State for the Environment, Food and Rural Affairs* [2006] 1 BCLC 601, Hart J was of the view that the public policy underlying CDDA 1986, was the protection of the public from those individuals who are not regarded as trustworthy persons to be involved in the management of a limited liability company. The relevant section of the public also consisted of, as a primary class, those who might extend credit to a company.

CDDA 1986 concerns civil proceedings against directors and the sanction is not penal, though the effect is to restrict individual freedom. Judicial attitudes have varied as to the nature of the conduct required to disqualify a director. It may include unethical behaviour towards third parties – a disregard to the interests of creditors or suppliers demonstrates values and conduct unbefitting a director. It may also include recklessness, incompetence, or breach of commercial morality towards wider stakeholders on the company.

11.5 According to Browne-Wilkinson VC in *Re Lo-Line Electric Motors Limited* [1988] 2 All ER 692:

> 'The primary purpose of the section is not to punish the individual but to protect the public against the future conduct of companies by persons whose past records as directors of insolvent companies have shown them to be a danger to creditors and others. Therefore, the power is not fundamentally penal. But, if the power to disqualify is exercised, disqualification does involve a substantial interference with the freedom of the individual. It follows that the rights of the individual must be fully protected. Ordinary commercial misjudgment is in itself not sufficient to justify disqualification. In the normal case, the conduct complained of must display a lack of commercial probity, although I have no doubt that in an extreme case of gross negligence or total incompetence disqualification could be appropriate'.

Under CDDA 1986, depending upon the grounds for disqualification, the court will either make a disqualification order or a disqualification undertaking.

Disqualification orders

11.6 A disqualification order is made by the court. In the circumstances specified below, a court may, and under CDDA 1986, ss 6 and 9A, must make against a person a disqualification order, that is to say an order that for a period specified in the order:

(a) he shall not be a director of a company, act as receiver of a company's property or in any way, whether directly or indirectly, be concerned or take part in the promotion, formation or management of a company unless (in each case) he has the leave of the court, and

(b) he shall not act as an insolvency practitioner: CDDA 1986, s 1(1).

The scope of the order is, therefore, broad and wide-ranging, and not just limited to a person being simply disqualified as a director. In *Re Gower Enterprises (No 2)* [1995] 2 BCLC 201, Robert Reid J was of the view that the word 'or' under CDDA 1986, s 1(1)(a) was intended to be conjunctive, and that the meaning of s 1(1) of the Act was that a disqualification order was an order that a person without the leave of the court, shall not be a director of a company, and shall not be a liquidator or an administrator of a company, and shall not be a receiver or manager of a company's property, and shall not be in any way, whether directly or indirectly be concerned and shall not take part in the promotion, formation or management of a company. Further, an order which did not prevent a person from doing all of those things, was not a disqualification order within the terms of s 1(1) of the Act. See too: *Re Seagull Manufacturing Co Ltd* [1996] 1 BCLC 51; and *Re Polly Peck International plc* [1994] 1 BCLC 574.

11.7 In each section of CDDA 1986 which gives a court power to or, as the case may be, imposes on it the duty to make a disqualification order, the Act specifies the maximum (and, in CDDA 1986, ss 6 and 8ZA, the minimum) period of disqualification, which may or (as the case may be) must be imposed by means of the order. Unless the court otherwise orders, the period of disqualification imposed, must begin at the end of the period of 21 days beginning with the date of the order: CDDA 1986, s 1(2) (as inserted by SBEEA 2015, Sch 7 Part 1).

Where a disqualification order is made against a person who is already subject to such an order or to a disqualification undertaking, the periods specified in those orders or, as the case may be, in the order and the undertaking will run concurrently: CDDA 1986, s 1(3).

11.8 A disqualification order may be made on grounds which are or include matters other than criminal convictions, notwithstanding that the person in respect of whom it is to be made, may be criminally liable in respect of those matters: CDDA 1986, s 1(4).

In making the disqualification order, the objective is to ensure that the director is prevented for a specified period of time, from engaging in management decisions or in any way connected with management matters within a company.

The term 'management' is broadly interpreted: it includes not just taking part in the company's affairs, but also holding a managerial post: *R v Campbell* [1984] 7 WLUK 16. See too: *Re Market Wizard Systems (UK) Ltd* [1998] 2 BCLC 282; *Drew v HM Advocate* 1996 SLT 1062.

Entering into contracts on the company's behalf is considered as taking part in the company's management: *Hill v Secretary of State for the Environment, Food and Rural Affairs* [2006] 1 BCLC 601.

11.9 Where an order is made under CDDA 1986, s 1, the courts are not required to select which aspect of the order to make: the order is made as a whole for all aspects of CDDA 1986, s 1(1)(a). In *R v Cole* [1998] 2 BCLC 234, the Court of Appeal stated that CDDA 1986, s 1(1) envisaged only one disqualification, with a number of different consequences, and not five different categories of disqualification. A pick and choose approach could not be adopted by the courts.

Disqualification undertakings

11.10 Whereas the disqualification order is made by the court, a disqualification undertaking may be agreed between the director and the Disqualification Unit of the Insolvency Service. There is no requirement for judicial proceedings. The disqualification undertaking has a similar effect to a disqualification order.

In the circumstances specified in CDDA 1986, ss 5A, 7, 8, 8ZC and 8ZE, the Secretary of State may accept a disqualification undertaking, that is to say an undertaking by any person that, for a period specified in the undertaking, the person:

(a) will not be a director of a company, act as receiver of a company's property or in any way, whether directly or indirectly, be concerned or take part in the promotion, formation or management of a company unless (in each case) he has the leave of a court, and

(b) will not act as an insolvency practitioner: CDDA 1986, s 1A(1) (as inserted by SBEEA 2015, Sch 7, Pt 1).

The maximum period which may be specified in a disqualification undertaking is 15 years; and the minimum period which may be specified in a disqualification undertaking under s 7 or 8ZC is two years: CDDA 1986, s 1A(2) (as inserted by SBEEA 2015, Sch 7, Pt 1).

11.11 Where a disqualification undertaking by a person who is already subject to such an undertaking or to a disqualification order is accepted, the periods specified in those undertakings or (as the case may be) the undertaking and the order will run concurrently: CDDA 1986, s 1A(3).

In determining whether to accept a disqualification undertaking by any person, the Secretary of State may take account of matters other than criminal convictions, notwithstanding that the person may be criminally liable in respect of those matters: CDDA 1986, s 1A(4).

The Secretary of State has discretion to decide whether or not to accept a disqualification undertaking: *Re Blackspur Group plc (No 3), Secretary of State for Trade and Industry v Davies (No 2)* [2002] 2 BCLC 263.

The court may on occasions decide to order a stay of a disqualification order, pending an appeal against the disqualification order: *Cathie v Secretary of State for Business, Innovation & Skills* [2011] EWHC 2234 (Ch).

11.12 In some situations, the court may make a disqualification order against a company director and then subsequently, the court grants permission for a disqualified director to act as a company director, on terms set out in the court order. The director may have contributed to the drafting of the court order. The issue arises as to whether the court is entitled to have regard to the intentions of the person drafting the order, for the purposes of its construction?

In *Feld v Secretary of State for Business, Innovation & Skills* [2014] EWHC 1383, the court stated that the principles of contractual interpretation were appropriate to be considered in the interpretation of a court order. It would give the court insight into the person's intention in drafting the order. See too: *R* v *Evans* [2004] EWCA Crim 3102.

In some circumstances, it may be possible for directors to have the length of their disqualification period reduced. In *R v Randhawa* [2008] EWCA Crim 2599, two directors were successful in having the length of their disqualification periods reduced. The directors gave undertakings under CDDA 1986, s 1A that that for a period of ten years from 2003, they would not take part in any company's management. Subsequently, they were disqualified for 12 years from 2007. Taking together the undertakings and disqualification orders, this meant that they would be disqualified from acting as directors for 16 years. They contended that 12 years was too long a period of disqualification. The Court of Appeal accordingly reduced the period of disqualification, taking account of the directors' undertakings and their acceptance of the gravity of the criminal offences they had committed.

Grounds for disqualification – disqualification for general misconduct in connection with companies

11.13 CDDA 1986 sets out various grounds for disqualification in connection with companies.

Disqualification on conviction of indictable offence

11.14 The court may make a disqualification order against a person where he is convicted of an indictable offence (whether on indictment or summarily) in connection with the promotion, formation, management, liquidation or striking off of a company with the receivership of a company's property or with his being an administrative receiver of a company: CDDA 1986, s 2(1).

In subsection (1), 'company' includes overseas company: CDDA 1986, s.2(1A) (as inserted by SBEEA 2015, Sch 7, Part 1).

11.15 The maximum period of disqualification under CDDA 1986, s 2 is:

(a) where the disqualification order is made by a court of summary jurisdiction, five years, and

(b) in any other case, 15 years: CDDA 1986, s 2(3).

Disqualification for persistent breaches of companies legislation

11.16 The court may make a disqualification order against a person, where it appears that he has been persistently in default in relation to provisions of the companies legislation, requiring any return, account or other document to be filed with, delivered to or sent to, or notice of any matter to be given to, the registrar of companies: CDDA 1986, s 3(1).

On an application to the court for an order to be made under CDDA 1986, s 3, the fact that a person has been persistently in default in relation to such provisions as are mentioned above, may (without prejudice to its proof in any other manner) be conclusively proved by showing that in the five years ending with the date of the application, he has been adjudged guilty (whether or not on the same occasion) of three or more defaults in relation to those provisions: CDDA 1986, s 3(2).

11.17 A person is to be treated under s 3(2) as being adjudged guilty of a default in relation to any provision of that legislation if:

(a) he is convicted (whether on indictment or summarily) of an offence consisting in a contravention of or failure to comply with that provision (whether on his own part or on the part of any company), or

(b) a default order is made against him, that is to say, an order under any of the following provisions:

   (i) CA 2006, s 452 (order requiring delivery of company accounts),

   (ia) CA 2006, s 456 (order requiring preparation of revised accounts),

   (ii) CA 2006, s 1113 (enforcement of company's filing obligations),

   (iii) the Insolvency Act 1986, s 41 (enforcement of receiver's or manager's duty to make returns), or

   (iv) the Insolvency Act 1986, s 170 (corresponding provision for liquidator in winding up),

   in respect of any such contravention of or failure to comply with that provision (whether on his own part or on the part of any company): CDDA 1986, s 3(3).

In this section, 'company' includes overseas company: CDDA 1986, s 3A (as inserted by SBEEA 2015, Sch 7, Pt 1).

The maximum period of disqualification under this section is five years: CDDA 1986, s 3(5).

Disqualification for fraud, etc, in winding up

11.18 The court may make a disqualification order against a person if, in the course of the company's winding up, it appears that he:

(a) has been guilty of an offence for which he is liable (whether he has been convicted or not) under CA 2006, s 993 (fraudulent trading), or

(b) has otherwise been guilty, while an officer or liquidator of the company, receiver of the company's property, or administrative receiver of the company, of any fraud in relation to the company, or of any breach of his duty as such officer, liquidator, receiver or administrative receiver: CDDA 1986, s 4(1).

The maximum period of disqualification under CDDA 1986, s 4 is 15 years: CDDA 1986, s 4(3).

A liquidator had standing to bring disqualification proceedings against a former liquidator of a company: *Wood v Mistry* [2012] EWHC 1899 (Ch). Newey J disqualified the liquidator for 12 years. The period of disqualification reflected the serious breaches of the liquidator's misconduct.

Disqualification on summary conviction

11.19 An offence counting for the purposes of CDDA 1986, s 5 is one of which a person is convicted (either on indictment or summarily) in consequence of a contravention of, or failure to comply with, any provision of the companies legislation requiring a return, account or other document to be filed with, delivered or sent, or notice of any matter to be given, to the registrar of companies (whether the contravention or failure is on the person's own part or on the part of any company): CDDA 1986, s 5(1).

Where a person is convicted of a summary offence counting for those purposes, the court by which he is convicted (or, in England and Wales, any other magistrates' court acting for the same petty sessions area) may make a disqualification order against him, if the circumstances specified in the next subsection are present: CDDA 1986, s 5(2).

11.20 Those circumstances are that, during the five years ending with the date of the conviction, the person has had made against him, or has been convicted of, in total not less than three default orders, and offences counting for the purposes of this section; and those offences may include that of which he is convicted as mentioned in CDDA 1986, s 5(2), and any other offence of which he is convicted on the same occasion: CDDA 1986, s 5(3).

The maximum period of disqualification under s 5 is five years: CDDA 1986, s 5(5).

New grounds for disqualification

Convictions abroad

Disqualification for certain convictions abroad

11.21 If it appears to the Secretary of State that it is expedient in the public interest, that a disqualification order under s 5A of CDDA 1986 should be made against a person, the Secretary of State may apply to the court for such an order: CDDA 1986, s 5A(1).

The court may, on an application under s 5A(1) of CDDA 1986, make a disqualification order against a person who has been convicted of a "relevant foreign offence": CDDA 1986, s 5A(2).

A 'relevant foreign offence' is an offence committed outside Great Britain:

(a) in connection with:

   (i) the promotion, formation, management, liquidation or striking off of a company (or any similar procedure),

   (ii) the receivership of a company's property (or any similar procedure), or

   (iii) a person being an administrative receiver of a company (or holding a similar position), and

(b) which corresponds to an indictable offence under the law of England and Wales: CDDA 1986, s 5A(3).

11.22 In *Re Genz Holdings Ltd; Secretary of State for Business, Energy and Industrial Strategy v Naqaweh* [2018] 2 BCLC 386, the defendants were convicted by the Swedish court of serious offences (gross false accounting, impeding a tax order and gross fraud), in connection with the management of Swedish branches of English companies. The issue for consideration was whether the Swedish offences had close similarity to or were analogous or equivalent in character to indictable English offences; and whether the Swedish offences were 'relevant foreign offences' under CDDA 1986, s 5A. The court held that the convictions of the defendants in Sweden were relevant foreign offences under CDDA 1986, s 5A(3) on which the Secretary of State could rely for disqualification of the defendants. This was because the offence which was committed overseas, 'corresponded' to an indictable offence for the purposes of CDDA 1986, s 5A(3)(b), if there was a close similarity, or the offences were analogous or equivalent in character. On the facts, the convictions in Sweden were relevant foreign proceedings corresponding to the indictable offences of failing to maintain accounting records contrary to CA 2006, ss 386–387 false accounting contrary to s.17 Theft Act 1968, s 17 and fraud contrary to Fraud Act 2006, ss 2 and 11. The court considered *per curiam* that the term 'management of a company' for the purposes of CDDA 1986, s 5A referred to both internal and external management of the company's affairs, and covered activity in relation to the whole history of the company. See too *R v Austen* (1985) 7 Cr App Rep (S) 214.

11.23 Where it appears to the Secretary of State that, in the case of a person who has offered to give a disqualification undertaking, (a) the person has been convicted of a relevant foreign offence, and (b) it is expedient in the public interest that the Secretary of State should accept the undertaking (instead of applying, or proceeding with an application, for a disqualification order), the Secretary of State may accept the undertaking: CDDA 1986, s 5A(4).

In CDDA 1986, s 5A the term 'company' includes an overseas company; and 'the court' means the High Court.

The maximum period of disqualification under an order under this section is 15 years: CDDA 1986, s 5A(5).

Disqualifications relating to unfit directors

Duty of court to disqualify unfit directors of insolvent companies

11.24 The court must make a disqualification order against a person in any case where, on an application under CDDA 1986, s 6, it is satisfied:

(a) that he is or has been a director of a company, which has at any time become insolvent (whether while he was a director or subsequently), and

(b) that his conduct as a director of that company (either taken alone or taken together with his conduct as a director of one or more other companies or overseas companies) makes him unfit to be concerned in the management of a company: CDDA 1986, s 6(1) (as inserted by SBEEA 2015, s 106(2)(a).

The references to a person's conduct as a director of any company or overseas company include, where that company or overseas company has become insolvent, references to that person's conduct in relation to any matter connected with or arising out of the insolvency: CDDA 1986, s 6(1A) (as inserted by SBEEA 2015, s 106(2)(b).

11.25 For the purposes of CDDA 1986, ss 6 and 7, a company becomes insolvent if:

(a) the company goes into liquidation at a time when its assets are insufficient for the payment of its debts and other liabilities, and the expenses of the winding up,

(b) an administration order is made in relation to the company, or

(c) an administrative receiver of the company is appointed: CDDA 1986, s 6(2) (as amended by SBEEA 2015, s 106(2)(c).

An overseas company becomes insolvent, if the company enters into insolvency proceedings of any description (including interim proceedings) in any jurisdiction: CDDA 1986, s 6(2A) (as inserted by SBEEA 2015, s 106(2)(d).

The term 'liquidation' is defined as the time when a company passes a resolution for the voluntary winding up of the company, or the time of the court order, where there is a compulsory winding up of the company: Insolvency Act 1986, s 247 (as incorporated under CDDA 1986, s 22(3)).

11.26 For the purposes of CDDA 1986, ss 6 and 7, 'director' includes a shadow director: CDDA 1986, s 6(3B).

Under s 6 the minimum period of disqualification is two years, and the maximum period is 15 years: CDDA 1986, s 6(4).

CDDA 1986, s 6 has given rise to much case law in the interpretation and legal and practical implications involved in the term "unfit", and is a significant section under which a large number of legal proceedings ensue, including disqualification orders and undertakings.

Section 6 applies to a *de jure* director, shadow director or a *de facto* director: CDDA 1986, s 6(3C); and *Re Kaytech International plc, Secretary of State for Trade and Industry v Kaczer* [1999] 2 BCLC 351. Rimer J decided that, in ascertaining whether an individual was a de facto director of a company, the crucial question was, whether he had assumed the status and functions of a company director, so as to make himself responsible under the CDDA 1986, as if he were a de jure director

Section 6 aims to protect the public from unfit directors, including protection of the creditors and other stakeholders of the company.

The court will have regard to the conduct of the director, regardless of whether he has been validly appointed, or is merely assuming to act as a director without any appointment at all, when deciding to make a disqualification order: *Re Lo-Line Electric Motors Ltd* [1988] 2 All ER 692.

11.27 In some situations, abdication of responsibility and duties may lead to a director being disqualified: *Secretary of State for Business Innovation and Skills v Reza* [2013] CSOH 86. Lord Malcolm stated:

> 'If someone accepts a directorship and then abdicates all responsibility for the affairs of the company, on any common sense view they have demonstrated unfitness for the office to a high degree … The public interest demands that directors of companies take an active interest in the affairs of the company, and are mindful of their personal responsibilities for the proper running of the business'.

See too: *Re Grayan Ltd* [1995] Ch 241, where Hoffmann LJ stated that the court should not shirk in its duty to disqualify a director, who has fallen below the required standard.

Determining 'unfitness'

11.28 The Secretary of State must demonstrate not only that the company is insolvent but that, at the time, the person was unfit. Typically, the directors would have been trading through the company, entering into transactions causing losses to the company and mounting debts, including tax debts and liabilities, and continues to trade while the company is insolvent. During this period, the directors may have paid themselves excessive remuneration, or diverted corporate funds for other purposes, which may have the effect of placing corporate assets beyond the reach of creditors, including preferential treatment of one creditor over another.

Some examples of 'unfitness'

11.29 The court will have regard to the evidence in the application to disqualify, to determine whether the 'unfitness' test has been met. In *Amaron Ltd, Secretary of State for Trade and Industry v Lubrani* [2001] 1 BCLC 562, the directors (husband and wife) carried on business of the company, sustaining losses and mounting Crown debts while the company was insolvent. Neuberger J held that the circumstances merited a disqualification order being made against them.

In *Secretary of State for Trade and Industry v Gray* [1995] 1 BCLC 276, the allegations against the directors were that they had: (1) caused the company to trade while insolvent; (2) failed to keep proper accounting records; (3) failed to file the appropriate year audited accounts on time; and (4) made preferential payments contrary to s 239 of the Insolvency Act 1986.

The Court of Appeal held that the question of whether a director's conduct made him unfit to be concerned in the management of a company within the meaning of CDDA 1986, s 6(1), was to be determined by reference to the matters and evidence relied on in the application for the disqualification order, and not by reference to whether, at the date of the hearing, the future protection of the public might or might not require a period of disqualification. CDDA 1986, s 6 imposed a duty on the court to disqualify a person whose conduct had shown him to be unfit. The purpose of making disqualification mandatory was to ensure that everyone whose conduct had fallen below the appropriate standard, was disqualified for at least two years (s 6(4)), whether in the individual case the court thought this was necessary in the public interest or not.

In *The Official Receiver v Watson* [2008] EWHC 64 (Ch), the director was disqualified on the basis of his acquiescence and participation in the corporate governance system involving breaches of company law.

The court is required to have regard to addressing the concept of 'unfitness', and not a breach of duty by a director, though a breach of duty could ultimately result in unfitness being demonstrated, but may not necessarily do so. The court will also consider whether any creditors were affected, particularly where phoenix companies are established and the previous companies still have unpaid creditors: *Re Travel Mondial (UK) Ltd* [1991] BCLC 120.

11.30 Unfitness may be demonstrated by mere incompetence or dishonesty: *Re Barings plc (No 5), Secretary of State for Trade and Industry v Baker (No 5)* [1999] 1 BCLC 433. See also [2000] 1 BCLC 523. See too: *Secretary of State for Business, Enterprise and Regulatory Reform v Sullman* [2009] 1 BCLC 397.

11.31 In considering whether a person is fit to be a director, the court will apply the facts of the case to the standard of conduct established by the courts, appropriate to a person fit to be a director – that being a question of mixed law and fact: *Secretary of State for Trade and Industry v Goldberg* [2004] 1 BCLC 597.

11.32 The court will also have regard to the conduct of the director when making the appropriate disqualification order. In *Re Bunting Electric Manufacturing Co Ltd, Secretary of State for Trade and Industry v Golby* [2006] 1 BCLC 550, Judge McCahill stated that although the focus of the CDDA 1986 was on the conduct of the director, not its consequences, the consequences were not irrelevant or immaterial, since they were relevant to the court's assessment of the seriousness or relative seriousness of the conduct complained of, and were important not only in considering whether an order for disqualification should be made, but also in determining any appropriate period of any disqualification. There was no unfairness in this approach to the defendant.

11.33 In some cases, the courts have stated that the disqualification procedure under CDDA 1986, s 6 is a two-stage procedure. In *Secretary of State for Trade and Industry v Swan* [2005] BCC 596, Etherton J stated that the determination of unfitness under CDDA 1986, s 6 was a two-stage process. First, the Secretary of State had to establish as facts, to the requisite standard of proof, namely on a balance of probabilities, the matters on which the allegation of unfitness was based. Second, the court had to be satisfied that the conduct alleged was sufficiently serious to warrant disqualification.

11.34 Other cases have decided that there is a three-stage process under CDDA 1986, s 6 in disqualifying a director. In *Official Receiver v Key* [2009] 1 BCLC 22, Mithani J held that in determining whether a defendant was unfit to be a director the decision whether the requirements of CDDA 1986, s 6(1)(b) were met involved a three stage process: first, did the matters relied on amount to misconduct; second, if so, did they justify a finding of unfitness; and, third, if so, what period of disqualification ought to be imposed. The court was required to take a broad brush approach in making a value judgment about the defendant's fitness or otherwise to be a director, and that required little more than a common sense decision about whether the facts of the case, when applied to the standard of conduct laid down by the court, ought to result in a finding of unfitness being made against the defendant.

11.35 The court will have regard to CDDA 1986, Sch 1 in connection with determining the director's conduct. In all cases, the following are taken into account:

1. Any misfeasance or breach of any fiduciary or other duty by the director in relation to the company.
2. Any misapplication or retention by the director of, or any conduct by the director giving rise to an obligation to account for, any money or other property of the company.
3. The extent of the director's responsibility for the company entering into any transaction liable to be set aside under Part XVI of the Insolvency Act 1986 (provisions against debt avoidance).
4. The extent of the director's responsibility for any failure by the company to comply with any of the following aspects of CA 2006, namely:
   - (a) s 113 (register of members);
   - (b) s 114 (register to be kept available for inspection);
   - (c) s 162 (register of directors);
   - (d) s 165 (register of directors' residential addresses);
   - (e) s 167 (duty to notify registrar of changes: directors);
   - (f) s 275 (register of secretaries);
   - (g) s 276 (duty to notify registrar of changes: secretaries);
   - (h) s 386 (duty to keep accounting records);
   - (i) s 388 (where and for how long accounting records to be kept);

(j) s 854 (duty to make annual returns);

(k) s 860 (duty to register charges); and

(l) s 878 (duty to register charges: companies registered in Scotland).

The extent of the director's responsibility for any failure by the directors of the company to comply with the following provisions of CA 2006:

(a) ss 394 or 399 (duty to prepare annual accounts);

(b) ss 414 or 450 (approval and signature of abbreviated accounts); and

(c) s 433 (name of signatory to be stated in published copy of accounts)

11.36 The court will take the following into account in determining unfitness where the company is insolvent:

- The extent of the director's responsibility for the causes of the company becoming insolvent.
- The extent of the director's responsibility for any failure by the company to supply any goods or services which have been paid for (in whole or in part).
- The extent of the director's responsibility for the company entering into any transaction or giving any preference, being a transaction or preference:

  (a) liable to be set aside under s 127 or ss 238 to 240 of the Insolvency Act 1986, or.

  (b) challengeable under s 242 or 243 of that Act
- The extent of the director's responsibility for any failure by the directors of the company to comply with s 98 of the Insolvency Act 1986 (duty to call creditors' meeting in creditors' voluntary winding up).
- Any failure by the director to comply with any obligation imposed on him by or under any of the following provisions of the Insolvency Act 1986.

  (a) s 22 (company's statement of affairs in administration);

  (b) s 47 (statement of affairs to administrative receiver);

  (c) s 66 (statement of affairs in Scottish receivership);

  (d) s 99 (directors' duty to attend meeting; statement of affairs in creditors' voluntary winding up);

  (e) s 131 (statement of affairs in winding up by the court);

  (f) s 234 (duty of any one with company property to deliver it up);

  (g) s 235 (duty to co-operate with liquidator, etc).

11.37 Other aspects of a director's conduct may be relevant in disqualification proceedings. In *Re Migration Services International Limited, Official Receiver v Webster* [2000] 1 BCLC 666, Neuberger J held that other aspects of a director's conduct could still be taken into account even though not mentioned specifically under CDDA 1986, Sch 1.

The Secretary of State is required to set out the factual basis of allegations of unfitness with supporting evidence. In *Secretary of State for Business, Innovation and Skills v Doffman*

[2011] 2 BCLC 541, Newey J held that in deciding whether the Secretary of State had satisfied the allegations of unfitness, the court was required to have regard to, but was not restricted to, the statutory matters in paras 1, 2 and 6 of Sch 1 to CDDA 1986 on which the Secretary of State relied, namely misfeasance or breach of fiduciary or other duty, misapplication or retention of, or failure to account for, money, and responsibility for the company's insolvency.

11.38 Under CA 2006, s 172(3), directors are required to take account of creditors' interests in promoting the company's success. The interests of creditors or failure to take account of their interests is one of the significant aspects for application under CDDA 1986, s 6 by the Secretary of State against a director. Typically, the allegation will be that the directors carried on business while the company was insolvent without regard to creditors' interests. *Mea Corporation Ltd, Secretary of State for Trade and Industry v Aviss* [2007] 1 BCLC 618.

11.39 Unfitness may be demonstrated by the company's insolvency and that the director knew that the company had no reasonable prospect of meeting creditors' claims: *Secretary of State v Creggan* [2002] 1 BCLC 99

Further, significant company debts and engaging in preferring a creditor could demonstrate unfitness: *Secretary of State for Trade and Industry v Collins* [2000] 2 BCLC 223.

11.40 Where the facts demonstrate competence and no dishonesty nor improper purpose, unfitness will not have been satisfied. In *Secretary of State for Trade and Industry v Gill* [2004] All ER 345, Blackburne J did not find that 'unfitness' had been established. There was no suggestion that the directors had not viewed seriously the professional advice they had received in connection with the company's business. There was also no suggestion that any part of the directors' motivation was to line their own pockets, or that they had some other dishonest or consciously improper purpose in mind in continuing to trade. Further, they had not acted incompetently. In these circumstances, the court did not make a disqualification order.

11.41 Disqualification orders fall into three main brackets depending upon the seriousness of the offence. This aspect was considered in *Re Sevenoaks Stationers (Retail) Limited* [1991] BCLC 325. The director in question had been a director of five companies which had gone into insolvent liquidation. The accounts of the companies had not been properly audited and with respect to one of the companies, the accounting records of the company were inadequate. There were other allegations of impropriety in the management of the company's affairs, and substantial Crown debts were owing. The director was disqualified for seven years, and he appealed against his sentence.

The Court of Appeal held that in determining the length of a disqualification order under CDDA 1986, s 6, the top bracket of disqualification should be reserved for serious cases. The minimum bracket of two to five years should be reserved for cases which were relatively not serious; and the middle bracket of six to ten years should apply to serious cases that did not deserve the maximum sentence. However, non-payment of Crown debts could not be treated as automatic grounds for disqualification.

Furthermore, it was of paramount importance that a director facing a disqualification order should know the charges that he had to meet. This may have implications for a director to plead the Human Rights Act 1998, and the European Convention on Human Rights including the right to a fair trial and natural justice concepts.

11.42 A lower standard of fairness is required in civil proceedings than criminal actions as disqualification proceedings are civil in nature: *R v Secretary of State for Trade and Industry ex p McCormick* [1998] BCC 379. See too *DC v United Kingdom (39031/97)* [2000] BCC 710.

11.43 The use in disqualification proceedings of statements obtained under s 235 of the Insolvency Act 1986 did not necessarily involve a breach of art 6(1) of the European Convention on Human Rights: *Official Receiver v Stern* [2000] 1 WLR 2230.

11.44 The court cannot make an order under IA 1986, s 236 for production of documents by third parties for subsequent use in disqualification proceedings – this would be an abuse of power by the Official Receiver: *Re Pantmaenog Timber Co Ltd* [2001] 4 All ER 588.

Disqualification orders under s 6: applications and acceptance of undertakings

11.45 If the Secretary of State is of the view that it is expedient in the public interest that a disqualification order under CDDA 1986, s 6 should be made against any person, an application for the making of such an order against that person may be made:

(a) by the Secretary of State, or

(b) if the Secretary of State so directs in the case of a person who is or has been a director of a company which is being or has been wound up by the court in England and Wales, by the official receiver: CDDA 1986, s 7(1).

Except with the leave of the court, an application for making a disqualification order against any person cannot be made after the end of the period of three years, beginning with the day on which the company of which that person is or has been a director became insolvent: CDDA 1986, s 7(2) (as inserted by SBEEA 2015, s 108(1)). Section 108(1) of SBEEA 2015 applies only to an application relating to a company which has become insolvent after the commencement of that subsection: SBEEA 2015, s 108(2). Section 6(2) of the CDDA 1986 (meaning of 'becoming insolvent') applies for the purposes of s 108(2) of SBEEA 2015 as it applies for the purposes of s 6 of that Act: SBEEA 2015, s 108(3).

11.46 If it appears to the Secretary of State that the conditions mentioned in CDDA 1986, s 6(1) are satisfied as regards any person who has offered to give him a disqualification undertaking, he may accept the undertaking, if it appears to him that it is expedient in the public interest that he should do so (instead of applying, or proceeding with an application, for a disqualification order): CDDA 1986, s 7(2A).

The issue of whether or not it is 'expedient' in the public interest for a disqualification order to be made, is a matter for determination by the Secretary of State and not by the court

In *Re Blackspur Group plc, Secretary of State for Trade and Industry v Davies* [1998] 1 BCLC 676, Lord Woolf MR set out the following points:

(1) The purpose of CDDA 1986 is the protection of the public, by means of prohibitory remedial action, by anticipated deterrent effect on further misconduct and by encouragement of higher standards of honesty and diligence

in corporate management, from those who are unfit to be concerned in the management of a company.

(2) Parliament has designated the Secretary of State as the proper public officer to discharge the function of making applications to the court for disqualification orders. There is a wide discretion to do so in cases where it appears, in the prescribed circumstances, that 'it is expedient in the public interest that a disqualification order should be made'. In any particular case it may be decided that the public interest is best served by making and continuing an application to trial; or by not making an application at all; or by not continuing a pending application to trial; or by not contesting at trial points raised by way of defence or mitigation. All these litigation decisions are made by the Secretary of State according to what is considered by her to be 'expedient in the public interest'. They are not made by the court or by other parties to the proceedings.

(3) Once proceedings have been brought to trial, it is for the court, not for the Secretary of State or for any other party, to decide whether a disqualification order should or should not be made. A court can only make a disqualification order if it is 'satisfied' on the prescribed statutory matters. As the court must be 'satisfied' of those matters, it is not appropriate for the court to act, or even for the court to be asked to act, as a rubber stamp on a proposed consent order, without regard to its factual basis.

However, this does not prevent the court from taking into account the agreement of the parties in concluding that it is satisfied that the case warrants disqualification and in determining the period of disqualification which is appropriate, thus allowing the issues to be determined by the court to be disposed of summarily.

(4) Applications under CDDA 1986 are not ordinary private law proceedings, even when heard and determined by a civil court. They are made, and can only be properly made, in cases where it is considered 'expedient in the public interest' to seek a disqualification order in the specified statutory form which, when made, has serious penal consequences. The unique form of the order and the special procedure for obtaining it are prescribed by CDDA 1986. Significantly, CDDA 1986 does not expressly equip the court with a discretion to deploy the armoury of common law and equitable remedies to restrain future misconduct (injunction or undertaking in lieu of injunction), to punish for disregard of restraints imposed by court order (contempt powers of imprisonment or fine), to compensate for past loss unlawfully inflicted (damages) or to restore benefits unjustly acquired (restitution).

11.47 The Secretary of State or the official receiver may require any person:

(a) to furnish him with such information with respect to that person's or another person's conduct as a director of a company, which has at any time become insolvent (whether while the person was a director or subsequently), and

(b) to produce and permit inspection of such books, papers and other records as are considered by the Secretary of State or (as the case may be) the official receiver, to be relevant to that person's or another person's conduct as such a director,

as the Secretary of State or the official receiver may reasonably require, for the purpose of determining whether to exercise, or of exercising, any function of his under CDDA 1986, s 7: CDDA 1986, s 7(4) (as inserted by DA 2015, Sch 6, Part 4).

The Secretary of State can also require a report on the conduct of directors to be sent by electronic means via the portal: see The Insolvent Companies (Reports on Conduct of Directors) (England and Wales) Rules 2016, SI No 2016/180. See too CDDA 1986, s 7A (office holder's report on the conduct of directors).

11.48 The Secretary of State and not the court is required to decide whether or not to bring disqualification proceedings before the court. In *Re Barings plc (No 3), Secretary of State for Trade and Industry v Baker* [1999] 1 BCLC 226, Chadwick LJ stated that the decisions whether or not to commence, and thereafter to pursue, applications to the court for disqualification orders, have been entrusted by Parliament to the Secretary of State. It is for her, and not for the court, to make those decisions.

Further, a court was not entitled to intervene and stay proceedings because it may take the view that the Secretary of State is acting in a manner that it may regard as over-zealous. That would be to substitute the court's view of what is expedient in the public interest for her view. That is no part of the court's role. The basis upon which the court can interfere, by granting a stay of proceedings, is to protect its own process from abuse.

11.49 An abnegation of responsibility by a director in the company's affairs was a significant failure rendering him unfit, and subject to disqualification proceedings. In *Secretary of State for Business, Innovation and Skills v Aaron & Ors* [2009] EWHC 3263 (Ch), the Secretary of State successfully brought proceedings for the disqualification of two directors under CDDA 1986, s 7 for breaches of the Financial Services rules.

The directors contended that their disqualification would be unfair, because their breaches of FSA rules were not connected with the general management of the company. Proudman J stated:

> 'The fact that he [the director] has not shown himself unfit to manage any business, or to undertake a different management role, is, like the likelihood or otherwise of offending again … a matter which goes to leave to be concerned in the management of a company under s 17 CDDA and to length of disqualification. It is not a matter which goes to disqualification itself. Secondly, there is the simple fact that the abnegation of responsibility by a director is a matter affecting the ability to conduct ordinary corporate governance. A director's failure to ensure that he was sufficiently concerned with relevant responsibilities is a grass roots failure'.

Office-holder's report on conduct of directors

11.50 The office-holder of an insolvent company, must prepare a report (a 'conduct report') about the conduct of each person who was a director of the company:

(a) on the insolvency date, or

(b) at any time during the period of three years ending with that date: CDDA 1986, s 7A(1) (as inserted by SBEEA 2015, s 107(2)).

A company is considered insolvent if:

(a) the company is in liquidation and at the time it went into liquidation, its assets were insufficient for the payment of its debts and other liabilities and the expenses of the winding up,

(b) the company has entered administration, or

(c) an administrative receiver of the company has been appointed;

and s 6(1A) applies for the purposes of this section as it applies for the purpose of that section: CDDA 1986, s 7A(2) (as inserted by SBEEA 2015, s 107(2)).

A conduct report must, in relation to each person, describe any conduct of the person which may assist the Secretary of State in deciding whether to exercise the power under section 7(1) or (2A) in relation to the person: CDDA 1986, s 7A(3) (as inserted by SBEEA 2015, s 107(2)).

The office-holder must send the conduct report to the Secretary of State before the end of:

(a) the period of three months beginning with the insolvency date, or

(b) such other longer period as the Secretary of State considers appropriate in the particular circumstances: CDDA 1986, s 7A(4) (as inserted by SBEEA 2015, s 107(2)).

If new information comes to the attention of an office-holder, the office-holder must send that information to the Secretary of State as soon as reasonably practicable: CDDA 1986, s 7A(5) (as inserted by SBEEA 2015, s 107(2)).

11.51 The term 'new information' is information which an office-holder considers should have been included in a conduct report prepared in relation to the company, or would have been so included had it been available before the report was sent: CDDA 1986, s 7A(6) (as inserted by SBEEA 2015, s 107(2)).

If there is more than one office-holder in respect of a company at any particular time (because the company is insolvent by virtue of falling within more than one paragraph of subsection (2) at that time), subsection (1) applies only to the first of the office-holders to be appointed: CDDA 1986, s 7A(7) (as inserted by SBEEA 2015, s 107(2)).

In the case of a company which is at different times insolvent by virtue of falling within one or more different paragraphs of subsection (2):

(a) the references in subsection (1) to the insolvency date are to be read as references to the first such date during the period in which the company is insolvent, and

(b) subsection (1) does not apply to an office-holder if at any time during the period in which the company is insolvent a conduct report has already been prepared and sent to the Secretary of State: CDDA 1986, s 7A(8) (as inserted by SBEEA 2015, s 107(2)).

The 'office-holder' in respect of a company which is insolvent is:

(a) in the case of a company being wound up by the court in England and Wales, the official receiver;

(b) in the case of a company being wound up otherwise, the liquidator;

(c) in the case of a company in administration, the administrator;

(d) in the case of a company of which there is an administrative receiver, the receiver: CDDA 1986, s 7A(9) (as inserted by SBEEA 2015, s 107(2)).

11.52 The 'insolvency date':

(a) in the case of a company being wound up by the court, means the date on which the court makes the winding-up order (see s 125 of IA 1986);

(b) in the case of a company being wound up by way of a members' voluntary winding up, means the date on which the liquidator forms the opinion that the company will be unable to pay its debts in full (together with interest at the official rate) within the period stated in the directors' declaration of solvency under s 89 of IA 1986;

(c) in the case of a company being wound up by way of a creditors' voluntary winding up where no such declaration under section 89 of that Act has been made, means the date of the passing of the resolution for voluntary winding up;

(d) in the case of a company which has entered administration, means the date the company did so;

(e) in the case of a company in respect of which an administrative receiver has been appointed, means the date of that appointment: CDDA 1986, s 7A(10) (as inserted by SBEEA 2015, s 107(2)).

Disqualification of director on finding of unfitness

11.53 If the Secretary of State makes a finding that it is expedient in the public interest that a disqualification order should be made against a person who is, or has been, a director or shadow director of a company, he may apply to the court for such an order: CDDA 1986, s 8(1).

The court may make a disqualification order against a person where, on an application under CDDA 1986, s 8, it is satisfied that his conduct in relation to the company (either taken alone or taken together with his conduct as a director or shadow director of one or more other companies or overseas companies), makes him unfit to be concerned in the management of a company: CDDA 1986, s 8(2) (as inserted by SBEEA 2015 s 106(3)(a)).

11.54 If the Secretary of State considers that, in the case of a person who has offered to give him a disqualification undertaking:

(a) the conduct of the person in relation to a company of which the person is or has been a director or shadow director (either taken alone or taken together with his conduct as a director or shadow director of one or more other companies or overseas companies), makes him unfit to be concerned in the management of a company, and

(b) it is expedient in the public interest that he should accept the undertaking (instead of applying, or proceeding with an application, for a disqualification order) he may accept the undertaking: CDDA 1986, s 8(2A) (as inserted by SBEEA 2015, s 106(3)(b)) and s 109(1)).

The maximum period of disqualification under this section is 15 years: CDDA 1986, s 8(4).

Other cases of disqualification

Participation in wrongful trading

11.55 Where the court makes a declaration under s 213 or 214 of the Insolvency Act 1986 that a person is liable to make a contribution to a company's assets, then, whether or not an application for such an order is made by any person, the court may, if it thinks fit, also make a disqualification order against the person to whom the declaration relates: CDDA 1986, s 10(1).

The maximum period of disqualification under this section is 15 years: CDDA 1986, s 10(2).

In this section 'company' includes overseas company: CDDA 1986, s 10(3) (as inserted by SBEEA 2015, Sch 7, Part 1).

Undischarged bankrupts

11.56 It is an offence for a person to act as director of a company or directly or indirectly to take part in or be concerned in the promotion, formation or management of a company, without the leave of the court, at a time when any of the circumstances mentioned in s 11(2) apply to the person: CDDA 1986, s 11(1) (as inserted by SBEEA 2015, s 113(1)).

The circumstances are:

(a) the person is an undischarged bankrupt in England;

(c) a debt relief restrictions order or undertaking is in force in respect of the person under the Insolvency Act 1986;

(d) a moratorium period under a debt relief order applies in relation to the person under the Insolvency Act 1986.

Determining unfitness etc: matters to be taken into account

11.57 CDDA 1986, s 12C applies where a court must determine:

(a) whether a person's conduct as a director of one or more companies or overseas companies makes the person unfit to be concerned in the management of a company;

(b) whether to exercise any discretion it has to make a disqualification order under any of s 2–4, 5A, 8 or 10;

(c) where the court has decided to make a disqualification order under any of those sections, or is required to make an order under section 6, what the period of disqualification should be: CDDA 1986, s 12C(1) (as inserted by SBEEA 2015, s 106(5)).

11.58 However, s 12C does not apply where the court in question is one mentioned in section 2(2)(b) or (c): CDDA 1986, s 12C(2) (as inserted by SBEEA 2015, s 106(5)).

This section also applies where the Secretary of State must determine:

(a) whether a person's conduct as a director of one or more companies or overseas companies makes the person unfit to be concerned in the management of a company;

(b) whether to exercise any discretion the Secretary of State has to accept a disqualification undertaking under s 5A, 7 or 8: CDDA 1986, s 12C(3) (as inserted by SBEEA 2015, s 106(5)).

11.59 In making any such determination in relation to a person, the court or the Secretary of State must:

(a) in every case, have regard in particular to the matters set out in paragraphs 1 to 4 of Sch 1;

(b) in a case where the person concerned is or has been a director of a company or overseas company, also have regard in particular to the matters set out in paragraphs 5 to 7 of that Schedule: CDDA 1986, s 12C(4) (as inserted by SBEEA 2015, s 106(5)).

In this section 'director' includes a shadow director: CDDA 1986, s 12C(5) (as inserted by SBEEA 2015, s 106(5)).

Matters to be taken into account in all cases

11.60 Under Schedule 1 to CDDA 1986 (as inserted by SBEEA 2015, s 106(6)), in determining unfitness of directors, the following matters will be taken into account:

- The extent to which the person was responsible for the causes of any material contravention by a company or overseas company of any applicable legislative or other requirement.
- Where applicable, the extent to which the person was responsible for the causes of a company or overseas company becoming insolvent.
- The frequency of conduct of the person which falls within Sch 1, para 1 or 2.
- The nature and extent of any loss or harm caused, or any potential loss or harm which could have been caused, by the person's conduct in relation to a company or overseas company.

11.61 The following are additional matters to be taken into account where person is or has been a director of a company:

- Any misfeasance or breach of any fiduciary duty by the director in relation to a company or overseas company.
- Any material breach of any legislative or other obligation of the director which applies as a result of being a director of a company or overseas company.
- The frequency of conduct of the director which falls within para 5 or 6.

Consequences of contravention

Criminal penalties

11.62 If a person acts in contravention of a disqualification order or disqualification undertaking or in contravention of CDDA 1986, s 12(2), 12A or 12B, or is guilty of an offence under s 11, he is liable:

(a) on conviction on indictment, to imprisonment for not more than two years or a fine, or both; and

(b) on summary conviction, to imprisonment for not more than six months or a fine not exceeding the statutory maximum, or both: CDDA 1986, s 13.

Offences by body corporate

11.63 Where a body corporate is guilty of an offence of acting in contravention of a disqualification order or disqualification undertaking or in contravention of CDDA 1986, s 12A or 12B, and it is proved that the offence occurred with the consent or connivance of, or was attributable to any neglect on the part of any director, manager, secretary or other similar officer of the body corporate, or any person who was purporting to act in any such capacity he, as well as the body corporate, is guilty of the offence and liable to be proceeded against and punished accordingly: CDDA 1986, s 14(1).

Where the affairs of a body corporate are managed by its members, CDDA 1986, s 14(1) applies in relation to the acts and defaults of a member in connection with his functions of management as if he were a director of the body corporate: CDDA 1986, s 14(2).

Personal liability for company's debts where person acts while disqualified

11.64 A person is personally responsible for all the relevant debts of a company if at any time:

(a) in contravention of a disqualification order or disqualification undertaking or in contravention of CDDA 1986, s 11, 12A or 12B he is involved in the management of the company, or

(b) as a person who is involved in the management of the company, he acts or is willing to act on instructions given without the leave of the court by a person whom he knows at that time:

  (i) to be the subject of a disqualification order or disqualification undertaking or a disqualification order under the Company Directors Disqualification (Northern Ireland) Order 2002; or

  (ii) to be an undischarged bankrupt: CDDA 1986, s 15(1).

11.65 Where a person is personally responsible under CDDA 1986, s 15 for the relevant debts of a company, he is jointly and severally liable in respect of those debts with the company and any other person who, whether under this section or otherwise, is so liable: CDDA 1986, s 15(2).

For the purposes of s 15 the relevant debts of a company are:

(a) in relation to a person who is personally responsible under paragraph (a) of s 15(1), such debts and other liabilities of the company as are incurred at a time when that person was involved in the management of the company, and

(b) in relation to a person who is personally responsible under paragraph (b) of that subsection, such debts and other liabilities of the company as are incurred at a time when that person was acting or was willing to act on instructions given as mentioned in that paragraph: CDDA 1986, s 15(3).

For the purposes of s 15, a person is involved in the management of a company if he is a director of the company or if he is concerned, whether directly or indirectly, or takes part, in the management of the company: CDDA 1986, s 15(4).

11.66 For the purposes of s 15 a person who, as a person involved in the management of a company, has at any time acted on instructions given without the leave of the court by a person whom he knew at that time to be the subject of a disqualification order or disqualification undertaking or to be an undischarged bankrupt is presumed, unless the contrary is shown, to have been willing at any time thereafter to act on any instructions given by that person: CDDA 1986, s 15(5).

Compensation orders and undertakings

11.67 The court may make a compensation order against a person on the application of the Secretary of State if it is satisfied that the conditions mentioned in s 15A(3) are met: CDDA 1986, s 15A(1) (as inserted by SBEEA 2015, s 110)).

If the Secretary of State considers that the conditions mentioned in s 15(3) are met in respect of a person who has offered to give the Secretary of State a compensation undertaking, the Secretary of State may accept the undertaking instead of applying, or proceeding with an application, for a compensation order: CDDA 1986, s 15A(2) (as inserted by SBEEA 2015, s 110)).

11.68 The conditions are that:

(a) the person is subject to a disqualification order or disqualification undertaking under this Act, and

(b) conduct for which the person is subject to the order or undertaking has caused loss to one or more creditors of an insolvent company of which the person has at any time been a director: CDDA 1986, s 15A(3) (as inserted by SBEEA 2015, s 110)).

An 'insolvent company' is a company that is or has been insolvent and a company becomes insolvent if:

(a) the company goes into liquidation at a time when its assets are insufficient for the payment of its debts and other liabilities and the expenses of the winding up,

(b) the company enters administration, or

(c) an administrative receiver of the company is appointed: CDDA 1986, s 15A(4) (as inserted by SBEEA 2015, s 110)).

11.69 The Secretary of State may apply for a compensation order at any time before the end of the period of two years beginning with the date on which the disqualification order referred to in paragraph (a) of s 15A(3) was made, or the disqualification undertaking referred to in that paragraph was accepted: CDDA 1986, s 15A(5) (as inserted by SBEEA 2015, s 110)).

In the case of a person subject to a disqualification order under section 8ZA or 8ZD, or a disqualification undertaking under section 8ZC or 8ZE, the reference in subsection (3)(b) to conduct is a reference to the conduct of the main transgressor in relation to which the person has exercised the requisite amount of influence: CDDA 1986, s 15A(6) (as inserted by SBEEA 2015, s 110)).

Amounts payable under compensation orders and undertakings

11.70 A compensation order is an order requiring the person against whom it is made to pay an amount specified in the order:

(a) to the Secretary of State for the benefit of:

(i) a creditor or creditors specified in the order;

(ii) a class or classes of creditor so specified;

(b) as a contribution to the assets of a company so specified: CDDA 1986, s 15B(1) (as inserted by SBEEA 2015, s 110)).

11.71 When specifying an amount the court (in the case of an order) and the Secretary of State (in the case of an undertaking) must in particular have regard to:

(a) the amount of the loss caused;

(b) the nature of the conduct mentioned in s 15A(3)(b);

(c) whether the person has made any other financial contribution in recompense for the conduct (whether under a statutory provision or otherwise): CDDA 1986, s 15B(3) (as inserted by SBEEA 2015, s 110)).

An amount payable by virtue of s 15B(2) under a compensation undertaking is recoverable as if payable under a court order: CDDA 1986, s 15B(4) (as inserted by SBEEA 2015, s 110)).

An amount payable under a compensation order or compensation undertaking is provable as a bankruptcy debt: CDDA 1986, s 15B(5) (as inserted by SBEEA 2015, s 110)).

Variation and revocation of compensation undertakings

11.72 The court may, on the application of a person who is subject to a compensation undertaking either reduce the amount payable under the undertaking, or provide for the undertaking not to have effect: CDDA 1986, s 15C(1) (as inserted by SBEEA 2015, s 110)).

On the hearing of an application, the Secretary of State must appear and call the attention of the court to any matters which he considers relevant, and may give evidence or call witnesses: CDDA 1986, s 15C(1) (as inserted by SBEEA 2015, s 110)).

Application for disqualification order

11.73 A person intending to apply for the making of a disqualification order or, in the case of an order under s 5A, the High Court ,shall give not less than ten days' notice of his intention to the person against whom the order is sought; and on the hearing of the application the last-mentioned person may appear and himself give evidence or call witnesses: CDDA 1986, s 16(1) (as inserted by SBEEA 2015, Sch 7, Part 1).

An application to a court for the making against any person of a disqualification order under any of ss 2–4 of CDDA 1986, may be made by the Secretary of State or the official receiver, or by the liquidator or any past or present member or creditor of any company or overseas company in relation to which that person has committed or is alleged to have committed an offence or other default: CDDA 1986, s 16(2) (as inserted by SBEEA 2015, Sch 7, Part 1).

11.74 On the hearing of any application under CDDA 1986 made by a person falling within CDDA 1986, s 16(4), the applicant must appear, and call the attention of the court to any matters which seem to him to be relevant, and may himself give evidence or call witnesses: CDDA 1986, s 16(3).

The persons referred to in s 16(3) are:

(a) the Secretary of State;

(b) the official receiver;

(c) the Competition and Markets Authority;

(d) the liquidator;

(e) a specified regulator (within the meaning of CDDA 1986, s 9E): CDDA 1986, s 16(4).

Register of disqualification orders and undertakings

11.75 Pursuant to CDDA 1986, s 18, the Secretary of State has enacted the *Companies (Disqualification Orders) Regulations 2009 SI 2009/2471*. The purpose of the Regulations is to require certain court officers to provide the Secretary of State with particulars of disqualification orders, and grants of leave in relation to such orders or disqualification undertakings made or accepted under CDDA 1986, and of any action taken by a court in consequence of which any such orders or undertakings are varied or cease to be in force. The instrument prescribes the particulars and form in which the particulars are to be provided by the court officers to the Secretary of State.

Foreign directors' disqualification

11.76 Part 40 of CA 2006 is concerned with company directors' foreign disqualification. It addresses a gap that previously existed under the law. Persons who had been disqualified from being a director, or from holding an equivalent position, or engaging in the management of a company in another State, were able to form a company in the UK, to appoint themselves a director of that company, and then operate that company either in the UK or in the State where they have been disqualified. The provisions in Part 40 give the Secretary of State a power to close the gap by making regulations to disqualify from being a director of a UK company, persons who have been disqualified in another State.

11.77 Part 40 is the first part which is outside the company law provisions of the Act. It does not, therefore, form part of the Companies Acts. This is due to the fact that the provisions in this part are linked with those of the Company Directors' Disqualification Act 1986. That Act is not part of the Companies Acts, because it has implications beyond companies to other bodies (such as NHS foundation trusts), and extends beyond persons covered by the Companies Acts to persons such as insolvency practitioners. The fact that Part 40 is not part of the Companies Acts has the consequence that the definitions in the earlier parts of the Act do not apply – hence the need to define the term 'the court' in s 1183. Similarly, the definitions for Part 40 are not listed in Sch 8 to the Act.

Persons subject to foreign restrictions

11.78 Section 1182 of CA 2006 defines what is meant by references in Part 40 to a person being subject to 'foreign restrictions': CA 2006, s 1182(1).

A person is subject to foreign restrictions if under the law of a country or territory outside the United Kingdom:

(a) he is, by reason of misconduct or unfitness, disqualified to any extent from acting in connection with the affairs of a company,

(b) he is, by reason of misconduct or unfitness, required:

  (i) to obtain permission from a court or other authority, or

  (ii) to meet any other condition,

  before acting in connection with the affairs of a company, or

(c) he has, by reason of misconduct or unfitness, given undertakings to a court or other authority of a country or territory outside the United Kingdom not to act in connection with the affairs of a company, nor restricting the extent to which, or the way in which, he may do so: CA 2006, s 1182(2).

11.79 The references in s 1182(2) to acting in connection with the affairs of a company are to do with being a director of a company; or acting as receiver of a company's property; or being concerned or taking part in the promotion, formation or management of a company: CA 2006, s 1183.

12 Derivative claims

Introduction

12.1 This chapter examines how a shareholder may be able to bring a derivative claim, including the causes of action and outcomes before the court. It also considers the legal and procedural aspects and the interaction between CA 2006 and Civil Procedure Rules that impact upon derivative claims.

This chapter addresses the following issues:

- the position of derivative actions at common law;
- an outline of the rule in *Foss v Harbottle*;
- statutory derivative claims; and
- the 'reflective loss' principle.

Derivative claims and proceedings by members

12.2 This section considers derivative claims in England from both a common law and a statutory position. It considers the rule in *Foss v Harbottle* including some of the exceptions to the *rule* and the procedural aspects under CA 2006 for a shareholder to bring derivative proceedings. Despite the availability of the statutory derivative claim under CA 2006 which has superseded *Foss v Harbottle*, the rule in *Foss v Harbottle* may still apply in certain circumstances – see **12.6**.

The position at common law: the rule in Foss v Harbottle

12.3 Traditionally at common law, the courts were reluctant to interfere in the internal affairs and management of the company. If the majority had decided on a particular course of action, the courts would not second-guess the decisions of the directors or shareholders. Judicial attitudes at the time were that the corporate decision makers were best qualified and experienced in management matters, and to address the company's best interest, when embarking on a particular transaction. The courts favoured the majority rule approach so that if the majority decided on a particular action or transaction, the minority would have to accept the majority decision. This became known as the 'rule in *Foss v Harbottle*', considered below. One of the principal issues with this rule was that it did not take proper account of the detriment, injustice, harm or injury that may be suffered by the company itself. The company's interests were not sufficiently protected, unless a shareholder could fall within certain exceptions to the rule. The combined effect of this rule and exceptions meant that it was legally and procedurally difficult to bring derivative claims at common law. See too Denning in *Wallersteiner v Moir (No 2)* [1975] 1 All ER 849.

12.4 At common law, the position regarding derivative claims was governed by the rule in *Foss v Harbottle* (1843) 2 Hare 461. The rule comprised two principles. First, where a wrong was allegedly done to a company, the proper claimant in legal proceedings was the company. Second, in respect of an alleged transaction, which may bind the company by a simple majority of the members, a shareholder may not bring any action or claim in respect of the alleged transaction. See too *Edwards v Halliwell* [1950] 2 All ER 1064; and the Law Commissions of England and Wales and Scotland report on *Shareholder Remedies (1997).*

The effect of CA 2006 on the rule in Foss v Harbottle

12.5 CA 2006 has effectively replaced the common law derivative action by the statutory code for derivative claims under CA 2006, Pt 11, Ch 1. The principles set out in the rule in *Foss v Harbottle,* and subsequent common law cases on derivative actions have largely been incorporated under the CA 2006.

12.6 In *Iesini and others v Westrip Holdings Ltd* [2011] 1 BCLC 498, Lewison J stated that: 'In the first place the statutory derivative claim has replaced the common law derivative action. A derivative claim may 'only' be brought under the Act'.

The procedural aspects of the derivative claim will therefore be governed by CA 2006 rather than the common law principles.

However, the statutory basis of the derivative claim does not mean that the rule in *Foss v Harbottle* is no longer applicable, or totally abrogated particularly in respect of multiple derivative actions. In *Waddington Ltd v Chan Chun Hoo Thomas* [2009] 2 BCLC 82, the Hong Kong Court of Final Appeal commented that the rule in *Foss v Harbottle* was not displaced by the Companies Acts (see Ribiero J and Lord Millett (particularly in respect of 'multiple derivative' actions, which are not addressed under the CA 2006, and therefore fall to be considered by the common law principles). See too: *Universal Project Management Services Ltd v Fort Gilkicker Ltd* [2013] Ch 551; and *Abouraya v Sigmund* [2014] All ER 208. See further **12.37–2.39**.

Statutory derivative claims – the position under CA 2006

12.7 The statutory derivative claim is governed by CA 2006, Pt 11, Ch 1 and Civil Procedure Rules Part 19, Practice Direction 19C – Derivative Claims. The Practice Direction applies to derivative claims under CA 2006, Pt 11, Ch 1 including permission to continue or take over such claims. It does not apply to claims or order under CA 2006, s 996 (unfair prejudicial conduct) for which a separate regime applies.

Definition of a 'Derivative Claim'

12.8 CA 2006 sets out the statutory definition of a 'derivative claim'. Part 11, Chapter 1 applies to proceedings in England by a member of a company:

(a) in respect of a 'cause of action' vested in the company; and

(b) seeking relief on behalf of the company.

This is referred to in Pt 11, Ch 1 as a 'derivative claim': CA 2006, s 260(1).

A derivative claim may only be brought:

(a) under Chapter 1; or

(b) in pursuance of an order of the court in proceedings under CA 2006, s 994 (proceedings for protection of members against unfair prejudice): CA 2006, s 260(2).

Establishing a cause of action

12.9

- A derivative claim under CA 2006, Pt 11, Ch 1 may be brought only in respect of a cause of action arising from an actual or proposed act or omission involving:
- negligence,
- default,
- breach of duty, or
- breach of trust by a director of the company.

The cause of action may be against the director or another person (or both): CA 2006, s 260(3). The term 'director' includes a former director; and a shadow director is treated as a director: CA 2006, s 260(5). There is no definition of 'another person', but this could include those assisting the director of the company, who have caused some wrongs to the company in terms of negligence, default, breach of duty or breach of trust. The 'another person' may include a third party against whom the derivative claim may be brought, rather than the director. It could include *de facto* directors too.

It is immaterial whether the cause of action arose before or after the person seeking to bring or continue the derivative claim became a member of the company: CA 2006, s 260(4).

A derivative claim only applies to present members. It excludes former shareholders. The term 'a member of a company' includes a person who is not a member, but to whom shares in the company have been transferred or transmitted by operation of law: CA 2006, s 260(5) – this usually operates on death or bankruptcy of a shareholder. The term 'member' will usually refer to a minority shareholder bringing the derivative claim and, very exceptionally, to a controlling shareholder. It also applies to a shareholder who is registered in the register of members.

The courts will also have regard to any fraud or abuse of power when considering derivative claims: *Cinematic Finance Ltd v Ryder* [2010] EWHC 3387 (Ch).

Application for permission to continue derivative claim

12.10 In deciding whether it is in the company's interests to bring derivative proceedings, the court will ultimately decide this issue. Upon issuing a claim form under the Practice Direction 19-C, a member of a company who brings a derivative claim under Part 11, Chapter 1 must apply to the court for permission to continue it: CA 2006, s 261(1). The objective is for the shareholder to obtain a quick decision by the court on whether it is in the company's interests to bring a derivative claim; and the court being satisfied that it is in the company's best interests for such proceedings to be brought.

There are various stages involved in the application for permission to continue the derivative claim. The shareholder must complete a claim form which must be headed 'Derivative Claim'. If the claimant seeks an order that the defendant company or other body concerned indemnify the claimant against liability for costs incurred in the permission application or the claim, this should be stated in the permission application or claim form or both, as the case requires: Practice Direction 19C – Derivative Claims, paras 2(1) and 2(2). The claimant will be the shareholder, and the co-defendants will be the director and the company: see 19C, para 4.

The first stage: establishing a prima facie case

12.11 At the first stage, only the shareholder will be before the court based on evidence filed, to establish a *prima facie* case for permission to continue the derivative claim. The decision whether the claimant's evidence discloses a *prima facie* case, will normally be made without submissions from or (in the case of an oral hearing to reconsider such a decision reached pursuant to r 19.9A(9)) attendance by the company. If without invitation from the court, the company volunteers a submission or attendance, the company will not normally be allowed any costs of that submission or attendance: Practice Direction 19C, para 5.

According to *Langley Ward Ltd v Trevor* [2011] All ER 78, the first stage process of examining a prima facie case cannot be side-stepped: the court will consider all evidence presented to it in deciding whether a prima facie case has been established.

12.12 If it appears to the court that the application and the evidence filed by the applicant in support of it do not disclose a *prima facie* case for giving permission (or leave), the court:

(a) must dismiss the application; and

(b) may make any consequential order it considers appropriate: CA 2006, s 261(2).

12.13 The potential defendants against whom a derivative claim may be brought are wide and not limited to directors: *Iesini and Others v Westrip Holdings Ltd* [2011] 1 BCLC 498. Lewison J stated that a derivative claim as defined by s 260(3) was not confined to a claim against the insiders. The cause of action may be against the director or another person (or both). The cause of action must arise from an actual or proposed act or omission involving negligence, default, breach of duty or breach of trust by a director of the company. However, since the cause of action must arise from his default (etc), a derivative claim brought under Pt 11, Ch 1 will not allow a shareholder to pursue the company's claim against a third party, where that claim depends on a cause of action that has arisen independently from the director's default (etc).

However, it is contended that the threshold for the *prima facie* case is far higher than required under s 261. There is no requirement under the CA 2006 to show a *prima facie* case both that the company has a good cause of action and that the cause of action arises out of a directors' default, breach of duty.

The second stage

12.14 At the second stage, if the application is not dismissed under s 261(2), the court:

(a) may give directions as to the evidence to be provided by the company; and

(b) may adjourn the proceedings to enable the evidence to be obtained: CA 2006, s 261(3).

12.15 On hearing the application, the court may:

(a) give permission (or leave) to continue the claim on such terms as it thinks fit;

(b) refuse permission (or leave) and dismiss the claim; or

(c) adjourn the proceedings on the application and give such directions as it thinks fit: CA 2006, s 261(4).

This second stage no longer involves a consideration of a *prima facie* case. In *FanmailUK.com v Cooper* [2008] EWHC 2198 (Ch), [2008] BCC 877 Robert Englehart QC, sitting as a deputy judge, stated that on an application under CA 2006, s 261, it would be 'quite wrong … to embark on anything like a mini-trial of the action'. However, in *Iesini and Others v Westrip Holdings Ltd* [2011] 1 BCLC 498, Lewison J was of the opinion that the court also had to form a view on the strength of the claim in order properly to consider the requirements of CA 2006, ss 263(2)(a) and 263(3)(b). Any view could only be provisional where the action had yet to be tried; but the courts would have to make a decision based on the material before them. In *Iesini*, the proceedings were adjourned to allow a dispute as to the company's ownership to be resolved before proceeding to any derivative claim.

Although the claimant was required under CA 2006, s 261 to show a prima face case that the company has a cause of action, s 263 did not require any such test, but was based upon various factors for the court's consideration: *Hughes v Weiss* [2012] All ER (D) 197.

The court will have regard to all the factors under CA 2006, s 263, in deciding whether or not to grant permission to continue the claim as a derivative claim: *Kiani v Cooper* [2010] All ER (D) 97; *Stainer v Lee* [2011] 1 BCLC 537.

In considering whether derivative proceedings should be brought, the court will have regard to the interests of independent board members and any independent shareholders: *Airey v Cordell* [2006] All ER (D) 111.

Permission to continue the derivative action may be refused where conduct complained of was authorised or ratified by the company: *Re Singh Brothers Contractors (North West) Ltd; Singh v Singh* [2013] EWHC 2138.

12.16 The position of a shareholder in a public limited company bringing a derivative action on the company's behalf was considered in *Bridge v Daley* (17 June 2015). The shareholder complained of mismanagement by the directors in the conduct of the company's affairs. Hodge J (sitting as a High Court judge) held that it was 'extraordinary' for a shareholder of a public company to bring such derivative proceedings. He refused the shareholder permission.

Application for permission to continue claim as a derivative claim

12.17 In this section, the position of the derivative claim is considered from the company's perspective, where the company has brought a claim against a director or another person.

Claim by the company

12.18 CA 2006, s 262 applies where:

- a company has brought a claim; and
- the cause of action on which the claim is based could be pursued as a derivative claim under Part 11, Chapter 1: CA 2006, s 262(1).

Application by the member

12.19 A member of the company may apply to the court for permission to continue the claim as a derivative claim on the ground that:

- the manner in which the company commenced or continued the claim amounts to an abuse of the process of the court;
- the company has failed to prosecute the claim diligently; and
- it is appropriate for the member to continue the claim as a derivative claim: CA 2006, s 262(2).

There is no definition of 'diligently', but the court will apply the ordinary, natural meaning to refer to persevering and all relentless efforts being used to prosecute the claim. The company will need to demonstrate that it prosecuted the claim in such manner.

Possible court orders

12.20 If it appears to the court that the application and the evidence filed by the applicant in support of it do not disclose a *prima facie* case for giving permission, the court:

(a) must dismiss the application; and

(b) may make any consequential order it considers appropriate: CA 2006, s 262(3).

If the application is not dismissed under s 262(3), the court:

(a) may give directions as to the evidence to be provided by the company; and

(b) may adjourn the proceedings to enable the evidence to be obtained: CA 2006, s 262(4).

On hearing the application, the court may:

(a) give permission to continue the claim as a derivative claim on such terms as it thinks fit;

(b) refuse permission and dismiss the application; or

(c) adjourn the proceedings on the application and give such directions as it thinks fit.

Should permission be given?

12.21 In deciding whether to give permission to a shareholder to continue a claim as a derivative claim, the court is required to have regard to various factors in arriving at its decision. Section 263 is, therefore, key to understanding the factors involved, the importance that the court attaches to these factors, and the connection to ss 261 and 262. There is no threshold to be achieved under s 263. The court is not required to consider whether there is a strong or a weak case.

The court can dismiss any application under s 261 if it is satisfied under s 263(2)(a) that a director acting in accordance with s 172 (duty to promote the success of the company), would not seek to continue the claim: *Franbar Holdings Limited v Patel* [2009] 1 BCLC 1.

In determining whether to grant permission for a derivative claim under the CA 2006, the court was required to refuse permission under s 263(2)(a), if the relevant facts showed that a notional director, acting in accordance with his duty to promote the success of the company, would consider that it was not in the company's interest for the claim to proceed: *Mission Capital plc v Sinclair* [2010] 1 BCLC 304.

Further, taking account of other factors in CA 2006, s 263, if a hypothetical director, acting reasonably in the interests of its members, would decide not to continue with its derivative claim, the claim cannot then be pursued by the member: *Stimpson and Others v Southern Private Landlords Association* [2009] EWHC 2072 (Ch).

12.22 The following provisions apply where a member of a company applies for permission under s 261 or 262: CA 2006, s 263.

Under CA 2006, the court must refuse permission by a member to continue the claim as a derivative claim in three situations:

First, permission must be refused if the court is satisfied that a person acting in accordance with s 172 (duty to promote the success of the company) would not seek to continue the claim. This aspect is sometimes referred to as the 'hypothetical director'. The court will not consider what a reasonable director would have done in the circumstances, nor what the court would have considered that a director would have done in this regard. The court is required to have regard to the fact that a director of a company, must act in the way he considers, in good faith, would be most likely to promote the success of the company, for the benefit of its members as a whole, and in doing so have regard (amongst other matters) to:

(a) the likely consequences of any decision in the long term;

(b) the interests of the company's employees;

(c) the need to foster the company's business relationships with suppliers, customers and others;

(d) the impact of the company's operations on the community and the environment;

(e) the desirability of the company maintaining a reputation for high standards of business conduct; and

(f) the need to act fairly as between members of the company: CA 2006, s 172.

12.23 In *Iesini v Westrip Holdings Ltd* [2011] 1 BCLC 498, Lewison J interpreted CA 2006, s 263(2)(a), as meaning that no director would seek to pursue the claim. Section 263(2)(a) is one of the main duties of loyalty that a director owes to the company, to act in the best interests of the company.

However, a distinction arises in an application for breach of s 172 and an application under s 263(2)(a). Under s 172, provided the director has acted in good faith in promoting the long term interests of the company, the courts will not second-guess directors' decisions. However, under s 263(2)(a), the courts will be required to interfere and determine whether a person acting in accordance with s 172 would not seek to continue the claim. In *Iesini*, Lewison J considered that this was 'essentially a commercial decision, which the court is ill-equipped to take except in a clear case'. The decision required a consideration of various factors, including that the court must refuse permission to continue the claim as a derivative claim, if it is satisfied that the hypothetical director would not seek to continue the claim. In some cases, the courts have concluded that having regard to s 172, a hypothetical director would seek to continue a claim.

A hypothetical director may conclude on the facts and evidence that a claim could have been brought as a derivative claim: *Kiani v Cooper* [2010] 2 BCLC 427, where Proudman J stated that a notional director, having regard to s 172, would conclude that disclosure of documentation was required, and that there was a case to be tried, owing to strong evidence of breach of fiduciary duties.

12.24 However, in *Kleanthous v Paphitis* [2011] EWHC 2287 (Ch), Newey J was of the view that in the light of established authority, the court could potentially grant permission for a derivative claim to be continued, without being satisfied that there was a strong case. The merits of the claim would be relevant to whether permission should be given, but there was no set threshold.

In this case, there were arguable claims against the respondents. However, the chances of them succeeding were significantly less than even. The claims against the fourth respondent were particularly weak. Applying s 263(2)(a) of the Act therefore, permission to continue the claim would be refused on the basis that 'a person acting in accordance with section 172 … would not seek to continue the claim'.

Accordingly, the court refused permission for the derivative claim to continue.

12.25 In the Scottish case of *Wishart v Castlecroft Securities Ltd* [2009] CSIH 65, the court concluded, having regard to the factors in CA 2006, s 263(3), that the claim should continue. In so doing, the court attached particular importance to the factors in s 268(2)(b) and (f). Under s 268(2)(b), the court was required to take into account the importance that a person acting in accordance with s 172 would attach to raising the derivative proceedings. Several factors might be relevant in that regard, including the prospects of success of the proposed proceedings. Having regard to the authorities on the fiduciary duties of company directors and the accessory liabilities of third parties, and taking into consideration the affidavits and productions, the proposed derivative proceedings were arguable. It was not apparent that there were any substantial countervailing factors which would lead a director acting in accordance with s 172, to attach little or no importance to raising them. Under s 268(2)(f), the court must consider whether the cause of action was one which the member could pursue in his own right rather than on behalf of the company.

12.26 The issue of authorisation or ratification by the company is also important in the court deciding whether or not the claim should continue as a derivative claim. Neither the company nor the shareholder may subsequently query the act or omission, once it has been ratified or authorised by the company. Authorisation or ratification will be an absolute bar to the continuation of the derivative claim. The provision does not state who should authorise or ratify – the directors or the shareholders – but in practice this will be a matter for the company's articles of association or the shareholders. The effect of authorisation is that there is no further breach of duty, and ratification means that if any breach of duty existed, it has been cured. In law, shareholders cannot ratify illegal or *ultra vires* acts or acts that are in breach of the company's articles of association. The court will also have regard to the interests of disinterested shareholders in arriving at its decision.

Factors for consideration in deciding whether the derivative claim should proceed

12.27 In considering whether to give permission to continue the derivative claim, the court must take into account six factors, which are non-exhaustive, in particular:

(a) Whether the member is acting in good faith in seeking to continue the claim:

The shareholder has the burden of showing the court that he is acting in good faith in wishing to continue the derivative claim. Motive is therefore an important consideration. If the motive is tainted by malice or frivolous or vexatious litigation, then good faith cannot be shown. Also, where a shareholder has personal interests to be derived from the litigation.

The court will have regard to the bona fides of the shareholder bringing the derivative claim. In *Stainer v Lee* [2011] 1 BCLC 304, Roth J considered that the shareholder had acted in good faith, and indeed had support from 35 other shareholders in the company.

There must be a 'real purpose' in bringing the derivative action. Once there is a 'real purpose' in bringing the derivative claim, the courts may accept the need for continuation of such claim: *Mission Capital plc v Sinclair* [2010] 1 BCLC 537. On the facts, Floyd J refused the shareholder permission to continue the claim as a derivative claim, taking account of the factors.

The court considers the interests of the company as a whole rather than personal motives or interests of the shareholder, in determining whether to agree to the continuation of the derivative claim by the shareholder: *Franbar Holdings Ltd v Patel* [2009] 1 BCLC 1; *Parry v Bartlett* [2011] EWHC 3146 (Ch).

The derivative claim must be brought bona fide for the company's benefit. In *Barrett v Duckett* [1995] 1 BCLC 243, Peter Gibson LJ stated that a shareholder would be allowed to bring a derivative action on behalf of a company, where the action was brought bona fide for the benefit of the company for wrongs to the company, for which no other remedy was available, and not for an ulterior purpose. Conversely, if the action was brought for an ulterior purpose or if another adequate remedy was available, the court would not allow the derivative action to proceed. The conduct of the shareholder and motives will be considered by the court. This aspect was previously addressed in *Nurcombe v Nurcombe* [1984] BCLC 557 by Lawton LJ.

(b) The importance that a person acting in accordance with s 172 (duty to promote the success of the company) would attach to continuing the derivative claim

Under this heading, the court will consider the position from the hypothetical director's viewpoint, in the manner he considers will most likely promote the success of the company. In *Franbar Holdings Ltd v Patel* [2009] 1 BCLC 1, Judge William Trower stated that the hypothetical director acting in accordance with s 172, would take into account a wide range of considerations when assessing the importance of continuing the claim. These include such matters as:

- the prospects of success of the claim,
- the ability of the company to make a recovery on any award of damages,
- the disruption which would be caused to the development of the company's business by having to concentrate on the proceedings,
- the costs of the proceedings and
- any damage to the company's reputation and business if the proceedings were to fail. This includes any potential claim for relief under s 994.

• The court may also consider the views of independent non-executive directors, as to whether or not a derivative claim should proceed: *Kleanthous v Paphitis* [2011] EWHC 2287 (Ch).

(c) Where the cause of action results from an act or omission that is yet to occur, whether the act or omission could be, and in the circumstances would be likely to be: authorised by the company before it occurs, or ratified by the company after it occurs.

The acts or omissions may include matters such as negligence, default, breach of duty or breach of trust. The court has the power to adjourn proceedings to allow for any ratification of the act or omission. The ratification will usually be by the shareholders at a general meeting. The issue is whether the effect of ratification is to improperly prevent the claimant from bringing a derivative claim on behalf of the company: see *Smith v Croft (No 2)* [1987] 3 All ER 909. The issue of authorisation may be given by board members who are not involved in the cause of action.

(d) Where the cause of action arises from an act or omission that has already occurred, whether the act or omission could be, and in the circumstances would be likely to be, ratified by the company:

The court will have regard to all applicable facts in determining whether ratification would be possible. This is not necessarily a bar to bringing the claim as a derivative claim, but only one of the factors for the court's consideration.

(e) Whether the company has decided not to pursue the claim:

This decision could be taken by either the directors or the shareholders. In this situation, they decide not to bring proceedings against the director, concerned but they do not ratify or authorise the act in question. If no decision has been taken, then the court could adjourn the proceedings for the company to decide whether or not to pursue the claim. In *Kleanthous v Paphitis* [2011] EWHC 2287, the fact that the board of directors had established a committee, which had resolved not to pursue any claim, was influential for the court in refusing the shareholder leave to continue the claim as a derivative claim.

(f) Whether the act or omission in respect of which the claim is brought gives rise to a cause of action that the member could pursue in his own right rather than on behalf of the company: CA 2006, s 263(3):

Under the heading, the court considers whether there is any possible action which a shareholder can bring in his own right, rather than as a derivative action, which arises from the same act or omission. In such circumstances, the shareholder may be able to bring a claim for unfair prejudicial conduct by those in control of the company. Although a shareholder may pursue the claim as a derivative claim, because the costs and expenses will be met by the company, the courts have shown reluctance to grant the shareholder damages owing to the reflective loss principle considered at 12.43.

In *Franbar Holdings Ltd v Patel* [2009] 1 BCLC 1, Judge William Trower was of the view that the cause of action should arise out of the same act or omission; where that act or omission gives rise to both a claim for unfair prejudice against a member, and a claim for breach of duty against a director, s 263(3)(f) is engaged. The adequacy of the remedy available to the member in his own right is, however, a matter which will go into the balance when assessing the weight of this consideration on the facts of the case. The judge decided that Franbar could pursue all its claims under s 994 as well as breach of the shareholders' agreement.

See too Proudman J in *Kiani v Cooper* [2010] 2 BCLC 427.

In some of the cases before the courts, where the shareholder is seeking leave to continue with the derivative claim, the courts have refused permission to continue with such claim where in effect, the shareholder is seeking a petitioner's relief for unfair prejudicial conduct under CA 2006, s 994.

In *Mission Capital plc v Sinclair* [2010] 1 BCLC 304, Floyd J decided that the appropriate action for the Sinclair was to seek to petition for unfair prejudicial conduct under CA 2006, s 994. He refused permission for the shareholders to continue with the claim as a derivative claim.

In *Kleanthous v Paphitis* [2011] EWHC 2287, Newey J refused to grant the shareholder permission to continue the claim as a derivative claim, on the basis that the shareholder could pursue an action under s 994 CA 2006, including the fact that much of the monies recovered from the respondents would be returned to them by way of a distribution.

12.28 There may be valid reasons for the shareholder not to pursue an action under s 994. First, the shareholder would have to show unfair prejudicial conduct in the affairs of the company, which affects the shareholder or some group of the shareholders. Second, the shareholder may not wish to be bought out and leave the company, as one of the remedies is for the shareholder's shares to be purchased by the company. Third, the shareholder may wish to continue in such capacity with the company for long-term gains to be made by the company. The shareholder therefore may not find pursuing a claim under s 994 an attractive one. The shareholder therefore tries to pursue a derivative claim in the hope of seeking some redress for the company, without the need to exit from the company.

12.29 In some circumstances, the derivative claim may be more beneficial than a claim for unfair prejudicial conduct: *Wishart v Castlecroft Securities Ltd* [2009] CSIH 615, where the Scottish Court considered whether an alternative remedy may be suitable having regard to s 263(3). The case concerned a diversion of corporate opportunity by a company director. The Court stated that proceedings under s 994 would however constitute, at best, an indirect means of achieving, what could be achieved directly by derivative proceedings. Further, the complainant's case was not that the company's affairs have been mismanaged. The relief the complainant sought was to have the company restored to the position in which it ought to be, by an order for restitution or damages; not that he should be bought out. In that regard, the Court noted that an order requiring him to be bought out at the time, when the commercial property market was depressed, would not be an attractive remedy. The order sought in the proposed derivative proceedings, that the properties in question be declared to be held upon a constructive trust for the company, would in reality be a more valuable remedy, since the claimant could then benefit from any rise in the value of his shareholding over the longer term, consequent upon a recovery in the market. Furthermore, any inquiry into whether there had been mismanagement, or into the price at which the claimant should be bought out, would require the court to establish the truth or otherwise of the claimant's allegations. The Court also noted that the company did not appear to be deadlocked, and that it continued to trade. In these circumstances, the availability of an alternative remedy under s 994 did not appear be a compelling consideration.

The possibility of winding up

12.30 In some cases, the courts have considered whether the winding up of the company may be the most appropriate outcome, rather than proceed by way of a derivative claim. The language under s 263(3) refers to a 'cause of action', and while such a term may not be appropriate for a shareholder to bring an action in his own right, it may be a relevant circumstance that the court may consider, in deciding whether or not to continue with the derivative proceedings.

In some circumstances, winding up a company may be the most preferred option. In *Langley Ward Ltd v Trevor* [2011] All ER (D) 78, the company was a quasi-partnership and was ultimately in a deadlock position, including having completed all its projects. Judge David Donaldson QC decided that the company was a natural candidate to be wound up on a just and equitable ground by either of the shareholders (see too *Re Yenidje Tobacco Co Ltd* [1916] 2 Ch 426; *Re Worldhams Park Golf Course Ltd, Whidbourne v Troth* [1998] 1 BCLC 554 at 556). Accordingly, the court proceeded on the basis that the company would almost certainly go into winding up by one route or another. It was therefore appropriate to consider the comparative merits of leaving all or some of the disputes to be dealt with by a liquidator, rather than by litigation in a derivative action, and factor those into the overall decision which the court had to reach under s 263 as regards each of the claims.

12.31 The list set out in s 263(3) is not exhaustive. Although it must have regard 'in particular' to the factors set out, the court may consider other aspects that may be relevant to a decision on whether or not a shareholder may continue with the derivative claim. This aspect incorporates one strand of the rule in *Foss v Harbottle*, that where independent shareholders do not wish to bring proceedings, then the courts would take this into account in deciding the derivative claim: *Smith v Croft (No 2)* [1988] Ch 114. The following additional aspects have been considered by the courts:

(1) **Costs and expenses of continuing the derivative claim**. In *Iesini v Westrip Holdings Limited* [2011] 1 BCLC 498, Lewison J considered that the potential liability for costs was a relevant consideration.

(2) **The interests of the company's employees**. In *Stimpson v Southern Private Landlords Association* [2010] BCC 387, Judge Pelling QC considered that the position of the remaining employees in the company remained bleak, and that this was a matter which the court should take into account: 'The significance of a point such as this is very fact sensitive, but it is nonetheless one that is relevant

here at least when considering whether to give permission because s 263(3) is not exhaustive and here a relatively small number of employees are at risk …'

(3) **Any monies recovered from the defendants would ultimately be returned to them by way of a distribution as they were the company's majority shareholders**: *Kleanthous v Paphitis* [2011] EWHC 2287 where the principal director/shareholder held 72% of the company's shares.

(4) **The court may also have regard to the merits of the claim**: *Wishart v Castlecroft Securities Limited* [2009] CSIH 615; and *Kleanthous v Paphitis* [2011] EWHC 2287.

In considering whether to give permission, the court must have particular regard to any evidence before it as to the views of members of the company who have no personal interest, direct or indirect, in the matter: CA 2006, s 263(4).

In this regard, the court will consider the views of disinterested shareholders as to whether the derivative action should be continued. In *Steiner v Lee* [2011] 1 BCLC 537, Roth J considered the interests of independent shareholders as important to the derivative claim proceedings.

The difficulty in practice is to identify who are the disinterested shareholders 'who have no personal interest, direct or indirect, in the matter' and then to ascertain how their views are to be obtained. According to Lewison J in *Iesini v Westrip Holdings Ltd* [2011] 1 BCLC 498, disinterested shareholders will be those who do not have a financial interest in the outcome, beyond their interests as shareholders in the company.

12.32 Once the court takes account of the views of disinterested members, the court thereafter has the power to grant permission for the continuation of the derivative claim. The court has, in some cases, had regard to costs that may be incurred of proceeding with the derivative claim: see **12.33**. In other cases, the courts have granted permission to a shareholder to continue with the derivative claim on a limited basis only, such as disclosure of certain documentation that would provide a clearer picture of the merits of the case: *Steiner v Lee* [2011] 1 BCLC 537; and *Kiani v Cooper* [2010] 2 BCLC 427; *Smith v Croft (No 3)* [1987] BCLC 355.

The court also has power to refuse permission or to adjourn proceedings and give such directions as it thinks fit.

'Wrongdoer control' of a company is not an absolute preclusive condition for bringing a derivative claim: *Bamford v Harvey* [2012] EWHC 2858 (Ch); [2012] WLR (D) 298. See too: *In Cinematic Finance Ltd v Ryder and Others* [2010] EWHC 3387 (Ch).

The issue of costs in derivative proceedings

12.33 Where the court hears a derivative claim, it may make an indemnity order requiring the company to indemnify the claimants for costs incurred in bringing the proceedings. Part 11 of the CA 2006 makes no reference to the issue of costs in respect of derivative claims. However, under 'Practice Direction 19C – Derivative Claims', if the claimant seeks an order that the defendant company or other body concerned indemnify the claimant against liability for costs incurred in the permission application or the claim, this should be stated in the permission application or claim form or both, as the case requires: para 2(2).

This may be a matter to which the court will have regard particularly taking account of the expenses involved, and whether the expense involved would justify continuation of the claim. It may also be an issue for the shareholder who may not have the financial means to commence litigation.

In *Wallersteiner v Moir (No 2)* [1975] 1 All ER 849, the Court of Appeal stated that it was open to the court in a minority shareholder's action, to order that the company should indemnify the claimant against the costs incurred in the action. Where the wrongdoers themselves controlled the company, a minority shareholder's action brought to obtain redress, whether brought in the claimant's own name or on behalf of himself and the other minority shareholders, and even though brought without the company's authority, was, in substance, a representative action on behalf of the company, to obtain redress for the wrongs done to the company. Accordingly, provided that it was reasonable and prudent in the company's interest for the claimant to bring the action, and it was brought by him in good faith, it was a proper exercise of judicial discretion or in accordance with the principles of equity, that the court should order the company to pay the claimant's costs down to judgment whether the action succeeded or not.

12.34 Normally a shareholder should be indemnified for his costs in bringing a derivative claim. In *Stainer v Lee* [2011] 1 BCLC 537, Roth J agreed with the principle set out in *Wallersteiner v Moir (No 2),* that a shareholder who received the sanction of the court to proceed with a derivative action, should normally be indemnified as to his reasonable costs by the company for the benefit of which the action would accrue. However, where the amount of likely recovery was presently uncertain, there was concern that his costs could become disproportionate. Accordingly, Roth J placed a ceiling on the costs for which he granted an indemnity for the future (ie excluding the costs of the present application) at £40,000 (exclusive of VAT). There would be liberty to apply to extend the scope of that indemnity.

12.35 The claimant to derivative proceedings should also accept the rise of costs in such claims. In *Kiani v Cooper* [2010] 2 BCLC 427, Proudman J was of the view that the claimant should also take part of the risks of costs associated with the derivative claim. While Proudman J was prepared to make an order that the claimant's costs should be borne by the company, he was not prepared to grant her an indemnity in respect of any adverse costs order: 'It seems to me that [the claimant] should be required to assume part of the risk of the litigation.'

12.36 In *Carlisle & Cumbria United Independent Supporters' Society Ltd v CUFC Holdings Ltd* [2010] All ER (D) 25 (May), the derivative claim had already been settled, and the case before the Court of Appeal concerned the claimant's costs of the proceedings, and whether he was entitled to claim these from the company. Arden LJ spoke of 'an expectation of [the Claimant] receiving its proper costs from the Companies on an indemnity basis if the action had gone forward'. The defendant director in question argued that he should be indemnified by the company for his costs in bringing the derivative claim, pursuant to the company's articles of association which provided that a director had a right of indemnity for acts done in the course of acting as a director. The Court of Appeal rejected the director's contention. According to Arden LJ, the provision in the articles of association was limited to expenditure reasonably and properly incurred by the director, and did not extend to costs in pursuing the derivative claim.

The possibility of bringing multiple derivative claims and claims against overseas companies

12.37 One issue that has not been addressed under Part 11, is whether there is scope for bringing multiple derivative claims under the CA 2006 where, for example, a parent company brings proceedings in respect of wrongs done to a subsidiary company. Multiple derivative actions have their origins under the common law.

12.38 Multiple derivative actions may be brought under common law by a parent company which was a member of its subsidiary. In *Waddington Ltd v Chan Chun Hoo Thomas* [2009] 2 BCLC 82, the Hong Kong Court of Final Appeal held that a shareholder could maintain a multiple derivative action at common law on behalf of a subsidiary of the company of which he was a member, since any depletion of the subsidiary's assets caused indirect loss to its parent company and its shareholders, which gave him a legitimate interest in the relief claimed, sufficient to justify him in bringing proceedings to recover the loss. Accordingly, where a wrongdoer defrauded a subsidiary or sub-subsidiary of a parent company, and his control of the parent company precluded an action by the subsidiary, in which the cause of action was vested, a shareholder in the parent company could bring a multiple derivative action against him.

See too *Renova Resources Private Equity Ltd v Gilbertson* [2009] CILR 268.

12.39 Part 11 of CA 2006 does not specify whether or not multiple derivative claims could be brought. In *Universal Project Management Services Ltd v Fort Gilkicker Ltd* [2013] Ch 551, it was held that the shareholder would be granted permission for the proceedings to continue. According to Briggs J, the derivative action was a procedural device designed by the common law to enable justice to be done, where the wrongdoer was in control of the entity in which the cause of action was vested. The device was a single piece of procedural ingenuity, which did not distinguish between ordinary, multiple or double derivative actions, and was sufficiently flexible to accommodate as the legal champion or representative of a company in wrongdoer control a would-be claimant who was either (and usually) a member of that company or (exceptionally) a member of its parent company, where that parent company was in the same wrongdoer control.

Briggs J stated that CA 2006, s 260, which had replaced the ordinary derivative action by a member of the allegedly wronged company, with the statutory derivative claim provided in Ch 1 of Pt 11 of that Act, had not abolished the whole of the common law derivative action, in relation to companies, and had left other instances of the application of the procedural device unaffected. Therefore, the common law multiple derivative action remained available as a means of dealing with wrongs done to the company. The precise nature of the corporate body which owned the wronged company's shares was of no legal relevance, provided that it was itself in wrongdoer control and had some members who were interested in seeing the wrong done to the company put right. Further, the second defendant's status as an equal owner of the LLP and as one of the only two directors of the first defendant, meant that there was wrongdoer control, that, accordingly, the court would grant permission for the continuation of the multiple derivative action, but that, in all the circumstances, the proceedings would be temporarily stayed for negotiations to take place.

Briggs J further held that the provisions of CA 2006, Pt 11 did not apply to double derivative actions, and had not implicitly or otherwise abolished the common law jurisdiction of the courts to entertain such actions.

See too *Halle v Trax BW Ltd* [2000] BCC 1020; *Trumann Investment Group v Societe Generale SA* [2002] EWHC 2621; and *Airey v Cordell* [2007] Bus LR 391; *Abouraya v Sigmund* [2014] EWHC 277 (Ch).

In *Bhullar v Bhullar* [2015] All ER (D) 130 (Jul), Morgan J held that it was settled law that the common law did provide for the possibility of a double (or multiple) derivative claim, and that the court's jurisdiction in that respect had not been taken away by ss 260 to 264 of the 2006 Act. Accordingly, applying settled law, the court had jurisdiction to permit a double derivative claim.

12.40 Another aspect for consideration is whether a derivative claim may be brought against overseas companies. However, s 1 excludes overseas companies from the definition of 'company'. It may be argued that although s 260(2) merely sets out the procedure for derivative claims that fall within s 260, it has not abolished the ability to bring derivative proceedings at common law against such companies.

Application for permission to continue derivative claim brought by another member

12.41 The CA 2006 also addresses a situation where an application for permission to continue a derivative claim which is brought by another shareholder. Section 264 applies where a member of a company ('the claimant'):

(a) has brought a derivative claim;

(b) has continued as a derivative claim a claim brought by the company; or

(c) has continued a derivative claim under this section: CA 2006, s 264(1).

Another member of the company ('the applicant') may apply to the court for permission to continue the claim on the ground that:

(a) the manner in which the proceedings have been commenced or continued by the claimant amounts to an abuse of the process of the court;

(b) the claimant has failed to prosecute the claim diligently; and

(c) it is appropriate for the applicant to continue the claim as a derivative claim: CA 2006, s 264(2).

12.42 If it appears to the court that the application and the evidence filed by the applicant in support of it do not disclose a *prima facie* case for giving permission (or leave), the court:

(a) must dismiss the application; and

(b) may make any consequential order it considers appropriate: CA 2006, s 264(3).

If the application is not dismissed under s 264(3), the court:

(a) may give directions as to the evidence to be provided by the company; and

(b) may adjourn the proceedings to enable the evidence to be obtained: CA 2006, s 264(4).

On hearing the application, the court may:

(a) give permission (or leave) to continue the claim on such terms as it thinks fit;

(b) refuse permission (or leave) and dismiss the application; or

(c) adjourn the proceedings on the application and give such directions as it thinks fit: CA 2006, s 264(5).

The reflective loss principle

12.43 In connection with derivative proceedings, on occasions the courts have also addressed the 'reflective loss' principle. In corporate terms, this applies where the losses of individual shareholders are inseparable from the general losses of the company (eg where a company suffers a loss owing to a breach of duty owed to it by a director). It arises where the company and the shareholder may have rights against the director arising from the same set of facts and circumstances. The 'reflective principle' is based on the concept that the losses suffered by the company, should also be reflected in the losses suffered by the shareholder.

It is based on the premise that a shareholder may also have suffered loss in terms of a diminution in the value of his shareholding as a result of the loss suffered by the company. Accordingly, the shareholder's loss is reflected in that of the company's loss. A company may bring proceedings against the wrongdoer to recover its loss. However, the legal issue has been whether a shareholder can also bring proceedings for any loss it may have suffered, owing to the breach of duty by the wrongdoer, as well as a breach of duty to the shareholder.

12.44 Where a shareholder only suffers a diminution in value of his shares, owing to losses suffered by the company, this is a wrong to the company preventing the shareholder from claiming any losses and bringing a personal action against the wrongdoer. In *Prudential Assurance Co Ltd v Newman Industries Limited (No 2)* [1982] 1 All ER 354, the Court of Appeal stated:

> '… It is also correct that, if directors convene a meeting on the basis of a fraudulent circular, a shareholder will have a right of action to recover any loss which he has been personally caused in consequence of the fraudulent circular; this might include the expense of attending the meeting. But what he cannot do is to recover damages merely because the company in which he is interested has suffered damage. He cannot recover a sum equal to the diminution in the market value of his shares, or equal to the likely diminution in dividend, because such a 'loss' is merely a reflection of the loss suffered by the company. The shareholder does not suffer any personal loss. His only 'loss' is through the company, in the diminution in the value of the net assets of the company.

Accordingly, the shareholder could not claim for any reflective loss.

Where the *Prudential* rule applies, the shareholder's claim against the wrongdoer is excluded, even if the company does not pursue its own right of action. The rationale is that the shareholder does not suffer a loss which is recognised in law as having an existence distinct from the company's loss. Therefore, such a claim by the shareholder is barred by the rule in *Foss v Harbottle* (1843) 2 Hare 461. See too *Edwards v Halliwell* [1950] 2 All ER 1064. The *Prudential* rule has no application to losses suffered by a shareholder which are distinct from the company's loss, or to situations where the company has no cause of action.

12.45 The courts are also of the view that as the director's act or omission is a wrong done to the company, only the company can properly recover for losses. In *Stein v Blake* [1998] 1 All ER 724, the Court of Appeal followed the *Prudential* case, and held that the loss sustained by a shareholder by a diminution in the value of his shares by reason of the misappropriation of the company's assets, was a loss recoverable only by the company and not by the shareholder, who had suffered no loss distinct from that suffered by the company. Accordingly, in this case only the companies concerned, and not the claimant, could bring an action for recovery of the loss.

12.46 Generally, a shareholder cannot recover a loss that is reflective of the company's loss. Until *Sevilleja v Marex Financial Limited* [2020] 2 AC 1, the leading case on the 'no reflective loss' principle was *Johnson v Gore Wood & Co* [2001] 1 BCLC 313. In that case, the House of Lords held that it was necessary to scrutinise the pleadings closely in order to ascertain whether the loss claimed appeared to be or was one which would be made good if the company had enforced its full rights against the party responsible; and whether the loss claimed was merely a reflection of the loss suffered by the company. Any reasonable doubt would have to be resolved in favour of the claimant. In carrying out that exercise, as in determining at trial whether the shareholder's claim should be upheld on the facts, the court was required, on the one hand, to respect the principle of company autonomy, ensure that the company's creditors were not prejudiced by the action of individual shareholders, and ensure that a party did not recover compensation for a loss which another party had suffered. On the other hand, the court had to be astute to ensure that the party who had in fact suffered loss was not arbitrarily denied fair compensation.

In the *Johnson* case, the claim for the diminution in the value of J's pension and majority shareholding in the company, was merely a reflection of the company's loss, and would therefore be struck out, in so far as it related to payments which the company would have made into a pension fund for J. However, that claim was not objectionable in principle in so far as it related to enhancement in the value of J's pension, if the payments had been duly made. As regards the other heads of claim, the claim for aggravated damages failed on the pleaded facts, while the claim for mental distress and anxiety (Lord Cooke dissenting) fell foul of the principle that damages for such loss were not generally recoverable in respect of a breach of contract.

Lord Bingham (which judgment was approved in the *Sevilleja* case but not approving Lord Millett's judgment) stated the following principles derived from cases addressing the no-reflective loss principle:

(1) Where a company suffers loss caused by a breach of duty owed to it, only the company may sue in respect of that loss. No action lies at the suit of a shareholder suing in that capacity and no other to make good a diminution in the value of the shareholder's shareholding where that merely reflects the loss suffered by the company. A claim will not lie by a shareholder to make good a loss which would be made good if the company's assets were replenished through action against the party responsible for the loss, even if the company, acting through its constitutional organs, has declined or failed to make good that loss. So much is clear from *Prudential Assurance Co Ltd v Newman Industries Ltd (No 2)* [1982] 1 All ER 354 at 366–367, [1982] Ch 204 at 222–223; *Heron International Ltd v Lord Grade* [1983] BCLC 244 at 261–262, *Fischer (George) (GB) Ltd* v *Multi-Construction Ltd* [1995] 1 BCLC 260 at 266 and 270–271, *Gerber Garment Technology Inc v Lectra Systems Ltd* [1997] RPC 443;and *Stein v Blake* [1998] 1 All ER 724 esp at 726–729.

(2) Where a company suffers loss but has no cause of action to sue to recover that loss, the shareholder in the company may sue in respect of it (if the shareholder has a cause of action to do so), even though the loss is a diminution in the value

of the shareholding. This is supported by *Lee v Sheard* [1955] 3 All ER 777 at 778, [1956] 1 QB 192 at 195–196, the *Fischer* case and the *Gerber* case.

(3) Where a company suffers loss caused by a breach of duty to it, and a shareholder suffers a loss separate and distinct from that suffered by the company caused by breach of a duty independently owed to the shareholder, each may sue to recover the loss caused to it by breach of the duty owed to it but neither may recover loss caused to the other by breach of the duty owed to that other. I take this to be the effect of *Lee v Sheard* [1955] 3 All ER 777 at 778, [1956] 1 QB 192 at 195–196; *Heron International Ltd v Lord Grade* [1983] BCLC 244 at 262; *Howard (RP) Ltd & Richard Alan Witchell v Woodman Matthews and Co (a firm)* [1983] BCLC 117 at 123, the *Gerber* case and *Stein v Blake* [1998] 1 All ER 724 at 726.

12.47 The rationale behind the rule against recovery of reflective loss is that there should be no double recovery, so a shareholder can only bring a derivative action for losses of the company, and may not allege she has suffered a loss in her personal capacity for a personal right. To this extent, the rights of the shareholder are subservient to those of the company. The objective is that the defendant should not have to compensate twice for the same loss. However, the reflective loss principle may apply where the company cannot for some reason enforce its claim or its claim is weak against the defendant, but that the shareholder may have a good claim and seek compensation for losses sustained.

12.48 The leading case on the reflective loss principle is the Supreme Court decision in *Sevilleja v Marex Financial Limited* [2020] UKSC 31. Mr Sevilleja ('S'), owned and controlled two companies ('the Companies') incorporated in the British Virgin Islands ("BVI"). Marex Financial Ltd ('Marex'), brought proceedings against the Companies for sums due under a contract. At first instance, Field J gave judgment for Marex for over US$5.5 million, including costs of £1.65 million. Subsequently in July 2013, S allegedly procured the offshore transfer of over US$9.5 million from the Companies' London accounts into his personal control. By the end of August 2013, the Companies' assets were just US$4,329.48, such that Marex could not receive payment of its judgment debt and costs.

In December 2013, S placed the Companies into liquidation in the BVI, their alleged debts exceeding US$30 million. Marex was the only creditor not connected to S. According to Marex, the liquidation process was effectively on hold, with the liquidator failing to investigate claims submitted to him, to locate Marex's missing funds, or to issue proceedings against S.

Marex now sought damages from S in tort for: (1) inducing or procuring the violation of its rights under Field J's judgment and orders; and (2) intentionally causing it to suffer loss by unlawful means. The sums claimed were: (1) the judgment debt, interest and costs awarded by Field J, less an amount Marex recovered in the US proceedings; and (2) costs incurred by Marex in its attempts to obtain payment. S contended that Marex's claim in respect of (1) was barred by the 'reflective loss' principle. That contention was upheld by the Court of Appeal.

The Supreme Court unanimously allowed Marex's appeal. The leading judgment was given by Lord Reed who examined the decisions giving rise to the 'reflective loss' principle including *Prudential* and *Johnson* and subsequent cases. Lord Reed decided that *Prudential* laid down a rule of company law: a diminution in the value of a shareholding or in distributions to shareholders, which was merely the result of a loss suffered by the company in consequence of a wrong done to it by the defendant, was not in the eyes of the law damage which was separate and distinct from the damage suffered by the company, and was therefore not recoverable. This rule was based on *Foss v Harbottle* (1843) 2 Hare 461, which would be subverted if the shareholder could pursue a personal action in those circumstances. That understanding of the rule was consistent with the judgment of Lord Bingham in *Johnson*. Lord Millett's speech, however, treated the 'reflective loss' principle as a wider principle of the law of damages, based on the avoidance of double recovery. Lord Reed reviewed subsequent cases in which the 'reflective loss' principle as explained by Lord Millett had developed, including *Giles v Rhind* [2002] EWCA Civ 1428, *Perry v Day* [2004] EWHC 3372 (Ch), and *Gardner v Parker* [2004] EWCA Civ 781 [6877]. This examination made clear the need to distinguish

> '(1) cases where claims are brought by a shareholder in respect of loss which he has suffered in that capacity, in the form of a diminution in share value or in distributions, which is the consequence of loss sustained by the company, in respect of which the company has a cause of action against the same wrongdoer, and (2) cases where claims are brought, whether by a shareholder or by anyone else, in respect of loss which does not fall within that description, but where the company has a right of action in respect of substantially the same loss'.

The first kind of case was barred by the rule in *Prudential*, regardless of whether the company recovers its loss in full. In the second kind of case, recovery was permissible in principle, although it may be necessary to avoid double recovery.

Accordingly, Lord Reed decided that the reasoning in *Johnson* (other than that of Lord Bingham) should be departed from, and that *Giles*, *Perry* and *Gardner* were wrongly decided. The rule in *Prudential* did not therefore apply to Marex, which was a creditor of the Companies, not a shareholder.

In *Broadcasting Investment Group Ltd v Smith* [2021] EWCA Civ 912, the Court of Appeal considered the reflective loss principle, in which the claimant shareholder alleged breach of contract by the defendant. The shareholder claimed for diminution in value of shares caused by actionable loss to the company. The Court of Appeal held that reflective loss principle will not bar a shareholder's claim, who is also a contractual promisee or beneficiary, in circumstances where the company in which the shares are owned, has acquired the right to bring a claim in respect of the same contract against the same wrongdoer under s.1 of the Contracts (Rights of Third Parties) Act 1999.

12.49 The Privy Council ('Board') in *Primeo Fund v Bank of Bermuda (Cayman) Ltd (Cayman Islands)* [2021] UKPC 22, restated the reflective loss principle, ie that the rule falls to be assessed as at the point in time when a claimant suffers loss, and not at the time proceedings are brought. According to the Board, a shareholder suffering a loss in the form of a diminution in value of its shareholding, which was not recoverable under the reflective loss rule, could not subsequently convert that loss into one which was recoverable by selling its shareholding. It stated that to find otherwise would lead to very 'odd results'. The Board stated that the reflective loss rule applied in relation to claims against a person who was a 'common wrongdoer', in the sense that they have by their action or omission, committed wrongs both against the claimant who is a shareholder in a company, and against the company itself. It is important to note that the reflective loss rule is, as was made clear in the majority judgments in *Marex*, a rule of substantive law associated with the rule in *Foss v Harbottle* and concerned with the recognition in law of particular types of loss. It is not a procedural rule concerned only with the avoidance of double recovery. Applied as a substantive rule of law, whether the reflective loss rule is applicable or not, falls to be assessed as at the point in time when the claimant suffers loss arising from some relevant breach of obligation by the relevant wrongdoer. The Board further stated that the decision of Flaux LJ in *Nectrus Ltd v UCP Plc* [2021] EWCA Civ 57 was wrong (the reflective loss principle falls to be assessed at the point of time the claim is made). Although not binding in English law, the influential panel sitting on the Board and their decision, will have a significant impact on future reflective loss cases on assessment of the reflective loss principle.

Checklist: derivative actions at common law

12.50 *This checklist sets out the position of derivative actions at common law and the situations when such actions may be brought. It should be noted that much of the common law on derivative actions has been replaced by the statutory derivative claim under CA 2006; and remnants of the common law principles may apply, for example, to 'multiple derivative actions' at common law*

No	*Issue*	*Reference*
1	Traditionally, the courts were reluctant to interfere in the company's internal management decisions – directors were best placed to decide corporate matters	*Burland v Earle* [1902] AC 83
2	Where a wrong is allegedly done to a company, the proper claimant in legal proceedings is the company	*Foss v Harbottle* (1843) 2 Hare 461
3	Where a majority decide on a particular transaction, this will bind the minority	*Foss v Harbottle* (1843) 2 Hare 461
4	The nature of the derivative action brought by a member must enable the company to enforce rights against the wrongdoers and claim remedies for the benefit of the company	
5	The company must establish a *prima facie* case that: the company is entitled to the relief claimed; and the action falls within the proper boundaries of the rule restricting members' actions on behalf of the company	*Prudential Assurance Co Limited Co Limited v Newman Industries Ltd (No 2)* [1982] 1 All ER 354
6	Exceptions to the rule in *Foss v Harbottle* allowing the claimant to bring an action include: ● fraud on the minority ● misuse or abuse of power	*Edwards v Halliwell [1950]* 2 All ER 1064 *Estmanco (Kilner House) Ltd v Greater London Council* [1982] 1 All ER 437
7	The court will take account of the views of independent shareholders as to whether or not the derivative action should proceed	*Smith v Croft (No 2)* [1987] 3 All ER 909
8	The common law position on multiple derivative actions has not been replaced by the CA 2006 and the common law principles will therefore apply The court will take account of the conduct of the claimant in bringing the action on behalf of the company	*Waddington Ltd v Chan Chun Hoo Thomas* [2005] 2 BCLC 8 *Universal Project Management Services Ltd v Fort Gilkicker Ltd* [2013] Ch 551 *Abouraya v Sigmund* [2014] EWHC 277 (Ch) *Nurcombe v Nurcombe* [1984] BCLC 557

9	In respect of the 'reflective loss' principle, the rule in *Prudential* was limited to claims by shareholders that, as a result of actionable loss suffered by their company, the value of their shares, or of the distributions they received as shareholders, had been diminished. Other claims, whether by shareholders or anyone else, should be dealt with in the ordinary way	*Sevilleja v Marex Financial Limited* [2020] UKSC 31

Checklist: practice and procedure of statutory derivative claims

12.51 *This checklist sets out the practice and procedure for commencing a derivative claim under CA 2006, Pt 11, Ch 1. It is essentially based on the CPR Rules.*

No	Issue	Reference
1	Only a member of a company may bring proceedings by way of a derivative claim	CA 2006, s 260(4) CA 2006, s 260(3)
2	There must be a 'cause of action'	
3	The cause of action must arise from actual or proposed act or omission involving: ● Negligence ● Default ● Breach of duty ● Breach of trust ● By a director or another person	CA 2006, s 260(3)
4	A claimant member completes a Claim Form headed 'Derivative Claim'	Practice Direction 19C para 2(1)
5	The company (including the director or another person) must be made a defendant to the claim	CPR 19.9(2)
6	Claimant must also file with the Claim Form: Application notice under Part 23 CPR for permission to continue the claim; and The written evidence on which the claimant relies in support of the permission application	CPR 19.9A(2)
7	The claimant must not make the company a respondent to the permission application	CPR 19.9A(3)
8	Claimant must notify the company of the claim and permission application by sending to the company as soon as reasonably practicable after the claim form is issued: ● A notice in the form set out in PD 19C ● Attach a copy of the provisions of the CA 2006 required by that form ● The application notice ● Copy of evidence filed by the claimant in support of the permission application	CPR 19.9A(4)
9	Claimant must thereafter send the notice and documents to the company under Part 6 CPR by way of service on the company	CPR 19.9A(5)
10	Claimant must file a witness statement confirming that claimant has notified the company	CPR 19.9A(6)

11	After issuance of the claim, the claimant must not take any further step in the proceedings without the court's permission other than: • A step permitted or required by rule 19.9A or 19.9C; or • Making an urgent application for interim relief	CPR 19.9 r (4)
12	At the first stage, the claimant must establish a *prima facie* case for application to continue the derivative claim	CA 2006, s 261(2)
13	The company's attendance will not be required at this hearing – but the court may take account of any voluntary submissions by the company of any evidence of documents	PD 19C r 5
14	Where an application is made to the High Court, it will be assigned to the Chancery Division and decided by a High Court judge	PD 19C r 6(1)
15	If the application is made to the county court, it will be decided by a circuit judge	PD 19C r 6(2)
16	At the second stage, if the application is not dismissed, the court will proceed to give directions on the evidence to be obtained by the company	CA 2006, s 261(4)
17	As an alternative to the s 261 derivative claim, the CA 2006 sets out a procedure for an application by a member to continue a claim as a derivative claim and the factors to which the courts will have regard in arriving at its decision	CA 2006, ss 262, 263

13 Unfair prejudicial conduct

Introduction

13.1

This Chapter addresses the following issues:

- the grounds for petitioning to the court.
- what constitutes 'unfair prejudicial conduct'?
- who may petition to the court? and
- the possible statutory orders that the court may make.

Petition by company member for unfair prejudice

13.2 CA 2006, Pt 30 sets out an important and frequently used remedy for a shareholder, who may be aggrieved about the functioning and operation of the company's affairs. A member of a company may apply to the court by petition for an order on either of two grounds:

(a) that the company's affairs are being or have been conducted in a manner that is unfairly prejudicial to the interests of members generally or of some part of its members (including at least himself); or

(b) that an actual or proposed act or omission of the company (including an act or omission on its behalf) is or would be so prejudicial: CA 2006, s 994(1).

13.3 Typically, it is the minority shareholder who will present the petition before the court for unfair prejudicial conduct. The issue usually arises where there is a deadlock situation, and one shareholder wishes to leave the company; or where the shareholder believed that he had a legitimate expectation to participate in the company's management, but has been so excluded from participation; or the shareholder may wish to exit from the company and disputes arise over valuation of the shares and at what price the exiting shareholder will obtain for the sale shares. Many disputes are usually settled where a fair offer is made for the shares to enable the shareholder to exit the company, without the need to proceed towards a hearing of the petition, or proceedings may be stayed if the parties are minded to reach an amicable settlement.

In other circumstances, the position of settlement of disputes may be governed by the shareholders' agreement, setting out the dispute settlement mechanism which may be by way of arbitration or reference to an expert. An issue has arisen before the courts as to whether parties to a dispute can contract out of the statutory right to petition for unfair prejudicial conduct under s 994. Disputes between shareholders may be the subject of arbitration proceedings. In *Fulham Football Club (1987) Ltd v Richards*

[2012] 1 All ER 414, the Court of Appeal held that disputes between shareholders can be subject to arbitration reference. Patten LJ stated that the statutory provisions about unfair prejudice contained in s 994, gave to a shareholder an optional right to invoke the assistance of the court in cases of unfair prejudice.

Shareholders considering entering into shareholders' agreements should consider retaining the right to petition to the court for unfair prejudicial conduct.

Who can petition?

13.4 Section 994 provides that only a "member" of the company may petition to the court –known as the petitioner. A person may only petition to the court in his capacity as a member of the company, and not in any other capacity: *Arrow Nominees Inc v Blackledge* [2000] 2 BCLC 167.

However, the provisions of Part 30 also apply to a person who is not a member of a company, but to whom shares in the company have been transferred or transmitted by operation of law: CA 2006, s 994(2): *Re a Company (No 007828 of 1985)* (1986) 2 BCCC 98951. An agreement to transfer or transmit is not sufficient. The transferor must execute a proper instrument of transfer and have this delivered to the transferee: *Re a Company (No 003160 of 1986)* (1986) BCLC 99276. A person must have proper standing to bring a petition under s 994. A blank transfer form is insufficient: see Mervyn J in *Re Quickdome Ltd* [1988] BCLC 370.

13.5 A petition may also be brought by a trustee in bankruptcy or a personal representative of the member: *Re McCarthy Surfacing Ltd* [2006] All ER 193. A person may still be able to petition despite the fact that the directors refused to register the petitioner's shares.

A nominee shareholder may also petition under s 994: *Atlasview Ltd v Brightview Ltd* [2004] 2 BCLC 191.

It is also possible for a petitioner to bring proceedings under s 994, where the company is insolvent: *Gamlestaden Fastigheter AB v Baltic Partners Ltd* [2008] 1 BCLC 468. Section 994 did not prevent the court from granting a remedy, even though there may be no financial benefit to the petitioner.

13.6 Although in most cases, the petitioner will be a minority shareholder, there is nothing to prevent a majority or controlling shareholder from bringing an action under s 994. However, in such situations, it may be difficult for the controlling shareholder to show that the affairs of the company were unfairly prejudicial, as the majority shareholder may elect to use his voting power to control the company's affairs: *Re Legal Costs Negotiators Limited* [1999] 2 BCLC 171. See too *Parkinson v Eurofinance Group Ltd* [2001] 1 BCLC 720.

In *Macom GmbH v Bozeat* [2021] EWHC 1661 (Ch), the court was required to consider whether a majority shareholder could bring proceedings for unfair prejudicial conduct under CA 2006. The petitioner held 60% shareholding and alleged breaches of directors' duties, and failure to observe the shareholders' agreement, and undermining the company's corporate governance system. The court accepted that a majority shareholder could petition under s 994 CA 2006. Further, that "prejudice" was not limited to cases where there was an actual, or potential, diminution in the value of the petitioner's shareholding. Rather, it may extend to a breakdown of the relationship of trust and confidence amongst the shareholders, as a result of the respondent's conduct of the company's affairs and failures of good administration. The court granted an order regulating the company's future affairs.

13.7 The courts may sometimes refuse to grant the petitioner standing to bring proceedings or order relief for the petitioner, on the ground of the petitioner's conduct in bringing the proceedings. In *Grace v Biagioli* [2006] 2 BCLC 70, a minority shareholder was removed from office as a director. However, he had been secretly negotiating to buy out a potential competitor. One issue before the court was whether the majority directors entitled to dismiss the minority director from office. It was held by the Court of Appeal that the appellant's conduct in attempting to negotiate the purchase of a potential competitor, which would have placed him in a position of conflict with his duties as a director, and his willingness to embark on such negotiations, without any prior disclosure or discussion with his fellow directors and shareholders, and his subsequent attempts to conceal his actions, all justified his dismissal as a director. See too *Richardson v Blackmore* [2006] All ER 345.

In *Re London School of Electronics Ltd* [1985] 2 BCLC 273, Nourse J held that s 994 empowered the court to grant such relief as it thought fit, provided that it was satisfied that the company's affairs were being, or had been, conducted in a manner unfairly prejudicial to the interests of some part of the members. Further, although the conduct of the petitioner could affect the relief which the court thought fit to grant under s 994, there was no independent or overriding requirement that it should be just and equitable to grant relief, or that the petitioner should come to court with clean hands. See too *R A Noble & Sons (Clothing) Ltd* [1983] BCLC 273.

13.8 Section 994 also refers to the conduct of the company's affairs that will be the subject of the petition. A dispute between shareholders, for example a shareholder not selling his shares in the company, was not conduct in connection with the company's affairs: *Re Legal Costs Negotiators Limited* [1999] 2 BCLC 171. Alternatively, the minority shareholder action can relate to another ground for the petition, namely, an actual or proposed act or omission of the company (including an act or omission on its behalf).

The scope of s 994 is wide to include the company's controllers, namely directors or shareholders, or both. It also includes the control of a subsidiary by its parent company, and the conduct of the subsidiary's business may be treated as that of its parent company. The 'affairs of a company' may include those of its subsidiary: *Gross v Rackind* [2005] 1 WLR 3505. See too *Re Dominion International Group (No 2)* [1996] 1 BCLC 572. The nature of control exercised by a parent over its subsidiary in such a way, may amount to unfair prejudicial conduct: *Nicholas v Soundcraft Electronics Ltd* [1993] BCLC 360 (on the facts however no unfair prejudice in the conduct of the company's affairs was proved). See too *Scottish Co-operative Wholesale Society Ltd v Meyer* [1959] AC 324.

On occasions, the courts have stated that the term 'affairs of the company' should be liberally interpreted: it could extend to matters which were capable of coming before the board for its consideration, and are not restricted merely to those that have actually been presented before the board: *Hawkes v Cuddy* [2009] 2 BCLC 427.

In *Oak Investment Partners XII v Broughtwood* [2010] 2 BCLC 459, mismanagement of the affairs of a company and conduct by one party to a quasi-partnership arrangement in respect of a jointly owned company that caused an irrevocable breakdown in the relationship of trust and confidence inherent in the arrangement were both capable of being unfairly prejudicial conduct.

13.9 The court will not entertain a petition by the petitioner when the conduct complained of has not materialised: *Re Astec (BSR) plc* [1998] 2 BCLC 556 (the mere voicing of dissentient views by a minority on the board could not found a petition under s 994).

What are the interests of the members?

13.10 Section 994(1) states that the conduct must be unfairly prejudicial to the 'interests of members generally or of some part of its members…'There is no statutory definition of 'interests'. The interests must however be in connection with the company's affairs, and not personal or other interests of the shareholder: *Gamlestaden Fastigheter AB v Batlic Partners Ltd* [2008] 1 BCLC 468.

The interests must apply to the members in their capacity as shareholders and not any other interest: *Re A Company (No 00314 of 1989), ex parte Estate Acquisition & Development Limited* [1991] BCLC 154, where Mummery J was of the view that s 994 applied to conduct which was unfairly prejudicial to the interests of the member qua member. It did not extend to conduct which was prejudicial to other interests of persons, who happened to be members of the company (see *Re a company* [1983] BCLC 126 at 135; and *Re a company (No 00477 of 1986)* [1986] BCLC 376 at 378).

13.11 The category as to what constitutes the interests of the members is not closed: but it is wide. In *O'Neill v Phillips* [1999] 2 BCLC 1, Lord Hoffmann stated that 'the requirement that prejudice must be suffered as a member should not be too narrowly or technically construed'. See too *Shepherd v Williamson* [2010] All ER 142.

In some circumstances the courts have been willing to grant the petitioner relief, where the petitioner could show that there was some close connection between the member's interests and those of the company, for example, where the shareholder is also a creditor of the company: *R & H Electrical Limited v Haden Bill Electrical Limited* [1995] 2 BCLC 280; see too Richards J in *Re Woven Rugs Limited* [2010] All ER 41.

What constitutes 'unfairly prejudicial'?

13.12 The conduct complained of must be 'unfairly prejudicial'. There is no statutory definition of this term, and much falls on case law to consider circumstances constituting unfairly prejudicial. Many of the cases on unfair prejudicial conduct have been concerned with small companies, where management is in the hands of a few key officers. These companies are similar to 'quasi-partnerships', because apart from their articles of association, their management functions and operations are sometimes governed by loose arrangements, and informal agreements on the management of a company's affairs. These 'informal' agreements or arrangements may be verbal or arising through conduct through a course of dealings. These can also give rise to some expectations on the part of the shareholder for his participation in the company. Issues tend to arise when such expectations are not met or disputed by the other party, which creates a conflict as to what exactly was agreed between the parties including their understanding.

The aspect of expectations may arise at the moment that the company is formed or it may arise subsequently: *Tay Bok Choon v Tahanson Sdn Bhd* [1987] 1 WLR 413; *Strahan v Wilcock* [2006] 2 BCLC 555.

If a company's board of directors make a bona fide decision not to effect a reduction of capital but to retain it within the company, the fact that this financially affects a shareholder does not mean that it is necessarily unfairly prejudicial: *Re a Company* [1986] BCC 990.

'Unfairly prejudicial' are flexible terms to meet various circumstances that could be faced by a petitioner: *Re Saul D Harrison and Sons plc* [1995] 1 BCLC 14. According to Neill LJ, the conduct must be both prejudicial (in the sense of causing prejudice or harm to the relevant interest), and also unfairly so: conduct may be unfair without being prejudicial or prejudicial without being unfair, and it is not sufficient if the conduct satisfies only one of these tests. In construing the word 'unfairly' in this context, account must be taken not only of the legal rights of the petitioner, but also whether there are any equitable considerations, such as the petitioner's legitimate expectations to be weighed in the balance. According to Neill LJ, in order to establish unfairness, it was not enough to show that some managerial decision may have prejudiced the petitioner's interest. A shareholder on joining a company, will be deemed to have accepted the risk that in the wider interests of the company decisions may be taken which will prejudice his own interests. It may be necessary for the directors to take steps which are prejudicial to some of the members, in order to secure the future prosperity of the company or even its survival: cf *Nicholas v Soundcraft Electronics Ltd* [1993] BCLC 360 at 372 per Ralph Gibson LJ. Although it was open to the court to find that serious mismanagement of a company's business constituted conduct that was unfairly prejudicial to the interests of the shareholders, the court would normally be very reluctant to accept that some managerial decisions could amount to unfairly prejudicial conduct: see *Re Elgindata Ltd* [1991] BCLC 959 at 993.

13.13 The test for determining unfairness is objective. According to Hoffmann LJ in *Saul*, in deciding what is fair or unfair for the purposes of s 994, it was important to bear in mind that fairness is being used in the context of a 'commercial relationship'. The articles of association are the contractual terms governing the relationships of the shareholders with the company, and each other. They determine the powers of the board and the company in general meeting, and everyone who becomes a member of a company is taken to have agreed to them. Since keeping promises and honouring agreements is probably the most important element of commercial fairness, the starting point in any case under s 994, will be to ask whether the conduct of which the shareholder complains, was in accordance with the articles of association. The powers which the shareholders have entrusted to the board are fiduciary powers, which must be exercised for the benefit of the company as a whole. If the board act for some ulterior purpose, they step outside the terms of the bargain between the shareholders and the company. As a matter of ordinary company law, this may or may not entitle the individual shareholder to a remedy.

Trivial or technical infringements of the articles were not intended to give rise to petitions under s 994. Hoffmann LJ, in *Saul*, stated that the very minimum required to make out a case of unfairness, was that the powers of management have been used for an unlawful purpose, or the articles otherwise infringed.

CA 2006, s 994 requires the petitioner to show both prejudice and unfairness: *Re Sunrise Radio Limited, Kohli v Lit* [2010] 1 BCLC 367. Prejudice will most often be established by reference to conduct having a depressive effect (actual or threatened) on the value of the petitioner's shareholding, which will in most cases be a minority holding, typically in a private company with restrictions on transfer.

Unfairness, in turn, is most often connoted some breach of the articles, statute, or general principles of company law. However, the operation of s.994 CA 2006 is not necessarily limited to such cases. The test is objective. There may be mutual understandings between shareholders giving rise to special rights of a quasi-partnership kind. Even without that, the conduct of the company's directors may, whether by reason of malevolence, crass stupidity, or something in between, fall so far short of the standards to be expected of them, as to lead to the conclusion that the petitioning shareholder cannot reasonably be expected to have the minimum of trust and confidence in the integrity or basic competence of the board, that any shareholder is entitled ordinarily to expect.

13.14 A member may be able to rely on equitable considerations might make it unfair for those conducting the affairs of the company, to rely on their strict legal powers. In the leading case of *O'Neill v Phillips* [1999] 2 BCLC 1, the House of Lords considered what constituted unfair prejudicial conduct, and decided that for the purposes of s 994, although a member of a company would not ordinarily be entitled to complain of unfairness, unless there had been some breach of the terms on which he had agreed that the company's affairs should be conducted, equitable considerations might make it unfair for those conducting the affairs of the company to rely on their strict legal powers. This would apply where the exercise of the power in question would conflict with the promises the parties had exchanged, and it was not necessary that such promises should be independently enforceable as a matter of contract. A promise may be binding as a matter of justice and equity, although for one reason or another (eg because in favour of a third party) it would not be enforceable in law.

According to Lord Hoffmann, unfairness may only be shown in either of the following two situations:

(a) a breach of agreed terms between the parties on how the company should be conducted; or

(b) establishing a complaint by reference to equitable considerations.

Lord Hoffmann rejected the test of 'legitimate expectations' as inappropriate to unfairness. This previously applied where a shareholder considered that he had a legitimate expectation

13.15 In some situations, the exercise of legal rights may be subject to equitable considerations of a personal character, that is, of a personal character arising between one individual and another. This may make it unjust, or inequitable, to insist on legal rights, or to exercise them in a particular way: *Ebrahimi v Westbourne Galleries Limited* [1972] 2 All ER 492.

13.16 A quasi-partnership relationship depends upon mutual trust and confidence, which if breached, would result in equitable considerations being taken into account, to determine unfairness. The parties in such circumstances may not have recorded the terms of their agreement in writing, as to how the affairs of the company should be conducted – instead relying upon the understandings of the parties within the company. A breach of mutual trust and confidence in a quasi-partnership may lead to unfair prejudicial conduct: *Re Astec (BSR) plc* [1998] 2 BCLC 556.

13.17 The understanding of the parties may not necessarily be in written form, but rather through promises or by conduct, usually connected with participation within the company. These aspects are likely to be taken into account by the courts in addressing equitable considerations. In *Strahan v Wilcock* [2006] 2 BCLC 555, Arden LJ stated that, in determining what equitable obligations arose between the parties, the court must look at all the circumstances, including the company's constitution, any written agreement between the shareholders and the conduct of the parties.

13.18 There are some cases where inability to participate in the company's management has been held to be unfairly prejudicial conduct: *Brownlow v G H Marshall Limited* [2000] 2 BCLC 655. See too *Apex Global Management Ltd v FI Call Ltd* [2015] EWHC 3269 (Ch).

In *Wootliff v Rushton-Turner (No 2)* [2018] 1 BCLC 479, the court held that in order to establish that the company was a quasi-partnership, in which equitable considerations made it unjust for the respondent to insist on their legal rights under the articles of association, or to exercise them by dismissing the petitioner, the petitioner had to show that he had a personal relationship with the respondents, involving mutual trust and confidence, in which equitable considerations which overlay the articles, gave him a legitimate expectation that he would not be dismissed. On the facts, however, the relationship between the parties was solely commercial, rather than an association formed on the basis of a personal relationship involving mutual trust and confidence. See too *Rembert v Daniel* [2018] 2 BCLC 156; *Waldron v Waldron* [2019] EWHC 115 (Ch); *Yusuf v Yusuf* [2019] EWHC 90 (Ch); *Toppin v Toppin* [2019] EWHC 46 (Ch); and *Re Edwardian Group Ltd; Estera Trust (Jersey) Ltd v Singh* [2019] 1 BCLC 171.

Case law examples of successful claims for unfair prejudicial conduct

13.19

Case	**Nature of conduct**
Grace v Biagioli [2006] 2 BCLC 70	Failure to pay dividend once declared.
Lloyd v Casey [2002] 1 BCLC 454	Director engaging in transactions for his personal gain to the company's detriment.
Irvine v Irvine (No 1) [2007] 1 BCLC 349	Director awarding himself excessive remuneration without board or shareholder approval to the minority shareholder's detriment as less dividends received.
Re Woven Rugs Limited [2010] All ER 41	A refinancing of the company resulted in benefit to the majority shareholders to the detriment of minority shareholders.
Re Little Olympian Each-Ways Ltd (No 3) [1995] 1 BCLC 636	Director transferring the company's assets to another company at an undervalue. The assets were subsequently sold to a third party for a gain.
Re Brenfield Squash Racquets Club Limited [1996] 2 BCLC 184	Company's assets were used to secure the debts of the majority shareholders.
Re McCarthy Surfacing Limited, Hequet v McCarthy [2009] 1 BCLC 622	A bonus agreement prevented minority shareholders from receiving dividends on a project.
Allmark v Burnham [2006] 2 BCLC 437	Majority shareholders establishing a business in competition with company to the minority shareholder's detriment.

13.20 According to CA 2006, for the purposes of s 994(1)(a), a removal of the company's auditor from office on grounds of divergence of opinions on accounting treatments or audit procedures; or on any other improper grounds, will be treated as being unfairly prejudicial to the interests of some part of the company's members: CA 2006, s 994(1A) (as inserted by the Statutory Auditors and Third Country Auditors Regulations 2007, SI 2007/3494, reg 42).

Powers of the court under Part 30

13.21 Section 996 sets out important remedies for a shareholder, once it has been demonstrated that there has been unfair prejudicial conduct under s 994. If the court is satisfied that a petition under Part 30 is well founded, it may make such order as it thinks fit for giving relief in respect of the matters complained of: CA 2006, s 996(1). The remedial orders are not granted by the court as of right and are discretionary, but the orders are wide-ranging. According to Patten J in *Grace v Biagioli* [2006] 2 BCLC 70, the court is 'entitled to look at the realities and practicalities of the overall situation, past, present and future'. The nature of the court's powers could include other remedies such as damages: *Gamlestaden Fastigheter AB v Baltic Partners Limited* [2008] 1 BCLC 468.

At times, the courts have also considered granting interim orders: *Pringle v Callard* [2008] 2 BCLC 505.

13.22 The courts may make the following orders:

- regulate the conduct of the company's affairs in the future (eg see *Re Harmer* [1958] 3 All ER 689, where the court ordered the father to be removed as chairman of the company, to allow his sons to participate in the company's management. The father was considered dictatorial, and refused to entertain any interference in the company's management by his sons);
- require the company:
  - to refrain from doing or continuing an act complained of, or
  - to do an act that the petitioner has complained it has omitted to do;
- authorise civil proceedings to be brought in the name and on behalf of the company by such person or persons and on such terms as the court may direct;
- require the company not to make any, or any specified, alterations in its articles without the leave of the court; and
- provide for the purchase of the shares of any members of the company by other members or by the company itself and, in the case of a purchase by the company itself, the reduction of the company's capital accordingly: CA 2006, s 996(2).

The remedy of purchase of shares is one of most common orders sought by many petitioners petitioning under s 994. There is a preference for a detachment from the company, so that the petitioner is brought out, and the company continues with the management of its business.

In some cases, the court may order a 'clean break' from participation in the company's management: *Petition of (1) Thomas Orr and (2) James Orr Petitioner for orders under section 996 of the Companies Act 2006 in respect of D S Orr & Sons (Holdings) Limited and DS Orr & Sons Limited* [2013] CSOH 116.

The court may also have regard to the long-term interests of the company in granting an appropriate remedy: *Grace v Biagioli* [2006] 2 BCLC 70, where buying out the petitioner was most applicable in the circumstances. It allowed the shareholder to finally exit from the company, and preserve the interests of existing shareholders for the future, by removing any other claims or difficulties in the future. See too *Re Coloursource Limited, Dalby v Bodilly* [2005] BCC 627.

13.23 Some issues can arise in relation to the valuation of shares where the court has ordered a buyout of the petitioner's shares.

Certain principles should be applied in the valuation of the exiting minority's shares. The starting point on valuation of shares is set out in *Re Bird Precision Bellows Limited* (1985) 1 BCC 99467. Bird Precision Bellows Ltd ('Company') was incorporated in 1975. The petitioners, who held 26% of the issued share capital of the company, alleged that the company was a quasi-partnership and that from the date of its incorporation there was an agreement or understanding that they would participate in the conduct of the company's affairs. This was challenged by the respondents, who held the remaining 74% of the company's issued share capital. The petitioners were removed from office as directors and wrongfully excluded from the company's business. The petitioners presented a petition under s 994 alleging that the affairs of the company had been conducted in a manner unfairly prejudicial to their interests as members and sought an order under s 996 that the respondents purchase their shares. At the first hearing of the petition before Vinelott J, it was ordered by agreement that the respondents purchase the shares of the petitioners 'at such a price as the court shall hereafter determine'. The petition came before Nourse J for determination of the price.

Nourse J established the following principles on valuation of shares, which was affirmed by the Court of Appeal (1985) 1 BCC 9467:

1. The price should be fixed pro rata according to the value of the shares as a whole, without any discount to reflect the fact that the shares constituted a minority holding.

2. The price fixed by the court under s 996 at which shares were to be purchased should be fair.

3. Although general guidelines could be given as to what constituted a fair price in cases of common occurrence, the issue could not, however, be conclusively determined until the facts in a particular case had been examined. There was no rule of universal application either that the price of a minority shareholding in a small private company should be fixed on a pro rata basis according to the value of the shares as a whole or, alternatively, that the price should be discounted to reflect the fact that the shares were a minority holding. Where the sale was being forced on the holder because of the unfairly prejudicial manner in which the affairs of the company were being conducted by the majority, and the shares to be valued had been acquired on the incorporation of a quasi-partnership company and it was thus expected that the holder would participate in the conduct of the company's affairs, as a general rule it was only fair that the price should be fixed pro rata without any discount. That general rule applied not only where there had been unfairly prejudicial conduct on the part of the majority but also where, as in the present case, there had been an agreement for the price to be determined by the court without any admission as to such conduct. Equally, as a general rule, if the order was for the purchase of the shares of a delinquent majority, the price should not contain a premium to reflect their

majority control. However, in the exceptional case where a shareholder had so acted as to deserve his exclusion, the price could be appropriately discounted since he could be treated as if he had elected to sell his shares, and such a sale would be at a discount.

On the facts, the company was a quasi-partnership since it had been set up on the understanding that the petitioners would participate in the conduct of its affairs and, although their conduct was not beyond reproach, they had not in the circumstances acted so as to deserve their exclusion. Accordingly, it was appropriate that the price to be paid for their shares should be fixed on a pro rata basis, without any discount to reflect the fact that the shares constituted a minority holding.

Since the agreement between the parties that the shares be purchased at a fair value to be determined by the court, did not contain any provision that the price should bear interest from some date prior to its determination, or that the petitioners should receive damages for the loss of the use of the purchase moneys, there was no basis for the award of interest before judgment.

Where shares in a quasi-partnership company had been acquired at a price which was discounted because they were a minority holding and the purchaser had acquired them as an investment, without any intention of participating in the company's affairs, it might well be fair that the shares should be bought out on the same basis where an order for their purchase is made under CA 2006 s 996.

13.24 Some of the cases tend to be in connection with quasi-management partnerships, where the courts have stated the valuation must be on a *pro rata* basis. Some established bases for valuation of the shares could be applied where a minority shareholder was to be bought out. In *CVC/Opportunity Equity Partners Ltd v Denarco Almeida* [2002] 2 BCLC 108, the Privy Council stated that the valuation should be based as a sale of the total business to a third party interested in purchasing the shares. According to Lord Millett, there were essentially three possible bases on which a minority holding of shares in an unquoted company could be valued. In descending order, these were: (i) as a rateable proportion of the total value of the company as a going concern without any discount for the fact that the holding in question is a minority holding; (ii) as before but with such a discount; and (iii) as a rateable proportion of the net assets of the company at their break up or liquidation value. Which of these should be adopted as the appropriate basis of valuation depended on all the circumstances. The choice must be fair to both parties. Further it was difficult to see any justification for adopting the break up or liquidation basis of valuation, where the purchaser intended to continue to carry on the business of the company as a going concern. This would give the purchaser a windfall at the expense of the seller.

According to Lord Millett, if the going concern value was adopted, a further question arose: whether a discount should be applied to reflect the fact that the holding was a minority one. An outsider would normally be unwilling to pay a significant price for a minority holding in a private company, and a fair price as between a willing seller and a willing purchaser might be expected to reflect this fact. It would seem to be unreasonable for the seller to demand a higher price from an unwilling purchaser than he could obtain from a willing one. Small private companies commonly had articles which restricted the transfer of shares by requiring a shareholder who was desirous of disposing of his shares to offer them first to the other shareholders at a price fixed by the company's auditors. It was the common practice of auditors in such circumstances to value the shares as between a willing seller and a willing buyer and to apply a substantial discount to reflect the fact that the shares represent a minority holding.

A non-discount basis of valuation of shares may be applied to an exiting minority shareholder where the company is a quasi-partnership: *Strahan v Wilcox* [2006] 2 BCLC 555.

The court has to fix a price for the shares that is fair in all the circumstances for the exiting and existing shareholders: *Attwood v Maidment* [2013] 2 BCLC 46.

13.25 If the company is not a quasi-partnership, the courts will value the minority shareholder's shares on a discounted basis, because the minority shareholder held the shares as an investment in the company. In *Irvine v Irvine (No 2)* [2007] 1 BCLC 445, the issue was whether the valuation should be on a *pro rata* basis or at a discount. Blackburn J held that a minority shareholding was to be valued as such (namely as a minority interest in the company), unless some good reason existed to attribute to it a *pro rata* share of the overall value of the company. Short of a quasi-partnership or some other exceptional circumstance, there was no reason to accord to it a quality which it lacked. In this case, there were no circumstances which could be described as exceptional. Accordingly, the minority shareholding should be valued on a discounted basis. See too *Strahan v Wilcock* [2006] 2 BCLC 555.

13.26 However, in *Re Sunrise Radio Ltd, Kohli v Lit* [2010] 1 BCLC 367, even though the company was not a quasi-partnership, the court ordered the valuation of the shares on a *pro rata* valuation basis. HHJ Purle QC stated that there was no rule of universal application excluding an undiscounted valuation, where there was no quasi-partnership. The court had a very wide discretion to do what was considered fair and equitable in all the circumstances of the case, in order to put right and cure for the future the unfair prejudice, which the petitioner had suffered at the hands of the other shareholders of the company.

13.27 An issue which has arisen in some cases is the effect of an unfair prejudicial petition of an earlier offer by the majority to purchase the minority shareholding of a petitioner. In *O'Neill v Philllips* [1999] 1 WLR 1092, Lord Hoffmann held that there had been no unfair prejudicial conduct in that case. He considered *obiter* the effect of the offer by Mr Phillips to buy the shares at a fair price. The offer had been made to Mr O'Neill when the petition proceedings had already been underway for almost three years. The offer was to buy the shares at a price to be agreed or in default of agreement to be fixed by a chartered accountant as a valuer, on a non-discounted basis. Lord Hoffmann decided that Mr O'Neill had been entitled to reject the offer, because it did not include his legal costs. He encouraged parties where at all possible for the majority, to make an offer to buy the shares which was plainly reasonable so that if the minority rejected it, the majority could apply to strike out the petition subsequently lodged. According to Lord Hoffmann, 'unfairness' did not lie in the exclusion from management alone but 'in exclusion without a reasonable offer'. In the course of his judgment, Lord Hoffmann set out the features of a 'reasonable offer'. The first is that it must be to purchase the shares at a fair value. That will normally be a valuation without a minority discount. Although there may be special circumstances in which it is fair to take a discounted value, it will seldom be possible for the court to strike out a petition based on such an offer. The value, if not agreed, should be determined by a competent expert acting as an expert consistent with the objective of economy and expedition 'even if this carries the possibility of a rough edge for one side or the other'. The offer should also provide for equality of arms between the parties in the sense that both parties should have access to information about the company which bears upon the value of the shares and both should have the right to make submissions to the expert.

Where the offer is made after a long period of litigation it should include an offer of costs, although the majority shareholder should be given a reasonable opportunity to make the offer, including time to explore the question of how to raise finance, before he becomes obliged to pay the petitioner's legal costs as part of the offer. See too *Harborne Road Nominees Ltd v Karvasaki* [2011] EWHC 2214 (Ch).

In *Prescott v Potamianos* [2019] EWCA Civ 932, the Court of Appeal stated that the terms of any offer made by the majority to purchase the petitioner's shares, the circumstances in which the offer was made, and the reasons why it was rejected, are one aspect of the overall consideration by the court of whether an unfair prejudice petition should succeed. The Court of Appeal endorsed the view of Arden LJ in *Maidment v Atwood: Re Tobian Properties Ltd* [2012] EWCA Civ 998, that the dominant characteristic of the unfair prejudice remedy was its adaptability, enabling the courts to produce a just remedy, where minority shareholders can show wrongdoing that prejudices their interests. The case law in this area has consistently declined to introduce 'bright lines' and the assessment of an offer to purchase was no exception to this flexible approach.

The Court of Appeal in *Prescott v Potamianos* set out a non-exhaustive list of the factors relevant to the court's assessment of the reasonableness of the offer, and the petitioner's rejection of it. It emphasised that there was no one feature of an offer that would make it automatically either reasonable or unreasonable. The non-exhaustive list is as follows:

- First, the value offered or the means proposed for arriving at that value will, of course, be important. An offer inviting the petitioner to join in the appointment of a mutually acceptable independent expert who will be given full access to relevant company documents and whose decision on the value will be binding on the parties is more likely to be a fair offer than a fixed figure presented on a 'take it or leave it' basis. But the offer of a fixed figure is not necessarily unfair. For example, if the fixed figure is based on recent approaches by third-party buyers for the whole of the company's share capital, then a court may find that a pro-rata valuation of the petitioner's holding was a fair valuation. Similarly, if the parties agree between themselves a method for valuing the shares and the offer is presented with a full and transparent explanation to the petitioner of how the figure has been arrived at, again a fixed figure may well be fair: see too *CVC/Opportunity Equity Partners Ltd and another v Demarco Almeida* [2002] 2 BCLC 108.

- The ability of the petitioner to be able to satisfy himself that the figure offered is reasonable before he has to decide whether to accept or reject the offer is an important factor. Any offer is likely to be made at a time when the relationship of trust and confidence between the quasi-partners has already come under strain. Suspicion and mutual recrimination may already characterise their relationship. When considering the fairness of a fixed figure, the point is not only whether it may ultimately be shown to have been a fair reflection of the value of the shares from the majority shareholder's perspective but whether that fact was reasonably apparent to the petitioner at the time the offer was made. A fixed price offer will rarely be fair if the minority shareholder or his advisers are not provided with access to company documents necessary to see how the price has been arrived at and to determine whether it is a reasonable valuation. Similarly, an offer to instruct an independent expert will not be reasonable if the majority is not prepared to open the company's books to that expert.

- The fairness of the value may also be linked with the substance of the unfair prejudice allegations. HHJ Cooke noted in *Harborne* at paragraph 31 that where the minority shareholder alleges that the majority have diverted business from the company or misapplied company assets, it may not be just to expect the minority shareholder to accept an expert valuation for his shares without an authoritative determination of the claim. This was also an important factor in *Re Woven Rugs Ltd* [2010] EWHC 230 (Ch). In that case, David Richards J (as he then was) held that some of the offers made to buy the minority's shares were made after the majority had procured two transactions which were alleged by the petitioner to have been detrimental to the company and which were part of the unfairly prejudicial conduct alleged: see paragraph 168. Any offers based on assessing the value of the company as diminished by those transactions could not be considered reasonable. In our view, disputes between the parties over matters which materially affect the valuation of the company may be relevant to the reasonableness of an offer even where ultimately the court decides the dispute against the minority shareholder. It may be unreasonable to expect the petitioner to accept an expert valuation based on an assumption that those disputes will or might be decided in a particular way.

- The second factor, after price or value, is the likelihood of the majority shareholder being able to implement the offer made. The Court of Appeal did not accept the view put forward by the petitioner that an offer is only reasonable if it can become binding immediately upon the petitioner's acceptance. However, the reasonableness of the offer and the petitioner's response to it may be affected by how likely it appeared at the time that the majority shareholder would follow through. In *Re Flex Associates Ltd* [2009] EWHC 3690 (Ch) the majority made an offer, expressed to be made pursuant to the guidelines in *O'Neill v Phillips*, to purchase the shares at fair value to be determined by an independent expert. That offer was expressed to be 'subject to affordability'. David Donaldson QC (sitting as a Deputy High Court Judge) found that there had been no unfairly prejudicial conduct but went on to consider the relevance of the offers if he had otherwise been persuaded to grant the petition. He said that the fact that it was conditional upon affordability meant that the defendants 'would have no obligation to buy at all, let alone at the price fixed by the expert': see paragraph 74. The offer would not have entitled the defendants to have the petition struck out and would not have provided a defence to a claim based on exclusion, had that claim otherwise been sound. See too *West v Blanchet* [2000] 1 BCLC 795 per Peter Leaver QC.

- A third factor is the proximity of the offer to the unfairly prejudicial conduct complained of. One of the offers relied on by the defendant in *Re Woven Rugs* to defeat the petition had been made some years before the unfairly prejudicial conduct. David Richards J stated that 'it cannot be relied on as a remedy for conduct yet to occur'. He commented that the defendant in that case 'appears to think that such an offer gives him carte blanche to behave in future as he wishes': paragraph 166. The Court of Appeal did not accept the view that there is a strict principle that an offer cannot render subsequent prejudicial conduct fair if it would otherwise be unfair. However, the timing of the offer may well be significant, depending on the nature of the prejudicial conduct alleged. Where the prejudicial conduct amounts to the exclusion of a quasi-partner from the management of the company, the question for the court is whether the offer made to purchase his shares means that the petitioner cannot then complain about that exclusion. That will depend on whether, at the time the offer was made, all the petitioner could reasonably expect was that he should be bought out so that he and his former business partners could go their separate ways. Where an offer is made before the relationship has broken down, the petitioner may act reasonably in refusing the offer if, for example, he still harbours a legitimate hope that the business can be got back on track and the quasi-partners can find a way of working together for the future. Similarly, his refusal may be reasonable if there is a prospect that the business can be sold to a third party for a sum larger than the value he is being offered. The acceptance of the offer amounts to the acceptance by the petitioner that he must walk away from a business that has been his full-time occupation and in which he has usually invested years of effort and skill. The fact that, with hindsight, the quasi-partners were unable to resolve their differences and the price he was being offered was fair, does not mean that an offer made before this in fact became apparent should have been accepted by the petitioner.

13.28 There may be circumstances where the petitioner seeks an order for the respondent to purchase his shares. In this situation, the issue arises whether the respondent has the financial means to purchase the petitioner's shares; or whether the court may invoke an 'escape clause', and order another remedy under CA 2006, s 996.

The court will not, however, include an 'escape clause' in considering the appropriate remedy to be granted under CA 2006, s 996: *Re Cumana Ltd* [1986] BCLC 430. According to Lawton LJ, the fact that a wrongdoer was impecunious, was no reason why judgment should not be given against him for the amount of compensation due to his victim. See too *Scottish Co-operative Wholesale Society Ltd v Meyer* [1958] 3 All ER 66 at 89, [1959] AC 324 at 369, per Lord Denning. Nicholls LJ stated that the 'difficulties in formulating and implementing an appropriate escape clause were such as to make this proposal impracticable and unsatisfactory'.

An escape clause is not an appropriate where it was conceded by the company that unfair prejudicial conduct had occurred: *Re Scitec Group Ltd* [2011] 1 BCLC 277.

Checklist: unfair prejudice

13.29 *This checklist sets out a checklist for unfair prejudicial conduct.*

No	*Issue*	*Reference*
1	A shareholder may petition to the court for relief on grounds that the company's affairs are being conducted in an unfair prejudicial manner; or that an actual or proposed act or omission of the company (including an act or omission on its behalf) is or would be so prejudicial.	CA 2006, s 994(1)
2	The provisions concerning the applications for unfair prejudicial conduct are set out in further detail by way of Statutory Instrument.	The Companies (Unfair Prejudice Applications) Proceedings Rules 2009 SI 2009/2469
3	Is the conduct unfairly prejudicial?	CA 2006, s 994(1)
4	Does it concern the interests of members?	CA 2006, s 994(1)
5	Does it involve the company's affairs?	CA 2006, s 994(1)
6	What relief is the petitioner looking for?	CA 2006, s 996
7	If a shareholder is exiting from the company by court order for the company to purchase the shares, what is the basis for valuation of the shares on exit?	CA 2006, s 996

14 Company secretaries

Introduction

14.1 This chapter addresses the following issues:

- the role and function of the company secretary;
- company secretary exemption for a private company;
- the requirements and qualifications for a company secretary for public companies;
- the application of the UK Corporate Governance Code to company secretaries;
- some key cases on the role of the company secretary; and
- checklists on the appointment and dismissal of the company secretary.

Duties and functions of a company secretary

14.2 The duties and functions of a company secretary are varied and wide-ranging under CA 2006, and generally under common law and the law of contract. These can include authority to bind the company. Some of the essential duties and functions of a company secretary include:

- ensuring compliance with the company's articles of association and memorandum of association;
- preparing background reports and research papers for board/shareholders' meetings;
- completing the statutory registers, including register of members (CA 2006, s 114); secretaries (CA 2006, s 265); directors (CA 2006, s 162); debenture holders (CA 2006, s 743); and company charges (CA 2006, ss 877 and 892);
- compliance with the statutory returns including company's reports and financial accounts; annual returns; appointment and removal of directors/secretary/auditor; filing amendments to the company's articles of association;
- ensuring compliance with the UK Corporate Governance Code as applicable to listed companies, including independent advice to the board on governance aspects;
- ensuring good communication flow between directors and shareholders within the corporate governance structure;
- assisting in ensuring that directors (executive and non-executive) receive induction and training on their duties, functions and liabilities;
- organising and convening board and shareholders' meetings which includes sending notices of meetings;

- preparing minutes of board and shareholders' meetings;
- where appropriate, ensuring that the company's website contains accurate and true information including details of any forthcoming meetings;
- ensuring that all proper and correct procedures are followed in connection with convening meetings, and matters to be attended to after the meetings;
- maintaining good shareholder communications generally, and attending to their queries on any corporate matters arising.

Private company exemption

14.3 Private companies are not required to appoint a company secretary: CA 2006, s 270(1).

CA 2006 defines a private company 'without a secretary', as a company which has taken advantage of the exemption under s 270(1): CA 2006, s 270(2).

For private companies without a secretary, the company has the capacity and power to serve and lodge documents itself. Any documents addressed to the company secretary, are treated as addressed to the company. Any functions of the company secretary can be undertaken by a director; or a person authorised generally or specifically in that behalf by the directors: CA 2006, s 270(3).

Alternative method of record-keeping

14.4 CA 2006 allows for an alternative method of record-keeping in the case of private companies: CA 2006, s 274A. See **14.5–14.10**.

Option to keep information in the central register

14.5 Private companies have the option to keep corporate information on the central register under CA 2006, ss 279A–279F.

Right to make an election

14.6 In order to exercise the option, an election may be made under CA 2006, s 279A by the subscribers wishing to form a private company; or by the private company itself, once it is formed and registered: CA 2006, s 279A(1).

The election is made by giving notice of election to the registrar: CA 2006, s 279A(2). If the election notice is given by subscribers wishing to form a private company, it must be given when the documents required to be delivered under CA 2006, s 9 are delivered to the registrar: CA 2006, s 279A(3).

Effective date of election

14.7 An election to keep corporate information on the central register is effective when the notice of election is registered by the registrar: CA 2006, s 279B(1). The election remains in force until either the company ceases to be a private company; or a notice of withdrawal sent by the company under section 279E CA 2006 is registered by the registrar, whichever occurs first: CA 2006, s 279B(2).

Effect of election on obligations under CA 2006, ss 275 and 276

14.8 While the election is in force under section 279A in respect of a company, the company's obligations are to keep and maintain a register of secretaries under CA 2006, s 275 and to notify the registrar of changes to it under CA 2006, s 276 during this period: CA 2006, s 279C.

Duty to notify registrar of changes

14.9 While the election is in force, the company must deliver to the registrar any information of which the company would, during that period, have been obliged to give notice under CA 2006, s 276 had the election not been in force; and any statement that would have had to accompany such a notice: CA 2006, s 279D(2).

The information (and any accompanying statement) must be delivered as soon as reasonably practicable after the company becomes aware of the information and, in any event, no later than the time by which the company would have been obliged under s 276 CA 2006, s 276 to give notice of the information: CA 2006, s 279D(3). Failure to comply with this section can lead to criminal penalties, such as a fine: CA 2006, s 279D(4) and (5).

Withdrawing the election

14.10 A company may withdraw an election made by it under CA 2006, 279A: CA 2006, s 279E(1). Withdrawal is achieved by giving notice of withdrawal to the registrar: CA 2006, s 279E(2). The withdrawal takes effect when the notice is registered by the registrar: CA 2006, s 279E(3).

The effect of withdrawal is that the company's obligation under CA 2006, s 275 to keep and maintain a register of secretaries, and its obligation under s 276, to notify the registrar of changes to that register, apply from then on with respect to the period going forward: CA 2006, s 279E(4).

This means that, when the withdrawal takes effect, the company must enter in its register of secretaries, all the information that is required to be contained in that register, in respect of matters that are current as at that time. However, the company is not required to enter in its register, information relating to the period when the election was in force that is no longer current: CA 2006, s 279E(5).

Public companies

14.11 A public company must appoint a company secretary: CA 2006, s 271. The secretary must be qualified to act as such: CA 2006, s 273.

Qualifications of secretaries of public companies

14.12 It is the duty of the directors of a public company to take all reasonable steps to secure that the secretary (or each joint secretary) of the company:

(a) has the requisite knowledge and experience to discharge the functions of company secretary; and

(b) has one or more stipulated qualifications as stated in CA 2006, s 273(1), which includes membership of a specified professional body.

Discharge of function where office vacant or secretary unable to act

14.13 If within the company, the office of secretary is vacant, or there is for any other reason no secretary capable of acting, anything required or authorised to be done by the secretary may be undertaken by an assistant or deputy secretary (if any). If there is no assistant or deputy secretary, or none capable of acting, then the company secretarial functions can be performed by any person authorised generally or specifically by the directors: CA 2006, s 274.

Duty to keep register of secretaries

14.14 A public company must keep a register of its secretaries. This must contain the required particulars (see CA 2006, ss 277–279) of the person or persons who are the company secretary or joint secretaries: CA 2006, s 275(2). The register must be kept available for inspection at the company's registered office; or at a place specified in regulations under s 1136: CA 2006, s 275(3).

The company must give notice to the registrar of the place at which the register is kept available for inspection. The registrar must also be notified of any change in that place, unless the register has at all times been kept at the company's registered office: CA 2006, s 275(4).

14.15 The register must be open to inspection by any member of the company without charge; and by any other person on payment of such fee as may be prescribed: CA 2006, s 275(5).

Criminal penalty fines can apply where the company, and any company officer refuses to allow inspection: CA 2006, s 275(7). Where there is a refusal of inspection of the register, the court may by order compel an immediate inspection of it: CA 2006, s 275(8).

Duty to notify registrar of changes

14.16 A company must, within a period of 14 days from a person becoming or ceasing to be its secretary or one of its joint secretaries; or the occurrence of any change in the particulars contained in its register of secretaries, give notice to the registrar of the change and of the date on which it occurred: CA 2006, s 276(1). Form CHO3 (Change of Secretary's Details) or Form CHO4 (Change of Corporate Secretary's details) should be used.

14.17 The notice of a person having become secretary, or one of joint secretaries, of the company must be accompanied by a statement by the company, that the person has consented to act as the secretary: CA 2006, s 276(2).

Failure to comply with the section can lead to a criminal conviction and a fine: CA 2006, s 276(4).

Particulars of secretaries to be registered: individuals

14.18 A company's register of secretaries must contain the following particulars: the name and any former name; and address: CA 2006, s 277(1).

14.22 The term 'name' means a person's Christian name (or other forename) and surname. However, for a peer; or an individual usually known by a title, the title may be stated instead of his Christian name (or other forename), and surname or in addition to either or both of them: CA 2006, s 277(2).

14.23 A 'former name' means a name by which the individual was formerly known for business purposes. Where a person is or was formerly known by more than one such name, each of them must be stated: CA 2006, s 277(3). There are however some exceptions under s 277(4) CA 2006.

14.24 The address required to be stated in the register is a service address. This may be stated to be 'The company's registered office': CA 2006, s 277(5). There is no requirement to provide the secretary's residential address.

Once the company is incorporated, the person(s) who are named are deemed to be appointed: CA 2006, s 16(6).

Particulars of secretaries to be registered: corporate secretaries and firms

14.25 A company's register of secretaries must contain the following particulars in the case of a body corporate, or a firm that is a legal person under the law by which it is governed:

(a) corporate or firm name;

(b) registered or principal office;

(c) in the case of a limited company that is a UK-registered company, the registered number.

(d) in any other case, particulars of:

  (i) the legal form of the company or firm and the law by which it is governed; and

  (ii) if applicable, the register in which it is entered (including details of the state) and its registration number in that register: CA 2006, s 278(1).

If all the partners in a firm are joint secretaries, it is sufficient to state the particulars that would be required if the firm were a legal person and the firm had been appointed secretary: CA 2006, s 278(2).

Significant cases on company secretaries

14.26 Earlier cases considered that a company secretary merely served an administrative purpose, with no authority to bind the company: *Barnett, Hoares & Co v South London Tramways Co* (1887) 18 QBD 815.

The duties of a secretary were limited to purely administrative matters: *George Whitechurch Ltd v Cavanagh* [1902] AC 117.

14.27 The modern judicial view is that a company secretary has wider responsibilities and duties. These are not limited to administrative matters: *Panorama Developments (Guildford) Ltd v Fidelis Furnishing Fabrics Ltd* [1971] 2 QB 711.

According to Lord Denning:

> 'But times have changed. A company secretary is a much more important person nowadays than he was in 1887. He is an officer of the company with extensive duties and responsibilities. This appears not only in the modern Companies Acts, but also by the role which he plays in the day-to-day business of companies. He is no longer a mere clerk. He regularly makes representations on behalf of the company and enters into contracts on its behalf which come within the day-to-day running of the company's business. So much so that he may be regarded as held out as having authority to do such things on behalf of the company. He is certainly entitled to sign contracts connected with the administrative side of a company's affairs, such as employing staff, and ordering cars, and so forth. All such matters now come within the ostensible authority of a company's secretary'.

See *Re Maidstone Buildings Provisions Ltd* [1971] 1 WLR 1085.

Applicability of the UK Corporate Governance Code to company secretaries

14.28 The UK Corporate Governance Code (2018) provides the following role of company secretaries in the corporate governance process:

> 'Provision 16:
>
> All directors should have access to the advice of the company secretary, who is responsible for advising the board on all governance matters. Both the appointment and removal of the company secretary should be a matter for the whole board.'

Checklist for appointing a company secretary

14.29 *Note: A company secretary is not required to be appointed for a private company limited by shares. The following checklist only applies if one is appointed, and it sets out the steps and procedures for appointment. The checklist also applies to the appointment of a company secretary in a public company. The appointment may be governed by a company's articles of association. If the company has adopted Table A 1985, regulation 99 provides for the appointment by the directors. However, the Model Articles for private and public companies do not set any provisions for the appointment of a company secretary. Companies established after 1 October 2009 may either need to amend their articles to include a provision for the appointment of a company secretary or modify the Model Articles to include such provision.*

A suggested provision would be:

'Subject to the provisions of the Companies Act 2006, the secretary shall be appointed by the directors for such term, at such remuneration and upon such conditions as they may think fit; and any secretary so appointed may be removed by them'.

The checklist set out below on the procedure will need to be adapted depending upon the procedures set out in the company's articles of association on convening a board meeting.

No	*Issue*	*Reference*
1	Prospective secretary to write to the company's board of directors of interest in acting as the company secretary. The company's auditor cannot act as the company's secretary.	CA 2006, s 1214
	The secretary of a public company must be qualified to act as a secretary of such company.	
	A person must consent to being appointed as the company's secretary.	CA 2006, s 276(2) (as inserted by SBEEA 2015, s 100(5))
2	Prepare a Board Agenda setting out details of the proposed appointment and terms upon which employment will be made. Board to convene a meeting on reasonable notice. Notice to state date, time and place of the meeting.	Articles of association. Employment contract or written particulars: Employment Rights Act 1996, s 1
3	Ensure quorum available at the board meeting.	Articles of association
4	Directors vote by simple majority at the board meeting on the appointment of the company secretary. Consider whether the company secretary will be remunerated and terms of remuneration and any employment contract or written particulars of employment. Also, whether the company secretary will be a signatory to any of the company's bank accounts and financial authority limits? Will any professional liability indemnity insurance be taken out in respect of the company secretary?	Employment Rights Act 1996, s 1
5	Consider dispensing with a board meeting if directors can pass a written resolution for the appointment of the company secretary.	Articles of Association
6	After the board meeting, prepare minutes of the meeting recording appointment of the company secretary.	Minutes
7	Update the company's statutory books. Complete the Register of Secretaries.	CA 2006, s 275
8	Secretary to also provide a service address which need not be the residential address. File at Companies House on the appointment of the company secretary.	CA 2006, s 277(1)
9	Details required for a non-corporate secretary are: • company number; • company name; • date of appointment; • date of birth; • full name of secretary; • full service address; • the signature of the new secretary.	Within 14 days, use Form IN01 (Application to register a company) for the first appointment upon incorporation of the company. For subsequent appointments use Form APO3 (Appoint a secretary) or AP04 (Appoint a corporate secretary): CA 2006, s 276

11	Consider a change to bank mandate forms and secretary as signatory to company bank account	Bank mandate forms

Checklist for company secretary's dismissal

14.30 *This checklist applies where a company secretary is to be dismissed from office. The matter is considered at the board meeting and not at a shareholders' meeting. CA 2006 does not address the position of removal of a secretary. Therefore, this aspect is considered to be within the authority of the directors.*

No	*Issue*	*Reference*
1	Prepare a Board Agenda setting out details of the proposed termination. Board to ensure it has considered applicable employment law issues on termination of the contract of employment and followed appropriate procedures for termination. Board to convene on reasonable notice. Notice to state date, time and place of meeting.	Articles of association Employment Rights Act 1996 (as amended) and/or other applicable employment legislation
2	Ensure quorum available at the board meeting.	Articles of association
3	Directors to consider the grounds for dismissal and whether a fair dismissal including carrying out proper steps and procedures of an investigative nature in connection with the performance or conduct of the company secretary. HR report should be obtained and any other supporting evidence of proposed dismissal.	HR report Employment/service contract
4	Consider also terms of the employment/service contract including any restrictive covenants and restraint of trade/non-solicitation clauses and their enforceability.	
5	Consider also whether a settlement agreement may be appropriate in the circumstances.	Settlement agreement
6	Directors vote by simple majority on a show of hands at the board meeting on the dismissal of the company secretary.	Articles of Association
7	Consider dispensing with a board meeting if directors can pass a written resolution for the dismissal of the company secretary.	Articles of Association
8	After the board meeting, prepare minutes of the meeting recording dismissal of the company secretary.	Minutes
9	Update the company's statutory books.	Register of Secretaries
10	File at Companies House on the termination of the company secretary. This will also apply on the company secretary's resignation. Note: In respect of public companies, if a public company does not appoint a company secretary, the Secretary of State can issue a direction requiring such appointment and the date within which the appointment must be made (within one to three months from the date of the Secretary of State's direction).	Within 14 days, use Form TM02 (Terminate an appointment of a Secretary) CA 2006, s 272

Prescribed forms for secretaries

14.31 *The following are the prescribed forms for secretaries, which are required to be registered at Companies House as appropriate.*

Form No:	Details
APO3:	Appoint a secretary
APO4:	Appoint a corporate secretary
TMO2:	Terminate an appointment of a secretary
CHO3:	Change the details of a secretary
CHO4:	Change in details of corporate secretary

15 Resolutions and meetings

Introduction

15.1 This Chapter addresses the following issues:

- the different forms of resolutions;
- the practice and procedure for convening meetings;
- the circumstances where meetings may be dispensed with; and
- the concept of informal unanimous consent of shareholders.

Resolutions

15.2 A distinction is made under CA 2006 between resolutions passed by a private company and those passed by a public company.

For a *private* company, a resolution must be passed either as a written resolution; or at a meeting of the members: CA 2006, s 281(1).

A resolution by members of a *public* company must be passed at a meeting of the members: CA 2006, s 281(2).

Ordinary resolutions

15.3 If a provision of the Companies Acts requires a resolution of a company, or of the members (or a class of members), and does not specify the type of resolution required, it will usually be an ordinary resolution. The exception is where the company's articles require a higher majority (or unanimity): CA 2006, s 281(3).

An ordinary resolution requires a simple majority: CA 2006, s 282(1).

It is however possible for a private company to dispense with convening a meeting by using a written resolution. This is passed by a simple majority by members representing a simple majority of the total voting rights of eligible members (see CA 2006, Pt 13, Ch 2): CA 2006, s 282(2).

A resolution which is passed at a meeting on a show of hands, can be passed by a simple majority of the votes cast by those entitled to vote: CA 2006, s 282(3).

A resolution which is passed on a poll taken at a meeting can be passed by a simple majority by members representing a simple majority of the total voting rights of members who (being entitled to do so) vote in person, by proxy or in advance (see CA 2006, s 322A) on the resolution: CA 2006, s 282(4).

Special resolutions

15.4 A special resolution requires a majority of not less than 75%: CA 2006, s 283(1).

A written resolution can be passed by 75% majority of members, representing not less than 75% of the total voting rights of eligible members (see CA 2006, Pt 13, Ch 2): CA 2006, s 283(2).

15.5 A written resolution which is proposed as a special resolution must specify this, and can only be passed as a special resolution CA 2006, s 283(3).

A resolution taken at a meeting on a show of hands by 75%, is effective if it is passed by not less than 75% of the votes cast by those entitled to vote: CA 2006, s 283(4).

A resolution taken on a poll at a meeting can be passed by 75%, if it is passed by members representing not less than 75% of the total voting rights of the members who (being entitled to do so) vote in person, by proxy or in advance (see CA 2006, s 322A) on the resolution: CA 2006, s 283(5).

15.6 Where members propose to pass a special resolution, the notice of the meeting must include the text of the resolution. It must also specify the intention to propose the resolution as a special resolution: CA 2006, s 283(6): *Moorgate Mercantile Holdings Limited* [1980] 1 All ER 40.

Votes: general rules

15.7 Generally, on a vote on a written resolution, every member has one vote: CA 2006, s 284(1).

On a vote on a resolution on a show of hands at a meeting, each member present in person has one vote: CA 2006, s 284(2).

Generally, where a vote on a resolution is taken by poll at a meeting, each member has one vote: CA 2006, s 284(3).

The above general rules may be modified by anything in the company's articles providing otherwise.

Voting by proxy

15.8 Generally, where a resolution is taken on a show of hands at a meeting, every proxy present who has been duly appointed by one or more members entitled to vote on the resolution, has one vote. There are exceptions set out in s 285(2): CA 2006, s 285(1).

Written resolution of private companies

15.9 A 'written resolution' means a resolution of a private company: CA 2006, s 288(1).

The following cannot be passed as a written resolution:

(a) a resolution under s 168 CA 2006 removing a director before the expiration of his period of office;

(b) a resolution under s 510 CA 2006 removing an auditor before the expiration of his term of office: CA 2006, s 288(2).

15.10 A resolution may be proposed as a written resolution by the directors of a private company (see s 291); or by the members of a private company (see ss 292–295): CA 2006, s 288(3).

15.11 A written resolution of a private company will have effect as if passed by the company in general meeting; or by a meeting of a class of members of the company: CA 2006, s 288(5).

Circulation of written resolutions proposed by directors

15.12 Where a written resolution is proposed, the company must send or submit a copy of the resolution to every eligible member. An 'eligible member' is a person who would have been entitled to vote on the resolution on the circulation date of the resolution (see CA 2006, s 290): CA 2006, s 289(1).

The company must send copies at the same time (so far as reasonably practicable) (a) to all eligible members in hard copy form, in electronic form or by means of a website. Alternatively, (b) if it is possible to do so without undue delay, by submitting the same copy to each eligible member in turn (or different copies to each of a number of eligible members in turn); or by sending copies to some members in accordance with paragraph (a) and submitting a copy or copies to other members in accordance with paragraph (b): CA 2006, s 292(3).

The copy of the resolution must be accompanied by a statement informing the member how to signify agreement to the resolution (see s 296); and as to the date by which the resolution must be passed if it is not to lapse (see s 297): CA 2006, s 291(4).

Members' power to require circulation of written resolution

15.13 Members of a private company may require the company to circulate a resolution which is proposed as a written resolution: CA 2006, s 292(1).

In the following circumstances, a resolution which is proposed as a written resolution will not be valid if:

(a) it would, if passed, be ineffective (whether by reason of inconsistency with any enactment or the company's constitution or otherwise); or

(b) it is defamatory of any person; or

(c) it is frivolous or vexatious: CA 2006, s 292(2).

15.14 Where the members require a company to circulate a resolution, they may require the company to circulate with it a statement of not more than 1,000 words on the subject matter of the resolution: CA 2006, s 292(3).

A company is then required to circulate the resolution and any accompanying statement, once it has received requests that it do so from members representing not less than 5% of the total voting rights of all members entitled to vote on the resolution: CA 2006, s 292(4); or such lower percentage as is specified in the company's articles: CA 2006, s 292(5). The request may be in hard copy form or in electronic form; it must identify the resolution and any accompanying statement; and must be authenticated by the person or persons making it: CA 2006, s 292(6).

Circulation of written resolution proposed by members

15.15 A company that is required under CA 2006, s 292 to circulate a written resolution must send or submit to every eligible member a copy of the resolution; and a copy of any accompanying statement. The copy of the resolution must be accompanied by guidance as to how to signify agreement to the resolution (see s 296); and the date by which the resolution must be passed if it is not to lapse (see s 297): CA 2006, s 293(4).

Expenses of circulation

15.16 The company's expenses in complying with CA 2006, s 293 must be paid by the members who requested the circulation of the resolution, unless the company resolves otherwise: CA 2006, s 294(1).

Application not to circulate members' statements

15.17 A company is not required to circulate a members' statement under CA 2006, s 293 if, on an application by the company or another person who claims to be aggrieved, the court is satisfied that the rights conferred by s 292, and that section are being abused: CA 2006, s 295(1).

The court may order the members who requested the circulation of the statement, to pay the whole or part of the company's costs on such an application, even if they are not parties to the application: CA 2006, s 295(2).

Procedure for signifying agreement to written resolution

15.18 A member signifies his agreement to a proposed written resolution when the company receives from him (or from someone acting on his behalf) an authenticated document by identifying the resolution to which it relates; and indicating his agreement to the resolution: CA 2006, s 296(1).

The document must thereafter be sent to the company in hard copy form or in electronic form: CA 2006, s 296(2). A member's agreement to a written resolution, once signified, may not be revoked: CA 2006, s 296(3). A written resolution is passed when the required majority of eligible members have signified their agreement to it: CA 2006, s 296(4).

Period for agreeing to written resolution

15.19 A proposed written resolution lapses if it is not passed before the end of the period specified in the company's articles; or if none is specified, the period of 28 days beginning with the circulation date: CA 2006, s 297(1).

The agreement of a member to a written resolution is ineffective if signified after the expiry of that period: CA 2006, s 297(2).

Sending documents relating to written resolution by electronic means

15.20 Where a company has given an electronic address in any document containing or accompanying a proposed written resolution, it is deemed to have agreed that any document or information relating to that resolution, may be sent by electronic means to that address (subject to any conditions or limitations specified in the document): CA 2006, s 298(1).

The term 'electronic address' means any address or number used for the purposes of sending or receiving documents or information by electronic means: CA 2006, s 298(2).

Publication of written resolution on website

15.21 CA 2006, s 299 applies where a company sends a written resolution; or a statement relating to a written resolution, to a person by means of a website: CA 2006, s 299(1).

The resolution or statement is not validly sent, unless the resolution is available on the website throughout the period beginning with the circulation date, and ending on the date on which the resolution lapses under s 297: CA 2006, s 299(2).

Resolutions at meetings

Resolutions at general meetings

15.22 A resolution of the members of a company is validly passed at a general meeting, if notice of the meeting and of the resolution is given; and the meeting is held and conducted, in accordance with the provisions of Ch 3 (and, where relevant, Ch 4 of Pt 13 of the CA 2006) and the company's articles: CA 2006, s 301.

The term 'meeting' in the context of company law is not defined by CA 2006. However, the ordinary meaning of the word 'meeting' denotes 'a coming together of two or more persons': *Re Altitude Scaffolding Ltd, Re T & N Limited* [2007] 1 BCLC 199 per David Richards J.

The rationale for meetings is to allow those attending to give informed consent (where possible) on company matters: *Byng v London Life Association Ltd* [1989] BCLC 400.

Directors' power to call general meetings

15.23 The directors of a company may call a general meeting of the company: CA 2006, s 302. The company's articles of association (or if applicable, the shareholders' agreement) may specify in detail how this meeting is to be called

Members' power to require directors to call general meeting

15.24 The company's members may require the directors to call a general meeting of the company: CA 2006, s 303(1).

The directors must call a general meeting once the company has received requests to do so from:

(a) members representing at least 5% of such of the paid-up capital of the company as carries the right of voting at general meetings of the company (excluding any paid-up capital held as treasury shares); or

(b) in the case of a company not having a share capital, members who represent at least 5% of the total voting rights of all the members having a right to vote at general meetings: CA 2006, s 303(2).

15.25 A request for a meeting must state the general nature of the business to be dealt with at the meeting; and may include the text of a resolution that may properly be moved, and is intended to be moved at the meeting: CA 2006, s 303(4). The request must be a valid one by the shareholders representing 5% of the total voting rights, if directors are to call the EGM: *Rose v McGivern* [1998] 2 BCLC 593; *Ball v Metal Industries Ltd* 1957 SC 315.

15.26 A resolution may properly be moved at a meeting unless:

(a) it would, if passed, be ineffective (whether by reason of inconsistency with any enactment or the company's constitution or otherwise);

(b) it is defamatory of any person; or

(c) it is frivolous or vexatious: CA 2006, s 303(5): *Kaye v Oxford House (Wimbledon) Management Company Ltd* [2019] EWHC 2181 (Ch).

15.27 A request may be in hard copy form or in electronic form; and must be authenticated by the person or persons making it: CA 2006, s 303(6).

Directors' duty to call meetings required by members

15.28 Directors required under CA 2006, s 303 to call a general meeting of the company, must call a meeting within 21 days from the date on which they become subject to the requirement. The meeting must be held on a date not more than 28 days after the date of the notice convening the meeting: CA 2006, s 304(1).

If the requests received by the company identify a resolution intended to be moved at the meeting, the notice of the meeting must include notice of the resolution: CA 2006, s 304(2). The business that may be dealt with at the meeting includes a resolution of which notice is given in accordance with s 304: CA 2006, s 304(3). If the resolution is to be proposed as a special resolution, the directors are treated as not having duly called the meeting, if they do not give the required notice of the resolution in accordance with s 283: CA 2006, s 304(4).

Power of members to call meeting at company's expense

15.29 If the directors are required under CA 2006, s 303 to call a meeting; and do not do so in accordance with s 304, the members who requested the meeting, or any of them representing more than one half of the total voting rights of all of them, may themselves call a general meeting: CA 2006, s 305(1).

15.30 Where the requests received by the company included the text of a resolution intended to be moved at the meeting, the notice of the meeting must include notice of the resolution: CA 2006, s 305(2). The meeting must be called for a date not more than three months after the date on which the directors become subject to the requirement to call a meeting: CA 2006, s 305(3). The meeting must be called in the same manner, as nearly as possible, as that in which meetings are required to be called by directors of the company: CA 2006, s 305(4).

The business which may be dealt with at the meeting includes a resolution of which notice is given in accordance with this section: CA 2006, s 305(5).

15.31 Any reasonable expenses incurred by the members requesting the meeting by reason of the failure of the directors duly to call a meeting, must be reimbursed by the company: CA 2006, s 305(6). Any sum reimbursed must be retained by the company out of any sums due or to become due from the company by way of fees or other remuneration, in respect of the services of such of the directors as were in default: CA 2006, s 305(7).

Power of court to order meeting

15.32 It is possible for the court to order a general meeting to be held. However, this is at the court's discretion. CA 2006, s 306 applies if for any reason it is impracticable to call a meeting of a company, in any manner in which meetings of that company may be called; or to conduct the meeting in the manner prescribed by the company's articles or this Act: CA 2006, s 306(1).

15.33 It is possible for the court may, either of its own motion or on the application of a director of the company; or of a member of the company who would be entitled to vote at the meeting, order a meeting to be called, held and conducted in any manner the court thinks fit: CA 2006, s 306(2). Where the court makes an order, it may give such ancillary or consequential directions as it thinks expedient: CA 2006, s 306(3). Such directions may include a direction that one member of the company present at the meeting is deemed to constitute a quorum: CA 2006, s 303(4). In this situation, a meeting called, held and conducted in accordance with the court order is deemed duly called, held and conducted: CA 2006, s 306(5).

15.34 Some of the cases under CA 2006, s 306 address the quorum requirements at general meetings, particularly where there is no requisite quorum at such meetings. In such situations, the applicant is seeking the court's permission to pass certain resolutions at an inquorate meeting, or where there is a deadlock at these meetings, and there is no provision in the articles of association or any shareholders' agreement to resolve such deadlock: *Monnington v Easier plc* [2006] 2 BCLC 283.

The fact that a petition for unfair prejudicial conduct under s 994 has been presented, does not necessarily prevent the court from considering applications under s 306. However, it will be a factor that the court will consider particularly where class rights are involved if they are set out in a shareholders' agreement: *Harman v BML Group Ltd* [1994] 2 BCLC 674.

The court may have regard to the interests of minority shareholders in respect of shareholder meetings: *Re Sticky Fingers Restaurant Limited* [1992] BCLC 84.

In *Might SA v Redbus Interhouse plc* [2004] 2 BCLC 449, the applicant applied under s 306 on the basis that the chairman to be appointed for the general meeting, would be one of the directors whom the shareholders proposed to remove from office; and if the director was to be appointed as chairman, he would have a conflict of interest and vested interest not to be removed. The issue was whether it was impracticable to hold a meeting. The court held that the fiduciary position of a company director did not prevent him assuming the position of chairman at the company's general meeting, regardless of any conflict of interest that may exist.

15.35 CA 2006, s 306 does not define 'impracticable'. Each case will be decided on its facts as to what is impracticable. The objective of s 306 is to allow for the continuity of the company's functioning and operations, without unnecessary hindrance. The concept of 'impracticable' signifies that there must be regard to all the circumstances, to determine the practicability of holding a meeting: *Re El Sombrero Ltd* [1958] Ch 900.

The court may make an order validating resolutions at a shareholders' meeting: *Vectone Entertainment Holding Limited v South Entertainment Ltd* [2004] 2 BCLC 224.

15.36 On occasions, the court has been involved under CA 2006, s 306 where actual or potential violence may be involved at a meeting: *Re British Union for the Abolition of Vivisection [1995] 2 BCLC 1.*

There have been occasions where shareholders have been absent from meetings or simply refuse to attend meetings, so that the meeting becomes inquorate. In such situations, the courts have intervened to allow meetings to be held. The court may order a meeting to be held where it is inquorate: *Re Opera Photographic Limited* [1989] BCLC 763.

15.37 In some situations, the court has not exercised its discretion to make an order under s 306. In *Ross v Telford* [1998] 1 BCLC 82, the Court of Appeal stated that s 306 was a procedural section: it was not designed to affect substantive voting rights, or to shift the balance of power between shareholders, particularly in a deadlock situation. It had no application to a board meeting. Also, *Union Music Ltd v Watson* [2003] 1 BCLC 453.

Notice required of general meeting

15.38 A general meeting of a private company (other than an adjourned meeting) must be called by notice of at least 14 days: CA 2006, s 307(1).

A general meeting of a public company (other than an adjourned meeting) must be called by notice of in the case of an annual general meeting, at least 21 days; and in any other case, at least 14 days: CA 2006, s 307(2). However, the company's articles may require a longer period of notice than that specified in s 307(1) or (2): CA 2006, s 307(3).

15.39 A general meeting may be called by shorter notice than that otherwise required, if shorter notice is agreed by the members: CA 2006, s 307(4). The shorter notice must be agreed to by a majority in number of the members having a right to attend and vote at the meeting, being a majority who:

(a) together hold not less than the requisite percentage in nominal value of the shares giving a right to attend and vote at the meeting (excluding any shares in the company held as treasury shares); or

(b) in the case of a company not having a share capital, together represent not less than the requisite percentage of the total voting rights at that meeting of all the members: CA 2006, s 307(5).

15.40 The requisite percentage is:

(a) in the case of a private company, 90% or such higher percentage (not exceeding 95%) as may be specified in the company's articles;

(b) in the case of a public company, 95%: CA 2006, s 307(6).

Subsections 307(5) and (6) of CA 2006 do not apply to an annual general meeting of a public company (see instead s 337(2)): CA 2006, s 307(7).

Manner in which notice to be given

15.41 Notice of a general meeting of a company must be given:

(a) in hard copy form;

(b) in electronic form; or

(c) by means of a website (see s 309),

or partly by one such means and partly by another: CA 2006, s 308.

Publication of notice of meeting on website

15.42 Notice of a meeting is not validly given by a company by means of a website, unless it is given in accordance with s 309: CA 2006, s 309(1).

When the company notifies a member of the presence of the notice on the website the notification must:

(a) state that it concerns a notice of a company meeting;

(b) specify the place, date and time of the meeting; and

(c) in the case of a public company, state whether the meeting will be an annual general meeting: CA 2006, s 309(2).

The notice must be available on the website throughout the period beginning with the date of that notification, and ending with the conclusion of the meeting: CA 2006, s 309(3).

Persons entitled to receive notice of meetings

15.43 Notice of a general meeting of a company must be sent to every member of the company; and every director: CA 2006, s 310(1).

15.44 In s 310(1), the reference to members includes any person who is entitled to a share in consequence of the death or bankruptcy of a member, if the company has been notified of their entitlement: CA 2006, s 310(2).

In s 310(2), the reference to the bankruptcy of a member includes the sequestration of the estate of a member: CA 2006, s 310(3).

15.45 CA 2006, s 310 is subject to any enactment; and any provision of the company's articles: CA 2006, s 310(4).

Contents of notices of meetings

15.46 Notice of a general meeting of a company must state the time and date of the meeting; and the place of the meeting: CA 2006, s 311(1).

Notice of a general meeting of a company must also state the general nature of the business to be dealt with at the meeting: CA 2006, s 311(2).

Section 311 CA 2006, s 311 is subject to any provision of the company's articles.

In respect of venues for the meetings, the Court of Appeal in *Byng v London Life Association Ltd* [1989] BCLC 400, stated that in order for a meeting of members to be validly constituted, it was not necessary for all the members to be physically present in the same room. A valid meeting could take place if the shareholders were in different places, provided all steps were taken to direct shareholders to the places other than the main venue where the meeting was to be held, and that there were adequate audio visual links to enable those in all the locations, to see and hear what was going on in the other rooms.

Resolution requiring special notice

15.47 Where any provision of the Companies Acts requires special notice of a resolution, the resolution is not effective, unless notice of the intention to move it has been given to the company, at least 28 days before the meeting at which it is moved: CA 2006, s 312(1).

The company must, where practicable, give its members notice of any such resolution in the same manner and at the same time as it gives notice of the meeting: CA 2006, s 312(2).

15.48 Where that is not practicable, the company must give its members notice at least 14 days before the meeting by advertisement in a newspaper having an appropriate circulation; or in any other manner allowed by the company's articles: CA 2006, s 312(3).

If, after notice of the intention to move such a resolution has been given to the company, a meeting is called for a date 28 days or less after the notice has been given, the notice is deemed to have been properly given, though not given within the time required: CA 2006, s 312(4).

Accidental failure to give notice of resolution or meeting

15.49 Where a company gives notice of a general meeting; or a resolution intended to be moved at a general meeting, any accidental failure to give notice to one or more persons, will be disregarded for the purpose of determining whether notice of the meeting or resolution (as the case may be) is duly given: CA 2006, s 313(1).

15.50 Except in relation to notice given under (a) s 304 (notice of meetings required by members); or (b) s 305 (notice of meetings called by members); or (c) s 339 (notice of resolutions at AGMs proposed by members), s 313(1) applies subject to any provision of the company's articles: CA 2006, s 313(2).

15.51 An accidental omission is distinguished from an omission. In the latter situation, proceedings at meetings will be declared void. In *Musselwhite v C H Musselwhite & Son Ltd* [1962] Ch 964, there was an omission to serve notice, arising from an error as to legal position of a shareholder's membership within the company.

Russell J held that that the omission to give notice of a meeting to the claimants, prima facie invalidated the meeting, and that an omission arising from an error was not accidental. The meeting was therefore a nullity.

Members' power to require circulation of statements

15.52 The members of a company may require the company to circulate, to members of the company entitled to receive notice of a general meeting, a statement of not more than 1,000 words with respect to a matter referred to in a proposed resolution to be dealt with at that meeting; or other business to be dealt with at that meeting: CA 2006, s 314(1).

15.53 A company is required to circulate a statement once it has received requests to do so from:

(a) members representing at least 5% of the total voting rights of all the members who have a relevant right to vote (excluding any voting rights attached to any shares in the company held as treasury shares); or

(b) at least 100 members who have a relevant right to vote and hold shares in the company on which there has been paid up an average sum, per member, of at least £100.

See also CA 2006, s 153 (exercise of rights where shares held on behalf of others): CA 2006, s 314(2).

15.54 The term a 'relevant right to vote' means:

(a) in relation to a statement with respect to a matter referred to in a proposed resolution, a right to vote on that resolution at the meeting to which the requests relate; and

(b) in relation to any other statement, a right to vote at the meeting to which the requests relate: CA 2006, s 314(3).

15.55 A request:

(a) may be in hard copy form or in electronic form;

(b) must identify the statement to be circulated;

(c) must be authenticated by the person or persons making it; and

(d) must be received by the company at least one week before the meeting to which it relates: CA 2006, s 314(4).

Company's duty to circulate members' statement

15.56 A company that is required under CA 2006, s 314, to circulate a statement, must send a copy of it to each member of the company entitled to receive notice of the meeting in the same manner as the notice of the meeting; and at the same time as, or as soon as reasonably practicable after, it gives notice of the meeting: CA 2006, s 315(1).

Section 315(1) of CA 2006 applies subject to s 316(2) (deposit or tender of sum in respect of expenses of circulation); and s 317 (application not to circulate members' statement): CA 2006, s 315(2).

15.57 Where there is a breach of CA 2006, s 315 an offence is committed by every officer of the company who is in default: CA 2006, s 315(3), which may lead a fine: CA 2006, s 315(4).

Expenses of circulating members' statement

15.58 The expenses of the company in complying with CA 2006, s 315 need not be paid by the members who requested the circulation of the statement if the meeting to which the requests relate is an annual general meeting of a public company; and requests sufficient to require the company to circulate the statement, are received before the end of the financial year preceding the meeting: CA 2006, s 316(1).

15.59 Otherwise the expenses of the company in complying with s 315 CA 2006 must be paid by the members who requested the circulation of the statement unless the company resolves otherwise. Further, unless the company has previously so resolved, it is not bound to comply with s 315, unless there is deposited with or tendered to it, not later than one week before the meeting, a sum reasonably sufficient to meet its expenses in doing so: CA 2006, s 316(2).

Application not to circulate members' statement

15.60 A company is not required to circulate a members' statement under CA 2006, s 315 if, on an application by the company or another person who claims to be aggrieved, the court is satisfied that the rights conferred by s 314 and s 315 are being abused: CA 2006, s 317(1).

The court may order the members who requested the circulation of the statement, to pay the whole or part of the company's costs on such an application, even if they are not parties to the application: CA 2006, s 317(2).

Quorum at meetings

15.61 In the case of a company limited by shares or guarantee and having only one member, one qualifying person present at a meeting is a quorum: CA 2006, s 318(1). In any other case, subject to the provisions of the company's articles, two qualifying persons present at a meeting are a quorum, unless:

(a) each is a qualifying person only because he is authorised under s 323 to act as the representative of a corporation in relation to the meeting, and they are representatives of the same corporation; or

(b) each is a qualifying person only because he is appointed as proxy of a member in relation to the meeting, and they are proxies of the same member: CA 2006, s 318(2).

15.62 The term a 'qualifying person' means:

(a) an individual who is a member of the company;

(b) a person authorised under s 323 (representation of corporations at meetings) to act as the representative of a corporation in relation to the meeting; or

(c) a person appointed as proxy of a member in relation to the meeting: CA 2006, s 318(3).

Where a resolution is passed at a meeting, which does not have the requisite quorum, it is void: see *Re Romford Canal Co, Pocock's Claims* (1883) 24 Ch D 85.

Chairman of meeting

15.63 A member may be elected to be the chairman of a general meeting by a resolution of the company passed at the meeting: CA 2006, s 319(1).

Section 319(1) is subject to any provision of the company's articles that states who may or may not be chairman: CA 2006, s 319(2).

At common law, a chairman has a duty to ensure proper conduct of meetings, and that those attending meetings have a right to be heard and vote at properly held meetings: *Byng v London Life Association Limited* [1989] BCLC 400.

15.64 In *National Dwellings Society v Sykes* [1894] 3 Ch 159, Chitty J held that it was the duty of a chairman to preserve order, conduct proceedings regularly, and take care that the sense of the meeting was properly ascertained with regard to any question before it.

Declaration by chairman on a show of hands

15.65 On a vote on a resolution at a meeting on a show of hands, a declaration by the chairman that the resolution has or has not been passed; or passed with a particular majority, is conclusive evidence of that fact without proof, of the number or proportion of the votes recorded in favour of or against the resolution: CA 2006, s 320(1).

An entry in respect of such a declaration in minutes of the meeting recorded in accordance with s 355, is also conclusive evidence of that fact without such proof: CA 2006, s 320(2). Section 320 does not apply if a poll is demanded in respect of the resolution (and the demand is not subsequently withdrawn): CA 2006, s 320(3).

Right to demand a poll

15.66 A provision of a company's articles is void, in so far as it would have the effect of excluding the right to demand a poll at a general meeting on any question other than the election of the chairman of the meeting; or the adjournment of the meeting: CA 2006, s 321(1).

15.67 A provision of a company's articles is void in so far as it would have the effect of making ineffective a demand for a poll on any such question which is made:

(a) by not less than five members having the right to vote on the resolution; or

(b) by a member or members representing not less than 10% of the total voting rights of all the members having the right to vote on the resolution (excluding any voting rights attached to any shares in the company held as treasury shares); or

(c) by a member or members holding shares in the company conferring a right to vote on the resolution, being shares on which an aggregate sum has been paid up equal to not less than 10% of the total sum paid up on all the shares conferring that right (excluding shares in the company conferring a right to vote on the resolution which are held as treasury shares): CA 2006, s 321(2).

Voting on a poll

15.68 On a poll taken at a general meeting of a company, a member entitled to more than one vote need not, if he votes, use all his votes or cast all the votes he uses in the same way: CA 2006, s 322.

Voting on a poll: votes cast in advance

15.69 A company's articles may contain provision to the effect that on a vote on a resolution on a poll taken at a meeting, the votes may include votes cast in advance: CA 2006, s 322A(1).

Notwithstanding CA 2006, s 322A, the company still has power to require reasonable evidence of the entitlement of any person who is not a member to vote: CA 2006, s 322A(2).

15.70 Any provision of a company's articles is void in so far as it would have the effect of requiring any document casting a vote in advance, to be received by the company or another person earlier than the following time:

(a) in the case of a poll taken more than 48 hours after it was demanded, 24 hours before the time appointed for the taking of the poll;

(b) in the case of any other poll, 48 hours before the time for holding the meeting or adjourned meeting: CA 2006, s 322A(3).

Rights to appoint proxies

15.71 A member of a company is entitled to appoint another person as his proxy, to exercise all or any of his rights to attend and to speak and vote at a meeting of the company: CA 2006, s 324(1).

In the case of a company having a share capital, a member may appoint more than one proxy in relation to a meeting, provided that each proxy is appointed to exercise the rights attached to a different share or shares held by him, or (as the case may be) to a different £10, or multiple of £10, of stock held by him: CA 2006, s 324(2).

Obligation of proxy to vote in accordance with instructions

15.72 A proxy must vote in accordance with any instructions given by the member by whom the proxy is appointed: CA 2006, s 324A.

Notice of meeting to contain statement of rights

15.73 In every notice calling a meeting of a company there must appear, with reasonable prominence, a statement informing the member of his rights under s 324; and any more extensive rights conferred by the company's articles to appoint more than one proxy: CA 2006, s 325(1).

Failure to comply with this section does not affect the validity of the meeting, or of anything done at the meeting: CA 2006, s 325(2).

15.74 If s 325 is not complied with respects any meeting, an offence is committed by every officer of the company who is in default: CA 2006, s 325(3). A person guilty of an offence is liable to a fine not exceeding: CA 2006, s 325(4).

Resolution passed at adjourned meeting

15.75 Where a resolution is passed at an adjourned meeting of a company, the resolution is for all purposes to be treated as having been passed on the date on which it was in fact passed, and is not to be deemed passed on any earlier date: CA 2006, s 332.

Sending documents relating to meetings etc in electronic form

15.76 Where a company has given an electronic address in a notice calling a meeting, it is deemed to have agreed that any document or information relating to proceedings at the meeting, may be sent by electronic means to that address (subject to any conditions or limitations specified in the notice): CA 2006, s 333(1).

Where a company has given an electronic address in an instrument of proxy sent out by the company in relation to the meeting, or in an invitation to appoint a proxy issued by the company in relation to the meeting, it is deemed to have agreed that any document or information relating to proxies for that meeting may be sent by electronic means to that address (subject to any conditions or limitations specified in the notice): CA 2006, s 333(2).

15.77 Under s 333(2), the documents relating to proxies include the appointment of a proxy in relation to a meeting; any document necessary to show the validity of, or otherwise relating to, the appointment of a proxy; and notice of the termination of the authority of a proxy: CA 2006, s 333(3).

The term 'electronic address' means any address or number, used for the purposes of sending or receiving documents or information by electronic means: CA 2006, s 333(4).

Records of resolutions and meetings

Records

15.78 Every company must keep records comprising:

(a) copies of all resolutions of members passed otherwise than at general meetings;

(b) minutes of all proceedings of general meetings; and

(c) details provided to the company in accordance with CA 2006, s 357 (decisions of sole member): CA 2006, s 355(1).

The records must be kept for at least ten years from the date of the resolution, meeting or decision (as appropriate): CA 2006, s 355(2).

If a company fails to comply with s 355, an offence is committed by every officer of the company who is in default: CA 2006, s 355(3).

A person guilty of an offence is liable to a fine: CA 2006, s 355(4).

Records as evidence of resolutions

15.79 CA 2006, s 356 applies to the records kept in accordance with s 355: CA 2006, s 356(1).

The record of a resolution passed otherwise than at a general meeting, if purporting to be signed by a director of the company or by the company secretary, is evidence of the passing of the resolution: CA 2006, s 356(2).

Where there is a record of a written resolution of a private company, the requirements of this Act, with respect to the passing of the resolution, are deemed to be complied with unless the contrary is proved: CA 2006, s 356(3).

The minutes of proceedings of a general meeting, if purporting to be signed by the chairman of that meeting or by the chairman of the next general meeting, are evidence of the proceedings at the meeting: CA 2006, s 356(4).

15.80 Where there is a record of proceedings of a general meeting of a company, then, until the contrary is proved:

(a) the meeting is deemed duly held and convened;

(b) all proceedings at the meeting are deemed to have duly taken place; and

(c) all appointments at the meeting are deemed valid: CA 2006, s 356(5).

Records of decisions by sole member

15.81 CA 2006, s 357 applies to a company limited by shares or by guarantee that has only one member: CA 2006, s 357(1).

Where the member takes any decision that may be taken by the company in general meeting; and has effect as if agreed by the company in general meeting, he must (unless that decision is taken by way of a written resolution) provide the company with details of that decision: CA 2006, s 357(2).

If a person fails to comply with s 357, he commits an offence: CA 2006, s 357(3), and may be subject to a fine: CA 2006, s 357(4).

Failure to comply with s 357 does not affect the validity of any decision referred to in CA 2006, s 357(2): CA 2006, s 357(5).

Inspection of records of resolutions and meetings

15.82 The records referred to in CA 2006, s 355 (records of resolutions etc) relating to the previous ten years must be kept available for inspection at the company's registered office; or at a place specified in regulations under CA 2006, s 1136: CA 2006, s 358(1).

15.83 The company must give notice to the registrar of the place at which the records are kept available for inspection; and of any change in that place, unless they have at all times been kept at the company's registered office: CA 2006, s 358(2).

15.84 The records must be open to the inspection of any member of the company without charge: s 358(3).

Any member may require a copy of any of the records on payment of such fee as may be prescribed: CA 2006, s 358(4).

If default is made for 14 days in complying with s 358(2) or an inspection required under s 358(3) is refused, or a copy requested under s 358(4) is not sent, an offence is committed by every officer of the company who is in default: CA 2006, s 358(5). A person may be subject to a fine: CA 2006, s 358(6).

In a case in which an inspection required under s 358(3) is refused or a copy requested under s 358(4) is not sent, the court may by order compel an immediate inspection of the records, or direct that the copies required be sent to the persons who requested them: CA 2006, s 358(7).

Informal unanimous consent of shareholders

15.85 Although CA 2006 sets out the law including rules and procedures for meetings to be convened and held, there has also at times been a recognition by the courts that not all the formalities may need to be complied with, if the shareholders unanimously assent informally to the passing of resolutions. The courts have held that such informal assent, provided it is unanimous, is equivalent to a validly convened meeting at which a resolution is passed. This has become known as the *'Duomatic principle'* based on the case below. The common law principle is now enshrined under the CA 2006, s 281(4)(a) states that '… nothing in this Part affects any enactment of rule of law as to things done otherwise than by passing a resolution'. Section 281(4)(c) states that 'nothing in this Part affects any enactment or rule of law as to ... cases in which a person is precluded from alleging that a resolution has not been duly passed.'

15.86 The *Duomatic* principle applies to both public and private companies, but may have less application to private companies, who may now use the written resolution procedure to pass certain resolutions. The principle is based on the rationale that as all members have validly and competently agreed on a matter affecting the company, the company should not be denied the free-will and decision making of all the shareholders: *Baroness Wenlock v River Dee Co* (1883) 36 Ch D 675; *Re New Cedos Engineering Co Ltd* [1994] 1 BCLC 797; and *Euro Brokers Holdings Ltd v Monecor (London) Ltd* [2003] 1 BCLC 506. The principle operates as a mechanism that waives the formal requirements for convening meetings.

The *Duomatic* principle does not permit shareholders to do informally what they could not have done formally by way of a written resolution or at a meeting: *Re New Cedos Engineering Co Ltd* [1994] 1 BCLC 797; *Atlas Wright (Europe) Ltd v Wright* [1999] BCC 163.

15.87 As long ago as 1920, in *Re Express Engineering Works Ltd* [1920] 1 Ch 466, the Court of Appeal considered a resolution to approve a debenture at a meeting which had not been convened in compliance with the Companies Acts. It held that as there was no suggestion of fraud involved, the company was bound in a matter *intra vires* by the unanimous agreement of its shareholders. Although the meeting was styled as a directors' meeting, all the five shareholders were present, and they might well have turned it into a general meeting, and transacted the same business. In these circumstances, the issue of the debentures was not invalid.

In *Parker & Cooper v Reading* [1926] Ch 975, Astbury J held that a company was bound in a matter *intra vires* the company by the unanimous agreement of all its corporators. If all the individual shareholders in fact assent to a transaction that is *intra vires* the company, though *ultra vires* the board, it was not necessary that they should hold a meeting in one room or one place to express that assent simultaneously. See too *Dickinson v NAL Realisations (Staffordshire) Ltd* [2019] EWCA Civ 2146.

15.88 This has become known as the *'Duomatic'* principle, which has given rise to subject of much case law in this area.

In *Re Duomatic Ltd* [1969] 1 All ER 161, Buckley J was of the view that although the shareholders did not take the formal step of formally convening a general meeting of the company, and passing a formal resolution approving the payment of directors' salaries, they had at the time of passing the accounts, applied their minds as to whether their drawings as directors, should be approved as being on account of remuneration payable to them as directors. Accordingly, their consent should be regarded as tantamount to a resolution of a general meeting. Only those shareholders who are entitled to vote at meetings can informally consent: shareholders who have no voting rights cannot assent.

15.89 The *Duomatic* principle has also been applied where there was no formal compliance with the CA 2006 for a meeting to be convened, particularly in respect of approval of long-term service contracts under s 188. In *Wright v Atlas Wright (Europe) Limited* [1999] 2 BCLC 301, Potter LJ in the Court of Appeal held that although the agreement between the claimant and the defendant did not comply with the requirements of s 188, the agreement was not rendered void under that provision. This was because the agreement was rendered enforceable by application of the principle in *Re Duomatic Ltd* [1969] 1 All ER 161, namely that the unanimous consent of all shareholders, who have a right to attend and vote at a general meeting of the company, can override formal, including statutory requirements in relation to the passing of resolutions at such meetings.

Further, in determining whether to apply the *Re Duomatic Ltd* principle, the court must examine the underlying purpose of the statutory provision. The underlying purpose of s 188 was limited, and did not exclude or render inappropriate the application of the *Re Duomatic Ltd* principle. Section 188 was for the benefit and protection of shareholders. It was to ensure that a company should not be bound by an obligation to employ a director for more than five years, unless its members had considered and approved the relevant term. The underlying intention of the section was to require unequivocal approval of the shareholders, regarding a long-term contract in respect of which there had been proper opportunity for the shareholders to consider the terms of the agreement approved.

Although s 188 set out the formality required as a precondition to the passing of the resolution, it was no more than a formality in the nature of a notice provision designed to ensure the opportunity for fully informed consent by the shareholders. It was thus amenable to waiver by the class for whose protection it was designed.

15.90 In *NBH Limited v Hoare* [2006] 2 BCLC 649, the court was required to consider whether the *Duomatic* principle also applied to substantial property transactions under CA 2006, s 190. Park J held that the principle of informal shareholder approval being as binding as a resolution in general meeting, applied to transactions affected by s 190, and therefore the shareholders' prior approval sufficed to meet the requirement of s 190.

15.91 In *Multinational Gas v Multinational Services* [1983] Ch 258, Lawton LJ stated that where approval was given to acts of directors by the shareholders, even though informally, the approval precluded the company asserting any liability against the director, because the adoption of the director's acts by the shareholders in agreement with each other, made the directors' acts the acts of the company itself.

15.92 However, there have been some situations where the court has not accepted the application of the *Duomatic* principle.

In *Schofield v Schofield* [2011] 2 BCLC 319, the Court of Appeal held that although assent could have been express or implied, verbal or by conduct, given at the time of the informal meeting or later, however, nothing short of unqualified agreement, objectively established, would suffice to establish assent within the *Duomatic* principle.

15.93 Before the *Duomatic* principle can apply, the shareholders must be properly appraised of all the facts. In *EIC Services Ltd v Phipps* [2004] 2 BCLC 589, the issue was whether the issue of shares and bonus shares, had been assented to by all the shareholders at an informal meeting, where some shareholders were not fully appraised of all relevant facts to provide an informed assent.

Neuberger J held that the *Duomatic* principle could not apply in such situations. He stated that the essence of the *Duomatic* principle was that, where the articles of a company required a course to be approved by a group of shareholders at a general meeting, that requirement could be avoided if all members of the group, being aware of the relevant facts, either gave their approval to that course, or so conducted themselves as to make it inequitable for them to deny that they had given their approval.

Whether the approval was given in advance or after the event, whether it was characterised as agreement, ratification, waiver, or estoppel, and whether members of the group gave their consent in different ways at different times, was irrelevant. However, before the *Duomatic* principle could be applied, the shareholders who were said to have assented or waived their objection had to have had the appropriate, or 'full', knowledge. Accordingly, where the directors merely informed shareholders of an intended (or past) action on the part of the directors, in circumstances in which neither the directors nor the shareholders were aware that the consent of the shareholders was required to that action, the shareholders could not be said, as a matter both of ordinary language and legal concept, to have 'assented' to that action for *Duomatic* purposes.

Quite apart from the fact that a shareholder could not be said to assent to a matter if he was merely told of it, he could not have the necessary full knowledge to enable him to assent, if he was not even aware that his assent was being sought in relation to the matter, let alone that the obtaining of his consent was a significant factor in relation to it.

On the facts, although the shareholders might well have been aware of the projected bonus issue their consent to the issue was neither sought nor given, and nor were they informed that the bonus issue would involve capitalisation of part of the company's share premium account.

15.94 The consent of the shareholders must be objectively established: *Schofield v Schofield* [2011] 2 BCLC 319. This may include agreement by the shareholder or some other mechanism that constitutes consent: *Re Bailey Hay & Co* [1971] 1 WLR 1357.

15.95 The *Duomatic* principle is, however, subject to some limitations.

In *Secretary of State for Business, Innovation and Skills v Doffman (No 2)* [2011] 2 BCLC 541, Newey J stated that the principle of ratification by informal shareholder approval, or conduct of a course of action requiring a resolution at a general meeting, was subject to the limitations that:

(a) unless it was inequitable for the shareholders to deny that they had given their approval, the principle did not apply if the shareholders had not addressed their minds to the matter in question;

(b) the principle did not apply if there was an unlawful distribution to shareholders; and

(c) the application of the principle was precluded if the company's financial circumstances were such, that the creditors were at risk and their interests overrode those of the shareholders.

In the Privy Council decision in *Ciban Management Corporation v Citco (BVI) Limited* [2020] UKPC 21, Lord Hodge was of the view that the *Duomatic* principle could operate to confer ostensible authority on a person. The principle was subject to certain recognised exceptions, namely: where there is dishonesty (see *Bowthorpe Holdings Ltd v Hills* [2002] EWHC 2331); where the shareholder had not consented to the relevant act (see *EIC Services Ltd v Phipps* [2003] EWHC 1507); and where the transaction would jeopardise the company's solvency or cause loss to creditors. Lord Hodge also referred to a further 'possible' qualification in the operation of the principle: where the consent is that of the beneficial owners rather than the registered shareholders. However, the correct view is that where the ultimate beneficial owner and not the registered shareholder is taking all the decisions in the relevant transactions, the *Duomatic* principle applies as regards the consent of (and authority given by) the ultimate beneficial owner (see *Shahar v Tsitsekkos* [2004] EWHC 2659 (Ch)).

15.96 There must be competence by the shareholder to assent to the meeting. The *Duomatic* principle cannot apply where the acts of other shareholders are required to affect the assent. In *Re New Cedos Engineering Co Ltd* [1994] 1 BCLC 797, Oliver J held that the *Duomatic* principle would not apply, where a shareholder had knowledge of the facts giving rise to any previous invalidity of meetings. Further, the principle would not apply, where all the shareholders entitled to attend and vote, assented to something *intra vires*, the company would be bound by that assent even though it was not given at a properly constituted meeting because the act of other shareholders was also required to assent.

The *Duomatic* principle cannot apply to relieve directors of liability in respect of transactions which are *ultra vires* the company (in the narrow or wider sense): *Rolled Steel Products* [1986] Ch 246.

The *Duomatic* principle will not apply to unlawful distribution of capital or unlawful payment of dividends: Re *Aveling Barford Ltd* [1989] 1 WLR 360; *Secretary of State for Business Innovation and Skills v Doffman* [2011] 2 BCLC 541.

15.97 The *Duomatic* principle can apply where breaches of duty by directors are ratified by the unanimous approval of the shareholders. The application of the *Duomatic* principle was considered in *Madoff Securities International Ltd v Raven* [2013] EWHC 3147 (Comm). Popplewell J was of the view that the principle was applicable if the directors honestly and reasonably believed the company to be solvent, notwithstanding that with the benefit of hindsight it could be shown to be insolvent or of doubtful solvency. The solvency of the company must however be objectively ascertained: *Lexi v Luqman (No 1)* [2007] EWHC 2652; *Tradepower (Holdings) Ltd v Tradepower (Hong Kong) Ltd* [2010] 1 HKC 380.

Popplewell J further stated that in order to rely on the *Duomatic* principle and for the shareholders to ratify a transaction, the transaction must be bone fide and honest: see *Re Bowthorpe Holdings Ltd* [2003] 1 BCLC 226. This involved a consideration of the legal and factual issues. On the facts, he found that directors had acted honestly and in good faith. According to Popplewell J:

> 'The legal issue is therefore whether the *Duomatic* principle is inapplicable where the directors are acting honestly but the shareholders approve the transaction acting in bad faith, in this case for the dishonest purposes of furthering a fraud. The factual issues depend upon the state of mind and intentions of the voting shareholders.'

On the facts, insofar as the transactions and payments involved a breach by the directors to act in what they perceived to be the interests of the company, or a failure to exercise reasonable care, skill and diligence, they were ratified by the shareholders unanimously. Accordingly, such ratification made such acts the acts of the company.

In *Ciban Management Corporation v Citco (BVI) Ltd* [2020] UKPC 21, the Privy Council held that where ultimate beneficial owners have been involved in relevant transactions and decisions, their consent (albeit informal) is also required. The *Duomatic* principle applies to the grant of ostensible authority as well as to actual authority.

Further, in *Satyam Enterprises Ltd v Burton* [2021] EWCA Civ 287, the Court of Appeal was required to consider the application of the *Duomatic* principle, and held that the ultimate beneficiary had provided express assent in connection with property transfer.

16 Auditors' Liability

Introduction

16.1 This Chapter addresses the following issues:

- how auditors are appointed in private companies;
- role of auditors;
- auditors' duties; and
- auditors' liability.

16.2 Part 16 of CA 2006 concerns the audited accounts and reports of a company. One objective is to demonstrate to the shareholders the financial position of the company, and the nature of the investments made by the shareholders in the company. Another objective is transparency of the information provided, to enable shareholders to make an informed decision on the company's financial status. It also provides a mechanism for directors' accountability towards the shareholders on the company's financial affairs. In this regard, auditors perform an essential function in auditing the company's accounts, and in the corporate governance system.

Appointment of auditors

Appointment of auditors of private companies: general

16.3 An auditor or auditors of a private company must be appointed for each financial year of the company, unless the directors reasonably resolve otherwise on the ground that audited accounts are unlikely to be required: CA 2006, s 485(1).

For each financial year for which an auditor or auditors is or are to be appointed (other than the company's first financial year), the appointment must be made before the end of the period of 28 days beginning with:

(a) the end of the time allowed for sending out copies of the company's annual accounts and reports for the previous financial year (see CA 2006, s 424); or

(b) if earlier, the day on which copies of the company's annual accounts and reports for the previous financial year are sent out under CA 2006, s 423.

This is the 'period for appointing auditors': CA 2006, s 485(2).

16.4 The directors may appoint an auditor or auditors of the company:

(a) at any time before the company's first period for appointing auditors;

(b) following a period during which the company (being exempt from audit) did not have any auditor, at any time before the company's next period for appointing auditors; or

(c) to fill a casual vacancy in the office of auditor: CA 2006, s 485(3).

16.5 The members may appoint an auditor or auditors by ordinary resolution:

(a) during a period for appointing auditors;

(b) if the company should have appointed an auditor or auditors during a period for appointing auditors but failed to do so; or

(c) where the directors had power to appoint under s 485(3), but have failed to make an appointment: CA 2006, s 485(4).

16.6 An auditor or auditors of a private company may only be appointed in accordance with CA 2006, s 485; or in accordance with s 486 (default power of Secretary of State).

This is without prejudice to any deemed re-appointment under s 487: CA 2006, s 485(5).

Term of office of auditors of a private company

16.7 An auditor or auditors of a private company hold office in accordance with the terms of their appointment. This is subject to the requirements that they do not take office until any previous auditor or auditors cease to hold office; and they cease to hold office at the end of the next period for appointing auditors unless re-appointed: CA 2006, s 487(1).

Fixing of auditor's remuneration

16.8 The CA 2006 distinguishes between remuneration of auditors appointed by various parties.

The remuneration of an auditor appointed by the members of a company, must be fixed by the members by ordinary resolution, or in such manner as the members may by ordinary resolution determine: CA 2006, s 492(1).

The remuneration of an auditor appointed by the company's directors must be fixed by the directors: CA 2006, s 492(2).

The remuneration of an auditor appointed by the Secretary of State must be fixed by the Secretary of State: CA 2006, s 492(3).

The term 'remuneration' includes sums paid in respect of expenses: CA 2006, s 492(4). It also applies in relation to benefits in kind as to payments of money: CA 2006, s 492(5).

Functions of the auditor

Auditor's report on company's annual accounts

16.9 A company's auditor must make a report to the company's members on all annual accounts of the company of which copies are, during his tenure of office, in the case of a private company, to be sent out to members under CA 2006, s 423: CA 2006, s 495(1).

16.10 The auditor's report must include:

(a) the identity of the company whose annual accounts are the subject of the audit;

(b) a description of the annual accounts that are the subject of the audit (including the period covered by those accounts);

(c) a description of the financial reporting framework that has been applied in the preparation of those accounts; and

(d) a description of the scope of the audit identifying the auditing standards in accordance with which the audit was conducted: CA 2006, s 495(2).

16.11 The report must state clearly whether, in the auditor's opinion, the annual accounts:

(a) give a true and fair view:

  (i) in the case of an individual balance sheet, of the state of affairs of the company as at the end of the financial year;

  (ii) in the case of an individual profit and loss account, of the profit or loss of the company for the financial year;

  (iii) in the case of group accounts, of the state of affairs as at the end of the financial year and of the profit or loss for the financial year of the undertakings included in the consolidation as a whole, so far as concerns members of the company;

(b) have been properly prepared in accordance with the relevant financial reporting framework; and

(c) have been prepared in accordance with the requirements of this Act (and, where applicable, Article 4 of the IAS Regulation).

16.12 The auditor's report:

(a) must be either unqualified or qualified;

(b) must include a reference to any matters to which the auditor wishes to draw attention by way of emphasis without qualifying the report;

(c) must include a statement on any material uncertainty relating to events that may cast significant doubt about the company's ability to continue to adopt the going concern basis of accounting; and

(d) must identify the auditor's place of establishment: CA 2006, s 495(4).

Where more than one person is appointed as an auditor:

(a) all the persons appointed must jointly make a report under this section and the report must include a statement as to whether all the persons appointed agree on the matters contained in the report; and

(b) if all the persons appointed cannot agree on the matters contained in the report, the report must include the opinions of each person appointed and give reasons for the disagreement: CA 2006, s 495(5).

The objective of the auditor's report demonstrates transparency and accountability of directors towards their shareholders: *Caparo Industries plc v Dickman* [1990] 1 All ER 568.

Duties and rights of auditors

16.13 One of the principal purposes for conducting an audit is to obtain evidence and verify details of the disclosures made in the company's financial statements. This ensures that the financial statements are free from misstatements, misrepresentations, error or fraud: In *Barings plc v Coopers & Lybrand* [1997] 1 BCLC 427, the Court of Appeal stated that auditors were required to conduct their audit in such a way as to make it probable that material misstatements in financial documents would be detected.

Previous case law considered that a low standard of diligence, skill and care in preparing the audit was required of an auditor. Early case law was particularly concerned with the extent to which the auditor could rely on management information that was being provided to the auditor, and limited the auditor's duties towards detecting any 'suspicious circumstances' in connection with the company's financial affairs. The auditors were given much flexibility in connection with the information provided by management. Auditors were not required to advise the company's management on transactional matters: *Re London & General Bank Limited (No 2)* [1895] 2 Ch 673. An auditor could rely upon statements made by the company's trusted employee in auditing the accounts: *Re Kingston Cotton Mill Co (No 2)* [1896] 2 Ch 279.

Auditors have a duty to report any fraud involving the company: *Sesea Finance Limited v KPMG* [2000] 1 BCLC 236.

However, a much higher standard of duty is now required of an auditor, particularly in respect of an audit client.

Auditors' liability

16.14 Like other professionals, auditors owe a duty of care to their clients in the performance of their work. There are various types of claims that may arise against auditors:

A contractual claim – in this case, the client alleges a breach of contractual duty by the auditor in the scope of work or services performed (eg, failure to complete the deliverables within a fixed time period).

A tortious claim – here the client may allege negligence, misleading, inaccurate or gross negligence in the performance of services by the auditor, which has caused loss to the client. In this situation, the client may be able to sue the auditors for damages.

A tortious claim by a third party against auditors – in this case there is no direct relationship between the third party and the auditors, but the third party's alleged reliance placed on the audited accounts prepared by the auditors, with a claim for damages. The claim can arise on the basis of an 'assumption of responsibility' in giving advice to the third party, for example, or meeting the tests set out in *Caparo Industries plc v Dickman* [1990] 1 All ER 568 of foreseeability, proximity and fairness. However, previously there was no one single test in determining the liability of auditors in negligence. In

Customs and Excise Commissioners v Barclays Bank [2006] 4 All ER 256, Lord Bingham stated that the emphasis should be on 'the detailed circumstances of the particular case and the particular relationship between the parties in the context of their legal and factual situation as a whole'. See too, *Standard Chartered Bank v Ceylon Petroleum* [2011] EWCH 1785 (Comm).

16.15 Some earlier cases on the scope of auditor's liability in negligence highlighted the standard of care required by an auditor in the performance of an audit. This included that an auditor must perform his duties with skill, care and caution: *Re Kingston Cotton Mill Co (No 2)* [1896] 2 Ch 279.

An auditor must also ensure that errors are not made in the course of providing services: *Fomento (Sterling Area) Ltd v Selsdon Fountain Pen Co* Ltd [1958] 1 All ER 11. An auditor's task is to conduct the audit as to make it probable that material misstatements in financial documents will be detected: *Barings plc v Coopers and Lybrand* [1997] 1 BCLC 427.

Claims by third parties

16.16 Some of the cases in respect of auditors' liability have concerned claims by third parties against auditors, based on a sufficient proximate relationship between the two parties, giving rise to a duty of care. The issue for the courts has been to determine what is the standard of duty of care owed by the auditors towards third parties, who claim negligence against the auditors? In this regard, the courts applied the common law principles of the tort of deceit to impose liability: it was necessary to show that the statement was falsely made, and reliance was placed by the third party on the false statement: *Derry v Peek* (1889) 14 App Cas 337. In an action of deceit, the claimant must prove actual fraud. Fraud is proved when it is shown that a false representation has been made knowingly, or without belief in its truth, or recklessly, without caring whether it be true or false. A false statement, made through carelessness and without reasonable ground for believing it to be true, may be evidence of fraud, but it does not necessarily amount to fraud. Such a statement, if made in the honest belief that it is true, is not fraudulent and does not render the person making it liable to an action of deceit.

Subsequently, the courts considered the application to auditors of the common law rules on negligent misstatements, which caused economic loss to the third party, based on the principles in *Hedley Byrne & Co Ltd v Heller & Partners Ltd* [1964] AC 465, where the House of Lords held that a negligent, though honest, misrepresentation, spoken or written, may give rise to an action for damages for financial loss caused thereby, apart from any contract or fiduciary relationship. This was because the law would imply a duty of care when a party seeking information from a party who had special skill, trusted him to exercise due care, and that party knew or ought to have known that reliance was being placed on his skill and judgment.

16.17 In order to demonstrate a duty of care owed by auditors towards third parties, three criteria were essential: the foreseeability of damage, proximity of relationship and the reasonableness or otherwise of imposing a duty. The leading case in this area is *Caparo Industries plc v Dickman* [1990] 1 All ER 568.

The respondents owned shares in a public company, F plc, whose accounts for the year ended 31 March 1984 showed profits far short of the predicted figure, which resulted in a dramatic drop in the quoted share price. After receipt of the audited accounts for the year ended 31 March 1984, the respondents purchased more shares in F plc, and later that year made a successful takeover bid for the company. Following the takeover, the respondents brought an action against the auditors of the company, alleging that the accounts of F plc were inaccurate and misleading, in that they showed a pre-tax profit of some £1.432 million for the year ended 31 March 1984, when in fact there had been a loss of over £400,000. The respondents alleged that the auditors had been negligent in auditing the accounts; that the respondents had purchased further shares and made their takeover bid in reliance on the audited accounts; and that the auditors owed them a duty of care either as potential bidders for F plc, because they ought to have foreseen that the 1984 results made F plc vulnerable to a takeover bid, or as an existing shareholder of F plc interested in buying more shares.

The House of Lords held that for a duty of care to arise, three aspects were required to be present:

- foreseeability of damage;
- proximity of relationship; and
- the reasonableness or otherwise of imposing a duty.

In determining whether there was a relationship of proximity between the parties, the court, guided by situations in which the existence, scope and limits of a duty of care had previously been held to exist rather than by a single general principle, would determine whether the particular damage suffered was the kind of damage which the defendant was under a duty to prevent, and whether there were circumstances from which the court could pragmatically conclude that a duty of care existed.

Where a statement put into more or less general circulation might foreseeably be relied on by strangers for any one of a variety of different purposes, which the maker of the statement had no specific reason to anticipate, there was no relationship of proximity between the maker of the statement, and any person relying on it unless it was shown that the maker knew that his statement would be communicated to the person relying on it, either as an individual or as a member of an identifiable class, specifically in connection with a particular transaction or a transaction of a particular kind, and that that person would be very likely to rely on it, for the purpose of deciding whether to enter into that transaction.

The auditor of a public company's accounts owed no duty of care to a member of the public at large, who relied on the accounts to buy shares in the company, because the court would not deduce a relationship of proximity between the auditor and a member of the public, when to do so, would give rise to unlimited liability on the part of the auditor. Furthermore, an auditor owed no duty of care to an individual shareholder in the company, who wished to buy more shares in the company, since an individual shareholder was in no better position than a member of the public at large; and the auditor's statutory duty to prepare accounts was owed to the body of shareholders as a whole. The purpose for which accounts were prepared and audited being to enable the shareholders as a body to exercise informed control of the company, and not to enable individual shareholders to buy shares with a view to profit. It followed that the auditors did not owe a duty of care to the respondents either as shareholders, or as potential investors in the company.

Lord Oliver was of the view that the provisions under CA 2006 on audits and auditors, required directors to be responsible for preparation of the company's accounts, and for the auditors to audit them. The audit was primarily for the company's benefit, but may at times be relied upon by other class of persons other than the company's shareholders. The company was entitled to rely upon them owing to the fiduciary relationship of directors towards the company; and the employment of auditors to prepare the accounts was based on a contractual relationship between the auditors and the company.

The provisions under CA 2006 concerning audits and auditors did not establish a formal relationship of a duty of care by auditors towards third parties, who required a copy of the audited reports or towards those who inspected the accounts at Companies House. A duty of care by the auditors under the Companies Act was only owed to the company's shareholders, but did not extend to a shareholder's decision to buy further shares in the company.

According to Lord Bridge, in order to establish a duty of care by the auditors towards other persons, there was a requirement to show a 'special relationship' with the third party who suffered loss. In this regard, the claimant was required to demonstrate that the auditors considered that the accounts and report:

> '… would be communicated to the plaintiff, either as an individual or as a member of an identifiable class, specifically in connection with a particular transaction or transactions of a particular kind (eg in a prospectus inviting investment) and that the plaintiff would be very likely to rely on it for the purpose of deciding whether or not to enter upon that transaction or upon a transaction of that kind.'

Liability for negligent misstatement

16.18 As regards an auditor's liability for negligent misstatement, according to the dissenting judgment of Lord Denning in *Candler v Crane, Christmas & Co* [1951] 2 KB 164 (which was approved in *Caparo Industries plc v Dickman* [1990] 2 AC 605), 'accountants owe a duty of care not only to their own clients, but also to all those whom they know will rely on their accounts in the transactions for which those accounts are prepared'. According to Lord Denning, accountants, exercising a calling which required knowledge and skill, owed a duty to use care in the work, which resulted in their accounts and reports, and also in the rendering of their accounts and reports. They owed that duty not only to their clients with whom they had contracted, but to any third person to whom they showed their accounts and reports or to whom they knew that their clients were going to show them, when, to the knowledge of the accountants that person would consider their accounts and reports with a view to the investment of money or taking other action to his gain or detriment. The duty only extended in respect of those transactions for which the accountants knew that their accounts were required. Lord Denning held that accountants would be liable for negligent misstatements even though there was no contractual relationship between the auditors and the third parties:

> 'First, what persons are under such duty? My answer is those persons such as accountants, surveyors, valuers and analysts, whose profession and occupation it is to examine books, accounts, and other things, and to make reports on which other people – other than their clients – rely in the ordinary course of business. Their duty is not merely a duty to use care in their reports. They have also a duty to use care in their work which results in their reports. Herein lies the difference between these professional men and other persons who have been held to be under no duty to use care in their statements, such as promoters who issue a prospectus and trustees who answer inquiries about the trust funds … Those persons do not bring, and are not expected to bring, any professional knowledge or skill into the preparation of their

> statements: they can only be made responsible by the law affecting persons generally, such as contract, estoppel, innocent misrepresentation or fraud. But it is very different with persons who engage in a calling which requires special knowledge and skill. From very early times it has been held that they owe a duty of care to those who are closely and directly affected by their work, apart altogether from any contract or undertaking in that behalf.'

With specific regard to accountants, he stated:

> 'They owe the duty, of course, to their employer or client; and also I think to any third person to whom they themselves show the accounts, or to whom they know their employer is going to show the accounts, so as to induce him to invest money or take some other action on them. But I do not think the duty can be extended still further so as to include strangers of whom they have heard nothing and to whom their employer without their knowledge may choose to show their accounts. Once the accountants have handed their accounts to their employer they are not, as a rule, responsible for what he does with them without their knowledge or consent.'

The principles concerning negligent misstatements established in *Hedley Byrne & Co Ltd v Heller & Partners Ltd* were further elucidated by Lord Bridge in *Caparo Industries plc v Dickman* [1990] 2 AC 605, where he stated that:

> '… that the defendant knew that his statement would be communicated to the plaintiff, either as an individual or as a member of an identifiable class, specifically in connection with a particular transaction or transactions of a particular kind (eg in a prospectus inviting investment) and that the plaintiff would be very likely to rely on it for the purpose of deciding whether or not to enter upon that transaction or upon a transaction of that kind.'

16.19 In this regard, the test is objective. Lord Oliver in *Caparo* set out the following test in establishing the necessary relationship between the maker of a statement or giver of advice ('the adviser') and the recipient who acts in reliance upon it ('the advisee'):

(1) the advice is required for a purpose, whether particularly specified or generally described, which is made known, either actually or inferentially, to the adviser at the time when the advice is given;

(2) the adviser knows, either actually or inferentially, that his advice will be communicated to the advisee, either specifically or as a member of an ascertainable class, in order that it should be used by the advisee for that purpose;

(3) it is known either actually or inferentially, that the advice so communicated is likely to be acted upon by the advisee for that purpose without independent inquiry, and

(4) it is so acted upon by the advisee to his detriment.

Modern judicial approaches on professional advisers' negligence towards clients

16.20 A modern judicial approach to a professional adviser's negligence has been considered in two Supreme Court cases which has implications for professional advisers, including auditors: *Khan v Meadows* [2021] UKSC 21 and *Manchester Building Society v Grant Thornton UK LLP* [2021] UKSC 20.

In *Khan v Meadows*, the Supreme Court was required to consider a claim for clinical negligence, where Dr Khan had led Ms Meadows to believe that she was not a carrier of haemophilia gene. Shortly after, she became pregnant and gave birth to a son, who was subsequently diagnosed as a haemophilia carrier. It was not disputed that the doctor was liable in negligence for the expenses that would be incurred by Ms Meadows in bringing up her son attributable to his haemophilia. The dispute between the parties arose from the fact that Ms Meadow's son was subsequently diagnosed with autism unrelated to haemophilia. The legal issue was whether Dr Khan was liable for all costs related to Ms Meadow's son's disabilities arising from her pregnancy, or only from haemophilia. In other words, what was Dr Khan's scope of duty in advising Ms Meadow's? The Supreme Court held that Dr Khan was only liable for losses falling within the scope of her duty of care, namely to advise Ms Meadows on whether or not she was a carrier of the haemophilia gene. She was not liable for the costs associated with Ms Meadow's son's autism. Her scope of duty did not extend to advising on the autism issue.

The Supreme Court identified six model questions that need to be addressed for application of the scheme of duty of care principle under the tort of negligence to apply:

(1) Is the harm (loss, injury and damage) which is the subject matter of the claim actionable in negligence? (the 'actionability question');

(2) What are the risks of harm to the claimant against which the law imposes on the defendant a duty to take care? (the 'scope of duty question');

(3) Did the defendant breach his or her duty by his or her act or omission? (the 'breach question');

(4) Is the loss for which the claimant seeks damages the consequence of the defendant's act or omission? (the 'factual causation question');

(5) Is there a sufficient nexus between a particular element of the harm for which the claimant seeks damages and the subject matter of the defendant's duty of care as analysed at stage 2 above? (the 'duty nexus question'); and

(6) Is a particular element of the harm for which the claimant seeks damages irrecoverable because it is too remote, or because there is a different effective cause or because the claimant has mitigated his or her loss or has failed to avoid loss which he or she could reasonably have been expected to avoid? (the 'legal responsibility question').

The second stage in the above scheme relates to the scope of duty principle. This provides that a defendant is liable only for losses which fall within the scope of his or her duty of care to the claimant. In addressing the scope of duty question, the court seeks to identify the purpose for which advice or information was given. It asks: "what was the risk which the advice or information was intended and was reasonably understood to address?'

In some cases, the answer to the scope of duty question also answers the duty nexus question (stage five). However, in cases where the scope of duty question is concerned with the quantification or extent of a particular kind of loss, the duty nexus question should be addressed separately, after the court has determined that there is a breach of duty and factual causation.

Applying the six step principles, there was no duty of nexus between Dr Khan's advice concerning haemophilia and Ms Meadow's son's autism. The law did not impose on Dr Khan any duty in respect of unrelated risks such as autism.

Manchester Building Society v Grant Thornton UK LLP [2021] concerned the scope of duty of care in the context of professional advice given by accountants in a contractual relationship with their client. The Supreme Court held that the Society suffered a loss falling with the scope of duty of care assumed by Grant Thornton, taking account of the purpose for which it gave the advice. The accountants were therefore liable for the loss the Society had suffered. However, there would be a reduction in damages of 50% for the Society's contributory negligence.

The Supreme Court stated that the duty of care assumed by a professional adviser was governed by the purpose of the duty. It was to be judged on an objective basis by reference to the reason why the advice was being given. One looks to see what risk the duty was supposed to guard against, and then look to see whether the loss suffered represented the fruition of that risk.

The Supreme Court considered that the focus should be more directly on the purpose for which the defendant gave the advice in question. There was no need to apply a counterfactual test (see *South Australia Asset Management Corpn v York Montague Ltd* [1997] AC 191 ('SAAMCO')) to arrive at the correct conclusion.

The loss suffered by the Society fell within the scope of the duty of care assumed by Grant Thornton, in light of the purpose of its advice. Grant Thornton's negligent advice was an effective cause of the loss. However, the Society's mismatching of mortgages and swaps in an overly ambitious application of the business model advised by Grant Thornton, amounted to contributory negligence.

Lord Leggatt framed the scope of duty principle in the language of causation. The question to be determined was whether there was a sufficient causal relationship between what made the information or advice wrong, and the 'basic loss' (ie the "factually caused loss"). He decided that there was a causal connection between Grant Thornton's negligent advice, and the Society's basic loss. The loss was caused by the lack of an effective hedging relationship between the swaps and the lifetime mortgages, which they were supposed to hedge, which Grant Thornton failed to appreciate and report to the Society, making its advice wrong.

These two Supreme Court decisions are significant in their application to professional advisers, which will include auditors' liability. In assessing the scope of duty of care of auditors, the English courts will apply the six steps or principles in *Khan v Meadows* to ascertain their liability in negligence, including contributory negligence which would have the effect of reducing the claimant's claim for damages. In *Manchester Building Society*, the Supreme Court stated that the use of terms 'information' and 'advice' should cease, and instead the focus should be on the need to identify with precision in any given case, the matters on which the professional person has undertaken responsibility to advise and, in the light of those matters, the risks associated with the transaction, which the adviser may fairly be taken to owe a duty of care, to protect the client against. This aspect is to be determined by identifying whether or not the adviser's contribution to the decision making process is limited. The SAAMCO analytical tool was now only considered as a 'useful cross-check' in some cases, to test whether the loss claimed fell within the scope of duty.

17 Company share capital

Introduction

17.1 This chapter considers following issues:

- a consideration of the company's share capital;
- procedure for allotment of shares by directors;
- pre-emption rights; and
- reduction of share capital for private companies.

Shares and share capital of a company

17.2 CA 2006, Pt 17, Ch 1 addresses the issue of shares and share capital of a company.

Shares

17.3 The term 'shares' in relation to a company means shares in the company's share capital: CA 2006, s 540(1). It includes stock (with some exceptions: CA 2006, s 540(4)). A company's shares may no longer be converted into stock: CA 2006, s 540(2).

Nature of shares

17.4 The shares or other interest of a member in a company are personal property, and are not in the nature of real estate. CA 2006, s 541.

Nominal value of shares

17.5 Shares in a limited company which have a share capital, must each have a fixed nominal value: CA 2006, s 542(1). An allotment of a share that does not have a fixed nominal value is void: CA 2006, s 542(2).

Shares in a limited company having a share capital may be denominated in any currency, and different classes of shares may be denominated in different currencies. But see s 765 (initial authorised minimum share capital requirement for public company to be met by reference to share capital denominated in sterling or euros): CA 2006, s 542(3).

If a company purports to allot shares in contravention of s 542, an offence is committed by every officer of the company who is in default: CA 2006, s 542(4). This may result in a fine being imposed on the officer: CA 2006, s 542(5).

Section 542 should be read together with s 9, which requires the application for registration of a company that is to be formed with a share capital, to include a 'statement of capital and initial shareholdings'. The contents of this statement are prescribed in s 10, and this includes a requirement to set out a total number of shares, and the aggregate nominal value of the shares, which are to be taken by the subscribers to the memorandum on formation.

Numbering of shares

17.6 Each share in a company which has a share capital, must be distinguished by its appropriate number: CA 2006, s 543(1). See CA 2006, s 543(2) for exceptions.

If at any time all the issued shares in a company are fully paid up and rank *pari passu* for all purposes; or all the issued shares of a particular class in a company are fully paid up and rank *pari passu* for all purposes, none of those shares need thereafter have a distinguishing number, so long as it remains fully paid up and ranks *pari passu* for all purposes with all shares of the same class for the time being issued and fully paid up: CA 2006, s 543(2).

Transferability of shares

17.7 The CA 2006 allows the shares or other interest of any member in a company, to be transferable in accordance with the company's articles: CA 2006, s 544(1).

This is subject to the Stock Transfer Act 1963 (c 18) (which enables securities of certain descriptions to be transferred by a simplified process); and regulations under Ch 2 of Pt 21 of this Act (which enable title to securities to be evidenced and transferred without a written instrument): CA 2006, s 544(2). See Pt 21 of this Act generally as regards share transfers: CA 2006, s 544(3).

Companies having a share capital

17.8 Section 545 provides that references in the Companies Acts to a company having a share capital are to a company that has power under its constitution to issue shares

Issued and allotted share capital

17.9 The term 'issued share capital' under CA 2006 refers to shares of a company that have been issued; and 'allotted share capital' refers to shares of a company that have been allotted: CA 2006, s 546(1). Issuance and allotment are two different aspects under CA 2006: *Clarke's Case* (1878) 8 Ch D 635.

In *National Westminster Bank plc v Inland Revenue Commissioners* [1994] 3 All ER 1, the House of Lords considered the distinction between 'issue of shares' and 'allotment'. It held that shares were 'issued' when an application had been followed by allotment, and notification and completed by entry on the register. The term 'issue' in relation to shares meant something distinct from allotment. It signified that some subsequent act had been done, whereby the title of the allottee had become complete. The Companies Acts have preserved the distinction in English law between an enforceable contract for the issue of shares (which contract is constituted by an allotment) and the issue of shares, which is completed by registration. Accordingly, the word 'issue' under the previous Income and Corporation Taxes Act 1988, was appropriate to indicate the whole process whereby unissued shares were applied for, allotted and finally registered.

Under the Companies Acts, any references to issued or allotted shares, or to issued or allotted share capital, include shares taken on the formation of the company by the subscribers to the company's memorandum: CA 2006, s 546(2).

Share capital

17.10 CA 2006 defines certain terms in connection with the company's share capital.

Called-up share capital

17.11 Section 547 defines a company's called-up share capital. In the Companies Acts 'called-up share capital', in relation to a company, means so much of its share capital as equals the aggregate amount of the calls made on its shares (whether or not those calls have been paid), together with any share capital paid up without being called; any share capital to be paid on a specified future date under the articles, the terms of allotment of the relevant shares or any other arrangements for payment of those shares; and 'uncalled share capital' is to be construed accordingly.

Equity share capital

17.12 Section 547 defines 'equity share capital' in relation to a company, as its issued share capital, excluding any part of that capital that, neither as respects dividends nor as respects capital, carries any right to participate beyond a specified amount in a distribution.

Allotment of shares: general provisions

17.13 CA 2006, Pt 17, Ch 2 sets out the provisions on allotment of shares.

Power of directors to allot shares

Exercise by directors of power to allot shares

17.14 Section 549 prohibits directors of a company from exercising any power of the company to allot shares in the company; or to grant rights to subscribe for, or to convert any security into, shares in the company, except in accordance with s 550 (private company with single class of shares) or s 551 (authorisation by company): CA 2006, s 549(1).

Section 549(1) does not apply to the allotment of shares in pursuance of an employees' share scheme; or to the grant of a right to subscribe for, or to convert any security into, shares so allotted: CA 2006, s 549(2).

In the event s 549 applies in relation to the grant of a right to subscribe for, or to convert any security into, shares, it does not apply in relation to the allotment of shares pursuant to that right: CA 2006, s 549(3).

A director or a person who knowingly contravenes, or permits or authorises a contravention of s 549 commits an offence: CA 2006, s 549(4), and may be subject to a fine: CA 2006, s 549(5).

However, s 549 does not affect the validity of an allotment or other transaction: CA 2006, s 549(6).

Power of directors to allot shares: private company with only one class of shares

17.15 Where a private company has only one class of shares, the directors may exercise any power of the company to allot shares of that class, or to grant rights to subscribe for or to convert any security into such shares. The exception is where to the extent directors are prohibited from doing so by the company's articles: CA 2006, s 550.

Section 550 therefore empowers the directors to allot shares (or to grant rights to subscribe for, or convert any security into shares), where the company is a private company which will have only one class after the proposed allotment. There is no requirement for the directors to have prior authority from the company's members for such an allotment of shares. In addition, the members may, if they wish, restrict or prohibit this power through the articles of association. The definition of 'classes of shares' is contained in s 808.

Power of directors to allot shares: authorisation by company

17.16 The company's directors may exercise a power of the company to allot shares in the company, or to grant rights to subscribe for or to convert any security into shares in the company. However, they must be authorised to do so by the company's articles or by resolution of the company: CA 2006, s 551(1).

The CA 2006 envisages various situations when authorisation may be given. The authorisation may be given for a particular exercise of the power, or for its exercise generally, and it may be unconditional or subject to conditions: CA 2006, s 551(2).

The authorisation must state the maximum number of shares that may be allotted under it. It must also specify the date on which it will expire, which must be not more than five years from: (i) in the case of authorisation contained in the company's articles at the time of its original incorporation, the date of that incorporation; and (ii) in any other case, the date on which the resolution is passed by virtue of which the authorisation is given: CA 2006, s 551(3).

17.17 The authorisation may be renewed or further renewed by resolution of the company for a further period not exceeding five years. It may also be revoked or varied at any time by a company resolution: CA 2006, s 551(4).

A resolution renewing authorisation must state (or restate) the maximum amount of shares that may be allotted under the authorisation or, as the case may be, the amount remaining to be allotted under it, and specify the date on which the renewed authorisation will expire: CA 2006, s 551(5).

In relation to rights to subscribe for or to convert any security into shares in the company, the references to the maximum amount of shares that may be allotted under the authorisation, are to the maximum amount of shares that may be allotted pursuant to the rights: CA 2006, s 551(6).

17.18 The directors may allot shares, or grant rights to subscribe for or to convert any security into shares, after authorisation has expired if the shares are allotted, or the rights are granted, in pursuance of an offer or agreement made by the company before the authorisation expired, and the authorisation allowed the company to make an offer or agreement which would or might require shares to be allotted, or rights to be granted, after the authorisation had expired: CA 2006, s 551(7).

A company resolution to give, vary, revoke or renew authorisation under s 551 may be an ordinary resolution, even though it amends the company's articles: CA 2006, s 551(8).

CA 2006, Pt 3, Ch 3 (resolutions affecting a company's constitution) also applies to a resolution under s 551: CA 2006, s 551(9).

Registration of allotment

17.19 A company must register an allotment of shares as soon as practicable, and in any event within two months after the date of the allotment: CA 2006, s 554(1).

This does not apply if the company has issued a share warrant in respect of the shares (see s 779): CA 2006, s 554(2).

If an election is in force under Pt 8, Ch 2A, the obligation to register the allotment of shares, is replaced by an obligation to deliver particulars of the allotment of shares to the registrar in accordance with that Chapter: CA 2006, s 554(2A) (as inserted by SBEEA 2015, Sch 5, Pt 2).

17.20 If a company fails to comply with s 544, an offence is committed by the company, and every officer of the company who is in default: CA 2006, s 554(3), who may then be liable to a fine: CA 2006, s 554(4).

For the company's duties as to the issue of share certificates etc, see Pt 21 (certification and transfer of securities): CA 2006, s 554(5).

Return of allotment

17.21 CA 2006, 555–557 are concerned with provisions dealing with return of allotment.

Return of allotment by limited company

17.22 Section 555 applies to a company limited by shares and to a company limited by guarantee, and having a share capital: CA 2006, s 551(1).The company must, within one month of making an allotment of shares, deliver to the registrar for registration a return of the allotment: CA 2006, s 551(2). This return must contain the prescribed information, and be accompanied by a statement of capital: CA 2006, s 551(3).

The statement of capital must state with respect to the company's share capital, at the date to which the return is made up, the total number of shares of the company, the aggregate nominal value of those shares; the aggregate amount (if any) unpaid on those shares (whether on account of their nominal value or by way of premium), and for each class of shares: (i) prescribed particulars of the rights attached to the shares, (ii) the total number of shares of that class, and (iii) the aggregate nominal value of shares of that class: CA 2006, s 555(4) (as amended by SBEEA 2015, Sch 6).

17.23 A return of allotments must be accompanied by a statement of capital. A statement of capital is in essence a 'snapshot' of a company's total subscribed capital at a particular point in time (in this context, the date to which the return of allotments is made up).

Offence of failure to make return

17.24 If a company makes default in complying with s 555 (return of allotment of shares by limited company, an offence is committed by every officer of the company who is in default: CA 2006, s 557(1), who may then be subject to a fine: CA 2006, s 557(2).

In the case of default in delivering to the registrar within one month after the allotment the return required by s 555, any person liable for the default may apply to the court for relief. The may grant relief if satisfied: (i) that the omission to deliver the document was accidental or due to inadvertence; or (ii) that it is just and equitable to grant relief. The court may make an order extending the time for delivery of the document, for such period as the court thinks proper: CA 2006, s 557(3).

When shares are allotted

17.25 Under the Companies Acts, shares in a company are allotted, when a person acquires the unconditional right to be included in the company's register of members (or, as the case may be, to have the person's name and other particulars delivered to the registrar under Pt 8, Ch 2A, and registered by the registrar) in respect of the shares: CA 2006, s 558 (as inserted by SBEEA 2015, Sch 5, Pt 2).

Provisions about allotment not applicable to shares taken on formation

17.26 The provisions of CA 2006, Pt 17, Ch 2 do not apply in relation to the taking of shares by the subscribers to the memorandum, on the formation of the company: CA 2006, s 559.

Allotment of equity securities: existing shareholders' right of pre-emption

17.27 CA 2006, Pt 17, Ch 3 is concerned with allotment of equity securities with reference to existing shareholders' rights of pre-emption.

Meaning of 'equity securities' and related expressions

17.28 The CA 2006 defines certain terms in relation to allotment of equity securities. 'Equity securities' refers to ordinary shares in the company, or rights to subscribe for, or to convert securities into, ordinary shares in the company. 'Ordinary shares' means shares other than shares that, as respects dividends and capital, carry a right to participate only up to a specified amount in a distribution: CA 2006, s 560(1).

The references to the allotment of equity securities in CA 2006, Pt 17, Ch 3 include the grant of a right to subscribe for, or to convert any securities into, ordinary shares in the company, and the sale of ordinary shares in the company, that immediately before the sale are held by the company as treasury shares: CA 2006, s 560(2).

Existing shareholders' right of pre-emption

17.29 A company must not allot equity securities to a person on any terms, unless it has made an offer to each person who holds ordinary shares in the company, to allot to him on the same or more favourable terms a proportion of those securities, namely, as nearly as practicable, equal to the proportion in nominal value held by him of the ordinary share capital of the company, and the period during which any such offer may be accepted has expired, or the company has received notice of the acceptance or refusal of every offer so made: CA 2006, s 561(1).

Securities that a company has offered to allot to a holder of ordinary shares may be allotted to him, or anyone in whose favour he has renounced his right to their allotment, without contravening s 561(1)(b): CA 2006, s 561(2).

If s 561(1) applies in relation to the grant of such a right, it does not apply in relation to the allotment of shares in pursuance of that right: CA 2006, s 561(3).

17.30 Shares held by the company as treasury shares are disregarded for the purposes of s 561. In this situation, the company is not treated as a person who holds ordinary shares, and the shares are not treated as forming part of the ordinary share capital of the company: CA 2006, s 561(4).

CA 2006, s 561 is subject to ss 564–566 (exceptions to pre-emption right), ss 567 and 568 (exclusion of rights of pre-emption), ss 569–573 (disapplication of pre-emption rights), and s 576 (saving for certain older pre-emption procedures): CA 2006, s 561(5).

Communication of pre-emption offers to shareholders

17.31 CA 2006 specifies the manner in which offers required by s 561 are to be made to holders of a company's shares: CA 2006, s 562(1). Such offers may be made in hard copy or electronic form: CA 2006, s 562(2).

The offer must state a period during which it may be accepted, and the offer must not be withdrawn before the end of that period: CA 2006, s 562(4).

The period must be at least 21 days beginning, in the case of an offer made in hard copy, with the date on which the offer is sent or supplied. In the case of an offer made in electronic form, with the date on which the offer is sent. In the case of an offer made by publication in the *Gazette*, with the date of publication: CA 2006, s 562(5).

Liability of company and officers in case of contravention

17.32 Where there is a contravention of s 561 (existing shareholders' right of pre-emption), or s 562 (communication of pre-emption offers to shareholders): CA 2006, s 563(1), the company and every one of its officers, who knowingly authorised or permitted the contravention, are jointly and severally liable to compensate any person to whom an offer should have been made, in accordance with those provisions for any loss, damage, costs or expenses, which the person has sustained or incurred by reason of the contravention: CA 2006, s 563(2).

No proceedings to recover any such loss, damage, costs or expenses can be commenced after the expiration of two years from the delivery to the registrar of companies of the return of allotment; or where equity securities other than shares are granted, from the date of the grant: CA 2006, s 563(3).

Exceptions to right of pre-emption

17.33 CA 2006, s 561(1) (existing shareholders' right of pre-emption) does not apply in relation to the allotment of bonus shares: CA 2006, s 564.

Further, s 561(1) does not apply to a particular allotment of equity securities, if these are, or are to be, wholly or partly paid up otherwise than in cash: CA 2006, s 565.

Exclusion of right of pre-emption

Exclusion of requirements by private companies

17.34 All or any of the requirements of s 561 or s 562, may be excluded by provision contained in the articles of association of a private company: CA 2006, s 567(1).

These provisions may be excluded generally in relation to the allotment by the company of equity securities, or in relation to allotments of a particular description: CA 2006, s 567(2).

17.35 Any requirement or authorisation contained in the articles of a private company, that is inconsistent with either s 561 or s 562, is treated as a provision excluding that section: CA 2006, s 567(3).

A provision to which s 568 applies (exclusion of pre-emption right: corresponding right conferred by articles) is not to be treated as inconsistent with s 561: CA 2006, s 567(4).

Exclusion of pre-emption right: articles conferring corresponding right

17.36 CA 2006, s 568 applies where, in a case in which s 561 (existing shareholders' right of pre-emption) would otherwise apply, a company's articles contain provision ('pre-emption provision') prohibiting the company from allotting ordinary shares of a particular class, unless it has complied with the condition that it makes such an offer as is described in s 561(1) to each person who holds ordinary shares of that class, and in accordance with that provision: (i) the company makes an offer to allot shares to such a holder; and (ii) he or anyone in whose favour he has renounced his right to their allotment accepts the offer: CA 2006, s 568(1).

In such a situation, s 561 does not apply to the allotment of those shares. The company may therefore allot them accordingly: CA 2006, s 568(2).

17.37 The provisions of s 562 (communication of pre-emption offers to shareholders) apply in relation to offers made, in pursuance of the pre-emption provision of the company's articles: CA 2006, s 568(3). This is subject to s 567 (exclusion of requirements by private companies).

If there is a contravention of the pre-emption provision of the company's articles, the company, and every officer of it who knowingly authorised or permitted the contravention, are jointly and severally liable to compensate any person to whom an offer should have been made under the provision for any loss, damage, costs or expenses which the person has sustained or incurred by reason of the contravention: CA 2006, s 568(4).

No proceedings to recover any such loss, damage, costs or expenses may be commenced after the expiration of two years from the delivery to the registrar of companies of the return of allotment, or where equity securities other than shares are granted, from the date of the grant: CA 2006, s 568(5).

Disapplication of pre-emption rights

Disapplication of pre-emption rights: private company with only one class of shares

17.38 The directors of a private company that has only one class of shares, may be given power by the articles, or by a special resolution of the company, to allot equity securities of that class, as if s 561 (existing shareholders' right of pre-emption) did not apply to the allotment, or applied to the allotment with such modifications as the directors may determine: CA 2006, s 569(1).

Where directors make an allotment under s 569, the provisions of Pt 17, Ch 3 apply: CA 2006, s 569(2).

Disapplication of pre-emption rights: directors acting under general authorisation

17.39 Where the company directors are generally authorised for the purposes of s 551 (power of directors to allot shares etc: authorisation by company), they may be given power by the articles, or by a special resolution of the company, to allot equity securities pursuant to that authorisation as if s 561 (existing shareholders' right of pre-emption) did not apply to the allotment, or applied to the allotment with such modifications as the directors may determine: CA 2006, s 570(1).

Where the directors make an allotment under s 570, the provisions of Ch 3 apply: CA 2006, s 570(2).

17.40 The power conferred by s 570 ceases to have effect, when the authorisation to which it relates is revoked, or would (if not renewed) expire. However, if the authorisation is renewed, the power may also be renewed, for a period not longer than that for which the authorisation is renewed, by a special resolution of the company: CA 2006, s 570(3).

Even where the power given by s 570 has expired, the directors may allot equity securities under an offer or agreement previously made by the company, if the power enabled the company to make an offer or agreement, that would or might require equity securities to be allotted after it expired: CA 2006, s 570(4).

Disapplication of pre-emption rights by special resolution

17.41 Where the directors of a company are authorised for the purposes of s 551 (power of directors to allot shares etc: authorisation by company), whether generally or otherwise, the company may by special resolution resolve that s 561 (existing shareholders' right of pre-emption) does not apply to a specified allotment of equity securities, to be made under that authorisation, or applies to such an allotment with such modifications as may be specified in the resolution: CA 2006, s 571(1).

Where such a resolution is passed, the provisions of Ch 3 apply accordingly: CA 2006, s 571(2).

17.42 A special resolution under s 571 ceases to apply when the authorisation to which it relates, is either revoked or would expire if not renewed: CA 2006, s 571(3). However, if the authorisation is renewed, the resolution may also be renewed, for a period not longer than that for which the authorisation is renewed, by a special resolution of the company.

Even where any such resolution has expired, the directors may allot equity securities in pursuance of an offer or agreement previously made by the company, if the resolution enabled the company to make an offer or agreement that would or might require equity securities to be allotted after it expired: CA 2006, s 571(4).

17.43 A special resolution under s 571, or a special resolution to renew such a resolution, must not be proposed, unless it is recommended by the directors, and the directors have complied with ss 571(6) and (7): CA 2006, s 571(5).

Before a special resolution is proposed, the directors must make a written statement setting out their reasons for making the recommendation, the amount to be paid to the company in respect of the equity securities to be allotted, and the directors' justification of that amount: CA 2006, s 571(6).

The directors' statement must, if the resolution is proposed as a written resolution, be sent or submitted to every eligible member at or before the time at which the proposed resolution is sent or submitted to him. Alternatively, if the resolution is proposed at a general meeting, it must be circulated to the members entitled to notice of the meeting with that notice: CA 2006, s 571(7).

Liability for false statement in the directors' statement

17.44 Section 572 applies in relation to a directors' statement under s 571 (special resolution disapplying pre-emption rights) that is sent, submitted or circulated under s 571(7): CA 2006, s 572(1).

A person who knowingly or recklessly authorises or permits the inclusion of any matter that is misleading, false or deceptive in a material particular in such a statement commits an offence: CA 2006, s 572(2). The person can be subject to imprisonment and/or fine: CA 2006, s 572(3).

Payment for shares

17.45 CA 2006, Pt 17, Ch 5 is concerned with the provisions dealing with payment for shares.

General rules

Shares not to be allotted at a discount

17.46 A company's shares must not be allotted at a discount: CA 2006, s 580(1). The allotment must not be less than the nominal value or par value of the shares. In *Ooregum Gold Mining Co of India v Roper* [1892] AC 125, the House of Lords held that a company had no power to issue shares as fully paid up, for a money consideration less than their nominal value.

According to Vaughan Williams LJ in *Re Innes & Co Ltd* [1903] 2 Ch 254, each transaction must be considered on its facts to see if there is any basis for a colourable transaction:

> 'It cannot be suggested that mere inadequacy of price was sufficient of itself to invalidate the contract. You must show that, these shares not having been paid for at all, the contract for purchase was a colourable transaction, and that in truth and in fact, qua value, these shares were not part of the consideration, but were a gift.'

In *Re White Star Line Ltd* [1938] 1 Ch 458, the Court of Appeal held that the consideration payable for the shares in money's worth by way of deferred creditors' certificates, which were less than the nominal value of the shares, was 'illusory' and did not amount to a payment under the Companies Acts

See too, *Welton v Saffery* [1897] AC 299; and *Re Eddystone Marine Insurance Co* [1893] 3 Ch 9.

If shares are allotted in contravention of CA 2006, s 580, the allottee is liable to pay the company an amount equal to the amount of the discount.

Provision for different amounts to be paid on shares

17.47 A company, if so authorised by its articles, may make arrangements on the issue of shares, for a difference between the shareholders in the amounts and times of payment of calls on their shares; accept from any member the whole or part of the amount remaining unpaid on any shares held by him, although no part of that amount has been called up; or pay a dividend in proportion to the amount paid up on each share, where a larger amount is paid up on some shares than on others: CA 2006, s 581(1).

General rule as to means of payment

17.48 Shares allotted by a company, and any premium on them, may be paid up in money or money's worth (including goodwill and know-how): CA 2006, s 582(1).

However, s 582 does not prevent a company from allotting bonus shares to its members, or from paying up, with sums available for the purpose, any amounts for the time being unpaid on any of its shares (whether on account of the nominal value of the shares or by way of premium): CA 2006, s 582(2).

Meaning of payment in cash

17.49 A share in a company is deemed paid up (as to its nominal value or any premium on it) in cash, or allotted for cash, if the consideration received for the allotment or payment up, is a cash consideration: CA 2006, s 583(2).

The term 'cash consideration' refers to cash received by the company, or a cheque received by the company in good faith, that the directors have no reason for suspecting will not be paid; or a release of a liability of the company for a liquidated sum (*Re Harmony and Montague Tin and Copper Mining Co, Spargo's Case* (1873) 8 Ch App 407); or an undertaking to pay cash to the company at a future date; or payment by any other means giving rise to a present or future entitlement (of the company or a person acting on the company's behalf) to a payment; or credit equivalent to payment, in cash: CA 2006, s 583(3).

17.50 In relation to the allotment or payment up of shares in a company, the payment of cash to a person other than the company, or an undertaking to pay cash to a person other than the company, counts as consideration other than cash: CA 2006, s 583(5).

This does not apply for the purposes of Ch 3 to Pt 17 of the CA 2006 (allotment of equity securities: existing shareholders' right of pre-emption). For the purpose of determining whether a share is or is to be allotted for cash, or paid up in cash, 'cash' includes foreign currency: CA 2006, s 583(6).

17.51 In *Wragg Ltd* [1897] 1 Ch 796, the Court of Appeal stated that in respect of a company limited by shares, the court will not enquire into the adequacy of the consideration for the shares, unless tainted by aspects such as fraud. The court stated that the liability of a shareholder to pay the company the price of his shares was a statutory liability. Provided that a company acted honestly and not colourably, and provided that it had not been so imposed upon as to be entitled to be relieved from its bargain, an agreement by the company to pay for property or services in fully paid-up shares, was valid and binding on the company and its creditors. Unless the transaction was impeached eg, on the ground of fraud – the value of the property or services paid for in shares could not be inquired into; the value of what was acquired by the company was measured by the price at which the company agreed to buy for the asset or services.

Liability of subsequent holders of shares

17.52 If a person becomes a holder of shares in respect of which there has been a contravention of any provision of CA 2006, Pt 17, Ch 5 and by virtue of that contravention, another is liable to pay any amount under the provision contravened, that person is also liable to pay that amount (jointly and severally with any other person so liable), subject as follows: CA 2006, s 588(1).

A person otherwise liable under s 587(1) is exempted from that liability, if either he is a purchaser for value and, at the time of the purchase, he did not have actual notice of the contravention concerned, or he derived title to the shares (directly or indirectly) from a person who became a holder of them after the contravention and was not liable under s 588(1): CA 2006, s 588(2).

17.53 The references in s 588 to a holder, in relation to shares in a company, include any person who has an unconditional right to be included in the company's register of members (or, as the case may be, to have the person's name and other particulars delivered to the registrar under Pt 8, Ch 2A and registered by the registrar), in respect of those shares, or to have an instrument of transfer of the shares executed in his favour: CA 2006, s 588(3) (as inserted by SBEEA 2015, Sch 5, Pt 2).

Share premiums

17.54 CA 2006, Pt 17, Ch 7 contains provisions on share premiums.

The share premium account

Application of share premiums

17.55 If a company issues shares at a premium, whether for cash or otherwise, a sum equal to the aggregate amount or value of the premiums on those shares, must be transferred to an account called 'the share premium account': CA 2006, s 610(1).

Where, on issuing shares, a company has transferred a sum to the share premium account, it may use that sum to write off the expenses of the issue of those shares; or any commission paid on the issue of those shares: CA 2006, s 610(2).

The company may use the share premium account to pay up new shares to be allotted to members as fully paid bonus shares: CA 2006, s 610(3).

Subject to s 610(2) and (3), the provisions of the Companies Acts relating to the reduction of a company's share capital apply, as if the share premium account were part of its paid up share capital: CA 2006, s 610(4).

Section 610 applies subject to s 611 (group reconstruction relief); s 612 (merger relief); and s 614 (power to make further provisions by regulations): CA 2006, s 610(5).

In *Henry-Head & Co Ltd v Ropner Holdings Ltd* [1951] 2 All ER 994, a holding company was formed to acquire shares of two associated companies and to effect amalgamation. A £1 share of the new company was issued for each £1 share in the two associated companies The company's assets were undervalued and were worth more than the nominal value of the shares.

Harman J held that the excess amount was rightly transferred to the share premium account under s 610.

See too: *Shearer (Inspector of Taxes) v Bercain Ltd* [1980] 3 All ER 295.

Judge Purle QC in *Re Sunrise Radio Ltd, Kohli v Lit* [2010] 1 BCLC 367 held that there had been a breach of directors' duties (by improper use of their powers), by issuing shares at par value, when they could have considered alternatives, such as issuing shares at a premium. This was unfairly prejudicial conduct to the minority shareholder.

Alteration of share capital

17.56 CA 2006, Pt 17, Ch 8 applies to alteration of share capital.

How share capital may be altered

Alteration of share capital of limited company

17.57 A limited company which has a share capital, may not generally alter its share capital: CA 2006, s 617(1). The exceptions are where a company is allotting new shares in accordance with Pt 17; or reducing its share capital in accordance with Ch 10: CA 2006, s 617(2).

The company may sub-divide or consolidate all or any of its share capital in accordance with s 618, or reconvert stock into shares in accordance with s 620: CA 2006, s 617(3).

The company may redenominate all or any of its shares in accordance with s 622, and may reduce its share capital in accordance with s 626 in connection with such a redenomination: CA 2006, s 617(4).

17.58 CA 2006, s 617 does not affect the power of a company to purchase its own shares, or to redeem shares, in accordance with Pt 18; or the power of a company to purchase its own shares in pursuance of an order of the court under s 98 (application to court to cancel resolution for re-registration as a private company), s 721(6) (powers of court on objection to redemption or purchase of shares out of capital), s 759 (remedial order in case of breach of prohibition of public offers by private company), or Pt 30 (protection of members against unfair prejudice); the forfeiture of shares, or the acceptance of shares surrendered in lieu, in pursuance of the company's articles, for failure to pay any sum payable in respect of the shares; the cancellation of shares under s 662 (duty to cancel shares held by or for a public company); the power of a company to enter into a compromise or arrangement in accordance with Pt 26 (arrangements and reconstructions), or to do anything required to comply with an order of the court on an application under that Part: CA 2006, s 617(5).

Sub-division or consolidation of shares

Sub-division or consolidation of shares

17.59 A limited company having a share capital may sub-divide its shares, or any of them, into shares of a smaller nominal amount than its existing shares, or consolidate and divide all or any of its share capital into shares of a larger nominal amount than its existing shares: CA 2006, s 618(1).

In any sub-division, consolidation or division of shares under s 618, the proportion between the amount paid and the amount (if any) unpaid on each resulting share, must be the same as it was in the case of the share from which that share is derived: CA 2006, s 618(2).

17.60 A company may exercise a power under s 618, only if its members have passed a resolution authorising it to do so: CA 2006, s 618(3).

A resolution under s 618(3) may authorise a company to exercise more than one of the powers under s 618; to exercise a power on more than one occasion; to exercise a power at a specified time or in specified circumstances: CA 2006, s 618(4). The company's articles may exclude or restrict the exercise of any power conferred by this section: CA 2006, s 618(5). The resolution may be an ordinary resolution; or a resolution requiring a higher majority (as the articles may require).

17.61 Consolidation of a company's share capital involves combining a number of shares into a new share of commensurate nominal value: for example, ten £1 shares may be combined to make one £10 share. Sub-division of a company's share capital involves dividing a share into a number of new shares with a smaller nominal value: for example, a £10 share may be sub-divided into ten £1 shares.

Notice to registrar of sub-division or consolidation

17.63 If a company exercises the power conferred by s 618 (sub-division or consolidation of shares), it must within one month after doing so, give notice to the registrar, specifying the shares affected: CA 2006, s 619(1). The notice must be accompanied by a statement of capital: CA 2006, s 619(2).

17.64 Immediately following the exercise of the power, the statement of capital must state with respect to the company's share capital: (a) the total number of shares of the company; (b) the aggregate nominal value of those shares; (c) for each class of shares (i) prescribed particulars of the rights attached to the shares, (ii) the total number of shares of that class, and (iii) the aggregate nominal value of shares of that class; and (d) the aggregate amount (if any) unpaid on those shares (whether on account of their nominal value or by way of premium),: CA 2006, s 619(3) (as inserted by SBEEA 2015, Sch 6).

17.65 If default is made in complying with s 619, an offence is committed by the company, and every officer of the company who is in default: CA 2006, s 619(4), who may be subject to a fine: CA 2006, s 619(5).

Classes of share and class rights

17.66 At common law, the term 'classes of shares' (or 'class rights') is usually used where the rights attaching to a particular share, relate to matters such as voting rights, a right to dividends and a right to a return of capital, when a company is wound up. Rights attach to a particular class of shares, if the holders of shares in that class enjoy rights that are not enjoyed by the holders of shares in another class.

Classes of shares

17.67 For the purposes of the Companies Acts, shares are of one class, if the rights attached to them are in all respects uniform: CA 2006, s 629(1).

The rights attached to shares are not regarded as different from those attached to other shares, by reason only that they do not carry the same rights to dividends, in the 12 months immediately following their allotment: CA 2006, s 629(2).

Variation of class rights

Variation of class rights: companies having a share capital

17.68 Rights attached to a class of a company's shares may only be varied in accordance with provision in the company's articles for the variation of those rights;

or where the company's articles contain no such provision, if the holders of shares of that class consent to the variation in accordance with s 630: CA 2006, s 630(2).

This is without prejudice to any other restrictions on the variation of the rights: CA 2006, s 630(3).

17.69 The consent required for the purposes of s 630 on the part of the holders of a class of a company's shares is consent in writing from the holders of at least three-quarters in nominal value of the issued shares of that class (excluding any shares held as treasury shares); or a special resolution passed at a separate general meeting of the holders of that class sanctioning the variation: CA 2006, s 630(4).

Any amendment of a provision contained in a company's articles for the variation of the rights attached to a class of shares, or the insertion of any such provision into the articles, is itself to be treated as a variation of those rights: CA 2006, s 630(5).

17.70 Under s 630 and (except where the context otherwise requires) in any provision in a company's articles for the variation of the rights attached to a class of shares, references to the variation of those rights include references to their abrogation: CA 2006, s 630(6).

Right to object to variation: companies having a share capital

17.71 Section 633 deals with the procedure or right to object to variation in respect of companies having a share capital. It applies where the rights attached to any class of shares in a company are varied under s 630 (variation of class rights: companies having a share capital): CA 2006, s 633(1).

The holders of not less in the aggregate than 15% of the issued shares of the class in question (being persons who did not consent to or vote in favour of the resolution for the variation), may apply to the court to have the variation cancelled: CA 2006, s 633(2).

If such an application is made, the variation has no effect unless and until it is confirmed by the court: CA 2006, s 633(3).

17.72 An application to the court must be made within 21 days after the date on which the consent was given or the resolution was passed (as the case may be); and may be made on behalf of the shareholders entitled to make the application by such one or more of their number as they may appoint in writing for the purpose: CA 2006, s 633(4).

17.73 The court, after hearing the applicant and any other persons who apply to the court to be heard, and appear to the court to be interested in the application, may, if satisfied having regard to all the circumstances of the case, that the variation would unfairly prejudice the shareholders of the class represented by the applicant, disallow the variation, and must if not so satisfied, confirm it.

The decision of the court on any such application is final: CA 2006, s 633(5).

Copy of court order to be forwarded to the registrar

17.74 The company must within 15 days after the making of an order by the court on an application under s 633 or 634 (objection to variation of class rights), forward a copy of the order to the registrar: CA 2006, s 635(1).

If default is made in complying with s 635 an offence is committed by the company; and every officer of the company who is in default: CA 2006, s 635(2), and may be subject to a fine: CA 2006, s 635(3).

Matters to be notified to the registrar

Notice of name or other designation of class of shares

17.75 Where a company assigns a name or other designation, or a new name or other designation, to any class or description of its shares, it must within one month from doing so deliver to the registrar, a notice giving particulars of the name or designation so assigned: CA 2006, s 636(1).

If default is made in complying with s 636, an offence is committed by the company; and every officer of the company who is in default: CA 2006, s 636(2).

Notice of particulars of variation of rights attached to shares

17.76 Where the rights attached to any shares of a company are varied, the company must within one month from the date on which the variation is made, deliver to the registrar a notice giving particulars of the variation: CA 2006, s 637(1).

If default is made in complying with this section, an offence is committed by the company; and every officer of the company who is in default: CA 2006, s 637(2), and may be subject to a fine: CA 2006, s 637(3).

Reduction of share capital

17.77 CA 2006, Pt 17, Ch 10 is concerned with reduction of capital.

Circumstances in which a company may reduce its share capital

17.78 A limited company which has a share capital may reduce its share capital:

(a) in the case of a private company limited by shares, by special resolution supported by a solvency statement (ss 642–644);

(b) in any case, by special resolution confirmed by the court (ss 645–651): CA 2006, s 641(1).

A company may not reduce its capital under s 641(1)(a) if as a result of the reduction, there would no longer be any member of the company holding shares other than redeemable shares: CA 2006, s 641(2).

A company may not reduce its share capital under CA 2006, s 641(1)(a) or (b)as part of a scheme by virtue of which a person, or a person together with its associates, is to acquire all the shares in the company, or (where there is more than one class of shares in a company) all the shares of one or more classes, in each case other than shares that are already held by that person or its associates: CA 2006, s 641(2A) (as inserted by the Companies Act 2006 (Amendment of Part 17) Regulations 2015, SI 2015/472, reg 3). There are exceptions to this under CA 2006, s 641(2B) (as inserted by the Companies Act 2006 (Amendment of Part 17) Regulations 2015, SI 2015/472, para 3).

Private companies: reduction of capital supported by solvency statement

Reduction of capital supported by solvency statement

17.79 A resolution for reducing share capital of a private company limited by shares is supported by a solvency statement if:

(a) the directors of the company make a statement of the solvency of the company in accordance with s 643 (a 'solvency statement'), not more than 15 days before the date on which the resolution is passed; and

(b) the resolution and solvency statement are registered in accordance with s 644: CA 2006, s 642(1).

17.80 Where the resolution is proposed as a written resolution, a copy of the solvency statement must be sent or submitted to every eligible member, at or before the time at which the proposed resolution is sent or submitted to him: CA 2006, s 642(2).

Where the resolution is proposed at a general meeting, a copy of the solvency statement must be made available for inspection by members of the company throughout that meeting: CA 2006, s 642(3).

The validity of a resolution is not affected by a failure to comply with s 642(2) or (3): CA 2006, s 642(4).

Solvency statement

17.81 A solvency statement is a statement that each of the directors:

(a) has formed the opinion, as regards the company's situation at the date of the statement, that there is no ground on which the company could then be found to be unable to pay (or otherwise discharge) its debts; and

(b) has also formed the opinion:

   (i) if it is intended to commence the winding up of the company within 12 months of that date, that the company will be able to pay (or otherwise discharge) its debts in full within 12 months of the commencement of the winding up; or

   (ii) in any other case, that the company will be able to pay (or otherwise discharge) its debts as they fall due during the year immediately following that date: CA 2006, s 643(1).

17.82 In forming those opinions, the directors must take into account all of the company's liabilities (including any contingent or prospective liabilities): CA 2006, s 643(2).

The solvency statement must be in the prescribed form and must state the date on which it is made; and the name of each director of the company: CA 2006, s 643(3).

17.83 If the directors make a solvency statement without having reasonable grounds for the opinions expressed in it, and the statement is delivered to the registrar, an offence is committed by every director who is in default: CA 2006, s 643(4), and may be subject to imprisonment and/or a fine: CA 2006, s 643(5).

Registration of resolution and supporting documents

17.84 Within 15 days after the resolution for reducing share capital is passed the company must deliver to the registrar a copy of the solvency statement; and a statement of capital.

This is in addition to the copy of the resolution itself, that is required to be delivered to the registrar under Ch 3 of Pt 3: CA 2006, s 644(1).

17.85 The statement of capital must state, with respect to the company's share capital, as reduced by the resolution:

(a) the total number of shares of the company;

(b) the aggregate nominal value of those shares;

(ba) the aggregate amount (if any) unpaid on those shares (whether on account of their nominal value or by way of premium); and

(c) for each class of shares:

  (i) prescribed particulars of the rights attached to the shares;

  (ii) the total number of shares of that class; and

  (iii) the aggregate nominal value of shares of that class: CA 2006, s 644(2) (as inserted by SBEEA 2015, Sch 6).

The registrar must register the documents delivered to him under s 644(1) on receipt: CA 2006, s 644(3). The resolution does not take effect until those documents are registered: CA 2006, s 644(4).

17.86 The company must also deliver to the registrar, within 15 days after the resolution is passed, a statement by the directors confirming that the solvency statement was made not more than 15 days before the date on which the resolution was passed; and provided to members in accordance with s 642(2) or (3): CA 2006, s 644(5).

17.87 The validity of a resolution is not affected by a failure to deliver the documents required to be delivered to the registrar under s 644(1) within the time specified in that subsection; or a failure to comply with s 644(5): CA 2006, s 644(6).

17.88 If the company delivers to the registrar a solvency statement that was not provided to members in accordance with s 642(2) or (3), an offence is committed by every officer of the company who is in default: CA 2006, s 644(7), who may be subject to a fine CA 2006, s 644(9).

Reduction of capital confirmed by the court

Application to court for order of confirmation

17.89 Where a company has passed a resolution for reducing share capital, it may apply to the court for an order confirming the reduction: CA 2006, s 645(1).

If the proposed reduction of capital involves either diminution of liability in respect of unpaid share capital; or the payment to a shareholder of any paid-up share capital, then s 646 (creditors entitled to object to reduction) applies unless the court directs otherwise: CA 2006, s 645(2).

17.90 The court may, if having regard to any special circumstances of the case it thinks proper to do so, direct that s 646 is not to apply as regards any class or classes of creditors: CA 2006, s 645(3).

The court may direct that s 646 is to apply in any other case: CA 2006, s 645(4).

Creditors entitled to object to reduction

17.91 Where s 646 applies (see s 645(2) and (4)), every creditor of the company who at the date fixed by the court is entitled to any debt or claim that, if that date were the commencement of the winding up of the company, would be admissible in proof against the company, is entitled to object to the reduction of capital: CA 2006, s 646(1).

The court must settle a list of creditors entitled to object: CA 2006, s 646(2).

For that purpose the court must ascertain, as far as possible without requiring an application from any creditor, the names of those creditors and the nature and amount of their debts or claims; and it may publish notices fixing a day or days within which creditors not entered on the list are to claim to be so entered or are to be excluded from the right of objecting to the reduction of capital: CA 2006, s 646(3).

17.92 If a creditor entered on the list whose debt or claim is not discharged or has not determined does not consent to the reduction, the court may, if it thinks fit, dispense with the consent of that creditor on the company securing payment of his debt or claim: CA 2006, s 646(4).

For this purpose the debt or claim must be secured by appropriating (as the court may direct) the following amount:

(a) if the company admits the full amount of the debt or claim or, though not admitting it, is willing to provide for it, the full amount of the debt or claim;

(b) if the company does not admit, and is not willing to provide for, the full amount of the debt or claim, or if the amount is contingent or not ascertained, an amount fixed by the court after the like enquiry and adjudication as if the company were being wound up by the court: CA 2006, s 646(5).

Offences in connection with list of creditors

17.93 If an officer of the company:

(a) intentionally or recklessly:

  (i) conceals the name of a creditor entitled to object to the reduction of capital; or

  (ii) misrepresents the nature or amount of the debt or claim of a creditor, or

(b) is knowingly concerned in any such concealment or misrepresentation,

he commits an offence: CA 2006, s 647(1), and may be liable to a fine CA 2006, s 647(2).

Court order confirming reduction

17.94 The court may make an order confirming the reduction of capital on such terms and conditions as it thinks fit: CA 2006, s 648(1). The court must not confirm the reduction unless it is satisfied, with respect to every creditor of the company who is entitled to object to the reduction of capital that either his consent to the reduction has been obtained; or his debt or claim has been discharged, or has determined or has been secured: CA 2006, s 648(2).

17.95 Where the court confirms the reduction, it may order the company to publish (as the court directs) the reasons for reduction of capital, or such other information in regard to it as the court thinks expedient, with a view to giving proper information to the public, and (if the court thinks fit) the causes that led to the reduction: CA 2006, s 648(3).

The court may, if for any special reason it thinks proper to do so, make an order directing that the company must, during such period (commencing on or at any time after the date of the order) as is specified in the order, add to its name as its last words the words 'and reduced'.

If such an order is made, those words are, until the end of the period specified in the order, deemed to be part of the company's name: CA 2006, s 648(4).

Registration of order and statement of capital

17.96 The registrar, on production of an order of the court confirming the reduction of a company's share capital, and the delivery of a copy of the order and of a statement of capital (approved by the court), must register the order and statement.

17.97 The statement of capital must state with respect to the company's share capital as altered by the order:

(a) the total number of shares of the company;

(b) the aggregate nominal value of those shares;

(ba) the aggregate amount (if any) unpaid on those shares (whether on account of their nominal value or by way of premium); and

(c) for each class of shares:

 (i) prescribed particulars of the rights attached to the shares;

 (ii) the total number of shares of that class; and

 (iii) the aggregate nominal value of shares of that class: CA 2006, s 649(2) (as inserted by SBEEA 2015, Sch 6).

17.98 The resolution for reducing share capital, as confirmed by the court's order, takes effect:

(a) in the case of a reduction of share capital that forms part of a compromise or arrangement sanctioned by the court under Pt 26 (arrangements and reconstructions):

 (i) on delivery of the order and statement of capital to the registrar; or

(ii) if the court so orders, on the registration of the order and statement of capital;

(b) in any other case, on the registration of the order and statement of capital: CA 2006, s 649(3).

17.99 Notice of the registration of the order and statement of capital must be published in such manner as the court may direct: CA 2006, s 649(4). The registrar must certify the registration of the order and statement of capital: CA 2006, s 649(5).

The certificate:

(a) must be signed by the registrar or authenticated by the registrar's official seal; and

(b) is conclusive evidence:

(i) that the requirements of this Act with respect to the reduction of share capital have been complied with; and

(ii) that the company's share capital is as stated in the statement of capital: CA 2006, s 649(6).

Effect of reduction of capital

Liability of members following reduction of capital

17.100 Where a company's share capital is reduced, a member of the company (past or present) is not liable in respect of any share to any call or contribution exceeding in amount the difference (if any) between:

(a) the nominal amount of the share as notified to the registrar in the statement of capital delivered under CA 2006, ss 644, 649, 1028A or 1032A of this Act or the Small Business, Enterprise and Employment Act 2015, Sch 4, para 7; and

(b) the amount paid on the share or the reduced amount (if any) which is deemed to have been paid on it, as the case may be: CA 2006, s 652(1) (as inserted by SBEEA 2015, Sch 4).

This is subject to s 653 (liability to creditor in case of omission from list): CA 2006, s 652(2).

Section 653 does not affect the rights of the contributories among themselves: CA 2006, s 652(3).

Liability to creditor in case of omission from list of creditors

17.101 Section 653 applies where, in the case of a reduction of capital confirmed by the court:

(a) a creditor entitled to object to the reduction of share capital is by reason of his ignorance:

(i) of the proceedings for reduction of share capital; or

(ii) of their nature and effect with respect to his debt or claim,

is not entered on the list of creditors; and

(b) after the reduction of capital the company is unable to pay the amount of his debt or claim: CA 2006, s 653(1).

17.102 Every person who was a member of the company at the date on which the resolution for reducing capital took effect under s 649(3), is liable to contribute for the payment of the debt or claim an amount not exceeding that which he would have been liable to contribute, if the company had commenced to be wound up on the day before that date: CA 2006, s 653(2).

If the company is wound up, the court on the application of the creditor in question, and proof of ignorance as mentioned in s 653(1)(a), may if it thinks fit settle accordingly a list of persons liable to contribute under s 653; and make and enforce calls and orders on them as if they were ordinary contributories in a winding up: CA 2006, s 653(3).

The reference in s 653(1)(b) to a company being unable to pay the amount of a debt or claim has the same meaning as in s 123 of the Insolvency Act 1986 (c 45): CA 2006, s 653(4).

Checklist: application and allotment of shares and pre-emption rights

17.103 *This checklist sets out the practice and procedure for an application and allotment of shares to a shareholder including pre-emption rights. It should be adapted depending upon the company's articles of association governing procedural meetings. It is concerned with a private company limited by shares.*

No	Issue	Reference
1	Some preliminary issues in connection with an application and allotment of shares include: • Before the company issues further shares, will alternative source of funding be considered? • Is the purpose of issuing shares to raise further funds? • Will the company need to increase its share capital to issue shares?	
2	The company's directors cannot allot shares unless there is authority to do so.	CA 2006, s 549
3	The authority to allot shares may either be: (a) in the articles of association; or (b) by an ordinary resolution	CA 2006, s 551
4	Check the private limited company's articles of association to see if there is authority for directors to allot shares	Articles of Association
5	Assuming that the private company limited by shares requires an ordinary resolution to be passed requiring authorisation to issue shares, the following procedure would apply: Before the Board meeting	 Articles of Association

5	• Call a Board meeting. Either a director or a secretary (if there is one) may call a Board meeting. Reasonable notice is required. • Prepare an Agenda setting out the terms and manner of redemption: At the Board meeting:	Articles of Association
	• Ensure that a quorum is present • Consider whether any directors' interests need to be declared • Chairman presides at the Board meeting • Voting will be on a show of hands	
	• The directors will vote to put the ordinary resolution to the EGM for authority to allot shares. The authority for allotment of the shares may be either specific relating to particular allotment of shares or general, or it may be unconditional or subject to conditions. The authority must be for a fixed duration not exceeding 5 years and must state the date on which it expires and the maximum number of shares involved. The authority may be revoked, varied or renewed at any time by ordinary resolution of the EGM • Consider if a Board meeting can be dispensed with by a written resolution procedure • In respect of pre-emption rights:	CA 2006, s 551(2), (3) and (4)
	– Consider any pre-emption rights of shareholders before issuing shares to the shareholders	CA 2006, ss 561–571
	– Consider whether any pre-emption rights of shareholders may be disapplied – Consider disapplication of pre-emption rights by special resolution proposed at the Board meeting and the EGM • Adjourn the Board meeting After the Board meeting: • Prepare minutes of the Board meeting • Call the EGM	Articles of Association
	• Notice of EGM to state: – date of the EGM – time – place – a note on proxy – the text of the ordinary resolution (allotment) and/or special resolution (disapplication of pre-emption rights) – consider whether the EGM can be dispensed with by written resolution • At the EGM:	Articles of Association
	– Ensure quorum is present	CA 2006, s 570

	– Chairman presides at the meeting – Voting will be on a show of hands unless a poll is demanded to pass the ordinary resolution and/or the special resolution	
	• After the EGM: – Prepare minutes of the EGM	
	• Reconvene the Board meeting: – Issue the shares – Issue the share certificates – Entry of shareholder in the register of members – File the resolutions at Companies House	
	– File SH01 (return of allotments of shares) within one month at Companies House	CA 2006, s 551(2)

18 Acquisition by limited company of its own shares

Introduction

18.1 This Chapter considers the following issues:

- acquisition by a private of its own shares;
- financial assistance for the acquisition of shares;
- redeemable shares; and
- purchase of own shares.

A traditional rule has existed at common law (now incorporated in the CA 2006), that a company must maintain its capital, in what has become known as the 'capital maintenance' doctrine. The effect of the doctrine is to protect the interests of shareholders, from an unlawful depletion of a company's capital, and to prevent any disguised gifts out of capital, such as payments by way of directors' remuneration; including an unlawful reduction of capital. The creditors' interests also intrude in such circumstances, by establishing safeguards for various financial transactions contemplated by the CA 2006.

A company may not acquire its own shares, as this would amount to a reduction of its capital. The doctrine of maintenance of capital was established in *Trevor v Whitworth* (1887) 12 App Cas 409. The protection of creditors was considered by the House of Lords as an important aspect of the maintenance of capital doctrine. The House of Lords held that capital of the company could only be returned through effecting a reduction under the Companies Acts, or on liquidation.

General provisions

General rule against limited company acquiring its own shares

18.2 The common law rule established in *Trevor v Whitworth* was consolidated under CA 2006, s 658.

CA 2006, Pt 18 applies to the acquisition by a limited company of its own shares. It is also supplemented by the Companies Act 2006 (Amendment of Part 18) Regulations 2015, SI 2015/532.

There is a general prohibition that a limited company must not acquire its own shares, whether by purchase, subscription or otherwise, except in accordance with Pt 18: CA 2006, s 658(1).

18.3 If a company purports to act in contravention of CA 2006, s 658, an offence is committed by the company, and every officer of the company who is in default. The purported acquisition is void: CA 2006, s 658(2). Failure to comply can lead to a fine and/or imprisonment.

18.4 Capital may only be returned to the company if sanctioned by the court. In *Barclays Bank plc v British & Commonwealth Holdings plc* [1996] 1 BCLC 1 (affirmed by the CA on other aspects [1996] 1 BCLC 27), Harman J stated that the principle established by *Trevor v Whitworth* was that a company could not return capital to its members, except by a reduction of capital sanctioned by the court. This principle applied even if the company's memorandum of association expressly provided for such a return. The principle was based upon 'grounds of public policy': see *MacDougall v Jersey Imperial Hotel Co Ltd* (1864) 2 Hem & M 528 at 535, 71 ER 568 at 571 per Page-Wood VC.

The capital maintenance doctrine is also associated with the rule that the company must not deplete its assets through a disguised gift out of capital, or through gratuitous payments: see *Re Halt Garage (1964) Ltd* [1982] 3 All ER 1016; *Brady v Brady* [1988] BCLC 20 (at first instance).

Exceptions to the general rule

18.5 There are, however, exceptions to the general prohibition. A limited company may acquire any of its own fully paid shares otherwise than for valuable consideration: CA 2006, s 659(1): see *Re Castiglione's Will Trust* [1958] Ch 549.

CA 2006, s 658 does not prohibit the following:

(a) the acquisition of shares in a reduction of capital duly made;

(b) the purchase of shares in pursuance of an order of the court under:

  (i) section 98 (application to court to cancel resolution for re-registration as a private company);

  (ii) section 721(6) (powers of court on objection to redemption or purchase of shares out of capital);

  (iii) section 759 (remedial order in case of breach of prohibition of public offers by private company); or

  (iv) Part 30 (protection of members against unfair prejudice);

(c) the forfeiture of shares, or the acceptance of shares surrendered in lieu, in pursuance of the company's articles, for failure to pay any sum payable in respect of the shares: CA 2006, s 659(3).

(d) The general prohibition under CA 2006, s 658 does not apply where the company acquired the shares through a nominee: CA 2006, s 660.

Financial assistance for purchase of own shares

Origins of financial assistance

18.6 The provisions on financial assistance are intended to protect against the general mischief, that the resources of the target company and its subsidiaries must not be used directly or indirectly to assist the purchaser financially to make the acquisition.

This may prejudice the interests of the creditors of the target or its group, and the interests of the shareholders, who do not accept the offer to acquire their shares, or to whom the offer was not made: *Chaston v SWP Group plc* [2003] 1 BCLC 675. The main objective of the provisions of Pt 18 have been to primarily protect the interests of shareholders and creditors from unlawful financial assistance transactions: punitive sanctions are secondary to this objective.

Previously, a common practice grew of purchasing the shares of a company having a substantial cash balance or realisable assets – the effect of which was to arrange for the purchase monies to be lent to the purchaser by the company: *Re VGM Holdings Ltd [1942]* 1 All ER 224.

Giving financial assistance

18.7 The provisions on financial assistance are set out in Ch 2 of Pt 18 which addresses the financial assistance for purchase of own shares.

Meaning of 'financial assistance'

18.8 The CA 2006 permits the giving of financial assistance in certain circumstances. However, the starting point in determining whether financial assistance has been given is to consider the statutory definition of the term. Section 677 defines 'financial assistance' as:

(a) financial assistance given by way of gift;

(b) financial assistance given:

  (i) by way of guarantee, security or indemnity (other than an indemnity in respect of the indemnifier's own neglect or default) (see: *Yeoman Credit Ltd v Latter* [1961] 2 All ER 294 on indemnity); or

  (ii) by way of release or waiver,

(c) financial assistance given:

  (i) by way of a loan or any other agreement under which any of the obligations of the person giving the assistance are to be fulfilled at a time when in accordance with the agreement any obligation of another party to the agreement remains unfulfilled; or

  (ii) by way of the novation of, or the assignment (in Scotland, assignation) of rights arising under, a loan or such other agreement; or

(d) any other financial assistance given by a company where:

  (i) the net assets of the company are reduced to a material extent by the giving of the assistance; or

  (ii) the company has no net assets: CA 2006, s 677(1).

The term 'net assets' means the aggregate amount of the company's assets less the aggregate amount of its liabilities: CA 2006, s 677(2).

CA 2006, s 677(1)(d) is wide in its scope and catches any other financial assistance other than those set out in s 677(1)(a)–(c).

For this purpose, a company's liabilities include (where it draws up Companies Act individual accounts) any provision of a kind specified for the purposes of s 677(3) by regulations under s 396; and (where it draws up IAS individual accounts) any provision made in those accounts: CA 2006, s 677(3).

In determining what constitutes financial assistance, the courts will look at the commercial realities of the transaction, and apply ordinary commercial meaning: *Charterhouse Investment Trust Ltd v Tempest Diesels Ltd* [1986] BCLC 1; *Barclays Bank plc v British & Commonwealth Holdings plc* [1996] 1 BCLC 1; *Chaston v SWP Group plc* [2003] 1 BCLC 675; and *MT Realisations Ltd v Digital Equipments Co Ltd* [2003] 2 BCLC 117.

There is no requirement to show any detriment to constitute financial assistance. See too *Belmont Finance Corp Ltd v Williams Furniture Ltd* [1980] 1 All ER 393. The detrimental aspect may, however, arise in relation to any other financial assistance given by a company where:

(i) the net assets of the company are reduced to a material extent by the giving of the assistance; or

(ii) the company has no net assets: CA 2006, s 677(1)(d).

18.9 A security provided for a loan was not financial assistance under the CA 2006: *Anglo Petroleum Ltd v TFB (Mortgages) Ltd* [2008] 1 BCLC 185.

18.10 If a company merely discharges a debt which it owes, this cannot amount to financial assistance: *Armour Hick Northern Limited v Armour Trust Ltd* [1980] 3 All ER 833; *and Re Uniq plc* [2012] 1 BCLC 783.

Circumstances in which financial assistance is prohibited

Assistance for acquisition of shares in a public company

18.11 CA 2006, s 678 sets out the principal prohibition on the giving of financial assistance and the timing of such assistance. It deals with the issue of assistance for the acquisition of shares in a public company.

Where a person is acquiring, or proposing to acquire, shares in a public company, it is not lawful either for that company, or one of its subsidiaries, to give financial assistance directly or indirectly for the purpose of the acquisition, before or at the same time as the acquisition takes place: CA 2006, s 678(1): See *Parlett v Guppys (Bridport) Ltd* [1996] 2 BCLC 34.

18.12 CA 2006, s 678(1) does not prohibit a company from giving financial assistance for the acquisition of shares in it or its holding company if:

(a) the company's principal purpose in giving the assistance is not to give it for the purpose of any such acquisition; or

(b) the giving of the assistance for that purpose is only an incidental part of some larger purpose of the company, and the assistance is given in good faith in the interests of the company: CA 2006, s 678(2).

18.13 Where a person has acquired shares in a company; and a liability has been incurred (by that or another person) for the purpose of the acquisition, it is not lawful for that company, or a subsidiary, to give financial assistance directly or indirectly for the purpose of reducing or discharging the liability if, at the time the assistance is given, the company in which the shares were acquired is a public company: CA 2006, s 678(3): *Arab Bank plc v Mercantile Holdings Limited* [1994] Ch 71.

18.14 There is, however, an exception to this general prohibition. Section 678(3) does not prohibit a company from giving financial assistance if:

(a) the company's principal purpose in giving the assistance is not to reduce or discharge any liability incurred by a person for the purpose of the acquisition of shares in the company or its holding company; or

(b) the reduction or discharge of any such liability is only an incidental part of some larger purpose of the company,

and the assistance is given in good faith in the interests of the company: CA 2006, s 678(4).

18.15 CA 2006, s 678 applies subject to ss 681 and 682 (unconditional and conditional exceptions to prohibition): CA 2006, s 678(5).

Once the financial assistance definition has been satisfied, it will be necessary to show that the exceptions to financial assistance set out in s 678 apply: *Charterhouse Investment Trust Ltd v Tempest Diesels Ltd* [1986] BCLC 1.

Payment of excessive rent cannot be said to be linked to the acquisition of shares in the company. In *Dyment v Boyden* [2005] 1 BCLC 163, a shareholder agreed to buy out other shareholders, by accepting a lease from them at an excessive rent. The payment of this rent materially reduced the company's net assets. The issue was whether the payment of excessive rent amounted to 'financial assistance', and whether this was given by the company directly or indirectly for purposes of acquiring shares. Was the company in fact discharging liabilities incurred by a shareholder for the purpose of acquiring shares?

The Court of Appeal held that although it was obvious that the respondents' objective in asking for and obtaining an excessive rent, was compensation for loss of earnings, that could not be deemed to be the purpose of the applicant and the company, since it could not be inferred that the respondents' purpose was also the purpose of the applicant and the company. Their purpose was to acquire the premises to keep the business going. In order to do that they had: (a) undertaken the obligation of procuring the company's entry into the lease; and (b) discharged that obligation by entering into the lease. In those circumstances the excessive rent demanded by the respondents could not be said to be linked to the acquisition of the shares. Accordingly, although the company's entry into the lease was 'in connection with' the acquisition of the respondents' shares by the applicant, it was not 'for the purpose of' that acquisition under s 678(2).

18.16 The exceptions to financial assistance set out in s 678(2) were considered by the House of Lords in *Brady v Brady* [1988] 2 All ER 617.

The House of Lords was required to consider whether the financial assistance in question from B Ltd to M Ltd was provided in the interests of the company, and as an incidental part of some larger purpose. It concerned a transfer of assets in return for fully paid up shares in a new company, and loan stock owing to a corporate reorganisation of the family company because of disputes between directors. The company transferred assets to a new company which in turn used the assets to pay off loan stock. The issue was whether the company provided financial assistance to a subsidiary to reduce the subsidiary's liability to company; and if so, whether the financial assistance was given in the interests of company and as an incidental part of some larger purpose.

The House of Lords took a narrow approach to the exceptions. It held that although the transaction involved the provision by B Ltd of financial assistance to M Ltd to reduce M Ltd's liability, the assistance had been provided 'in good faith in the interests of the company', within s 678(2)(b), as not only was the proposed transfer calculated to advance B Ltd's corporate and commercial interests and the interests of its employees, but it was also in the interest of the company and its creditors, that it should continue under proper management with the differences between the directors resolved.

However, the financial assistance had not been provided by B Ltd as 'an incidental part of some larger purpose of the company', and therefore the transaction was not saved by s 678(2)(b) from being prohibited by s 678(1), since a 'larger purpose' was not the same as a 'more important reason' and therefore the financial or commercial advantages flowing from the transaction, although possibly the most important reason for providing the assistance, could not constitute part of the larger purpose of the company. In the circumstances, the benefits accruing from the proposed transaction in the form of breaking the management deadlock, were not part of the larger purpose of the financial assistance, but were the essence of the scheme itself. Accordingly, the financial assistance was *prima facie* unlawful.

However, the transaction was saved as it was a private company which could give financial assistance out of capital (previously CA 1985, s 155).

18.17 Although *Brady v Brady* interpreted narrowly the exceptions where financial assistance would be permissible, there have been situations where the court has been prepared to admit the exception under s 678(2).

Payments made by a company in order to obtain release of its actual and prospective liabilities, was not financial assistance: it was incidental to a larger purpose and given in good faith: *Re Uniq plc* [2012] 1 BCLC 783.

Assistance by public company for acquisition of shares in its private holding company

18.18 CA 2006, s 679 states that where a person is acquiring or proposing to acquire shares in a private company, it is not lawful for a public company that is a subsidiary of that company to give financial assistance directly or indirectly for the purpose of the acquisition before or at the same time as the acquisition takes place: CA 2006, s 679(1).

Section 679(1), however, does not prohibit a company from giving financial assistance for the acquisition of shares in its holding company if:

(a) the company's principal purpose in giving the assistance is not to give it for the purpose of any such acquisition; or

(b) the giving of the assistance for that purpose is only an incidental part of some larger purpose of the company, and

the assistance is given in good faith in the interests of the company: CA 2006, s 679(2).

18.19 Where a person has acquired shares in a private company; and a liability has been incurred (by that or another person) for the purpose of the acquisition, it is not lawful for a public company that is a subsidiary of that company to give financial assistance directly or indirectly for the purpose of reducing or discharging the liability: CA 2006, s 679(3).

18.20 However, CA 2006, s s 679(3) does not prohibit a company from giving financial assistance if:

(a) the company's principal purpose in giving the assistance is not to reduce or discharge any liability incurred by a person for the purpose of the acquisition of shares in its holding company, or

(b) the reduction or discharge of any such liability is only an incidental part of some larger purpose of the company, and

the assistance is given in good faith in the interests of the company: CA 2006, s 679(4).

Section 679 applies subject to ss 681 and 682 (unconditional and conditional exceptions to prohibition): CA 2006, s 679(5).

Prohibited financial assistance an offence

18.21 CA 2006, s 680 creates a criminal offence for unlawful financial assistance. If a company contravenes either s 678(1) or (3) or s 679(1) or (3) (prohibited financial assistance), an offence is committed by the company, and every officer of the company who is in default: CA 2006, s 680(1). The penalty is a fine and/or imprisonment: CA 2006, s 680(2). The objective of these sanctions is to uphold the protection of shareholders and the creditors: *Selangor Rubber Estates Ltd v Cradock (No 3)* [1968] 1 WLR 1555; *Heald v O'Connor* [1971] 1 WLR 497; *Wallersteiner v Moir* [1974] 3 All ER 217; and *Arab Bank plc v Mercantile Holdings Limited* [1994] Ch 71.

Exceptions from prohibition

Unconditional exceptions

18.22 The financial assistance prohibitions do not apply to the following types of situations (s 681(1)), which are unconditional exceptions:

(a) a distribution of the company's assets by way of:

  (i) dividend lawfully made; or

  (ii) distribution in the course of a company's winding up;

(b) an allotment of bonus shares;

(c) a reduction of capital under Ch 10 of Pt 17;

(d) a redemption of shares under Ch 3 to Pt 18 or a purchase of shares under Ch 4 to Pt 18;

(e) anything done in pursuance of an order of the court under Pt 26 (order sanctioning compromise or arrangement with members or creditors);

(f) anything done under an arrangement made in pursuance of s 110 of the Insolvency Act 1986;

(g) anything done under an arrangement made between a company and its creditors that is binding on the creditors by virtue of Pt 1 of the Insolvency Act 1986: CA 2006, s 680(2).

Conditional exceptions

18.23 The financial assistance prohibitions do not apply in the following circumstances, and are considered conditional exceptions:

(a) if the company giving the assistance is a private company; or

(b) if the company giving the assistance is a public company and:

  (i) the company has net assets that are not reduced by the giving of the assistance; or

  (ii) to the extent that those assets are so reduced, the assistance is provided out of distributable profits: CA 2006, s 682(1).

18.24 The transactions to which s 682 applies are:

(a) where the lending of money is part of the ordinary business of the company, the lending of money in the ordinary course of the company's business;

(b) the provision by the company, in good faith in the interests of the company or its holding company, of financial assistance for the purposes of an employees' share scheme;

(c) the provision of financial assistance by the company for the purposes of or in connection with anything done by the company (or another company in the same group) for the purpose of enabling or facilitating transactions in shares in the first-mentioned company or its holding company between, and involving the acquisition of beneficial ownership of those shares by:

  (i) bona fide employees or former employees of that company (or another company in the same group); or

  (ii) spouses or civil partners, widows, widowers or surviving civil partners, or minor children or step-children of any such employees or former employees;

(d) the making by the company of loans to persons (other than directors) employed in good faith by the company with a view to enabling those persons to acquire fully paid shares in the company or its holding company to be held by them by way of beneficial ownership: CA 2006, s 682(2).

The term 'net assets' refers to the amount by which the aggregate of the company's assets exceeds the aggregate of its liabilities: CA 2006, s 682(3).

18.25 For this purpose:

(a) the amount of both assets and liabilities shall be taken to be as stated in the company's accounting records immediately before the financial assistance is given; and

(b) 'liabilities' includes any amount retained as reasonably necessary for the purpose of providing for a liability the nature of which is clearly defined and that is either likely to be incurred or certain to be incurred but uncertain as to amount or as to the date on which it will arise: CA 2006, s 682(4).

For the purposes of s 679(2)(c), a company is in the same group if it is a holding company or subsidiary of that company or a subsidiary of a holding company of that company: CA 2006, s 682(5).

Civil consequences of giving prohibited financial assistance

18.26 One civil consequence flowing from the prohibition on giving financial assistance is that as between the parties, the transaction is unenforceable and void at common law: *Brady v Brady* [1988] 2 All ER 617.

Another civil consequence is that there may have been a breach of directors' duties in giving such assistance. The company may bring an action against the directors in these circumstances: *Steen v Law* [1964] AC 287and *In A Flap Envelope Co Ltd* [2004] 1 BCLC 64.

The company may also be able to bring an action against third parties for the unlawful financial assistance: *Belmont Finance v Williams Furniture* [1979] Ch 250.

Sometimes, the courts have resorted to severing the illegal aspect of the transaction, so as to save the agreement to the extent possible. In *Carney v Herbert* [1985] 1 All ER 438, Lord Brightman considered that the illegal provisions could be severed from the agreement thereby making the agreement enforceable.

Any misapplication of assets or property of the company may result in breach of trust, and an account to the company for profits made by the director: *JJ Harrison (Properties) Ltd v Harrison* [2002] 1 BCLC 162.

Redeemable shares

Introduction

18.27 CA 2006, Pt 18, Ch 3 is concerned with redeemable shares.

Power of limited company to issue redeemable shares

18.28 A limited company which has a share capital, may issue shares that are to be redeemed or are liable to be redeemed, at the option of the company or the shareholder ('redeemable shares'), subject to the following provisions: CA 2006, s 684(1).

The articles of association of a private limited company may exclude or restrict the issue of redeemable shares: s 684(2). For private companies only, it removes the requirement for prior authorisation in the company's articles for a proposed allotment of redeemable shares. If they wish, the members may, however, restrict or prohibit the authority given to a company by s 684, by including a provision to this effect in the company's articles.

Terms and manner of redemption

18.29 The directors of a limited company may determine the terms, conditions and manner of redemption of shares, if they are authorised to do so by the company's articles of association; or by a resolution of the company: CA 2006, s 685(1).

A resolution under s 685(1)(b) may be an ordinary resolution, even though it amends the company's articles: CA 2006, s 685(2).

18.30 Where the directors are authorised under s 685(1) to determine the terms, conditions and manner of redemption of shares, they must do so before the shares are allotted. Further, any obligation of the company to state in a statement of capital the rights attached to the shares extends to the terms, conditions and manner of redemption: CA 2006, s 685(3).

Where the directors are not so authorised, the terms, conditions and manner of redemption of any redeemable shares must be stated in the company's articles of association: CA 2006, s 685(4).

Payment for redeemable shares

18.31 Section 686 states that redeemable shares in a limited company may not be redeemed unless they are fully paid: CA 2006, s 686(1).

The terms of redemption of shares in a limited company may provide that the amount payable on redemption may, by agreement between the company and the holder of the shares, be paid on a date later than the redemption date: CA 2006, s 686(2). Unless redeemed in accordance with a provision authorised by CA 2006, s 686(2), the shares must be paid for on redemption: CA 2006, s 686(3).

Financing of redemption

18.32 A private limited company may redeem redeemable shares out of capital in accordance with CA 2006, Pt 18, Ch 5: CA 2006, s 687(1). Subject to that, redeemable shares in a limited company may only be redeemed out of distributable profits of the company; or the proceeds of a fresh issue of shares made for the purposes of the redemption: CA 2006, s 687(2).

Any premium payable on redemption of shares in a limited company, must be paid out of distributable profits of the company, subject to the following provision: CA 2006, s 687(3).

18.33 If the redeemable shares were issued at a premium, any premium payable on their redemption may be paid out of the proceeds of a fresh issue of shares made for the purposes of the redemption, up to an amount equal to:

- (a) the aggregate of the premiums received by the company on the issue of the shares redeemed; or
- (b) the current amount of the company's share premium account (including any sum transferred to that account in respect of premiums on the new shares),

whichever is less: CA 2006, s 687(4).

The amount of the company's share premium account is reduced by a sum corresponding (or by sums in the aggregate corresponding) to the amount of any payment made under s 687(4): CA 2006, s 687(5). Section 687 is subject to s 735(4) (terms of redemption enforceable in a winding up): CA 2006, s 687(6).

Redeemed shares treated as cancelled

18.34 Where shares in a limited company are redeemed, the shares are treated as cancelled, and the amount of the company's issued share capital is diminished accordingly by the nominal value of the shares redeemed: CA 2006, s 688.

Notice to registrar of redemption

18.35 If a limited company redeems any redeemable shares, it must within one month after doing so give notice to the registrar, specifying the shares redeemed: CA 2006, s 689(1).

The notice must be accompanied by a statement of capital: CA 2006, s 689(2).

18.36 The statement of capital must state with respect to the company's share capital immediately following the redemption:

(a) the total number of shares of the company;

(b) the aggregate nominal value of those shares;

(ba) the aggregate amount (if any) unpaid on those shares (whether on account of their nominal value or by way of premium); and

(c) for each class of shares:

   (i) prescribed particulars of the rights attached to the shares;

   (ii) the total number of shares of that class; and

   (iii) the aggregate nominal value of shares of that class: CA 2006, s 689(3) (as inserted by SBEEA 2015, Sch 6).

Failure to comply with CA 2006, s 689 can result in a fine: CA 2006, s 689(5).

Purchase of own shares

Power of limited company to purchase own shares

18.37 A limited company having a share capital may purchase its own shares (including any redeemable shares), subject to the following provisions of Ch 5 to Pt 18 and any restriction or prohibition in the company's articles: CA 2006, s 690(1).

A limited company may not purchase its own shares if as a result of the purchase there would no longer be any issued shares of the company other than redeemable shares or shares held as treasury shares: CA 2006, s 690(2).

Payment for purchase of own shares

18.38 A limited company may not purchase its own shares unless they are fully paid: CA 2006, s 691(1). Where a limited company purchases its own shares, the shares must be paid for on purchase: CA 2006, s 691(2).

However, s 691(2) does not apply in a case where a private limited company is purchasing shares for the purposes of or pursuant to an employees' share scheme: CA 2006, s 691(3).

Financing of purchase of own shares

18.39 A private limited company may purchase its own shares out of capital in accordance with CA 2006, Pt 18, Ch 5: CA 2006, s 692(1).

If authorised to do so by its articles of association, a private limited company may purchase its own shares out of capital, otherwise than in accordance with Ch 5, up to an aggregate purchase price in a financial year of the lower of:

(a) £15,000; or

(b) the nominal value of 5% of its fully paid share capital as at the beginning of the financial year: CA 2006, s 692(1ZA) (as inserted by the Companies Act 2006 (Amendment of Part 18) Regulations 2015, SI 2015/532, reg 3(2)).

The terms of purchase of own shares must set out the payment provisions: *BDG Roof-Bond Ltd v Douglas* [2000] 1 BCLC 401.

Authority for purchase of own shares

Authority for purchase of own shares

18.40 CA 2006, s 701 distinguishes between two types of purchase of own shares.

A limited company may only purchase its own shares:

(a) by an *off-market purchase* authorised in accordance with s 693A or in pursuance of a contract approved in advance in accordance with s 694; or

(b) by a *market purchase*, authorised in accordance with s 701: CA 2006, s 693(1).

18.41 A purchase is 'off-market' if the shares are purchased otherwise than on a recognised investment exchange; or are purchased on a recognised investment exchange, but are not subject to a marketing arrangement on the exchange: CA 2006, s 693(2).

18.42 For this purpose. a company's shares are subject to a marketing arrangement on a recognised investment exchange if:

(a) they are listed under Pt 6 of the Financial Services and Markets Act 2000 (c 8); or

(b) the company has been afforded facilities for dealings in the shares to take place on the exchange:

(i) without prior permission for individual transactions from the authority governing that investment exchange; and

(ii) without limit as to the time during which those facilities are to be available: CA 2006, s 693(3).

18.43 A purchase is a 'market purchase', if it is made on a recognised investment exchange, and is not an off-market purchase by virtue of s 693(2)(b): CA 2006, s 693(4). The term 'recognised investment exchange' means a recognised investment exchange (within the meaning of the Financial Services and Markets Act 2000, Pt 18) other than an overseas exchange (within the meaning of that Part): CA 2006, s 693(5).

Authority for off-market purchase

Authority for off-market purchase

18.44 Subject to CA 2006, s s 693A, a company may only make an off-market purchase of its own shares in pursuance of a contract approved prior to the purchase in accordance with s 694: CA 2006, s 694(1).

Either:

(a) the terms of the contract must be authorised by a resolution of the company before the contract is entered into; or

(b) the contract must provide that no shares may be purchased in pursuance of the contract until its terms have been authorised by a resolution of the company: CA 2006, s 694(2).

The contract may be a contract entered into by the company and relating to shares in the company, that does not amount to a contract to purchase the shares, but under which the company may (subject to any conditions) become entitled or obliged to purchase the shares: CA 2006, s 694(3).

18.45 The authority conferred by a resolution under CA 2006, s s 694 may be varied, revoked or from time to time, renewed by a special resolution of the company: CA 2006, s 694(4).

A resolution conferring, varying, revoking or renewing authority under s 694 is subject to s 695 (exercise of voting rights), and s 696 (disclosure of details of contract): CA 2006, s 694(6).

Section 695 addresses the exercises of voting rights in relation to a resolution authorising off-market purchase.

Resolution authorising off-market purchase: disclosure of details of contract

18.46 CA 2006, s 696 applies in relation to a resolution to confer, vary, revoke or renew authority for the purposes of s 694 (authority for off-market purchase of own shares): CA 2006, s 696(1).

A copy of the contract (if it is in writing) or a memorandum setting out its terms (if it is not), must be made available to members:

(a) in the case of a written resolution, by being sent or submitted to every eligible member at or before the time at which the proposed resolution is sent or submitted to him;

(b) in the case of a resolution at a meeting, by being made available for inspection by members of the company both:

  (i) at the company's registered office for not less than 15 days ending with the date of the meeting; and

  (ii) at the meeting itself: CA 2006, s 696(2).

18.47 A memorandum of contract terms so made available, must include the names of the members holding shares to which the contract relates: CA 2006, s 696(3).

A copy of the contract so made available, must have annexed to it a written memorandum specifying those names that do not appear in the contract itself: CA 2006, s 696(4).

The resolution is not validly passed if the requirements of s 696 are not complied with: CA 2006, s 696(5).

CA 2006, s 687addresses variation of contract for off-market purchase.

Authority for market purchase

Authority for market purchase

18.48 A company may only make a market purchase of its own shares, if the purchase has first been authorised by a company resolution: CA 2006, s 701(1). That authority may be general or limited to the purchase of shares of a particular class or description, and may be unconditional or subject to conditions: CA 2006, s 701(2).

The authority must specify the maximum number of shares authorised to be acquired, and determine both the maximum and minimum prices that may be paid for the shares: CA 2006, s 701(3).

The authority may be varied, revoked or from time to time renewed by a resolution of the company: CA 2006, s 701(4). A resolution conferring, varying or renewing authority, must specify a date on which it is to expire, which must not be later than five years after the date on which the resolution is passed: CA 2006, s 701(5).

18.49 A company may make a purchase of its own shares after the expiry of the time limit specified if the contract of purchase was concluded before the authority expired; and the terms of the authority permitted the company to make a contract of purchase that would or might be executed wholly or partly after its expiration: CA 2006, s 701(6).

18.50 A resolution to confer or vary authority under CA 2006, s s 701 may determine either or both the maximum and minimum price for purchase by specifying a particular sum; or providing a basis or formula for calculating the amount of the price (but without reference to any person's discretion or opinion): CA 2006, s 701(7).

CA 2006, Pt 3, Ch 3 (resolutions affecting a company's constitution) applies to a resolution under s 701: CA 2006, s 701(8).

Copy of contract or memorandum to be available for inspection

18.51 CA 2006, s 702 applies where a company has entered into a contract approved under s 694 (authorisation of contract for off-market purchase); or a contract for a purchase authorised under s 701 (authorisation of market purchase): CA 2006, s 702(1). The company must keep available for inspection a copy of the contract or, if the contract is not in writing, a written memorandum setting out its terms: CA 2006, s 702(2).

18.52 The copy or memorandum must be kept available for inspection from the conclusion of the contract until the end of the period of ten years beginning with the date on which the purchase of all the shares in pursuance of the contract is completed; or the date on which the contract otherwise determines: CA 2006, s 702(3). The copy or memorandum must be kept available for inspection at the company's registered office, or at a place specified in regulations under s 1136: CA 2006, s 702(4).

18.53 The company must give notice to the registrar of the place at which the copy or memorandum is kept available for inspection, and of any change in that place, unless it has at all times been kept at the company's registered office: CA 2006, s 702(5).

Every copy or memorandum required to be kept under s 702 must be kept open to inspection without charge by any member of the company, and in the case of a public company, by any other person: CA 2006, s 702(6). Section 702 also applies to a variation of a contract, as it apply to the original contract: CA 2006, s 702(7).

Enforcement of right to inspect copy or memorandum

18.54 Failure to comply with CA 2006, s 702(2), (3) or (4), or default is made for 14 days in complying with s 702(5), or an inspection required under s 702(6) is refused, an offence is committed by the company, and every officer of the company who is in default: CA 2006, s 703(1), who may be subject to a fine: CA 2006, s 703(2).

In the case of refusal of an inspection required under s 702(6), the court may by order compel an immediate inspection: CA 2006, s 703(3).

Return to registrar of purchase of own shares

18.55 Where a company purchases shares under CA 2006, Pt 18, Ch 4, it must deliver a return to the registrar within the period of 28 days beginning with the date on which the shares are delivered to it: CA 2006, s 707(1).

The return must distinguish:

(a) shares in relation to which s 724 (treasury shares) applies and shares in relation to which that section does not apply; and

(b) shares in relation to which that section applies:

  (i) that are cancelled forthwith (under s 729 (cancellation of treasury shares); and

  (ii) that are not so cancelled: CA 2006, s 707(2).

18.56 The return must state, with respect to shares of each class purchased, the number and nominal value of the shares, and the date on which they were delivered to the company: CA 2006, s 707(3).

18.57 If default is made in complying with CA 2006, s 707, an offence is committed by every officer of the company who is in default: CA 2006, s 707(6). A person guilty of an offence under this section will be liable to a fine: CA 2006, s 707(7).

Notice to registrar of cancellation of shares

18.58 If on the purchase by a company of any of its own shares in accordance with CA 2006, Pt 18:

(a) section 724 (treasury shares) does not apply (so that the shares are treated as cancelled), or

(b) that section applies, but the shares are cancelled forthwith (under s 729 (cancellation of treasury shares),

the company must give notice of cancellation to the registrar, within the period of 28 days beginning with the date on which the shares are delivered to it, specifying the shares cancelled: CA 2006, s 708(1).

18.59 The notice must be accompanied by a statement of capital. The exception is where the statement of capital would be the same as a statement of capital that is required to be delivered to the registrar under s 720B(1): CA 2006, s 708(2) The statement of capital must state with respect to the company's share capital immediately following the cancellation:

(a) the total number of shares of the company;

(b) the aggregate nominal value of those shares;

(ba) the aggregate amount (if any) unpaid on those shares (whether on account of their nominal value or by way of premium); and

(c) for each class of shares:

  (i) prescribed particulars of the rights attached to the shares;

  (ii) the total number of shares of that class;

  (iii) the aggregate nominal value of shares of that class: CA 2006, s 708(3) (as inserted by SBEEA 2015, Sch 6).

18.60 If default is made in complying with s CA 2006, s 708, an offence is committed by the company, and every officer of the company who is in default, and they may be subject to a fine: CA 2006, s 708(4), (5)..

Redemption or purchase by private company out of capital

18.61 CA 2006, Pt 18, Ch 5 is concerned with the redemption or purchase by private company out of capital.

Power of private limited company to redeem or purchase own shares out of capital

18.62 A private limited company may, in accordance with CA 2006, Pt 18, Ch 5, but subject to any restriction or prohibition in the company's articles, make a payment in respect of the redemption or purchase of its own shares otherwise than out of distributable profits or the proceeds of a fresh issue of shares: CA 2006, s 709(1).

The references in Ch 5 to payment out of capital are to any payment so made, whether or not it would be regarded apart from s 709 as a payment out of capital: CA 2006, s 709(2).

The permissible capital payment

18.63 The payment that may be made by a company out of capital in respect of the redemption or purchase of its own shares is such amount as, after applying for that purpose, any available profits of the company; and the proceeds of any fresh issue of shares made for the purposes of the redemption or purchase, is required to meet the price of redemption or purchase: CA 2006, s 710(1). That is referred to as 'the permissible capital payment' for the shares: CA 2006, s 710(2).

Available profits

18.64 The available profits of the company, in relation to the redemption or purchase of any shares, are the profits of the company that are available for distribution (within the meaning of Pt 23): CA 2006, s 711(1). However, the issue whether a company has any profits so available, and the amount of any such profits, are determined in accordance with s 712 instead of in accordance with ss 836–842 in that Part: CA 2006, s 711(2).

Requirements for payment out of capital

18.65 A payment out of capital by a private company for the redemption or purchase of its own shares, is not lawful unless the requirements of the following sections are met, namely:

- CA 2006, s 714 (directors' statement and auditor's report);
- s 716 (approval by special resolution);
- s 719 (public notice of proposed payment); and
- s 720 (directors' statement and auditor's report to be available for inspection): CA 2006, s 713(1).

This is subject to s 720A and to any order of the court under s 721 (power of court to extend period for compliance on application by persons objecting to payment): CA 2006, s 713(2).

Directors' statement and auditor's report

18.66 The company's directors must make a statement in accordance with CA 2006, s 714: CA 2006, s 714(1). This must specify the amount of the permissible capital payment for the shares in question: CA 2006, s 714(2). It must state that, having made full inquiry into the affairs and prospects of the company, the directors have formed the opinion:

(a) as regards its initial situation immediately following the date on which the payment out of capital is proposed to be made, that there will be no grounds on which the company could then be found unable to pay its debts; and

(b) as regards its prospects for the year immediately following that date, that having regard to:

   (i) their intentions with respect to the management of the company's business during that year; and

   (ii) the amount and character of the financial resources that will in their view be available to the company during that year,

the company will be able to continue to carry on business as a going concern (and will accordingly be able to pay its debts as they fall due) throughout that year: CA 2006, s 714(3).

18.67 In forming their opinion for the purposes of CA 2006, s 714(3)(a), the directors must take into account all of the company's liabilities (including any contingent or prospective liabilities): CA 2006, s 714(4).

The directors' statement must be in the prescribed form, and must contain such information with respect to the nature of the company's business as may be prescribed: CA 2006, s 714(5).

It must, in addition, have annexed to it a report addressed to the directors by the company's auditor stating that:

(a) he has inquired into the company's state of affairs;

(b) the amount specified in the statement as the permissible capital payment for the shares in question is in his view properly determined in accordance with ss 710–712; and

(c) he is not aware of anything to indicate that the opinion expressed by the directors in their statement as to any of the matters mentioned in s 714(3) above is unreasonable in all the circumstances: CA 2006, s 714(6).

Directors' statement: offence if no reasonable grounds for opinion

18.68 If the directors make a statement under CA 2006, s 714, without having reasonable grounds for the opinion expressed in it, an offence is committed by every director who is in default: CA 2006, s 715(1). They can be subject to a fine and/or imprisonment: CA 2006, s 715(2).

Payment to be approved by special resolution

18.69 The payment out of capital must be approved by a special resolution of the company: CA 2006, s 716(1). This must be passed on, or within the week immediately following, the date on which the directors make the statement required by s 714: CA 2006, s 716(2).

A resolution under s 716 is subject to s 717 (exercise of voting rights) and s 718 (disclosure of directors' statement and auditors' report): CA 2006, s 716(3).

Resolution authorising payment: disclosure of directors' statement and auditor's report

18.70 CA 2006, s 718 applies to a resolution under s 716 (resolution authorising payment out of capital for redemption or purchase of own shares): CA 2006, s 718(1).

A copy of the directors' statement and auditor's report under s 714 must be made available to members:

(a) in the case of a written resolution, by being sent or submitted to every eligible member at or before the time at which the proposed resolution is sent or submitted to him;

(b) in the case of a resolution at a meeting, by being made available for inspection by members of the company at the meeting: CA 2006, s 718(2).

The resolution is ineffective if this requirement is not complied with: CA 2006, s 718(3).

Public notice of proposed payment

18.71 Within the week immediately following the date of the resolution under CA 2006, s 716 the company must publish a notice in the Gazette:

(a) stating that the company has approved a payment out of capital for the purpose of acquiring its own shares by redemption or purchase or both (as the case may be);

(b) specifying:

    (i) the amount of the permissible capital payment for the shares in question, and

    (ii) the date of the resolution,

(c) stating where the directors' statement and auditor's report required by s 714 are available for inspection; and

(d) stating that any creditor of the company may at any time within the five weeks immediately following the date of the resolution apply to the court under s 721 for an order preventing the payment: CA 2006, s 719(1).

18.72 Within the week immediately following the date of the resolution, the company must also either cause a notice to the same effect as that required by CA 2006, s 719(1) to be published in an appropriate national newspaper, or give notice in writing to that effect to each of its creditors: CA 2006, s 719(2).

The term 'an appropriate national newspaper' means a newspaper circulating throughout the part of the UK in which the company is registered: CA 2006, s 719(3).

Not later than the day on which the company first publishes the notice required by s 719(1), or if earlier, first publishes or gives the notice required by s 719(2), the company must deliver to the registrar a copy of the directors' statement and auditor's report required by s 714: CA 2006, s 719(4).

Directors' statement and auditor's report to be available for inspection

18.73 The directors' statement and auditor's report must be kept available for inspection throughout the period:

(a) beginning with the day on which the company:

   (i) first publishes the notice required by s 719(1); or

   (ii) if earlier, first publishes or gives the notice required by s 719(2); and

(b) ending five weeks after the date of the resolution for payment out of capital: CA 2006, s 720(1).

18.74 They must be kept available for inspection at the company's registered office, or at a place specified in regulations under CA 2006, s 1136: CA 2006, s 720(2).

The company must give notice to the registrar of the place at which the statement and report are kept available for inspection, and of any change in that place, unless they have at all times been kept at the company's registered office: CA 2006, s 720(3). They must be open to the inspection of any member or creditor of the company without charge: CA 2006, s 720(4).

18.75 If default is made for 14 days in complying with CA 2006, s 720(3), or an inspection under s 720(4) is refused, an offence is committed by the company and every officer of the company who is in default: CA 2006, s 720(5), and may be subject to a fine: CA 2006, s 720(6).

In the case of a refusal of an inspection required by s 720(4), the court may by order compel an immediate inspection: CA 2006, s 720(7).

Checklist: issuing redeemable shares

18.76 *This checklist sets out the practice and procedure for a company issuing redeemable shares. It is covered by the regime under CA 2006, Pt 18, Ch 3. It should be adapted depending upon the company's articles of association governing meetings.*

No	*Issue*	*Reference*
1	Must be a limited company having a share capital.	CA 2006, s 684(1)
2	The company may issue shares that are redeemed, or liable to be redeemed at the option of the company or the shareholder.	CA 2006, s 684
3	Check the private limited company's articles of association to see if they exclude or restrict the issuance of redeemable shares.	CA 2006, s 684(2)
4	A public company may only issue shares if expressly provided for in its Articles of Association.	CA 2006, s 684(3)
5	A company may not issue redeemable shares at a time when there are no issued shares of the company that are not redeemed.	CA 2006, s 684(4)

6	Check the Articles of Association of a limited company to see if the directors are authorised to determine the terms, conditions and manner of redemption.	CA 2006, s 685(1)
7	If the directors are not so authorised, call a Board meeting. Either a director or a secretary (if there is one) may call a Board meeting. Reasonable notice is required.	Articles of Association
8	Prepare an Agenda setting out the terms and manner of redemption: At the Board meeting: • Ensure that a quorum is present • Consider whether any directors' interests need to be declared • Chairman presides at the Board meeting • Voting will be on a show of hands • The directors will vote to put the ordinary resolution to the EGM to approve the terms and manner of redemption • Consider if a Board meeting can be dispensed with by a written resolution procedure. After the Board meeting: • Prepare minutes of the Board meeting • Call the EGM • Notice of EGM to state: – date of the EGM – time – place – a note on proxy – the text of the ordinary resolution – consider whether the EGM can be dispensed with by written resolution attaching the manner and terms of redemption. • At the EGM: – Ensure quorum is present – Chairman presides at the meeting – Voting will be on a show of hands unless a poll is demanded to pass the ordinary resolution. • After the EGM: – Prepare minutes of the EGM.	Articles of Association
9	Ensure that shares in a limited company are not redeemed unless they are fully paid.	
10	Where shares in a limited company are redeemed the shares are treated as cancelled, and the amount of the company's issued share capital is diminished accordingly by the nominal value of the shares redeemed.	

11	If a limited company redeems any redeemable shares it must within one month after doing so give notice to the registrar, specifying the shares redeemed.	CA 2006, s 689(1) Form SHO2 (Notice of consolidation, sub-division, redemption of shares or re-conversion of stock into shares)
	The notice must be accompanied by a statement of capital.	
	The statement of capital must state with respect to the company's share capital immediately following the redemption:	
	(a) the total number of shares of the company;	CA 2006, s 689(2)
	(b) the aggregate nominal value of those shares;	
	(c) for each class of shares:	
	(i) prescribed particulars of the rights attached to the shares;	
	(ii) the total number of shares of that class; and	
	(iii) the aggregate nominal value of shares of that class; and	
	(d) the amount paid up and the amount (if any) unpaid on each share (whether on account of the nominal value of the share or by way of premium.	CA 2006, s 689(3)

19 Company charges

Introduction

19.1 This Chapter considers the following issues:

- the concept of a fixed and floating charge;
- requirement to register charges; and
- the register of charges.

CA 2006, Pt 25 is concerned with company charges. It provides a scheme for the registration of charges created by a company. The aim of the registration is not only to set out all of the company's charges, but more fundamentally 'to warn unsuspecting creditors that the debtor company has charged its assets': *Re Welsh Irish Ferries Limited* [1985] BCLC 327, per Nourse J.

Fixed and floating charges

19.2 In English company law, a distinction is made between a fixed and floating charge. A fixed charge is a charge over, for example, a tangible asset or a charge over book debt. It evidences a debt due by the debtor to the creditor over a security interest, such as the debtor's property. The relationship between the debtor and creditor is contractual, which sets out the responsibilities and obligations of the parties. The fixed charge will typically restrict the debtor's right to dispose of the asset while the charge is secured. On the debtor's insolvency, the asset may be sold to realise funds for the creditor, and discharge the loan made to the debtor. Any excess balance funds are then usually paid back to the debtor.

A floating charge is a charge that is secured over assets, but which has the flexibility that the debtor is free to deal with the assets in the ordinary course of business until an event occurs (such as 'crystallisation' for example on the company's winding up). The effect of crystallisation is that the assets subject to the floating charge will be identified, and become a fixed charge at a particular point in time, with the objective of realising funds for the creditor. The assets may take the form of stock in trade.

A classic definition of a floating charge was set out by Romer LJ in *Re Yorkshire Woolcombers Association Ltd* [1903] 2 Ch 284, as comprising three characteristics:

- there must be an intention to create a charge on a class of assets both present and future;
- the assets are such that are changing in the ordinary course of business; and
- the company has flexibility to deal with the assets that are charged in the ordinary course of business.

See too: *Ilingworth v Houldsworth* [1904] AC 355.

19.3 The modern judicial attitudes towards floating charges demonstrate the flexibility of the charge, for the company to deal with the charged assets in the ordinary course of business.

The fact that a charge is described as a 'fixed' charge is not conclusive. The court will construe the document giving rise to the charge to determine the nature of the charge.

19.4 In *Agnew v Commissioner for Inland Revenue* [2001] 2 AC 710, in the Privy Council, Lord Millet stated that the critical feature which distinguished a floating from a fixed charge was in the chargor's ability, freely and without the chargee's consent, to control and manage the charged assets and withdraw them from the security. In deciding whether a charge is a fixed charge or a floating charge, the court is engaged in a two-stage process. At the first stage, it must construe the instrument of charge and seek to gather the intentions of the parties from the language they have used. The object at this stage of the process is not to discover whether the parties intended to create a fixed or a floating charge: it is to ascertain the nature of the rights and obligations which the parties intended to grant each other in respect of the charged assets. Once these have been ascertained, the court can then embark on the second stage of the process, which is one of categorisation. This is a matter of law. It does not depend on the intention of the parties. If their intention, properly gathered from the language of the instrument, is to grant the company rights in respect of the charged assets which are inconsistent with the nature of a fixed charge, then the charge cannot be a fixed charge, however they may have chosen to describe it.

In Re Spectrum Plus Limited [2005] 2 BCLC 269, the court stated that a floating charge was distinguished from a fixed charge, by its flexibility in allowing a debtor to deal freely with assets in the ordinary course of business. The House of Lords held that the essential characteristic of a floating charge, distinguishing it from a fixed charge, was that the asset subject to the charge was not finally appropriated as a security for the payment of the debt, until the occurrence of some future event. In the meantime, the chargor was left free to use the charged asset and to remove it from the security.

Companies registered in England and Wales – requirement to register company charges

Charges created by a company

19.5 A company that creates a charge must deliver the prescribed particulars of the charge, together with the instrument (if any) by which the charge is created or evidenced, to the registrar for registration before the end of the period allowed for registration: CA 2006, s 860(1).

Registration of a charge may instead be effected on the application of a person interested in it: CA 2006, s 860(2). Where registration is effected on the application of some person other than the company, that person is entitled to recover from the company the amount of any fees properly paid by him to the registrar on registration: CA 2006, s 860(3). A fine and/or imprisonment can be imposed on every officer of the company who is in default, for failure to comply with s 860: CA 2006, s 860 (4), (5). Section 860(4) does not apply if registration of the charge has been effected on the application of some other person: CA 2006, s 860(6).

19.6 Not all types of charges (such as a retention of title agreement or seller's lien: *London and Cheshire Insurance Co Ltd v Laplagrene Property Co Ltd* [1971] Ch 499) are registerable. Under s 860, only the following charges are registerable at Companies House:

(a) a charge on land or any interest in land, other than a charge for any rent or other periodical sum issuing out of land. However, the holding of debentures entitling the holder to a charge on land is not, for the purposes of s 860(7)(a), an interest in the land: CA 2006, s 861(1). It is immaterial for the purposes of Ch 1 to Pt 25 where land subject to a charge is situated: CA 2006, s 861(2);

(b) a charge created or evidenced by an instrument which, if executed by an individual, would require registration as a bill of sale;

(c) a charge for the purposes of securing any issue of debentures;

(d) a charge on uncalled share capital of the company;

(e) a charge on calls made but not paid;

(f) a charge on book debts of the company;

(g) a floating charge on the company's property or undertaking;

(h) a charge on a ship or aircraft, or any share in a ship; and

(i) a charge on goodwill or on any intellectual property: CA 2006, s 860(7). the term 'intellectual property' means any patent, trademark, registered design, copyright or design right; any licence under or in respect of any such right: CA 2006, s 861(4);

(j) The deposit by way of security of a negotiable instrument given to secure the payment of book debts is not, for the purposes of s 860(7)(f), a charge on those book debts: CA 2006, s 861(3).

Charges existing on property acquired

19.7 CA 2006, s 862 applies where a company acquires property which is subject to a charge of a kind which would, if it had been created by the company after the acquisition of the property, have been required to be registered under Pt 25, Ch 1: CA 2006, s 862(1). The company must deliver the prescribed particulars of the charge, together with a certified copy of the instrument (if any) by which the charge is created or evidenced, to the registrar for registration: CA 2006, s 862(2). A fine can be imposed on the company, and every officer of it who is in default for failure to comply with s 862: CA 2006, s 862(4), (5).

Special rules about debentures

19.8 There are special rules applicable to debentures set out in CA 2006, ss 863–865.

The register of charges

19.9 CA 2006, ss 869–873 govern the register of charges.

Register of charges to be kept by registrar

19.10 With respect to each company, the registrar must keep a register of all the charges requiring registration under Ch 1 to Pt 25, Ch 1: CA 2006, s 869(1).

In the case of a charge to the benefit of which holders of a series of debentures are entitled, the registrar is required to enter in the register the required particulars specified in s 863(2): CA 2006, s 869(2).

In the case of a charge imposed by the Enforcement of Judgments Office under Art 46 of the 1981 Order, the registrar must enter in the register the date on which the charge became effective: CA 2006, s 869(3).

19.11 In the case of any other charge, the registrar must enter in the register the following particulars:

(a) if it is a charge created by a company, the date of its creation and, if it is a charge which was existing on property acquired by the company, the date of the acquisition;

(b) the amount secured by the charge;

(c) short particulars of the property charged; and

(d) the persons entitled to the charge: CA 2006, s 869(4).

The registrar will give a certificate of the registration of any charge registered under CA 2006, Pt 25, Ch 1 stating the amount secured by the charge: CA 2006, s 869(5).

19.12 The certificate must be signed by the registrar or authenticated by the registrar's official seal. It then becomes conclusive evidence that the requirements of Pt 25, Ch 1 as to registration have been satisfied: CA 2006, s 869(6). The registrar's certificate is also conclusive even where the certificate was issued by mistake or error by the registrar, or that the charge was not validly registered: *Ali v Top Marques Car Rental Ltd* [2006] EWHC 109 (Ch); and must be accepted by all who have notice of the charge, including liquidators: *National Provincial and Union Bank of England v Charnley* [1924] 1 KB 431. In *Re C L Nye Ltd* [1971] Ch 442, Harman LJ stated that the certificate was conclusive evidence of registration of a charge. The hub point of creating the register under s 869, was to give security to persons relying on the certificate.

Challenging the registrar's certificate?

19.13 Once the registrar grants a certificate under CA 2006, s 869, can his decision be the subject of a challenge by judicial review? The court will not entertain judicial review proceedings owing to the conclusivity of the certificate. This will be the case even where the charge was registered in error, or that the charge contains errors or is inaccurate: *Ali v Top Marques Car Rental Ltd* [2006] EWHC 109 (Ch); and *National Provincial and Union Bank v Charnley* [1924] 1 KB 431. In some cases, the courts have held that the registrar is unlikely to be subject to an action for damages, despite the conclusivity particularly where third parties may be misled: *Ministry of Housing and Local Government v Sharp* [1970] 2 QB 223; and *Davis v Radcliffe* [1990] 1 WLR 821.

However, there may be some exceptions to this rule, such as fraud. Where fraud is apparent, it may vitiate the conclusivity of the Registrar's certificate: *R v Registrar of Companies ex parte Central Bank of India* [1986] QB 1114. In this case, Slade LJ considered that the Registrar at Companies House had certain functions entrusted to him by Parliament, in issuing the conclusivity certificate. The registrar would be required to ask himself a number of questions (being a mixture of fact and law) before issuing the certificate. This could include the true date for creation of the charge. The registrar would be required to answer this question to the best of his ability, for the purpose of determining whether or not the charge was eligible for registration.

The registrar was also required to consider some special cases before issuing the certificate. First, where a purported certificate given by the registrar under s 869 of the CA 2006 disclosed an error on the face of it. In such situation, the registrar may not be able to correct the error. The second special situation might arise, where the certificate had been obtained by fraud. Even in that case, a direct attack on the certificate would, at least prima facie, be ruled out (see *Re Eric Holmes (Property) Ltd* [1965] Ch 1052, 1072 per Pennycuick J), though the court may act *in personam* against the fraudulent party, so as to prevent him taking advantage of the fraudulently obtained certificate (see, for example, *Lazarus Estates Ltd v Beasley* [1956] 1 QB 702). Furthermore, a creditor personally damaged by the fraud might be able to take proceedings for damages: see *Re C L Nye Ltd* [1971] Ch 442, 474, per Russell LJ.

The register kept in pursuance of s 869 must be open to inspection by any person: CA 2006, s 869(7).

The period allowed for registration

19.14 The period allowed for registration of a charge created by a company is:

(a) 21 days beginning with the day after the day on which the charge is created; or

(b) if the charge is created outside the UK, 21 days beginning with the day after the day on which the instrument by which the charge is created or evidenced (or a copy of it) could, in due course of post (and if despatched with due diligence) have been received in the UK: CA 2006, s 870(1).

19.15 The period allowed for registration of a charge to which property acquired by a company is subject is:

(a) 21 days beginning with the day after the day on which the acquisition is completed; or

(b) if the property is situated and the charge was created outside the UK, 21 days beginning with the day after the day on which the instrument by which the charge is created or evidenced (or a copy of it) could, in due course of post (and if dispatched with due diligence) have been received in the UK: CA 2006, s 870(2).

The period allowed for registration of particulars of a series of debentures as a result of s 863 is, if there is a deed containing the charge mentioned in s 863(1), 21 days beginning with the day after the day on which that deed is executed, or if there is no such deed, 21 days beginning with the day after the day on which the first debenture of the series is executed: CA 2006, s 870(3).

Registration of enforcement of security

19.16 If a person obtains an order for the appointment of a receiver or manager of a company's property, or appoints such a receiver or manager under powers contained in an instrument, he must within seven days of the order or of the appointment under those powers, give notice of the fact to the registrar: CA 2006, s 871(1).

Where a person appointed receiver or manager of a company's property under powers contained in an instrument, ceases to act as such receiver or manager, he must, on so ceasing, give the registrar notice to that effect: CA 2006, s 871(2).

The registrar must enter a fact of which he is given notice under s 871 in the register of charges: CA 2006, s 871(3). Failure to comply with s 871 by a person who makes a default can result in a fine: CA 2006, s 871(5).

Entries of satisfaction and release

19.17 CA 2006, s 872(2) applies if a statement is delivered to the registrar verifying with respect to a registered charge:

(a) that the debt for which the charge was given has been paid or satisfied in whole or in part; or

(b) that part of the property or undertaking charged has been released from the charge or has ceased to form part of the company's property or undertaking: CA 2006, s 872(1).

The registrar may enter on the register a memorandum of satisfaction in whole or in part, or of the fact part of the property or undertaking has been released from the charge, or has ceased to form part of the company's property or undertaking (as the case may be): CA 2006, s 872(2).

Where the registrar enters a memorandum of satisfaction in whole, the registrar must, if required, send the company a copy of it: CA 2006, s 872(3).

Rectification of register of charges

19.18 The court may allow rectification of a charge if it is satisfied:

(a) that the failure to register a charge before the end of the period allowed for registration, or the omission or mis-statement of any particular, with respect to any such charge or in a memorandum of satisfaction:

  (i) was accidental or due to inadvertence or to some other sufficient cause; or

  (ii) is not of a nature to prejudice the position of creditors or shareholders of the company; or

(b) that on other grounds it is just and equitable to grant relief: CA 2006, s 873(1).

19.19 The court may, on the application of the company or a person interested, and on such terms and conditions as seem to the court just and expedient, order that the period allowed for registration shall be extended or, as the case may be, that the omission or mis-statement shall be rectified: CA 2006, s 873(2).

The court, however, requires the applicant to act quickly in effecting the charge: *Re Telematic Ltd* [1994] 1 BCLC 90. In respect of omissions or mis-statements, the court does not have power to remove an entry, nor the removal of information volunteered by the company, which was not required to be provided: *Exeter Trust Ltd v Screenways Ltd* [1991] BCLC 888; and *Igroup Ltd v Ocwen* [2004] 1 WLR 451.

This is a discretionary power which the courts may exercise, and full details must be provided as to the reasons for non-registration or as to mistaken registration, and not merely that it was due to inadvertence. In *Re Kris Cruisers Ltd* [1949] Ch 138, the court stated that the term 'some other sufficient cause', were words which would be satisfied, if it were proved that the secretary of a company had been wrongly advised by his solicitor or counsel, that registration need not be sought. Vaisey J considered this section to be 'a benevolent section in this sense, that it appears to give the mortgagee or the charge, a complete and unfettered opportunity for repentance, and really to place him in the same position exactly as if he had been careful and not careless, diligent and not negligent'.

The courts have also considered other grounds where it would be 'just and equitable to grant relief': *Re Braemar Investments Limited* [1989] Ch 54. These include situations where on quickly learning of the failure to register, the charge is registered, but the overriding consideration is whether it is just and equitable to extend the period for registration.

19.20 The power of rectification given to the court includes the correction of certain omissions or misstatements. The court does not have power to delete the whole registration: *Exeter Trust Ltd v Screenways Ltd* [1991] BCLC 888 (per Nourse LJ).

Normally, the court will not make an order for rectification once liquidation commences, or the company is insolvent: *Re s Abrahams and Sons* [1902] 1 Ch 695; and *Re Ashpurton Estates Ltd* [1983] Ch 110. However, in exceptional circumstances, the court may grant such an order: *Barclays Bank plc v Stuart Landon Ltd* [2001] 2 BCLC 316; and *RM Arnold & Co Ltd* [1984] BCLC 535.

The power of rectification is limited to correcting mistakes or omissions, or omission in the entry of any particulars, with respect to a mortgage or charge or in a memorandum of satisfaction, made by the registrar on the register of charges maintained by the registrar under the Companies Acts. It does not extend to mistakes otherwise than in a particular entered on the register, and accordingly did not extend to the information particulars entered on prescribed mortgage or charge forms submitted to Companies House by an applicant: *Igroup Ltd v Owen* [2004] 2 BCLC 61. The court does not have any inherent power of rectification, as such a power would be wholly inconsistent with the limited statutory jurisdiction to order rectification under the Companies Acts.

Avoidance of certain charges

Consequence of failure to register charges created by a company

19.21 If a company creates a charge under CA 2006, s 860, the charge is void (so far as any security on the company's property or undertaking is conferred by it) against:

(a) a liquidator of the company;

(b) an administrator of the company; and

(c) a creditor of the company,

unless s 860 is complied with: CA 2006, s 874(1).

In *Smith v Bridgend County Borough Council* [2002] 1 AC 336, the Supreme Court held that the term 'void against the liquidator', meant void against a company acting by its liquidator.

19.22 If a creditor has a registered charge which is subject to an unregistered charge, that creditor has a priority to the unregistered charge, regardless of whether the company is in liquidation or administration, and even where he had knowledge that the unregistered charge existed: *Re Monolithic Building Co* [1915] 1 Ch 643.

Section 874(1) is subject to the provisions of Ch 1 to Pt 25: CA 2006, s 874(2).

Section 874(1) is without prejudice to any contract or obligation for repayment of the money secured by the charge; when a charge becomes void under this section, the money secured by it immediately becomes payable: CA 2006, s 874(3).

Companies' records and registers

Companies to keep copies of instruments creating charges

19.23 A company must keep available for inspection a copy of every instrument creating a charge requiring registration under Pt 25, Ch 1. This includes any document delivered to the company under s 868(3)(b): CA 2006, s 875(1).

In the case of a series of uniform debentures, a copy of one of the debentures of the series is sufficient: CA 2006, s 875(2).

A company's register of charges

19.24 Every limited company must keep available for inspection a register of charges and enter in it all charges specifically affecting property of the company; and all floating charges on the whole or part of the company's property or undertaking: CA 2006, s 876(1).

The entry must, in each case, give a short description of the property charged, the amount of the charge and, except in the cases of securities to bearer, the names of the persons entitled to it: CA 2006, s 876(2). If an officer of the company knowingly and wilfully authorises or permits the omission of an entry required to be made in pursuance of s 876, he commits an offence: CA 2006, s 876(3), and will be subject to a fine CA 2006, s 876(4).

Instruments creating charges and register of charges to be available for inspection

19.25 CA 2006, s 877 applies to:

(a) documents required to be kept available for inspection under s 875 (copies of instruments creating charges); and

(b) a company's register of charges kept in pursuance of s 876: CA 2006, s 877(1).

19.26 The documents and register must be kept available for inspection at the company's registered office, or at a place specified in regulations under s 1136: CA 2006, s 877(2). The company must give notice to the registrar of the place at which the documents and register are kept available for inspection, and of any change in that place, unless they have at all times been kept at the company's registered office: CA 2006, s 877(3). The documents and register must be open to the inspection of any creditor or member of the company without charge, and of any other person on payment of such fee as may be prescribed: CA 2006, s 877(4). If default is made for 14 days in complying with s 877(3) or an inspection required under s 877(4) is refused, an offence is committed by the company, and every officer of the company who is in default: CA 2006, s 877(5), resulting in a fine being imposed: CA 2006, s 877(6).

If an inspection required under s 877(4) is refused, the court may, by order, compel an immediate inspection: CA 2006, s 877(7).

The register of charges

Register of charges to be kept by registrar

19.27 The registrar must keep, with respect to each company, a register of all the charges requiring registration under CA 2006, Pt 25, Ch 2: CA 2006, s 885(1).

In the case of a charge to the benefit of which holders of a series of debentures are entitled, the registrar must enter in the register the required particulars specified in s 882(2): CA 2006, s 885(2).

19.28 In the case of any other charge, the registrar must enter in the register the following particulars:

(a) if it is a charge created by a company, the date of its creation and, if it is a charge which was existing on property acquired by the company, the date of the acquisition;

(b) the amount secured by the charge;

(c) short particulars of the property charged;

(d) the persons entitled to the charge; and

(e) in the case of a floating charge, a statement of any of the provisions of the charge and of any instrument relating to it which prohibit, restrict or regulate the company's power to grant further securities ranking in priority to, or *pari passu* with, the floating charge, or which vary or otherwise regulate the order of ranking of the floating charge in relation to subsisting securities: CA 2006, s 885(3).

19.29 The registrar must give a certificate of the registration of any charge registered in pursuance of CA 2006, Pt 25, Ch 2, stating the name of the company, and the person first-named in the charge among those entitled to the benefit of the charge (or, in the case of a series of debentures, the name of the holder of the first such debenture issued), and the amount secured by the charge: CA 2006, s 885(4).

The certificate must be signed by the registrar or authenticated by the registrar's official seal. This is conclusive evidence that the requirements of Ch 2 to Pt 25 as to registration have been satisfied: CA 2006, s 885(5). The register kept in pursuance of s 885 must be open to inspection by any individual: CA 2006, s 885(6).

The period allowed for registration

19.30 The period allowed for registration of a charge created by a company is 21 days, beginning with the day after the day on which the charge is created. If the charge is created outside the UK, 21 days beginning with the day after the day on which a copy of the instrument by which the charge is created or evidenced could, in due course of post (and if despatched with due diligence) have been received in the UK: CA 2006, s 886(1).

The period allowed for registration of a charge to which property acquired by a company is subject is 21 days, beginning with the day after the day on which the transaction is settled. If the property is situated and the charge was created outside the UK, this is 21 days beginning with the day after the day on which a copy of the instrument by which the charge is created or evidenced could, in due course of post (and if despatched with due diligence) have been received in the UK: CA 2006, s 886(2).

The period allowed for registration of particulars of a series of debentures as a result of s 882 is, if there is a deed containing the charge mentioned in s 882(1), 21 days beginning with the day after the day on which that deed is executed, or if there is no such deed, 21 days beginning with the day after the day on which the first debenture of the series is executed: CA 2006, s 886(2).

Entries of satisfaction and relief

19.31 CA 2006, s 887 states that s 887(2) applies if a statement is delivered to the registrar verifying (with respect to any registered charge) that the debt for which the charge was given has been paid or satisfied in whole or in part, or that part of the property charged has been released from the charge or has ceased to form part of the company's property: CA 2006, s 887(1).

If the charge is a floating charge, the statement must be accompanied by either: (a) a statement by the creditor entitled to the benefit of the charge, or a person authorised by him for the purpose, verifying that the statement mentioned in s 887(1) is correct; or (b) a direction obtained from the court, on the ground that the statement by the creditor mentioned in paragraph (a) could not be readily obtained, dispensing with the need for that statement: CA 2006, s 887(2).

19.32 The registrar may enter on the register, a memorandum of satisfaction (in whole or in part) regarding the fact contained in the statement mentioned in s 887(1): CA 2006, s 887(3).

Where the registrar enters a memorandum of satisfaction in whole, he must, if required, furnish the company with a copy of the memorandum: CA 2006, s 887(4).

The company is not required to submit particulars with respect to the entry in the register of a memorandum of satisfaction where the company, having created a floating charge over all or any part of its property, disposes of part of the property subject to the floating charge: CA 2006, s 887(5).

Rectification of register of charges

19.33 CA 2006, s 888 states that s 888(2) applies if the court is satisfied:

(a) that the failure to register a charge before the end of the period allowed for registration, or the omission or mis-statement of any particular with respect to any such charge or in a memorandum of satisfaction:

(i) was accidental or due to inadvertence or to some other sufficient cause; or

(ii) is not of a nature to prejudice the position of creditors or shareholders of the company, or

(b) that on other grounds it is just and equitable to grant relief: CA 2006, s 888(1).

The court may, on the application of the company or a person interested, and on such terms and conditions as seem to the court just and expedient, order that the period allowed for registration shall be extended or, as the case may be, that the omission or mis-statement shall be rectified: CA 2006, s 888(2).

Avoidance of certain charges

Charges void unless registered

19.34 If a company creates a charge to which CA 2006, s 878 applies, the charge is void (so far as any security on the company's property or any part of it is conferred by the charge) against:

(a) the liquidator of the company;

(b) an administrator of the company; and

(c) any creditor of the company unless that section is complied with: CA 2006, s 889(1).

Section 889(1) is without prejudice to any contract or obligation for repayment of the money secured by the charge; and when a charge becomes void under s 889 the money secured by it immediately becomes payable: CA 2006, s 889(2).

Checklist: board approval to a charge

19.35 *This checklist provides procedural aspects for approval to a charge by the company's Board of Directors. This checklist should be adapted depending on the company's articles of associations on procedural aspects.*

No	Issue	Reference
1	Consider the type of charge that is being created and the terms of the charge (including negative pledge clauses and crystallisation).	CA 2006, s 860
2	The essential characteristic of a floating charge is its ability for flexibility and freedom of movement of assets.	*Re Spectrum Plus Limited* [2005] 2 BCLC 269
3	Prepare an Agenda for the Board Meeting.	Agenda
4	Call a Board meeting – on reasonable notice setting out date, time and place of meeting.	Notice
5	Consider if Board Meeting may be dispensed with by a written resolution procedure?	Written resolution
6	Directors to declare any interest in the charge.	CA 2006, ss 177, 182

No	Issue	Reference
7	Ensure quorum present and consider whether Chairman has a casting vote in the event of a deadlock.	Articles of Association
8	Directors vote on a show of hands by simple majority to approve the charge.	Articles of Association
9	Prepare minutes of the Board meeting.	Minutes
10	Lodge the charge at Companies House using prescribed form and fee.	Form MR [ ] (see Companies House Forms as to the appropriate form to be used)
11	Obtain certificate of registration from Registrar.	Certificate
12	Update register of charges/director's interests.	Statutory register

20 Certification, transfer of securities and people with significant control

Introduction

20.1 This Chapter addresses the following issues:

- the legal nature of a share certificate;
- requirement for directors to register shares on allotment and effect;
- transfer of securities; and
- person with significant control and the maintenance of a public register.

Share certificate as evidence of title

20.2 Where a company is registered in England, a certificate under the common seal of the company, specifying any shares held by a member, is prima facie evidence of his title to the shares: CA 2006, s 768(1).

Issue of certificates on allotment

Duty of company as to issue of certificates on allotment

20.3 A company must, within two months after the allotment of any of its shares, debentures or debenture stock, complete and have ready for delivery:

(a) the certificates of the shares allotted;

(b) the debentures allotted; or

(c) the certificates of the debenture stock allotted: CA 2006, s 769(1).

There are exceptions to CA 2006, s 769(1) which are set out in s 769(2).

20.4 If there is noncompliance with CA 2006, s 769(1), an offence is committed by every officer of the company who is in default: CA 2006, s 769(3), who may be subject to a fine: CA 2006, s 769(4).

Transfer of securities

Registration of transfer

20.5 A company may not register a transfer of shares in or debentures of the company unless:

(a) a proper instrument of transfer has been delivered to it, or

(b) the transfer:

  (i) is an exempt transfer within the Stock Transfer Act 1982 (c 41); or

  (ii) is in accordance with regulations under Ch 2 of Pt 21: CA 2006, s 770(1).

Section 770(1) of CA 2006 does not affect any power of the company to register as shareholder or debenture holder, a person to whom the right to any shares in or debentures of the company has been transmitted by operation of law: CA 2006, s 770(2).

Procedure on transfer being lodged

20.6 When a transfer of shares in or debentures of a company has been lodged with the company, the company must either register the transfer; or give the transferee notice of refusal to register the transfer, together with its reasons for the refusal, as soon as practicable, and in any event, within two months after the date on which the transfer is lodged with it: CA 2006, s 771(1).

If the company refuses to register the transfer, it must provide the transferee with such further information about the reasons for the refusal as the transferee may reasonably request. This does not include copies of minutes of meetings of directors: CA 2006, s 771(2).

20.7 If a company fails to comply with CA 2006, s 771 an offence is committed by the company; and every officer of the company who is in default: CA 2006, s 771(3), who may be subject to a fine: CA 2006, s 771(4).

There are exceptions to s 771 which are set out in s 779.

20.8 CA 2006, s 771 and articles of association with similar provisions have given rise to a number of cases. In *Re Hackney Pavilion Ltd* [1924] 1 Ch 276, the Board's right to decline registration of shares is required to be actively exercised by a vote of the Board:

A failure by directors to exercise the right to refuse transfer of shares, may result in rectification of the register, in favour of the applicant: *Moodie v Shepherd (Bookbinders) Limited* [1949] 2 All ER 1044.

The powers conferred by the company's articles of association on the directors to refuse to register the transfer, must be exercised within a reasonable time: *Re Swaledale Cleaners Ltd* [1968] 3 All ER 619. According to Harman LJ, a reasonable time within which directors must make up their minds either to accept a transfer or to refuse, must be the two months within which they have to answer under CA 2006, s 771(1).

Provided the decision to refuse registration was taken with a reasonable time, failure to comply with the statutory notice period did not render directors' decision to refuse transfer of shares as invalid. In *Popley v Planarrive Ltd* [1997] 1 BCLC 8, P submitted shares for registration in his name, which, if registered, would have given him control of the company as a shareholder. If P obtained such control, he would use his power to obtain control of the board. The articles of association provided that the directors of the company had an absolute discretion to refuse to register a transfer of shares. The articles (Art 25 of Table A of the Companies Act 1985) also provided that, if the directors refused to register a transfer of shares, they should send to the transferee, within two months after the date on which the transfer was lodged, notice of their refusal to register the transfer. The directors refused to register the ten shares in P's name, but did not inform P of their decision as they were obliged to do under Art 25.

Laddie J held that the court was willing to proceed on the basis that the directors' refusal to register the shares in P's name, was taken within two months of his request having been submitted to the company. Accordingly, there were no grounds for applying the principle in *Re Swaledale Cleaners Ltd* [1968] 3 All ER 619. All that the principle in *Re Swaledale Cleaners Ltd* decided was that, if the directors failed to exercise their discretion within a reasonable time, they lost their power to refuse registration. However, different considerations applied where the decision was taken within a reasonable time, but there was a failure to inform the transferee of the decision. Such a failure may well expose the directors to civil or criminal liability, but could not relate back to turn the proper exercise of the directors' powers into a nullity. Accordingly, on the facts, the failure to comply with Art 25 could not result in the directors' refusal to register being ineffective. Laddie J also held that in exercising their power to refuse to register a transfer of shares, the directors must act bona fide in the interests of the company. The onus was on P to show that they had not done so.

Transfer of shares on application of transferor

20.9 On the application of the transferor of any share or interest in a company, the company must enter in its register of members, the name of the transferee (or, as the case may be, deliver the name of the transferee to the registrar under Ch 2A of Pt 8), in the same manner and subject to the same conditions, as if the application for the entry (or delivery) were made by the transferee: CA 2006, s 772 (as inserted by the SBEEA 2015, Sch 5, Pt 2).

Execution of share transfer by personal representative

20.10 An instrument of transfer of the share or other interest of a deceased member of a company may be made by his personal representative although the personal representative is not himself a member of the company; and is as effective as if the personal representative had been such a member at the time of the execution of the instrument: CA 2006, s 773.

This is known as transmission by operation of law: it may apply on death of the shareholder. There is no requirement for a proper instrument of transfer before registration can be effected. The next further process is for the personal representative of the deceased to be registered as a member.

Evidence of grant of probate

20.11 The production to a company of any document that is by law sufficient evidence of the grant of:

(a) probate of the will of a deceased person;

(b) letters of administration of the estate of a deceased person; or

(c) confirmation as executor of a deceased person,

must be accepted by the company as sufficient evidence of the grant: CA 2006, s 774.

Certification of instrument of transfer

20.12 The certification by a company of an instrument of transfer of any shares in, or debentures of, the company is to be taken as a representation by the company to any person acting on the faith of the certification, that there have been produced to the company such documents as on their face show a *prima facie* title to the shares or debentures, in the transferor named in the instrument: CA 2006, s 775(1).

The certification is not to be taken as a representation that the transferor has any title to the shares or debentures: CA 2006, s 775(2).

Where a person acts on the faith of a false certification by a company made negligently, the company is under the same liability to him as if the certification had been made fraudulently: CA 2006, s 775(3).

20.13 Certain rules apply for the purposes of complying with CA 2006, s 775:

(a) an instrument of transfer is certificated if it bears the words 'certificate lodged' (or words to the like effect);

(b) the certification of an instrument of transfer is made by a company if:

   (i) the person issuing the instrument is a person authorised to issue certificated instruments of transfer on the company's behalf; and

   (ii) the certification is signed by a person authorised to certificate transfers on the company's behalf or by an officer or employee either of the company or of a body corporate so authorised;

(c) a certification is treated as signed by a person if:

   (i) it purports to be authenticated by his signature or initials (whether handwritten or not); and

   (ii) it is not shown that the signature or initials was or were placed there neither by himself nor by a person authorised to use the signature or initials for the purpose of certificating transfers on the company's behalf: CA 2006, s 775(4).

Issue of certificates on transfer

Duty of company as to issue of certificates on transfer

20.14 A company must, within two months after the date on which a transfer of any of its shares, debentures or debenture stock is lodged with the company, complete and have ready for delivery:

(a) the certificates of the shares transferred;

(b) the debentures transferred; or

(c) the certificates of the debenture stock transferred: CA 2006, s 776(1).

20.15 The term 'transfer' means a transfer duly stamped and otherwise valid; or an exempt transfer within the Stock Transfer Act 1982. However, it does not include a transfer that the company is for any reason entitled to refuse to register, and does not register: CA 2006, s 776(2).

There are exceptions to CA 2006, s 776 which are set out in s 776(3).

20.16 If default is made in complying with CA 2006, s 776(1), an offence is committed by every officer of the company who is in default: CA 2006, s 776(5), who may be subject to a fine: CA 2006, s 776(6).

Information about people with significant control

Introduction

20.17 The SBEEA 2015 (by inserting Pt 21A into CA 2006), introduced a number of measures to increase the accountability of companies, by facilitating the process of seeing who owns or controls companies, and the persons who may make decisions on the operation and functioning of companies. This is achieved principally through the establishment of a central register of people with significant control ('PSC'). The effect of this register is to capture and see who owns the shares in the company, and also who influences or controls a company discretely. Companies will still need to keep their own register of people with significant control. The objective is to increase trust, provide some transparency and encourage investment in the UK. They are required to send the information to Companies House, with their confirmation statement or as part of the incorporation package. Companies House will make all information from companies available for free, in a central, searchable register of people with significant control. Not all companies will need to record the people with significant control information, as there are certain exemptions for such companies set out in the SBEEA 2015.

20.18 CA 2006, Pt 21A is supplemented by the Register of People with Significant Control Regulations 2016, SI 2016/339. The Regulations set out details of the applicability of the register to specific persons, and to the protection regime to ensure that the information on the register is not misused.

CA 2006, Sch 1A defines what is meant by 'a person with significant control' ('PSC'). It sets out a company's requirements to obtain required information on such people, and hold it in a register kept available for public inspection (the 'PSC register'). Schedule 1A also sets out the obligations that apply to people with significant control and certain legal entities; and the requirement for companies to provide information in the PSC register to the registrar in the context of their confirmation statement under Pt 24 of the CA 2006. The registrar will make the information public with limited exceptions.

20.19 The objective of CA 2006, s 790A (as inserted by the SBEEA 2015, s 81 and Sch 3) is to provide an overview of the operation and function of the CA 2006, Pt 21A for ease of navigation of the various sections. This includes the purpose and objective of Part 21A and its interrelationship with other sections of the CA 2006. Part 21A is arranged as follows:

(a) the remaining provisions of Ch 1 to Pt 21A of the CA 2006 identify the companies to which P 21A applies, and explain some key terms, including what it means to have 'significant control' over a company;

(b) Ch 2 to Pt 21A of the CA 2006 imposes duties on companies to gather information, and on others to supply information, to enable companies to keep the register required by Ch 3 to Pt 21A;

(c) Ch 3 to Pt 21A requires companies to keep a register, referred to as a 'register of people with significant control over the company' and to make the register available to the public;

(d) Ch 4 to Pt 21A gives private companies the option of using an alternative method of record-keeping; and

(e) Ch 5 to Pt 21A makes provision for excluding certain material from the information available to the public.

Companies to which Pt 21A applies

20.20 CA 2006, Pt 21A applies to companies other than DTR5 issuers; and companies of any other description specified in the Register of People with Significant Control Regulations: CA 2006, s 790B(1).

20.21 In deciding whether to specify a description of the company, the Secretary of State is to have regard to the extent to which companies of that description are bound by disclosure and transparency rules (in the UK or elsewhere) broadly similar to the ones applying to DTR5 issuers: CA 2006, s 790B(2).

A 'DTR5 issuer' is an issuer to which Ch 5 of the Disclosure Rules and Transparency Rules sourcebook, made by the Financial Conduct Authority (as amended or replaced from time to time) applies: CA 2006, s 790B(3).

Key terms

20.22 CA 2006, s 790C explains some key terms used in Pt 21A: CA 2006, s 790C(1).

The references to a person with (or having) 'significant control' over a company, are to an individual who meets one or more of the specified conditions in relation to the company: CA 2006, s 790C(2).

The 'specified conditions' are those set out in Pt 1 of Sch 1A: CA 2006, s 790C(3). This provides that a person with significant control over a company, is an individual (X) who meets one or more of the 'specified conditions' in relation to the company.

THE SPECIFIED CONDITIONS (SCHEDULE 1A)

References to People with Significant Control over a Company

Introduction

1. This Part of this Schedule specifies the conditions, at least one of which must be met by an individual ('X'), in relation to a company ('company

Y'), in order for the individual to be a person with 'significant control' over the company.

Ownership of shares

2. The first condition is that X holds, directly or indirectly, more than 25% of the shares in company Y.

Ownership of voting rights

3. The second condition is that X holds, directly or indirectly, more than 25% of the voting rights in company Y.

Ownership of right to appoint or remove directors

4. The third condition is that X holds the right, directly or indirectly, to appoint or remove a majority of the board of directors of company Y.

Significant influence or control

5. The fourth condition is that X has the right to exercise, or actually exercises, significant influence or control over company Y.

Trusts, partnerships etc

6. The fifth condition is that:

(a) the trustees of a trust or the members of a firm that, under the law by which it is governed, is not a legal person meet any of the other specified conditions (in their capacity as such) in relation to company Y, or would do so if they were individuals, and

(b) X has the right to exercise, or actually exercises, significant influence or control over the activities of that trust or firm.

Part 2 concerns holding an interest in a company. Part 3 deals with power to amend thresholds.

20.23 Individuals with significant control over a company are either 'registrable' or 'non-registrable' in relation to the company:

(a) they are 'non-registrable' if they do not hold any interest in the company, except through one or more other legal entities over each of which they have significant control. and each of which is a 'relevant legal entity' ('RLE') in relation to the company;

(b) otherwise, they are 'registrable'.

The references to a 'registrable person' in relation to a company, are to an individual with significant control over the company, who is registrable in relation to that company: CA 2006, s 790C(4).

20.24 A 'legal entity' is a body corporate, or a firm that is a legal person under the law by which it is governed: CA 2006, s 790C(5).

In relation to a company, a legal entity is a 'relevant legal entity' if:

(a) it would have come within the definition of a person with significant control over the company if it had been an individual; and

(b) it is subject to its own disclosure requirements: CA 2006, s 790C(6).

20.25 A legal entity is 'subject to its own disclosure requirements' if:

(a) Part 21A of CA 2006 applies to it (whether by virtue of s 790B or another enactment that extends the application of this Part);

(b) it is a DTR5 issuer;

(c) it is of a description specified in regulations under CA 2006, s 790B (or that section as extended); or

(d) it is of a description specified in the Register of People with Significant Control Regulations 2016: CA 2006, s 790C(7).

20.26 A relevant legal entity is either 'registrable' or 'non-registrable' in relation to a company:

(a) it is 'non-registrable' if it does not hold any interest in the company except through one or more other legal entities over each of which it has significant control and each of which is also a relevant legal entity in relation to the company;

(b) otherwise, it is 'registrable'.

The references to a 'registrable relevant legal entity' in relation to a company, are to a relevant legal entity which is registrable in relation to that company: CA 2006, s 790C(8).The effect of the terminology is to determine whether or not the individual's or RLE's details must be entered or noted in the company's PSC register.

20.27 For the purposes of CA 2006, s 790C(4) and (8):

(a) whether someone:

 (i) holds an interest in a company; or

 (ii) holds that interest through another legal entity,

 is to be determined in accordance with Pt 2 of Sch 1A;

(b) whether someone has significant control over that other legal entity, is to be determined in accordance with s 790C(2) and (3) and Pt 1 of Sch 1A, reading references in those provisions to the company, as references to that other entity: CA 2006, s 790C(9).

20.28 The effect of provisions in respect of RLE's is that, if for example, company A is owned by company B, and company B maintains a PSC register under Part 21A, a person ('P') with significant control over both B and A as a result of the same shareholding (held through B), need not be registered as a PSC in relation to A, provided that P has no other interest in the company through any other means. Instead, B will be noted in A's PSC register as an RLE. Those looking at A's register will be able then to look at B's register to identify P. The objective is to avoid, where appropriate, ownership disclosure arrangements are in place, duplicative reporting.

Example of Relevant Legal Entities required to keep information on the register of PSC

Relevant Legal Entity X

↓

Relevant Legal Entity Y

↓

Company Z

In some cases, a legal entity rather than a person may fulfil one or more of the conditions above. Entities that fulfil one of the conditions and that are required to hold a PSC register or disclose information, for example, as a DTR5 issuer, are referred to as 'relevant legal entities'. Not all relevant legal entities should be recorded on the register. By not requiring all entities to look through their ownership chain in these circumstances, makes it easier for an entity to maintain its own register, whilst still ensuring that information on all people with significant control will be available on the public register.

In the above example, three UK registered companies are involved. Company Z is fully owned by Company Y, and Company Y is fully owned by Company X. Companies X and Y are both relevant legal entities (they both keep a PSC register) who own more than 25% of the share capital of Z (Y directly and X indirectly). In order to avoid duplication of information on the register, Company Z would include only the first relevant legal entity (here Company Y) in its PSC register, and should not include Company X. Any person who is interested to look further would need to search Company Y's PSC register which would identify Company X. In this example, the first relevant legal entity in the chain is Company Y, which will be a registerable relevant legal entity. Company X will be a non-registerable relevant legal entity, and should not be included in Company Z's PSC register.

20.29 The register that a company is required to keep under s 790M (register of people with significant control over a company), is referred to as the company's 'PSC register': CA 2006, s 790C(10). Part 3 of the 2016 Regulations makes provision about the particulars to be noted in a company's register of persons with significant control, concerning the nature of a person's control over the company: reg 7.

In deciding whether to specify a description of legal entity under s 790C(7)(d) of the CA 2006, , the Secretary of State is to have regard to the extent to which entities of that description are bound by disclosure and transparency rules (in the United Kingdom or elsewhere), broadly similar to the ones applying to an entity falling within any other paragraph of that subsection: CA 2006, s 790C(11).

Company's duty to investigate and obtain information

20.30 Certain duties are imposed on companies and PSCs. A company to which Pt 21A applies must take reasonable steps:

(a) to find out if there is anyone who is a registrable person or a registrable relevant legal entity in relation to the company; and

(b) if so, to identify them: CA 2006, s 790D(1).

A company to which Pt 21A applies, must give notice to anyone whom it knows or has reasonable cause to believe to be a registrable person, or a registrable relevant legal entity in relation to it: CA 2006, s 790D(2).

20.31 The notice, if addressed to an individual, must require the addressee to state whether or not he or she is a registrable person in relation to the company (within the meaning of Pt 21A); and if so, to confirm or correct any particulars of his or hers that are included in the notice, and supply any that are missing: CA 2006, s 790D(3).

20.32 The notice, if addressed to a legal entity, must require the addressee to state whether or not it is a registrable relevant legal entity in relation to the company (within the meaning of Pt 21A); and if so, to confirm or correct any of its particulars that are included in the notice, and supply any that are missing: CA 2006, s 790D(4).

20.33 A company to which Pt 21A applies, may also give notice to a person if it knows or has reasonable cause to believe that the person:

(a) knows the identity of someone who falls within s 790D(6); or

(b) knows the identity of someone likely to have that knowledge: CA 2006, s 790D(5). The aim of this section is to provide the company with the means to obtain information on registerable persons and RLE's, where it does not itself know their identity. This includes entities in the ownership chain which are not RLE's, but which might know the identity of a registerable person or RLE. For example, a company may know that a person (X) is acting on behalf of PSC (P), but may not know any of P's details. The company may serve notice on X in order to obtain information on P.

It would be possible for a company to serve notice on a lawyer under s 790D(5) to obtain information. In this case, the issue would be whether the information held by a lawyer about PSC's or RLE's would be subject to legal professional privilege. If so, the lawyer would be exempt from providing such information under s 790D(12).

20.34 The persons who fall within s 790D(6) are:

(a) any registrable person in relation to the company;

(b) any relevant legal entity in relation to the company;

(c) any entity which would be a relevant legal entity in relation to the company but for the fact that s 790C(6)(b) does not apply in respect of it: CA 2006, s 790D(6).

20.35 A notice under s 790D(5) may require the addressee:

(a) to state whether or not the addressee knows the identity of:

  (i) any person who falls within s 790D(6); or

  (ii) any person likely to have that knowledge, and

(b) if so, to supply any particulars of theirs that are within the addressee's knowledge, and state whether or not the particulars are being supplied with the knowledge of each of the persons concerned: CA 2006, s 790D(7).

The notice must state that the addressee is to comply with the notice by no later than the end of the period of one month, beginning with the date of the notice: CA 2006, s 790D(8).

As the company's duty to provide information under s 790D is on-going and continuous, there is no defined period within which steps must be taken or notice given.

20.36 The Secretary of State may by regulations make further provision about giving notices under this section. This includes the form and content of any such notices and the manner in which they must be given: CA 2006, s 790D(9). This is set out under the Register of People with Significant Control Regulations 2016, SI 2016/339, which provides that a warning notice given under Sch 1B, para 1 to the Act must:

(a) specify the date on which the warning notice is given;

(b) be accompanied by a copy of the notice given under s 790D or 790E of the Act to which the warning notice relates;

(c) identify the addressee's relevant interest in the company by reference to the shares or right in question;

(d) state that the company will consider reasons provided to it as to why the addressee failed to comply with the notice given under s 790D or 790E of the Act;

(e) explain the effect of a restrictions notice; and

(f) state that, by virtue of a restrictions notice, certain acts or failures to act may constitute an offence.

This will tell them that the company will issue them with a restriction notice. The effect of a restriction notice is to freeze the person or entity's interest in the company, until the company obtains the information it needs and lifts the restrictions. Further, the holder of the interest in the shares will not be able to sell, transfer or receive any benefit from the rights, or exercise the rights attached to them.

20.37 A restrictions notice issued under Sch 1B, para 1 to the Act must:

(a) specify the date on which the restrictions notice is issued;

(b) be accompanied by a copy of the warning notice which preceded the restrictions notice;

(c) identify the addressee's relevant interest in the company by reference to the shares or right in question;

(d) explain the effect of the restrictions notice;

(e) state that, by virtue of the restrictions notice, certain acts or failures to act may constitute an offence; and

(f) state that an aggrieved person may apply to the court for an order directing that the relevant interest cease to be subject to restrictions: SI 2016/339, reg 19.

20.38 Under SI 2016/339, reg 20, a company must take account of any incapacity of the addressee, in deciding what counts as 'valid reason' sufficient to justify the addressee's failure to comply with the notice.

Regulation 21 addresses the withdrawal and effect of withdrawal of the restrictions notice.

A company is not required to take steps or give notice under s 790D(11) with respect to a registrable person or registrable relevant legal entity if:

(a) the company has already been informed of the person's status as a registrable person or registrable relevant legal entity in relation to it, and been supplied with all the particulars; and

(b) in the case of a registrable person, the information and particulars were provided either by the person concerned or with his or her knowledge: CA 2006, s 790D(11). The objective of s 790D(11) is to ensure that individuals are in all cases aware of their entry in the company's PSC register. This is important, for example, in the event that the individual wants to apply for their information to be protected from disclosure, and to ensure that the individual knows to update the company should their personal details change.

20.39 A person to whom a notice under s 790D(5) is given, is not required by that notice to disclose any information in respect of which a claim to legal professional privilege could be maintained in legal proceedings: CA 2006, s 790D(12).

A reference to knowing the identity of a person, includes knowing information from which that person can be identified.

The term 'particulars' means:

(i) in the case of a registrable person or a registrable relevant legal entity, the required particulars (see s 790K), and

(ii) in any other case, any particulars that will allow the person to be contacted by the company: CA 2006, s 790D(13).

Company's duty to keep information up-to-date

20.40 CA 2006, s 790E applies if particulars of a registrable person or registrable relevant legal entity are stated in a company's PSC register: CA 2006, s 790E(1).

The company must give notice to the person or entity, if the company knows or has reasonable cause to believe that a relevant change has occurred: CA 2006, s 790E(2).

In the case of a registrable person, a 'relevant change' occurs if:

(a) the person ceases to be a registrable person in relation to the company; or

(b) any other change occurs as a result of which the particulars stated for the person in the PSC register are incorrect or incomplete: CA 2006, s 790E(3).

20.41 In the case of a registrable relevant legal entity, a 'relevant change' occurs if:

(a) the entity ceases to be a registrable relevant legal entity in relation to the company; or

(b) any other change occurs as a result of which the particulars stated for the entity in the PSC register are incorrect or incomplete: CA 2006, s 790E(4).

20.42 The company must give the notice as soon as reasonably practicable, after it learns of the change or first has reasonable cause to believe that the change has occurred: CA 2006, s 790E(5).

The notice must require the addressee:

(a) to confirm whether or not the change has occurred; and

(b) if so:

 (i) to state the date of the change; and

 (ii) to confirm or correct the particulars included in the notice, and supply any that are missing from the notice: CA 2006, s 790E(6).

CA 2006, s 790D(8)–(10) apply to notices under s 790E as to notices under that section: CA 2006, s 790E(7).

20.43 A company is not required to give notice under s 790E if the company has already been informed of the relevant change; and in the case of a registrable person, that information was provided either by the person concerned or with his or her knowledge: CA 2006, s 790E(8).

Failure by company to comply with information duties

20.44 If a company fails to comply with a duty under the CA 2006, s 790D or 790E to take steps or give notice, an offence is committed by the company; and every officer of the company who is in default: CA 2006, s 790F(1), who may be subject to imprisonment and/or fine.

Duty to supply information

20.45 CA 2006, ss 790G and 790H apply to duty on others on information gathering.

CA 2006, s 790G complements s 790D, with the aim of ensuring that registerable persons and RLE's, who are not known to or identified by the company under s 790D, are nevertheless entered in the company's PSC. The duty to supply information under s 790G, is partly based on the regulations under the Financial Services and Markets Act 2000 (implementing the Transparency Directive 2013/50/EU) which places a disclosure obligation on investors in certain public listed companies.

CA 2006, s 790G applies to a person if:

(a) the person is a registrable person or a registrable relevant legal entity in relation to a company;

(b) the person knows that to be the case or ought reasonably to do so;

(c) the required particulars of the person are not stated in the company's PSC register;

(d) the person has not received notice from the company under s 790D(2); and

(e) the circumstances described in paras (a) to (d) have continued for a period of at least one month: CA 2006, s 790G(1).

20.46 The person must:

(a) notify the company of the person's status (as a registrable person or registrable relevant legal entity) in relation to the company;

(b) state the date, to the best of the person's knowledge, on which the person acquired that status; and

(c) give the company the required particulars (see s 790K): CA 2006, s 790G(2).

The duty under s 790G(2) must be complied with by the end of the period of one month, beginning with the day on which all the conditions in sub-s (1)(a)–(e) were first met with respect to the person: CA 2006, s 790G(3).

Duty to update information

20.47 CA 2006, s 790H complements s 790E in connection with a registerable person or RLE, to notify the company of relevant changes to information in the PSC register. The objective is to ensure that changes to information in the PSC register that are not known to or identified by the company, are nevertheless recorded which will support the accuracy of the company's PSC register.

Section 790H applies to a person if:

(a) the required particulars of the person (whether a registrable person or a registrable relevant legal entity) are stated in a company's PSC register;

(b) a relevant change occurs;

(c) the person knows of the change or ought reasonably to do so;

(d) the company's PSC register has not been altered to reflect the change; and

(e) the person has not received notice from the company under s 790E by the end of the period of one month beginning with the day on which the change occurred: CA 2006, s 790H(1).

20.48 The person must notify the company of the change; state the date on which it occurred; and give the company any information needed to update the PSC register: CA 2006, s 790H(2).

20.49 The duty under s 790H(2) must be complied with by the later of the end of the period of two months beginning with the day on which the change occurred; and the end of the period of one month beginning with the day on which the person discovered the change: CA 2006, s 790H(3).

The term 'relevant change' has the same meaning as in s 790E: CA 2006, s 790H(4).

Compliance

Enforcement of disclosure requirements

20.50 CA 2006, Sch 1B contains provisions for when a person (whether an individual or a legal entity) fails to comply with a notice under s 790D or 790E or a duty under s 790G or 790H: CA 2006, s 790I.

Exemption from information and registration requirements

Power to make exemptions

20.51 The Secretary of State may exempt a person (whether an individual or a legal entity) under s 790J: CA 2006, s 790J(1). Sections 790J(2) and (3) sets out the effect of an exemption.

Required particulars

20.52 CA 2006, s 790K sets out the information that must be held by the company in respect of registerable persons (both individuals and legal entities) and RLEs. It also sets out what should be recorded on the register. The information set out below should provide for a unique identification of individuals registered.

The 'required particulars' of an individual who is a registrable person are:

(a) name;

(b) a service address;

(c) the country or state (or part of the United Kingdom) in which the individual is usually resident;

(d) nationality;

(e) date of birth;

(f) usual residential address;

(g) the date on which the individual became a registrable person in relation to the company in question;

(h) the nature of his or her control over that company (see Sch 1A); and

(i) if, in relation to that company, restrictions on using or disclosing any of the individual's PSC particulars are in force under regulations under s 790ZG, that fact: CA 2006, s 790K(1). This will enable the register available for public inspection to indicate that information has been withheld from public disclosure.

20.53 Under SI 2016/339, reg 7 the particulars required by ss 790K(1)(h), 790K(2)(e) and 790K(3)(f) of the Act (particulars as to nature of control over the company), are every statement listed in Sch 1 that is true in relation to the person in question. Regulation 7 and Sch 1 require the register to show which of the five conditions the PSC satisfies. The five conditions are set out above.

20.54 In the case of a person in relation to which CA 2006, Pt 21A has effect by virtue of s 790C(12) as if the person were an individual, the 'required particulars' are:

(a) name;

(b) principal office;

(c) the legal form of the person and the law by which it is governed;

(d) the date on which it became a registrable person in relation to the company in question; and

(e) the nature of its control over the company (see Sch 1A): CA 2006, s 790K(2).

20.55 The 'required particulars' of a registrable relevant legal entity are:

(a) corporate or firm name;

(b) registered or principal office;

(c) the legal form of the entity and the law by which it is governed;

(d) if applicable, the register of companies in which it is entered (including details of the state) and its registration number in that register;

(e) the date on which it became a registrable relevant legal entity in relation to the company in question; and

(f) the nature of its control over that company (see Sch 1A): CA 2006, s 790K(3).

CA 2006, s 163(2) (particulars of directors to be registered: individuals) applies for the purposes of s 790K(1): CA 2006, s 790K(4).

20.56 The Secretary of State may by regulations make further provision about the particulars required by s 790K(1)(h), (2)(e) and (3)(f): CA 2006, s 790K(5): see SI 2016/339, Part 4.

Power to amend required particulars

20.57 The Secretary of State may by regulations amend s 790K so as to add to or remove from any of the lists of required particulars: CA 2006, s 790L.

Register of people with significant control

20.58 CA 2006, Pt 21A, Ch 3 is concerned with the register of people with significant control. The SBEEA 2015, Sch 3 amends the CA 2006 to require companies to keep a register of people who have significant control over the company, as part of transparency within the company: SBEEA 2015, s 81. The requirements and meaning of a 'person with significant control' are set out in that Schedule. The Secretary of State must carry out a review of Pt 21A and related provisions of CA 2006 inserted by the SBEEA 2015 within three years of the SBEEA 2015, s 92 coming into force. Section 92 makes provision for information in the PSC register to be delivered to the registrar of companies ('registrar'). It is considered appropriate for the review to take account of both the company's requirement to maintain a register (Pt 21A), and the requirement to provide this information to the registrar and to make it publicly available: SBEEA 2015, s 82.

Duty to keep register

20.59 A company to which Pt 21A applies, must keep a register of people with significant control over the company: CA 2006, s 790M(1). This will be one of the registers that companies are required to keep under the CA 2006, together with others including the register of members and directors (CA 2006, ss 113 and 162 respectively). These registers will provide publicly available information on the management, ownership and control arrangements of the company.

The required particulars of any individual with significant control over the company who is 'registrable' in relation to the company, must be entered in the register once all the required particulars of that individual have been confirmed: CA 2006, s 790M(2).

The company must not enter any of the individual's particulars in the register, until they have all been confirmed: CA 2006, s 790M(3). The objective is to avoid the inclusion of partial data in the PSC register, which may make it more difficult to identify where a company or individual has failed to comply with its duty under Ch 2 to Pt 21A of the CA 2006.

20.60 Particulars of any individual with significant control over the company who is 'non-registrable' in relation to the company must not be entered in the register: CA 2006, s 790M(4).

But the required particulars of any entity that is a registrable relevant legal entity in relation to the company, must be noted in the register once the company becomes aware of the entity's status as such: CA 2006, s 790M(5).

If the company becomes aware of a relevant change (within the meaning of s 790E), with respect to a registrable person or registrable relevant legal entity whose particulars are stated in the register:

(a) details of the change and the date on which it occurred must be entered in the register; but

(b) in the case of a registrable person, the details and date must not be entered there until they have all been confirmed: CA 2006, s 790M(6).

The Secretary of State may by regulations require additional matters to be noted in a company's PSC register: CA 2006, s 790M(7). This would ensure clarity for those searching the register. SI 2016/339, Part 4 sets out additional information to be included in a company's register of persons with significant control, where there are no registerable persons; there is an unidentified registerable person; there are unconfirmed details of a registerable person; a company's investigations are on-going; and where there have been failures to comply with requirements to provide information under CA 2006, ss 790D and 790E: see SI 2016/339, regs 10–17.

20.61 A person's required particulars, and the details and date of any relevant change with respect to a person, are considered for the purposes of s 790M(8) to have been 'confirmed' if:

(a) the person supplied or confirmed them to the company (whether voluntarily, pursuant to a duty imposed by Pt 21A or otherwise);

(b) another person did so but with that person's knowledge; or

(c) they were included in a statement of initial significant control delivered to the registrar under s 9 by subscribers wishing to form the company: CA 2006, s 790M(9). This will ensure that individuals are aware of their inclusion in the register particularly if they want to apply for their information to be protected from disclosure.

20.62 In the case of someone who was a registrable person or a registrable relevant legal entity in relation to the company on its incorporation:

(a) the date to be entered in the register as the date on which the individual became a registrable person, or the entity became a registrable relevant legal entity, is to be the date of incorporation; and

(b) in the case of a registrable person, that particular is deemed to have been 'confirmed': CA 2006, s 790M(10).

20.63 For the purposes of CA 2006, s 790M(11):

(a) if a person's usual residential address is the same as his or her service address, the entry for him or her in the register may state that fact instead of repeating the address (but this does not apply in a case where the service address is stated to be 'The company's registered office');

(b) s 126 (trusts not to be entered on register) does not affect what may be entered in a company's PSC register or is receivable by the registrar in relation to people with significant control over a company (even if they are members of the company);

(c) see s 790J (exemptions) for cases where a person does not count as a registrable person or a registrable relevant legal entity: CA 2006, s 790M(11).

20.64 If a company makes default in complying with s 790M, an offence is committed by the company; and every officer of the company who is in default: CA 2006, s 790M(12), who may be subject to a fine: CA 2006, s 790M(13).

A company to which Pt 21A applies is not by virtue of anything done for the purposes of this section affected with notice of, or put upon inquiry as to, the rights of any person in relation to any shares or rights in or with respect to the company: CA 2006, s 790M(14).

Register to be kept available for inspection

20.65 CA 2006, ss 790N–790V provide how a company must maintain and make the PSC register available. These provisions are based on CA 2006, ss 114–121 and 125, which make similar provisions to a company's register of members. These two registers will then provide a complete picture of the company's ownership and control.

A company's PSC register must be kept available for inspection at its registered office; or at a place specified in regulations under s 1136: CA 2006, s 790N(1).

This is based on CA 2006, s 114 (register to be kept available for inspection).

20.66 A company must give notice to the registrar of the place where its PSC register is kept available for inspection and of any change in that place: CA 2006, s 790N(2).

No such notice is required if the register has, at all times since it came into existence, been kept available for inspection at the company's registered office: CA 2006, s 790N(3).

20.67 If a company makes default for 14 days in complying with s 790N(2), an offence is committed by the company; and every officer of the company who is in default: CA 2006, s 790N(3), who may be subject to a fine: CA 2006, s 790N(3).

Rights to inspect and require copies

20.68 The CA 2006, s 790O applies to companies that hold their own PSC register (as they have not elected to hold their own PSC register at Companies House). A company's PSC register must be open to the inspection of any person without charge: CA 2006, s 790O(1). Section 790O is based on CA 2006, s 114 (register to be kept available for inspection).

Any person may require a copy of a company's PSC register, or any part of it, on payment of such fee as may be prescribed: CA 2006, s 790O(2). The Register of People with Significant Control Regulations 2016 sets the fee at £12.00: see reg 6(1).

20.69 A person seeking to exercise either of the rights conferred by this section must make a request to the company to that effect: CA 2006, s 790O(3).

The request must contain the following information in the case of an individual, his or her name and address; in the case of an organisation, the name and address of an individual responsible for making the request on behalf of the organisation; and the purpose for which the information is to be used: CA 2006. s 790O(3).

20.70 The request must be for a proper purpose. There is no definition of 'proper purpose', but the term is intended to have and wide interpretation and application. The purpose of the register is to provide transparency of company ownership and control, and a person may inspect the register in the interests of finding out that information. This could, for example, arise in the context of investigative journalism.

CA 2006, s 790O is based on the s 116 (right to inspect and take copies). However, unlike the register of members, it is considered important that any person may inspect the register free of charge due to the scope of those who may be registerable persons of RLE's in respect of a company and may therefore wish to inspect a company's register.

PSC register – response to request for inspection or copy

20.71 CA 2006, s 790P is based on the s 117 (register of members: response to request for inspection or copy). It sets out how a company must respond to a request made under s 790O.

Where a company receives a request under s 790O, it must within five working days either comply with the request; or apply to the court: CA 2006, s 790P(1).

If it applies to the court, it must notify the person making the request: CA 2006, s 790P(2).

20.72 If on an application under this section, the court is satisfied that the inspection or copy is not sought for a proper purpose:

(a) it must direct the company not to comply with the request; and

(b) it may further order that the company's costs on the application be paid in whole or in part by the person who made the request, even if that person is not a party to the application: CA 2006, s 790P(3). The term 'proper purpose' is not defined, but this may be read in light of the fact that the purpose of the

PSC register, is to provide public information about a company's ownership and control.

20.73 If the court makes such a direction and it appears to the court that the company is or may be subject to other requests made for a similar purpose (whether made by the same person or different persons), it may direct that the company is not to comply with any such request.

The order must contain such provision as appears to the court appropriate to identify the requests to which it applies: CA 2006, s 790P(4).

If on an application under s 790P, the court does not direct the company not to comply with the request, the company must comply with the request immediately upon the court giving its decision or, as the case may be, the proceedings being discontinued: CA 2006, s 790P(5).

PSC register – refusal of inspection or default in providing copy

20.74 CA 20906, s 790Q is based on the s 118 (register of members: refusal of inspection or default in providing copy).

If an inspection required under s 790O is refused or default is made in providing a copy required under that section, otherwise than in accordance with an order of the court, an offence is committed by the company; and every officer of the company who is in default: CA 2006, s 790Q(1), who may be subject to a fine: CA 2006, s 790Q(2).

In the case of any such refusal or default, the court may by order compel an immediate inspection or, as the case may be, direct that the copy required be sent to the person requesting it: CA 2006, s 790Q(3).

PSC register – offences in connection with request for or disclosure of information

20.75 It is an offence for a person knowingly or recklessly to make in a request under CA 2006, s 790O, a statement that is misleading, false or deceptive in a material particular: CA 2006, s 790R(1).

It is an offence for a person in possession of information obtained by exercise of either of the rights conferred by that section:

(a) to do anything that results in the information being disclosed to another person; or

(b) to fail to do anything with the result that the information is disclosed to another person,

knowing, or having reason to suspect, that person may use the information for a purpose that is not a proper purpose: CA 2006, s 790R(2).

20.76 A person guilty of an offence under CA 2006, s 790R is liable to a fine and/or imprisonment: CA 2006, s 790R(3).

CA 2006, s 790R is based on s 119 (register of members: offences in connection with request for or disclosure of information).

Information as to state of register

20.77 This is based on CA 2006, s 120 (information as to state of register and index).

Where a person inspects the PSC register, or the company provides a person with a copy of the register or any part of it, the company must inform the person of the most recent date (if any) on which alterations were made to the register, and whether there are further alterations to be made: CA 2006, s 790S(1).

If a company fails to provide the information required under s 790S(1), an offence is committed by the company; and every officer of the company who is in default: CA 2006, s 790S(2), who may be subject to a fine: CA 2006, s 790S(3).

Protected information

20.78 The objective of CA 2006, s 790T is to make clear that a company is under a duty to keep its PSC register available for inspection. It does not extend to information protected from public disclosure under regulations made under CA 2006, Pt 21A, Ch 5.

Sections 790N and 790O(1) and (2) are subject to:

(a) s 790ZF (protection of information as to usual residential address); and

(b) any provision of regulations made under s 790ZG (protection of material): CA 2006, s 790T(1).

Section 790T(1) is not to be taken to affect the generality of the power conferred by virtue of s 790ZG(3)(f): CA 2006, s 790T(2).

Removal of entries from the register

20.79 An entry relating to an individual who used to be a registrable person, may be removed from the company's PSC register after the expiration of ten years from the date on which the individual ceased to be a registrable person, in relation to the company: CA 2006, s 790U(1).

An entry relating to an entity that used to be a registrable relevant legal entity, may be removed from the company's PSC register, after the expiration of ten years from the date on which the entity ceased to be a registrable relevant legal entity in relation to the company: CA 2006, s 790U(2).

Power of court to rectify register

20.80 CA 2006, s 790V is based on CA 2006, s 125 (power of court to rectify register). If:

(a) the name of any person is, without sufficient cause, entered in or omitted from a company's PSC register as a registrable person or registrable relevant legal entity; or

(b) is made or unnecessary delay takes place in entering on the PSC register the fact that a person has ceased to be a registrable person or registrable relevant legal entity, the person aggrieved or any other interested party, may apply to the court for rectification of the register: CA 2006, s 790V(1).

The court may either refuse the application, or may order rectification of the register and payment by the company of any damages sustained by any party aggrieved: CA 2006, s 790V(2).

20.81 On such an application, the court may decide any question as to whether the name of any person who is a party to the application should or should not be entered in or omitted from the register; and more generally, decide any question necessary or expedient to be decided for rectification of the register: CA 2006, s 790V(3).

In the case of a company required by this Act to send information stated in its PSC register to the registrar of companies, the court, when making an order for rectification of the register, must by its order direct notice of the rectification to be given to the registrar: CA 2006, s 790V(4).

20.82 The reference in CA 2006, s 790V to 'any other interested party' is to any member of the company; and any other person who is a registrable person or a registrable relevant legal entity in relation to the company: CA 2006, s 790V(5).

Alternative method of record-keeping

20.83 CA 2006, Pt 21A, Ch 4 is concerned with alternative methods of record keeping.

Chapter 4 sets out rules allowing private companies to keep information on the register kept by the registrar instead of entering it in their PSC register: CA 2006, s 790W(1).

The register kept by the registrar (see s 1080) is referred to in Ch 4 as 'the central register': CA 2006, s 790W(2).

Chapter 3 must be read with Ch 4: CA 2006, s 790W(3).

Ch 4 does not affect the duties imposed by Ch 2: CA 2006, s 790W(4).

Where an election under s 790X is in force in respect of a company, references in Ch 2 to the company's PSC register, are to be read as references to the central register: CA 2006, s 790W(4).

Right to make an election

20.84 A private company may elect to keep its PSC register on the central register.

An election may be made under CA 2006, s 790X by the subscribers wishing to form a private company under this Act; or by the private company itself once it is formed and registered: CA 2006, s 790X(1).

20.85 The election is of no effect unless notice of the intention to make the election was given to each eligible person at least 14 days before the day on which the election was made; and no objection was received by the subscribers or, as the case may be, the company from any eligible person within that notice period: CA 2006, s 790X(2).

20.86 A person is an 'eligible person' if:

(a) in a case of an election by the subscribers wishing to form a private company, the person's particulars would, but for the election, be required to be entered in the company's PSC register on its incorporation; and

(b) in the case of an election by the company itself:

(i) the person is a registrable person or a registrable relevant legal entity in relation to the company; and

(ii) the person's particulars are stated in the company's PSC register: CA 2006, s 790X(3).

An election under this section is made by giving notice of election to the registrar: CA 2006, s 790X(4).

20.87 If the notice is given by subscribers wishing to form a private company, it must be given when the documents required to be delivered under CA 2006, s 9 are delivered to the registrar; and it must be accompanied by a statement confirming that no objection was received as mentioned in s 790X(2): CA 2006, s 790X(5).

20.88 If the notice is given by the company, it must be accompanied by a statement confirming that no objection was received as mentioned in CA 2006, s 790X(2); and a statement containing all the information that is required to be contained in the company's PSC register as at the date of the notice in respect of matters that are current as at that date: CA 2006, s 790X(6).

20.89 The company must where necessary, update the statement sent under CA 2006, s 790X(6)(b) to ensure that the final version delivered to the registrar contains all the information that is required to be contained in the company's PSC register as at the time immediately before the election takes effect (see s 790Y), in respect of matters that are current as at that time: CA 2006, s 790X(7).

The obligation in s 790X(7) to update the statement includes an obligation to rectify it (where necessary), in consequence of the company's PSC register being rectified (whether before or after the election takes effect) : CA 2006, s 790X(8).

20.90 If default is made in complying with s 790X(7), an offence is committed by the company; and every officer of the company who is in default. For this purpose a shadow director is treated as an officer of the company: CA 2006, s 790X(9). The person concerned may be subject to a fine: CA 2006, s 790X(10).

20.91 A reference in CA 2006, Pt 21A, Ch 4 to matters that are current as at a given date or time is a reference to persons who are a registrable person or registrable relevant legal entity in relation to the company as at that date or time and whose particulars are required to be contained in the company's PSC register as at that date or time; and any other matters that are current as at that date or time: CA 2006, s 790X(11).

Effective date of election

20.92 An election made under s 790X takes effect when the notice of election is registered by the registrar: CA 2006, s 790Y(1).

The election remains in force until either the company ceases to be a private company; or a notice of withdrawal sent by the company under s 790ZD is registered by the registrar, whichever occurs first: CA 2006, s 790Y(2).

Effect of election on obligations under Ch 3

20.93 The effect of an election under CA 2006, s 790X on a company's obligations under Ch 3 is as follows: CA 2006, s 790Z(1).

The company's obligation to maintain a PSC register does not apply with respect to the period when the election is in force: CA 2006, s 790Z(2).

This means that, during that period:

(a) the company must continue to keep a PSC register in accordance with Ch 3 (an 'historic' register), containing all the information that was required to be stated in that register as at the time immediately before the election took effect; but

(b) the company does not have to update that register to reflect any changes that occur after that time: CA 2006, s 790Z(3).

The provisions of Ch 3 (including the rights to inspect or require copies of the PSC register) continue to apply to the historic register during the period when the election is in force: CA 2006, s 790Z(4).

20.94 The company must place a note in its historic register:

(a) stating that an election under s 790X is in force;

(b) recording when that election took effect; and

(c) indicating that up-to-date information about people with significant control over the company is available for public inspection on the central register: CA 2006, s 790Z(5).

Section 790M(12) and (13) apply if a company makes default in complying with s 790Z(5), as they apply if a company makes default in complying with that section: CA 2006, s 790Z(6).

The obligations under s 790Z with respect to an historic register do not apply in a case where the election was made by subscribers wishing to form a private company: CA 2006, s 790Z(7).

Duty to notify registrar of changes

20.95 The duty under s 790ZA(2) applies during the period when an election under s 790X is in force: CA 2006, s 790ZA(1).

The company must deliver to the registrar any information that the company would during that period have been obliged under Ch 3 to enter in its PSC register, had the election not been in force: CA 2006, s 790ZA(2).

The information must be delivered as soon as reasonably practicable after the company becomes aware of it and, in any event, no later than the time by which the company would have been required to enter the information in its PSC register: CA 2006, s 790ZA(3).

20.96 If default is made in complying with this section, an offence is committed by the company; and every officer of the company who is in default. For this purpose a shadow director is treated as an officer of the company: CA 2006, s 790ZA(4). The person concerned may be subject to a fine: CA 2006, s 790ZA(5).

Information as to state of central register

20.97 When a person inspects or requests a copy of material on the central register relating to a company in respect of which an election under s 790X is in force, the person may ask the company to confirm that all information that the company is required to deliver to the registrar under this Chapter has been delivered: CA 2006, s 790ZB(1).

If a company fails to respond to a request under s 790ZB(1), an offence is committed by the company; and every officer of the company who is in default: CA 2006, s 790ZB(2), who may be subject to a fine: CA 2006, s 790ZB(3).

Power of court to order company to remedy default or delay

20.98 CA 2006, s 790ZC applies if:

(a) the name of a person is without sufficient cause included in, or omitted from, information that a company delivers to the registrar under this Chapter concerning persons who are a registrable person or a registrable relevant legal entity in relation to the company; or

(b) default is made or unnecessary delay takes place in informing the registrar under this Chapter that a person:

 (i) has become a registrable person or a registrable relevant legal entity in relation to the company; or

 (ii) has ceased to be a registrable person or a registrable relevant legal entity in relation to it: CA 2006, s 790ZC(1).

The person aggrieved, or any other interested party, may apply to the court for an order requiring the company to deliver to the registrar the information (or statements) necessary to rectify the position: CA 2006, s 790ZC(2).

The court may either refuse the application, or may make the order and order the company to pay any damages sustained by any party aggrieved: CA 2006, s 790ZC(3).

20.99 On such an application the court may decide:

(a) any question as to whether the name of any person who is a party to the application should or should not be included in or omitted from information delivered to the registrar under this Chapter about persons who are a registrable person or a registrable relevant legal entity in relation to the company; and

(b) any question necessary or expedient to be decided for rectifying the position: CA 2006, s 790ZC(4).

Section 790ZC does not affect a person's rights under ss 1095 or 1096 (rectification of register on application to registrar or under court order): CA 2006, s 790ZC(5).

20.100 The reference in s 790ZC to 'any other interested party' is to any member of the company; and any other person who is a registrable person or a registrable relevant legal entity in relation to the company): CA 2006, s 790ZC(6).

Withdrawing the election

20.101 A company may withdraw an election made by or in respect of it under CA 2006, s 790X: CA 2006, s 790ZD(1). Withdrawal is achieved by giving notice of withdrawal to the registrar: CA 2006, s 790ZD(2). The withdrawal takes effect when the notice is registered by the registrar: CA 2006, s 790ZD(3).

The effect of withdrawal is that the company's obligation under Ch 3 to maintain a PSC register applies from then on with respect to the period going forward: CA 2006, s 790ZD(4).

20.102 This means that, when the withdrawal takes effect:

(a) the company must enter in its PSC register all the information that is required to be contained in that register, in respect of matters that are current as at that time;

(b) the company must also retain in its register all the information that it was required under s 790Z(3)(a), to keep in an historic register while the election was in force; but

(c) the company is not required to enter in its register information relating to the period when the election was in force that is no longer current: CA 2006, s 790ZD(5).

20.103 The company must place a note in its PSC register:

(a) stating that the election under s 790X has been withdrawn;

(b) recording when that withdrawal took effect; and

(c) indicating that information about people with significant control over the company relating to the period when the election was in force that is no longer current is available for public inspection on the central register: CA 2006, s 790ZD(6).

Section 790M(12) and (13) apply if a company makes default in complying with s 790ZD(6), as they apply if a company makes default in complying with that section: CA 2006, s 790ZD(7).

Protection of information as to usual residential address

20.104 The provisions of CA 2006, ss 240–244 (directors' residential addresses: protection from disclosure) apply to information within s 790F(2) as to protected information within the meaning of those sections: CA 2006, s 790ZF(1).

The information within s 790ZF(2) is:

(a) information as to the usual residential address of a person with significant control over a company; and

(b) the information that such a person's service address is his or her usual residential address: CA 2006, s 790ZF(2).

Section 790ZF(1) does not apply to information relating to a person if an application under regulations made under s 790ZG has been granted with respect to that information and not been revoked: CA 2006, s 790ZF(3).

20.105 Regulations under CA 2006, s 790ZG may make provision as to:

(a) who may make an application;

(b) the grounds on which an application may be made;

(c) the information to be included in and documents to accompany an application;

(d) how an application is to be determined;

(e) the duration of and procedures for revoking the restrictions on use and disclosure;

(f) the operation of ss 790N–790S in cases where an application is made, and

(g) the charging of fees by the registrar for disclosing PSC particulars where the regulations permit disclosure, by way of exception, in prescribed circumstances: CA 2006, s 790ZG(3).

20.106 Provision under s 790ZG(3)(d) and (e) may in particular:

(a) confer a discretion on the registrar;

(b) provide for a question to be referred to a person other than the registrar for the purposes of determining the application or revoking the restrictions: CA 2006, s 790ZG(4).

Nothing in s 790ZG or in regulations made under it affects the use or disclosure of particulars of a person in any other capacity (for example, the use or disclosure of particulars of a person in that person's capacity as a member or director of the company): CA 2006, s 790ZG(6).

20.107 This section concerns the regime to protect information about people in exceptional circumstances. The provisions in the SBEEA 2015, Sch 3 together with the Register of People with Significant Control Regulations 2016, SI 2016/339, regs 22–32 establish a regime that provides the following protections:

- the residential address of all people with significant control will be kept by the company, but will never appear on the registers that companies make available to the public or the central public register. This information would only be accessible by specified public authorities and credit reference agencies (CRAs) which satisfy the conditions specified in Sch 3 to the Regulations;

- a company's own PSC register will show the full date of birth of a person with significant control, but the day of the date of birth will not appear on the central register. It will only do so where a company has specifically chosen to keep its PSC information solely at Companies House;

- some people may feel that they or somebody they live with would be at serious risk of violence or intimidation due to the activities of a company they are involved with. Although a PSC's residential address will not be on a public register, these people will be able to apply to Companies House to prevent their residential address from being disclosed to CRAs. Company directors are currently able to apply for this level of protection also;

- the Regulations also make provision for a second type of protection available to PSC's who feel that if their wider PSC information was on a public register they or somebody they live with would be at serious risk of violence or intimidation due to the activities of a company they are involved with. Alternatively they may feel at risk as a result of a particular characteristic or attribute specific to themselves taken together with the company they are involved with. These PSCs will be able to apply to Companies House to stop all of their PSC information from appearing on any public register;
- people are able to apply to Companies House for these protections from January 2016. Their details will be suppressed from the register until the outcome of their application and any appeal. If the application is granted, the details will continue to be suppressed;
- if an application for protection is not granted the decision can be appealed on specified grounds, including that the decision is unlawful, irrational or unreasonable.

Checklist: certification and transfer of securities

20.108 *This Checklist sets out an overview of the regulatory framework governing certification and transfer of securities.*

No	*Issue*	*Act reference*
1	The certificate prepared by the company setting out shares held by a shareholder is prima facie evidence of his title to the shares, unless the contrary is shown.	CA 2006, s 768
2	A company must, within two months after the allotment of any of its shares, debentures or debenture stock, complete and have ready for delivery: (a) the certificates of the shares allotted; (b) the debentures allotted; or (c) the certificates of the debenture stock allotted	CA 2006, s 769
3	A company may not register a transfer of shares in or debentures of the company unless: (a) a proper instrument of transfer has been delivered to it, or (b) the transfer: (i) is an exempt transfer within the Stock Transfer Act 1982 (c 41); or (ii) is in accordance with regulations under Ch 2 of Pt 21.	CA 2006, s 770
4	When a transfer of shares in or debentures of a company has been lodged with the company, the company must either: (a) register the transfer; or (b) give the transferee notice of refusal to register the transfer, together with its reasons for the refusal, as soon as practicable and in any event within two months after the date on which the transfer is lodged with it. Failure to comply may lead to criminal penalties.	CA 2006, s 771 *Moodie v Shepherd (Bookbinders) Limited* [1949] 2 All ER 1044; *Popley v Planarrive Ltd* [1997] 1 BCLC 8

5	On an application for transfer of shares by the transferor, the company must register in the register of members the same interest for the transferee.	CA 2006, s 772
6	On a transmission of shares on death, a personal representative may apply to be registered as a member and upon evidence of probate.	CA 2006, s 773
7	The certification of instrument of transfer evidence prima facie title to the shares or debentures, but not a representation that the transferor has any title to the shares or debentures.	CA 2006, s 775
8	A company must issue a certificate for shares/debentures within two months after the date on which the transfer is made.	CA 2006, s 776

21 Information about interests in a company's shares

Introduction

21.1 This Chapter considers the following issues:

- the legal aspects, practice and procedure enabling a company to seek information from a person about interests in its shares;
- application for seeking a court order imposing restrictions on a person's shares; and
- how the shareholders can require the company to act in connection with information about interests in the company's shares.

Companies to which CA 2006, Pt 22 applies

21.2 CA 2006, Pt 22 applies only to public companies: CA 2006, s 791. It is concerned with information about interest in a company's shares. The provisions of Part 22 address a public company's right to investigate who has an interest in its shares. This may be important for various reasons, such as knowing the true identity of the person holding the shares, as in some cases, shares may be held by a nominee and the identity may not be initially clear. Another factor may be that the person in question is progressively building up a shareholding in the company that may have the effect of ultimately launching a takeover bid for the company, or to build up a sizeable percentage to block the passing of resolutions, that are not in the interests of the individual concerned.

Shares to which CA 2006, Pt 22 applies

21.3 CA 2006, Pt 22 refers to a 'company's shares'. This is a reference to the company's issued shares of a class, carrying rights to vote in all circumstances at general meetings of the company (including any shares held as treasury shares): CA 2006, s 792(1).

The temporary suspension of voting rights in respect of any shares does not affect the application of Pt 22 in relation to interests in those or any other shares: CA 2006, s 792(2).

CA 2006, s 792 addresses the type of shares for which a CA 2006, s 793 notice may be issued. These are shares carrying the rights to vote in all circumstances at general meetings. Shares held by a company 'in treasury' following a purchase of its own shares, (as an alternative to cancelling such shares on purchase), are included in the definition.

Notice requiring information about interests in shares

Notice requirements

21.4 A public company may give notice to any person whom the company knows or has reasonable cause to believe to be interested in the company's shares; or to have been so interested at any time during the three years immediately preceding the date on which the notice is issued: CA 2006, s 793(1).

21.5 The notice may require the person to confirm that fact or (as the case may be) to state whether or not it is the case; and if he holds, or has during that time held, any such interest, to give such further information as may be required in accordance with s 793 below: CA 2006, s 793(2).

21.6 The notice may require the person to whom it is addressed, to give particulars of his own present or past interest in the company's shares (held by him at any time during the three-year period mentioned in CA 2006, s 793(1)(b)).

The notice may require the person to confirm that fact or (as the case may be) to state whether or not it is the case, and if he holds, or has during that time held, any such interest, to give such further information as may be required in accordance with the following provisions of s 793: CA 2006, s 793(2).

21.7 The notice may require the person to whom it is addressed, to give particulars of his own present or past interest in the company's shares (held by him at any time during the three-year period mentioned in s 793(1)(b)): CA 2006, s 793(3)

The notice may require the person to whom it is addressed, where his interest is a present interest and another interest in the shares subsists; or another interest in the shares subsisted during that three-year period at a time when his interest subsisted, to give, so far as lies within his knowledge, such particulars with respect to that other interest as may be required by the company's notice: CA 2006, s 793(4).

21.8 The particulars referred to in under CA 2006, s 793(3) and (4) include:

(a) the identity of persons interested in the shares in question; and

(b) whether persons interested in the same shares are or were parties to:

  (i) an agreement to which CA 2006, s 824 applies (certain share acquisition agreements); or

  (ii) an agreement or arrangement relating to the exercise of any rights conferred by the holding of the shares: CA 2006, s 793(5).

21.9 The notice may require the person to whom it is addressed, where his interest is a past interest, to give (so far as lies within his knowledge) particulars of the identity of the person who held that interest immediately upon his ceasing to hold it: CA 2006, s 793(6).

The objective of CA 2006, s 793 is to seek information about a person's 'interest' in the company's shares, whether past or present: *Re TR Technology Investment Trust plc* [1988] BCLC 256. An issue arose in this case as to how much information the company could require the other party to provide. Section 793 allows the company to ask for whatever particulars it thinks fit, provided that they are 'with respect to that other interest'. There are two safeguards against abuse by the company. First, the company's only remedy for failure to comply is an application for restrictions under CA 2006, Pt 22; and the grant of that remedy is within the discretion of the court. Second, it is a defence to any criminal proceedings that the requirement was frivolous or vexatious.

21.10 The information required by the notice must be given within such reasonable time as may be specified in the notice: CA 2006, s 793(7).

The concept of 'reasonable time' should allow the person sufficient time to seek advice and assistance in connection with notice served by the company: *Re Lonrho plc (No 2)* [1989] BCLC 309. In this case, Lonrho was required to pay the respondent's costs, because reasonable time was not given to respond to the notice particulars.

21.11 The company has power under CA 2006, s 793 to send notices to persons domiciled in another jurisdiction, even where there is no link with the UK: *Re F H Lloyd Holdings plc* [1985] BCLC 293 per Nourse J.

The objective of s 793 is that it allows a public company to issue a notice requiring a person who it knows, or has reasonable cause to believe, has an interest in its shares (or to have had an interests in the previous three years), to confirm or deny the fact, and if the former, to disclose certain information about the interest, including information about any other person with an interest in the shares.

CA 2006, s 793(3) and (4) enable the company to require details to be given of a person's past or present interest, and to provide details of any other interest subsisting in the shares of which he is aware. These provisions allow the company to pursue information through a chain of nominees, by requiring each in the chain to disclose the person for whom they are acting. Under s 793(6), where the addressee's interest is a past one, a company can ask for information concerning any person by whom the interest was acquired immediately subsequent to their interest. Particulars may also be required by way of seeking information of any share acquisition agreements, or any agreement or arrangement as to how the rights attaching to those shares should be exercised (CA 2006, ss 824 and 825).

21.12 CA 2006, s 793 enables companies to discover the identity of those with voting rights (direct or indirect), that fall below the thresholds for automatic disclosure, and it also enables companies (and members of the company) to ascertain the underlying beneficial owners of shares.

The notice is not required to be in hard copy (under the general provisions on sending or supplying documents or information in CA 2006, Pt 37). Notices, and responses thereto, may be given in electronic form. A response must be given in "reasonable" time. What is reasonable has not been defined so as to allow flexibility according to the circumstances, but if the time given is not reasonable, the company will not have served a valid notice.

21.13 In the leading Supreme Court case on CA 2006, s 793, *Eclairs Group Limited v JKX Oil & Gas plc; Glengary Overseas Ltd v JKX Oil and Gas plc* [2015] UKSC 71, JKX was a public company with shares listed on the London Stock Exchange. The company also had a Ukrainian subsidiary with interests in oil and gas. Eclairs and Glengary were claimants who through nominee companies, held a beneficial interest in JKX of 39%.

Eclairs required JKX to convene an EGM under CA 2006, s 303, to consider resolutions to remove two executive directors and replace them with three new ones. JKX's Board was concerned that the effect of the EGM was an attempt to conduct a raid and gain control of JKX by the Ukrainian and Russian individuals.

In such event, JKX served notices pursuant to a power contained in its articles of association (Article 42), seeking information about the share ownerships and arrangements between the two shareholders including details about:

- number of shares held;
- nature of interest in the shares; and
- whether they were parties to any agreement or arrangement relating to the acquisition of shares in JKX or the exercise of voting rights.

Once JKX received responses to its notices, it considered them materially inaccurate, and subsequently served restriction notices under its articles of association the effect of which was to prevent the voting and transfer of Eclairs' and Glengary's shares. The claimants brought proceedings challenging the restriction notices. They contended that the notices requiring information about their shares were invalid for non-compliance with CA 2006 and articles of association. Further, the directors were not entitled to impose restrictions, as they did not have reasonable cause to believe that the responses to the notices were inadequate; and that the directors had acted for an improper purpose in imposing the restrictions.

The issue before the Supreme Court was whether the proper purpose rule applied to Article 42, and the scope of the rule in its application to directors' duties including the impact of s 793 notices. On the issue of CA 2006, s 793, the Supreme Court held that the objective of the s 793 notices was for the company to obtain information which the company did not have, and in circumstances of which the company was not entirely cognisant. The restrictions under Part 22 of the CA 2006 were set out as a sanction to compel the provision of information to which the company was entitled. Accordingly, any power to restrict the rights attaching to shares in the articles of association (Article 42), was wholly ancillary to the statutory power to call for information under s 793 of the CA 2006. The Supreme Court stated that the proper purpose rule was concerned with abuse of power. A company director must not, subjectively, act for an improper reason (See Chapter 9 on directors' duties and proper purposes rule).

Notice requiring information: order imposing restrictions on shares

21.14 Where a notice under CA 2006, s 793 (notice requiring information about interests in company's shares) is served by a company on a person who is or was interested in shares in the company, and that person fails to give the company the information required by the notice within the time specified in it, the company may apply to the court for an order directing that the shares in question be subject to restrictions.

For the effect of such an order see s 797: CA 2006, s 794(1).

If the court is satisfied that such an order may unfairly affect the rights of third parties in respect of the shares, it may, for the purpose of protecting those rights and subject to such terms as it thinks fit, direct that such acts by such persons or descriptions of persons and for such purposes as may be set out in the order, shall not constitute a breach of the restrictions: CA 2006, s 794(2).

The interests of third parties should be considered before the court makes an order under s 794 of the CA 2006. In *Lonhro plc (No 4)* [1990] BCLC 151, Peter Gibson J stated that in exercising its jurisdiction to make an order under CA 2006, s 794, the court would take into consideration the interests of innocent third parties in deciding whether or not such an order should be made. However, once the court determined that an order should be made, the order had to take the form set out in CA 2006, s 797 and the court had no jurisdiction to make a modified order which would qualify the restrictions set out in that section.

21.15 On an application under s 794, the court may make an interim order. Any such order may be made unconditionally or on such terms as the court thinks fit: CA 2006, s 794(3).

CA 2006, ss 798–802 make further provision about orders under s 794: CA 2006, s 794(4).

The effect of s 794 is to allow the court to make a 'freezing order' in respect of the shares.

A person to whom notice is served must give full and truthful responses. In some circumstances, the court may make an order freezing the shares of the real owner including a restriction order: *Re TR Technology Investment Trust plc* [1988] BCLC 256.

21.16 The courts are of the view that an application for restriction orders, should not be considered as a fertile ground for applicants to seek further information of persons, for the purposes of gaining further advantage over them.

Once information required by the company is provided, the restriction order is no longer effective: *Re Ricardo Group plc* [1989] BCLC 766. Millett J was of the view that restriction orders were not to be used as weapons to gain a temporary advantage over an opponent in a contested takeover bid. Their only legitimate purpose was to coerce a recalcitrant respondent into providing the requisite information.

Notice requiring information: offences

21.17 A person who:

(a) fails to comply with a notice under CA 2006, s 793 (notice requiring information about interests in company's shares);

(b) in purported compliance with such a notice:

- (i) makes a statement that he knows to be false in a material particular; or
- (ii) recklessly makes a statement that is false in a material particular, commits an offence: CA 2006, s 795(1),

commits an offence.

A person does not commit an offence under s 795(1)(a) if he proves that the requirement to give information was frivolous or vexatious: CA 2006, s 795(2).

A person guilty of an offence under s 795 is liable to a fine and/or imprisonment: CA 2006, s 795(3).

Orders imposing restrictions on shares

Consequences of order imposing restrictions

21.18 The effect of an order made under CA 2006, s 794, that shares are subject to restrictions is as follows, namely:

(a) any transfer of the shares is void;

(b) no voting rights are exercisable in respect of the shares;

(c) no further shares may be issued in right of the shares or in pursuance of an offer made to their holder;

(d) except in a liquidation, no payment may be made of sums due from the company on the shares, whether in respect of capital or otherwise: CA 2006, s 797(1).

21.19 Where shares are subject to the restriction in CA 2006, s 797(1)(a), an agreement to transfer the shares is void. This does not apply to an agreement to transfer the shares on the making of an order under s 800 made by virtue of s 800(3)(b) (removal of restrictions in case of court-approved transfer): CA 2006, s 797(2).

Where shares are subject to the restriction in s 797(1)(c) or (d), an agreement to transfer any right to be issued with other shares in right of those shares, or to receive any payment on them (otherwise than in a liquidation), is void. This does not apply to an agreement to transfer any such right on the making of an order under CA 2006, s 800 made by virtue of CA 2006, s 797(3)(b) (removal of restrictions in case of court-approved transfer): CA 2006, s 797(3).

Penalty for attempted evasion of restrictions

21.20 CA 2006, s 798 applies where shares are subject to restrictions by virtue of an order under s 794: CA 2006, s 798(1).

A person commits an offence if he:

(a) exercises or purports to exercise any right:

 (i) to dispose of shares that to his knowledge, are for the time being subject to restrictions; or

 (ii) to dispose of any right to be issued with any such shares; or

(b) votes in respect of any such shares (whether as holder or proxy), or appoints a proxy to vote in respect of them,

(c) being the holder of any such shares, fails to notify of their being subject to those restrictions a person whom he does not know to be aware of that fact but does know to be entitled (apart from the restrictions) to vote in respect of those shares whether as holder or as proxy, or

(d) being the holder of any such shares, or being entitled to a right to be issued with other shares in right of them, or to receive any payment on them (otherwise than in a liquidation), enters into an agreement which is void under s 797(2) or (3): CA 2006, s 798(2).

21.21 If shares in a company are issued in contravention of the restrictions, an offence is committed by the company; and every officer of the company who is in default: CA 2006, s 798(3), who may be subject to a fine: CA 2006, s 798(4).

The provisions of CA 2006, s 798 are, however, subject to any directions under s 794(2) (directions for protection of third parties); or s 799 or 800 of the CA 2006 (relaxation or removal of restrictions), and in the case of an interim order under CA 2006, s 794(3), to the terms of the order: CA 2006, s 798(5).

Relaxation of restrictions

21.22 An application may be made to the court on the ground that an order directing that shares will be subject to restrictions, unfairly affects the rights of third parties in respect of the shares: CA 2006, s 799(1). An application for an order may be made by the company or by any person aggrieved: CA 2006, s 799(2).

If the court is satisfied that the application is well-founded, it may, for the purpose of protecting the rights of third parties in respect of the shares, and subject to such terms as it thinks fit, direct that such acts by such persons or descriptions of persons and for such purposes as may be set out in the order, do not constitute a breach of the restrictions: CA 2006, s 799(3).

Removal of restrictions

21.23 An application may be made to the court, for an order directing that the shares will cease to be subject to restrictions: CA 2006, s 800(1). The application may be made by the company or by any person aggrieved: CA 2006, s 800(2).

The court must not make an order unless:

(a) it is satisfied that the relevant facts about the shares have been disclosed to the company, and no unfair advantage has accrued to any person as a result of the earlier failure to make that disclosure, or

(b) the shares are to be transferred for valuable consideration and the court approves the transfer: CA 2006, s 800(3).

21.24 An order made by virtue of CA 2006, s 800(3)(b) may continue, in whole or in part, in respect of the restrictions set out in s 797(1)(c) and (d) (restrictions on issue of further shares or making of payments), so far as they relate to a right acquired or offer made before the transfer: CA 2006, s 800(4).

Where any restrictions continue in force under CA 2006, s 800(4):

(a) an application may be made under s 800 for an order directing that the shares will cease to be subject to those restrictions, and

(b) section 800(3) does not apply in relation to the making of such an order: CA 2006, s 800(5).

Order for sale of shares

21.25 The court may order that the shares subject to restrictions be sold, subject to the court's approval as to the sale: CA 2006, s 801(1). The application may only be made by the company: CA 2006, s 801(2). Where the court has made such order, it may make such further order relating to the sale or transfer of the shares as it thinks fit: CA 2006, s 801(3).

The persons who can make the application are the company, or the person appointed by or in pursuance of the order to effect the sale, or by any person interested in the shares: CA 2006, s 801(4).

On making an order under s 801(1) or (3), the court may order that the applicant's costs be paid out of the proceeds of sale: CA 2006, s 801(5).

Application of proceeds of sale under court order

21.26 Where shares are sold pursuant to a court under CA 2006, s 801, the proceeds of the sale, less the costs of the sale, must be paid into court for the benefit of the persons, who are beneficially interested in the shares: s 802(1) CA 2006.

A person who is beneficially interested in the shares may apply to the court for the whole or part of those proceeds to be paid to him: CA 2006, s 802(2).

21.27 On such an application, the court must order the payment to the applicant of the whole of the proceeds of sale, together with any interest on them, or if another person had a beneficial interest in the shares at the time of their sale, such proportion of the proceeds and interest as the value of the applicant's interest in the shares bears to the total value of the shares. This is subject to the following qualification: CA 2006, s 802(3).

If the court has ordered under s 801(5) that the costs of an applicant under that section are to be paid out of the proceeds of sale, the applicant is entitled to payment of his costs out of those proceeds, before any person interested in the shares receives any part of those proceeds: CA 2006, s 802(4).

Power of members to require company to act

Power of members

21.28 The members of a company may require it to exercise its powers under CA 2006, s 793 (notice requiring information about interests in shares): CA 2006, s 803(1).

A company is required to do so, once it has received requests (to the same effect) from members of the company holding at least 10% of such of the paid-up capital of the company, as carries a right to vote at general meetings of the company (excluding any voting rights attached to any shares in the company held as treasury shares): CA 2006, s 803(2).

A request may be in hard copy form or in electronic form. It must

(i) state that the company is requested to exercise its powers under CA 2006, s 793;

(ii) specify the manner in which the company is requested to act; and

(iii) give reasonable grounds for requiring the company to exercise those powers in the manner specified; and

(iv) must be authenticated by the person or persons making it: CA 2006, s 803(3).

Duty of company to comply with requirement

21.29 A company that is required under CA 2006, s 803 to exercise its powers under s 793 (notice requiring information about interests in company's shares) must exercise those powers in the manner specified in the requests: CA 2006, s 804(1).

If default is made in complying with s 804(1), an offence is committed by every officer of the company who is in default: CA 2006, s 804(2), with the person subject to a fine: CA 2006, s 804(3).

Report to members on outcome of investigation

21.30 On the conclusion of an investigation carried out by a company pursuant to a requirement under CA 2006, s 803, the company must prepare a report of the investigation.

The report must be made available for inspection within a reasonable period (not more than 15 days) after the conclusion of the investigation: CA 2006, s 805(1).

Where a company undertakes an investigation pursuant to a requirement under s 803, and the investigation is not concluded within three months after the date on which the company became subject to the requirement, the company must prepare in respect of that period, and in respect of each succeeding period of three months ending before the conclusion of the investigation, an interim report of the information received during that period: CA 2006, s 805(2).

Each such report must be made available for inspection within a reasonable period (not more than 15 days) after the end of the period to which it relates: CA 2006, s 805(3).

21.31 The reports must be retained by the company for at least six years from the date on which they are first made available for inspection. They must be kept available for inspection during that time at the company's registered office, or at a place specified in regulations under CA 2006, s 1136: CA 2006, s 805(4).

The company must give notice to the registrar of the place at which the reports are kept available for inspection, and of any change in that place, unless they have at all times been kept at the company's registered office: CA 2006, s 805(5).

The company must within three days of making any report prepared under s 805 available for inspection, notify the members who made the requests under s 803 where the report is so available: CA 2006, s 805(6).

An investigation carried out by a company pursuant to a requirement under s 803 is concluded when: (a) the company has made all such inquiries as are necessary or expedient for the purposes of the requirement; and (b) in the case of each such inquiry (i) a response has been received by the company, or (ii) the time allowed for a response has elapsed: CA 2006, s 805(7).

Report to members: offences

21.32 If default is made for 14 days in complying with CA 2006, s 805(5) (notice to registrar of place at which reports made available for inspection), an offence is committed by the company, and every officer of the company who is in default: CA 2006, s 806(1), and the person may be subject to a fine: CA 2006, s 806(2).

If default is made in complying with any other provision of s 805 (report to members on outcome of investigation), an offence is committed by every officer of the company who is in default, who may be subject to a fine: CA 2006, s 806(3).

Right to inspect and request copy of reports

21.33 Any report prepared under CA 2006, s 805 must be open to inspection by any person without charge: CA 2006, s 807(1).

Any person is entitled, on request and on payment of such fee as may be prescribed, to be provided with a copy of any such report or any part of it. The copy must be provided within ten days after the request is received by the company: CA 2006, s 807(2).

21.34 If an inspection required under s 807(1) is refused, or default is made in complying with s 807(2), an offence is committed by the company, and every officer of the company who is in default: CA 2006, s 807(3), who may be subject to a fine: CA 2006, s 807(4).

In the case of any such refusal or default, the court may by order compel an immediate inspection or, as the case may be, direct that the copy required be sent to the person requiring it: CA 2006, s 807(5).

Register

Register of interests disclosed

21.35 The company must keep a register of information received by pursuant to a requirement imposed under CA 2006, s 793 (notice requiring information about interests in company's shares): CA 2006, s 808(1).

A company which receives any such information must, within three days of the receipt, enter in the register the fact that the requirement was imposed, and the date on which it was imposed, and the information received pursuant to the requirement: CA 2006, s 808(2).

The information must be entered against the name of the present holder of the shares in question or, if there is no present holder or the present holder is not known, against the name of the person holding the interest: CA 2006, s 808(3).

The register must be made up so that the entries against the names entered in it appear in chronological order: CA 2006, s 808(4).

21.36 If default is made in complying with CA 2006, s 808 an offence is committed by the company and every officer of the company who is in default: CA 2006, s 808(5), who may be subject to a fine: CA 2006, s 808(6).

21.37 The company is not by virtue of anything done for the purposes of s 808, affected with notice of, or put upon inquiry as to, the rights of any person in relation to any shares: CA 2006, s 808(7).

Register to be kept available for inspection

21.38 The register kept under CA 2006, s 808 (register of interests disclosed) must be kept available for inspection at the company's registered office, or at a place specified in regulations under s 1136: CA 2006, s 809(1).

A company must give notice to the registrar of companies of the place where the register is kept available for inspection, and of any change in that place: CA 2006, s 809(2). However, no such notice is required if the register has at all times been kept available for inspection at the company's registered office: CA 2006, s 809(3).

21.39 If default is made in complying with s 809(1), or a company makes default for 14 days in complying with s 809(2), an offence is committed by the company, and every officer of the company who is in default: CA 2006, s 809(4), who may be subject to a fine: CA 2006, 809(5).

Associated index

21.40 Unless the register kept under CA 2006, s 808 (register of interests disclosed) is kept in such a form as itself to constitute an index, the company must keep an index of the names entered in it: CA 2006, s 810(1). The company must make any necessary entry or alteration in the index within ten days after the date on which any entry or alteration is made in the register: CA 2006, s 810(2).

The index must contain, in respect of each name, a sufficient indication to enable the information entered against it to be readily found: CA 2006, s 810(3).

The index must be at all times kept available for inspection at the same place as the register: CA 2006, s 810(4).

21.41 If default is made in complying with s 810, an offence is committed by the company, and every officer of the company who is in default: CA 2006, s 810(5), who may be subject to a fine: CA 2006, s 810(6).

Rights to inspect and require copy of entries

21.42 The register required to be kept under CA 2006, s 808 (register of interests disclosed), and any associated index must be open to inspection by any person without charge: CA 2006, s 811(1).

Any person is entitled, on request and on payment of such fee as may be prescribed, to be provided with a copy of any entry in the register: CA 2006, s 811(2). A person seeking to exercise either of the rights conferred by s 811 must make a request to the company to that effect: CA 2006, s 811(3).

21.43 The request must contain the following information:

(a) in the case of an individual, his name and address;

(b) in the case of an organisation, the name and address of an individual responsible for making the request on behalf of the organisation;

(c) the purpose for which the information is to be used; and

(d) whether the information will be disclosed to any other person, and if so:

   (i) where that person is an individual, his name and address,

   (ii) where that person is an organisation, the name and address of an individual responsible for receiving the information on its behalf, and

   (iii) the purpose for which the information is to be used by that person: CA 2006, s 811(4).

Court supervision of purpose for which rights may be exercised

21.44 Where a company receives a request under CA 2006, s 811 (register of interests disclosed: right to inspect and require copy), it must comply with the request if it is satisfied that it is made for a proper purpose, and refuse the request if it is not so satisfied: CA 2006, s 812(1). If the company refuses the request, it must inform the person making the request, stating the reason why it is not satisfied: CA 2006, s 812(2). A person whose request is refused may apply to the court: CA 2006, s 812(3).

If an application is made to the court, the person who made the request must notify the company. The company must then use its best endeavours to notify any persons whose details would be disclosed, if the company were required to comply with the request: CA 2006, s 812(4).

21.45 If the court is not satisfied that the inspection or copy is sought for a proper purpose, it must direct the company not to comply with the request: CA 2006, s 812(5).

If the court makes such a direction, and it appears to the court that the company is or may be subject to other requests made for a similar purpose (whether made by the same person or different persons), it may direct that the company is not to comply with any such request.

The order must contain such provision as appears to the court appropriate to identify the requests to which it applies: CA 2006, s 812(6).

21.46 If the court does not direct the company not to comply with the request, the company must comply with the request immediately upon the court giving its decision or, as the case may be, the proceedings being discontinued: CA 2006, s 812(7).

Register of interests disclosed: refusal of inspection or default in providing copy

21.47 If an inspection required under CA 2006, s 811 (register of interests disclosed: right to inspect and require copy) is refused or default is made in providing a copy required under that section, otherwise than in accordance with the CA 2006, s 812, an offence is committed by the company, and every officer of the company who is in default: CA 2006, s 813(1) (as inserted by SBEEA 2015, s 83), who may be subject to a fine: CA 2006, s 813(2).

In the case of any such refusal or default, the court may by order compel an immediate inspection or, as the case may be, direct that the copy required be sent to the person requesting it: CA 2006, s 813(3).

Register of interests disclosed: offences in connection with request for or disclosure of information

21.49 It is an offence for a person knowingly or recklessly to make in a request under CA 2006, s 811 (register of interests disclosed: right to inspect or require copy) a statement that is misleading, false or deceptive in a material particular: CA 2006, s 814(1).

It is an offence for a person in possession of information obtained by exercise of either of the rights conferred by that section to do anything that results in the information being disclosed to another person, or to fail to do anything with the result that the information is disclosed to another person, knowing, or having reason to suspect, that person may use the information for a purpose that is not a proper purpose: CA 2006, s 814(2). A person guilty of an offence will be subject to a fine: CA 2006, s 814(3).

Entries not to be removed from the register

21.50 Entries in the register kept under CA 2006, s 808 (register of interests disclosed) must not be deleted except in accordance with s 816 (old entries), or s 817 (incorrect entry relating to third party): CA 2006, s 815(1). If an entry is deleted in contravention of s 815(1), the company must restore it as soon as reasonably practicable: CA 2006, s 815(2).

If default is made in complying with s 815(1) or (2), an offence is committed by the company, and every officer of the company who is in default: CA 2006, s 815(3), who may be subject to a fine: CA 2006, s 815(4).

Removal of entries from register: old entries

21.51 A company may remove an entry from the register kept under CA 2006, s 808 (register of interests disclosed) if more than six years have elapsed since the entry was made: CA 2006, s 816.

Meaning of interest in shares

General

21.52 CA 2006, s 820 applies to determine for the purposes of Pt 22 of the Act whether a person has an 'interest in shares': CA 2006, s 820(1).

In Pt 22, a reference to an interest in shares includes an interest of any kind whatsoever in the shares, and any restraints or restrictions to which the exercise of any right attached to the interest is or may be subject will be disregarded: CA 2006, s 820(2).

Where an interest in shares is comprised in property held on trust, every beneficiary of the trust is treated as having an interest in the shares: CA 2006, s 820(3).

21.53 A person is treated as having an interest in shares if: (a) he enters into a contract to acquire them; or (b) not being the registered holder, he is entitled (i) to exercise any right conferred by the holding of the shares, or (ii) to control the exercise of any such right: CA 2006, s 820(4).

For the purposes of s 820(4)(b), a person is entitled to exercise or control the exercise of a right conferred by the holding of shares if he has a right (whether subject to conditions or not) the exercise of which would make him so entitled, or is under an obligation (whether subject to conditions or not) the fulfilment of which would make him so entitled: CA 2006, s 820(5).

A person is treated as having an interest in shares if he has a right to call for delivery of the shares to himself or to his order, or he has a right to acquire an interest in shares or is under an obligation to take an interest in shares. This applies whether the right or obligation is conditional or absolute: CA 2006, s 820(6).

Persons having a joint interest are treated as each having that interest: CA 2006, s 820(7). It is immaterial that shares in which a person has an interest are unidentifiable: CA 2006, s 820(8).

In *Re TR Technology Investment Trust plc* [1988] BCLC 256 at 261, the court stated that the term 'interest in shares' was widely defined, as an interest of any kind whatsoever in the shares and included beneficial ownership, as well as direct ownership. The court described this wide definition as being designed 'to counter the limitless ingenuity of persons who prefer to conceal their interest behind trusts and corporate entities' (Hoffmann J).

Interest in shares: right to subscribe for shares

21.54 CA 2006, s 793 (notice by company requiring information about interests in its shares) applies in relation to a person who has, or previously had, or is or was entitled to acquire, a right to subscribe for shares in the company as it applies in relation to a person who is or was interested in shares in that company: CA 2006, s 821(1).

Checklist

21.55 *This checklist sets out the regulatory framework concerning information about interests in a company's shares with particular reference to CA 2006, Pt 22 where a company serves notice on a person and the consequences ensuing from such notice.*

No	Issue	Act reference
1	The provisions concerning information about interests in a company's shares are only applicable to public companies.	Part 22, CA 2006, s 791
2	A company may serve notice requiring interests in its shares, where it knows or has reasonable cause to believe that a person is interested in its shares; or has been so interested at any time during the three years before the notice was served.	CA 2006, s 793
3	The s 793 notice may require the person to confirm whether or not he has interest in the shares; and to give information as to his own present and past interest in the company's shares.	CA 2006, s 793
4	Consider the nature of questions that may be asked, and ensure they relate solely to the person's interest in the shares, and that the power under the articles of association is not exercised for a wrong purpose.	*Eclairs Group Ltd v JKX Oil and Gas plc* [2015] UKSC 71

No	Issue	Act reference
5	The term 'interest' in shares has a wide meaning and should not be interpreted narrowly.	*Re TR Technology Investment Trust plc* [1988] BCLC 256
6	The information required by the notice must be given within such reasonable time as specified in the notice.	CA 2006, s 793; *Re Lonhro plc (No 2)* [1989] BCLC 309
7	An application may be made to the court by the company for an order imposing restrictions on the person's shares where that person fails to give information under the notice within a reasonable time.	CA 2006, s 794
8	In considering whether to make a restriction order, the court must take account of interests of third parties.	*Re Lonhro plc (no 2)* [1989] BCLC 309
9	The effect of the application by the company to the court is to obtain a 'freezing order' in respect of the person's shares.	*Re TR Technology Investment Trust plc* [1988] BCLC 256
10	Failure to comply with the notice requiring information or making a false or reckless statement is a criminal offence.	CA 2006, s 795
11	The effect of an order imposing restrictions on shares is that any transfer of shares is void; no voting rights are exercisable in respect of the shares; no further shares may be issued to the person.	CA 2006, s 797
12	Criminal penalties apply for attempted evasion of restrictions, by a person any exercising any right to dispose of shares that are the subject of restrictions or failure to notify that the shares are subject to restrictions.	CA 2006, s 798
13	An application may be made to the court by the company or an aggrieved person, on the ground that the order directing that the shares be subject to restrictions, unfairly affects the rights of third parties in respect of the shares.	CA 2006, s 799(1) and (2)
14	The court has power to make such order as it thinks fit in connection with the relaxation of the restrictions imposed, including protecting the rights of third parties in respect of the shares and direct that the acts of such persons set out in the order do not constitute a breach of restrictions.	CA 2006, s 799(3)
15	The court has power to order that the shares subject to restrictions be sold, subject to the court's approval as to the sale, including such other order that they court may think fit – the court has a wide discretion.	CA 2006, s 801
16	Any proceeds from sale of the shares must be paid into court for the benefit of the persons beneficially interested in the shares.	

22 Dissolution and restoration to the register

Introduction

22.1 This chapter addresses the following issues:

- the procedure for striking off a company from the register;
- how the concept of voluntary striking off operates;
- the position regarding property of the dissolved company; and
- the different forms of restoration and the effect of restoration.

Dissolution and restoration to the register – striking off

22.2 CA 2006, Pt 31, Ch 1 is concerned with striking off. It examines the registrar's role in striking off a defunct company and voluntary striking off. In practice, this can be a useful mechanism for the Registrar to remove the company from the list of companies maintained at Companies House. It also allows for a speedier process from an administrative viewpoint, rather than for companies to proceed towards liquidation, which may take time including costs involved. The registrar's power to strike off a company, gives the company an opportunity to file its accounts and rectify its filing obligations with Companies House.

Registrar's power to strike off a defunct company

Power to strike off a company not carrying on business or in operation

22.3 The registrar has power to effect an accelerated procedure for striking off defunct companies. If the registrar has reasonable cause to believe that a company is not carrying on business or is not in operation, the registrar may send a letter to the company inquiring whether it is carrying on business or is in operation: CA 2006, s 1000(1).

There is no statutory definition of 'not carrying on business' or 'in operation'. In practice, the registrar may take into account all facts and circumstances, including failure to lodge accounts or to respond to letters, or failure by the company to communicate with the registrar in response to any requests made the by the registrar. The registrar may take this view if, for example:

- he has not received documents from a company that should have been sent them to him;

- mail that the registrar has sent to a company's registered office is returned undelivered; or
- the company has no directors.

22.4 Before striking the company off the register, the registrar is required to write two formal letters and send notice to the company's registered office, to ascertain whether the company is still carrying on business or in operation.

If the registrar does not within 14 days of sending the letter receive any answer, the registrar must, within 14 days after the expiration of that period, send to the company by post a registered letter referring to the first letter, and stating:

(a) that no answer to it has been received; and

(b) that if an answer is not received to the second letter within 14 days from its date, a notice will be published in the *Gazette* with a view to striking the company's name off the register: CA 2006, s 1000(2) (as inserted by SBEEA 2015, s 103(2)(a)).

22.5 If the registrar receives an answer to the effect that the company is not carrying on business or in operation, or does not within 14 days after sending the second letter receive any answer, the registrar may publish in the *Gazette*, and send to the company by post, a notice that at the expiration of two months from the date of the notice the name of the company mentioned in it will, unless cause is shown to the contrary, be struck off the register and the company will be dissolved: CA 2006, s 1000(3) (as inserted by SBEEA 2015, s 103(2)(b)).

At the expiration of the time mentioned in the notice the registrar may, unless cause to the contrary is previously shown by the company, strike its name off the register: CA 2006, s 1000(4).

The registrar must publish a notice in the *Gazette* stating that the company's name has been struck off the register: CA 2006, s 1000(5).

On the publication of the notice in the *Gazette*, the company is dissolved.

22.6 However, the liability (if any) of every director, managing officer and member of the company continues, and may be enforced as if the company had not been dissolved. The court still has the power to wind up a company which has been struck off the register: CA 2006, s 1000(7).

It is, therefore, advisable for the company's officers to promptly reply to any formal inquiry by the Registrar, and deliver any outstanding documents at Companies House.

As to the application to LLPs, see the Limited Liability Partnerships (Application of Companies Act 2006) Regulations 2009, SI 2009/1804, as amended by the Companies and Limited Liability Partnerships (Filing Requirements) Regulations 2015, SI 2015/1695.

Duty to act in case of the company being wound up

22.7 In some circumstances, the registrar has a duty to act in case of a company being wound up. If, in such circumstances,

(a) the registrar has reasonable cause to believe:

   (i) that no liquidator is acting; or

(ii) that the affairs of the company are fully wound up; and

(b) the returns required to be made by the liquidator have not been made for a period of six consecutive months,

the registrar must publish in the *Gazette,* and send to the company or the liquidator (if any) a notice that at the expiration of two months from the date of the notice the name of the company mentioned in it will, unless cause is shown to the contrary, be struck off the register and the company will be dissolved: CA 2006, s 1001(1) (as inserted by SBEEA 2015, s 103(3)).

22.8 At the expiration of the time mentioned in the notice the registrar may, unless cause to the contrary is previously shown by the company, strike its name off the register: CA 2006, s 100s 1001(2).

The registrar must publish notice in the *Gazette* of the company's name having been struck off the register: CA 2006, s 1001(3). On the publication of the notice in the *Gazette*, the company is effectively dissolved: CA 2006, s 1001(4).

However, the liability (if any) of every director, managing officer and member in CA 2006, s 1001 affects the power of the court to wind up a company the name of which has been struck off the register: CA 2006, s 1001(5). As to service of letter or notice see s.1002 CA 2006.

Voluntary striking off

Striking off on application by a company

22.9 An alternative to the registrar striking off a company from the register, is the voluntary striking off by the company as the applicant. This provides another speedy and effective mechanism to terminate the company's existence, subject to certain procedures being followed.

A company may apply to the registrar to be voluntarily struck off the register and dissolved. The company can do this if it is no longer needed. For example, the directors may wish to retire and there is no one to take over from them; or it is a subsidiary whose name is no longer needed; or it was set up to exploit an idea that turned out not to be feasible. Some companies who are dormant or non-trading choose to apply for strike off. Where a decision is taken by the company's directors that they no longer want to retain the company and wish to have it struck off, the registrar will not normally pursue any outstanding late filing penalties, unless the company is restored to the register at a later stage.

This procedure is not an alternative to formal insolvency proceedings where these are appropriate. Even if the company is struck off and dissolved, creditors and others could still apply for the company to be restored to the register.

CA 2006, s 1003 applies to striking off on application by a company, also known as 'voluntary striking off'. On application by a company, the registrar of companies may strike the company's name off the register: CA 2006, s 1003(1).

22.10 The application must be made on the company's behalf by its directors or by a majority of them, and must contain the prescribed information: CA 2006, s 1003(2). The applicant must complete Form DS01 'Striking off application by a company'. The form must be signed and dated by:

- the sole director, if there is only one;
- by both, if there are two;
- by all, or the majority of directors, if there are more than two.

The registrar may not strike a company off under s 1003 until after the expiration of two months from the publication by the registrar in the *Gazette* of a notice. The notice must state that the registrar may exercise the power to strike off in relation to the company and inviting any person to show cause why that should not be done: CA 2006, s 1003(3) (as inserted by the SBEEA 2015, s 103(4)).

22.11 The registrar must publish a notice in the *Gazette* of the company's name having been struck off: CA 2006, s 1003(4). On the publication of the notice in the *Gazette*, the company is dissolved: CA 2006, s 1003(4).

However, the liability (if any) of every director, managing officer and member of the company continues, and may be enforced as if the company had not been dissolved. The court still has power to wind up a company, the name of which has been struck off the register: CA 2006, s 1003(6). Therefore, liability issues are still preserved despite the company no longer existing.

CA 2006 deals with the circumstances where an application cannot be made for a voluntary striking off as set out under ss 1004 and 1005.

Copy of application to be given to members, employees, etc

22.12 CA 2006 sets out some safeguards for those likely to be affected by a company's dissolution. The persons listed below should be warned before applying for voluntary striking off, as any of them may object to the company being struck off. A company may notify any other organisation or party who may have an interest in the company's affairs, otherwise they might later object to the application. Examples include Her Majesty's Revenue and Customs, local authorities, especially if the company is under any obligation involving planning permission or health and safety issues, training and enterprise councils and government agencies.

A person who makes an application under s 1003 (application for voluntary striking off) on behalf of a company must secure that, within seven days from the day on which the application is made, a copy of it is given to every person who at any time on that day is:

(a) a company member;

(b) an company employee;

(c) a company creditor;

(d) a company director;

(e) a manager or trustee of any pension fund established for the benefit of employees of the company; or

(f) a person of a description specified for the purposes of this paragraph by regulations made by the Secretary of State: CA 2006, s 1006(1).

There is also an obligation to give a copy of the application to new members: CA 2006, s 1007.

22.13 There is no requirement to give a copy of the application to a director who is a party to the application: CA 2006, s 1006(2).

The duty imposed by s 1006 does not apply if the application is withdrawn before the end of the period for giving the copy application: CA 2006, s 1006(3).

A person who fails to perform the duty imposed on him by s 1006 commits an offence. If he does so with the intention of concealing the making of the application from the person concerned, he commits an aggravated offence: CA 2006, s 1006(4).

In proceedings for an offence under s 1006 it is a defence for the accused to prove that he took all reasonable steps to perform the duty: CA 2006, s 1006(5).

22.14 A person guilty of an offence under CA 2006, s 1006 (other than an aggravated offence) is liable on conviction on indictment, to a fine: CA 2006, s 1006(6). A person guilty of an aggravated offence under this section will be subject to a fine and/or imprisonment.

Copy of application: provisions as to service of documents

22.15 A document, for the purposes of CA 2006, ss 1006 and 1007, is treated as having been given to a person, if it is delivered to him, left at his proper address or sent by post to him at that address: CA 2006, s 1008(2).

Circumstances in which an application is to be withdrawn

22.16 CA 2006, s 1009 lists the circumstances in which an application can be withdrawn.

Form DS02 should be used to withdraw the application if directors change their mind, or the company ceases to be eligible for striking off. An interested party may object to the dissolution by making objections or complaints in writing to the Registrar with any supporting evidence, such as copies of invoices that may prove that the company is trading. Other reasons for withdrawal could include:

- if the company has broken any of the conditions of its application, for example, it has traded, changed its name or become subject to insolvency proceedings during the three-month period before the application, or afterwards
- if the directors have not informed interested parties
- if any of the declarations on the form are false
- if some form of action is being taken, or is pending, to recover any money owed (such as a winding-up petition or action in a small claims court)
- if other legal action is being taken against the company
- if the directors have wrongfully traded or committed a tax fraud or some other offence.

22.17 A person who is a director of the company at the end of a day on which any of the events mentioned in s 1009(1) occurs, must secure that the company's application is withdrawn immediately: CA 2006, s 1009(2). An application under s 1003 is withdrawn by sending a notice to the registrar: CA 2006, s 1010.

For the purposes of s 1009(1)(a), a company is not treated as trading or otherwise carrying on business, by virtue only of the fact that it makes a payment in respect of a liability incurred in the course of trading or otherwise carrying on business: CA 2006, s 1009(3).

22.18 A person who fails to perform the duty imposed on him by s 1009 commits an offence, which can result in a fine and/or imprisonment: CA 2006, s 1009(5).

Property of dissolved company

22.19 CA 2006, Pt 31, Ch 2 is concerned with the property of the dissolved company once the company has been struck off.

Property of dissolved company to be bona vacantia

22.20 When a company is dissolved, all property and rights whatsoever vested in or held on trust for the company immediately before its dissolution (including leasehold property, but not including property held by the company on trust for another person), are deemed to be *bona vacantia. In such circumstances, the property* belongs and vests in the Crown, or to the Duchy of Lancaster or to the Duke of Cornwall for the time being (as the case may be): CA 2006, s 1012(1).

Therefore, all property, cash and other assets owned by a company when it is dissolved automatically pass to the Crown. However, liabilities do not pass to the Crown on dissolution, and they are normally extinguished.

22.21 Dealing with dissolved companies' assets depends on the last registered office address; or where the asset is situated.

If the company's last registered office and the asset was in England or Wales, but not in the Duchies of Lancaster or Cornwall, its assets are dealt with by the Treasury Solicitor.

If the company's last registered office and the asset was in the Duchies of Cornwall or Lancaster, its assets fall to be dealt with by the Duchies' solicitors.

The Duchy of Cornwall comprises the County of Cornwall. The Duchy of Lancaster comprises the Counties of Lancashire, Merseyside and parts of Greater Manchester, Cheshire and Cumbria. Further details as to the precise boundaries of the Duchy can be obtained from the Duchy Office.

Duchy Office
1 Lancaster Place
Strand
London WC2E 7ED
Tel: 020 7836 8277

22.22 If the last registered office and the asset are in different jurisdictions, the location of the last registered office will usually determine who deals with the asset.

The asset types include:

- land and interests in land in England and Wales
- bank accounts

- other forms of cash (such as insurance policies, tax refunds or sums paid into court)
- copyrights
- trademarks
- patents and other intellectual property
- the benefit of mortgages where sums are owed to a dissolved company
- the benefit of other assets or agreements that the company entered into

The government's Bona Vacantia Division does not deal with assets which are held by a dissolved company as a trustee for someone else.

22.23 The Treasury Solicitor cannot undertake the following:

- pay the liabilities of dissolved companies
- manage or insure property or assets
- take formal possession of assets before selling them
- sell assets for less than market value
- sell where it is not cost effective to do so
- give any form of title guarantee when selling – the risk of buying a *bona vacantia* asset is with the purchaser
- provide any legal advice
- help resolve problems where there is no value for the Crown or where it would not be cost effective to do so

Crown disclaimer of property vesting as bona vacantia

22.24 Where property vests in the Crown under CA 2006, s 1012, the Crown's title to it under that section may be disclaimed by a notice signed by the Crown representative (ie the Treasury Solicitor): CA 2006, s 1013(1). The right to execute a notice of disclaimer under s 1013 may be waived by or on behalf of the Crown either expressly or by taking possession: CA 2006, s 1013(2).

22.25 A notice of disclaimer must be executed within three years after the date on which the fact that the property may have vested in the Crown under s 1012 first comes to the notice of the Crown representative; or if ownership of the property is not established at that date, the end of the period reasonably necessary for the Crown representative to establish the ownership of the property: CA 2006, s 1013(3).

If an application in writing is made to the Crown representative by a person interested in the property requiring him to decide whether he will or will not disclaim, any notice of disclaimer must be executed within 12 months after the making of the application, or such further period as may be allowed by the court: CA 2006, s 1013(4).

22.26 A notice of disclaimer under CA 2006, s 1013 is of no effect if it is shown to have been executed after the end of the period specified by s 1013(3) or (4): CA 2006, s 1013(5). A notice of disclaimer must be delivered to the registrar and retained and registered by him: CA 2006, s 1013(6). Copies of it must be published in the *Gazette* and sent to any persons who have given the Crown representative notice that they claim to be interested in the property: CA 2006, s 1013(7).

The Crown, therefore, has a statutory power to give up its interest in *bona vacantia*.

22.27 If the government's Bona Vacantia Division disclaim an asset, it means that a particular asset is treated as never having passed to the Crown as *bona vacantia*. It can disclaim any kind of asset, at any time. The power to disclaim is frequently used in relation to difficult or problematic land or land which has limited value, or where it would not be cost effective to dispose of it.

As soon as the Bona Vacantia Division have evidence that an asset has vested in the Crown, they will consider whether it should be disclaimed before taking further steps. They will continue to consider whether the asset should be disclaimed as the case progresses.

22.28 The Bona Vacantia Division usually disclaim the following:

- land used in common, such as private roads, service yards, amenity land, or the common parts of an estate or a block of flats;
- property subject to onerous covenants or other potential liabilities;
- property which is contaminated or has buildings, trees, or other items which are in a dangerous state and condition;
- property in negative equity;
- property subject to a dispute or competing claims;
- low value property;
- commercial leases that pass to the Crown as bona vacantia;
- assets which are the subject of dispute or litigation.

If the Bona Vacantia Division decide to disclaim an asset, they will issue a notice of disclaimer. A copy of the disclaimer notice will be published in the London Gazette and a copy sent to the Registrar of Companies and anyone who has given Bona Vacantia Division notice that they claim to be interested in the asset. Any Leasehold title is extinguished on disclaimer. If the property disclaimed is freehold land, the freehold title will be extinguished.

Effect of Crown disclaimer

22.29 Where notice of disclaimer is executed within England and Wales in respect of any property, that property is deemed not to have vested in the Crown under CA 2006, s 1012: CA 2006, s 1014(1).

General effect of disclaimer

22.30 The Crown's disclaimer operates so as to terminate, as from the date of the disclaimer, the rights, interests and liabilities of the company in or in respect of the property disclaimed: CA 2006, s 1015(1).

It does not, except so far as is necessary for the purpose of releasing the company from any liability, affect the rights or liabilities of any other person: CA 2006, s 1015(2).

Disclaimer of leaseholds and vesting orders are addressed under ss 1016 and 1017 CA 2006.

Restoration to the register

22.31 CA 2006, Pt 31, Ch 3 (ss 1024–1028) addresses issues concerned with the restoration of the register.

Application for administrative restoration to the register

22.32 Under certain conditions, where a company was dissolved because it appeared to be no longer carrying on business or in operation, a former director or member may apply to the registrar to have the company restored. This is called 'administrative restoration'. If the registrar restores the company, it is deemed to have continued in existence as if it had not been dissolved and struck off the register.

An application may be made to the registrar to restore to the register a company that has been struck off the register under CA 2006, s 1000 or 1001 (power of registrar to strike off defunct company): CA 2006, s 1024(1).

22.33 An application under CA 2006, s 1024 may be made whether or not the company has in consequence been dissolved: CA 2006, s 1024(2). Such application may only be made by a former director or former member of the company: CA 2006, s 1024(3). It may not be made after the end of the period of six years from the date of the dissolution of the company. For this purpose an application is made when it is received by the registrar: CA 2006, s 1024(4).

Requirements for administrative restoration

22.34 On an application under CA 2006, s 1024, the registrar must restore the company to the register if, and only if, the following three conditions are met: CA 2006, s 1025(1).

The first condition is that the company was carrying on business or in operation at the time of its striking off: CA 2006, s 1025(2).

The second condition is that, if any property or right previously vested in or held on trust for the company has vested as *bona vacantia*, the Crown representative has signified to the registrar in writing consent to the company's restoration to the register: CA 2006, s 1025(3).

It is the applicant's responsibility to obtain that consent and to pay any costs of the Crown representative in dealing with the property during the period of dissolution, or in connection with the proceedings on the application, that may be demanded as a condition of giving consent: CA 2006, s 1025(4).

The third condition is that the applicant has delivered to the registrar such documents relating to the company as are necessary to bring up to date the records kept by the registrar, and paid any penalties under s 453 or corresponding earlier provisions (civil penalty for failure to deliver accounts), that were outstanding at the date of dissolution or striking off: CA 2006, s 1025(5).

Application to be accompanied by statement of compliance

22.35 An application under CA 2006, s 1024 (application for administrative restoration to the register) must be accompanied by a statement of compliance: CA 2006, s 1026(1). This is a statement that the person making the application has standing to apply (see s 1024(3)), and that the requirements for administrative restoration (see s 1025) are met: CA 2006, s 1026(2). The registrar may accept the statement of compliance as sufficient evidence of those matters: CA 2006, s 1026(3). Form RT01 (Application for Administrative Restoration) should be used to make an application to the Registrar accompanied by the statement of compliance and a fee of £100.

22.36 The applicant must meet the Crown representative's costs or expenses (if demanded). The company must pay any statutory penalties for late filing of accounts delivered to the registrar outside the period allowed for filing. The penalties that may be due are:

- unpaid penalties outstanding on accounts delivered late before the company was dissolved
- penalties due for accounts delivered on restoration, if the accounts were overdue at the date the company was dissolved.

The company must also pay the appropriate filing fee on submission of any outstanding documents.

Registrar's decision on application for administrative restoration

22.37 The registrar must give notice to the applicant of the decision on an application under CA 2006, s 1024 (application for administrative restoration to the register): CA 2006, s 1027(1). If the decision is that the company should be restored to the register, the restoration takes effect as from the date that notice is sent: CA 2006, s 1027(2). In the case of such a decision, the registrar must enter on the register a note of the date as from which the company's restoration to the register takes effect, and cause notice of the restoration to be published in the *Gazette*: CA 2006, s 1027(3). The notice under s1027(3)(b) must state the name of the company or, if the company is restored to the register under a different name (see s 1033), that name and its former name, the company's registered number, and the date as from which the restoration of the company to the register takes effect: CA 2006, s 1027(4).

Effect of administrative restoration

22.38 The general effect of administrative restoration to the register is that the company is deemed to have continued in existence, as if it had not been dissolved or struck off the register: CA 2006, s 1028(1). The company is not liable to a penalty under s 453 or any corresponding earlier provision (civil penalty for failure to deliver accounts) for a financial year in relation to which the period for filing accounts and reports ended after the date of dissolution or striking off, and before the restoration of the company to the register: CA 2006, s 1028(2).

In *Bridgehouse (Bradford No. 2) Ltd v BAE* [2020] EWCA Civ 759, the Court of Appeal was required to consider the effect of CA 2006, s 1028 in connection with an administrative restoration. The claimant company and the defendant company entered into an agreement for the sale and purchase of properties. Subsequently, the claimant company's name was struck off the register of companies by the Companies House registrar under powers set out in CA 2006, s 1000 on the basis that the company was not carrying on business or in operation, as the company had failed to submit accounts on time. The defendant company, believing that there was an event of default under the agreement by virtue of a clause in the agreement providing for such termination event, served a notice terminating the agreement. Later, the claimant applied for administrative restoration to the register under CA 2006, s 1024, which application was granted and the company was restored to the register. The claimant then commenced arbitration proceedings challenging the validity of the defendant's termination of the agreement. The issue was: what effect did the restoration have on the defendant's termination of the agreement? The arbitrator determined that the agreement had been validly terminated, and that the termination was not affected by the claimant's subsequent restoration to the register. The claimant appealed on the grounds of whether the effect of CA 2006, s 1028 was that the defendant's termination had to be re-assessed retrospectively as a result of the claimant's restoration to the register such that the termination notice was to be regarded as ineffective. The High Court dismissed the claimant's appeal, stating that the restoration to the register did not undo the termination of the agreement. The Court of Appeal held that the parties' dispute fell within the arbitration, and was capable of arbitration. See too *Fulham Football Club (1987) Ltd v Richards* [2011] EWCA Civ 855, [2012] Ch 333.

22.39 The court may give such directions and make such provision as seems just, for placing the company and all other persons in the same position (as nearly as may be) as if the company had not been dissolved or struck off the register: CA 2006, s 1028(3). An application to the court for such directions or provision may be made any time within three years after the date of restoration of the company to the register: CA 2006, s 1028(4).

Restoration to the register by the court

22.40 This is governed by CA 2006, ss 1029–1032.

Application to the court for restoration to the register

22.41 An application may be made to the court to restore to the register a company:

(a) that has been dissolved under Ch 9 of Pt 4 of the Insolvency Act 1986 or Ch 9 of Pt 5 of the Insolvency (Northern Ireland) Order 1989, SI 1989/2405) (dissolution of company after winding up);

(b) that is deemed to have been dissolved under para 84(6) of Sch B1 to that Act or para 85(6) of Sch B1 to that Order (dissolution of company following administration); or

(c) that has been struck off the register:

  (i) under s 1000 or 1001 (power of registrar to strike off defunct company); or

(ii) under s 1003 (voluntary striking off);

whether or not the company has in consequence been dissolved: CA 2006, s 1029(1).

22.42 The application may be made by:

(a) the Secretary of State;

(b) any former director of the company;

(c) any person having an interest in land in which the company had a superior or derivative interest;

(d) any person having an interest in land or other property:

(i) that was subject to rights vested in the company; or

(ii) that was benefited by obligations owed by the company;

(e) any person who but for the company's dissolution would have been in a contractual relationship with it;

(f) any person with a potential legal claim against the company;

(g) any manager or trustee of a pension fund established for the benefit of employees of the company;

(h) any former member of the company (or the personal representatives of such a person);

(i) any person who was a creditor of the company at the time of its striking off or dissolution;

(j) any former liquidator of the company;

(k) where the company was struck off the register under s 1003 (voluntary striking off), any person of a description specified by regulations under s 1006(1)(f) or 1007(2)(f) (persons entitled to notice of application for voluntary striking off);

or by any other person appearing to the court to have an interest in the matter: CA 2006, s 1029(2).

When an application to the court may be made

22.43 An application to the court for restoration of a company to the register, may be made at any time for the purpose of bringing proceedings against the company for damages for personal injury: CA 2006, s 1030(1).

No order can be made on such an application if it appears to the court that the proceedings would fail by virtue of any enactment as to the time within which proceedings must be brought: CA 2006, s 1030(2).

In making that decision the court must have regard to its power under s 1032(3) (power to give consequential directions etc) to direct that the period between the dissolution (or striking off) of the company and the making of the order is not to count for the purposes of any such enactment: CA 2006, s 1030(3).

In any other case an application to the court for restoration of a company to the register may not be made after the end of the period of six years from the date of the dissolution of the company, subject as follows: CA 2006, s 1030(4).

22.44 The application is made to the court by completing a Pt 8 claim form. The Registrar at the Companies Court in London, usually hears restoration cases in chambers once a week. Cases are also heard at the District Registries. Alternatively, an application may be made to the county court that has authority to wind up the company.

The court will require:

- evidence that the originating document was served
- written confirmation that the solicitor dealing with the *bona vacantia* assets has no objection to the restoration of the company (there should be attached a copy of the solicitor's letter to the affidavit or witness statement this does not apply in Scotland)
- when the company was incorporated and the nature of its objects (there should be attached a copy of the certificate of incorporation and the memorandum of association and, if appropriate, the articles of association)
- its membership and officers
- its trading activity and, if applicable, when it stopped trading
- an explanation of any failure to deliver accounts, annual returns or notices to the registrar
- details of the striking-off and dissolution
- comments on the company's solvency
- any other information that explains the reason for the application.

22.45 In England and Wales, the above information must be provided in an affidavit or witness statement. The registrar will provide information to assist in an application to the court. Before the court hearing, the registrar will normally require the delivery of any statutory documents to bring the company's public file up to date. These documents should be sent at least five working days before the hearing, to allow the registrar sufficient time to process or return them for amendment.

Decision on application for restoration by the court

22.46 On an application under CA 2006, s 1029, the court has a discretion to order the restoration of the company to the register:

(a) if the company was struck off the register under s 1000 or 1001 (power of registrar to strike off defunct companies) and the company was, at the time of the striking off, carrying on business or in operation; or

(b) if the company was struck off the register under s 1003 (voluntary striking off) and any of the requirements of ss 1004–1009 were not complied with; or

(c) if, in any other case, the court considers it just to do so: CA 2006, s 1031(1).

If the court orders restoration of the company to the register, the restoration takes effect on a copy of the court's order being delivered to the registrar: CA 2006, s 1031(2). The registrar must cause to be published in the *Gazette* notice of the restoration of the company to the register: CA 2006, s 1031(3). The notice must state the name of the company or, if the company is restored to the register under a different name (see s 1033), that name and its former name, the company's registered number, and the date on which the restoration took effect: CA 2006, s 1031(3).

Effect of court order for restoration to the register

22.47 Under the CA 2006, the general effect of an order by the court for restoration to the register is that the company is deemed to have continued to exist as if it had not been dissolved or struck off the register: CA 2006, s 1032(1).

The company is not liable to a penalty under s 453 or any corresponding earlier provision (civil penalty for failure to deliver accounts) for a financial year in relation to which the period for filing accounts and reports ended after the date of dissolution or striking off, and before the restoration of the company to the register: CA 2006, s 1032(2).

22.48 The court may give such directions and make such provision as seems just for placing the company and all other persons in the same position (as nearly as may be) as if the company had not been dissolved or struck off the register: CA 2006, s 1032(3): see *Pickering v Davy* [2017] EWCA Civ 30.

The court may also give directions as to:

(a) the delivery to the registrar of such documents relating to the company as are necessary to bring up to date the records kept by the registrar;

(b) the payment of the costs of the registrar in connection with the proceedings for the restoration of the company to the register; and

(c) where any property or right previously vested in or held on trust for the company has vested as *bona vacantia*, the payment of the costs of the Crown representative:

  (i) in dealing with the property during the period of dissolution; or

  (ii) in connection with the proceedings on the application: CA 2006, s 1032(4).

22.49 The registrar will normally restore a company with the name it had before it was struck off and dissolved. However, if at the date of restoration the company's former name is the same as another name on the registrar's index of company names, he cannot restore the company with its former name. A check should be made as to whether the company's name is the same as another on the register by using the WebCheck service.

If the name is no longer available, the court order may state another name by which the company is to be restored. On restoration, Companies House will issue a change of name certificate as if the company had changed its name.

Alternatively, the company may be restored to the register as if its registered company number is also its name. The company then has 14 days from the date of restoration to pass a resolution to change the name of the company. There must be delivered a copy of the resolution and a 'notice of change of name by resolution of directors' (Form NM05) to Companies House with the appropriate fee. Companies House will then issue a change of name certificate. It is an offence if the company does not change its name within 14 days of being restored with the number as its name. The change of name does not take effect until we have issued the certificate.

22.50 There are also costs or penalties involved. Where property has become *bona vacantia*, the Court may direct that the claimant meets costs of the Crown representative in dealing with the property during the period of dissolution or in connection with the proceedings. The Court may also direct that the claimant meets the registrar's costs in connection with the proceedings for the restoration.

The company must normally pay any statutory penalties for late filing of accounts delivered to the registrar outside the period allowed for filing. The penalties that may be due are:

- unpaid penalties outstanding on accounts delivered late before the company was dissolved
- penalties due for accounts delivered on restoration, if the accounts were overdue at the date the company was dissolved.

The appropriate filing fee must also be paid on submission of outstanding documents.

The level of any late filing penalty depends on how late the accounts are when Companies House receives them. For example, a set of accounts that should have been delivered two months before a private company was dissolved are normally regarded as two months late, if they are delivered on restoration and the relevant penalty must be paid. The company is not liable for late filing penalties for accounts received on restoration but which became due while the company was dissolved.

A court order under CA 2006, s 1032 is retrospective: *Tyman's Limited v Craven* [1952] 2 QB 100.

22.51 In *RLoans v The Registrar of Companies* [2013] All ER 180, the court held that the court's power to order restoration was discretionary, but in the absence of special circumstances restoration should normally follow. The general effect of an order by the court for restoration to the register was that the company was deemed to have continued in existence as if it had not been dissolved or struck off the register. The company was not liable to a civil penalty for failure to deliver accounts for a financial year in relation to which the period for filing accounts and reports ended: (i) after the date of dissolution or striking off, and (ii) before the restoration of the company to the register. The court might give such directions and make such provision as seems just for placing the company and all other persons in the same position, as if the company had not been dissolved or struck off the register. See too *Peaktone Limited v Joddrell* [2013] 1 All ER 13.

Checklist: regulatory structure for dissolution and restoration of a company

22.52 *This checklist provides an overview of the regulatory structure governing dissolution and restoration of a company. It considers the different methods of removing a company from the register at Companies House and the different forms of seeking company restoration.*

No	Issue	Reference
1	The Registrar of Companies House has power to strike off a defunct company. This applies where the company is no longer carrying on business or in operation. Examples include where the company has no directors or where the Registrar has not received documents back from the company.	CA 2006, s 1000(1)
2	Alternatively, a voluntary striking off may be applied for. The proper applicant will be the company. It usually applies where the company is no longer needed or all directors wish to retire. The removal of the company will be by the Registrar. Form DS01 'Striking off application by a company'.	CA 2006, s 1003(1)
3	The court can order restoration to the register in certain circumstances. An application is made to the court. The effect is that the company is deemed to have continued to exist as if it had not been dissolved or struck off.	CA 2006, ss 1029(1) and 1032; *R Loans v The Registrar of Companies* [2013] All ER 180
4	Restoration may also take place by administrative restoration provided certain conditions are satisfied. This allows a former director or member to apply to the Registrar to have the company restored. Form RT01 is used for the Administrative Restoration.	CA 2006, s 1024(1)
5	The assets and property of the company goes to the Crown *bona vacantia* except any of the company's liabilities	CA 2006, s 1012(1)
6	The Crown can disclaim property vesting as *bona vacantia*. Typical examples including disclaiming onerous property covenants, property in negative equity, assets which are the subject of litigation	CA 2006, s 1011(1)

23 Registrar of companies

Introduction

23.1 This Chapter addresses the following issues:

- the registration regime under CA 2006 in its application to registrars;
- the appointment of the company registrar;
- functions of the registrar;
- dealings with Companies House and the registrar; and
- proposed changes by the Government to filing requirements.

The Registrar of Companies occupies an important position within the regulatory structure of the company's establishment, operation and functioning process. The registrar has duties that require compliance with CA 2006 including regulations and enforcement mechanisms to ensure companies comply with the laws. Part 35 of CA 2006 (as amended by SBEEA 2015) governs the duties and functions of the registrar.

In December 2020, the government undertook a consultation, *Corporate Transparency and Register Reform*, which considered the options available to enhance the role of Companies House, increase the transparency of UK corporate entities, and enhance the powers of the registrars. The government's vision is for the register at Companies House to be built upon relevant and accurate information and ensure greater corporate transparency. To this end, the following is proposed to enhance the power of registrars at Companies House:

- Introducing *a new power to query information* – There is a proposal to introduce a new power for the Registrar to query information. It sets out the scope, the risk-based approach, and scenarios for when the power may be used by the Registrar. It also covers the proposed approach for how the querying power may apply to company names.
- *Reform of the Registrar's existing powers* – The government proposes to introduce reform to some of the Registrar's existing powers. This includes greater powers for the Registrar to administratively remove information from the register, and to close current loopholes, such as the rectification of a registered office address. It also sets out proposals for conferring the power to require documents to be delivered by electronic means only from the Secretary of State to the Registrar.
- *Rules governing company registers* – There are proposals related to changing parts of the rules governing the registers kept by companies themselves. The government proposes removing the requirement to keep a Register of Directors. It also seeks views on the impact of making amendments to other company registers and on the election regime which was introduced in 2016.

- *Implementing the ban on corporate directors* – There are proposals to tackle opaque corporate structures. The government also proposes that appointing corporate directors will be prohibited by companies, unless their own boards comprise all natural persons, and those natural persons have their identities verified.
- *Improving the quality and value of financial information on the UK companies register* – The government is considering: (i) how companies might in future be able to file accounts once only with government, instead of separately to Companies House, HMRC and other agencies; (ii) the filing options available to small companies with the aim of achieving a better balance between minimising burdens and ensuring the information provided is valuable; (iii) the proposal that all companies should file accounts digitally with Companies House; and (iv) additional checks Companies House could carry out on accounts filings.

See the Corporate Transparency and Register Reform White Paper policy overview and response to final consultations, presented to Parliament by the Secretary of State for Business, Energy and Industrial Strategy (February 2022).

The registrar

23.2 The registrars are appointed by the Secretary of State: CA 2006, s 1060(2).

There is a separate registrar of companies for England and Wales; Scotland and Northern Ireland: CA 2006, s 1060(1).

The registrar's functions

23.3 The registrar is obliged to perform the functions conferred on him by the Companies Act; and perform functions as directed by the Secretary of State: CA 2006, s 1061(1).

The registrar is required to have an official seal for the authentication of documents in connection with the performance of his functions: CA 2006, s 1062.

23.4 One of the registrar's functions is to publish in the *Gazette,* or in accordance with s 1116, to provide alternative means of giving public notice, in connection with notice of the issue of any certificate of incorporation of a company: CA 2006, s 1064(1). Any person may require the registrar to provide him with a copy of any certificate of incorporation of a company, either signed by the registrar or authenticated by the registrar's seal: CA 2006, s 1065.

Registrar's requirements as to form, authentication, and manner of delivery

23.4 CA 2006 requires various forms and documents to be delivered to the registrar at Companies House. The registrar may impose requirements as to the form, authentication and manner of delivery of documents required or authorised to be delivered to the registrar under any enactment: CA 2006, s 1068(1).

As regards the form of the document, the registrar may require the contents of the document to be in a standard form; or impose requirements to enable the document to be scanned or copied: CA 2006, s 1068(2). Companies House scans the documents and paper forms that are delivered to it to produce an electronic image. It then stores the original, paper documents and uses the electronic image as the working document.

When a customer searches the company record, they see the electronic image reproduced online. Companies House specifies that the original must be legible and that it can also produce a clear copy. When a document is submitted electronically, Companies House automatically creates an electronic image from the data provided by the customer.

Documents filed through WebFiling are formatted in accordance with specifications set out by the registrar in his rules on electronic filing as published on the Companies House website.

With regard to paper documents, generally, every paper document sent to Companies House must state the registered name and number of the company in a prominent position. There are a few exceptions to this rule, which are set out in the published registrar's rules. Paper documents should be on A4 size, plain white paper with a matt finish. The text should be black, clear, legible, and of uniform density. Letters and numbers must be clear and legible so that the Companies House can make an acceptable copy of the document. Failure to follow these guidelines is likely to result in the document being rejected. The following guidelines may assist in the preparation and filing of paper documents:

As regards authentication, the registrar may require the document to be authenticated by a particular person or a person of a particular description; specify the means of authentication; and require the document to contain or be accompanied by the name or registered number (or both) of the company (or other body) to which it relates: CA 2006, s 1068(3).

Agreement for delivery by electronic means

23.5 The registrar may agree with a company (or other body) that documents relating to the company (or other body) that are required or authorised to be delivered to the registrar, can be delivered by electronic means, except as provided for in the agreement; and they must conform to such requirements as may be specified in the agreement or specified by the registrar.

Document not delivered until received

23.6 A document is not delivered to the registrar until it is received by the registrar: CA 2006, s 1071(1).

The register

23.7 The registrar must keep records of the information contained in documents delivered to the registrar under any enactment; and certificates issued by the registrar under any enactment: CA 2006, s 1080(1). The records relating to companies are referred to collectively in the Companies Acts as 'the register': CA 2006, s 1080(2).

Information contained in documents delivered to the registrar may be recorded and kept in any form the registrar thinks fit, provided it is possible to inspect and produce a copy of it: CA 2006, s 1080(4).

This is sufficient compliance with any duty of the registrar to keep, file or register the document or to record the information contained in it: CA 2006, s 1080(5).

The records kept by the registrar must be such that information relating to a company or other registered body is associated with that body, in such manner as the registrar may determine, so as to enable all the information relating to the body to be retrieved: CA 2006, s 1080(6).

Preservation of original documents

23.8 The originals of documents delivered to the registrar in hard copy form must be kept for three years after they are received by the registrar. Thereafter, they may be destroyed provided the information contained in them has been recorded. This is subject to s 1087(3) (extent of obligation to retain material not available for public inspection): CA 2006, s 1083(1).

The registrar is under no obligation to keep the originals of documents delivered in electronic form, provided the information contained in them has been recorded: CA 2006, s 1083(2).

Inspection of the register

23.9 Any person may inspect the register: CA 2006, s 1085(1). This right of inspection extends to the originals of documents delivered to the registrar in hard copy form if, and only if, the record kept by the registrar of the contents of the document is illegible or unavailable.

The period for which such originals are to be kept is limited by s 1083(1): CA 2006, s 1085(2).

Right to copy of material on the register

23.10 Any person may ask to copy any material on the register: CA 2006, s 1086(1).

The fee for any such copy of material derived from an enhanced disclosure document (see CA 2006, s 1078), whether in hard copy or electronic form, must not exceed the administrative cost of providing it: CA 2006, s 1086(2).

Section 1086 is subject to s 1087 (material not available for public inspection) and s 1087ZA (required particulars available for public inspection for limited period): CA 2006, s 1086(3).

Material not available for public inspection

23.11 CA 2006 sets out a list of information that is prohibited from public inspection. The following material must not be made available by the registrar for public inspection:

(a) the contents of any document sent to the registrar containing views expressed pursuant to s 56 (comments on proposal by company to use certain words or expressions in company name);

(b) protected information within s 242(1) (directors' residential addresses: restriction on disclosure by registrar) or any corresponding provision of regulations under s 1046 (overseas companies);

(ba) representations received by the registrar in response to a notice under:

(i) s 245(2) (notice of proposal to put director's usual residential address on the public record), or

(ii) any corresponding provision of regulations under s 1046 (overseas companies);

(bb) information to which ss 240–244 are applied by s 790ZF(1) (residential addresses of people with significant control over the company) or any corresponding provision of regulations under s 1046 (overseas companies);

(bc) information that, by virtue of regulations under s 790ZG or any corresponding provision of regulations under s 1046, the registrar must omit from the material on the register that is available for inspection: (as inserted by SBEEA 2015, Sch 3, Part 2);

(c) any application to the registrar under s 1024 (application for administrative restoration to the register) that has not yet been determined or was not successful;

(d) any document received by the registrar in connection with the giving or withdrawal of consent under s 1075 (informal correction of documents);

(da) information falling within s 1087A(1) (information about a person's date of birth) (as inserted by SBEEA 2015, s 96(2));

(e) any application or other document delivered to the registrar under s 1088 (application to make address unavailable for public inspection) and any address in respect of which such an application is successful;

(f) any application or other document delivered to the registrar under s 1095 (application for rectification of register);

(g) any court order under s 1096 (rectification of the register under court order) that the court has directed under s 1097 (powers of court on ordering removal of material from the register) is not to be made available for public inspection;

(ga) any application or other document delivered to the registrar under s 1097A (rectification of company registered office) other than an order or direction of the court;

(h) the contents of:

(i) any instrument creating or evidencing a charge; or

(ii) any certified or verified copy of an instrument creating or evidencing a charge,

delivered to the registrar under Pt 25 (company charges) or regulations under s 1052 (overseas companies);

(i) any e-mail address, identification code or password deriving from a document delivered for the purpose of authorising or facilitating electronic filing procedures or providing information by telephone;

(j) the contents of any documents held by the registrar pending a decision of the Regulator of Community Interest Companies under:

(i) s 36A of the Companies (Audit, Investigations and Community Enterprise) Act 2004 (eligibility for registration as community interest company);

(ii) s 38 of that Act (eligibility for conversion to community interest company); or

(iii) s 55 of that Act (eligibility for conversion from community interest company to charity),

and that the registrar is not later required to record;

(k) any other material excluded from public inspection by or under any other enactment: CA 2006, s 1087(1) (as inserted by SBEEA 2015, s 99(2)).

A restriction applying by reference to material deriving from a particular description of document does not affect the availability for public inspection of the same information contained in material derived from another description of document in relation to which no such restriction applies: CA 2006, s 1087(2).

Material to which s 1087 applies need not be retained by the registrar for longer than appears to the registrar reasonably necessary for the purposes for which the material was delivered to the registrar: CA 2006, s 1087(3).

Information about a person's date of birth

23.12 CA 2006, s 1087A (as inserted by SBEEA 2015, s 96(3) is concerned with information about a person's date of birth. Information falls within CA 2006, s 1087(1) at any time ('the relevant time') if:

(a) it is DOB information;

(b) it is contained in a document delivered to the registrar that is protected at the relevant time as regards that information;

(c) the document is one in which such information is required to be stated; and

(d) if the document has more than one part, the part in which the information is contained is a part in which such information is required to be stated: CA 2006, s 1087A(1).

'DOB information' is information as to the day of the month (but not the month or year) on which a relevant person was born: CA 2006, s 1087A(2).

23.13 A 'relevant person' is an individual:

(a) who is a director of a company, or

(b) whose particulars are stated in a company's PSC register as a registrable person in relation to that company (see Part 21A): CA 2006, s 1087A(3).

A document delivered to the registrar is 'protected' at any time unless:

(a) it is an election period document;

(b) s 1087A(7) applies to it at the time; or

(c) it was registered before this section comes into force: CA 2006, s 1087A(4).

23.14 As regards DOB information about a relevant person in his or her capacity as a director of the company, each of the following is an 'election period document':

(a) a statement of the company's proposed officers delivered under s 9 in circumstances where the subscribers gave notice of election under s 167A (election to keep information on central register) in respect of the company's register of directors when the statement was delivered;

(b) a document delivered by the company under s 167D (duty to notify registrar of changes while election in force): CA 2006, s 1087A(5).

23.15 As regards DOB information about a relevant person in his or her capacity as someone whose particulars are stated in the company's PSC register, each of the following is an 'election period document':

(a) a statement of initial significant control delivered under s 9 in circumstances where the subscribers gave notice of election under s 790X in respect of the company when the statement was delivered;

(b) a document containing a statement or updated statement delivered by the company under s 790X(6)(b) or (7) (statement accompanying notice of election made after incorporation);

(c) a document delivered by the company under s 790ZA (duty to notify registrar of changes while election in force): CA 2006, s 1087A(6).

23.16 CA 2006, s 1087(7) applies to a document if:

(a) the DOB information relates to the relevant person in his or her capacity as a director of the company;

(b) an election under s 167A is or has previously been in force in respect of the company's register of directors;

(c) the document was delivered to the registrar at some point before that election took effect,

(d) the relevant person was a director of the company when that election took effect; and

(e) the document was either:

 (i) a statement of proposed officers delivered under s 9 naming the relevant person as someone who was to be a director of the company, or

 (ii) notice given under s 167 of the relevant person having become a director of the company: s 1087A(1) (CA 2006: s 1087A(7)).

Information about a person does not cease to fall within s 1087A(1) when he or she ceases to be a relevant person and, to that extent, references in this section to a relevant person include someone who used to be a relevant person: CA 2006, s 1087A(8).

Section 1087A(1) does not oblige the registrar to check other documents or (as the case may be), other parts of the document to ensure the absence of DOB information: CA 2006 s 1087A(8).

Disclosure of DOB Information

23.17 The registrar must not disclose restricted DOB information unless:

(a) the same information about the relevant person (whether in the same or a different capacity) is made available by the registrar for public inspection as a result of being contained in another description of document in relation to which no restriction under s 1087 applies (see sub-s (2) of that section); or

(b) disclosure of the information by the registrar is permitted by sub-s (2) or another provision of this Act: CA 2006, s 1087B(1).

The registrar may disclose restricted DOB information:

(a) to a public authority specified for the purposes of this subsection by regulations made by the Secretary of State; or

(b) to a credit reference agency: CA 2006, s 1087B(2).

The Companies (Disclosure of Date of Birth Information) Regulations 2015, SI 2015/1694 specify the conditions for disclosure of date of birth information (defined as 'DOB information' in CA 2006, s 1087A to public authorities and credit reference agencies under CA 2006, s 1087B.

23.18 The registrar may disclose restricted DOB information to a specified public authority where the conditions specified in SI 2015/1694, Sch 2, paras 2 and 3 are satisfied: reg 2(1).

A specified public authority shall deliver to the registrar such information or evidence as the registrar may direct for the purpose of enabling the registrar to determine in accordance with these Regulations whether to disclose restricted DOB information to a specified public authority: reg 2(2).

The registrar may require such information or evidence to be verified in such manner as the registrar may direct: reg 2(3).

The specified public authority must inform the registrar immediately of any change in respect of any statement delivered to the registrar pursuant to Sch 2 or information or evidence provided for the purpose of enabling the registrar to determine whether to disclose restricted DOB information: reg 2(4).

23.19 The public authorities specified for the purposes of CA 2006, s 1087B(2) are set out in SI 2015/1694, Sch 1: reg 2(5).

Regulation 3 provides that the registrar may disclose restricted DOB information to a credit reference agency where the conditions specified in Sch 2, paras 6–10 are satisfied: reg 3(1).

The registrar may rely on a statement delivered to the registrar by a credit reference agency under of Sch 2, para 10 as sufficient evidence of the matters stated in it: reg 3(2).

Notwithstanding paragraph (2), a credit reference agency must deliver to the registrar such information or evidence in addition to the statement required by of Schedule 2, para 10 as the registrar may direct for the purpose of enabling the registrar to determine in accordance with these Regulations whether to disclose restricted DOB information to a credit reference agency: reg 3(3).

The registrar may require such information or evidence to be verified in such manner as the registrar may direct: reg 3(4).

23.20 The credit reference agency must inform the registrar immediately of any change in respect of any statement delivered to the registrar pursuant to SI 2015/1694,

Sch 2 or information or evidence provided for the purpose of enabling the registrar to determine whether to disclose restricted DOB information: reg 3(5).

CA 2006, s 243(3)–(8) (permitted use or disclosure of directors' residential addresses etc by the registrar) apply for the purposes of s 1087B(2) as for the purposes of that section (reading references there to protected information as references to restricted DOB information): CA 2006, s 1087B(3).

CA 2006, s 1087B does not apply to restricted DOB information about a relevant person in his or her capacity as someone whose particulars are stated in the company's PSC register, if an application under regulations made under s 790ZG (regulations for protecting PSC particulars) has been granted with respect to that information and not been revoked: CA 2006, s 1087B(4).

'Restricted DOB information' means information falling within s 1087A(1): CA 2006, s 1087B(5).

Application to register to make address unavailable for public inspection

23.21 The Secretary of State may make provision by regulations requiring the registrar, on application, to make an address on the register unavailable for public inspection: CA 2006, s 1088(1). The regulations may make provision as to:

(a) who may make an application;

(b) the grounds on which an application may be made;

(c) the information to be included in and documents to accompany an application;

(d) the notice to be given of an application and of its outcome; and

(e) how an application is to be determined: CA 2006, s 1088(2).

Provision under s 1088(2)(e) may in particular:

(a) confer a discretion on the registrar; and

(b) provide for a question to be referred to a person other than the registrar for the purposes of determining the application: CA 2006, s 1088(3).

Provision was made by the Companies (Disclosure of Address) (Amendment) Regulations 2009, SI 2009/214. The 2009 Regulations permit applications from individuals where there is a serious risk that they, or a person living with them, will be subject to violence or intimidation owing to the activities of the company with which they are involved. Under the 2009 Regulations, applications could only be made in respect of information filed with the Registrar on or after 1 January 2003 and not before that date. Further, the test under the 2009 Regulations of 'serious risk of violence or intimidation' was related solely to the company's activities and not any other wider activities unrelated to the company. Applications under the 2009 Regulations did not permit persons who were at risk from fraud or identity theft to have their residential address withheld. The 2009 Regulations have been amended by the Companies (Disclosure of Address) (Amendment) Regulations 2018, SI 2018/528 which came into force on 25 April 2018. The 2018 Regulations provide that an individual director whose usual residential address is on the register at Companies House, can apply under CA 2006, s 1088 to the registrar to make the address unavailable for public inspection on the companies register. The 2018 Regulations remove the requirement that individual directors must show a serious risk of violence or intimidation arising from a company's activities. It also allows applications in respect of information filed before 1 January 2003 but requires certain details set out in the 2018 Regulations to be provided with such an application.

The 2009 Regulations allow a company to apply to the Registrar for the suppression of residential address information of all its members. However, the 'serious risk of violence or intimidation' test will still apply for such applications due to the potential effect on corporate transparency of large scale redactions of historic information.

The 2018 Regulations allow a member of a company to make an application for suppression of the residential address, without having to show a serious risk of violence or intimidation in the same manner as an individual director.

The test of 'serious risk of violence or intimidation' will still however apply in respect of an application by a person who registers a charge.

An individual who is required to maintain a current address on the register (such as a current director of a live company) will have to provide a service address instead. This will be publicly available on the register instead of their home address. An individual who is not subject to this requirement (such as a former director of a live company) will not need to provide a service address. Their residential address will instead be partially suppressed to show only the first half of the post code.

23.22 An application must specify the address to be removed from the register and indicate where it is on the register: CA 2006, s 1088(4).

The regulations may provide:

(a) that an address is not to be made unavailable for public inspection under s 1088 unless replaced by a service address; and

(b) that in such a case the application must specify a service address: CA 2006, s 1088(5).

Registrar's notice to resolve inconsistency in the register

23.23 Where it appears to the registrar that the information contained in a document delivered to the registrar is inconsistent with other information on the register, the registrar may give notice to the company to which the document relates:

(a) stating in what respects the information contained in it appears to be inconsistent with other information on the register; and

(b) requiring the company to take steps to resolve the inconsistency: CA 2006, s 1093(1).

23.24 The notice must:

(a) state the date on which it is issued; and

(b) require the delivery to the registrar, within 14 days after that date, of such replacement or additional documents as may be required to resolve the inconsistency: CA 2006, s 1093(2).

23.25 If the necessary documents are not delivered within the period specified, an offence is committed by the company; and every officer of the company who is in default: CA 2006, s 1093(3), who may be subject to a fine: CA 2006, s 1093(4).

Administrative removal of material from the register

23.26 The registrar may remove from the register anything that there was power, but no duty, to include: CA 2006, s 1094(1).

This power is exercisable, in particular, so as to remove:

(a) unnecessary material within the meaning of s 1074; and

(b) material derived from a document that has been replaced under:

- s 1076 (replacement of document not meeting requirements for proper delivery); or
- s 1093 (notice to remedy inconsistency on the register): CA 2006, s 1094(2).

23.27 CA 2006, s 1094 does not authorise the removal from the register of:

(a) anything whose registration has had legal consequences in relation to the company as regards:

- its formation;
- a change of name;
- its re-registration;
- its becoming or ceasing to be a community interest company;
- a reduction of capital;
- a change of registered office;
- the registration of a charge;
- its dissolution; or
- a change in its membership particulars of which were delivered to the registrar under section 128E (duty to notify registrar of changes while election to keep information on central register is in force);

(b) an address that is a person's registered address for the purposes of s 1140 (service of documents on directors, secretaries and others): CA 2006, s 1094(3).

23.28 On or before removing any material under CA 2006, s 1094 (otherwise than at the request of the company), the registrar must give notice:

(a) to the person by whom the material was delivered (if the identity, and name and address of that person are known); or

(b) to the company to which the material relates (if notice cannot be given under para (a) and the identity of that company is known): CA 2006, s 1094(4).

The notice must:

(a) state what material the registrar proposes to remove, or has removed, and on what grounds; and

(b) state the date on which it is issued: CA 2006, s 1094(5).

Rectification of register on application to registrar

23.29 The registrar must remove from the register any material:

(a) that derives from anything that the court has declared to be invalid or ineffective, or to have been done without the authority of the company; or

(b) that a court declares to be factually inaccurate, or to be derived from something that is factually inaccurate, or forged;

and that the court directs should be removed from the register: CA 2006, s 1096(1).

23.30 The court order must specify what is to be removed from the register and indicate where on the register it is: CA 2006, s 1096(2).

The court must not make an order for the removal from the register of anything the registration of which had legal consequences as mentioned in s 1094(3) unless satisfied:

(a) that the presence of the material on the register has caused, or may cause, damage to the company, and

(b) that the company's interest in removing the material outweighs any interest of other persons in the material continuing to appear on the register: CA 2006, s 1096(3).

Where in such a case the court does make an order for removal, it may make such consequential orders as appear just with respect to the legal effect (if any) to be accorded to the material by virtue of its having appeared on the register: CA 2006, s 1096(4).

A copy of the court's order must be sent to the registrar for registration: CA 2006, s 1096(5).

23.31 CA 2006, s 1096 applies to both companies and LLPs (Limited Liability Partnerships (Application of Companies Act 2006 Regulations 2009, SI 2009/1804). However, there is no similar provision applicable to limited liability partnerships established under the Limited Partnerships Act 1907 (LPA 1907).

In *Bank of Beirut SAL v HRH Prince Adel El-Hashemite* [2015] EWHC 1451 (Ch), two banks claimed to be victims of a fraud carried out by a person claiming to be HRH Price Adel El-Hashemite by forging documents and registering certain documents at Companies House under the LPA 1907, giving the appearance of the banks as a general partner and the Prince as a limited partner. The registrar (registrar) registered the limited partnership based on the documents received. The issue was whether the court had power to order rectification of the register and to order the registrar to delete the registration of the limited partnerships. In this regard the registrar was joined as a defendant in the action. The difficulty was that under LPA 1907, s 8C the certificate of registration issued by the registrar is 'conclusive evidence' that the limited partnership came into existence on the date of registration. Nugee J held that the establishment of fraud or forgery by themselves were not sufficient to go behind the conclusiveness of the certificate issued by the registrar. The registrar had acted in good faith in registering the limited partnership. He concluded that he had no authority under the LPA 1907 to require the registrar to remove the entries relating to the limited partnerships at Companies House. Further, it was not the court's function to micromanage the process at Companies House. Moreover, the registrar had not been in breach of his public law functions in declining to remove the partnerships as if they had never existed. To do so would cause more confusion and the most appropriate course of action which the registrar had taken was to mark the register so that anyone searching was reasonably alerted to the position.

23.32 Where the court makes an order for the removal of anything from the register under CA 2006, s 1096 (rectification of the register), it may give directions as set out under s 1097 CA 2008: CA 2006, s 1097(1).

The court may direct that any note on the register that is related to the material that is the subject of the court's order must be removed from the register CA 2006, s 1097(2).

It may direct that its order must not be available for public inspection as part of the register: CA 2006, s 1097(3).

It may direct that no note must be made on the register as a result of its order, or that any such note must be restricted to such matters as may be specified by the court: CA 2006, s 1097(4).

The court must not give any direction under s 1097 unless it is satisfied:

(a) that:

  (i) the presence on the register of the note or, as the case may be, of an unrestricted note, or

  (ii) the availability for public inspection of the court's order, may cause damage to the company; and

(b) that the company's interest in non-disclosure outweighs any interest of other persons in disclosure: CA 2006, s 1097(5).

Rectification of register under court order

23.33 The registrar must remove from the register any material that derives from anything that the court has declared to be invalid or ineffective, or to have been done without the authority of the company; or that a court declares to be factually inaccurate, or to be derived from something that is factually inaccurate, or forged, and that the court directs should be removed from the register: CA 2006, s 1096(1).

The court order must specify what is to be removed from the register and indicate where on the register it is: CA 2006, s 1096(2).

The court must not make an order for the removal from the register of anything the registration of which had legal consequences as mentioned in s 1094(3) unless satisfied that the presence of the material on the register has caused, or may cause, damage to the company; and that the company's interest in removing the material outweighs any interest of other persons in the material continuing to appear on the register: CA 2006, s 1096(3).

Where the court does make an order for removal, it may make such consequential orders as appear just with respect to the legal effect (if any) to be accorded to the material, by virtue of its having appeared on the register: CA 2006, s 1096(4). A copy of the court's order must be sent to the registrar for registration: CA 2006, s 1096(5).

Powers of the court on ordering removal from the register

23.34 Where the court makes an order for the removal of anything from the register under CA 2006, s 1096 (rectification of the register), it may give certain directions: CA 2006, s 1097(1). It may direct that any note on the register that is related to the material that is the subject of the court's order, must be removed from the register: CA 2006, s 1097(2).

It may direct that its order must not be available for public inspection as part of the register: CA 2006, s 1097(3). It may also direct that no note shall be made on the register as a result of its order; or that any such note shall be restricted to such matters as may be specified by the court: CA 2006, s 1097(4).

The court must not give any direction unless it is satisfied:

(a) that the presence on the register of the note or, as the case may be, of an unrestricted note; or the availability for public inspection of the court's order; may cause damage to the company; and

(b) that the company's interest in non-disclosure outweighs any interest of other persons in disclosure: CA 2006, s 1097(5).

The registrar's index of company names

23.35 The registrar of companies must keep an index of the names of the companies and other bodies to which CA 2006, s 1099 applies. This is known as 'the registrar's index of company names': CA 2006, s 1099(1). It applies to UK-registered companies; any body to which any provision of the Companies Acts applies by virtue of regulations under s 1043 (unregistered companies); and overseas companies that have registered particulars with the registrar under s 1046, other than companies that appear to the registrar not to be required to do so: CA 2006, s 1099(2).

It also applies to:

(a) limited partnerships registered in the UK;

(b) limited liability partnerships incorporated in the UK;

(c) European Economic Interest Groupings registered in the UK;

(d) open-ended investment companies authorised in the UK;

(e) societies registered under the Industrial and Provident Societies Act 1965 (c 12) or the Industrial and Provident Societies Act (Northern Ireland) 1969 (c 24 (NI)): CA 2006, s 1099(3).

Right to inspect index

23.36 Any person may inspect the registrar's index of company names: CA 2006, s 1100.

Documents to be drawn up and delivered in English

23.37 The general rule is that all documents required to be delivered to the registrar must be drawn up and delivered in English: CA 2006, s 1103(1). This is subject to:

- s 1104 (documents relating to Welsh companies); and
- s 1105 (documents that may be drawn up and delivered in other languages): CA 2006, s 1103(2).

Documents that may be drawn up and delivered in other languages

23.38 Documents may be drawn up and delivered to the registrar in a language other than English, but when delivered to the registrar they must be accompanied by a certified translation into English: CA 2006, s 1105(1).

This applies to:

(a) agreements required to be forwarded to the registrar under Ch 3 of Pt 3 (agreements affecting the company's constitution);

(b) documents required to be delivered under s 400(2)(e) or s 401(2)(f) (company included in accounts of larger group: required to deliver copy of group accounts);

(c) instruments or copy instruments required to be delivered under Pt 25 (company charges);

(d) documents of any other description specified in regulations made by the Secretary of State: CA 2006, s 1105(2). These include:

- a memorandum of association;
- a company's articles;
- a valuation report required to be delivered to the registrar under s 94(2)(d);
- any order made by a competent court in the UK or elsewhere (see the Registrar of Companies and Applications for Striking Off Regulations 2009, SI 2009/1803, reg 7).
- certified copy of a debenture or other instrument creating or evidencing a charge over the property of an overseas company;
- certified copy of the company's constitution;
- copy of accounting documents; and
- copy of accounts (see the Overseas Companies (Execution of Documents and Registration of Charges) Regulations 2009, SI 2009/1917, regs 8, 9, 14, 15, 27, 32, 40, 45, 46 and 55).

Voluntary filing of translations

23.39 A company may deliver to the registrar one or more certified translations of any document relating to the company that is or has been delivered to the registrar: CA 2006, s 1106(1).

The Secretary of State may by regulations specify:

(a) the languages; and

(b) the descriptions of documents,

in relation to which this facility is available: Overseas Companies (Execution of Documents and Registration of Charges) Regulations 2009, s 1106(2).

23.40 The regulations must provide that it is available as from 1 January 2007:

(a) in relation to all the official languages of the European Union; and

(b) in relation to all documents subject to the Directive disclosure requirements (see s 1078): Overseas Companies (Execution of Documents and Registration of Charges) Regulations 2009; CA 2006, s 1106(3).

The power of the registrar to impose requirements as to the form and manner of delivery includes power to impose requirements as to the identification of the original document and the delivery of the translation in a form and manner enabling it to be associated with the original: CA 2006, s 1106(4).

Section 1106 does not apply where the original document was delivered to the registrar before this section came into force: CA 2006, s 1106(6).

Certified translations

23.41 The term 'certified translation' means a translation certified to be a correct translation: CA 2006, s 1107(1).

In the case of any discrepancy between the original language version of a document and a certified translation:

(a) the company may not rely on the translation as against a third party; but

(b) a third party may rely on the translation unless the company shows that the third party had knowledge of the original: CA 2006, s 1107(2).

A 'third party' means a person other than the company or the registrar: CA 2006, s 1107(3).

Registrar's requirements as to certification or verification

23.42 Where a document required or authorised to be delivered to the registrar under any enactment is required:

(a) to be certified as an accurate translation or transliteration; or

(b) to be certified as a correct copy or verified,

the registrar may impose requirements as to the person, or description of person, by whom the certificate or verification is to be given: CA 2006, s 1111(1).

The power conferred by s 1068 (registrar's requirements as to form, authentication and manner of delivery) is exercisable in relation to the certificate or verification as if it were a separate document: CA 2006, s 1111(2).

Requirements imposed under s 1111 must not be inconsistent with requirements imposed by any enactment with respect to the certification or verification of the document concerned: CA 2006, s 1111(3).

General false statement offence

23.43 It is an offence for a person knowingly or recklessly to deliver or cause to be delivered to the registrar, for any purpose of the Companies Acts, a document; or to make to the registrar, for any such purpose, a statement, that is misleading, false or deceptive in a material particular: CA 2006, s 1112(1).

23.44 A person guilty of an offence under, s 1112 will be liable to imprisonment and/or fine: CA 2006, s 1112(2).

In March 2018, a company director was fined for deliberately falsifying information about his firms, in what is thought to be the first-ever conviction of its kind. The director in question was ordered to pay a fine of over £12,000, after he pleaded guilty to filing false information on the UK's company register. Deliberately filing false information on the UK register is a serious offence and people who have been found to have knowingly done so can face prosecution.

Enforcement of company's filing obligations

23.45 CA 2006, 1113 applies where a company has made default in complying with any obligation under the Companies Acts to deliver a document to the registrar; or to give notice to the registrar of any matter: CA 2006, s 1113(1).

The registrar, or any member or creditor of the company, may give notice to the company requiring it to comply with the obligation: CA 2006, s 1113(2).

23.46 If the company fails to make good the default within 14 days after service of the notice, the registrar, or any member or creditor of the company, may apply to the court for an order directing the company and any specified officer of it, to make good the default within a specified time: CA 2006, s 1113(3).

The court's order may provide that all costs of or incidental to the application are to be borne by the company or by any officers of it responsible for the default: CA 2006, s 1113(4).

Section 1113 does not affect the operation of any enactment making it an offence, or imposing a civil penalty, for the default: CA 2006, s 1113(5).

The court's control over the registrar

23.47 There has been some judicial authority for the view that even in the absence of statutory powers, the court has some control over the powers of the registrar. In *Re Calmex Limited* [1989] 1 All ER 485, the registrar had registered a winding up order which was made against Calmex Ltd. This order was made by mistake, as it was intended to wind up an unconnected company. The court was required to consider whether it could make an order that the winding up order be removed from the register? Hoffmann J held that the court could make the order on the basis that the purpose of the register was not simply to chronicle events, but to record information which might be useful to persons dealing with the company. Accordingly, he could not see any purpose in recording that the company had been the victim of mistaken identity, and that the existence of the record was serious injustice to the company.

However, *Re Calmex* has been distinguished in other cases. In *Igroup Ltd v Ocwen* [2003] EWHC 2431, the mortgage companies had delivered for registration forms containing particulars of charges, to which were scheduled details of their customers' personal information. Lightman J did not make an order requiring the Registrar to remove or replace the schedules. The documents delivered to the Registrar were valid and the Registrar was under no duty to rectify them.

23.48 In *Re a Company (No 004766 of 2003)* [2004] EWHC 35, the company had delivered annual accounts for registration containing a reference to an offer under the civil procedure rules, in respect of on-going litigation. The judge refused to make an order permitting the filing of revised accounts, and held that the filed accounts were not a nullity and could not be said to be improperly filed.

23.49 An issue which arises is whether there can be a claim against the Registrar for negligence and breach of statutory duty, where the Registrar has made an error that amounts to negligence? In *Sebry v Companies House The Registrar of Companies* [2015] EWHC 115, the claimant was a managing director in a company called 'Taylor and Sons Limited' (Company). Another company was registered at Companies House under the name 'Taylor and Son Limited', and a winding up order was made by the Chancery Court against this latter company, but the order did not include the company number, and was received by Companies House, which by error registered the order against 'Taylor and Sons Limited' instead of against 'Taylor and Son Limited'. Communications between the Companies House and the claimant led to the ultimate removal of the winding up order against Taylor and Sons Limited, but the damage had already been inflicted by the Company's creditors and suppliers having knowledge of this order, which led to the Company's administration. Edis J considered both the common law and statutory breach of duty by the Registrar.

With regard to the common law duty of care, Edis J considered that there were three approaches to the determination of the existence or otherwise of a duty of care at law: (a) 'incrementalism' (based on legal precedent); (b) assumption of responsibility; and (c) the 'three stage Caparo test'. Where the Registrar undertook to alter the status of a company on the Register which it was his duty to keep, in particular by recording a winding up order against it, he assumed a responsibility to that company (but not to anyone else), to take reasonable care to ensure that the winding up order is not registered against the wrong company. That special relationship between the Registrar and the company arose because it was foreseeable that if a company was wrongly said on the Register to be in liquidation, it would suffer serious harm. The system placed a degree of trust therefore in the Registrar's staff to ensure that it did not damage companies which had no way of defending themselves against errors. When such an exercise was performed in private and behind closed doors, those doing it had truly assumed responsibility for it. A registrar owed a duty of care when entering a winding up order on the register, to take reasonable care to ensure that the order was not registered against the wrong company. That duty was owed to any company which was not in liquidation, but which was wrongly recorded on the register as having been wound up by order of the court. See too: *Hedley Byrne v Heller* [1963] 2 AC 465 and subsequently developed in *Caparo Industries v Dickman* [1990] 2 AC 605, *Murphy v*

Brentwood [1991] 1 AC 398 and *Commissioners of Customs & Excise v Barclays Bank plc* [2007] 1 AC 181.

Applying each of the three tests for the existence of a duty of care, Edis J concluded that on the facts there was a relationship between the company and Companies House, at the time when the liquidation document examiner entered the winding up order against it, which was a 'special' one. It followed that there was an assumption of responsibility and that the company was entitled to succeed on the duty issue. In the instant case, foreseeability of harm was obvious. Therefore, the limbs of the 'three stage Caparo test' which were in play were proximity and whether it was fair, just and reasonable to impose a duty. Given that a duty was owed to one individual company whose identity was readily discoverable by the liquidator document examiner, meant that it was fair and just to impose a duty. The class was limited and its members ascertainable at the stage when treatment was given. Further it was fair, just and reasonable to impose the duty of care. The evidence was that the company had gone into administration as a direct result of the false information published, and therefore on the evidence causation had been proved.

24 Company investigations

Introduction

24.1 This Chapter addresses the following issues:

- the regime governing company investigations;
- some principal reasons why company investigations may take place;
- formal investigations by government appointed inspectors;
- the powers of officers in the conduct of company investigations;
- the application of 'natural justice' and human rights; and
- sanctions for non-compliance with the company investigations.

Although the system of corporate governance relies to some extent on self-regulation by companies, in ensuring that there are effective and proper systems in place to monitor directors' actions, and their accountability towards shareholders, self-regulation mechanisms alone cannot be the basis of an effective governance system. The maintenance of a high standard of corporate governance, and the need to prevent an abuse of directors' powers and duties requires, in some cases, the need for legislation to intervene in corporate affairs supplemented by self-regulation. Shareholders cannot continuously monitor directors' activities and, they may not have the resources or the time to undertake a detailed investigation into the company's affairs. In the UK, company law legislation adds another dimension to the corporate governance system, by empowering some governmental and regulatory authorities to conduct company investigations, where there may be evidence of abuse of power or suspected criminal activity. This may in some circumstances require the interaction and coordination between the Secretary of State for Department for Business, Energy and Industrial Strategy, the Serious Fraud Office, the Crown Prosecution Service and the police and other regulatory authorities.

24.2 Company investigations involve a process of intervention into the company's affairs. It may involve the appointment of investigation officers and inspectors by BEIS, to determine whether or not a company under investigation may be involved in any unscrupulous activities, and to prevent such activities from taking place. The process of investigation can be rigorous and encroaches on the boundaries of civil and criminal law. It may involve principles of natural justice and fair play, in ensuring inspectors act with the utmost fairness towards those under investigation. The nature of the investigation and its outcome may have an adverse effect on the company's reputation, and the reputation of its directors and key officers, including the chairman and chief executive. It could lead to civil or criminal sanctions against these officers concerned. The trust and confidence which the shareholders have in their company may be eroded quickly leading to a major collapse of the company. Increasingly, company investigations also involve human rights issues invoking the European Convention of Human Rights and the Human Rights Act 1998, owing to the exercise of wide powers vested in inspectors, the exercise of which could contravene the human rights legislation.

The Department for Business, Energy and Industrial Strategy in 2018 consulted on insolvency and corporate governance aspects (see Insolvency and Corporate Governance – 20 March 2018). The Government proposes that the scope of the current investigation and enforcement regime be extended to include former directors of dissolved companies. This may be achieved by introducing a new power for investigation into the conduct of individuals, who were directors of companies which have been dissolved, and to take action against former directors who are found to have acted in breach of their legal obligations. In particular, the Government also considering whether the Secretary of State should have power to:

(a) require any person to provide such information as may reasonably be requested to allow the Insolvency Service to investigate the conduct and actions of former directors of a dissolved company;

(b) seek an order disqualifying a former director from being a director of any other company;

(c) seek an order that the former director financially compensates creditor(s), where the director's actions caused identifiable losses; and

(d) seek a prosecution where there is evidence of criminal conduct.

24.3 At the heart of the debate on company investigations thereby maintaining an effective corporate governance system, is the need to protect the public. One of the objectives of company investigations is to protect investors, suppliers, creditors, consumers and the wider public, from misconduct and the unscrupulous practices of corporations. The Secretary of State for the BEIS has wide powers of investigation where such practices are suspected; depending upon the outcome of the investigation, the Secretary of State can prosecute offenders or take other appropriate action, where necessary, to ensure that those who need protection are, in fact, protected. Although the Secretary of State has the discretion to decide whether or not an investigation is appropriate, he will look at the following aspects:

- the possibility of a practical outcome from the use of BEIS powers;
- the possibility of documents being available to support the complaint; and
- the wider public interest in the matter complained of.

The powers contained in CA 1985 are used to investigate alleged complaints against companies. However, under the Financial Services and Markets Act 2000, the Secretary of State also has power to investigate partnerships, companies and individuals. The investigations are usually carried out by officials from BEIS or by private sector lawyers, accountants and other specialists.

24.4 This Chapter considers the BEIS process in company investigations by considering some of the key legislative provisions regulating this area. It addresses the main grounds upon which an investigation may take place. Depending upon the nature of the ground that may be invoked, the Secretary of State for the BEIS may appoint inspectors to undertake the investigation. The inspectors' powers are considered and as well as the issue of whether they can be challenged on the basis that they have exceeded the powers given to them. An analysis of the concept of natural justice is considered with particular reference to case law. Human rights legislation is also at the heart of company investigations and various cases are considered with particular regard to Art 6 of the European Convention on Human Rights.

Regulatory framework of company investigations

24.5 Company investigations are regulated by the following regime:

- **Part XIV of the Companies Act 1985** – the principal provisions governing company investigations are still retained under CA 1985, which has been amended from time to time.
- **Companies Act 1989** – amended CA 1985 to add further powers concerning search warrants.
- **Companies (Audit, Investigations and Community Enterprise) Act 2004** – amended CA 1985 to add further powers on right of entry.
- **Criminal Justice and Police Act 2001** – amended CA 1985 to take account of decisions of the European Court of Human Rights on subsequent use of material and documents obtained following the investigation.
- **Human Rights Act 1988** and the **European Convention of Human Rights** – addresses aspects of fairness of a trial of an individual and which impacts on the powers of inspectors and officers under CA 1985.
- **Insolvency Act 1986, s 124A** – allows the Secretary to petition for the company's winding up where having obtained a report following the investigation of a company, it appears expedient to wind up the company in the public interest.
- **Company Directors Disqualification Act 1986, s 8** – allows the Secretary of State to petition on the grounds of unfitness of a director subsequent to the follow up investigation into the company's affairs.

Procedure for company investigations

24.6 Company investigations are empowered to be undertaken by the Secretary of State for Business, Energy and Industrial Strategy ('BEIS') through its Companies Investigation unit. Whilst the vast majority of enquiries conducted by BEIS are confidential enquiries under CA 1985, s 447, over the years the Secretary of State for BEIS has appointed Inspectors under other sections of the Act (or earlier legislation) that allow for the publication of a report.

Inspections are normally carried out where the company involved is a major plc and the matters subject to enquiry are of significant public interest. BEIS investigations are usually confidential. It can neither confirm nor deny that an investigation is taking place, and by law, BEIS cannot provide a person with any details of its findings. It will however take action or make the information available to other regulators and enforcement agencies if it has any concerns.

24.7 BEIS assess all complaints made to it which are capable of being addressed by its powers, and decide whether or not it is in the public interest to investigate the companies against which they have been made. As part of that process, it may obtain further information from the complainants, and carry out our own background research. It does not approach the companies at that stage.

It may then decide that there is no basis for an investigation.

However, if BEIS is satisfied that there is sufficient 'good reason', and that it is in the public interest to do so, it will normally conduct an investigation. The decision to investigate is entirely at its discretion.

If BEIS does not investigate the matter itself, it may pass the information provided to another public body, that may be in a better position to investigate or act on the concerns that have been raised.

BEIS's investigations are fact-finding in nature and largely inquisitorial. They are not criminal investigations as such, although they may address conduct which could amount to criminal behaviour. It does not have to restrict its enquiries solely to what was in the original complaint. It also issues press releases when follow up action is successfully completed.

Matters on which BEIS cannot assist

24.8 BEIS cannot assist with the following aspects:

- investigate unincorporated partnerships or sole traders.
- investigate companies which do not carry on business in England
- investigate companies which have been dissolved or in compulsory liquidation.
- resolve any differences a person may have with a company, such as a dispute over the quality of goods or services provided.
- recover any money that is owed to a person.
- intervene in any dispute between a company and its shareholders. In particular, the fact that some shareholders are unhappy with decisions made by the directors is not a basis for an enquiry.
- intervene in any dispute between the company's directors.
- give any advice or guidance on what course of action a person could or should take if he is in dispute with a company.
- comment on whether or not a company is reputable, or provide references (credit, or otherwise) for a particular company.

BEIS Investigation Procedure

24.9 When BEIS receives a complaint, it first sees whether or not the organisation complained about is one which it can investigate. Thereafter, it will see what other information it can obtain about the company, both from the person who has complained and from other sources, and assess the extent to which the activities of the company may pose a threat to the public in general. This process is known as 'vetting'. Where BEIS decides that there is sufficient good reason to investigate, and that an investigation is in the wider public interest, it will appoint investigators.

Although this appointment is made by the Secretary of State for BEIS, the appointment document will be signed by a Departmental official who has the authority to do so. Investigations are usually carried out by BEIS staff. They may however be carried out by other professionals with the necessary expertise, but under the supervision of BEIS. The investigators will, if required, produce copies of their authorities and identity cards.

24.10 The investigator(s) will then call at the company's premises (often unannounced) and talk to the company's officers. They will ask questions of those who appear to be in charge, and require sight of documents which they feel will be useful in the enquiry, taking photocopies of anything they consider to be important. The investigator also has the facility to obtain electronic copies of information held on computers.

Investigators can demand detailed information not only from the company's directors, but also from other company employees and third parties who may be in possession of relevant documents and information.

24.11 The time taken to investigate will depend on many factors, but in particular the complexity of the issues and the extent of co-operation received. Once its investigators are satisfied that all the necessary information has been obtained, they will consider it with a view to recommending whether or not the Department needs to take follow up action. If necessary, they will obtain legal advice. Any appropriate follow up action is then identified and agreed will be taken.

Possible outcomes following BEIS investigations

24.12 BEIS may decide that there is insufficient good reason or that it is not in the wider public interest to investigate. However, it may decide to investigate:

- Where the investigation shows that the company's business is being operated contrary to the public interest (eg in a manner likely to cause harm, detriment or loss to third party consumers, investors and traders), BEIS can ask the court to make a winding up order. This will put the company into compulsory liquidation and thereby prevent it from further trading. This is the follow up action that BEIS is most likely to take.

  However, this does not stop the individuals involved with the company from trading through another company, or on their own. The objective is to stop the immediate mischief or undesirable trading activities as soon as possible.

- If the behaviour of the directors is such that they appear 'unfit' to be directors, BEIS can apply to the court for them to be disqualified from acting as company directors, or provide information to colleagues in the Insolvency Service (who investigate companies that have become insolvent) to assist with their disqualification effort.

  The objective is to stop individuals running companies in the future, but this will not stop them trading on their own or in partnership. However, they will lose the privilege of 'limited liability' and will be personally responsible for the debts they incur.

- The information that BEIS obtains, may be passed to BEIS Prosecution Lawyers, police or other investigation agencies, with a view to them carrying out a criminal investigation, where it appears that criminal offences have been committed by the company or its officers. Where appropriate, a formal warning letter may be sent instead of prosecution.

This is more likely where breaches are capable of being remedied and there has been no obvious harm. For example, failure to record the required company details on business correspondence. However, the decision not to prosecute will be reconsidered if the same or further offences come to the BEIS's attention.

- The investigation may provide BEIS with information which it can pass on to another regulatory organisation which has powers to deal with what BEIS have found.
- Exceptionally, where BEIS has concerns about a company's trading activities or the administration of its affairs, but there is no basis for formal action or the management appear capable of remedying the position, BEIS may take some other action such as an 'informal warning' letter. This will set out its concerns and the improvement expected. BEIS may ask for proof that appropriate action is being taken.

However, it is not BEIS's role to monitor the affairs of any company or to provide feedback to a company following an enquiry. This exceptional step will be taken only if it is the appropriate outcome in the wider public interest. BEIS may have a 'second look' to confirm that improvements have been made, particularly if further complaints are received.

The investigation may show that the original concerns were unfounded, and no other concerns have arisen, in which case no further action will be taken.

Reasons for company investigations

24.13 From a consideration of past inspectors' reports on company investigations, the following key reasons typically give rise to company investigations:

- Where fraudulent trading may be involved.
- Where there is any information to suggest that the company may be involved in a pattern of misconduct.
- The nature of investigations may ensure that directors and other officers are accountable for their actions given the wide powers available to the inspectors.
- Inspections serve to indirectly protect the interests of various 'stakeholders' within the corporation including creditors, shareholders and employees against corporate misconduct.
- Inspections may serve as a deterrent effect in demonstrating to other companies and organisations of the penalties that may be imposed on them, including the adverse publicity that disclosure may bring.
- The reputation of directors and key officers may be seriously affected, and in some cases may lead to a disqualification under CDDA 1986. In other cases, directors and other key officers as well as non-executive officers may go to jail depending upon the gravity of the offence.
- Inspections must be conducted with the utmost fairness and impartiality: a failure to do so may compel an applicant to invoke the European Convention of Human Rights.

An overview of the investigation powers

Complaint

24.14

Fraud? Public interest? Shareholder interest? Policy holder interest? Other wrongdoing?	No		
Yes ↓			
Does another regulator have an interest? Is information available?			
↓			
Is any other investigatory body making inquiries?	Yes →	Do they want assistance?	No →
No ↓	Yes		
Information to support allegations?	No →	Is there other cause for concern?	No →
Yes ↓	Yes		
Is there a civil remedy available to complainant?	Yes →	A matter of great public interest?	No →
↓	Yes		
Acceptable for inquiry		Not acceptable for inquiry	

The scope of investigation of companies

24.15 CA 1985 establishes a mechanism for allowing company investigations to be carried out, depending upon the ground being invoked and the corporate abuse that may have taken place. It will be seen that the most frequently invoked powers are under CA 1985, ss 432 and 447, depending on the nature and complexity of the investigation involved. Applications under ss 431 and 432 are relatively rare in practice.

Application of CA 1985, s 431: formal investigations

Appointment

24.16 CA 1985, s 431 allows the Secretary of State for Business, Energy and Industrial Strategy to appoint one or more competent inspectors to investigate a company's affairs, and to report on the result of their investigations to him: CA 1985, s 431(1). This is a formal investigation by the inspectors. It is an investigation of a company on its own application or that of its members.

Inspectors do not sit in public. In *Hearts of Oak Assurance Co Ltd v Attorney-General* [1932] AC 392, the House of Lords held that an inspector appointed (under another

Act) for the purpose of examining into and reporting on the affairs of an industrial assurance company, was not entitled to conduct the inspection in public. However, this did not prevent him from admitting from time to time any persons such as witnesses, the presence of whom was reasonably necessary to enable him to carry out his duty under the statute.

Potential applicants

24.17 In order to invoke CA 1985, s 431 appointment of inspectors, the following persons may be the potential applicants:

(a) in the case of a company having a share capital, on the application either of:

  (i) not less than 200 members; or

  (ii) members holding not less than one-tenth of the shares issued (excluding any shares held as treasury shares);

(b) in the case of a company not having a share capital, on the application of not less than one-fifth in number of the persons on the company's register of members; and

(c) in any case, on the application of the company: CA 1985, s 431(2).

Security for costs

24.18 In the above cases however, the Secretary of State may, before appointing inspectors, require the applicant(s) to give security, to an amount not exceeding £5,000, or such other sum as he may by order specify, for payment of the investigation costs: CA 1985, s 431(4).

Supporting application

24.19 The application by any of the above applicants must be supported by such evidence as the Secretary of State may require, for the purpose of showing that the applicant(s) has a good reason for requiring the investigation: CA 1985, s 431(3).

Those complainants requesting an investigation must satisfy the Secretary of State that there is a good reason for an investigation and they may have to pay all or some of the costs of the investigation. This provision is rarely used in practice owing to the standing of persons who can apply, and the sanction of costs and expenses involved becomes counter-productive for the potential applicants.

Application of CA 1985, s 432 – other company investigations

24.20 This is another main provision used to initiate the investigation and the appointment of inspectors to look into a company's activities. The appointment will normally be as a result of some adverse publicity surrounding the company, which is likely to involve a complex investigation.

Appointment

24.21 Under s 432, the Secretary of State must appoint one or more competent inspectors to investigate the company's affairs; inspectors must report the result of their investigations to him, if the court by order declares that its affairs ought to be so investigated: CA 1985, s 432(1).

A company's 'affairs' includes all aspects concerning the company and the term is widely construed by giving it a natural meaning: *R v Board of Trade Ex parte St Martin Preserving Co* [1965] 1 QB 603. The term included its goodwill, its profit and loss, its contracts and investments and assets, including its shareholding in and ability to control a subsidiary or sub-subsidiary and those of the liquidator and debenture holder.

Grounds

24.22 The Secretary of State may make such an appointment if it appears to him that there are circumstances suggesting that:

(a) the company's affairs are being or have been conducted with intent to defraud its creditors, or the creditors of any other person, or otherwise for a fraudulent or unlawful purpose, or in a manner which is unfairly prejudicial to some part of its members. In this case, reference to a company's 'members' includes any person who is not a member but to whom shares in a company have been transferred by operation of law;

(b) any actual or proposed act or omission of the company (including an act or omission on its behalf) is or would be so prejudicial, or that the company was formed for any fraudulent or unlawful purpose – grounds (a) and (b) above are similar to the unfair prejudicial ground under CA 2006, s 994;

(c) persons concerned with the company's formation or the management of its affairs have in connection therewith been guilty of fraud, misfeasance or other misconduct towards it or towards its members; or

(d) the company's members have not been given all the information with respect to its affairs which they might reasonably expect: CA 1985, s 432(2). This section does not entitle the Secretary of State to appoint inspectors merely because the directors may have breached their duties of skill, care and diligence: *SBA Properties Ltd v Cradock* [1967] 1 WLR 716.

Inspectors may be appointed under s 432(2) of the CA 1985 on terms that any report they may make is not to be published (CA 1985, s 432A); and in such a case, s 437(3) of the CA 1985 (availability and publication of inspectors' reports) does not apply (CA 1985, s 432(2A)).

CA 1985, s 432(1) and (2) are without prejudice to the powers of the Secretary of State under s 431; and the power conferred by s 432(2) is exercisable with respect to a body corporate notwithstanding that it is in course of being voluntarily wound up: (CA 1985, s 432(3)).

Inspectors' powers during investigation

24.23 Inspectors who are appointed to investigate the company's affairs can also, where they believe it is necessary to do so, investigate a connected body corporate, such as the subsidiary or the holding company. They can report on the affairs of the connected body corporate so far as the affairs are relevant to the company's investigation which the BEIS inspectors were first investigating: CA 1985, s 433. The investigation powers may also extend to unincorporated associations if they are in any way associated with the corporate body.

Publication of documents and evidence to inspectors

24.24 The BEIS inspectors have wide powers to require the company's officers or agents:

(a) to produce all documents of or relating to the company which are in their custody or power;

(b) to attend before the inspectors when required to do so; and

(c) to give inspectors all assistance in connection with the investigation as they are reasonably able to give: CA 1985, s 434(1).

Inspectors were not entitled to require a person to sign a confidentiality undertaking, which went further than was either reasonable or necessary in the circumstances. In *Re An Inquiry into Mirror Group Newspapers plc* [1999] 1 BCLC 690, the court was required to consider the 'reasonableness' of assistance that could be given to inspectors under CA 1985, s 434(1). Kevin Maxwell ('M'), an ex-director, refused to give a confidentiality undertaking sought by the inspectors or to answer questions. The issue was whether the inspectors were entitled to require a confidentiality undertaking; whether the ex-director was justified in refusing to answer the questions; and whether there were any limits on the right of inspectors to require assistance.

Sir Richard Scott V-C held that inspectors appointed under Pt XIV of the 1985 Act owed no duty to those from whom they had obtained information or documents that might inhibit them in the use of that information or those documents for the purposes of their statutory inquiry. Nor did they have any legal obligation to such persons to insist on confidentiality undertakings being given by others before whom, for the purposes of their inquiry, they wished to put the material, since confidentiality could be protected simply by making the confidential character of the information and documents known. It followed that in the absence of any express statutory power to do so, the inspectors had not been entitled to require M to sign the confidentiality undertaking, which in any event went further than was either reasonable or necessary. Accordingly, M's refusal to sign the undertaking did not represent a failure on his part to give the inspectors any assistance he was reasonably able to give.

The purpose of Pt XIV inspections, where there were grounds that suggested some irregularity or impropriety in the conduct of the affairs of a company had occurred, was to discover what had happened. However, inspectors could not place demands on persons that were unreasonable, whether as to the time they had to expend or the expense they had to incur in preparation for the questions or in any other respect. In the instant case, having regard to the extent of the interrogations that M had already undergone, the potential burden that the questioning might place on him risked going beyond that which an unrepresented individual could reasonably be required to accept. Accordingly, until steps were taken by the inspectors to reduce that burden, M's refusal to answer questions did not constitute a breach of his statutory obligations under s 434.

24.25 If the inspectors consider that an officer or agent of the company or other body corporate, or any other person, is or may be in possession of information relating to a matter which they believe to be relevant to the investigation, they may require him:

(a) to produce to them any documents in his custody or power relating to that matter;

(b) to attend before them;

(c) otherwise to give them all assistance in connection with the investigation which he is reasonably able to give,

and it is that person's duty to comply with the requirement: CA 1985, s 434(2).

It is the duty of the company's officer or agent to comply with the above requirements. The references to 'officers' or 'agents' include those past as well as present. 'Agents' in relation to a company or other body corporate include its bankers and solicitors and persons employed by it as auditors, whether these persons are or are not officers of the company or other body corporate: CA 1985, s 434(4).

An inspector may, for the purposes of the investigation, examine any person on oath, and may also administer an oath: CA 1985, s 434(3).

An answer given by a person to a question put to him in exercise of the powers conferred upon the BEIS inspectors, may be used in evidence against him: CA 1985, s 434(5).

Unless certain documents are excluded from disclosure on the ground that they are confidential documents, which the public interest required to be protected from disclosure, they would under the general law, be admissible in evidence. In practice, inspectors will usually put questions to a person under investigation. The answers may then be used in evidence against him: CA 1985, s 434(5). The evidence given by a person to inspectors in the course of an investigation may be admissible in civil proceedings: *London & County Securities Ltd v Nicholson* [1980] 3 All ER 861.

Transcripts of evidence given by the witnesses could be disclosed but only after prior notification to the witnesses, and subject to any application by the witnesses to set aside the order to disclose: *Soden v Burns* [1996] 3 All ER 967.

Application of natural justice to company investigations

24.26 Although the concept of natural justice does not feature in CA 1985 provisions dealing with company investigations, it has been addressed by the courts in connection with some of the procedural aspects of corporate investigations. The term 'natural justice' has been used in a variety of legal contexts, but generally refers to 'fair play' – the opportunity to be heard; the right to make representations; the fact that the inspector must not perform the combined role of judge, jury and executioner; that there will be no bias in arriving at a decision that is fair and properly applies the applicable laws to the facts under consideration.

Although the proceedings before the inspectors were only administrative and inquisitorial in nature, and not judicial or quasi-judicial, yet the characteristics of the proceedings required the inspectors to act fairly: *Re Pergamon Press [1971] Ch 388.*

One of the first cases to apply the concept of natural justice was in *Re Pergamon Press,* where the Court of Appeal was required to address the procedural fairness of the powers of the inspectors in conducting their investigation, balanced against the interests of the individual(s) under investigation. The Court of Appeal held that although the proceedings before the inspectors were only administrative, and not judicial or quasi-judicial, yet the characteristics of the proceedings required the inspectors to act fairly. If they were disposed to condemn or criticise anyone in a report, they must first give him a fair opportunity to correct or contradict the allegation, for which purpose an outline of the charge would usually suffice.

Except for the requirement to act fairly, the inspectors should not be subject to any set rules of procedure, and should be free to act at their own discretion. Accordingly, as the inspectors had shown that they intended to act fairly and had given every assurance that could reasonably be required, the directors' refusal to give evidence was unjustified: *R v Gaming Board for Great Britain, ex parte Benaim* [1970] 2 All ER 528.

The Court of Appeal further stated that the inspectors (who were under a duty to act fairly and to give anyone whom they proposed to condemn or criticise in their report a fair opportunity to answer what was alleged against him) had acted perfectly properly and the directors had no right to demand further assurances: see dicta of Lord Reid in *Ridge v Baldwin* [1964] AC 40, 65; and *Reg v Gaming Board for Great Britain, Ex parte Benaim and Khaida* [1970] 2 QB 417.

24.27 Subsequent cases have highlighted that natural justice does have a part to play in company investigations particularly the procedural aspects.

Where inspectors are holding an inquiry under s 432 of the CA 1985, it is sufficient for them to put to the witnesses what had been said against them by other persons, or in documents, to enable them to deal with those criticisms in the course of the inquiry: *Maxwell v Department of Trade and Industry [1971 M No 2901]*, [1974] QB 523.

24.28 For further application of the 'natural justice' principles see: *F Hoffmann-La Roche & Co AG and others v Secretary of State for Trade and Industry* [1974] 2 All ER 1128.

In Norwest Holst Ltd v Department of Trade [1978] 3 All ER 280, the court stated that the decision of the Secretary of State to appoint inspectors under s 432 of the CA 1985 was no more than an administrative decision, and a full application of natural justice did not apply:

Under Pt XIV of CA 1985, company investigations should be conducted in private and that the inspectors should not make public information disclosed to them in the course of the investigation: *Re An Inquiry Into Mirror Group Newspapers* [2000] Ch 194.

Application of human rights to company investigations

24.29 An issue that has arisen in respect of the powers of the inspectors to obtain documents and raise questions to the person concerned could self-incriminate that person in subsequent proceedings? Further, whether any responses to the inspectors would be a breach of Article 6 of the European Convention of Human Rights? Article 6 provides:

> '1. In the determination of his civil rights and obligations or of any criminal charge against him, everyone is entitled to a fair and public hearing within a reasonable time by an independent and impartial tribunal established by law. Judgment shall be pronounced publicly but the press and public may be excluded from all or part of the trial in the interest of morals, public order or national security in a democratic society, where the interests of juveniles or the protection of the private life of the parties so require, or the extent strictly necessary in the opinion of the court in special circumstances where publicity would prejudice the interests of justice.
>
> 2. Everyone charged with a criminal offence shall be presumed innocent until proved guilty according to law.
>
> 3. Everyone charged with a criminal offence has the following minimum rights:
>
> (a) to be informed promptly, in a language which he understands and in detail, of the nature and cause of the accusation against him;
>
> (b) to have adequate time and the facilities for the preparation of his defence;

(c) to defend himself in person or through legal assistance of his own choosing or, if he has not sufficient means to pay for legal assistance, to be given it free when the interests of justice so require;

(d) to examine or have examined witnesses against him and to obtain the attendance and examination of witnesses on his behalf under the same conditions as witnesses against him;

(e) to have the free assistance of an interpreter if he cannot understand or speak the language used in court.'

The European Court of Human Rights has established various jurisprudential principles with regard to the application of human rights and its application to company investigations.

The right of an individual not to incriminate himself, which is central to the notion of a fair procedure inherent in Art 6(1) of the EHRC, is primarily concerned with the right of an accused to remain silent. Accordingly, it is not therefore confined to statements of admission of wrongdoing or to remarks which are directly incriminating: *Saunders v United Kingdom* [1998] 1 BCLC 362.

The functions of Inspectors is administrative and inquisitorial in nature; and the right of access to a court was not absolute, but may be subject to implied limitations: *Fayed v United Kingdom* (1994) 18 EHRR 393.

A person has a right not to incriminate himself: *IJL v United Kingdom* (2001) 33 EHRR 11.

24.30 However, in criminal proceedings where that person is charged with an offence to which s 434(5A) applies:

(a) no evidence relating to the answer may be adduced; and

(b) no question relating to it may be asked,

by or on behalf of the prosecution, unless evidence relating to it is adduced, or a question relating to it is asked, in the proceedings by or on behalf of that person.

24.31 CA 1985, s 434(5A) applies to any offence other than an offence under Perjury Act 1911, s 2 or 5 (false statements made on oath otherwise than in judicial proceedings or made otherwise than on oath).

24.32 The term 'document' includes information recorded in any form: CA 1985, s 434(6).

The power under CA 1985, s 434 to require production of a document includes power, in the case of a document not in hard copy form, to require the production of a copy of the document in hard copy form; or in a form from which a hard copy can be readily obtained: CA 1985, s 434(7).

An inspector may take copies of or extracts from a document produced in pursuance of s 434: CA 1985, s 434(8).

Obstruction of inspectors treated as contempt of court

24.33 If any person:

(a) fails to comply with the production of documents and assist inspectors with evidence in connection with the company's affairs under s 434(1)(a) or (c);

(b) refuses to comply with a requirement under s 434(1)(b) or (2); or

(c) refuses to answer any question put to him by the inspectors for the purposes of the investigation,

the inspectors may certify that fact in writing to the court: CA 1985, s 436(1).

The court can then enquire into the case; and after hearing any witnesses who may be against or on behalf of the alleged offender, and after hearing any statement which may be offered in defence, the court may punish the offender in like manner as if he had been guilty of contempt of the court: CA 1985, s 436(2).

Inspectors' reports

24.34 The inspector may, but if so directed by the Secretary of the State must, make interim reports to the Secretary of State. On conclusion of the investigation, the inspector must make a final report to the Secretary of State: CA 1985, s 437(1).

Any persons who have been appointed under s 431 or 432 may at any time and, if the Secretary of State directs them to do so, must inform him of any matters coming to their knowledge as a result of their investigations: CA 1985, s 437(1A).

If the inspectors were appointed under s 432 in pursuance of an order of the court, the Secretary of State must furnish a copy of any report of theirs to the court: CA 1985, s 437(2).

24.35 In any case the Secretary of State may, if he thinks fit:

(a) forward a copy of any report made by the inspectors to the company's registered office;

(b) furnish a copy on request and on payment of the prescribed fee to:

  (i) any member of the company or other body corporate which is the subject of the report;

  (ii) any person whose conduct is referred to in the report;

  (iii) the auditors of that company or body corporate;

  (iv) the applicants for the investigation;

  (v) any other person whose financial interests appear to the Secretary of State to be affected by the matters dealt with in the report, whether as a creditor of the company or body corporate, or otherwise; and

(c) cause any such report to be printed and published: CA 1985, s 437(3).

In exercising the discretion conferred on him by s 437(3)(c) of the CA 1985 the Secretary of State was required to act in the public interest: *Lonrho plc v Secretary of State for Trade and Industry* [1989] 2 All ER 609. The House of Lords held that having regard to the circumstances, the Secretary of State had properly exercised his discretion in deciding to defer publication of the report, on the ground that early publication might be prejudicial to the SFO's investigation and to a fair trial. Since arriving at his decision, he had acted independently and had only confirmed his decision after careful consideration of the appellant's arguments.

Expenses of investigating a company's affairs

24.36 These investigations by the BEIS inspectors will inevitably involve expense and costs to the state. The expenses of an investigation will be defrayed in the first instance by the Secretary of State. However, he will recover those expenses from the persons liable. Expenses of the investigation include such reasonable sums as the Secretary of State may determine in respect of general staff costs and overheads: CA 1985, s 439(1).

A person who is convicted on a prosecution instituted as a result of the investigation may in the same proceedings be ordered to pay those expenses to such extent as may be specified in the order: CA 1985, s 439(2).

A body corporate dealt with by an inspectors' report, where the inspectors were appointed otherwise than of the Secretary of State's own motion, is liable except where it was the applicant for the investigation, and except so far as the Secretary of State otherwise directs: CA 1985, s 439(4).

24.37 Where inspectors were appointed:

(a) under CA 1985, s 431; or

(b) on an application under s 442(3),

the applicant or applicants for the investigation is or are liable to such extent (if any) as the Secretary of State may direct: CA 1985, s 439(5).

The report of inspectors appointed otherwise than of the Secretary of State's own motion may, if they think fit, and must if the Secretary of State so directs, include a recommendation as to the directions (if any) which they think appropriate, in the light of their investigation, to be given under s 439(4) or (5): CA 1985, s 439(6).

Any liability to repay the Secretary of State imposed by s 439(2) above is (subject to satisfaction of his right to repayment) a liability also to indemnify all persons against liability under s 439(4) and (5): CA 1985, s 439(8).

A person liable under any one of those subsections is entitled to a contribution from any other person liable under the same subsection, according to the amount of their respective liabilities under it: CA 1985, s 439(9).

Expenses to be defrayed by the Secretary of State under s 439 shall, so far as not recovered under it, be paid out of money provided by Parliament: CA 1985, s 439(10).

Inspectors' report to be evidence

24.38 A copy of any report of inspectors certified by the Secretary of State to be a true copy, is admissible in any legal proceedings as evidence of the opinion of the inspectors in relation to any matter contained in the report and, in proceedings on an application under Company Directors' Disqualification Act 1986, s 8 as evidence of any fact stated therein: CA 1985, s 441(1).

A document purporting to be a certificate as set out above shall be received in evidence and be deemed to be such a certificate, unless the contrary is proved: CA 1985, s 441(2).

The BEIS investigative powers under CA 1985, s 432 are wider than those under s 447. Whereas under s 432 the investigation is undertaken where there is suspected malpractice and there are complex issues involved, thereby requiring BEIS to probe further into the company and require persons to attend to the inspection to answer questions, s 447 does not require such attendance, and is limited to document production and a search of premises for documents, as well as an explanation of the documentation. Both ss 432 and 437 have, as their objective, to allow the BEIS to investigate the facts and determine the nature of the allegations made against the company.

Power to investigate company ownership

24.39 CA 2006 enables the Secretary of State to appoint inspectors to investigate the company's ownership, where the position is unclear. Usually this is undertaken at the request of shareholders or of the companies themselves. Companies have a legal right to know who owns the shares.

Where it appears to the Secretary of State that there is good reason to do so, he may appoint one or more competent inspectors to investigate and report on the membership of any company, and otherwise with respect to the company, for the purpose of determining the true persons who are or have been financially interested in the success or failure (real or apparent) of the company or able to control or materially to influence its policy: CA 1985, s 442(1).

24.40 If an application for investigation under CA 1985, s 442 with respect to particular shares or debentures of a company is made to the Secretary of State by members of the company, and the number of applicants or the amount of shares held by them is not less than that required for an application for the appointment of inspectors under s 431(2)(a) or (b), then, subject to the following provisions, the Secretary of State must appoint inspectors to conduct the investigation applied for: CA 1985, s 442(3).

The Secretary of State must not appoint inspectors if he is satisfied that the application is vexatious; where inspectors are appointed, their terms of appointment must exclude any matter in so far as the Secretary of State is satisfied that it is unreasonable for it to be investigated: CA 1985, s 442(3A).

24.41 The Secretary of State may, before appointing inspectors, require the applicant or applicants to give security, to an amount not exceeding £5,000, or such other sum as he may by order specify, for payment of the costs of the investigation.

An order under s 442(3B) shall be made by statutory instrument which shall be subject to annulment in pursuance of a resolution of either House of Parliament: CA 1985, s 442(3B).

If on an application under s 442(3) it appears to the Secretary of State that the powers conferred by s 444 are sufficient for the purposes of investigating the matters which inspectors would be appointed to investigate, he may instead conduct the investigation under that section: CA 1985, s 442(3C).

Subject to the terms of their appointment, the inspectors' powers extend to the investigation of any circumstances suggesting the existence of an arrangement or understanding which, though not legally binding, is or was observed or likely to be observed in practice and which is relevant to the purposes of the investigation: CA 1985, s 442(4).

Provisions applicable on investigation under s 442

24.42 For purposes of an investigation under CA 1985, s 442, ss 433(1), 434, 436 and 437 apply with the necessary modifications of references to the affairs of the company or to those of any other body corporate, subject however to the following subsections: CA 1985, s 443(1).

Those sections apply to:

(a) all persons who are or have been, or whom the inspector has reasonable cause to believe to be or have been, financially interested in the success or failure or the apparent success or failure of the company or any other body corporate whose membership is investigated with that of the company, or able to control or materially influence its policy (including persons concerned only on behalf of others); and

(b) any other person whom the inspector has reasonable cause to believe possesses information relevant to the investigation,

as they apply in relation to officers and agents of the company or the other body corporate (as the case may be): CA 1985, s 443(2).

If the Secretary of State is of the opinion that there is good reason for not divulging any part of a report made by virtue of s 442 and s 443(3), he may under s 437 disclose the report with the omission of that part; he may cause to be kept by the registrar of companies a copy of the report with that part omitted or, in the case of any other such report, a copy of the whole report: CA 1985, s 443(3).

Power to obtain information as to those interested in shares

24.43 If it appears to the Secretary of State that there is good reason to investigate the ownership of any shares in or debentures of a company, and that it is unnecessary to appoint inspectors for the purpose, he may require any person whom he has reasonable cause to believe to have or to be able to obtain any information as to the present and past interests in those shares or debentures and the names and addresses of the persons interested and of any persons who act or have acted on their behalf in relation to the shares or debentures to give any such information to the Secretary of State: CA 1985, s 444(1).

For this purpose a person is deemed to have an interest in shares or debentures if he has any right to acquire or dispose of them or of any interest in them, or to vote in respect of them, or if his consent is necessary for the exercise of any of the rights of other persons interested in them, or if other persons interested in them can be required, or are accustomed, to exercise their rights in accordance with his instructions: CA 1985, s 444(2).

24. 44 A person who fails to give information required of him under s 444, or who in giving such information makes any statement which he knows to be false in a material particular, or recklessly makes any statement which is false in a material particular, commits an offence: CA 1985, s 444(3). A fine and/or imprisoned can be imposed in such circumstances: CA 1985, s 444(4).

Power to impose restrictions on shares and debentures

24.45 If in connection with an investigation under either CA 1985, s 442 or 444, it appears to the Secretary of State that there is difficulty in finding out the relevant facts about any shares (whether issued or to be issued), he may by order that the shares shall, until further order, be subject to the restrictions of CA 1985, Pt XV: CA 1985, s 445(1).

If the Secretary of State is satisfied that an order under s 445(1) may unfairly affect the rights of third parties in respect of shares then the Secretary of State, for the purpose of protecting such rights and subject to such terms as he thinks fit, may direct that such acts by such persons or descriptions of persons and for such purposes as may be set out in the order, shall not constitute a breach of the restrictions of CA 1985, Pt XV: CA 1985, s 445(1A).

Section 445 and Pt XV in its application to orders under it, apply in relation to debentures as in relation to shares save that s 445(1A) shall not so apply: CA 1985, s 445(2).

General powers to give directions

24.46 In exercising his functions an inspector must comply with any direction given to him by the Secretary of State under CA 1985, s 446A: CA 1985, s 446A(1).

The Secretary of State may give an inspector appointed under s 431, 432(2) or 442(1) a direction:

(a) as to the subject matter of his investigation (whether by reference to a specified area of a company's operation, a specified transaction, a period of time or otherwise); or

(b) which requires the inspector to take or not to take a specified step in his investigation: CA 1985, s 446A(2).

24.47 The Secretary of State may give an inspector appointed under any provision of this Part a direction requiring him to secure that a specified report under CA 1985, s 437:

(a) includes the inspector's views on a specified matter;

(b) does not include any reference to a specified matter;

(c) is made in a specified form or manner; or

(d) is made by a specified date: CA 1985, s 446A(3).

24.48 A direction under CA 1985, s 446A:

(a) may be given on an inspector's appointment;

(b) may vary or revoke a direction previously given; and

(c) may be given at the request of an inspector: CA 1985, s 446A(4).

The reference to an inspector's investigation includes any investigation he undertakes, or could undertake, under s 433(1) (power to investigate affairs of holding company or subsidiary). The term 'specified' means specified in a direction under s 446A: CA 1985, s 446A(5).

Direction to terminate investigation

24.49 The Secretary of State may direct an inspector to take no further steps in his investigation: CA 1985, s 446B(1). The Secretary of State may give a direction under s 446B to an inspector appointed under s 432(1) or 442(3) only on the grounds that it appears to him that:

(a) matters have come to light in the course of the inspector's investigation which suggest that a criminal offence has been committed; and

(b) those matters have been referred to the appropriate prosecuting authority: CA 1985, s 446B(2).

24.50 Where the Secretary of State gives a direction under CA 1985, s 446, any direction already given to the inspector under s 437(1) to produce an interim report and any direction given to him under s 446A(3) in relation to such a report, will cease to have effect: CA 1985, s 446B(3).

Where the Secretary of State gives a direction under this section, the inspector must not make a final report to the Secretary of State unless:

(a) the direction was made on the grounds mentioned in s 446B(2) and the Secretary of State directs the inspector to make a final report to him; or

(b) the inspector was appointed under s 432(1) (appointment in pursuance of order of the court): CA 1985, s 446B(4).

An inspector must comply with any direction given to him under s 446B: CA 1985, s 446B(5).

Under s 446B, a reference to an inspector's investigation includes any investigation he undertakes, or could undertake, under s 433(1) (power to investigate affairs of holding company or subsidiary): CA 1985, s 446B(6).

Resignation and revocation of appointment

24.51 An inspector may resign by notice in writing to the Secretary of State: CA 1985, s 446C(1).

Also, the Secretary of State may revoke the appointment of an inspector by notice in writing to the inspector: CA 1985, s 446C(2).

Appointment of replacement inspectors

24.52 Where:

(a) an inspector resigns;

(b) an inspector's appointment is revoked; or

(c) an inspector dies,

the Secretary of State may appoint one or more competent inspectors to continue the investigation: CA 1985, s 446D(1).

24.53 An appointment under CA 1985, s 446D(1) will be treated for the purposes of Pt XIV of the CA 1985 (apart from this section) as an appointment under the provision of Pt XIV of the CA 1985 under which the former inspector was appointed: CA 1985, s 446D(2). The Secretary of State must exercise his power under s 446D(1) so as to secure that at least one inspector continues the investigation: CA 1985, s 446D(3).

Section 446D(3) does not apply if:

(a) the Secretary of State could give any replacement inspector a direction under s 446B (termination of investigation); and

(b) such a direction would (under s 446D(4)) result in a final report not being made: CA 1985, s 446D(4).

In s 446D, references to an investigation include any investigation the former inspector conducted under s 433(1) (power to investigate affairs of holding company or subsidiary): CA 1985, s 446D(5).

Obtaining information from former inspectors

24.54 CA 1985, s 446E applies to a person who was appointed as an inspector:

(a) who has resigned; or

(b) whose appointment has been revoked: CA 1985, s 446E(1).

Section 446E also applies to an inspector to whom the Secretary of State has given a direction under s 446B (termination of investigation): CA 1985, s 446E(2).

24.55 The Secretary of State may direct a person to whom CA 1985, s 446E applies to produce documents obtained or generated by that person during the course of his investigation to the Secretary of State; or an inspector appointed under CA 1985: CA 1985, s 446E(3).

The power under s 446E(3) to require production of a document includes the power, in the case of a document not in hard copy form, to require the production of a copy of the document in hard copy form; or in a form from which a hard copy can be readily obtained: CA 1985, s 446E(4).

The Secretary of State may take copies of or extracts from a document produced in pursuance of s 446E: CA 1985, s 446E(5).

24.56 The Secretary of State may direct a person to whom CA 1985, s 446E applies to inform him of any matters that came to that person's knowledge as a result of his investigation: CA 1985, s 446E(6).

A person must comply with any direction given to him under s 446E: CA 1985, s 446E(7).

The references to the investigation of a former inspector or inspector include any investigation he conducted under s 433(1) (power to investigate affairs of holding company or subsidiary). The term 'document' includes information recorded in any form: CA 1985, s 446E(8).

Power to require documents and information: Informal Investigations

24.57 As formal investigations in the appointment of inspectors is rarely used in practice, the most common type of informal investigation is under s CA 1985, s 447 and the appointment of CI investigators by the Secretary of State for BEIS. The Secretary of State may act under s 447(2) and (3) in relation to a company: CA 1985, s 447(1).

The Secretary of State may give directions to the company requiring it to produce such documents (or documents of such description) as may be specified in the directions; or to provide such information (or information of such description) as may be so specified: CA 1985, s 447(2).

24.58 The Secretary of State may authorise a person (an investigator) to require the company or any other person:

(a) to produce such documents (or documents of such description) as the investigator may specify;

(b) to provide such information (or information of such description) as the investigator may specify: CA 1985, s 447(3).

A person on whom a requirement under s 447(3) is imposed may require the investigator to produce evidence of his authority: CA 1985, s 447(4).

A requirement under s 447(2) or (3) must be complied with at such time and place as may be specified in the directions or by the investigator (as the case may be): CA 1985, s 447(5).

The production of a document in pursuance of s 447 does not affect any lien which a person has on the document: CA 1985, s 447(6).

24.59 The Secretary of State or the investigator (as the case may be) may take copies of or extracts from a document produced in pursuance of s 447.

A 'document' includes information recorded in any form: CA 1985, s 447(8).

The power under s 447 to require production of a document includes power, in the case of a document not in hard copy form, to require the production of a copy of the document in hard copy form; or in a form from which a hard copy can be readily obtained: CA 1985, s 447(9).

There must be a genuine and bona fide decision exercised by the Secretary of State in exercising his powers to obtain certain documents, as part of a company's investigation under the CA 1985.In *R v Secretary of State for Trade and Industry, ex parte Perestrello* [1981] QB 19, the court stated that the Secretary of State's powers to obtain documents must not be exercised for any ulterior motive.

See too *Attorney-General's Reference No 2 of 1998* [1999] BCC 590.

Information provided: evidence

24.60 A statement made by a person in compliance with a requirement under CA 1985, s 447 may be used in evidence against him: CA 1985, s 447A(1). Subsequent use of the testimony obtained by the inspectors may be used in proceedings under s 8 of the CDDA 1986: *R v Secretary of State for Trade and Industry ex parte McCormick* [1998] BCC 379.

24.61 The disqualification proceedings under the CDDA 1986 are not criminal proceedings but civil in nature.

But in criminal proceedings in which the person is charged with a relevant offence :

(a) no evidence relating to the statement may be adduced by or on behalf of the prosecution; and

(b) no question relating to it may be asked by or on behalf of the prosecution,

unless evidence relating to it is adduced or a question relating to it is asked in the proceedings by or on behalf of that person: CA 1985, s 447A(2).

A relevant offence is any offence other than the following: an offence under s 451; or an offence under Perjury Act 1911, s 5 (false statement made otherwise than on oath).

Entry and search of premises

24.62 A justice of the peace may issue a warrant under CA 1985, s 448 if satisfied on information on oath given by or on behalf of the Secretary of State, or by a person appointed or authorised to exercise powers under this Part, that there are reasonable grounds for believing that there are on any premises documents whose production has been required under this CA 1985, Pt 14 and which have not been produced in compliance with the requirement: CA 1985, s 448(1).

24.63 A justice of the peace may also issue a warrant under CA 1985, s 448 if satisfied on information on oath given by or on behalf of the Secretary of State, or by a person appointed or authorised to exercise powers under this Part:

(a) that there are reasonable grounds for believing that an offence has been committed for which the penalty on conviction on indictment is imprisonment for a term of not less than two years and that there are, on any premises, documents relating to whether the offence has been committed,

(b) that the Secretary of State, or the person so appointed or authorised, has power to require the production of the documents under this Part, and

(c) that there are reasonable grounds for believing that if production was so required the documents would not be produced but would be removed from the premises, hidden, tampered with or destroyed: CA 1985, s 448(2).

24.64 A warrant under this CA 1985, s 448 shall authorise a constable, together with any other person named in it and any other constables:

(a) to enter the premises specified in the information, using such force as is reasonably necessary for the purpose;

(b) to search the premises and take possession of any documents appearing to be such documents as are mentioned in s 448(1) or (2), as the case may be, or to take, in relation to any such documents, any other steps which may appear to be necessary for preserving them or preventing interference with them;

(c) to take copies of any such documents; and

(d) to require any person named in the warrant to provide an explanation of them or to state where they may be found: CA 1985, s 448(3).

If in the case of a warrant under s 448(2) the justice of the peace is satisfied on information on oath that there are reasonable grounds for believing that there are also on the premises other documents relevant to the investigation, the warrant shall also authorise the actions mentioned in s 448(3) to be taken in relation to such documents: CA 1985, s 448(4).

24.65 A warrant under CA 1985, s 448 shall continue in force until the end of the period of one month beginning with the day on which it is issued: CA 1985, s 448(5).

Any documents of which possession is taken under s 448 may be retained:

(a) for a period of three months; or

(b) if within that period proceedings to which the documents are relevant are commenced against any person for any criminal offence, until the conclusion of those proceedings: CA 1985, s 448(6).

Any person who intentionally obstructs the exercise of any rights conferred by a warrant issued under this section or fails without reasonable excuse to comply with any requirement imposed in accordance with s 448(3)(d) is guilty of an offence: CA 1985, s 448(7).

24.66 A person guilty of an offence under s 448 will be liable on conviction on indictment, to a fine: CA 1985, s 448(7A) CA 1985.

For the purposes of ss 449 and 451A (provision for security of information), documents obtained under s 448 shall be treated as if they had been obtained under the provision of this Part under which their production was or, as the case may be, could have been required: CA 1985, s 448(8).

Under s 448, the term 'document' includes information recorded in any form: CA 1985, s 448(10).

Protection in relation to certain disclosures: information provided to Secretary of State

24.67 A person who makes a relevant disclosure is not liable by reason only of that disclosure in any proceedings relating to a breach of an obligation of confidence: CA 1985, s 448A(1).

A relevant disclosure is a disclosure which satisfies each of the following conditions:

(a) it is made to the Secretary of State otherwise than in compliance with a requirement under Pt XIV of the CA 1985;

(b) it is of a kind that the person making the disclosure could be required to make in pursuance of Pt XIV of the CA 1985;

(c) the person who makes the disclosure does so in good faith and in the reasonable belief that the disclosure is capable of assisting the Secretary of State for the purposes of the exercise of his functions under Pt XIV of the CA 1985;

(d) the information disclosed is not more than is reasonably necessary for the purpose of assisting the Secretary of State for the purposes of the exercise of those functions; and

(e) the disclosure is not one falling within s 448A(3) or (4): CA 1985, s 448A(2).

A disclosure falls within s 448A(3) if the disclosure is prohibited by virtue of any enactment whenever passed or made: CA 1985, s 448A(3).

24.68 A disclosure falls within CA 1985, s 448A(4) if it is made by a person carrying on the business of banking or by a lawyer; and it involves the disclosure of information in respect of which he owes an obligation of confidence in that capacity: CA 1985, s 448A(4).

Under s 448A, the term 'enactment' has the meaning given by CA 2006, s 1293: CA 1985, s 448A(5).

Provision for security of information obtained

24.69 CA 1985, s 449 applies to information (in whatever form) obtained:

(a) in pursuance of a requirement imposed under s 447;

(b) by means of a relevant disclosure within the meaning of s 448A(2); and

(c) by an investigator in consequence of the exercise of his powers under s 453A: CA 1985, s 449(1).

Such information must not be disclosed unless the disclosure is made to a person specified in Sch 15C; or is of a description specified in Sch 15D: CA 1985, s 449(2).

A person who discloses any information in contravention of s 449 is guilty of an offence: CA 1985, s 449(6). A person guilty of an offence under s 449 will be liable to a fine and/or imprisonment.

Any information which may by virtue of s 449 be disclosed to a person specified in Sch 15C, may be disclosed to any officer or employee of the person: CA 1985, s 449(8).

Section 449 does not prohibit the disclosure of information if the information is or has been available to the public from any other source: CA 1985, s 449(9).

For the purposes of s 449, information obtained by an investigator in consequence of the exercise of his powers under s 453A, includes information obtained by a person accompanying the investigator in pursuance of s 449(4) in consequence of that person's accompanying the investigator: CA 1985, s 449(10).

Section 449 does not authorise the making of a disclosure in contravention of the data protection legislation: CA 1985, s 449(11) (see the Data Protection Act 2018).

Punishment for destroying, mutilating, etc company documents

24.70 An officer of a company who:

(a) destroys, mutilates or falsifies, or is privy to the destruction, mutilation or falsification of a document affecting, or relating to the company's property or affairs, or

(b) makes, or is privy to the making of, a false entry in such a document,

is guilty of an offence, unless he proves that he had no intention to conceal the state of affairs of the company or to defeat the law: CA 1985, s 450(1).

Section 450(1) applies to an officer of an authorised insurance company which is not a body corporate as it applies to an officer of a company: CA 1985, s 450(A1).

A person who, as mentioned above, fraudulently parts with, alters or makes an omission in any such document or is privy to fraudulent parting with, fraudulent altering or fraudulent making of an omission in, any such document, is guilty of an offence: CA 1985, s 450(2). The person may be subject to a fine and/or imprisonment: CA 1985, s 450(3).

Under s 450, the term 'document' includes information recorded in any form: CA 1985, s 450(5).

Punishment for furnishing false information

24.71 A person commits an offence if in purported compliance with a requirement under s 447 to provide information, he provides information which he knows to be false in a material particular; or he recklessly provides information which is false in a material particular: CA 1985, s 451(1).

A person guilty of an offence under s 451 is liable to a fine and/or imprisonment: CA 1985, s 451(2).

Disclosure of information by Secretary of State or inspector

24.72 CA 1985, s 451A applies to information obtained:

(a) under ss 434–446E;

(b) by an inspector in consequence of the exercise of his powers under s 453A: CA 1985, s 451A(1).

The Secretary of State may, if he thinks fit:

(a) disclose any information to which this section applies to any person to whom, or for any purpose for which, disclosure is permitted under s 449; or

(b) authorise or require an inspector appointed under Pt XIV of the CA 1985 to disclose such information to any such person or for any such purpose: CA 1985, s 451A(2).

24.73 Information to which CA 1985, s 451A applies may also be disclosed by an inspector appointed under Pt XIV to:

(a) another inspector appointed under Pt XIV of the CA 1985;

(b) a person appointed under:

 (i) s 167 of the Financial Services and Markets Act 2000 (general investigations);

 (ii) s 168 of that Act (investigations in particular cases);

 (iii) s 169(1)(b) of that Act (investigation in support of overseas regulator);

 (iv) s 284 of that Act (investigations into affairs of certain collective investment schemes); or

 (v) regulations made as a result of s 262(2)(k) of that Act (investigations into open-ended investment companies),

 to conduct an investigation; or

(c) a person authorised to exercise powers under:

 (i) s 447 of this Act; or

 (ii) s 84 of the Companies Act 1989 (exercise of powers to assist overseas regulatory authority): CA 1985, s 451A(3).

Any information which may by virtue of s 451(3) be disclosed to any person may be disclosed to any officer or servant of that person: CA 1985, s 451A(4).

24.74 The Secretary of State may, if he thinks fit, disclose any information obtained under s 444 to:

(a) the company whose ownership was the subject of the investigation;

(b) any member of the company;

(c) any person whose conduct was investigated in the course of the investigation;

(d) the auditors of the company; or

(e) any person whose financial interests appear to the Secretary of State to be affected by matters covered by the investigation: CA 1985, s 451A(5).

For the purposes of s 451A, information obtained by an inspector in consequence of the exercise of his powers under s 453A includes information obtained by a person accompanying the inspector in pursuance of s 451A(4) in consequence of that person's accompanying the inspector: CA 1985, s 451A(6).

The reference to an inspector in s 451A(2)(b) includes a reference to a person accompanying an inspector in pursuance of s 453A(4): CA 1985, s 451A(7).

Checklist: power to enter and remain on premises

24.75 *This checklist sets out the procedural aspects governing the power of investigators and inspectors appointed by the Secretary of State for BEIS to enter and remain on premises.*

Part 1 of CAICE amended (inter alia) CA 1985, Pt 14 and introduced (in s 453A(2)) the power for inspectors and investigators who are duly authorised by the Secretary of State to enter premises used by a company and remain there for as long as is necessary in order to exercise their statutory functions.

CA 1985, s 453B(4) and (6) (as amended) provide that (i) as soon as practicable after exercising the power to enter and remain on premises 'appropriate recipients' are to be given a statement of powers, rights and obligations ('the statement'); and (ii) as soon as reasonably practicable after the exercise of the power a written record of the visit ('the record') is to be sent to anyone entitled to request a copy who asks for it. By virtue of s 453B(4) and (7), the content of the statement and the record are to be prescribed by regulations. The statutory instrument governing the power to enter and remain on premises sets out procedural rules under para 2 dealing with the statement, and para 3 with the record.

The amendments to CA 1985 effected by CAICE came into force on 6 April 2005 including the statutory instrument.

No	Issue	Act reference
1	The provisions concerning the power of investigators and inspectors appointed by the Secretary of State for BIS to enter and remain on premises are set out in further detail by way of Statutory Instrument	The Companies Act 1985 (Power to Enter and Remain on Premises: Procedural) Regulations 2005, SI 2005/684

2	**Prescribed contents of the written statement given under s 453B(4) or sent under s 453B(5) of the CA 2006** Under para 2 of the regulations, the written statement which s 453B(4) of the CA1985 requires the inspector or investigator to give to an appropriate recipient (or which s 453B(5), where it applies, requires him to send to the company) must contain the following information: (a) a statement that the inspector or investigator has been appointed or (as the case may be) authorised by the Secretary of State to carry out an investigation and a reference to the enactment under which that appointment or authorisation was made; (b) a statement that the inspector or investigator has been authorised by the Secretary of State under s 453A(1) to exercise the powers in that section; (c) a description of the conditions which are required by s 453A(1) to be satisfied before an inspector or investigator can act under s 453A(2); (d) a description of the powers in sub-s 453A(2); (e) a statement that the inspector or investigator must, at the time he seeks to enter premises under s 453A, produce evidence of his identity and evidence of his appointment or authorisation (as the case may be); (f) a statement that any person accompanying the inspector or investigator when the inspector or investigator seeks to enter the premises must, at that time, produce evidence of his identity; (g) a statement that entry to premises under s 453A may be refused to an inspector, investigator or other person who fails to produce the evidence referred to (in the case of an inspector or investigator) in para (e) or (in the case of any other person) in para (f); (h) a statement that the company, occupier and the persons present on the premises may be required by the inspector or investigator, while he is on the premises, to comply with any powers the inspector or investigator may have by virtue of his appointment or authorisation (as the case may be) to require documents or information; (i) a statement that the inspector or investigator is not permitted to use any force in exercising his powers under s 453A and is not permitted during the course of his visit to search the premises or to seize any document or other thing on the premises; (j) a description of the effect of s 453C(2) as it relates to a requirement imposed by an inspector or investigator under s 453A; (k) a statement that it is an offence under s 453A(5) intentionally to obstruct an inspector, investigator or other person lawfully acting under s 453A; (l) a description of the inspector's or investigator's obligations under s 453B(6) and (7) to prepare a written record of the visit and to give a copy of the record, when requested, to the company and any other occupier of the premises; and (m) information about how any person entitled under s 453B(6) to receive a copy of that record can request it.	Paragraph 2

3	**Prescribed contents of the written record prepared under s 453B(6) of the CA 1985** Under para 3 of the regulations, the written record which s 453B(6) of the CA 1985 requires an inspector or investigator to prepare must contain the following information: (a) the name by which the company in relation to which the powers under s 453A were exercised was registered at the time of the authorisation under s 453A(1)(a); (b) the company's registered number at that time; (c) the postal address of the premises visited; (d) the name of the inspector or investigator who visited the premises and the name of any person accompanying him; (e) the date and time when the inspector or investigator entered the premises and the duration of his visit; (f) the name (if known by the inspector or investigator) of the person to whom the inspector or investigator and any person accompanying him produced evidence of their identity under s 453B(3); (g) the name (if known by the inspector or investigator) of the person to whom the inspector or investigator produced evidence of his appointment or authorisation (as the case may be) as required by s 453B(3); (h) if the inspector or investigator does not know the name of the person to whom he produced evidence of his identity and appointment or authorisation as required by s 453B(3), an account of how he produced that evidence under that section; (i) if the inspector or investigator does not know the name of the person to whom any person accompanying the inspector or investigator produced evidence of his identity under s 453B(3), an account of how that evidence was produced under that section; (j) the name (if known by the inspector or investigator) of the person who admitted the inspector or investigator to the premises or, if the inspector or investigator does not know that person's name, an account of how he was admitted to the premises; (k) the name (if known by the inspector or investigator) of every appropriate recipient to whom the inspector or investigator, while on the premises, gave a written statement of powers, rights and obligations as required by s 453B(4); (l) if the inspector or investigator does not know the name of a person referred to in paragraph (k), an account of how the written statement was given to that person; (m) the name (if known by the inspector or investigator) of any person physically present on the premises (to the inspector's or investigator's knowledge) at any time during the inspector's or investigator's visit (other than another inspector or investigator, a person accompanying the inspector or investigator or a person referred to in para (k)) and with whom the inspector or investigator communicated in relation to the inspector's or investigator's presence on the premises;	Paragraph 3

	(n) a record of any apparent failure by any person during the course of the inspector's or investigator's visit to the premises to comply with any requirement imposed by the inspector or investigator under Pt 14 of the 1985 Act; and (o) a record of any conduct by any person during the course of the inspector's or investigator's visit to the premises which the inspector or investigator believes amounted to the intentional obstruction of him, or anyone accompanying him, in the lawful exercise of the power to enter and remain on the premises under s 453A.	

25 Legal aspects of corporate social responsibility

Introduction

25.1 This chapter considers the following issues:

- definition and attributes of corporate social responsibilities;
- regulating corporate social responsibilities;
- judicial attitudes towards the concept; and
- the statutory regulation of corporate social responsibilities.

One of the primary difficulties in dealing with the legal aspects of corporate social responsibility is that no identifiable and acceptable definition of the concept can be found. Consequently, both the dimensions and the nature of the concept remain unclear, although its role in the corporate world and the business world at large cannot be denied. In this section, an attempt is made to examine various definitions of corporate social responsibility.

There seems to be a broad consensus among many commentators that a definition of 'corporate social responsibility' contains two main principles: the philanthropic and the trusteeship principles. When a company discharges a social service role, it is then concerned with corporate philanthropy. In such circumstances, companies participate in society by engaging in social activities themselves and by encouraging philanthropic activities in the form of the resolution of chosen social problems of the community without any direct monetary benefits.

25.2 The trusteeship principle perceives directors as trustees for shareholders, creditors, employees, consumers and the wider community. However, there seems to exist an apparent hierarchy between these groups. For example, directors' responsibilities towards shareholders and creditors of the company primarily relate to the protection of their monetary interests. The nature of the interests to be protected in respect of employees, consumers and the wider community seems to be of a much broader nature, and may be impossible to quantify in monetary terms.

Corporate philanthropy is, therefore, concerned with the company's role in society. The trusteeship principle is, however, more concerned with the awareness of a sense of responsibility on the part of directors towards the various groups with whom they are directly concerned.

The concept of corporate social responsibilities may not, therefore, be accurately defined; it may only be described.

Features of corporate social responsibility

25.3 One of the features of corporate social responsibility is to provide a 'good service' to the community and to the various 'stakeholders' in a company. This idea was advanced by Berle and Means in the 1930s in *The Modern Corporation and Private Property*, although they never expressly refer to the concept in their work. They thought the modern corporation should be a 'social institution' involving the interrelation of a wide diversity of economic interests. These 'interests' included the owners who supply capital, the workers who 'create' and the consumers who give credence to the company's products. Social pressure requires companies to exercise their power equally for the benefit of all these groups. Berle and Means claimed that directors, therefore, held their power in trust for these groups. This was:

> 'a wholly new concept of corporate activity. The various affected groups had placed the company in a position to demand that the modern corporation serve not only the shareholders but also society. The interests of the community were paramount'.

In his later writing, Berle believed that corporate social responsibility had 'revolutionalised' the modern company. Management provided a social service and a 'good life' for the community. Corporate social responsibility required the management of a company to have an orientation which contributed to a corporation's philanthropic activities and those based on the trusteeship principle. There is also a voluntary commitment by corporations to pursuing social objectives. The spill-over effect of such a commitment should automatically improve the quality of management, and thereby contribute to the welfare of society. This 'voluntary assumption' of responsibilities includes corporate involvement in charitable contributions, community service, employee welfare, charging reasonable prices, improving existing products and introducing new ones, locating plants according to community needs, providing for the conservation of natural resources and promoting fundamental scientific research for the benefit of the community.

Corporate social responsiveness

25.4 The concept of corporate social responsiveness developed in the 1970s in response to the vagueness of the concept of social responsibility. Some critics argued that the emphasis on motivation alone was not sufficient. Instead, corporate social responsiveness should be identified with the managerial task of implementing social policies within the financial framework of the company's activities. Managers should be required to restructure their companies and to adapt corporate behaviour, to ensure that it is socially responsive to the community and other groups in society.

25.5 This perspective emerged as a result of increasing demands from various consumer pressure groups, employees, trade unions and other interest groups. It involves three basic phases. The first is the 'identification phase' which reflects the process of companies identifying current social issues and formulating future developments. The second phase is the 'commitment stage', when companies select specific social issues requiring responsive action and they specify their level of commitment to them. The final phase is 'implementation', which focuses on the initiation and execution of the agreed social policies.

Without awareness amongst the general public as to corporate social responsibility, corporate social responsiveness may not be effectively achieved. In this sense, there is a correlation between corporate social responsiveness and an awareness of corporate social responsibility in the general public.

Corporate social rectitude

25.6 Corporate social rectitude is concerned with the ethical aspects of corporate social behaviour. Although the concept is close to the general features of corporate social responsibility, nevertheless it is possible to identify the meaning of corporate social rectitude and its role in developing and activating general corporate social responsibility.

As the expression suggests, it is concerned with the ethical dimensions of corporate activities. In other words, corporate social rectitude provides the foundation of corporate social responsibility. Corporate social rectitude apparently conflicts with the attitudes maintained by profit maximisers, but a standard of responsible behaviour for corporate bodies requires that the concept of corporate social rectitude is maintained.

25.7 Corporate social rectitude is based on the developments that took place in the business community in the US under the pioneering movement launched by the pressure groups, including the US Chamber of Commerce, initially in the field of consumer protection, but which gradually extended to the protection of the environment and other related areas. The ethical aspects of corporate social rectitude are linked to the value element. This emphasises the need for directors to adopt ethical values towards shareholders, creditors, employees and other persons having a legal interest in the company which may be enshrined in corporate codes of conduct and mission statements formulated by some companies.

Corporate social performance

25.8 This concept refers to a system of assessing a company's performance in achieving its social objectives, based on social policies of a participatory nature. One method of assessing the social performance of companies is to measure the social objectives they are implementing. This requires a system to measure and report on social issues and ultimately assessing the performance of directors in achieving the company's social objectives.

Corporate social performance may be assessed either by financial accounting procedures or by social audit systems. A social audit system could measure social issues such as equal employment opportunity programmes, conditions of work in the workplace, pollution control, job satisfaction and the quality of working life, the ethical performance of corporate executives, as well as community and urban redevelopment programmes by companies. The data extrapolated from social auditing could be useful for companies in assessing their social performance over the years.

The term corporate social performance is a relative term in that, in a dynamic society, its dimensions will change alongside society's perceptions, attitudes and understandings of the concept. Effective social audit may suffer unless a socially responsible society has articulated what is expected of a corporation in terms of its corporate social responsibilities. Government initiatives in this regard are essential for developing corporate social responsibility to assess corporate social performance.

The legal regulation of corporate social responsibility

25.9 One aspect of corporate social responsibility involves corporate philanthropy – the use of corporate funds for social or charitable purposes. It is not concerned with political donations as these are separately regulated by UK legislation on the control of political donations by companies (see CA 2006, Pt 14).

In most companies, directors control corporate funds. They are vested with powers delegated to them by shareholders, to use corporate funds in the best interests of their company. In this respect, directors must exercise their powers and discretion bona fide for the company's best interests, not for improper purposes. However, directors cannot embark on philanthropic activities by depleting corporate funds at their discretion. They must comply with the legal framework which is intended to safeguard the interests of both creditors and investors from the unauthorised use of corporate funds, including observing their duties under CA 2006, in both equity and at common law.

25.10 This section considers the legal regulation of corporate philanthropy and gratuitous distributions. The starting point is a consideration of the *ultra vires* doctrine. Although the doctrine is now largely of historical interest, the purpose of considering it here is to demonstrate its influence on the development of corporate social responsibility in UK law and practice. The impact of the doctrine on corporate philanthropy is also considered. The existence of various judicial approaches reveals the inconsistency with which the courts have applied the doctrine in this area. The statutory regime under CA 2006 for regulating corporate philanthropy is considered.

Although companies are regulated to some extent as to how they may pursue social obligations, there has been no attempt to date to consolidate this very fragmented and piecemeal legal framework under a unifying regulatory system. There is a need for a coherent legal framework on corporate philanthropy and gratuitous distributions.

Ultra vires doctrine

25.11 The legal implications of and judicial approaches to corporate philanthropy can only be explained and understood by reference to the *ultra vires* doctrine. This section outlines the historical development of the doctrine and the sequence of reforms culminating in the enactment of CA 2006. It also looks at the courts' application of the doctrine and suggests that in some cases, it has been misunderstood and incorrectly applied. This has resulted in a series of inconsistent judicial approaches in some of the cases on corporate philanthropy.

History and nature of the ultra vires doctrine – the position before 2006

25.12 The aim of the *ultra vires* doctrine as it applied to companies was to protect investors and creditors against unauthorised corporate activities and depletion of their funds. In the strict sense of the term, any transaction which was beyond the company's capacity as defined in its objects clause in the memorandum of association, would be void and could not be ratified by the members.

25.13 The *ultra vires* doctrine was first applied in its strict sense to registered and statutory companies in the mid-nineteenth century, with particular application to the railway and public utility companies. In the landmark decision of *Ashbury Railway Carriage and Iron Company v Riche* (1875) LR 7 HL 653, the House of Lords was concerned with the effect of the railway company entering into a transaction which was not permitted by its objects clause. It held that a company incorporated under the Companies Acts had capacity to do only those acts which were expressly or impliedly authorised by its memorandum of association. The House of Lords clearly distinguished acts which were *ultra vires* the directors, because they were beyond the powers delegated to them under their company's articles and, therefore, capable of ratification by the members, from those acts which were *ultra vires* the company, because they were beyond the objects as expressed in the memorandum. These latter acts were correctly termed *ultra vires* and not ratifiable by the members in general meeting.

25.14 The strict rule in the *Ashbury* case was relaxed in subsequent cases, which had gradually diminished the scope of the doctrine. Various devices were used to mitigate the extreme effects of the doctrine. In *A-G v Great Eastern Railway Company* (1880) 5 App Cas 473, the House of Lords concluded that, in addition to the express powers given to the company under its memorandum, a company had implied powers to do whatever was reasonably incidental to the carrying out of the express objects. Lord Selborne LC stated that 'the doctrine ought reasonably, and not unreasonably to be understood and applied …'. The doctrine could also be circumvented by the corporate practice of providing an extensive list of objects and powers in the memorandum and allowing companies the freedom to engage in a wide range of activities without being restricted by the doctrine. Although the House of Lords in *Cotman v Brougham* [1918] AC 514 viewed this activity as 'pernicious practice: confusing power with purpose', Lord Wrenbury felt he had to 'yield to it' but nevertheless expressed his dissatisfaction: 'It has arrived now at a point at which the fact is that the function of the memorandum is taken to be not to specify, not to disclose, but to bury beneath a mass of words the real object or objects of the company, with the intent that every conceivable form of activity shall be found included somewhere within its terms.'

25.15 This issue was resolved by the judicial practice of analysing and construing various objects and powers in the memorandum and defining the main as opposed to the ancillary objects of the company's activities. The courts applied the 'ejusdem generis' rule of construction by deciding that the powers could only be used in relation to the company's objects. This became known as the 'main objects rule of construction'. *In Re Haven Gold Mining Company* (1882) 20 ChD 151, the court held that where the company's objects were expressed in a series of paragraphs, the court would look for those paragraphs which contained the company's main objects. All other sub-paragraphs would be considered ancillary to its main objects.

25.16 Some companies, nevertheless, evaded the distinction between powers and objects and thereby avoided the application of the *ultra vires* rule. This was achieved by the practice of including a provision at the end of the objects clause which stated that the objects should not be construed restrictively and that both paragraphs should be interpreted as a separate and an independent object. This was known as the *Cotman v Brougham* clause ([1918] AC 514). The courts subsequently took a restrictive view of this form of clause. In *Re Introductions Limited v National Provincial Bank Limited* [1970] Ch 199, Harman J considered that not all powers could be objects: 'You cannot have an object to do every mortal thing you want, because that is to have no object at all.'

25.17 The legal rationale of allowing the main objects rule of construction to defeat the *ultra vires* doctrine was extended to subjective objects clauses. These were drafted to empower a company 'to carry on any other trade or business whatever, which can in the opinion of the board of directors, be advantageously carried on by, in connection with, or ancillary to, any of the above businesses or general business of the company'. The validity of this clause was upheld by the Court of Appeal in

Bell Houses Ltd v City Wall Properties Ltd [1966] 1 QB 207, where the court applied a 'natural and ordinary meaning' to the clause and concluded that as long as the directors honestly and genuinely formed the view that a particular business could be carried on advantageously, any activity undertaken in reliance of such a clause would be within the company's capacity.

The doctrine sometimes impacted unfairly on innocent third parties to the transaction because of the doctrine of constructive notice which deems a party to have notice of the company's objects and capacity.

Reform of the law

25.18 In 1986 the Department of Trade and Industry commissioned Dr DD Prentice to review the *ultra vires* doctrine with a view to making recommendations in this area. A Consultative Document was produced to seek comments from various interested parties. According to the Department of Trade and Industry, 'in practice, it (ie the *ultra vires* doctrine) represents an obstacle to enterprise and works so capriciously that it is doubtful whether it offers any real protection to anyone'.

The Prentice Report recommended the complete abolition of the *ultra vires* doctrine since it no longer served any useful purpose. His recommendations, inter alia, were that a company should have the capacity to do any act whatsoever; a third party dealing with a company should not be affected by the contents of any document merely because it was registered with the registrar of companies or with the company (this could be made the subject of appropriate exceptions); a company should be bound by the acts of its board or an individual director; a third party should be under no obligation to determine the scope of the authority of a company's board or an individual director, or the contents of a company's articles or memorandum.

25.19 Although CA 1989 had virtually repealed the *ultra vires* doctrine, the Act has not adopted the recommendations proposed by Prentice. It instead inserted a new s 3A into CA 1985 ('Statement of Company's Objects'). This provided that where the memorandum states that the company's object is to carry on business as a 'general commercial company', the company can carry on any trade or business whatsoever. It also had the power to do all such things as are incidental or conducive to the carrying on of any trade or business by it, including philanthropic acts. CA 1985, s 3A was intended to encourage companies to use the 'short form' objects clause rather than the 'long form' objects clause which was widely drafted to avoid the *ultra vires* doctrine.

Further steps towards the virtual abolition of the *ultra vires* doctrine were achieved by substituting the original s 35 above (CA 2006, ss 35, 35A and 35B as amended), which sections have now been transposed under CA 2006 by replacing these provisions under CA 1985 and CA 1989: CA 2006, s 39.

Judicial approaches to corporate philanthropy and gratuitous distributions

25.20 Some complex legal issues can arise where a company engages in corporate philanthropy or gratuitous distributions in the form of gifts to institutions, or by way of remuneration and pensions to directors, which are of an altruistic nature. The cases show that the courts have, over the years, viewed such payments with no great enthusiasm, and sometimes with outright hostility.

In some cases, the courts have misapplied the doctrine by referring to the term *ultra vires* as an abuse or misuse of power by directors rather than to the company's capacity. This section considers the various judicial approaches that the courts have taken in addressing corporate philanthropy and gratuitous distributions, including the circumstances when they are permissible or declared as *ultra vires*.

Business judgment approach

25.21 This approach was one of the first to be applied by the English courts to some cases on corporate philanthropy. It allows corporate gifts to be made where decisions are taken by directors bona fide, as to what they consider (not what the court considers) is in the best interests of their company. It appears that the courts are reluctant to interfere with directors' business decisions, as they are best placed to manage their company's business. This approach is also concerned with the extent to which the wishes of the majority can be questioned by minority shareholders. The courts will not generally entertain any shareholders' proceedings against a company under the rule in *Foss v Harbottle* (1843) 2 Hare 461.

In what has come to be regarded as a seminal exposition of the rule, Jenkins LJ in *Edwards v Halliwell* [1950] 2 All ER 1064, stated that it was based upon two propositions: first, the proper claimant in an action in respect of a wrong alleged to be done to a company is prima facie the company; and second, only the majority of the shareholders can decide to bring proceedings where a wrong has been done to the company.

Directors should not be prevented from carrying on business in a manner most conducive to the company's welfare. One of the earliest English applications of the business judgment approach to corporate philanthropy is *Taunton v Royal Insurance Company* (1864) 2 H & M 135. A minority shareholder in the insurance company attempted to restrain the company and its directors from offering to pay compensation to 80 householders in Liverpool whose houses were damaged by a gunpowder explosion on board a vessel. He also sought a declaration that the directors were personally liable to account for any payments already made to those affected by the explosion. The company's articles of association gave directors the power to settle and adjust claims and also general powers to conduct the company's business – including insurance – against any form of casualty according to their discretion as might be for the company's welfare. Counsel for the plaintiff argued that the payments by the insurance company to the owners of the houses were not covered by such risks under the terms of the insurance policy. Relying on *Foss v Harbottle*, the defendants, however, contended that the payment of compensation to those affected by the explosion was an internal business arrangement with which the court should not interfere. Counsel for the defendants argued: 'Could not the directors give a Christmas Box? If either the directors or the company in general meeting can do this, the Plaintiff is out of court on the principle of *Foss v Harbottle*.'

Vice-Chancellor, Sir Page Wood, stated that it was not in the interests of companies that the conduct of their business should be 'needlessly hampered'. Directors should not be prevented from carrying on business in a manner most conducive to the company's welfare. The expenditure of corporate funds was 'designed to secure to the company the largest possible amount of profit in its own proper business'. The Vice-Chancellor stated that the payment was made not on the ground of legal liability but because the directors thought it 'judicious' to do so. The action therefore failed. There was also concern for the company's welfare and reputation in the community if these payments were not made. The company wished to avoid any questions which its customers could raise at law as to its strict obligations or any imputation on its liberality when paying compensation for the losses which were incurred: 'It is said that the payment is a mere gratuity. Let it be so called, it does not follow that it is beyond the power of the company if to give such gratuities be the generally received method of conducting such a business.'

This business judgment approach was followed in *Hampson v Price's Patent Candle Company* (1876) 45 LJ Ch 437, where as a matter of factory management policy, the directors had proposed to make one week's ex-gratia payment (in addition to the usual wages) to their employees 'in recognition of the fact that their exertions have helped to make the company's profits larger than they have been for the last sixteen years'. These payments were for employees who had 'worked there with good character throughout the year'. There was no express power in the memorandum to pay these gratuities. A majority of the shareholders had approved the payments, but the plaintiff, who was one of the dissenting shareholders, brought an action against the company.

Jessel MR decided that the company's articles gave wide powers of management to its directors. They could, therefore, lawfully exercise all the powers of the company. In approving the payments he reasoned: 'Can anything be more reasonable than that, when the employer has had a very good year through the exertions of the workmen employed by him, he should give them something more than their ordinary wages by encouraging them to exert themselves for the future?'

The directors had clearly acted bona fide by seeking approval for the payment from their shareholders. The court would not interfere where directors had decided that the proposed payment to their employees would encourage them to work for the company's benefit. This was the 'best mode' of conducting the company's affairs as determined by the directors and 'no judge ought to give an opinion on matters of this kind, which he does not understand'. Jessel MR concluded that: '… the managers and directors of the company whose business it is, and who ought to know how to conduct the business to the most advantage, ought to be allowed to judge whether what is about to be done is advantageous and reasonable or not'.

Liberal approach

25.22 A liberal approach has, on occasions, been applied by the English courts in allowing companies to engage in corporate philanthropy. In the absence of an express power in the company's constitution to make gratuitous payments, the courts have, in some cases, implied a power to make these donations provided they are reasonably incidental or conducive to the company's business. In 1962, the Jenkins Committee on Company Law Reform reasserted this liberal approach and went so far as to say that: 'The practice, which has developed, of companies (without express powers) making donations to general charities of no direct interest to the companies' business has never been challenged in the courts in this country and we venture to think that this practice, which is regarded by businessmen as necessary to create or preserve goodwill for their companies, would on that ground, be acceptable to the court today.'

The case of *Evans v Brunner Mond* [1921] 1 Ch 359 is one of the first applications of this liberal approach. One of the company's objects, in clause 3 of its memorandum, stated that it could do 'all such business and things as may be incidental or conducive to the attainment of the above objects, or any of them'. The shareholders had passed a resolution authorising their directors to distribute £100,000 to various universities and scientific institutions in furtherance of scientific education and research. A dissenting shareholder sought an injunction to restrain the company from making this payment claiming a declaration that the resolution was *ultra vires* the objects and powers of the company.

Eve J construed the company's objects as permitting donations for the furtherance of scientific education and research. He appreciated the past practice by the courts of distinguishing between objects and powers, but thought that it was not now necessary to distinguish between the two. It was merely sufficient to interpret the extent and scope of the company's objects. His Lordship concluded: 'The wide and general objects are to be construed as ancillary to the company's main purpose, and I apprehend that the act to be intra vires must be one which can fairly be regarded as incidental or conducive to the main or paramount purpose for which the company was formed.'

25.23 However, in *Tomkinson v South-Eastern Railway Company* (1887) 35 ChD 675, at a meeting of the shareholders of a railway company (which was established by statute), a resolution was passed authorising the directors to subscribe a sum of £1,000 out of the company's funds by way of a donation towards the Imperial Institute for the purposes of exhibitions and sporting events. Kay J held that the proposed donation to the Imperial Institute was not within the objects of the railway company, nor was it reasonably incidental to the company's main purpose. Kay J stated: 'To say…that any expenditure which may indirectly conducive to the benefit of the company, is *intra vires*, seems to me to be extravagant'. Accordingly an injunction was granted to prevent such donation.

The liberal approach has also been applied in some US cases on corporate philanthropy. In *AP Smith Manufacturing v Barlow* (1953) 13 NJ 145, the directors proposed to donate '$1,500 to Princeton University and a further contribution towards its maintenance'. Some of the minority shareholders brought an action to prevent this distribution of corporate funds on the ground that the company's objects did not expressly permit such donations. Further, there was no implied power to make them.

Jacobs J reviewed the historical literature on corporate social responsibility, and observed that the early corporate charters referred to services to the public in their recitals: 'The corporate object was the public one of managing and ordering the trade as well as the private one of profit for the members.' He upheld the validity of the donation because it was reasonably incidental to the company's objectives and benefited the company's reputation by establishing a closer relationship with local educational institutions. The court also upheld the donation on the general grounds of a company's wider obligations to the community. Jacobs J stated:

> 'Modern conditions require that corporations acknowledge and discharge social as well as private responsibilities as members of the communities within which they operate.'

The liberal approach, therefore, justifies corporate philanthropy by referring to its role in contributing to the socio-economic health of the community.

The restrictive approach

25.24 Where the company is no longer a 'going concern' because of its insolvency or near insolvency, and is not in a position to exercise corporate philanthropy nor is capable of discharging any social obligations, the courts have applied a restrictive approach. The expenditure of corporate funds in these circumstances would, therefore, be *ultra vires*. The rationale for this approach is protection of the interests of creditors and shareholders investing in the company against the unlawful depletion of corporate funds by directors. A further justification for this restrictive approach is that a company which is in the process of winding up cannot be in a position to maximise profits for the shareholders. This approach reflects the traditional economic perspective that the only social responsibilities of companies are to maximise profits for the benefit of their shareholders.

This restrictive approach was applied in the English case of *Hutton v West Cork Railway Company* (1883) 23 ChD 654. An action was brought by the holder of a debenture stock who did not approve of a resolution by the company to make certain payments to the company's officers. The court was required to decide whether the sum of £1,050 could lawfully be paid by the company as compensation to its managing director and other officers for loss of their employment. It was also required to determine whether another sum of £1,500 could be paid to directors as remuneration for their past services in circumstances where the company was no longer a going concern. The Court of Appeal held that a power to make these payments could not be implied after the company had ceased to be a going concern. The powers could be implied only as incidental to the company's business but not where the company was moribund.

Cotton LJ distinguished this case from the *Taunton* and *Hampson* cases where payments were made by companies which were going concerns. In the present case, the company was no longer a going concern. The proposed payment of £1,050 to the company's directors was a gratuity but without any prospect of it being in any way reasonably conducive to the company's benefit. His lordship considered that payment as *ultra vires*. The other proposed payment of £1,500 to the directors was not a reasonable sum as remuneration for their past services. It was instead 'a sum which might with reasonable generosity be paid to them taking into consideration the fact that they never received anything during the years when they carried on the railway'. This payment was also held to be beyond the company's powers and *ultra vires*.

Bowen LJ sympathised with the directors' dilemma, but felt that their interests must be balanced against the interests of the dissenting shareholders:

> 'They can only spend money which is not theirs but the company's, if they are spending it for purposes which are reasonably incidental to the carrying on of the business of the company.'

Bowen LJ reasoned that bona fides could not be the sole test 'otherwise you might have a lunatic conducting the affairs of the company, and paying away its money with both hands in a matter perfectly bona fide yet perfectly irrational'. The test was whether the payment was reasonably incidental to and within the reasonable scope of carrying on the company's business. In the absence of any express provisions in the company's articles, the payments to the directors would amount to a gratuity. Thus:

> 'A railway company, or the directors of the company, might send down all the porters at a railway station to have tea in the country at the expense of the company. Why should they not? It is for the directors to judge, provided it is a matter which is reasonably incidental to the carrying on of the business of the company; and a company which always treated its employees with Draconian severity, and never allowed them a single inch more than the strict letter of the bond, would soon find itself deserted – at all events, unless labour was very much more easy to obtain in the market than it often is …
>
> It is no charity sitting at the board of directors because … charity has no business to sit at the board of directors qua charity. The law does not say that there are to be no

cakes and ale, but there are to be no cakes and ale except such as are required for the benefit of the company.'

25.25 This statement by Bowen LJ clearly suggests that a company has the sole authority to determine what would be regarded as being for the benefit of the company. However, where the company had ceased to be a going concern it could not derive any benefit from the gratuitous distribution. The company had a special and limited business 'and that business was to preside at its own funeral, to wind itself up and to carry on its own internal affairs'.

The restrictive policy was applied in *Parke v Daily News Limited* [1962] Ch 927. The defendant company was in the process of selling its two main associated newspapers which had incurred losses, to Associated Newspapers. The directors of the Daily News had intended to distribute the proceeds of the sale to the company's employees who were to be made redundant. Before a meeting of Daily News shareholders could be convened to approve the proposed payment to the employees, the plaintiff brought an action against the company claiming that the proposed payment was *ultra vires* the company.

Plowman J decided that the directors were not acting in the best interests of their shareholders. The directors' decision was actuated by other motives, predominant among which was 'a desire to treat the employees generously beyond all legal entitlement'.

In considering the directors' affidavits which provided substantive evidence that 'the employees had claims to consideration' which it was proper for the company to consider, Plowman J accepted:

> 'The view that directors, in having regard to the question "what is in the best interests of their company" are entitled to take into account the interests of the employees, irrespective of any consequential benefit to the company, is one which may be widely held.'

However, in answer to the affidavit of the Daily News accountant that companies had an obligation to their employees, Plowman J replied 'but no authority to support that proposition as a proposition of law was cited to me. I know of none, and in my judgment, such is not the law'. The directors were prompted by motives which, however laudable and however enlightened from the point of view of industrial relations, were such that the law would not recognise as sufficient the justification for making the proposed payments to the employees. This was based on the reasoning that the Daily News would cease to be a going concern after the business was sold to Associated Newspapers.

The 'three pertinent questions' approach

25.26 When considering the nature of corporate transactions (including corporate philanthropic and gratuitous distributions), the court should consider three questions in determining the validity of such transactions.

This approach derives from *Re Lee Behrens & Company Limited* [1932] 2 Ch 46, in which the company's directors had resolved to provide an annuity for a period of five years to the widow of the company's former managing director on his death. The company's constitution contained an express power to that effect. At a later date, a resolution was passed for a voluntary winding up of the company. The widow lodged a proof in winding up for the capitalised value of the annuity. Counsel for the widow argued that the pension payment was not *ultra vires* since there was power under the company's articles to provide for the welfare of persons employed or formerly employed by the company, including the employees' widows and children. But the company's liquidator argued that the annuity payment granted to the widow was a gratuitous payment.

Eve J held that the transaction was not 'for the benefit of the company or reasonably incidental to the company's business'. The power to provide for the annuity was not within the terms of the company's articles. The company had failed to seek the approval of the shareholders in a general meeting and it was, consequently, *ultra vires*. According to Eve J, whether or not payments could be made under an express or implied power depended upon the answers to 'three pertinent questions', namely:

(1) Is the transaction reasonably incidental to the carrying on of the company's business?

(2) Is it a bona fide transaction?

(3) Is it done for the benefit, and to promote the prosperity, of the company?

He decided that the predominant and only consideration in the minds of the directors was a desire to provide for the widow without considering whether any benefit could be derived by the company as a result. Another ground for rejecting the pension payment was that it was a gift from the company's assets by the directors. They could not use corporate assets unless authorised to do so by the company's constitution. However, it is submitted that if Eve J's decision related to the company's capacity, then it is erroneous since there was an express power to provide the pension in this case. This case misapplied the *ultra vires* rule. The decision can only be defended on the grounds that there was of a breach of duty by the directors.

In *Re W & M Roith Limited* [1967] 1 All ER 427, the company's articles were altered to enable the directors to award pensions and annuities to certain persons including widows of directors. There was a service agreement between Roith in his capacity as a director and the company, whereby Roith was appointed as a general manager for the remainder of his life and devoted the whole of his time and abilities to the company's business. One of the provisions of his service agreement provided for payments to his wife in the event of his death. A few months after his death, the company went into a creditors' voluntary liquidation. However, Plowman J held that the true inference from the circumstances was that the service agreement was not reasonably incidental to the carrying on of the company's business nor was it entered into bona fide for the benefit, and to promote the prosperity, of the company. He applied the three tests enumerated by Eve J in *Re Lee Behrens*. He decided that the whole object of these payments was to benefit the widow, not the company. The payments were, therefore, *ultra vires* the company. In light of subsequent cases, Re Roith must now be regarded as dubious authority.

25.27 The decision in *Re Lee Behrens* (and the cases which have applied this test) is now largely of historical interest as it was criticised and distinguished by Pennycuick J in *Charterbridge Corporation Limited v Lloyds Bank Limited* [1970] Ch 62, as inappropriate to the scope of express powers. This case concerned a group guarantee. Lloyds Bank had advanced money to the property development subsidiary in a group, provided that each other company in the group gave a guarantee of the indebtedness secured by a debenture on its assets. The issue in this case was whether the guarantees and debentures given by the other companies were *ultra vires*. The objects clause contained an express power providing for the giving of guarantees and debentures by the companies. In commenting on the three tests in the *Behrens* case, Pennycuick J stated that the first of the three pertinent questions posed by Eve J was only appropriate to the scope of the implied powers of a company which did not have an express power. The second test was appropriate in part to the duties of directors and not corporate capacity. The third test was wholly inappropriate to the scope of express powers and notwithstanding the words 'whether they may be made under an express or implied power' at the beginning of the power. He doubted whether Eve J really intended the last test to apply to express powers. Pennycuick J stated:

> 'Apart from authority, I should feel little doubt that where a company is carrying out the purposes expressed in its memorandum, and does an act within the scope of a power expressed in its memorandum, that act is an act within the powers of the company. The memorandum of a company sets out its objects and proclaims them to persons dealing with the company and it would be contrary to the whole function of a memorandum that objects unequivocally set out in it should be subject to some implied limitation by reference to the state of mind of the parties concerned. Where directors misapply the assets of their company, that may give rise to a claim based on breach of duty. Again, a claim may arise against the other party to the transaction, if he has notice that the transaction was effected in breach of duty. Further, in a proper case, the company concerned may be entitled to have the transaction set aside. But all that results from the ordinary law of agency and has not of itself anything to do with the corporate powers of the company.'

The *Behrens* three questions approach has now been finally laid to rest in *Rolled Steel Products (Holdings) Limited v British Steel Corporation* [1986] Ch 246. The Court of Appeal stated that the Behrens case was of no assistance and 'positively misleading when the relevant question is whether a particular gratuitous transaction was within a company's corporate capacity'. The Court of Appeal stated that the confusion had arisen from the misuse of the term *ultra vires*. In the correct usage of the term, it referred to acts in excess of the company's capacity in which case the transaction would be void and not capable of ratification. Those acts which were in excess or an abuse of the power of directors were not *ultra vires* and could be ratified by the members in general meeting. Both the Behrens and the Roith decisions were concerned with the latter aspect.

Modern approaches

25.28 There have been a series of decisions in the 1980s on gratuitous distributions in which the propriety of the application of the *ultra vires* doctrine have been considered. These cases have concerned express provisions in the company's constitution enabling such payments to be made.

In *Re Halt Garage (1964) Limited* [1982] 3 All ER 1016, the company's general meeting resolved to award remuneration to both the husband and wife who were its only directors. Its articles provided an express power, inter alia, to award remuneration to directors. Oliver J held that the competence of the company to award the remuneration pursuant to the company's express power depended upon whether the payments were 'genuine directors' remuneration' as opposed to a 'disguised gift out of capital'. Therefore, if a transaction was intra vires, the test was to consider the genuineness and honesty of the transaction including the exercise of that power. He rejected the test that payments were required to be for the 'benefit of the company' and considered the previous cases on the application of the *ultra vires* principle to gratuitous distributions to be incorrect. The test of 'bona fide' or 'benefit to the company' was only appropriate to the question of propriety of the exercise of a power rather than the capacity to exercise it.

Oliver J stated:

> 'In the absence of fraud on the creditors or on minority shareholders, the quantum of such remuneration is a matter for the company. There is no implication or requirement that it must come out of profits only and, indeed, any requirement that it must be so restricted would, in many cases, bring businesses to a halt and prevent a business which had fallen on hard times from being brought round ... I cannot help thinking, if I may respectfully say so, that there has been a certain confusion between the requirements for a valid exercise of the fiduciary powers of directors (which have nothing to do with the capacity of the company but everything to do with the propriety of acts done within that capacity), the extent to which powers can be implied or limits be placed, as a matter of construction, on express powers, and the matters which the court will take into consideration at the suit of a minority shareholder in determining the extent to which his interests can be overridden by a majority vote. These three matters, as it seems to me, raise questions which are logically quite distinct but which have sometimes been treated as if they demanded a single, universal answer leading to the conclusion that, because a power must not be abused, therefore, beyond the limit of propriety it does not exist ...
>
> The real test must, I think, be whether the transaction in question was a genuine exercise of the power. The motive is more important than the label. Those who deal with a limited company do so on the basis that its affairs will be conducted in accordance with its constitution, one of the express incidents of which is that the directors may be paid remuneration. Subject to that, they are entitled to have the capital kept intact. They have to accept the shareholders' assessment of the scale of that remuneration, but they are entitled to assume that, whether liberal or illiberal, what is paid is genuinely remuneration and that the power is not used as a cloak for making payments out of capital to the shareholders as such.'

In *Re Horsley and Weight Limited* [1982] Ch 442, the Court of Appeal was also required to consider the applicability of the *ultra vires* rule to gratuitous distributions. It held that if an act which was expressed in the company's memorandum was capable of being an 'independent substantive object', it could not be *ultra vires* because it was by definition something which the company was established to do. Buckley LJ appeared to sanction gratuitous distributions for philanthropic purposes provided they were expressly stated in the objects clause:

> 'The objects of a company do not need to be commercial; they can be charitable or philanthropic; indeed they can be whatever the original incorporators wish, provided that they are legal. Nor is there any reason why a company should not part with its funds gratuitously or for non-commercial reasons if to do so is within its objects.'

25.29 In *Aveling Barford Ltd v Perion Ltd* [1989] BCLC 626, the company's balance sheet (which was now in liquidation) showed that, on a going concern basis, its assets exceeded its liabilities but that it had an accumulated deficit on its profit and loss account and therefore was not in a position to make any distribution to its shareholders. The company sold property, valued by an independent valuer at £650,000, to the first defendant company, a company which was controlled by L who also controlled the plaintiff company. The purchase price of the property was £350,000. The purchase was to be financed in part by a mortgage and the mortgagee company valued the property at £1,150,000. It also appeared that the company and the defendant had agreed that should the defendant sell the property within a year of the transaction then the defendant would pay the company £400,000 if the sale price exceeded £800,000. Within a year of the transaction the defendant sold the property for £1,526,000. The company obtained judgment in default on the ground that the first defendant was a constructive trustee of the proceeds of the sale of the property. The first defendant sought to have the judgment set aside. It was held by the court that as L knew that the property was worth £650,000, it was a breach of L's fiduciary duty to arrange to sell the property for £350,000 and, since the first defendant was aware of the facts constituting the breach, it was accountable as a constructive trustee. The sale to the defendant was not a genuine exercise of the power of the plaintiff to sell its property. It was a sale at an undervalue for the purpose of enabling L, the sole beneficial owner of the plaintiff, to obtain an unauthorised return of capital and hence was *ultra vires* and unratifiable.

25.30 Hoffmann J stated:

> 'So it seems to me in this case that looking at the matter objectively, the sale to Perion was not a genuine exercise of the company's power under its memorandum to sell its assets. It was a sale at a gross undervalue for the purpose of enabling a profit to be realised by an entity controlled and put forward by its sole beneficial shareholder. This was as much a dressed-up distribution as the payment of excessive interest in Ridge Securities or excessive remuneration in Halt Garage. The company had at the time no distributable reserves and the sale was therefore *ultra vires* and incapable of validation by the approval or ratification of the shareholder.'

In *Commissioners of Inland Revenue v Richmond and Jones*, [2003] EWCA 999 (Ch), the court decided that directors who caused their company to make *ultra vires* payments were in the same position as trustees who make payments in breach of trust, and are liable to make good the money so applied: see too *Re Lands Allotment Company* [1894] 1 Ch 616.

The courts will also have regard to the genuineness of the transaction: *Progress Property Co Ltd v Moorgarth Group Ltd* [2010] 1 BCLC 1.

For a wider interpretation as to 'capacity' in an international conflict of laws perspective to enter into transactions, see *Haugesund Kommune and another v Depfa ACS Bank (Wikborg Rein & Co, Part 20 defendant)* [2011] 1 All ER (Comm) 985.

Statutory regime for corporate social responsibility

25.31 The starting point for a consideration of legal aspects of companies exercising corporate social responsibility is the CA 2006. The following form the statutory basis for regulation of corporate social responsibilities:

Objects clause

25.32 Under CA 2006, s 31(1), 'unless a company's articles specifically restrict the objects of the company, its objects are unrestricted'. The effect of this section is that a company's objects are unlimited: it can carry on any trade or business or service. The objects must, however, be legal and the company must be established for a legal purpose. A company may not be so formed for an unlawful purpose: CA 2006, s 7(2). The effect of having an unrestricted objects clause is that it allows contractual freedom for the company to enter into transactions internally and externally with third parties. It obviates any barriers or obstacles that may previously have existed. Companies do not need to amend their articles of association to add other business activities: the very nature of the unrestricted objects means that, practically, the company is able to engage in transactions and conclude agreements in a timely manner.

25.33 Although a company may have unrestricted objects, s 31(1) still allows it specifically to restrict the company's objects if it so requires. So, although certain objects may be permitted to be conducted by the company, other activities or acts may be expressly prohibited. For example, the company's objects may provide the following:

> 'The company's objects shall be unrestricted except that it shall not be engaged in any charitable or philanthropic donations.'

Here, the company specifically restricts its capacity to provide these activities. It would be open to interpretation as to what exactly constituted 'charitable' or 'philanthropic' donations as the objects here do not define these terms. Would, for example, the provision of corporate facilities (such as the use of a hall for events/workshop training) to a voluntary organisation constitute a charitable donation? Is the term 'donation' strictly limited to financial contributions? Or does it include other forms of charitable services including voluntary work within the community? The terms may need to be further defined or refined to ensure, with absolute clarity, the nature of the activities or services that were to be restricted (eg financial donations may be expressly prohibited, but not other forms of voluntary services).

25.34 The revised objects clause may then appear as follows:

> 'The company's objects shall be unrestricted except that it shall not be engaged in any charitable or philanthropic donations. The term "donations" in this context shall mean any financial contributions by the Company, but shall exclude any voluntary services or assumption of voluntary responsibilities by the Company in relation to charitable or philanthropic activities.'

The extent of the restriction can therefore be set out and defined as required by the company depending upon the circumstances and such restrictions, if any, will be set out in the company's articles of association, and not the memorandum of association.

Company's capacity

25.35 Assuming that there is a restriction in the company's objects clause as set out in the articles of association on the corporate or philanthropic donations and the company, in breach of this restriction, engages in providing donations to a charity or for a charitable cause. Is the provision of the financial donation beyond the company's capacity?

CA 2006, s 39(1) provides that the validity of an act done by a company shall not be called into question on the ground of lack of capacity by reason of anything in the company's constitution. This means that the 'act' (ie the financial contribution to a charity or for a philanthropic cause) will not be beyond the company's capacity. The company still has the capacity to undertake this prohibited or restricted act. It will not be *ultra vires*. It cannot be challenged as exceeding the company's capacity. As between the third party and the company, the financial contribution is valid and cannot be questioned even where the company lacked the capacity to do so in its articles of association.

The effect is that there is no longer any *ultra vires* (external effects) to be invoked to prevent the financial contribution being made. Companies have the flexibility and freedom to engage in such prohibited transactions with third parties. For further analysis, see Chapter 7 on corporate capacity and related matters.

Power of directors to bind the company

25.36 However, as between the company and the directors, the internal effects of the *ultra vires* doctrine still survive and apply to directors.

CA 2006, s 40(1) begins with a presumption of 'good faith' in favour of a person dealing with the company. The power of the directors to bind the company, or authorise others to do so, is deemed to be free of any limitation under the company's constitution. The term 'constitution' includes the company's articles of association. For this purpose:

(a) a person 'deals with' a company if he is a party to any transaction or other act to which the company is a party;

(b) a person dealing with a company:

  (i) is not bound to enquire as to any limitation on the powers of the directors to bind the company or authorise others to do so;

  (ii) is presumed to have acted in good faith unless the contrary is proved; and

  (iii) is not to be regarded as acting in bad faith by reason only of his knowing that an act is beyond the powers of the directors under the company's constitution.

25.37 The third party is not bound to enquire into the company's constitution as to any limitations or restrictions or powers of authority. The third party can assume that the directors have the powers to act on the company's behalf.

The references above to limitations on the directors' powers under the company's constitution include limitations deriving:

(a) from a resolution of the company or of any class of shareholders; or

(b) from any agreement between the members of the company or of any class of shareholders.

However, as between the directors and the shareholders, CA 2006, s 40 does not affect any right of a member of the company to bring proceedings to restrain the doing of an action that is beyond the powers of the directors. But no such proceedings lie in respect of an act to be done in fulfilment of a legal obligation arising from a previous act of the company. The right of a member to bring proceedings applies to any present or future actions in which the directors have engaged and which was beyond their powers. A member will not be able to bring an action where the company was already bound to fulfil a legal obligation which also includes any contractual obligation which the company was bound to fulfil.

25.38 In practice, it may be very difficult for shareholders to ascertain the future intentions of directors on donations or directors' policy on corporate philanthropy. Directors still have obligations to the company under CA 2006, s 40, which states, inter alia, that 'it remains the duty of the directors to observe any limitations on their powers flowing from the company's memorandum'. If any loss to the company is caused by their entering into a legal obligation (eg a cash donation) they may be liable to their company for a breach of their fiduciary duties. Therefore, irrespective of shareholders' application for an injunction, the requirement for directors to perform their fiduciary duties properly operates as a blocking mechanism in this regard.

In the context of corporate philanthropy, the 'transaction' could be a contract entered into with, for example, a charitable institution and the 'act' could include directors making gratuitous distributions or ex-gratia payments. The act or transaction which is entered into must be approved by the board of directors acting collectively or by any person authorised by them. Section 40 also provides that a third party will not be acting in bad faith by reason of his knowing that the act is beyond the powers of directors under the company's constitution. A third party will be presumed to have acted in good faith unless the contrary is proved: *Barclays Bank Limited v TOSG Trust Fund* [1984] BCLC 1.

25.39 Any 'limitations' imposed upon the powers of directors will be ineffective as against the third party. These are limitations in the company's memorandum or articles of association including those imposed by the resolutions of the general meeting. If an act or transaction is beyond the powers of directors or any other person, it could be ratified by an ordinary resolution: *Grant v UK Switchback Rys* (1880) 40 ChD 135. The third party is further protected by the abolition of the doctrine of constructive notice and will not be required to inquire whether the act or transaction with the company is valid under the company's constitution.

Section 40 does not affect any liability incurred by the directors, or any other person, by reason of the directors' exceeding their powers. For further analysis, see Chapter 7 on corporate capacity and related matters.

General duties of directors

25.40 Directors must still, nevertheless, observe any restrictions placed on their powers when engaging in, for example, corporate social responsibility. CA 2006, s 171 requires a director to act in accordance with the company's constitution. Further, the director must only exercise powers for the purposes for which they were conferred.

When considering whether to engage in corporate philanthropy, there will be a duty on a director to ensure that, in any given case, he acts in a way he decides in good faith would be most likely to promote the company's success for the benefit of the members as a whole: CA 2006, s 172. The courts will apply a subjective test in deciding whether the director in question exercised good faith in promoting corporate success by engaging in corporate philanthropic activities. They are likely to question the motive of a director in the transaction and how the company has benefited by the transaction including shareholder welfare.

25.41 In the context of corporate philanthropy, in deciding whether this would promote the company's success, the director is required to take account, in good faith, all the 'material factors' that it is practicable in the circumstances for him to identify. A consideration of the 'material factors' means: (i) the likely consequences (short and long term) of the actions open to a director, so far as a person of care and skill would consider them relevant; and (ii) all such factors as a person of care and skill would consider relevant. It is generally accepted within some companies that corporate philanthropy, in whatever form, may be beneficial to the corporation in the long term as it may enhance the company's reputation in the local community and may also benefit the community in some way. Again, motives of a director will be considered by the courts who will in particular have regard to the following matters that a director would have considered (among others) before engaging in corporate philanthropy:

- The company's need to foster its business relationships, including those with its employees and suppliers and the customers for its products and services. A director may be justified in making a gratuitous payment to its employees because the company has performed well over the years as this would foster its business relations with its employees. A company may second some of its employees to a supplier or a particular customer which could be justified as fostering business relationships as part of the social responsibilities of companies.
- The company's need to have regard to the impact of its operations on the communities affected and on the environment. Although this may suggest any adverse effects of the corporation's activities on communities and the environment, it also includes the beneficial effects of, for example, a donation made by the company towards the establishment of a school or hospital for the community. It is unlikely to be disputed that this was for the company's as well as the local community's benefit. This should be compared to a situation where a company proposes to build a chemical plant where the chemicals and facilities used at the plant are considered hazardous and dangerous to both the local community and environment. The exercise of corporate philanthropy requires a consideration by the directors as to how the local community and the environment would benefit from the company's operations.
- The company's need to maintain a reputation for high standards of business conduct. Directors must not deplete corporate assets to either the company's detriment, or its shareholders or creditors. From the viewpoint of corporate philanthropy, a company must engage in such activities with the highest standards of ethics and conduct that can be expected and not for any wrongful or fraudulent motives that could affect the company's future. So, for example, a company that engages in money laundering activities and uses some of the proceeds for philanthropic purposes would have violated the high standard of conduct and ethics by engaging in such criminal activities. It is not denied that a company must engage in profit maximisation but not at any cost and only ethically in the best interests of the corporation.
- The company's need to achieve outcomes that are fair as between its members. Although directors have the discretion to decide whether or not to engage in philanthropic activities, they should ensure that such activities are transparent to shareholders and appropriate disclosure is made to demonstrate that these activities are bona fide in the best interests of the company.

25.42 A director must also exercise independent judgement: CA 2006, s 173.

The courts are also likely to have regard to other aspects of the directors' general duties under the CA 2006 in considering the validity of corporate philanthropy. They include exercising care, skill and diligence when engaging in philanthropic transactions by a consideration of the knowledge, skill and experience which may reasonably be expected of a director in his position and any additional knowledge, skill and experience that the director has: CA 2006, s 174.

Further, the director must not be involved in any philanthropic transactions that would involve a conflict of interest: CA 2006, s 175.

25.43 Corporate philanthropy may involve use of corporate funds or services to third parties. The courts may have regard to any personal use by the director of the company's property, information or opportunity whereby the director benefits from such use in the performance of his functions. Any benefits or rewards received by a director or former director from third parties in respect of the philanthropic activities may be challenged as contrary to directors' duties: CA 2006, s 176.

It is, however, possible for more than one of the general duties to apply in any given case: CA 2006, s 179.

The consequences of breach (or threatened breach) of ss 171–177 are the same as would apply if the corresponding common law rule or equitable principle applied. The duties in those sections (with the exception of s 174 (duty to exercise reasonable care, skill and diligence)) are, accordingly, enforceable in the same way as any other fiduciary duty owed to a company by its directors: CA 2006, s 178.

Other legal mechanisms to regulate corporate social responsibility

25.44 At times, the courts have resorted to other legal mechanisms to regulate corporate social responsibility, particularly when faced with a depletion or misapplication of corporate funds (especially in light of the virtual abolition of the *ultra vires* doctrine).

Breach of directors' fiduciary duties

25.45 The courts could declare that directors have acted unconstitutionally by exceeding their authority, or by abusing their powers, they may have acted in breach of their fiduciary duties: *ANZ Executors and Trustees Co Ltd v Quintex Ltd* (1990) 8 ACLC 980. The transaction may then be set aside. The third party in receipt of corporate funds and with knowledge of the misapplication of funds by directors, may be treated as a constructive trustee and therefore liable to reimburse the company for any sums received: *Selangor United Rubber Estates Ltd v Craddock (No 3)* [1968] 1 WLR 1555; *Belmont Finance Corp Ltd v Williams Furniture Ltd (No 2)* [1980] 1 All ER 393. Some breaches of directors' duties, however, will not be capable of ratification: *Kinsela v Russell Kinsela Pty Ltd* (1986) 10 ACLR 395; *Polly Peck International plc v Nadir (No 2)* [1993] BCLC 187.

Disguised gifts out of capital

25.46 The courts may resort to the capital maintenance doctrine by holding that the company's capital cannot be reduced without complying with the procedures under CA 2006, otherwise the payments by the company will be 'dressed-up gifts of capital'. The courts may, therefore, declare the payments *ultra vires*. In *Ridge Securities Ltd v IRC* [1964] 1 All ER 275, Pennycuick J stated:

> 'A company can only lawfully deal with its assets in furtherance of its objects. The corporators may take assets out of the company by way of a dividend or, with leave of the court, by way of a reduction of capital, or in a winding up. They may of course acquire them for full consideration. They cannot take assets out of the company by way of a voluntary disposition, however described, and if they attempt to do so, the disposition is *ultra vires* the company.'

Insolvency aspects

25.47 Where the company is insolvent, the courts may set aside certain transactions under the Insolvency Act 1986 (IA 1986), s 212 which states, inter alia, that if in the course of a company's winding up, it appears that a director has 'misapplied or retained or become accountable for, any money or other property of the company, or been guilty of any misfeasance or breach of any fiduciary or other duty in relation to the company', the court can compel the director to repay the money or property or to personally contribute to the company's assets as the court thinks just. Donations by directors for philanthropic purposes would be caught by this provision.

25.48 Corporate donations could also be set aside where directors have been involved in fraudulent trading under IA 1986, s 213. This applies where, in the course of a company's winding up, it appears that any business of the company has been carried on with intent to defraud the company's creditors or any other person, or for any fraudulent purpose. The company's liquidator can apply to the court for a declaration that any persons who were 'knowingly parties' to fraudulent trading, should make such contributions (if any) to the company's assets as the court thinks proper: *Re Augustus Barnett & Sons Ltd* [1986] BCLC 170; *Re Gerald Cooper Chemicals Ltd* [1978] Ch 262; *Re Patrick & Lyon Ltd* [1933] Ch 786.

25.49 The courts could also apply IA 1986, s 214 to set aside corporate donations on grounds of wrongful trading. This applies where an insolvent company has gone into liquidation, and at some time before the commencement of the company's winding up, the director knew or ought to have concluded that there was no reasonable prospect that the company would avoid going into insolvent liquidation. The company's liquidator can apply to the court for a declaration that the director should make such contribution (if any) to the company's assets as the court thinks proper: *Re Produce Marketing Consortium Ltd (No 2)* [1989] BCLC 520; *Re DKG Contractors Ltd* (1990) BCC 903.

25.50 It is submitted that corporate donations may also be set aside as transactions at an undervalue under IA 1986, s 238. A company enters into a transaction at an undervalue if:

> '(a) the company makes a gift to that person or otherwise enters into a transaction with that person on terms that provide for the company to receive no consideration, or
>
> (b) the company enters into a transaction with that person for a consideration the value of which, in money or money's worth, is significantly less than the value, in money or money's worth, of the consideration provided by the company.'

However, the court will not declare a transaction to be at an undervalue if it is satisfied that the company entered into the transaction in good faith and for the purpose of carrying on its business and that at the time it did so, there were reasonable grounds for believing that the transaction would benefit the company. Another alternative which the judiciary might resort to would be to declare the philanthropic donations as a transaction defrauding creditors under IA 1986, ss 423–425. This applies where a company enters into a transaction at an undervalue with the intention of putting the company's assets beyond the reach of creditors. This transaction can be set aside whenever it was made by the company. It is to be emphasised that the above procedures are available only in respect of insolvent companies.

Unfair prejudicial conduct

25.51 Where, however, shareholders have not been granted an injunction under CA 2006, s 40(4) by virtue of the company already entering into a contractual obligation with a third party, it is arguable that shareholders could petition the court under CA 2006, s 994 on grounds that 'the company's affairs are being or have been conducted in a manner which is unfairly prejudicial to the interests of its members generally or some part of its members …' Shareholders may argue that the unlawful depletion or misapplication of corporate funds by directors for philanthropic activities constitutes unfair prejudicial conduct.

25.52 If a shareholder succeeds in demonstrating unfair prejudicial conduct under CA 2006, s 994, the court could make one or more orders under s 996, which may take the form of:

(a) regulating the future conduct of the company's affairs by, for example, imposing a limit on the amount companies could donate for philanthropic purposes; or

(b) by requiring the company to refrain from doing or continuing an act complained of by the petitioner by, for example, preventing the company from engaging in specific philanthropic activities; or by requiring the company to do an act which the petitioner has complained the company has omitted to do; or

(c) by authorising civil proceedings to be brought in the name and on behalf of the company by such person or persons and on such terms as the courts may decide; or

(d) require the company not to make any or any specified alterations in its articles without the leave of the court; or

(e) provide for the purchase of shares of any members of the company by other members, or by the company itself and, in the case of a purchase by the company itself, the reduction of the company's capital accordingly.

In the case of (a), the company may only be ordered to reduce its donation but not refrain from making it altogether or order the company not to make the donation, whereas under the second alternative, it is possible for the court to order the company to change the beneficiary of the corporate social responsibilities. Under (c), however, the petitioner could bring civil proceedings on the company's behalf where, for example, the company has engaged in corporate social responsibilities and this has unfairly prejudiced the shareholder.

Derivative action

25.53 There may be a challenge to corporate philanthropy or corporate social responsibility by a shareholder bringing a statutory derivative claim under CA 2006, Pt 11, Ch 1 where: (a) a cause of action is vested in the company; and (b) the shareholder is seeking relief on the company's behalf: CA 2006, s 260.

The shareholder is required to apply to the court for permission to continue the derivative action. At the first stage, if it appears to the court that the application and evidence filed by the applicant in support of it does not disclose a *prima facie* case for giving permission, the court must dismiss the application; and may make any consequential order it considers appropriate: CA 2006, s 261(2).

25.54 At the second stage, if the application is not dismissed under s 262(2), the court may give directions as to the evidence to be provided by the company; and it may adjourn proceedings to enable the evidence to be obtained: CA 2006, s 261(3).

Upon hearing the application, the court may give permission to continue the claim on such terms as it thinks fit; or refuse permission and dismiss the claim; or adjourn the proceedings on the application and give such directions as it thinks fit: CA 2006, s 261(4).

The application by the shareholder for permission to continue the claim as a derivative claim, will apply where a company has brought a claim; and the cause of action on which the claim is based could be pursued as a derivative claim: CA 2006, s 262. The shareholder must satisfy one of the grounds for application under s 262(2) with the court's powers set out under s 262(3). See further Chapter 18 on derivative claims.

Checklist: legal aspects of corporate social responsibility

25.55 *This checklist sets out the key issues likely to be encountered in respect of the legal aspects of corporate social responsibility. It also addresses possible challenges to the validity or legality of companies engaging in this area.*

No	Issue
1	Develop a policy and strategy towards corporate social responsibility.
2	What are the social issues affecting the company that require immediate attention?
3	Consider the interests of shareholders and shareholder maximisation with long-term interests of other potential claimants on the corporation.
4	What are the concerns of shareholders that require immediate action (eg directors' remuneration, corporate leadership and direction)?
5	Nominate senior independent director for accountability to shareholders on specific issues.
6	Ensure transparency and openness towards shareholders by channels including IT and use of website and links for shareholder communication.
7	Consider interests of employees and appropriate corporate disclosure to employees.
8	Consider whether employees may be involved in indirect participation in corporate decision-making.
9	Identify interests of creditors and for corporations to avoid any transactions that impact adversely on the interests of creditors.
10	Identify the interests of the consumers and the wider public in the high quality and services provided to these groups and how the company can be ethically responsible towards them.
11	What is the company's environmental policy? Consider steps to minimise any harm to the environment.
12	How does the company integrate within the community? Consider ways in which the company can benefit the community such as sponsorship programmes.
13	Does the company have a policy on political or charitable donations? Identify criteria for the donations.
14	Has the company produced a code of ethics? Identify the key issues with which the company will comply and to which it will adhere.

No	Issue
15	Company to review its policy on transparency, openness and disclosure of information towards the potential claimants on the corporation.
16	Consider other philanthropic activities of the corporation, such as helping the disadvantaged, secondments of employees to worthy organisations, free advice and assistance to beneficial organisations.
17	Consider whether nominee directors may be suitable for appointment to the board.
18	Identify induction courses for directors with emphasis on corporate social policy issues.
19	Identify tax advantages in corporate philanthropic activities.
20	Consider corporate social policy at a European level particularly where company is multinational – ensure uniformity and consistency in application of social policies at a European level.
21	Consider possible challenges to corporate social responsibility: • Is it a disguised gift out of capital? • Is it a breach of directors' general duties (including any fiduciary and common law)? • Will the act of CSR have any implications upon the company's insolvency including the setting aside of a CSR transaction? • Could the transaction be considered as unfair prejudicial conduct? • Could the shareholder bring a derivative claim?

Index

[*all references are to paragraph number*]